Simone Weil

Simone Weil
A Life

Simone Pétrement

Translated from the French
by Raymond Rosenthal

PANTHEON BOOKS
New York

English Translation Copyright © 1976 *by Random House, Inc.*

All rights reserved under International and Pan-American Copyright Conventions. Published in the United States by Pantheon Books, a division of Random House, Inc., New York, and simultaneously in Canada by Random House of Canada Limited, Toronto. Originally published in France as La Vie de Simone Weil by Librairie Arthème Fayard, Paris, France. The present edition has been condensed from the two volumes published by Fayard.

Library of Congress Cataloging in Publication Data

Pétrement, Simone.
Simone Weil: A Life.

Translation of La Vie de Simone Weil.
Includes bibliographical references and index.
    1. *Weil, Simone, 1909-1943.* 2. *Philosophers—France—Biography.*
B2430. W474P4613   194 B   76-9576
ISBN 0-394-49815-1

Grateful acknowledgment is made to the following for permission to reprint previously published material:

Librairie Arthème Fayard and Routledge and Kegan Paul Ltd.: Excerpts from *Simone Weil As We Have Known Her* by Gustave Thibon and R. P. Perrin. Originally published in French as *Simone Weil telle que nous l'avons connue* by Editions Fayard, English translation published by Routledge & Kegan Paul Ltd.

Mr. Dwight Macdonald: Excerpts from "The Iliad, or The Poem of Force" by Simone Weil, translated by Mary McCarthy. Reprinted from *Politics*, November 1945. Copyright 1945 by Dwight Macdonald.

Oxford University Press: Selected excerpts from *Selected Essays 1934–1943, Seventy Letters,* and *First and Last Notebooks* by Simone Weil, translated by Sir Richard Rees and published by Oxford University Press. (First published in French by Editions Gallimard.)

G. P. Putnam's Sons: Excerpts from *Waiting for God* by Simone Weil, translated by Emma Craufurd. Copyright 1951 by G. P. Putnam's Sons.

Manufactured in the United States of America

24689753

*Blessed are those
who hunger and thirst
for justice.*

—*The Gospel According
to St. Matthew*

Preface

In the last letter Simone Weil wrote to Father Perrin, she asked him to turn his attention and charity from herself to the thoughts she had borne within her, which, she liked to think, had far greater value than her mere person. And in a letter to her parents, almost the last letter she wrote before her death, she let us see how distressed she was by people who praised her intelligence instead of asking themselves the question: "Is what she says true?" Thus she would have preferred that people did not take a particular interest in her person and her life. On the contrary, she wanted them to examine her ideas and make an effort to find out whether or not they were true. A writer's life can never explain in what way his thought is true, just as it cannot explain why his work is beautiful.

It is true, however, that in Simone Weil's case her life had an especial value of its own, indeed an incredible value! But to aim at presenting a somewhat faithful picture of it is a hopelessly difficult task. To begin with, it took place too close to us; the picture is bound to be blurred and the story hampered and confused by the many subjective impressions, the multitude of facts that can still be tracked down, not to mention the host of vivid memories so many people have kept of this extraordinary being. From the perspective of today it is hard to discern what deserves to be told and what can safely be neglected—that is, to select from among all the fortuitous, superficial, and ephemeral strokes, those strokes that will form an enduring portrait and will assume ever greater importance. To all this must be added—and this is perhaps the greatest obstacle—that it is well-nigh impossible to describe this life in a purely external manner, sticking to the bare events; inevitably one tries to understand these events and, while recounting them, to suggest certain central themes. But in order to understand them one should be her equal, or close to it. In his excellent book on Simone Weil, Richard Rees has rightly observed that it would require "a very exceptional biographer and critic" to do justice to both her life and her work.

To write of her life means to deal with her work, for the bond between her life and her thought was inconceivably close. Nobody has more heroically endeavored to bring her actions into accord with her ideas. So a biographer cannot be satisfied with describing the externals, and the upshot is that the enterprise becomes one of truly redoubtable proportions. But the main thing is still to be said—for, confronted by so pure a life, one hesitates to speak of it out of a fear of not being able to present it without changing it in terms of one's own inadequacies. There are few men or women who would not feel unworthy to touch such a life. So the question must be asked: Who am I that I dare to speak out?

Indeed, that is why I hesitated for so long before undertaking the work that Simone's mother, Mme. Selma Weil, wanted to entrust to me. She had asked me to write a biography of her daughter; unfortunately, I was not able to give her this satisfaction before her death. But since she had told me many of her memories and had given me a great many documents, a time came when I thought that I could not allow all this material she had confided in me to be buried with me and that I must write it down in some way, to the best of my ability.

In order to complement Mme. Weil's memories and my own, I have made a number of inquiries and questioned many people who knew Simone Weil intimately. The job of getting some order into what I had collected was a long one, and I was afraid that if I put off publishing what I know, the book would never be completed and this information would be lost.

Furthermore, publishing this biography as I have written it, imperfect as it may be, will permit numerous witnesses who have known Simone Weil to call attention to whatever inaccuracies and important omissions they may find in it. The longer one waits, the more the number of such witnesses decreases.

I have done this work with small hope of satisfying everyone. Simone Weil's life and thought were rich in many and varied aspects; each person will see these matters in his own way and will reproach me for having distorted, neglected, or insufficiently emphasized this or that aspect that he regards as essential. An element of subjective evaluation is inevitable and the biographer must always correct his particular attitudes by keeping in mind the work of the person who is the subject of the biography—if that person has left us a body of work. Fortunately, Simone Weil has done so; and so I have let her speak in her own voice as often as possible, and if this book is useful, I believe that it is especially so because of the unpublished documents it contains and the effort I have made to put these documents in order, establishing more or less accurately the date of each document. Simone Weil's letters rarely bear dates; and a great number of the unpublished documents were written on separate, undated sheets. In comparing them to other documents, I think I have been able to establish approximate dates for certain letters, essays, and fragments. It is a contribution to a task that must be continued.

Many of these unpublished manuscripts have not been used in this book, either because the date is uncertain or because certain limits had to be set. Thus there remains a large open field for future research. It is vain to hope to present a complete story (even relatively complete) when one is dealing with a contemporary life, particularly a life that, although quite brief, has been so fecund in both thought and action and touched the lives of so many people and so many different spheres. It is possible even that I yielded too much to the desire to present as complete a picture as possible, not omitting anything that was told me or that I thought I myself knew. But short introductions to Simone Weil's life and work are available; I address myself here to those who want to know more. Retaining only that which was the most significant while eliminating the rest would have meant a series of choices that I am afraid would have been arbitrary. In most instances, I have preferred to leave to those who are wiser than I the care and possibility of choosing the essential.

I want to thank all those who have helped me, either by the information they gave me, or by the authorization to use certain documents. Above all I want to thank André Weil for having authorized the publication of many of his sister's unpublished writings. I also want to express my gratitude to Urbain and Albertine Thévenon, who permitted me to consult and to quote fully from the letters that Simone wrote to them; to Jean Duperray, who gladly allowed me to reproduce large extracts from his accounts; to Dr. Louis Bercher, who, besides the information he gave me, also sent me his unpublished notes; to Jean Rabaut, who has let me read an unpublished article and thanks to whom a text undoubtedly written by Simone was rediscovered; to Jean Tortel, who was kind enough to write a page of reminiscences for me; and to Louis Closon, who authorized me to publish an important letter. Among those who have also given me assistance I want to thank Mme. Jeanne Michel Alexandre, Mme. Suzanne Aron, Jean Ballard, Jean Beaufret, René Belin, Mme. Simone Canguilhem, François Carpentier, Ferdinand Charbit, Michel Collinet, Mother Colombe, O.S.B., Mother François Copeau, O.S.B., Pierre Dantu, Mme. Adèle Dubreuil, Jean-Paul Finidori, Eugène Fleuré, Mme. Forestier, Robert Gaillardot, Jacques Ganuchaud, Julián Gorkin, Dr. Jacqueline Grenet, Daniel Guerin, Guillaume Guindey, Pierre Guiral, Max Hugueny, Dom Clément Jacob, O.S.B., Gilbert Kahn, René Lefeuvre, Mme. Letourneux, Camille Marcoux, Mlle. Geneviève Mathiot, Louis Mercier, Mlle. May Mesnet, Mme. Raymonde Nathan, Abbé René de Naurois, Nguyen Van Danh, Miss Ebba Olsen, Aimé Patri, Alain de Possel, Jean Prader, Mlle. Clémence Ramnoux, Jacques Redon, Mme. Rosin, Maurice Schumann, Mme.

France Serret, Boris Souvarine, Canon Fernand Vidal, Jean Wahl, Mme. Eveline Weil, and Yvon.

I would also like to mention here some of those to whom I am indebted for information and documents and who are now dead. First of all, Dr. Bernard Weil and his wife, whose memories have been the basis for most of the material in the chapter entitled "Family and Childhood." Among others I would like to mention especially Lucien Cancouët, René Château, Mme. Thérèse Closon, Pierre and Hélène Honnorat, and Pierre Monatte.

More than once I have used the books by Jacques Cabaud, *L'Expérience vécue de Simone Weil* (Paris: Plon, 1957) and *Simone Weil à New York et à Londres* (Paris: Plon, 1967), the first of which has been translated into English with the title *Simone Weil: A Fellowship in Love* (New York: Channel Press, 1964), after having been corrected and amplified in the English version. Cabaud has the great merit of being the first to attempt a difficult job, gathering in many different places a great deal of information. His research and mine do not entirely overlap; when I found in his work some interesting fact that I had not encountered elsewhere, I have mentioned it by referring to his books.

In the chapters that cover the Marseilles period I have often referred to the book of memoirs written by Father Perrin and Gustave Thibon, *Simone Weil As We Knew Her* (London: Routledge & Kegan Paul, 1953).

Contents

List of Illustrations

Men and women workers at the Alsthom plant where Simone Weil worked for several months in 1934–1935. This photo was taken during the famous sit-in strikes in 1936.

Simone Weil, photograph for identity card at the Renault plant, 1935.

Simone skiing, most likely at Montana, 1935.

Two photos of Simone Weil in Spain after her return from the front, 1936.

Simone and her mother at Sitges, 1936.

The Terramar Palace, which was turned into a hospital during the Spanish Civil War and where Simone Weil was treated at Sitges. (*Photo L. Roison.*)

Crucifix in the Basilica of Santa Chiara at Assisi. This is the image of Christ which, it is said, spoke to St. Francis. Simone Weil visited Assisi in 1937.

The Abbey of Saint-Pierre at Solesmes. Simone attended all the holy services there during the Easter week of 1938.

Venice, Riva degli Schiavoni, on the Grand Canal. To the right the Pensione Bucintoro, where Simone Weil stayed in June 1938.

"Love" by George Herbert, copied by Simone Weil. It was while reciting this poem that she experienced, no doubt in November 1938, the feeling of Christ's presence.

Simone Weil in Marseilles, spring, 1941.

Simone in Marseilles, spring, 1941, sitting in a café with Jean Lambert.

Simone in Marseilles, spring, 1941, with Lanza del Vasto.

Saint-Julien-de-Peyrolas, in the Gard area, where Simone Weil worked as a grape harvester in 1941.

Simone Weil, date unknown.

Hélène Honnorat (1913–1967).

Ruins of Montségur, last bastion of Occitan and Cathar resistance.

Simone Weil in New York, 1942.

Simone Weil's pass in London. (*Snark International.*)

Simone Weil

1
Family and Childhood
(1909-1925)

Dr. Bernard Weil, Simone's father, was born in Strasbourg on April 7, 1872. His family had been established for a long time in Alsace. His father, Abraham Weil, was married twice. With his first wife, he had at least three children (perhaps four). With his second wife, who was the sister of his first, he had three sons: Bernard, Oscar, and a third son who died at the age of thirty-six. This grandfather's descendants were very numerous. Businessmen or merchants, there were not many intellectuals among them, save for the doctor himself. A certain number of them must have settled in Paris, for they would sometimes visit the Weils when the children, André and Simone, were still very young. They would usually come in a group and it was hard for the children to sort them out. One day they asked Simone to tell them who each one of them was. Simone was very young—she must have been five or so. Of one extremely elegant lady, she said, "Oh, you, you're the lady's maid."

When Simone manifested her revolutionary inclinations, it was not very pleasing to this side of the family. They admired André, who from early youth had distinguished himself by his intellectual gifts and his scholastic successes, but Simone shocked them. She had a few furious arguments over social problems with her uncle Oscar.

The doctor's father died before André was born. His mother, Eugénie Weil, lived to the age of ninety-three. She died in 1932. She lived in Paris, on rue de Paradis, and spent the summer months at Montmorency. Except for the last two years of her life, she was always lively and in good health.

She was a very pious Jew. When she visited the doctor—she came almost every Sunday—she would follow Mme. Weil into the kitchen to make sure that she didn't cook anything contrary to Jewish dietary laws.

The doctor's father had also been very pious, though not so strict. The doctor's mother, it appears, went so far as to say that she would rather see her granddaughter dead than married to a man who was not a Jew. The doctor himself, however, was an agnostic, a convinced atheist

3

even. But he felt that he had to be tactful about his mother's religious feelings.

Mme. Bernard Weil, Simone's mother, was born in Rostov-on-Don on January 13, 1879. Her father, Adolphe Reinherz, had come from Galicia, in southern Poland. Her mother, Herminia Reinherz, née Sternberg, was born in Vienna, though her family had also originated in Galicia. Simone would sometimes joke about her mother's origins; she would say to her, "You come from a suspect nationality."

(This would be the place to recall an anecdote that the Weil family found very amusing. One of Mme. Reinherz's relations, having arrived in France after the First World War, had to fill out certain papers at the central police station. She had a great deal of trouble answering the questions they asked about her nationality. Having been born in Galicia, she had at first been Austrian, but after the country had been partitioned, she was not quite sure where her particular region had ended up. The police superintendent, finally at his wit's end, wrote down: "Nationality suspect.")

Mme. Weil had been given the first name of Salomea, in memory of a grandfather who was named Solomon. But she gave herself the name Selma, an abbreviated form of Salomea. Yet she did not like this name either, abbreviated or not. Her husband never used it, while her children and her friends called her "Mime."

Her parents lived in Russia for twelve years. She had a Cossack nurse, a beautiful woman, from what they told her later on. She spoke Russian at the age of two, but afterward completely forgot it. Her parents had a staff of seventeen servants in Russia and had guests almost every day. Starting about four in the afternoon, they would begin to arrive. They all sat down to a meal and were served enormous platters of food, and then would stay on talking and arguing until midnight. They would sleep on the sofas. The next morning they would all be served breakfast and would then leave.

When the Reinherzes emigrated from Russia in 1882, they settled in Antwerp. Adolphe Reinherz had great success in the import-export business, so much so that he was honored as a "leading naturalized Belgian." So his children were all Belgian nationals.

Mme. Weil had an older sister and brother and a younger sister. Her older sister was named Julie; she married Dr. Henri Neumand and had four children (three sons and a daughter named Maguitte). The Neumand family, after having lived for a while in Paris, settled in the Jura. Her other sister, Jenny, became Mme. Phillipsohn and lived in Frankfort on the Maine; she had two children, a daughter Olga and a son Max. Mme. Weil's brother died at twenty of typhoid fever. Two other Reinherz children, both boys, had died very young.

The Reinherzes were a cultured, musical, and artistic family. Adolphe Reinherz was a poet; he wrote poetry in Hebrew that was said to be very beautiful; and he also collected books in Hebrew. His wife came from a musical milieu; the pianist Denise Sternberg was her niece, while she herself was an excellent pianist. Mme. Weil took singing lessons and sang very well. (A famous singing teacher, who had given her lessons, told her at the end, "There's nothing more I can teach you.") She, too, played the piano and had an extensive knowledge of music and unerring taste. Her brother, perhaps the most talented of all the Reinherz children, had given promise of being so good a violinist that his maestro, when he died, had left him his precious Guadagnini violin. He could also draw very well, and had studied to be a lawyer.

Unlike the doctor's parents, Mme. Weil's parents were not religious. Most likely deists, they were liberal Jews who did not observe any of the religious practices.

Adolphe Reinherz died in Paris in 1906. He had known André, who was born that very year on May 6. He called him *"l'enfant,"* as though he were the only baby in the world. It was in his memory that Simone was named Adolphine (her given names were Simone-Adolphine).

Mme. Reinherz died in April 1929. She lived with the Weils. I knew her and would sometimes play the piano with her. She gave me some advice on how to play and in fact, during the last year of her life, actually gave me piano lessons, certainly the most useful and best piano lessons I have ever received. She was a small, quiet woman, gracious, very intelligent, with a sweet, pale face and white hair.

Dr. Weil, whose wife and children called him Biri, was a small, rather thin, very handsome man. Simone looked a great deal like him.

In his youth he had been an anarchist or, more precisely, he had been sympathetic to their ideas. When I met him his political sympathies had for some time been transferred to the Radical party. When he had decided to become a French national, he was obliged to recommence part of his studies so as to obtain the French diplomas that would permit him to practice medicine in France.

He was a taciturn man. Although he liked to crack jokes and laugh, he easily became overwrought and anxious, suffering torments over things that seemed negligible to the other members of his family. He was very gentle, kind, and modest. He was utterly unselfish and went out of his way to please others, to do what they asked of him. In all the hospitals in which he worked, when he left his colleagues were always sorry to see him go and gave him touching tokens of their affection. Yet he could suddenly become annoyed or irritated and, since he was very sensitive, he remembered for a long time afterward what had wounded him. He was very frank, sometimes beyond conventional bounds. In all matters of judgment he had a kind of inner resistance often common among Jews: he would carefully examine the matter in all of its aspects and was not easily convinced. His face wore a rather ironic, good-natured expression, a look of the utmost honesty.

Mme. Weil was a trifle smaller than her husband and looked more vigorous. When she was a baby, her brother had called her *"Dicke,"* that is, "the Big One." But she had never really been big. Her face breathed both intelligence and energy, a passion for life, an interest in everything, a desire for happiness. Her conversation was both amusing and full of wisdom. She could persuade one with so much ardor and so pleasantly that one felt overwhelmed. Extremely generous, she devoted herself unstintingly to her family and her friends, always making plans for them, advising, helping, indefatigably active. Her affection and her ability to organize were so overpowering that one was tempted to submit to her, to let her take over. But she did not want to take over; she only wanted to serve and be useful. Her authority was felt despite a real desire on her part to be effacing. She imposed herself naturally because of her courage (her daring, even), her acumen, her passionate love of her dear ones and her noble ambitions for them, her desire for and discernment of what could improve life, impelled by a kind of "practical genius." (This last expression is Gustave Thibon's.) She would have been an unusual person even if she had not had such unusual children.

It was the happiest and most united of marriages. I can never recall seeing them argue or disagree. Simone used to say to them, "I have caused trouble in many families"—she was joking, of course, for nothing of the kind had ever taken place—"it is only yours that I have failed to upset."

At mealtimes André would be amused to see how each of his parents would always leave for the other what he or she liked the most, thinking that the other also preferred it. As a result, he said, both of them always ate what they liked least and no one gained.

They were engaged on April 1, 1905, and married the same year, on May 22.

When she was a young girl and lived in Belgium, Mme. Weil had wanted to study medicine, but her father would not permit it. However, since her husband often talked about his patients and medicine, she had ended up knowing almost as much as he did. It was she who would often decide what treatment to give the children when they got sick. The doctor would leave home early to see his patients and was often absent when they needed his advice. In keeping with their habit of affectionate banter, the children often used to say, "Our mother treats us. She's the one who makes the wrong diagnoses."

This family, though so intelligent and very free to make ironic fun of each other, was pervaded by such a feeling of warmth and love that I was immediately struck by it when I first got to know them. The most natural, simple emotions were not at all muffled by the refinements of culture. Family ties were very strong; despite a pretended rudeness that sometimes appeared in their banter, a delicate, attentive tenderness united all the members of the family; and their welcome to friends was always generous and devoted.

I have said that Mme. Weil had noble ambitions for her family, and this was certainly true of the doctor, too. As one will see, nothing was neglected in the education of the children, so as to provide them with the highest forms of knowledge available and therefore the best possibilities for pursuing their chosen work. Yet Mme. Weil would later on say to an acquaintance (Renoult) who spoke to her of Simone's fame, "Ah, how much I would have preferred her to have been happy!"

Simone was born on February 3, 1909, in Paris in her parents' apartment at 19 boulevard de Strasbourg. (This house was demolished in 1912, when rue de Metz was cut through it.) She was born early, a month before term, but she was a fine infant, who developed well until the age of six months. In the month of August, however, when the family was living in Saint-Germain, Mme. Weil had an attack of appendicitis. Forced to stay in bed and to undergo rigorous treatment, she nevertheless continued to nurse her baby. From that moment on Simone did not fare so well and her progress was slow and rather painful. Years later she used to joke about this precocious decline, apparently due to the fact that her mother's milk had been affected by her illness. With a smile, she would complain that she had been poisoned in infancy. "That's why," she would say, "I am such a failure."

In January her grandmother, Mme. Reinherz, convinced them to wean her. But after this the infant became seriously ill. It was thought at first that she had some sort of poisoning owing to the change in diet, but it was soon realized that she, too, had most likely had an attack of appendicitis. After this crisis, Simone remained sickly and did not grow or develop properly. When she was sixteen months old, she wanted to be fed only by the bottle. When her mother tried to feed her with a spoon, she pushed it away. As a result, she became extremely weak. An English doctor who lived at Paris-Plage declared, "This baby cannot survive." A specialist was consulted; he said that a baby's wishes should not be opposed. From then on all her food was given her by bottle; large holes were pierced in the nipple so that more solid food could pass through. Every day Mme. Weil would take her to the Luxembourg Gardens so that she could breathe purer air than on the boulevard where they lived. With Simone, André, and the maid, Mme. Weil would take the double-decker streetcar and always sat on top, where there were fewer people, for she was afraid of exposing Simone to the chance of infection. It was from the signs along the boulevard de Strasbourg, seen from the streetcar's top deck, that André learned how to read.

So Simone was sick from her eleventh to her twenty-second month, and they had scant hopes of her becoming a normal child. When she was two years old, she had trouble with her adenoids. She coughed at night; they had to sing to her to get her to fall asleep. Many times Mme. Weil would leave, thinking she had gone to sleep, but Simone's eyes would open and she would say, "Again."

André, who was two years and nine months older than Simone, was given some children's books, the so-called little pink books, a series published by Larousse, one of which contained stories about the ancient Greeks and Romans. Simone heard them talking about these stories. One day when she was alone in her crib and been given one of these books so she could look at the pictures, they heard her say, "Is it true that Romans exist? I am afraid of the Romans!"

One of their cousins always gave Simone very expensive gifts. One day she visited Simone and presented her with a ring set with a large jewel. Simone said, "I do not like luxury." This made everyone laugh a lot and became a famous family joke, for Simone was barely three years old at the time.

When she was three and a half, she had a violent attack of appendicitis. One night Mme. Weil feared for her life. She was alone with the children; the doctor was taking a cure in the south of France and Mme. Reinherz had gone there to keep him company. Of the two doctors her husband had recommended, the first called by Mme. Weil made an incorrect diagnosis and his mistake had put the child in danger, since he said that she could drink. When the illness got much worse, Mme. Weil called the second doctor, whose diagnosis was correct but very upsetting, for he said that she had a very serious case of appendicitis. Finally, in the morning, Simone suddenly said, "Bad Mama, bad, bad." Mme. Weil and the maid embraced each other joyously, for they realized that if she spoke like that, it was because she was getting better. During this period operations were never performed immediately, so Simone stayed in bed for some time. She finally underwent an operation at a hospital in Auteuil called the Villa Molière and directed by Dr. Goldmann, where her mother had had her operation in 1910 and also her brother in 1911 or 1912.

In a letter dated December 30, 1912, Mme. Weil wrote: "My little daughter was operated on this Saturday; she is doing as well as can be expected and I hope to be able to bring her home next Saturday."

Yet, though André had had a quick convalescence, Simone's recovery was slow and she had to stay in the hospital for three weeks.

Dr. Goldmann, who had heard her talk while she was under the chloroform and had examined her several times during her convalescence, later told Mme. Weil that he didn't think she could survive. It seemed to him that a four-year-old capable of saying all the things that she had said could not possibly continue to live. He meant by this that she was too extraordinary to go on living.

Mme. Weil had carried her in her arms to the door of the operating room, telling her that they were going to show her a Christmas tree. Simone later reproached her mother in a grave, sad voice for having tricked her.

When they went to the hospital, they had passed the Eiffel Tower. For some time after, whenever Simone would catch sight of the Eiffel Tower on their walks, she would burst into tears. And for long after the operation she had a horror of doctors; she did not want to see them (except for her father, of course). When she saw a stranger enter the room, she did not want to stay there, fearful that he might turn out to be a doctor.

It was during her convalescence in the hospital that Mme. Weil, to entertain her, had told her the story "Marie in gold and Marie in tar." The heroine of this fairy tale, who was sent by her stepmother into the forest, reaches a house where she is asked whether she wants to enter by the door in gold or the door in tar. "For me," she replies, "tar is quite good enough." This was the right answer and a shower of gold fell on her. When her stepmother saw her bring back the gold, she then sent her own daughter into the forest. But when asked the same question, her daughter chose the golden door and was deluged with tar. Simone later said that this fairy tale had had an influence on her entire life.

During the summer of 1913, the whole family spent the month of August at Ballaigues in Switzerland, with Jenny, Olga, and Max Phillipsohn; and then for the month of September they went to the seaside, at Villers.

While at Ballaigues Mme. Weil wrote to Mlle. Chaintreuil, a teacher of the tenth grade at the Lycée Montaigne, who had been André's teacher during the previous year. "Simone," she wrote, "has developed in an incredible fashion. She follows André everywhere, takes an interest in everything he does, and feels, like him, that the days are too short. They have an excellent influence on each other; he protects her, helps her crawl over the difficult spots, and often gives way to her, while she, at his side from morning to night, has become livelier, gayer, more enterprising. Whenever the weather permits, we spend our days with them on the large open fields surrounded by pine trees that are the special charm of this region. The children pick flowers, catch butterflies (but they free them immediately, because they are full of pity for all forms of wildlife), and above all go on what they call 'exploratory journeys.' In fact they are only truly happy when they are far enough away so that they can imagine themselves all alone in the midst of nature."

They returned to Paris in October and subsequently moved to an apartment at 37 boulevard Saint-Michel, where they were to remain until 1929. André attended the Lycée Montaigne. Simone fell ill in October with a touch of the flu. But it was a little later, it seems, that she caused her parents some anxiety, which, fortunately, was short-lived. In an undated letter, which must however be from this period, Mme. Weil says: "The poor little thing has worried us a lot these last few days, because she suddenly began to limp. . . . But fortunately a surgeon, a friend of my husband's who examined her, assured us that it was nothing at all, just a bit of fatigue because she has grown too fast, and with a little rest it should soon disappear. . . . It is touching to see how she has resigned herself to staying in bed and doesn't even complain!" In fact she soon was well again.

She had begun to learn the alphabet and during the short period she had to stay in bed spent entire days bent over her reading primer.

When she was fully recovered, she began taking walks again and often, with her mother, would accompany her brother to and from school. André would tell Simone what he had learned in class or by himself. While riding on the streetcar, he would explain astronomy to her. One day a lady got off the streetcar in a huff, saying that she could no longer bear to hear children parroting their lessons; she could not believe that they really knew what they were talking about.

In May 1914 they both caught the measles, first André and then Simone. She was sick throughout the last week of May. In June, to make sure they recovered fully, Mme. Weil took them to a family pension at Plessis-Piquet. It had a garden with wide lawns and large, beautiful trees. Simone, who was still rather nervous and irritable as a result of the measles, gradually regained her usual gay spirits. By July she was once again in good health and was enjoying herself immensely. She liked to talk with the students who were staying at the pension and had befriended her. Although Mme. Weil frowned on these friendships, feeling that the students flattered and made too much of her, Simone would run to see them whenever she could. One student was born in Syria and once he told her that the French didn't welcome Syrians and that Syrian students weren't treated like Frenchmen. Simone exclaimed, "Well, so far as I can see, you are a pure-blooded Frenchman!"

The students wanted to give her a ride on a donkey. She immediately fell off and was dragged for some distance. They rushed to help her; she was sobbing and kept saying, "I want to get back on the donkey."

They all then went to Carolles, where they stayed in a small hotel; but they remained there only a few days. Mme. Weil was overcome by a deep feeling of depression that was unusual for her and that she regarded later as a premonition of the war just about to start. They left Carolles to go to Jullouville, where Mme. Weil's older sister was vacationing and where they rented a small villa. It was there that André, finding a geometry book that belonged to one of his older cousins, began studying it by himself, for the pleasure of it. He was soon able, at the age of nine, to solve difficult problems, and his family began to suspect that he had a genius for mathematics.

Simone was ecstatic about the sunsets. Whenever she heard that she could see a sunset, she would drop everything to run and see it.

They once went to visit an old doctor who had invited them to his house. He made as if to kiss Simone's hand, and she started to cry, shouting, "Water! Water!" She wanted to wash. The intimacy with the famous bacteriologist, Élie Metchnikov, a friend of the Weils, and their general contact with medical science, had developed among them an extreme fear of microbes. Mme. Weil did not want people to kiss the children. Before all the meals, their hands had to be rigorously cleaned; and if André had to open a door after having washed his hands, he would use his elbow. These family habits had given Simone certain strong feelings of repugnance. She did not like to be kissed, or to eat and touch certain things. Sometimes she did not want to touch something that had been handled by other people. She spoke of her "disgustingness." When it was a question of doing certain things, she would say, "I can't, because of my disgustingness."

She had great admiration and a warm feeling of friendship for her brother. She considered it an honor to follow him in all his boyish pranks. One day they both went around, holding each other by the hand, and knocked at the doors of some of the neighboring villas. To those who came to the door they said, "We're dying of hunger; our parents are letting us die of hunger." "Poor children!" the people exclaimed and immediately gave them cake and candy. They came back home stuffed and very satisfied. When their parents found out what they had done, they were overwhelmed with shame and indignation.

They tried to keep the children busy and amused, for they were absolutely unbearable when they were bored.

The family was still at Jullouville when war was declared.

The doctor showed up one day in uniform. Mme. Reinherz, who did not understand what was happening, said to her daughter, "I think your husband has gone crazy." He left at the beginning of August and was at first attached to an ambulance corps in the Meuse, but was later sent to Neufchâteau to work in a typhoid hospital.

At Neufchâteau officers were forbidden to bring along their wives. Nevertheless, Mme. Weil went there and settled in with the entire family. One officer told the others, "Weil has not only brought his wife, but also his children, his mother-in-law, and her dog." The authorities closed their eyes to this, yet appearances had to be kept up. The doctor visited his family on the sly; his official residence was in a boarding house and he ate his meals there with the other officers.

On December 14, 1914, Mme. Weil wrote to Mlle. Chaintreuil: "The hospitals are packed to overflowing with sick and wounded, and since up till now my husband has refused to let me help him in his work, I devote all the time not spent with the children making warm clothes, sewing up bed sheets, nightshirts, and so on. We also go almost every day to the hospitals to bring the patients oranges, crackers, and newspapers. And despite all this, one is ashamed to do so little when faced by such boundless misery!''

It was at Neufchâteau that Simone began to read. She already knew the alphabet but could not yet read fluently when at the beginning of December André got an idea. "Simone," he said, "should learn how to read for the New Year; it will be Biri's present." He would make her work at it for hours on end. When the doctor was there, they would both hide under the tablecloth and continue their work. On New Year's Day André said to his father, "Do you want Simone to read the newspaper to you?" She knew how to read, but she was completely worn out.

The doctor had an attack of angina and was forced to stay in his boarding house. Mme. Weil would go to see him there. Whenever the landlady saw a uniform approaching, she would bang on the floor with a broom and Mme. Weil would hide in a closet. One officer was in on the secret; when he came to the house, he would go straight to the closet and open it himself.

The family had to move because they were living in the center of the town and had become too noticeable. They did it on a very cold day when there was snow on the ground. Simone suddenly discovered that the bundle her brother was carrying was heavier than hers. She sat down in the snow and refused to move until they gave her a heavier bundle.

The doctor's angina turned into bronchitis and in February he was sent to Menton to be treated in a hospital, just when the prohibition against officers having their families with them was done away with.

The doctor left Neufchâteau in a hospital train and was en route for two days and two nights. His family rejoined him at Menton. They arrived there at almost the same time he did.

He should have been put in an army hospital, but he preferred staying with his family. Since this was not authorized, a male nurse would come to get him when an inspection was about to take place. At the end of February he was feeling better and started taking walks. Mme. Weil wrote on March 1: "He is much better, and since it's quite possible that we will not return soon to this lovely place, he wants to see as much of it as possible now. All of our cases of grippe are cured; Simone's was very tenacious and it's only been the last two days that she could begin going out."

The children were very happy in this beautiful town. Due to the war, many of the hotels were deserted. The hotel they had gone to was high up; the garden, having grown half wild, was full of splendid flowers and in the distance they could see snow-covered mountains beneath a blue sky. Simone, who loved flowers, was transported with joy when they went for walks. There was also a small summer house at the top of the hill. Once the children were there, they did not want to leave. When they were told they had to go back, there were terrible scenes of protest and despair, for they would have liked to stay there till dark so that they could see the moonlight.

In a letter dated March 1, Mme. Weil mentions Simone: "At the moment she has a favorite occupation, reading *Cyrano de Bergerac,* many passages of which she knows by heart, and she recites them with a rhetorical emphasis that makes us laugh till tears come to our eyes."

André knew all of *Cyrano* by heart. Simone and he would recite it together, taking the various parts in turn. Simone above all loved to recite the end, and they would all laugh when they heard her declaim, with great conviction,

> "Farewell Roxane, I go to die!
> I think it will be this evening, my beloved!"

The doctor was then assigned to Mayenne. They arrived there in April 1915 and managed to rent a house whose garden was full of many different kinds of roses, since the owner's husband, who had just died, had had a passion for roses. It was in this garden that they took the charming photograph of Simone sitting on her father's knee. It was in Mayenne, too, that a lady called André and Simone, respectively, "the genius and the beauty."

At the beginning of their stay there Simone seemed to be going through a period of whims and caprices and gave evidence of an indomitable will that astonished her parents. Mme. Weil wrote about it to Mlle. Chaintreuil on June 26: "She is going through a period of irritability and caprices that I can't understand, since nothing in her physical condition explains it. She is indomitable, impossible to control, with an indescribable stubbornness that neither I nor her father can make a dent in. She stands up to us with an aplomb and assurance that are by now rather comic (my husband can't keep from bursting into laughter in the middle of one of these scenes), but that, if continued, will be distressing. . . . I have certainly spoiled her too much, and even now, when she is good, I can't help but fondle and kiss her much more than I should. And my husband behaves just as I do, because this Simonette is a real woman and is marvelously capable of using her charm when it pleases her to do so."

At the age of nine André began doing equations. Simone had become enthusiastic about patriotic poems. Mme. Weil wrote: "We can't help but be a trifle annoyed and anxious, my husband and I, at the absorbing passion André shows for algebra. Some way or other he got hold of a book that I let him keep out of weakness, and since then he has succeeded (by his own resources, since nobody has ever given him any help), in solving equations of the first and second degree, and he is so happy that he has given up all play and spends hours immersed in his calculations. . . . Simonette is completely taken up with her passion for patriotic poems, which have dethroned *Cyrano* in her heart. She has a book by Déroulède that she knows almost by heart and that she recites to anyone who will listen and with an enthusiasm that is very amusing."[1]

At the beginning of October she wrote: "Simone reads a great deal, but aside from that, I don't make her work at all because she continues to grow enormously and I much prefer to see her playing and running about in the garden than bent over her exercise books. Also, she has barely learned to write; but I am sure that she will quickly make up for the time she has lost."

At Mayenne André and Simone began corresponding with adopted godchildren; these were soldiers who had no families, and those who wanted to help them adopted them as "godsons" and sent them packages of food and clothes. The children sent their godsons most of their sugar and all of their chocolate. Once they both got a present of a huge chocolate Easter egg; they refused to touch them and sent them immediately to their godsons.

Simone insisted on working for her adopted soldier. She gathered some wood and tied it into small bundles, for which her parents would pay her, and the money she earned was spent on purchases to fill the godson's packages.

In April or May 1916 one of the children's cousins, Raymonde, the daughter of Oscar Weil, eight or nine months younger than Simone, came to live with them. She had just lost her mother, who had died at twenty-nine. When they heard that she was coming, Simone said to her brother, "We must do everything that she wants, because she is an orphan."

On May 16 Mme. Weil wrote: "Simone has become so sweet! She is very affectionate and maternal toward her little cousin and gives way to her in everything, being filled with pity for her!"

The two cousins had always known each other, but their friendship became closer when they lived together at Mayenne. However, with her two cousins, Raymonde often felt faced by an almost impenetrable world. Their conversations and their games, always full of literary allusions, passed over her head, as they did with other children. "They had a universe of their own," she says, "to which their mother was admitted."

For the two children the passion for literature had grown tremendously. It was at Mayenne that they began to recite whole scenes from Corneille and Racine, and the one who made a mistake or forgot a line would get a slap from the other. Simone often recited Camille's imprecations against Rome. At Mayenne they also began to play the game of set rhymes, that is to say, composing very quickly little poems in which the rhyming words were agreed upon in advance.

For them, all play had become intellectual play and involved various kinds of knowledge. Thus the "game of families" had, with their mother's help, been transformed into a game of great men; instead of the families of the baker or the grocer, they had the family of the orators, of the poets, and so on.

According to Raymonde, Simone had generally little interest in games for children of her own age. She did play a bit, but almost her entire interest was focused on books.

In the summer Mme. Weil, who had been out of sorts for some time, went to take a cure at Luxeuil. In September, the day after she returned from Luxeuil, the doctor learned that he was being transferred to Algeria.

In the fall Mme. Weil and Mme. Reinherz settled in Paris again, with the children. For about three months Simone studied with Mlle. Chaintreuil at the Lycée Montaigne. She would write a little later, "I don't think that one often loves one's teacher as everyone in my class loved Aunt Gabrielle."

At the same time, in the same lycée, André studied under Andraud, a remarkable teacher of Latin, Greek, and French literature. André had begun to learn Latin.

It was probably at this time that André decided not to wear knee-socks. He wanted to become tougher. Simone imitated him. In the street people would stare at the two children with astonishment. Mme. Weil, terribly embarrassed by this, tried to put knee-socks on Simone at least. But the children had learned how to cry at will, and their mother, defeated by their tears, gave up trying to persuade them. One day a huge woman, seeing Simone's legs almost blue from the cold, bore down on Mme. Weil and hissed, "You wretch!"

Then they invented the trick of making their teeth chatter while they were on the streetcar, saying over and over, "I'm cold, I'm cold. Why don't our parents want to buy us knee-socks?" The other passengers would stare at Mme. Weil with fury in their eyes.

In Algeria the doctor fell ill and returned to France in December. He was soon assigned to Chartres, where his family accompanied him. The children were very unhappy about leaving their lycée in Paris. But the climate at Chartres, despite the cold weather, was good for them and Simone soon looked much healthier there than in Paris.

Mme. Weil had to undergo an operation. Toward the end of March she went to Laval to be operated on. During this separation Simone wrote to her, "I ardently desire your return." The operation was completely successful.

Some time after Mme. Weil's return, Simone's godson arrived unexpectedly one morning, on May 29. He was on leave and had come to spend it with the Weils. For Simone it was a great delight, a feast of friendship. Holding hands, the little girl and her big adopted soldier would take walks all through the day. The soldier did not stay very long.

They never saw him again, for soon after his leave he was killed in action.

At Chartres the Weil family had an old servant who had worked for the Abbé Langlois, the librarian at the Catholic Institute. She had been a nurse under Dr. Weil at Mayenne and he had recommended her. One day this old nurse said, "Simone is a saint." This undoubtedly was the first time that this word was used to describe her.

The surgeon Alexandre, who had operated on Mme. Weil, took Dr. Weil into his section at Laval. So it was decided that the rest of the family would move to Laval, and they left Chartres in August or September 1917.

André was sent to the boys' lycée, entering the fourth form. Since he was too advanced in mathematics, even for the fourth form, he only studied literature at the lycée. At the same time he took violin lessons. As for Simone, at first they thought they'd have her take special lessons, the lycée for girls being too far from their house on rue Hoche. But on October 15 they decided to send her to the lycée. On the twenty-third Mme. Weil wrote: "We made up our minds about eight days ago to put Simone in the girls' lycée. She has been bored ever since André started going to school and is happy to be with the other children." She was placed in the second year of elementary school. "As much as I can judge until now," Mme. Weil wrote, "she is very uneven, too advanced in certain things and backward in others. For example, she writes very slowly and almost never finishes at the same time as her classmates." In fact this slowness in writing did not indicate backwardness but rather a certain weakness and awkwardness of her hands, from which Simone was to suffer throughout her life. Her hands were too small for the size of her body. Even when she was fully grown she had the hands and wrists of a child. Never were hands less like those of a factory worker.

A month later, on November 24, Mme. Weil wrote: "I work every day with her from five to seven. . . . We live so far from the lycée that she never gets home before noon, so she can't do her homework until five o'clock, and she writes too slowly to be finished in time if she has to do it herself. Her teacher told me that she is very satisfied with her; she thinks she is very talented and tractable. But in certain things Simone still has some trouble catching up, since she worked quite irregularly the past year. What troubles me somewhat is that I can see she is always inclined to doubt and mistrust herself. Even when she knows the lesson she always has the nervous fear of failing to remember it. I fight this tendency as much as I can, because I'm afraid she'll suffer from it later on. How different André is! For him interrogations or compositions are a real joy, and without the slightest vanity, for he's sure of himself when he has learned something."

While taking the courses at the lycée, Simone also took piano lessons and her mother made her practice the piano at home.

The spring of 1918 had not brought the marvelous blossoming of the apple trees that they had seen at Mayenne. "The apple trees had very few blossoms, and the rain soon stripped the trees of these, too." But the greenery was lovely, and Mme. Weil was sorry that the children were too busy with their studies to find the time to go on walks. Simone was deeply involved with her schoolwork, and her success had encouraged her. "We thought a bit about taking Simone out of school for the summer months, but she refuses to hear of it. She has made enormous progress and is now at the head of her class, both in her marks and her compositions."

At the end of the school year both children were awarded the prize of best in their class, as well as many other prizes. But Simone could not be present at the ceremony at which the prizes were distributed, for that day she was in bed with whooping cough.

They were supposed to go to the seashore, at Penthièvre. Their trunks were already packed. Simone's whooping cough, which was painful and tenacious, forced them to put off the trip; but finally they were able to leave, and the family stayed at Penthièvre until September 15.

When they returned to Laval in October, the children did not go back to school. Their parents were afraid to send them because of the terrible flu epidemic that was then at its height and was causing so many deaths. They decided to have them take special lessons at home.

The war finally ended. Mme. Weil wrote on October 12: "What joy we feel over the news we've just received! Is it truly the end of this atrocious slaughter? How happy we would be if it were not for the thought of all the frightful gaps that can never be filled." But the doctor was not demobilized immediately, and the family remained in Laval until January 1919.

When they had moved back to Paris, Simone took special lessons with a woman teacher who had been recommended by the headmistress of the Lycée Fénelon. This woman thought Simone diligent but lacking in imagination.

That summer the family returned to Penthièvre. At the end of September Simone was enrolled in the Lycée Fénelon. She entered it on October 3, in the first form A, which was designated with an "A" because it had Latin and Greek as part of the curriculum. She was very unhappy at first. She was particularly disliked by the teachers in charge of the study hour because she did not have the habit of discipline and did everything wrong. In spite of herself, she was already an occasion for scandal. And often, at home, they would see her sitting with her head in her hands, as if utterly crushed; it was painful for her to say to herself, "Tomorrow I will have to go to the lycée." Then she grew accustomed to it and so much so that she even cried when she could not go.

Simone's class had two teachers she was very fond of: Mlle. Sapy, who taught letters and composition, and Mlle. Cotton, who taught mathematics. Both of them felt that Simone was greatly gifted. Her parents were astonished that she was also good at mathematics; they thought that André was the only one who was talented in this respect.

That year Mlle. Sapy assigned as the first subject for a composition "A Visit to the Louvre." Simone decided to describe the Egyptian statue "A Seated Scribe." Mlle. Sapy found the composition remarkable, and Simone's classmates also admired it. At least one of them, Geneviève Mathiot, borrowed it so that she could take it home and have it read by her family. This composition remained famous in the class.

Another time, Mlle. Sapy gave them the subject "What do you want to do in life?" There were so many things that Simone wanted to do that Mlle. Sapy was a bit dismayed.

Afterward she told Simone, "Don't forget that plants must develop not only like this" (she indicated the height with her hands) "but also like this" (she gestured to indicate breadth). Simone was to write during the last days of her life, "A tree only dies from the top"[2] and: "The leaves and fruits are simply a waste of energy if one wants only to go higher."[3] Mlle. Sapy's admonition proves that Simone already gave the impression of thinking in this way when still a child.

There were two subjects in which she could not succeed despite all her efforts: drafting maps in geography and drawing; and each time the tragedy began all over again. She had to do the maps on Thursday; Simone would spend almost all of Thursday on the map and even then got the lowest mark. The school finally excused her after her parents had requested it, although they had promised her a reward if she were last in the cartography class. In drawing, too, the defeat was heartbreaking. Mme. Weil finally went to see the teacher, an old maid, and explained to her that Simone had poor circulation and so her hands were swollen and awkward. The teacher replied by first striking her hand: "It is not this that is at fault," and then striking her forehead: "It's this." Simone was amused by this reply for the rest of her life. She would often say to her mother, striking her forehead: "It's here that the fault lies."

She was also excused from the class in manual work. Thanks to the intelligence of her parents, who were able to distinguish between the useful and the useless, she could almost do only those things that interested her. In certain cases, she did not write the compositions. It is also probable that she did not take the test for the certificate for secondary studies. She was very free as regards her obligations as a student.

She had become more and more interested in politics. One of her classmates declared that she was a communist. Simone said, "I'm a Bolshevik." This was not a word that was in the air. No doubt she knew very little then about Bolshevism, but it is certain that, while still a child, she tended toward "those organizations that appeal to the despised layers in the social hierarchy."[4] However, the Versailles Treaty, which was signed in June 1919, seemed to her to express "the desire to humiliate the defeated enemy."[5] The feeling of shame she experienced, together with her sympathy for the victims, led her for a long time to repudiate the patriotism of her childhood. She began to cherish the idea of revolution, which she renounced later on not without some inner struggle and a great feeling of regret.

It was at about this period that she learned of the existence of Jews and Gentiles. Her parents had not told her about this. When she was younger and read Balzac, she had thought that the word Jew was the name given to usurers.

On other subjects her parents did not hide the truth from their children. At Laval some little girls had asked Simone, "And what about you, were you born in a cabbage or a rose?" Simone had answered, "I was born in my mother's belly." This was the Metchnikov method.

Since they had returned to Paris, to help Mme. Weil they had hired a young Danish woman, Ebba Olsen, who several years before had been Raymonde's governess. She stayed with them for two years. She would spend the evenings with the grandmother, reading French books with her. She also took Simone to the lycée.

I once met Ebba Olsen, who has lived for many years in Copenhagen. According to her, Simone never played with a doll. There were no toys or playthings in the house, except for a ball. Moreover, she didn't want to sew. At Penthièvre in 1919 Ebba seems to have gotten Simone to make a small handkerchief with an open-work lace border for her mother, but this, she said, was the only sewing she ever did in her life.

When he came back from the lycée, André would plunge into his books. Simone passionately loved books, too. She knew long passages from certain poems and recited them "with her heart."

Ebba also said that Simone thought a lot and that this took up a great deal of her time. She wanted to understand and know, like André, and she would eventually get there but she was much slower. André learned everything at once, right off; but Simone had to take pains. She would wake up at night to do her homework. She was too conscientious.

She talked a lot with André, admired and was proud of him, and was never jealous of him. Yet sometimes the two children would fight. Simone was strong when she was very angry. She wasn't afraid of André and didn't want to give in to him. When she thought that something was just, she refused to back down.

(For her part, Mme. Weil described these battles as follows: they would fight as quietly as possible, so as not to arouse the attention of their parents, who would have separated them. They would hear something more like shuffling feet, not cries. They would go into the room and find them with stark white faces clutching and pulling each other by the hair.)

Ebba also said that Simone was very sweet and gay, but had a strong will and a definite character. She also had a sense of humor and would play pranks and jokes, but they were never malicious or nasty.

She did not think only of her studies; she was also concerned about the fate of the poor. One day there was a demonstration by the unemployed on boulevard Saint-Michel. Simone had disappeared. Mme. Reinherz told Ebba, "Go down and see if she's in the street." Simone had gone to the meeting of the unemployed. She was eleven years old.

When she knew that Ebba was alone in the kitchen she would go to keep her company and, to entertain her, she would recite some verses for her.

She did not like to dress too well. She said, "It would be better if everyone was dressed in the same way and for a *sou*. That way people could work and no differences would be apparent among them." She went to a wedding in a pretty dress that Mme. Weil and Ebba had made together; she looked lovely but was very vexed by it. It was at this reception that she saw people dancing together for the first time. She found it ridiculous—these grown-ups who were "pushing each other about" in this fashion. Like her, André was greatly irked by this wedding and swore that never again would he go to a wedding, not even his own.

As mentioned before, Simone did not like to be touched or kissed. One day when Ebba was with her, she met one of her teachers on the street, a woman, who kissed her. Simone didn't say a word but went red with anger.

(Jacqueline Cazamian also says that Simone didn't like to be kissed, even by her mother, and that in her relations with her friends she would avoid all demonstrations of affection and had "a more than touchy sense of modesty.")

Since her parents felt that Simone was overworked and exhausted, they did not send her to the lycée for the school year of 1920–1921, when she would have been in the fifth form. She took private lessons with Mlle. Sapy and Mlle. Cotton and made great progress. Mlle. Sapy lived in L'Île Saint-Louis, at the corner of a small street and the quay that Simone called the "Sapy Quay." It was perhaps at this time that Simone began to love the quays along the Seine. There were not many places she liked as much.

It was probably during the course of this winter (1920–1921) that she wrote the poetic tale "The Fire Imps,"[6] in which the flames become dancing and fighting characters, die away, and again flare up into life. (Mme. Weil thought that she had written it when she was eleven, that is to say between February 1920 and February 1921, and since it is a winter's tale, imagined no doubt before some fireplace filled with burning wood, it must date from the end of the 1919–1920 winter or, more probably, from the beginning of the following winter.) It was written for

Mlle. Sapy. The Greek words in this fairy tale had undoubtedly been taught to Simone by André.

She returned to the Lycée Fénelon in October 1921, but stayed there for only three months. She was in the fifth form A and no longer had Mlle. Sapy as her main teacher, but Mlle. P., a person who was often ironic and disagreeable and enjoyed criticizing and disparaging. When they saw that Simone was overtired after the first term, her parents tried to get her into the Sévigné, where the students didn't work so hard. But she stayed only for a term. She found that life there was too easygoing, that the strict discipline at Fénelon, once you got used to it, was better for you, and that at Sévigné they paid too many compliments.

She finished this year by taking private lessons, among others some lessons from Andraud, the teacher at Montaigne who had had André as a student in 1916, when he was in the second form, and had afterward continued to work with him by correspondence when the Weil family was at Chartres. It was probably with him that she began to study Greek.

At the end of the school year and after only a year of *cagne*,* André presented himself for the competitive examination for the Ecole Normale in the department of sciences and was accepted. He was then only sixteen. At fourteen he had passed his first university entrance examination, or *bachot.* He had always been accepted with the mention "very good," and in elementary mathematics he had a point total that is rarely attained. These successes of his, combined with Mlle. P.'s contempt, gave Simone an inferiority complex. She felt that she was very stupid compared to her brother.

That summer the Weil family took a trip in Belgium. They stayed for a while at Saint-Idesbald. While they were there, Simone disappeared one day at lunchtime. She finally reappeared about two or half past two; she had forgotten the time while reading *Crime and Punishment* in the dunes.

They also went to Knokke-le-Zoute. It was there that they took the snapshot in which Simone, sitting at a table out of doors next to André, is laughing so gaily, with all her heart.

Simone resumed the courses at Fénelon in October 1922. She did the whole year of the third form of upper school, still with the disagreeable Mlle P. as her teacher. This was the year that she fell into a "bottomless despair" because she thought she was not very gifted.

She thought seriously of dying. "I didn't mind having no visible successes, but what did grieve me was the idea of being excluded from that transcendent kingdom to which only the truly great have access and wherein truth abides. I preferred to die rather than live without that truth."[7] Yet in the depths of her despair she found a certitude that gave

---

*Class that prepares students to compete for entrance to the Ecole Normale.

her the strength to surmount it. She suddenly got the conviction that when it is a question of spiritual gifts, he who desires and makes every effort can finally obtain what he longs for. "After months of inner darkness, I suddenly had the everlasting conviction that any human being whatsoever, though practically devoid of natural gifts, can penetrate to the kingdom of truth reserved for genius, if only he longs for truth and perpetually concentrates all his attention upon its attainment. . . . Under the name of truth I also included beauty, virtue, and every kind of goodness. . . . The conviction that had come to me was that when one hungers for bread, one does not receive stones." She added, "But at that time I had not read the Gospels."[8]

In a photograph that appears to date from this period and that shows her among the students of her class, one can see that her legs were still bare and she wore short socks. She looks much younger than most of her classmates and gives an impression of vigor and gaiety. Only her hands betray some manual awkwardness. She already wore glasses.

At the beginning of the school year of 1923–1924, Simone, still at Fénelon, took the courses given in the fourth form A. These courses in principle make one eligible for a higher certificate, but in this class it was also possible to prepare for the *bachot.* However, Simone left the lycée at the end of December and prepared for the *bachot* by taking private lessons. But she also went regularly with her mother to hear Bédier's lectures on literature at the Collège de France. So when, at the oral *bachot,* she was questioned on the *Chanson de Roland,* the face of the old, bearded examiner lit up as she continued to answer his questions. She was accepted with the honorable mention of "very good."

According to a passage in her *Notebooks,*[9] it was when she was fifteen years old, that is, probably in 1924, which was the year of her first *bachot,* that Simone formed in her mind the image of an "unknown friend." She had a vital need of friendship; not finding among her acquaintances this ideal friend—she perhaps never would find him or her—she conjured up the figure of a distant, hidden, secret friend who she thought would be revealed to her one day.

The professor of philosophy at Fénelon had the reputation of being mediocre. Simone had heard people say that Le Senne, the professor at Victor-Duruy, was a fine philosopher. She enrolled in this lycée and soon became Le Senne's best pupil. He was to write on her student's exercise book that she could be numbered among the five or six most brilliant students he had encountered in the course of his career. A disciple of Hamelin, he professed an absolute idealism that Simone seemed to agree with. Yet he was chiefly interested in psychology, whereas Simone's keenest interest at the time was sociology; the author she studied most that year was Durkheim.

Already concerned with the study of character traits, Le Senne once defined Simone's character as "a secondary active emotional type," that is, "passionate." Simone was indignant because of this last word.

When she arrived at Duruy, she was disagreeably surprised by this lycée's worldly atmosphere. In comparison, at Fénelon, the social classes had been more mixed together and there were few rich girls. However, Simone made a close friend at Duruy. Among her classmates she met a girl named Suzanne Gauchon, who later married Raymond Aron, the well-known sociologist. Simone was very attached to her. Outside her family she was certainly one of the two or three persons for whom Simone had the warmest and deepest feelings, at least until about her twenty-fifth year. At that time, that is to say about 1934, she would again advise herself to return to the idea of the unknown friend.[10] But as late as 1932, when she was teaching at Le Puy, she sent Suzanne Gauchon a photograph showing her with her students and on the back she wrote Coûfontaine's words in Claudel's play *L'Otage* [The Hostage]: "My sharing was with my comrades, my faith and my hope, and my heart rested in a heart made like mine."[11]

It should be said that by uttering these words, Coûfontaine expresses a regret; he has never really shared. Suzanne Aron later said about Simone, "She had a desperate desire for tenderness, communion, friendship, and she didn't always discover the secret of how to obtain what she desired so deeply." She thought that Simone as the years went by became more and more solitary, but that in a sense she had always been solitary.

Through Suzanne, Simone got to know Edwige Copeau, whom her friends called Edi, and who in the Catholic Church has become Mother François Copeau, General Superior of the Benedictine missionaries. She had been a student at Duruy until her first *bachot*, but that year she was living in Bourgogne, where her father, Jacques Copeau, the famous playwright and director, had retired with a small group of disciples. Simone was not to meet her until the end of the school year, or perhaps only in the fall of 1925. For several years they met from time to time, at Suzanne's house, and they would then have discussions about religion.

Having been accepted for the *bachot* exams in philosophy at the end of June 1925, Simone took a trip with her parents and her brother to the Alps. At nineteen, her brother had just been accepted at the very top of the list in the competitive examination for teaching posts in mathematics. They stayed at Lanskevillard, in the Maurienne region. It was perhaps at the Evettes ice field that she saw the mountain landscape that gave her so profound an impression of the concept of purity.[12]

During this summer the Weils also stayed at the Hôtel du Château in Challes-les-Eaux. Mme. Weil took the cure. Simone established friendly relations with the chambermaids, the porter, the desk clerk, the bellhop, and the other employees at the hotel. She told them that they were being made to work too hard and advised them to organize a union. In the evening they would gather in the garden to talk together while the hotel's guests, among them her parents and Senator Lisbonne, who had Dr. Weil as his doctor, chatted in the hotel's salon. One evening a furious guest at the hotel said in a very loud voice, as he entered the salon, "If a person has such ideas, what is she doing at the Hôtel du Château?"

In October Simone became a first-year student in the upper form at Henri IV Lycée. It is the class that students call *la cagne,* or the preparatory course for the exams for the Ecole Normale. Since the previous year, girls were now being admitted. Like André, Simone wanted to enter the Ecole Normale at rue d'Ulm and above all she wanted to attend Alain's lectures.

2

The Encounter with Alain

Simone always thought of Le Senne with esteem, affection, and gratitude, but his philosophy does not appear to have had a lasting effect on her. On the other hand, it seems certain to me that she owes to Alain an essential part of her thought. For this reason a kind of boundary line can be marked out here, a new birth. Just as every artist starts from a work of art and not from the direct apprehension of nature, so every philosopher derives from a previous philosophy. This is true even of the greatest ones. It was, in my opinion, in Alain's class that Simone's philosophy began to take shape.

Yet from a certain point of view she had already chosen her road. The revolt against the social order, the feelings of indignation and severity toward the powers-that-be, the choice of the poor as comrades and companions—all this had not come from Alain. These are almost innate characteristics that linked her to him in advance. Besides, he did not preach violent revolt; on the contrary, in most situations he preached obedience; he believed that revolt almost always ended by reinforcing the powers-that-be and making the citizen more of a slave. But he did spread a spirit of inquiry, of resistance, the determination to judge freely and to keep the powers-that-be—which in Alain's view *always* want to tyrannize—within their just limits through the force of control exerted by opinion. Perhaps Simone owes to him the deepening of her feeling of revolt, the discernment of the real causes of tyranny, and the rejection of false solutions that lead to an even more onerous tyranny. She certainly owed him some part of the lucidity and forceful-ness of the thought that she later displayed in her political writings. Without him, she most likely would have wasted her devotion in the service of some political party. But in her determination to be always on the side of the slave she joined hands with her teacher rather than having formed this attitude on the basis of his doctrine. This was in her, as in him, an instinctive emotion and character trait that existed prior to any philosophical belief.

What's more, her character had in general already been formed. The stories about her childhood show her to have been sociable, passionately loving friendship and a loyal friend, very charitable, indignant against injustice but not against those injustices of which she personally was the victim; courageous, patient, and capable of unshakable will; intelligent, yet without her brother's extraordinary facility; achieving knowledge to some extent by strength of will and conscientious work, because of a determined effort to learn and a desire to do well; slow at manual work, where she encountered her greatest difficulties; interested in all the major problems and already exhibiting an avidity to know about everything that mattered and to gather the necessary instruments to solve all the great problems as fully as possible, and to concentrate solely on what she considered to be essential, which in fact was her most remarkable trait. While still a child, she had resolutely determined to make something out of her life and she feared above all to fail or "waste" her death.

Her appearance, when she entered Henri IV, was already pretty much what it would be for the rest of her life. A small, thin face, which seemed to be devoured by her hair and glasses. A fine-boned delicate nose, dark eyes that looked out boldly, a neck that strained forward and gave the impression of a burning, almost indiscreet curiosity; but her full mouth gave one a feeling of sweetness and good nature. Looking at them carefully, her features do not lack charm and even beauty; it was a face at once insolent and tender, bold in asking questions but with a timid smile that seemed to mock itself. But what about those heavy, rather forbidding eyeglasses or that air of always inquiring, knowing, judging? Her charm remained hidden from most people, who saw in Simone only a totally intellectual being. Her body was thin, her gestures lively but also clumsy. She wore clothes with a masculine cut, always the same outfit (a kind of suit with a very wide skirt and a long, narrow jacket), and always flat-heeled shoes. She never put on a hat, which at this time in the upper middle class was very unusual. All this made for a singular personality that evoked the image of the revolutionary intelligentsia and that, for this or some other reason, had the power to irritate many people, sometimes to the point of fury, and still does irritate them.

At the start Alain himself perhaps had a feeling of peasant distrust in the presence of a creature so little of the earth and so strange. I learned later that he called her "the Martian" (I don't know whether she ever knew of this). Much later he explained that this meant "that she had nothing of us and sovereignly judged us all."[1] But perhaps at first he had thought of H. G. Wells's Martians, who are all eyes and brain. I recall that when she handed in her first composition in class, which he thought to be good in some respects, he reproached her for a lack of style and observed of her manner of writing that it was the "style of a typewriter." There was a harshness in this observation that he certainly regretted, for at her very next composition he did not forget to say that she had a style like everyone else and even went out of his way to insist on this. But his initial judgment had perhaps been somewhat influenced or provoked by the impression that many people first had when confronted by Simone, the impression that some element of common humanity was missing in her—the very thickness of nature, so to speak.

Indeed, one senses that many of her old classmates, when they finally read her writings, were surprised to discover that she was so human. I myself was astonished by the incredible sensitivity she revealed. Certainly, when it came to generosity, a concern and pity for others, nobody has ever denied that she had these qualities, and in the highest, most selfless forms. In this sense, she was more human than anyone else. But what was hard to believe was that she had the ordinary human frailties. One might even think that she didn't have the same needs or the same desires as others, that she was not wounded or hurt by the same things. She forbade herself all weakness with such firm determination that one could mistake for a peculiarity of her nature what was in truth a product of her will.

As for the plans she had already formed, her whole conception of what she wanted to do with her life, it was—as she herself later said— a great misfortune to have been born a female. So she had decided to reduce this obstacle as much as possible by disregarding it, that is to say, by giving up any desire to think of herself as a woman or to be regarded as such by others, at least for a set period of time. It was perhaps this that made many people consider her in some way inhuman. A woman is expected, to the extent that she is natural, to let us see her feminine nature. But Simone wanted to express this side of herself as little as possible.

Her family would chaff her affectionately about her wish to be treated as a boy, and she too made jokes about it. Her parents called her "Simon," "our son number two," and "our *cagne* boy." When Simone wrote to her mother while at Henri IV, she even went so far as to speak of herself in the masculine gender and to sign her letters "your respectful son." There was in all this a touch of playfulness and a sign of extreme youth. But if it had been only a game, it would not have gone on for so long. Behind this game lay serious reasons, that is, the tasks that Simone had envisaged for herself and that would above all demand of her masculine qualities and strengths. It is not always possible to prevent the inner, profounder resolution from making its outward appearance.

It should furthermore be said that Mme. Weil had tried to develop masculine virtues in her daughter instead of a feminine personality. In a letter to Mlle. Chaintreuil, speaking of a little girl who was with them in the family pension at Plessis-Piquet, Mme. Weil had written: "This is the kind of little girl I have come across many times, the kind that leads me to like and esteem boys much more! The levity, the lack of forth-rightness, all these little posturings and grimaces in the eyes of the world. ... I shall always prefer the good little boys, boisterous and sincere, as I see them coming out of the Lycée Montaigne. And I do my best to encourage in Simone not the simpering graces of a little girl but the forthrightness of a boy, even if this must at times seem rude."[2]

Simone's determination to live like a man partly explains her unusual dress, for which some people still criticize her. It is true that there were other reasons. The most important was undoubtedly the lack of time, the fact that this outfit did not require much preparation or forethought. This was the reason she herself presented later on. One day in London, when Maurice Schumann told her in a kindly way that her insistence on being so different and unusual in her style of life and the way she dressed could be misunderstood, even by her friends, she argued, with tears starting in her eyes, in her defense, pointing to her poor state of health, her perpetual struggle with headaches, and the fact that she had very little energy at her disposal. And, indeed, when one thinks of all that she accomplished in her short life, it is understandable that she didn't have the leisure to shop for dresses.

In any event, her way of dressing became more and more that of a poor person or a monk, who dresses as cheaply as possible and devotes the least amount of time he can to it. I also have the feeling that it came to shock people less and less, either because it seemed less and less a willfully unusual costume or because women's dress itself evolved in such a way as to resemble it.

But when she was still young there was some element of willfulness in her manner of dressing; in fact, it seems to me that she really liked to dress like this. I remember once that her mother wanted her to go to the Opéra, and Simone agreed to have made for her not an evening gown but a tuxedo—a jacket and skirt in black cloth, the jacket being quite similar to that of a man's suit. This certainly cost as much as an evening gown and she undoubtedly had to have a fitting for it. It was therefore a deliberate act based on premeditated prejudices. It was certainly not an affectation. But it should be recognized that she was determined to be a man as much as possible. This resolve could seem childish if it had not been linked with specific, profoundly willed projects, and, moreover, projects that were actually carried out.

(There are perhaps still other reasons: the peculiar ideas that doctors' families often have about dress; Simone's revolutionary inclinations, combined with her contempt for bourgeois customs and her sense of mischief, which sometimes gave her pleasure in shocking people. And, finally, it might be thought that since she felt she was ugly, she had in her youth definitively renounced the normal life of a woman. This last reason does not seem to me to be a valid one, whereas I feel that there is some element of truth in all the others. As one can see from a letter to one of her students that Simone wrote later on,[3] she had decided not to think of love until she felt satisfied that what she wanted to do in her life had been fully achieved. So it was a matter of vocation; and she was not certain that she did not have another vocation. She was too shy to think that she could be loved as a woman, but instead tended to think that she could not. But nothing allows us to suppose that she had made up her mind about this in her early youth, and whatever her humility may have been, it is not likely that it was due to a kind of despair that she turned away from the customary path.)

Thus several motivations, and especially her desire to accomplish something for the good of humanity, had led her to adopt this dress that astonished and scandalized so many people. But on the other hand, one might truly consider her extreme intellectual rigor, her merciless logic, and the intransigent will she expressed in everything she did as alien to our everyday world. And all this could summon up the image of an inflexible, cold intellectual mechanism. This no doubt is the source of the observation made by an old *cagne* classmate, whom Marie-Magdeleine Davy quotes: "I knew Simone Weil at Henri IV; she was completely aloof and unsociable."[4]

However, this was an extreme reaction. Most of her classmates did not consider her unsociable, or at least not for long. At the start they were more tempted to make fun of her; it seems that she was actually the butt of a practical joke.[5] But if some students were for a long time mildly amused by certain things about her, the malicious mockery stopped quite soon. Yet they were amazed by her and inclined to regard her as rather odd. Though certainly she was not an "intellectual monster," as someone has remarked. She had both a very ardent and a very pure sensibility. (At bottom she was overly sensitive and actually had to *create* her courage.) In plain fact, she was a strange mixture of coldness and passion; on the one hand, there was in her something reasonable, rigorous, calm, and slow, while, on the other, there were lively, often awkward, often naive and charming impulses, together with a blaze of enthusiasm and long moments of violent indignation. But it was precisely in her sensitivity that she could seem different from most people, no doubt because to a rare degree she seemed to forget all personal interest or desire and became excited only for noble causes and with no concern for herself, giving rein to her violence solely for the general welfare and the truth. In a sense, her pride was great, but she was not thin-skinned; she was not concerned about wounds to her feeling of self-esteem, and even sought out those who did not like her. She seemed without resentment or anger for everything that involved only herself; she did not try to please and consequently was not timid in her relations with her classmates. Even her clumsiness seemed to spring from the fact that she was not made out of the same crude materials as the rest of us. She was truly different in the sense that she was already well above the common level, owing to the purity of her emotions and the strength of her character even more than to her intelligence.

Yet one senses that she was not always kind and gentle. She seemed to think that she had to be rough. Besides, she could be thoughtless and disproportionate in her reactions, still being very young, after all. Her violence could hurt people more and in a different way from what she would have wished. During the years at Henri IV and the Ecole Normale, there no doubt existed in her, fed by the fires of youth, too great a feeling of scorn. It would take her some time before she got rid of the habit of cutting, peremptory judgments, lofty condemnations, and disdain for the outward forms of courtesy. Some people thought that they could still detect arrogance in the objections that she later brought against the Catholic Church, but, on the contrary, those who knew her at the time of her studies find in these objections a measure and prudence, a feeling of consideration that were not part of her usual manner when she was younger. Later on, she allowed people to see more of her real nature, and spoke more about herself and her deepest desires, so that one could imagine what she was suffering and even that she was after all a woman. This grain of weakness added to her abiding intransigent will and rigorous intelligence would in some curious fashion make her more perfect. So, in this sense, it would be true to say that when she was a student, she had not yet attained full humanity. But what she achieved since that time was perhaps the most difficult thing to achieve, and at the beginning she had to cultivate her courage and forbid herself any weakness, so that afterward her weakness, or the slight traces of weakness, became even more moving and beautiful.

But now we must return to Alain's class.

I believe that Simone's philosophy was built at the start on Alain's and extends it, even when it appears to be opposed to it. So it seems to me quite necessary to explain Alain's philosophy.

One feels some shame in trying to summarize it, since Alain himself looked askance at all such attempts. He thought that a system is a paltry thing and that a thinker's strength can be best seen in the way he tackles specific problems. He never tried to sum up his doctrine; on the contrary, he seems to have taken precautions to make sure that it can never be torn from the body of his entire work. His thought, scattered over thousands of his brief essays called *Propos,* was always tied to a particular situation, a particular object, a style, and that's how he wanted it to be, having only contempt for that which can be put in summary form. Furthermore, he most likely would have denied that he had a doctrine. He did not claim to be saying anything new but simply that he understood what had been said for a long time and is in fact common thought. (The same attitude can be found in Simone, who writes: "Not to understand the new but to succeed by the strength of patience, effort and method to understand the obvious truths with all of one's being."[6]) Nevertheless, there was something that Alain's disciples called "the doctrine." These were certain ideas that they thought they had to defend and by which one recognized Alain's disciples. (And, by the way, the examiners at the competitive examinations for the Ecole Normale were never in any doubt about this.) This doctrine, which at least existed among his disciples, was it they who had fabricated it and would all of them have fabricated the same one? In fact, Alain did indeed have a doctrine, whether he wanted to or not. But how can one convey a form of teaching whose first article is that it must not be summarized? Nevertheless, we had an idea of it at the time, whether it was true or false, and it is this idea that is important for our purpose. So it is necessary to try to recall what this "doctrine" meant for us.

To begin with, it seems to me that it was contained in a certain number of bold and paradoxical affirmations that ran counter to the most widespread philosophical teachings of this period. One should certainly not conclude from this that Alain was greatly taken up with polemics. It was above all in presenting what was true that he rejected what was false, and the greatness of his teaching can be found in what is positive in it: a profound analysis of perception, admirable lessons in reading the great philosophers (and in general the great writers), and a method for learning how to think by means of a severe act of attention brought to bear on the art of writing. But I am trying to say what this teaching was *for us* and what we had in mind when we called it "the doctrine." It seems to me that for us it was profoundly distinct from other ways of teaching, and if we had been asked to define it, it is probable that we would have defined it first of all by comparing it to the other methods. The critical aspect of Alain's thought was important for his students, who, moreover, had a tendency to go beyond him, to exaggerate; it was certainly important for Simone. With regard to the great themes of philosophy, Alain based his teaching on a series of affirmations that attacked head-on all the reigning commonplaces and clichés. For example, he affirmed that:

—psychology cannot be a science in the ordinary sense of the word; there cannot be, properly speaking, *facts* of consciousness, or indeed there is only one, which is thought as a whole;

—thought is not produced by starting with the sensations, but instead it is sensation that is elaborated by means of all of our thought;

—the inferior degrees of consciousness do not exist except through the superior degrees;

—the unconscious does not exist as a psychological phenomenon; what is unconscious pertains to the body alone;

—psychological consciousness cannot be separated from moral conscience; there is only one consciousness and it is born when one poses the moral question; there is no consciousness without scruples; the idea of the good is the supreme idea, which gives birth to all others;

—the will for the good, or simply the will, involves the entire life of the mind;

—there is no such thing as an evil will; will and evil mutually exclude each other; the alternative is not between willing good and willing evil but between willing and not willing;

—the beginning of morality is even more "I want" than "I must," since what I must do is to be free, that is to say, to will;

—there is no will that is not free; if it is not free, it does not exist; what is not free does not have will but rather desire and passion;

—to will without doing does not exist; intention is not will, resolution is not will; the will does not exist except in action;

—there is no problem of choice; the function of the will is not to choose; the action has always already begun; the function of the will is to settle on a choice and to make it count;

—one can change the evil past into a good by the way one continues it; every man begins by fooling himself and by being a slave to passion, but even error and passion can be the material out of which one can fashion freedom;

—the imagination does not exist, in one sense; it is imaginary itself; we do not produce in our minds images that are akin to photographs of the objects; what we call the image is only the consciousness of certain movements of our bodies that lead us to believe that we are before objects and see them, when in reality we see nothing;

—the dream does not exist as a distinct phenomenon; we have only some more or less elaborated perceptions; the dream is a perception aborning and still very imperfect;

—there is no problem about the existence of the exterior world; the mind can think only by perceiving; it thinks only that which exists (whether or not it represents it to itself more or less accurately);

—nevertheless the forms and principles by which man seizes what exists come from him and not from things; and the more he is himself and faithful to himself, faithful to his principles, the better he knows things as they really are;

—the forms and principles of science are simply the principles of perception, and science is valuable only when joined to perception;

—judgment joined to perception has more value and is truer than reasoning;

—the project, for the artist, is a paltry thing and has no artistic value; the artist does not create beauty by copying an interior model that would be even more beautiful than the work realized, but he acts first of all and looks at what he does, and he continues according to what he has done, in this way gradually discovering, thanks to work and in the work itself, a beautiful form that he could not foresee;

—so it is by work and judgment that one attains the beautiful, not by some mysterious faculty of invention;

—genius in the arts and in thought lies above all in the will; it is of the same nature as heroism and saintliness; there is no profound distinction between the man of thought, the man of action, and the artist;

—there is a doubt that is not a hesitation among several beliefs but a way of being free, of stepping back to look at one's beliefs, without necessarily wanting to change them;

—faith, which is will, is not incompatible with doubt, quite the contrary; doubt is found in all true thought, and is the sign of reason;

—an idea is not true by itself, independent of the thinker: it is not right to speak of a true idea but rather of true thoughts, of true men (which does not mean that the truth is subjective and relative);

—attention is not, as one ordinarily describes it, the fact of being filled and as though hypnotized by a single object, a single thought; on the contrary, true attention is vibrant with doubt and freedom;

—attention is contemplation and exerts itself chiefly when one cannot change the object; ordinarily, one does not know the object on which one can act; the slave knows the master, not the master the slave; science has not come principally from the professions, trades, and external action but from religious contemplation;

—habit properly so-called is not something that enchains but that delivers; custom enchains, whereas habit is the possession of oneself that springs from exercise, etc.

Thus, for us, "the doctrine" meant rejecting and refuting many weak, false ideas that filled the textbooks as well as the courses of a good many professors. But contempt does not nourish the soul. Indeed, it was much more admiration than contempt that nourished Alain's disciples. For he admired the great and true philosophers just as much as he scorned the false ones. He especially worshipped Plato, Descartes, and Kant, and also Lagneau, who had been his teacher. One of his most energetic denials was that of the idea of progress in philosophy. He thought that Plato not only had not been left behind but was far ahead of us. He saw in the great thinkers heroes of the will even more than princes of the intelligence, or rather they were princes of the intelligence because they were heroes of the will. He wanted them to be right in everything, even in their mistakes. For a vigorous mind does not delude itself in the way that a weak mind does, and even in its error one can find some truth. He found a way to salvage the theory of the pineal gland in Descartes, and the blasting of the fig tree in the Gospels. He certainly had his prejudices, but he knew it and wanted them. He had absolutely no respect for those who changed their party or their religion; once a choice was made or given, he thought that one must stick to it and should strive to make it good. It is in this that the will consists, not in choice, which is a matter of chance. This was his attitude to religion, and he approved of Comte for having said, about the *Imitation*, that understanding must follow faith and not precede it or, even less, disrupt it. He even went so far as to say, "Only the stupid change their opinions," and "Only the man who believes thinks." As he put it, "Attention is religious or it is nothing."

But it was not only in this way that he was religious, and people have usually contrasted his thought too sharply to Simone's. It is true that in his lectures he spoke little about religion, avoiding everything that might shock believers or nonbelievers. He did not speak much about God, except when he commented on the philosophers and the other writers whom he dealt with. But it was clear that if he was anticlerical, he was not at all anti-Christian—rather the exact opposite. To define what his Christianity actually was would have been difficult for us since we were not very familiar with his writings, and even for those who knew his writings this was still an extremely difficult problem. But it was known that he approved of his teacher Lagneau, who on the one hand had taught that "God cannot be said to exist" and, on the other, that one cannot form any thought if the reality of God is not postulated in some manner. One could understand that he distinguished on one hand a "God-object," which is not the true God, and, on the other, the true God that is fundamentally mind, value, and perfection. The God that exists in the exterior world was for him the God-object ("what is it to exist if not to be caught in the context of experience?"[7]); the true God *must be* instead of existing, properly speaking; he is the perfection to which it is necessary to conform, whether or not he exists in the world of things. He manifestly believed in the soul as distinct from the body, while refusing to affirm what that would mean in terms of the survival of the soul after death (simply saying, with Socrates: "It is a fine risk to run"). He used the expression "save his soul," but in the sense that one must save one's soul in this life itself, at each instant. Finally, he sometimes evoked, with visible admiration, the images that Christianity had rendered popular: the Crucified One, the Virgin and Child, and the saints. He found in them an inexhaustible source of truth. To have been able, despite the social condemnation, to recognize in an executed criminal the highest value was in his eyes a moment of intelligence and insight that could not be surpassed. André Maurois could write with complete justification: "Alain was most likely anticlerical, yet he was certainly religious. Few men have been able to speak more intelligently about Christianity. Indeed, he was the first man to reveal to me the greatness of Christian doctrine and induce me to accept so large a part of it."[8]

His philosophy course was held three times a week, each time for two hours. Two times out of the three he started out by talking for about an hour on some philosophical or literary work. At the beginning of each school year, Alain would choose two great authors whom we studied, an hour a week devoted to each throughout almost the entire year. One author was a philosopher, the other a poet, novelist, or essayist. In 1925 we studied Plato and Balzac, most of the dialogues of the former and most of the novels of the latter. In 1926–1927, the works commented upon were, I believe, Kant's *Critiques* and Homer's *Iliad*—perhaps also, at the end of the year, Marcus Aurelius's *Meditations* and Lucretius' poem. In 1925–1926 the course dealt with psychology (understood in Alain's particular way, that is to say, openly involving logic, morality, and metaphysics). The following year it dealt with the history of philosophy. I know that the next year he gave a course on Hegel, but I don't know whether this involved commentary on a particular work of Hegel's or was the main course. I had then left Henri IV, because I had entered the lycée a year before Simone and got out a year before her.

During the hour when we studied a given work, a student would present a brief description of what we had had to read for that day, and then would read the passages he had chosen or Alain had pointed out to him. But after this Alain spoke, and he alone. There were no questions and no discussions. Sometimes he would call a student to the blackboard to write out a plan for a dissertation, but the role of the student was soon confined to writing what was dictated to him. So Alain spoke without being interrupted, giving the impression of reflecting as he went along and not thinking of us, his blue eyes looking as though they had withdrawn far into the distance, and never more naive, innocent, and purposeless than when his mind was preparing to throw out a piercing remark, whereupon he was suddenly most alert, sharp, and mischievous.

The essays we wrote for him at our pleasure were called *topos* or "topical essays" and were on subjects freely chosen by us. He urged us to write as much as possible, convinced that to learn how to write well was to learn how to think well. Besides regularly assigning us (about every three weeks) dissertations on subjects he chose, he advised us to get down on paper the ideas that occurred to us on any subject whatsoever and to show him this work.

Some of the *topos* or rough drafts for *topos* that Simone preserved are dated, which permits us to know to some extent what thoughts she had formed and in what order she formed them during the years when she was in Alain's class.

Even those of her compositions that do not bear dates can sometimes be dated approximately, thanks to the handwriting or some other circumstance. It is thus that one can regard as the oldest of all, with great probability, a composition whose beginning is missing but whose handwriting shows that it was written during the first term of the 1925–1926 school year, and, moreover, from its contents one can see that it was probably a dissertation on "The Imagination in Perception"; in fact,

Alain assigned us that subject in October 1925—it was the first dissertation of the year. In this fragment Alain's influence is already as obvious as it will be in the subsequent work. The idea expressed in it is that the "images" created by our imagination do not have the form of objects and are not kinds of painting but consist solely in the movements of our bodies, in an attitude and gestures, and actually are not images and change nothing in the appearances of things. The examples Simone presents are generally the same as Alain's. The thought still seems hesitant and the beautifully worded definitions or formulas, which Alain would approve of in the margin by a *t.b.* (*très bien*), are still rare.

But after this, the next oldest composition is no doubt a short *topo* that is dated November 1925 and is remarkable. It is, I believe, the first of Simone's essays that Alain judged to be excellent. Its subject is "The Fairy Tale of the Six Swans in Grimm," which tells the story of six brothers whose stepmother, a witch, had changed them into swans. To restore them to human form their sister must spin and sew six nightshirts for them out of white anemones and cannot speak at all while the work is going on. She takes six years to make the shirts. Her silence puts her in great danger, for she is exposed to accusations to which she cannot reply. Finally, when she is on the point of being sent to the gallows, the swans appear, she throws the shirts made of anemones on them, and once again they assume human form; so she is saved, for now she can justify herself. This is how Simone comments on this story: "To act is never difficult: we always act too much and scatter ourselves ceaselessly in disorderly deeds. To make six shirts from anemones and to keep silent: this is our only way of acquiring power. . . . Whoever spends six years sewing white anemones cannot be distracted by anything; they are perfectly pure flowers; but above all anemones are almost impossible to sew into shirts, and this difficulty prevents any other action from altering the purity of this six-year silence. The sole strength in the world is purity; all that which is without admixture is a fragment of the truth. Never have iridescent silks been worth as much as a beautiful diamond. . . . The sole strength and sole virtue is to cease from acting. . . ."

It will be observed that Simone depicts the sister's work as an abstention, a non-acting, rather than a directly useful action. It seems that for her it was the silence that saved rather than the shirts, the sacrifice more than the result of the sacrifice. "Here pure abstention acts," she says. The sufferings of the innocent redeem by themselves; a pure being acts through his mere existence; one is saved without apparent action. She will rediscover the same idea in her last writings. And one cannot help but think of the sacrifice that probably led to her death, that was not directly useful and was not an action, an intervention, but a refusal, an insistence on purity and loyalty to oneself. Besides, it is quite clear that though she usually seems to have pursued another ideal, having acted a great deal, in all of her acts she above all maintained the pure form of her soul, never yielding anything in spite of external obstacles.

One finds the same inspiration in the next *topo,* "The Beautiful and the Good," a long essay dated February 1926 and on which Alain has written as his comment "very beautiful."[9] At first she maintains that the moral act is not an act that conforms to this or that rule but is a free, unpredictable act, a creation like a work of art. She then says that this act is simply an act of purity and fidelity to oneself. But the center of the essay is a meditation on the story of Alexander, who, while crossing the desert and suffering from thirst like his soldiers, pours out on the ground, so as not to be more favored than they, the water that someone has brought him in a cask from a great distance away. "Nobody, much less Alexander, would have dared predict this astonishing deed; but once the deed is accomplished, there is nobody who does not have the feeling that it had to be like this." Therefore good and duty are created by the free will; they are not imposed on it. Simone then observes that ostensibly Alexander's act is not useful to anyone; it only safeguards Alexander's purity and humanity; but it is in this way that it is useful to everyone. "His well-being, if he had drunk, would have separated him from his soldiers. . . . Everything takes place in Alexander's soul, and for him it is simply a matter of taking the stance of a man. . . . So it suffices to be just and pure to save the world, which is an idea expressed by the myth of the Man-God who redeemed the sins of men by justice alone, without any political action. It is necessary therefore to save oneself, save the Spirit in oneself, of which external humanity is the myth. Sacrifice is the acceptance of pain, the refusal to obey the animal in oneself, and the will to redeem suffering men through voluntary suffering. Every saint has poured out the water; every saint has rejected all well-being that would separate him from the suffering of men. . . ." Words like these foreshadow Simone's entire life.

In these two *topos* one can find many of Alain's ideas. He taught that duty is above all to oneself and that in doing one's duty to oneself one cannot help but do it toward everyone. Like Diogenes, he felt that duty is defined by freedom (that is to say, self-mastery) and that there is no moral law that is imposed externally on man. For example, what is ugly in the lie is its cowardice, for a courageous lie like Sister Simplice's in *Les Misérables* is not ugly. So duty is not defined by an external law, by a rule such as "Do not lie," but by inner disposition. "If you could steal without the superior part of your soul being subjected to the inferior part, the theft would not be unjust." Moreover, he praises purity not only in human conduct but even in things, showing, for example, that there is beauty, even in a sense truth, in a pure color or a pure sound. Under certain conditions, he praises the person who abstains from acting in the external world, saying that, for instance, to think is to keep from acting, and that methodical experimentation, as opposed to blind experience, consists in acting as little as possible. One could even say that in certain cases he admired voluntary suffering. For example, he considered beautiful and human the custom of the savage who imposes suffering on himself while his wife is giving birth. He thought it laudable to impose certain tests on oneself. So a great part of the ideas here come from Alain. But it is not by chance that Simone was attracted principally to that part of the doctrine that concerned morality. Her own passion for the good and the moral met that of her teacher. She owed him something, but not everything.

One can speak of a sort of passion on Alain's part for morality. Though he was so mocking, so far from insipid, boring moralists, he was still as unskeptical as possible about morality itself. He naively and passionately admired beautiful deeds and could speak about them in an absolutely unique fashion, without any rhetoric. Perhaps he never taught anything but morality. In any event, for him the truth always was related to duty. According to him, those philosophical doctrines were true that implied the will to conduct oneself well, or, quite simply, the will in its pure state. Thus from this point of view, the Cartesian split between thought and extension (what is called Cartesian dualism) was true because it implies the will not to presume the existence in the body of any thought or mystery and to run it as resolutely as one runs a machine. For him, all greatness and beauty had a connection with duty. Simone had understood this. It appears that in a letter to Edi Copeau, which she wrote during her first months at Henri IV, she tried to explain Alain's doctrine to her friend by telling her that for him all greatness is moral. In those few words his doctrine was summed up as well as it could be.

In her second *topo,* Simone had said: "Sacrifice is the acceptance of pain." Sometime later while at Poët she said to me, "Alain's short-coming is to have rejected pain." I myself do not think that Alain rejected pain, but Simone wound up understanding it in this way, and no doubt that is how many people understand it. Yet during the period of her study under Alain, at least for the first year, it appears that she understood it quite differently. Or did she want to oppose him in this *topo*? It does not seem plausible to me and I have no recollection of her ever trying to oppose him in class, at least as regards philosophical problems. (In politics she had perhaps at times already criticized him.) In any event, in these compositions we find the first impression she had gotten of Alain's morality, and this first impression was perhaps the most correct one. It is evident moreover that Alain had completely approved the compositions she had written. These two *topos,* and especially the passages I have quoted, bear many marks of approbation in his handwriting. The entire last passage I have quoted, from after "it suffices therefore to be just and pure," has the letters "t.b." in the margin.

Simone was to put the cult of will and self-mastery into practice even more fully than can be imagined from what she wrote or said. It was owing to this that she changed her handwriting while studying at Henri IV. Instead of a rather sloppy, almost careless, scrawled handwriting she developed a square, perpendicular, constructed, designed, and completely willed handwriting, which as time went on became progressively less rigid and more supple and, finally, attained the pure, beautiful script of her last years. This abrupt break occurred about the third or fourth month at Henri IV; she must have decided then to compel her weak hands to overcome their awkwardness. But there were other, more dismaying signs of her strength of will. For example, for a long time we saw a round, deep wound, like a burn, on the back of her left hand, which took a number of months to heal. She did not want to tell us what had caused it, but something made me think then—and I am still convinced of it—that in the course of one of her nights of work she had burned herself with a cigarette that she had had to hold steadily and firmly against her hand, either to test her will or to punish herself for some shortcoming that to someone else would doubtless seem unimportant.

Of all the great philosophers, it was certainly Descartes whom Simone then preferred and would prefer for a long time. Of course she also had a deep esteem for Plato and Kant, but it is Descartes whom she will choose as the subject for her diploma dissertation. During her first year of teaching at Le Puy, the large volumes of the Adam-Tannery edition were always open on the floor of her room. She would kneel down in order to be able to read them without moving them, and when she was preparing her lecture for class, she would crawl from volume to volume.

It is clear, however, that she had also reflected on Spinoza and in fact never condemned him as she did Aristotle. She admired in him the courageous, pure, and proud man who was poverty-stricken and independent—and also the serenity of the man who said, "Confronted by human emotions, one must neither laugh nor weep nor grow indignant, but understand," and "I will consider men's actions and appetites as though they were a matter of lines, surfaces, and volumes." Finally, she unquestionably owed something to Spinoza: his definition of the "third type of knowledge," the knowledge at once intuitive and rational that was in her opinion the perfect knowledge. What Spinoza says about this kind of knowledge made a great impression on her. She endeavored as much as possible through the mind alone to perceive each thing by apprehending all the rational relationships that form it and could be called its essence. She speaks later on in her *Notebooks* of this "ultra-Spinozist form of meditation" that she practiced while at Henri IV and that consisted of "contemplating an object fixedly with the mind, asking

39

myself, 'What is it?' without thinking of any other object or relating it to anything else, for hours on end."[10]

Reading her compositions, it becomes quite clear that Simone was sympathetic to Christianity and especially to Catholicism. She quotes some passages from the Old and New Testaments (she must surely have read at least the New Testament during her first year at Henri IV, if she hadn't read it earlier); sometimes she quotes a sentence from Pascal or Saint Augustine; she invokes Christian dogmas; and in everything, both the passages and the dogmas, she makes an effort to discover a real meaning. No doubt she generally interpreted them symbolically, but in the end she tried to find a point of agreement with them.

People's memories of her confirm what we know directly from her writings. She liked to visit churches, and not only the beautiful ones. Like Alain, she believed that the Church and its ceremony did the soul good by wisely predisposing and preparing the body. Edi Copeau, who since 1926 had been taking instruction in the Catholic religion and in 1927 had decided to become a nun, testifies that Simone through all this time surrounded her with "an ardent, almost tender approbation." In a postcard to Simone written in 1920 but alluding to a discussion that certainly had taken place when Simone was still in *cagne,* Edi Copeau said: "Recalling our discussion with Mme. G., in which we were both defenders of the Apostolic Roman Church." When Simone first entered the Ecole Normale, it is said that Professor Bouglé described her as "a combination of anarchist and church fanatic." I have been told that after having read a paper before him somewhat later, he said, "After that, mademoiselle, there is nothing left for you but to enter a convent." Raymonde Nathan, Simone's cousin, remembers that at the period which was probably that of *cagne,* or the first year of the Ecole Normale, she talked with Simone about Pascal's conversion and expressed her indignation at what seemed a ridiculous weakness in him, saying, "I don't understand how one can believe in God"—she was quite young —and Simone replied, "What I can't understand is how one cannot believe in God."

Here, however, we must be on our guard, for Simone wrote later on: "Since adolescence, I saw the problem of God as a problem the data for which are lacking here below and I decided that the only way of being sure not to reach a false solution, which seemed to me the greatest possible evil, was not to pose it at all. So I did not pose it. I neither affirmed nor denied."[11] Besides, she even goes so far as to say that she had professed atheism: "In order to obey God, one must receive his commands. How did it happen that I received them in adolescence, while I was professing atheism?"[12] Her reply to Raymonde Nathan simply meant that she agreed with Descartes when he said that one can be assured of nothing so long as one is not assured of the existence of God, and that she approved of Lagneau, who, while he thought that the word "existence" was badly chosen, found a real meaning in Descartes's statement. Simone certainly approved of Descartes and also of Lagneau, for whom Alain had communicated to us so much enthusiasm that several of us were, because of Alain, more disciples of Lagneau than of Alain himself. So she had faith in God, in a sense—but this God was only the perfect thought, the God of the philosophers, a God who can be sought but who never seeks for you.

Among the essays she wrote while in *cagne,* there is one that demonstrates quite well the significance and limits of her belief in God. "I would agree to call God my freedom," she writes. "This convention has the advantage of delivering me completely from the God-object and at the same time it establishes the fact that the mode of God's reality is not existence or essence but what Lagneau called value. On the other hand, it is clear that God, if he was not and did not exist, would be less than an abstraction, since an abstraction is at least thought, whereas God cannot be abstract. Now if God is my freedom, he is and exists every time that my freedom is manifested in my ideas and my movements, that is to say, every time that I think. But this is only a matter of words, and I am as alone with this God as without him."

Alain's appraisals of the student Simone Weil, which he formulated at the end of each trimester over a period of three years are worth quoting.

For the first trimester of the year 1925–1926: "She has cogency, lucidity, and often wit and distinction in her powers of analysis. Her overall perspectives are less clear; she has to learn how to construct a coherent argument. She already shows an inventive mind and much may be expected of her."

For the second trimester: "Excellent student, who learns, forms herself, and develops with admirable rapidity and assurance. Her style lags a trifle behind her ideas, but one can predict brilliant results that may well prove astonishing."

For the third trimester: "An excellent student, who is capable of far-ranging ideas and whose appreciation of the best authors is of the utmost originality. The results are almost always of the first order, though not without a certain lees of obscurity from which she will eventually free herself."

For the first trimester of the year 1926–1927: "Very fine student, greatly gifted, who should, above all, be on her guard against over-abstruse reflections expressed in almost impenetrable language. She knows perfectly well, however, how to compose her essays, elucidate her arguments, and arrange her thoughts in writing. Her success depends upon herself."

For the second trimester: "Progress with respect to the examination. She has made an effort to give another direction to her profound and abstract subtleties of thought, which are for her a game, and to concentrate them on direct analysis. Her style is healthy and strong. Her success seems to me unquestioned."

For the third trimester: "Considerable power and consistency, though at times a trifle arid and abstract, and sometimes goes too fast and without sufficient preparation. Her examination thesis cannot fail to be outstanding."

For the first trimester of the year 1927–1928: "An already quite broad culture; a powerful and rare mind. Her thoughts at times outdistance her class exercises. As a consequence, an understandable abstruseness, which at times paralyzes her capacity for giving form and structure to her thoughts. Nevertheless, one can predict a brilliant success."

For the second trimester: "Brilliant in her reflections, great force. Her development of ideas sometimes a bit abstract. Laudable effort to conform to the rules of the student exercises. Excellent student."

For the third trimester: "Excellent student. I look forward to a brilliant success."[13]

3

Preparing for the Examination for the Ecole Normale (1925-1928)

I soon became Simone's friend. I do not know how this happened because I had nothing that could please her and still did not understand her very well. But her serious search for the truth attracted to her all those who were searching for it too, even if with much less energy. She would drag you into a discussion, force you to clarify what you thought, and soon you found yourself embarked on a common enterprise. In a short while I also became aware of her generosity, her courage, and the purity of her interests and concerns. My parents were rather unhappy about my friendship with her, for people said that she was a communist, and one day it just popped into my head to say to them that she was a saint, and when I thought about it later I realized that it was true.

Sometimes we would take walks together (very infrequently, for I lived on the outskirts of Paris and was almost always in a rush to catch the train at the Gare du Nord, to which I would go by subway). I can see her again in the street, heedless of the cars and escaping them by sheer chance (she claimed that a charm protec'ed her from them). Sometimes we walked to the Luxembourg Gardens. She showed me a path that was almost always deserted, in a corner of the park that was wilder than the rest. She loved this path and had named it after Jean-Jacques Rousseau. She loved Jean-Jacques, as I did, too.

There were times when she would ride in the subway with me. One day in the subway she looked at some workers and said to me, "It's not only out of a spirit of justice that I love them. I love them naturally. I find them more beautiful than the bourgeois." She was very sensitive to ugliness and the absurdity of what passed for beautiful among the bourgeois.

She would come to visit me at Soisy-sous-Montmorency, where I then lived. My father one day absent-mindedly called her Mlle. Levy, which made her blush. On another occasion it was I who was very clumsy. Some students in the Latin Quarter were shouting the name of the newspaper they were selling and added, "Anti-foreigner and antiyid." I hadn't heard them clearly and asked her what they had said. She told me and explained, "It's a name they give the Jews," and then blushed. I hope that that was the only time I hurt her by such thoughtless behavior.

She took me to her home. I was charmed by her parents' kindness and marveled at their culture, intelligence, freedom of opinion, and obvious talent for organizing their lives. Their gaiety charmed me, too. They had a lively, pretty maid named Suzanne who would tell everyone that the whole family was crazy, and when she said it, the Weils would all laugh.

Once I went to visit them in the country at Chevreuse. With Simone, I paddled a canoe on a small, very narrow stream that crossed the property of her family's friends. This was the first time I had ever paddled a canoe. We also went for walks. She showed me paths that plunged deep into the woods and said, "Unfortunately, there's always a sign that prohibits you from taking them." She told me that there were many nightingales in this wood and that you could hear them singing in the evening. The garden that surrounded their house was very large but uncultivated; the grass was high and the bushes grew wild, but they liked it that way.

One day when I had come with my mother to see Mme. Weil, she told us that Simone had been very upset in her childhood when she discovered that she, her mother, sometimes lied. These were little white lies of no importance, the kind you tell for convenience, such as saying that you're out when you didn't want to receive visitors. Simone insisted on the truth in small as well as large matters. It should also be said that when she was very young, she was not concerned about being polite, whereas her mother wanted her to be polite and behave properly.

Simone felt that there should not be the slightest discrepancy between one's beliefs and one's way of life. One day she said to me, when we were talking about people who do not live in accordance with their principles, "What I cannot bear is that they compromise." In those days she would make a horizontal, cutting gesture with her hand that seemed to express the very essence of her intransigence. This gesture cut sharply between high and low, repudiating everything that was low.

She was very severe with writers, and often a writer's single statement or action would be enough for her to regard his entire work with distrust. It was at this time that we began to discuss Pascal. While admiring some of his observations, she reproached him for having said somewhere that without the miracles one would not be obliged to believe. She could not forgive Vergil for having eliminated the praise of Gallus in one of his Georgics at a time when Gallus had fallen into disgrace and was sentenced to death. And she found it hard to forgive Racine for having been so skillful a courtier.

In class my seat was right next to hers. I can see her again, crouched slightly over her note paper, her fingers often covered with ink stains, writing very slowly and painfully, but quick to turn her head, attentive to everything, observing things ardently from behind her thick glasses. Because of the slowness with which she wrote she could take only very imperfect notes of Alain's lectures, and so she often borrowed her friends' notes. She was absentminded in certain matters, suffering the distractions natural to those who are absorbed in their own thoughts. I remember one day there were large splotches of ink on her clothes because she had put her bottle of Waterman's ink in her pocket and had forgotten to close it properly; she had placed the bottle in its cardboard box but hadn't screwed on the cap.

She would make little drawings on her papers. I told her that they looked like ectoplasms. They were fantastic or ghostly creatures—slender, undulant forms like soft substances that could be stretched or like flames.

She was not only friendly with me. Simone had even closer ties of friendship with several classmates and chiefly three of them: René Château, Jacques Ganuchaud and Pierre Letellier. Ganuchaud was no longer in *cagne,* but was already attending the Ecole Normale. He had entered *cagne* at the same time as Château, Letellier, and I, had presented himself for the entrance examination after his first year, and had been accepted. But he would often return to see his old classmates. This trio—Simone, Château, and Ganuchaud—liked to have discussions in the cafés. They often held their sessions in a bistro on the rue des Canettes. Simone drank black coffee; she also at times tried to drink wine, as she did later with the workers, so as not to be too different from the others and because she wanted to be able to "take" everything that men can "take," but she didn't like it at all and could drink only a small amount without getting sick. But she really liked to smoke. Sometimes the three friends would bring along a loaf of bread, paté, and cheese and dine in the café, where they were only served wine. They would then stay there talking and arguing until the café closed, which was about one or two in the morning. Sometimes they would roam about the streets until dawn, discussing all through the night. Once or twice they went to watch the dawn come up in a café in the Halles market. Men in full-dress and women in evening gowns would come there at the end of the night to eat fried potatoes; meanwhile they would be talking in a corner.

Letellier, who was also one of Simone's best friends, perhaps the one for whom she felt the greatest affection, was the son of Léon Letellier, a disciple of Lagneau's, called by Alain "the man of God" because he had published a book of his notes on Lagneau's precious series of lectures "on the existence of God." So Pierre Letellier was doubly tied to Lagneau—through his father and Alain. That meant a great deal to Simone, who deeply admired Lagneau. Moreover, she felt at this time that the most accomplished and most human man was the man who was both a manual worker and a thinker. Léon Letellier realized this ideal. The son of Norman peasants, he had left home at sixteen to work on a fishing boat that went to Newfoundland banks, and then had traveled all over the world as a seaman on ocean liners before going to school later in life and, when he was about thirty, becoming a student of Lagneau's. He had finally returned to settle down in his native Normandy as a farmer and raiser of livestock. Simone was eager to meet him, but he died during the early part of 1926. To make some sort of contact with his memory she had gone in the summer of 1927 to spend her vacation near the farm—La Martinière at Saint-Malo-de-la-Lande—where his life had ended.

Château and Letellier were very close friends and Simone thought very highly of their friendship. I cannot help but think that she perhaps had some special feeling for Pierre. If she was in love with anyone in *cagne,* it was surely with him. One day, just before the war, she seemed to want to tell me that she had fallen in love with one of our classmates when we were in *cagne.* We were talking about love (which we rarely did), and she said to me, speaking of herself, "Didn't you guess anything when we were in *cagne?*" I said that I hadn't, and she didn't insist. But in fact I had had the impression that she liked Letellier more than anyone else. I also think that if my supposition is correct and she had a feeling of more than friendship for him, it's unlikely that he himself had ever known about it and no doubt she had never told it to anyone. For she was terribly shy and certainly hid emotions of this sort, if indeed she ever did experience them. And that she once may have felt these emotions, in secret and with no sign of weakness, would not at all diminish her, it seems to me, but rather just the contrary.

The small group formed by Simone, Château, Ganuchaud, and Letellier was not only passionately interested in philosophy but also in politics. Simone had never been and never became a member of the Communist party, but she was more attracted to it than to any other political party. She might even have considered herself a communist, if one takes the word in its broadest sense. Indeed, if one does not mean by communist a member of the Communist party, one could say that she was a communist. During her years in *cagne* and at the Ecole Normale, and even after that, she would often draw the hammer and sickle on her letters, rough drafts, and other papers. She read *L'Humanité* regularly. In a letter she wrote to her mother in 1926, while her mother was taking a cure in Challes and was staying at the Hotel Du Château, she spoke of her own activity in this hotel the year before and called it "communism." ("You can see that communism, if it is not always advisable for senators. . . .* The fact is that the senators and guests have much less

*This sentence was not completed.

power to make life agreeable or disagreeable than the servants in the place where one is living." This came up because of the special attention the servants in the hotel lavished on Mme. Weil due to their fond memories of Simone.)

Later on at Le Puy in February 1932, she will write: "I am becoming less and less of a communist," which would suggest that she had been a communist to some extent. Monatte says that when he knew her in 1931, "she was a communist like all the rest of us." By communist he does not mean a member of the party, since in 1931 he and his friends had been outside the party for a number of years. He was then sympathetic to the "communist oppositions" (that is, the dissident communists who considered themselves the true communists). The Trotskyists were one of the dissident groups, and from about 1933 on orthodox communists thought of Simone as a Trotskyist. This was a mistake in one sense, for her opinion of Trotsky was far from being entirely favorable, and when she actually got an opportunity to speak to him in December 1933, they had a fierce argument. But if one were to say that she was a communist, though a dissident one, this was not untrue.

Had she ever tried to join the party? André Weil told me that for quite a long time he had seen lying about her room a letter requesting admission to the Communist party, which began somewhat like this: "Moved by a powerful feeling of solidarity . . .," but he didn't know whether she had ever sent it. (Apparently, she never did.) Simone Canguilhem declares that at Le Puy Simone still was uncertain whether one should act only through the trade unions or if one also had to belong to a party, which would then have been the Communist party. She appears to have discussed this with her teacher friends, Vidal and Delhermet, and they dissuaded her from joining the party.[1] After her trip to Germany, she will declare that she has lost all the respect that, despite herself, she still felt for the party. So she had respected it, despite herself. Boris Souvarine says that when he first met Simone at the end of 1932, she was a dissident communist like himself and his friends, and he is convinced that if the Communist party had been run in a different manner, she would have ended by joining it, despite her general hostility to political parties.

As for me I find it hard to believe that Simone, starting from the time she was at Henri IV, could have wholeheartedly become a member of any party, whatever it might be. I recall that about the time I entered the Ecole Normale in 1927, she bawled me out for having maintained that organization into a party could be useful and good under certain circumstances, and that all you had to do was limit the common action and clearly define its goals. (Château was with us and supported her views.) She had understood Alain's distrust of all organization and shared it, pushing it even further, since despite his distrust he was still associated with the Radical party. It seems impossible to me that she would have been able to accept any limitation on her freedom of thinking, speaking, and acting. The same scruples that prevented her from entering the Church would have also kept her, I believe, from joining the party. The idea of joining the Communist party, if it did not come before *cagne,* must have been formed in a moment of indignation and quickly abandoned. If it is true that at Le Puy she posed the problem of whether one should or should not join, this would prove that she had not done so yet, and finally she never did.

If she really had been tempted to do so when she was at Le Puy, I believe it could have been only with the intention of carrying on oppositional work in the party and of attempting to reform it. But she knew that one could not carry on opposition work without immediately being expelled. So I tend to think that if she did discuss this matter with Vidal and Delhermet, it was simply to force them to define their ideas more clearly, in some way playing the devil's advocate so as to push the discussion to its very limits, which she had a habit of doing.[†]

As is generally known, communism is one of the modes of socialism. Now Alain taught us that socialism was ineffective at really defending the individual and really establishing equality. His objections were strong ones and perhaps he alone had the intellectual means to convince us. For he was obviously at least as much of an advocate of equality as the socialists and obviously had just as much courage as they. While recognizing that certain socialist measures were indispensable, he thought that a kind of radicalism was more effective than socialism in protecting men against the abuses of power and giving them as much equality as possible. One must say "a kind of radicalism" because it must be made clear that radicalism as he conceived it could not be identified with the policy of the Radical party, whose name from that period on might appear very badly chosen (radical actually means extremist). Perhaps only Alain represented a radicalism that it was not absurd to call by this name, since his radicalism was in truth more violent and more shocking than that of a socialist. He no doubt had experienced strong emotions on the occasion of certain political events, from the Dreyfus case, when he had supported Dreyfus, to the First World War, when he had had the greatest sorrow of his life and had gone through the war as a volunteer at the same time that he detested it. (He had wanted to share the common misfortune; he had also believed that he had to pay this price in order to be able to continue thinking freely.) The war had made him an even more ardent and convinced pacifist, and for him the chief goal of political action was the preservation of peace. Not revolution, because he thought that war makes us into greater slaves than capitalism ever could. (What, he argued, is the power of a capitalist

---

[†]It is in this same sense that her letter to Louzon, from which I shall quote later on (pp. 125–126), should be interpreted.

compared to that of a simple lieutenant in wartime? What is the slavery of a worker when set alongside that of a soldier?) His disciples were therefore resolved to be pacifists before all else and to spread the spirit of resistance to war as much as possible.

In March 1927, Michel and Jeanne Alexandre began publishing the second series of *Libres Propos,* a magazine they had founded after the war so that Alain could freely express his opinions on current events as they occurred. They were deeply devoted to Alain and eager to work for peace. Several students or ex-students from Henri IV intended to write for this magazine—Château and Ganuchaud among others. Simone only wrote for it a little later, but from the beginning she did everything to support it and thought about what she would write for it.

A small group of pacifists, the Will for Peace, was formed at the end of 1927. Its secretary and I believe chief organizer was Madeleine Vernet. Its headquarters was at the Quakers' meeting place at 121 rue Guy-de-la-Bresse, in the fifth *arrondissement.* It published a monthly newspaper. People began to support this newspaper and to work for it. Ganuchaud would write it all practically by himself. Simone probably wrote for it too, but I can't be sure of this. In any event, she was one of those who helped to paste on the wrappers and write out the addresses; she even recruited her parents when they needed extra people to get out the mailing. They also had leaflets printed for the Will for Peace, which they pasted up all over Paris.

One of Alain's war comrades, Lucien Cancouët, worked for the national railways at the Left Bank–Paris depot and was active in the C.G.T. (General Confederation of Labor) railroad workers' union. He wanted to help his fellow workers become more educated and to facilitate their advancement by preparing them for the exams for the jobs of forwarding agent and clerk at the railroad's central offices. For their part, some of Alain's disciples, among them Simone, dreamed of renewing the attempt to set up people's universities. They realized that education is a form of power ("perhaps the principal form of power in our epoch," Simone will say), and that without this power the people will not really be able to govern. They also saw that it was more disheartening to deprive certain people of the mind's wealth than of material wealth, especially when they had enough material goods on which to live. But the people's universities had failed. A new start had to be made on a more modest base, connecting the people's school to some practically useful enterprise. Thus it came about that Cancouët and some of Alain's students organized lectures for the workers, some of which were intended to prepare them for the competitive exams while others were aimed at broad cultivation of the mind and a free inquiry into ideas.

For this purpose they had to form an association, which was called the Social Education Group. Ganuchaud signed the association's legal declaration on August 11, 1927. Cancouët announced the creation of the lecture courses in *La Tribune confédérée* on September 15. Classes were held at a municipal school on rue Falguière. There were courses in French, mathematics, and physics (industrial electricity), and a course in social education that was given every fifteen days on Sunday mornings. At the start the teachers were Ganuchaud, Château, and Guindey. At one point André Weil also gave a course in mathematics. Later on Simone and Marcoux came to reinforce the team of teachers and they gradually replaced all the others. This instruction was given for several years (until the year 1930–1931). At the beginning, there were about thirty students. The Sunday morning lectures were always attended by twenty-five to thirty students. These dealt chiefly with problems of sociology and political economy—for example, technology, property, the place of intellectuals in the city (should the people nourish the intellectuals?), and the war. Resumes of some of these lectures can be found in *Libres Propos,* starting from January 1928 on.

A certain number of railroad employees who attended these lectures succeeded in passing the tests and the competitive examinations and so improved their positions. Cancouët thought that this instruction had also helped them to improve their ability to think and their judgment, particularly in political matters; he came to this opinion on the basis of what they accomplished afterwards. He felt that the young teachers, above all Ganuchaud, Château, and Guindey, had had a profound influence on their students. He said that Simone could take a little less of the credit. They had all liked her as a good comrade, but she shocked and astonished people, and they thought her ideas were too farfetched and paradoxical and did not always accept them.

The first time that she took the entrance examination for the Ecole Normale, in June 1927, Simone failed in large part because of the low mark she received in history. So the next year, for most of the final trimester, she went to live with a friend of her parents, Mme. Letourneux, who ran a boarding school for young girls at Chasseneuil in the Charente region. Simone wanted to study quietly what she still had to learn about history. At the lycée they thought she was sick.

These were weeks of very hard work. People had to argue with her to convince her to get enough sleep. Otherwise, she would have gone to bed at all hours. Mme. Letourneux also scolded her because she smoked too much, but Simone could not work without smoking. She did not want anyone to go into her room to clean it. Each day she granted herself an hour to get some fresh air and used it either to learn how to play tennis or to take a stroll with some of the women in charge of the girls. The girls considered her an odd character, and they would watch her go past with looks of amazement, staring at her strange gait and her pockets bulging with the makings for cigarettes.

Despite all her work she found time to make friends with the gardener and other servants around the school. These friendships were not well received by the people in charge, since they thought that this would spoil the discipline. Simone gave the gardener some cigarettes and, with her usual contempt for opinion, was not afraid to take him to her room when she wanted to discuss something with him. The gardener's wife had black, terrible suspicions.

Elections were being held in the town. Simone became interested. On election day she did not want to go with her bourgeois friends, but instead left arm in arm with the gardener and other workers.

It was not without some apprehension that she again took the competitive examination. Though she had small hopes of being accepted, she was, and even did brilliantly.

At the same time that she was preparing for the examination for the Ecole Normale, she studied during her first two years in *cagne* for the four certificates that as a group constitute the license to teach philosophy. These examinations are held at the Sorbonne, though attending the Sorbonne's courses is not obligatory and it is quite possible that Simone rarely attended them. Alain's courses must have seemed more useful to her, and they actually were. She prepared herself chiefly through her reading; in particular, she made a thorough study of Dumas's psychology textbook. Yet she did sometimes go to the Sorbonne. Simone de Beauvoir, in her *Memoirs of a Dutiful Daughter,* remembers that she met her there.

"While preparing to enter the Normale," she says, "she was taking the same examinations at the Sorbonne as I. She intrigued me because of her great reputation for intelligence and her bizarre outfit; she would stroll around in the courtyard of the Sorbonne attended by a group of Alain's old students; she always carried in one pocket a copy of *Libres Propos* . . . and in the other a copy of *L'Humanité.* A great famine had broken out in China, and I was told that when she heard the news she had wept: these tears compelled my respect much more than her gifts as a philosopher. I envied her for having a heart that could beat right across the world. I managed to get near her one day. I don't know how the conversation got started; she declared in no uncertain tones that only one thing mattered in the world today: the Revolution that would feed all the starving people on the earth. I retorted, no less peremptorily, that the problem was not to make men happy, but to find the reason for their existence. She looked me up and down: 'It's easy to see that you've never gone hungry,' she snapped. Our relationship did not go any further. I realized that she had classified me as 'a high-minded little bourgeoise,' and this annoyed me. . . . I believed that I had freed myself from the bonds of my class. . . ."[2]

In June 1926 Simone passed the tests for the two certificates for "Morality and Sociology" and "Psychology," in March 1927 the certificate for "The History of Philosophy," and in June 1927 the certificate for "General Philosophy and Logic." I believe that she passed these tests brilliantly, especially the last two. According to Simone de Beauvoir, among the candidates who received the certificate of "General Philosophy and Logic," she stood at the very top of the list.[3]

4

The Ecole Normale
(1928-1931)

She would have liked to go work during the summer in the "Civilian Service" located in the principality of Lichtenstein. This organization had been founded by a Swiss named Pierre Cérésole and was intended gradually to replace military service and, by coexisting with it, give young people who were averse to an apprenticeship in war a chance nevertheless to devote themselves to their country or to humanity. It brought together volunteers from many different countries and usually put them to work repairing ruins or the damages left behind by floods and avalanches. In 1929 it had established its workshops in Lichtenstein, in the towns of Schaan and Vaduz. Château had gone there in August and Ganuchaud was to go there after him. Simone wanted to accompany Ganuchaud, but she wanted to work digging in the earth like the men (a plan that upset her parents very much). Now the women—or the "sisters," as they were called—were not allowed into the organization except to work in the kitchen. Simone stated in her application the kind of work she wanted to do and since she did not go, Cérésole must have turned down her request.

The Kellogg Peace Pact "outlawing" war was signed in Paris on August 27, 1928. Even though they doubted the efficacy of this agreement, those who condemned war greeted it with sympathy. In September the Will for Peace published a manifesto in which it invited the public to realize the significance of this political act and to bring pressure to bear on the governments to compel them to keep to their commitments. This manifesto called for "complete and immediate disarmament" as well as "the destruction of all war matériel and the cessation of all public or private manufacture of arms." Certainly naive demands when put in this form, for what is an arm? Peacetime industries can, if necessary, be quickly converted into war industries. Yet at that time every effort for peace appeared to be a duty that had to be supported. Simone did her best to spread the manifesto and on her return from vacation tried to get her friends to spread it too.

At the Ecole Normale, Simone was the only girl in her group of accepted candidates. The year before three girls had been accepted in the department of literature: Suzette Moline, Clémence Ramnoux, and I. The administration had assigned us a "den" on the Ecole's first floor. Simone joined us. Since she already had her license and only had to go to the Ecole for three years, whereas we had to go for four, she joined us to find herself just as far advanced in her studies as we; she only had to prepare for her diploma and her licenses to teach in the lycées and universities. There was nothing compulsory at the Ecole Normale for day students (save for military training, which did not concern girls, and the obligation to bring books back to the library before the Easter and summer vacations). When you had to prepare for exams, most of the courses were given at the Sorbonne, but, again, you did not attend them unless you wanted to. If you preferred to work alone and at home, you could very well do so. (I almost always worked at home; I also saw much less of Simone during the years at the Ecole than during the two years I had been with her at Henri IV.)

Simone was even freer, since, as I have said, she already had her license in philosophy. So in her first year she did not have to take any exams. Her second year, she had only the diploma exam and the P.C.N. physics exam.[1] Now it is very rare that one fails to get the diploma, and the P.C.N. physics exam was not difficult.

So there began for her a period of freedom, in which she certainly did a great deal of work but on things that she wanted to work on.

Among those who had enthusiastically supported the manifesto of the Will for Peace were members of the League for the Rights of Man. For a long time, the League seemed to have gone to sleep, but this appeal stirred it into life. Some of the rank-and-file members of the League began to accuse their Central Committee of doing little for peace. Soon after, the Central Committee, in answer to this prod, issued a protest against the budget for 1929 that had been passed by the Chamber of Deputies and included an increase in military expenditures. Encouraged by this success, some pacifists, who, I believe, were chiefly Alain's followers, devised a plan for entering one section of the League in large numbers to compel it to vote for a motion and so afterward be able to present it at the League Congress, which was to take place in the spring of 1929. It was without a doubt in January or the beginning of February 1929 that the move was made to get as large a number as possible to join the Fourteenth Section in Paris, which was presided over by the mathematician Hadamard, one of those in the League opposed to our pacifism. Simone not only joined herself but also induced her parents to join. They also brought along some railroad men from rue Falguière. I recall a meeting at which Victor Basch, the president of the League, who had come to fight us, made a speech in which he criticized exaggerated demands and systematic opposition to the government. When the government behaved justly and reasonably, he said, one should not be against it. That seemed to be obvious. Nevertheless the government rarely runs short of arguments to prove that it has acted justly and reasonably. A certain distrust and sometimes a certain a priori resistance, aimed at testing its arguments, is necessary if one really wants to control it. It is also true that what seems unreasonable and impossible might be perfectly possible and reasonable if one attempts to achieve it and wants it very strongly. Such is without a doubt the meaning of Alain's doctrine on "the citizens against the government." (If the resistance of the citizen did not ceaselessly counterbalance the constant effort of the powers-that-be to aggrandize themselves, the world would become one great tyranny.) But this doctrine at first sight seemed not quite right and Simone felt the need to justify our position against that of Victor Basch and so wrote it out.

In fact, a fragment has been found that she unquestionably wrote in the interval between this meeting and the League Congress and that begins as follows: "For the League. What should the attitude of the League be toward the government? . . . Should the League be an arbiter between the people and the government, or the organ of the people against the government?" To this question, she replies: "The League was founded . . . in order to defend the rights of man. . . . Certain people say that the League, weighing the arguments of the people and the government, must be an impartial arbiter between the citizens and the powers-that-be. Now . . . the government, which is the only force that can work through the State, is also the only one that knows the conditions of action. . . . It is therefore impossible to check on the arguments of the government. . . . To remain faithful to its name and its origins, the League must not be impartial . . . but rather, deaf to the arguments of the rulers, must systematically support the people."

Despite Basch and Hadamard, on February 4 the motion of the pacifists won in the balloting of the Fourteenth Section. This motion declared that the League is "an organ for the defense of the individual against all the powers-that-be" and that henceforward it would be "mobilized against war"; it demanded that the government finally and immediately take "real steps toward peace, such as: acceptance of universal and obligatory arbitration; a sincere attempt at disarmament, at least equal to that of Germany," etc.; and finally it called upon the people to realize "the Franco-German union, which has been compromised for the last ten years by unjust and absurd refusals (such as to evacuate German territory without delay and annul the humiliating Article 231 of the Versailles Treaty, etc.)."

All this may seem the height of folly when one thinks of Hitler. But perhaps if such steps had been taken by France, Hitler would have had less success in Germany. Didn't he have his first great successes in

September 1930? At the beginning of 1929, there was perhaps still time. And who can know what was folly and what was wisdom in these attempts to save the peace, when the world had not yet definitively plunged in the direction of war? (And, after all, to voluntarily adopt liberal measures toward Germany would have been more honorable and no doubt less dangerous than to wait until the Germans forced them on you. And when you have done everything possible to maintain peace, you fight the war, if you are forced to fight it, with a better conscience and firmer resolution.)

Hadamard now found himself a minority in his own section. He was kept on as president, but neutralized by a pacifist executive. At the Congress, which was held at Rennes on March 31, the motion was put to a vote. It did not get a majority, but it did receive five hundred and thirteen votes, which represented about a third of the League's membership. The Central Committee had based its fight against it on the issue of confidence and had threatened to resign. However, it changed its own motion, introducing into it certain key slogans of the opposition, and Basch publicly vowed from then on to prosecute the struggle for peace "with renewed energy and audacity."[2]

Simone's grandmother died of cancer in April 1929. Dr. Weil gave her progressively larger doses of morphine, so that she suffered very little. In fact, she did not suffer till the very end. She was seventy-nine years old. During her last moments she said, "It's not hard to die when you are surrounded by all those you love."

Until the last days of her life, she had had a mistaken view of Simone's character. She changed her mind in the course of her last illness. Simone made great efforts to distract and comfort her, even to the point of falling ill herself. She read *Les Misérables* to her and had long conversations with her, after which the old lady seemed to be calmer and less oppressed. She helped her, Mme. Weil believed, to bear the idea of dying.

It was some months before this that Simone had urged me to go once a week and play the piano with her grandmother. She had to insist a great deal, for the hour she proposed was that of a course in mathematics which I had just started to take and which interested me. She finally succeeded in persuading me. She undoubtedly thought that it would be a diversion for her grandmother and that at bottom music interested me more than mathematics. That is how I played the piano with Mme. Reinherz until she became too sick to continue.

On the first of May we were in our den at the Ecole, Simone and I, when we learned that Chiappe, the prefect of police in Paris, had ordered numerous preventive arrests to assure the failure of announced demonstrations. This time I was as indignant as Simone (I must admit that often I was much less so). To arrest people who had not yet done anything and of whom one could only suspect their intention on the basis of uncertain and arbitrary signs (it was said that among the men who reached the places where the processions were forming for the demonstration, they arrested all those who wore caps, on the theory, I suppose, that these men were workers) seemed to us outrageous. Simone took one of the large sheets of yellow paper that were given to us at the Ecole and wrote on it roughly as follows: "The undersigned, students and professors, protest the arrest of presumed demonstrators." We did not take too much time to consider this statement; we both left immediately to try to gather signatures. We went to the Sorbonne straightaway, and one of the first people we found there was Victor Basch, who was giving his course that day. He pounced on the phrase, "students and professors," which Simone had thoughtlessly used. He commented at length on the impertinence of this statement in which students were named before the professors. Then, after having thoroughly torn the thing apart, he showed that he was a decent fellow and signed, since he had no basic objections to the protest.

But I can no longer recall what led us to give up our project. Probably we realized that we had to gather a great number of signatures very quickly and that that was hardly possible. Or perhaps we wanted to wait and see what Chiappe would do with the people he had arrested. So we did nothing with this statement or with the signatures we had already obtained.

At the Ecole Normale Simone made the acquaintance of Marcoux, a first-year student like herself. He was from Poitiers and was also studying philosophy. Though not directly a student of Alain's, he had been taught by Bénézé, a disciple and friend of Alain's; in short, he was one of Alain's grandchildren. He soon became one of Simone's best friends. Since we were often not in the den, she installed Marcoux, who was happy to find a quiet corner where he could work.

They would sometimes talk at La Bonbonnière on rue Saint-Jacques, while having a *café crème*. Marcoux was interested in mathematics, a subject in which Simone was becoming more and more involved. He loaned her Hadamard's geometry textbook. She "pillaged" the book, as Marcoux put it, reducing it to a sorry state because of all the use she put it to; some pages had even been torn out. She did not agree with Hadamard and seemed to think that he had committed certain crimes against geometry.

They both participated in the school at rue Falguière. Marcoux taught mathematics, while Simone took care of the literary department. She may also have taught physics. But both of them wound up doing almost everything. After their courses, they would go at times to eat at the Cancouëts on rue Mayet.

Cancouët lived at that time at 16 A, rue Mayet. He had a very small dining room into which his friends would somehow manage to squeeze —not very comfortably. Simone, Ganuchaud, Château, and Marcoux often came for supper, Afterward, they would have impassioned discussions. Simone once or twice told the Cancouëts that they were no longer proletarians and were in fact already bourgeois, which made Mme. Cancouët very indignant.

Most likely it was for the course at rue Falguière that Simone wrote certain essays that appear to date from this period—essays dealing with economic and sociological subjects, for example, on money, equality of salaries, and equality in education. They could have been written for the course in social education.

She sometimes went with Marcoux to the area near the Jardin des Plantes. Beneath the Austerlitz bridge, on the right bank, barges unloaded large freestone blocks. Simone liked to get in among these stones to do her geometry. At this particular spot there were not many people about, except for some very gentle Parisian bums, who were indifferent to the outside world and ignored her completely. When Marcoux would reach the bridge, he would see her sitting there or kneeling (she would often work on her knees), her hair falling around her face; from time to time she would light a cigarette and smoke for a while, as she reflected on something. All this must have happened in the spring or at the beginning of the summer of 1929, for Marcoux believes he remembers that sunlight was always flooding the freestone blocks.

One day, as they were walking past the Halles wine market, Simone suddenly told him that she wanted to go into the Halles and try to get a job corking wine bottles. Marcoux thought that this could be dangerous for her and that she could easily lose a finger, since he knew she was quite clumsy. He steered her into a café and managed to dissuade her.

(So at times there would surface in her, as when she tried to work as a day laborer with pick and shovel, her profound desire to do manual work.)

Simone did not have many friends at the Ecole Normale, even among the students. Many of them feared or were in awe of her. "They tried to avoid her in the corridors because of the blunt, thoughtless way she had of confronting you with your responsibilities by asking for your signature on a petition. . . . or a contribution for some trade union strike fund."[3]

People would crack jokes about her, and not always friendly ones. There was a scheme to write a satirical revue in which, instead of taking as its targets the authorities of the Ecole, its directors and professors, as was the annual custom, they were going to make Simone the chief and perhaps only butt of their wit. But her friends intervened and the revue was never put on. I don't know whether she ever became aware of this plan. There was certainly no point in running the risk of hurting her by speaking to her about it.

But it was obviously the school's administration that was least tolerant of her. Simone was never very tactful toward those who wielded power of any kind. In Cabaud's book one can find the account of her impertinences to Bouglé, assistant director of the Ecole and particularly in charge of the students in the literature department. (Vessiot, the director, was a scientist and had very little contact with us.) I didn't witness the lecture where the question at issue was patriotism and where Simone, so it seems, after having let Bouglé speak, stood up and read without comment a speech (by Poincaré?) she had found in the *Official Gazette* of 1912. The author of this speech seems to have said that, if it were necessary, France would have to invade Belgium. "When she had finished, there was a moment of silence. Bouglé took out his watch and said, 'It is twelve o'clock; it's time for lunch.' This reply quickly became a catchword among the students, repeated, with the appropriate gesture, whenever a student couldn't find an answer to a disconcerting question."[4]

I wasn't there, but this story was told to me in pretty much the same terms. This also is true of the story Cabaud tells of her asking Bouglé for a contribution for the unemployed. He gave her twenty francs, but warned her that his gift must remain anonymous. She immediately put up a sign on the school bulletin board or "forum" (the name given at the Ecole Normale to a corridor where notices addressed to the other students could be posted). "Follow your director's example. Be an anonymous donor to the unemployment benefit fund."

Shortly before she died, Simone's grandmother had been able to go and see (partly climbing up a ladder) the still unfinished apartment at rue Auguste-Comte, behind the Luxembourg Gardens, that the Weils had bought on the blueprints. She had admired the beautiful view that spreads out below from these rooms on the sixth and seventh floors in a rather high section of town (the Montagne Sainte-Geneviève). Standing there one can see across the way the Sacré Coeur in Montmartre, which appears to be on the same level but from which one is separated by the whole center of Paris, which extends lower down in a broad valley and then climbs in a gentle slope toward the two heights. From the terrace one can see on the left the Eiffel Tower, the Chaillot Palace, the dome of the Invalides, the top of the Arc de Triomphe, Sainte-Clotilde, the towers of Saint-Sulpice, the roof of the Opéra, and the roofs of the Louvre; and on the right the steeple of Sainte-Chapelle, the Saint-Jacques tower, the church of the Sorbonne, the Panthéon, and Saint-Jacques du Haut-Pas. One has a good, commanding view of both the Luxembourg Palace and the Gardens quite close by, while just below the apartment stands the building of the School of Mines and the hothouses of the Luxembourg Gardens, with the fine old house in which Leconte de Lisle died.

The Weils began to move into the apartment in May 1929. The work had not yet been completed; there were still no staircase, no windows, no electricity, and no concierge. Every evening, Simone would climb up the unfinished stairs by the light of a lantern. There was still no elevator, or it did not function due to the lack of electrical current. Moreover, the keys had been packed by mistake in the shipping cases and for the first days they were there the Weils could not lock their door. The furniture movers, who were happy with their tips, told them, "You should move again soon." In fact, they did not move again for as long as they lived in Paris.

During this first year at the Ecole Normale, Simone frequently returned to hear Alain's lectures at Henri IV. I don't know how she could have done this without getting into trouble with the monitor. The previous year, after leaving the school, a certain number of us came back to hear Alain, even bringing along classmates who had never been students at the lycée, and one day the monitor noticed it. Having come by chance into the class, he was surprised to find it filled with many more students than it should have had. After the class ended, he had followed and stopped us, forbidding us ever to come back. The courses at the lycée not being public, it is true that we didn't have the right to attend Alain's lectures. We were advised to request a special authorization from the ministry; we wrote a letter asking for this authorization, which was refused. (The rumor was that an important functionary at the Department of Public Education had said, "Alain is giving a course in communism, and he has quite enough students.") The monitor personally saw to it that the prohibition was respected. Did his surveillance relax the following year? Perhaps he did not see Simone come to the lycée, or he despaired of preventing her from doing what she set her mind to? Or he became indignant the year before only because it was such a massive invasion? I don't know which of these circumstances was the case.

It was during her first year at the Ecole, when she was still going to Henri IV, that Maurice Schumann sat next to her in class. Since he was considered the best student because of a composition he had written, Alain, to honor him, had him sit next to her.

She continued to submit *topos* and Alain corrected them as before. That is why some of Simone's *topos* corrected by Alain are written on the Ecole Normale's large yellow sheets.

Several of the *topos* Simone wrote for Alain while she was at the Ecole deal with political philosophy or sociology. For example, there is one essay entitled "Concerning an Antinomy of the Law"; another is called "Some Different Meanings of the Word 'Order.' " In this last essay the problem discussed is the different meaning the word "order" has in politics compared to its meaning in mathematics or the Cartesian method. Simone felt very strongly about this difference, for she admired Cartesian order but had no sympathy for social order. "How is it," she asks, "that the same word expresses both the triumph and slavery of the mind?"

It is clear that she is trying to reconcile her political with her philosophical ideas. In the *topo* "Concerning an Antinomy of the Law," she tries to understand the law (social right) by comparing it to a straight line. Just as there is no straight line in nature, so straightness and rightness—that is, the law—are a creation of the human mind. Yet the law is not created by the mind independent of sensible intuition (here one recognizes the Kantian idea). Similarly, the law, although it is something other than an act, being, or power, is nevertheless not completely independent of these. For this reason, the essay begins with a quotation from Spinoza: "The law is measured by power." Simone finally thought the law is measured not by power but by work, by the action on nature —a Marxist idea. Law that is not sustained by work is meaningless. Law that only consists in pure ideas, or in power that is not exercised effectively, is a nullity.

One can see Simone searching for a definition of work in two articles she published in 1929: "Concerning Perception, or the Adventure of Proteus" and "Concerning Time." These two articles appeared in the May and August issues of *Libres Propos,* respectively.[5] The article on time was at first a *topo* submitted in class to Alain, which he had corrected.

"What is work?" she asks in "Proteus." She replies: "Work, as opposed to reflection, persuasion, and magic, is a series of actions that have no direct relation to either the original emotion or the goal pursued, or the former with the latter. Thus for a man who takes shelter in a cave and wishes to stop up the entrance with a large rock, the rule is first of all that the movements that permit him to do this have no relation to the spontaneous movements that, for example, cause him to fear ferocious beasts, and are even their direct opposite. Furthermore, when he has carried the rock halfway, the movement he must make is the same as if he had found the rock at this spot, the same as if he had reached his goal; and at every moment of his work, his movements are thus alien to his finished movements, his planned movements, as well as to his desires. . . . The law of work . . . is to be constantly indifferent to what precedes it as well as to what must follow it." So work is essentially *indirect* action, action applied to the *means.* If I stretch my hand toward that which pleases or interests me, this is not work. It is work from the moment that, in order to procure what interests me, I must go toward what does not interest me, make a detour, pass through intermediaries. In real work there is no immediate compensation; to learn how to work is to learn to make an effort in the *void,* as she would say later on. Besides, the means or intermediaries are just as indifferent and external to each other as they are to one's desires.

In the second article, she observed that work is a force exerted on oneself, but that it is also an indirect force. "To act is nothing else, for me, than changing myself, changing that which I am or that which I feel; but for this change in myself that I wish, it is not enough to wish it to obtain it. I can only obtain it indirectly. . . . If I suffer, I have no authority over my suffering but only the power to change it through the intermediary of other changes, which by themselves are usually indifferent to me. . . ."

So work presupposes an *action that is divided,* an action made of parts at once tied together and distinct, tied together but indifferent to each other, inseparable and separable. And that signifies, for Simone, that work implies an *extended* world. She thought that the representation of work is that it cuts out a space for us, distances the future from us, permits us therefore to figure forth space and time for ourselves. What makes the object appear to us as existing at a certain distance and the future appear as something that cannot be attained immediately, is the fact that we think of the act of work as intermediate acts between the object of our desire and ourselves.

So work plays an essential role in the formation of our consciousness. It is only by the test of work that we are given, and always together, time and extension, time as a condition, extension as the object of our action.

By this theory of work, Simone could at once exalt the worker and provide a moral basis for knowledge. This justified both her political program and her philosophy. The conclusion of her first article is: "Geometry, perhaps like all thought, is the child of courage and work." And the second article ends: "Let us awaken again to the world, that is, to work and perception, while still having the courage to observe this rule . . . to lower our body to the rank of a tool, our emotions to the rank of signs."

It was probably also during this first year at the Ecole Normale that she wrote the rough draft in which she discusses the duties of a representative of the people. She wrote it on white paper, but the handwriting is the same as that of the years spent at the Ecole. Or perhaps it was written at Chasseneuil on the occasion of the election campaign, just before the examination for the Ecole Normale—or, again, perhaps while she was on vacation, or right after the exam. Simone was faithful to Alain's ultra-democratic ideal and she even carried his ideas, with intrepid logic, to their ultimate consequences. Among other things, she condemned the political parties. She maintained that certain rigorous conditions must be applied to the functions of a deputy. She conceived of the laws as essentially negative (for example, "There will be no war," and "There will be no torture"). For her, the law is meant to guarantee that the human personality will be respected, that the powers of government and the other powers (the rich) will not go beyond certain limits. So the people don't have to govern (this is Alain's doctrine), but they must impose the laws, that is, set certain limits to the government and appoint certain guardians, the deputies, whose business it is to make sure that these limits will be maintained.

"But precautionary steps must be taken so that these guardians remain citizens without ever organizing themselves into a group. . . . Their function of surveillance must not become a profession, like the function of an administrator. They should never make judgments in accordance with a doctrine formed in advance, but should have a new judgment for each occasion. . . . Through the ballot, the people should make the deputies understand that their only function is that of denouncing the government if it does not abolish the injustices that it can abolish, and furthermore, that everything which makes the deputies a group and the function of deputy a career—meetings, parties, the posts given to deputies—should be abolished. . . . The deputies . . . should not be members of any political party. As for their opinions, they cannot have any contrary to the people's judgment; therefore they absolutely cannot have any temporal power or aspire to obtaining it. Thus a general, the manager of a factory, or a banker can never represent the people, nor can a priest who demands temporal power for the Church. But among those who have not and do not desire any power, the choice can only be made in terms of their firmness of character and judgment and their lack of political passion. There should not be any candidacy, since running for election is inevitably tied to political parties. . . . No man should ever dare to say: Vote for me because I am firm, courageous. . . ." The good deputy is not the man who tries to convince people to make him one, but the man who is sought out by the people.

During the summer of 1929 Simone wanted to participate in the farmers' work in the fields. She spent part of the summer at Marnoz in the Jura region with one of her aunts, her mother's older sister. This aunt's husband was a doctor, but the family owned property that it maintained and worked. The letters Simone wrote from Marnoz to her parents are not dated and so it is difficult to put them in the proper order. It is clear, however, that she must have been there in August and September. But only later was it discovered how hard she had worked, for example, digging potatoes for ten hours a day. In her letters she does not mention this hard work; instead, she dwells on everything that could reassure her parents—her "excursions" with her cousin Maguitte and the parties at which she learned how to dance; and she tries to amuse them with stories of her awkwardness and her moments of bewilderment or absent-mindedness.

At the end of her vacation she returned to Paris, where she saw her brother. He had just accepted a position as professor at the Moslem university at Aligarh, in India. He had to leave so as to take up his duties at the end of 1929.

During the school year of 1929–1930, Simone earned her diploma to teach in the lycées and university. As is known, this diploma is awarded for a dissertation, a kind of small thesis on which one works all year in almost complete freedom. For her subject she chose "Science and Perception in Descartes," and for her thesis director Brunschvicg (whom she rarely consulted). At the same time, she was preparing for the physics test of the P.C.N. It was then that I would see her. We would go to do practical exercises together near the Jardin des Plantes, and we would return by way of place de la Contrescarpe and rue de L'Estrapade. If I remember rightly, Letellier and Cécile Joint were with us. That year Simone also took instruction in pedagogy, that is, a certain number of courses in a lycée under the direction of a teacher. I believe, without being sure of it, that she took these courses at Janson-de-Sailly under the direction of Marcel Drouin.

Simone's diploma dissertation has been published in a collection of essays entitled *Sur la science.* [6] It is an essay that is more dogmatic than historical. In order to understand Descartes, Simone believes that one must oneself renew his whole enterprise. So the principal section of the essay is composed of a long meditation in the course of which she, like Descartes, tries to find the foundations of true knowledge. This search proceeds somewhat in the same order as Descartes': she begins with absolute doubt, and then from there gradually discovers a few certainties. First of all, the certainty of one's own existence, then that of the existence of God, and, finally, that of the existence of the world. But the formulas she employs are often very different from those of Descartes.

For example, there is a *cogito,* but in the form "I can, therefore I am." "To exist, to think, to know are only aspects of a single reality: to be able to act. . . . From the moment that I act, I make myself exist. . . . What I am is defined by what I can do." [7] Simone would no doubt say, like Goethe's Faust, "At the beginning was the act."

The self is power, the ability to act, and Simone above all affirms that "all real power is infinite." Yet after this she says: "If there exists only the self, there exists only this absolute power; I depend solely on my will, I do not exist except insofar as I create myself, I am God. . . . But that is not true. I am not God. . . . I must recognize the limits of this power; my sovereignty . . . disappears when I must give myself something to think about. Freedom is the sole power that is absolutely mine. Hence there is something besides myself that exists. . . ." [8]

I am free to reject what comes from my mind, but not to give it to myself, not *to begin* a thought. My life and my thoughts are first given without my willing them, given by an emotion "of pleasure and pain combined," which is the sign of an existence that I do not govern. It is the idea of God, the idea of the all-powerful, which has set this other existence before my eyes, making me realize that I am not an all-powerful being. Therefore this idea has great importance for the construction of my universe. But furthermore, Simone thinks that the object of this idea exists, that the all-powerful exists in itself.

"The idea of God alone has been able to bear witness to existence. Also the idea of God alone was the idea of a veritable and consequently real power; veritable power could not be imaginary. If the all-powerful could be a fiction of my mind, I could myself be a fiction, for I do not exist except insofar as I participate in the all-powerful."[9]

Therefore God exists for her. But one is astonished that this God is defined by his all-powerfulness rather than by benevolence, goodness, and perfection. For later on she defined God as being essentially the Good. Besides, the existence of God is proven at the same time as that of the world, more tied to the things of this world than in Descartes. Here the idea of God is that which makes man realize that he is not God, and this knowledge is at the same time knowledge of the world. Certain statements, however, explain this closer bond. Simone says that to become wise is the same as becoming master of oneself, and that in order to become master of oneself one must know that one is not God. Now to know that one is not God is to posit God in a certain fashion. The belief in God is expressed by the right thought on the subject of the world.

The world, here, is above all that which is opposed to freedom; it is the obstacle, oppression. "I remain impenetrable to myself to the extent that I do not create myself by the act of thinking, that is to say, insofar as I am subjected to the world's imprint. This world presses upon me with all the weight of aversion, desire, belief, leaving me, as I must recognize, no other power but that of rejection."[10]

But this world that oppresses me is not the world insofar as it is external to me. It exists insofar as it is interior to me, it is through my passions that it dominates me. "The impressions of the senses reach my thought and trouble it and, far from being an intelligence to which the senses are added like telephonists are linked to staff headquarters, I am first of all only imagination."[11]

How can one escape imagination save by a pure and simple repudiation? If I consider the objects that I conjure up for myself, I see that there is in them, among them, that which seems to be independent from this confused, impassioned, errant, and capricious imagination, this changing pressure of the world. There is in them that which is seemingly constructed voluntarily and clearly by me, according to an order that escapes my desires and my fears, an unchanging order. These are the objects of mathematics, simple objects, which I can complicate progressively in accordance with simple laws. Order is the alteration of which the mind disposes. Order and clear ideas are my only support.

Correct knowledge will therefore be the progressive knowledge of the world that is constructed when one adheres to order, without ever deviating from it, proceeding from the simple to the complex by only accepting clear ideas. This will be a physics in mathematical form that by its method will necessarily be analogous to Cartesian physics.

Nonetheless, "I am always double: on one hand, the passive being who is subjected to the world, and, on the other, the active being who has a grip on it; geometry and physics lead me to conceive how these two beings can be joined, but they do not join them. Certainly I cannot unite them directly . . .; but I can bring them together indirectly, since that is precisely what action consists of. Not this appearance of action by which the unchecked imagination leads me blindly to overturn the world by means of my disorderly desires, but true action, indirect action, action that conforms to geometry or, to give it its real name, work."[12]

"It is through work that reason seizes hold of the world."[13] Work teaches us to use the world insofar as it is an external obstacle in order to resist the world insofar as it is an interior enemy. "I must be tricky, cunning, I must hamper myself with obstacles that lead me to where I want to go."[14]

So here again we find in the conclusion the praise of work. It was to this that the entire essay tended; it was written to show that the science whose method is based on manual work is truer than the science of the modern experts, which disdains certain common notions and is based completely on abstract analysis.

Brunschvicg was far from enchanted by this essay. He gave it a mark of ten out of twenty; this was the lowest mark he could give without flunking the candidate. (He didn't want to flunk her; to flunk in one's work for the degree meant being dismissed from the Ecole Normale.)

One can find among Simone's manuscripts a certain number of fragments that are related to the preparation for the diploma. It seems that among them should be placed several rough drafts on the subject of the God of Descartes.

Descartes's God is also Simone's, for at that time she trusted entirely in Descartes. So it is her own belief that she is trying to define, and if there are many rough drafts, this is because she has some difficulty in defining it simply. At first only two things are evident: on one hand, that she does not like priests, theologians, and respectable people; on the other, that she wants to understand the belief in God and does not reject it, at least in one sense.

The true God of Descartes is not, in her view, the God of the theologians. "This God not only does not resemble the God of the theologians, but he is even that which reassures me as against theology; he is what there is of the infallible in myself. In fact I deceive myself, but by rights I should never deceive myself in the sense that it is up to me not to deceive myself."

The true God, she says, is what is infallible in myself. Actually, thought is infallible in its essence and it is that which proves that the perfect thought exists. "A perfect thought is an independent thought and nothing else. Now thought is independent. I know this, whatever I might know of my own shortcomings. . . . Because this knowledge implies the idea of an infallible thought. But as regards thought, neither existence nor perfection can be simply possible, since nothing, except thought itself, can confer on thought either existence or perfection. . . . For thought, value and existence are the same thing. . . . A simply possible idea does not contain either truth or value. This is what the *cogito* expresses and indeed what ontological proof expresses."

So here again we find a demonstration of the existence of God, and the proof offered consists in the fact that value and existence are one and the same thing in respect to thought. Insofar as it exists thought has value, and insofar as it has value it exists. If a thought has value, it is because it is truly a thought, because it exists as a thought and cannot not exist; and, reciprocally, if it exists as thought, it has value. This returns to Alain's idea that there is no such thing as a mediocre thought.

We can better comprehend here the proof of the existence of God than in the way she presented it in her dissertation. There she had proven the existence of God by the fact that we would not know how to begin a thought, that our thought is not entirely action, that at the beginning there is passion in it, and that we must recognize the existence of an external world. According to this, one might believe that the existence of God was known through the existence of the external world; and is it not the God-object that is known through the existence of the external world as being the cause of this world? Could Simone be returning to the God-object? Not at all, for in the dissertation God was not proven to be the cause, the creator of the external world, but only as not being dependent on the external world. His existence was proven directly by the idea of the all-powerful. Yet, even so, this God who is primarily power seems to us to be very different from the God Simone spoke of later on, and would even be different from the God Alain could believe in. But we can see more clearly now that the power she refers to was not at all a material, external power, a power analogous to that of the world, but only the power of the mind, thought insofar as it is action, will, and freedom. It is as absolute freedom that God exists, as absolute action bereft of all passion.

Yet there are still certain difficulties. Freedom in us is liberation, detachment from that which is undergone; thought begins with passion, as Simone recognizes. Is a thought that would be wholly action possible? Let us admit that if it is possible it exists, but is it possible?

On the other hand, Simone felt that thought insofar as it exists has value, and insofar as it has value it exists. If this is so, thought, insofar as it exists, would always be perfect and infallible. And indeed this is pretty much what she says in a fragment that also seems to date from the Ecole Normale years. Wherever there is freedom, she says in this fragment, there perfect knowledge can be found. Our thought, to the extent that it really exists, would therefore be identical with the divine thought.

Now Simone recognizes that it would be unfaithful to Descartes to identify God with the human mind. Perhaps she would like to take this step, as Sartre will later take it, but her respect for Descartes forbids it.

"Never has Descartes explicitly reduced God to the human mind. Certainly I find in myself the sign of God whose work I am, and this sign is enough to give me a value quite superior to that of the inanimate universe—but as perfect as the work may be, it could never equal the worker in value."

Therefore, for Descartes and, consequently, for Simone, God remains beyond man. How does she explain this transcendence of God? It seems that she sees it in relation to what is incomprehensible in the union of the soul and the body, in the accord (for there is a certain accord, unexpected, inexplicable) between the mind and nature.

"If God is a belief, that is so because there is indeed something here that is impenetrable to reason: the union of the soul and body. If I understood how the moral law excites an interest in me, I would know God. Yet this is a fact. A fact of a strange kind, a fact that one must create. Hence a new kind of proof. Causality was proven by the impossibility of believing in it.* God is proven in some way by the extreme difficulty of believing in him. One does not believe what one wishes; or rather one believes what one wishes, but it is necessary to will it. To will it—not to desire it. Since the idea of God can only express this incomprehensible accord between the realm of the mind and the realm of nature, I have only one way of proving this accord—it is to compel the world, by my actions, not to oppose my law. . . . God is presupposed and posited by the right action, and in no other way. There is not even an appearance of proof. One must deserve to believe in God.

"But it is a reasonable faith. . . . There is no certitude only in the sense that the idea of God does not impose itself as does (according to Kant) the idea of causality. All I would require is to have a little less courage to cease believing that God is. In this sense—and only in this sense—there is an opposition between belief and knowledge, not in the sense that the belief would be less certain or of less value, but just the contrary."

*A slip no doubt for "not believing in it."

And she adds in the margin: "On the contrary, belief is of much greater value, as regards the mind, and even more certain in the sense that it is related to the universal (the noumenon)."

To tell the truth, these fragments are only attempts, rough drafts, and perhaps successive, disconnected attempts. It would be imprudent to draw a doctrine from them, as if they were parts that were intended to form a whole. They merely show in what particular directions Simone was searching.

All that one can conclude is that she seems to identify religion with morality. At this period, to believe in God is for her simply to act correctly. "God is presupposed and posited by the right action, and in no other way." Belief is more the effect than the condition of courage and virtue. Morality is primary and unconditioned.

Simone outlined a formidable program of work for her last year at the Ecole Normale in preparation for the competitive exams. As regards morality, she noted, for example:

"To study thoroughly: Aristotle, Bentham, Schopenhauer, and Nietzsche.

"To brush up on: the Stoics, Epicureans, Skeptics (Montaigne), and Descartes, Pascal, Rousseau, Proudhon, Comte, Lagneau, Marx, and Tolstoy.

"To review carefully: Machiavelli, Hobbs, Leibnitz, Wolf, Bergson, Schelling, Fichte, Hegel, and Lenin.

"To review quickly: Plotinus, the Middle Ages, Bacon (?), Malebranche, Voltaire, and Encyclopedists.

"To study systematically: the Pre-Socratics, the Sophists, Socrates, Plato, Locke, Hume, Berkeley, Spinoza, Kant, and Maine de Biran.

"To learn by heart in the third trimester: scientific morality (sociological, psychological, and biological—Metchnikov); independent morality (Belot, Rauh . . .).

"Get hold of Rey's textbook of logic and morality that is used in *cagne* (and a trifle of idiotic gen. philo. [general philosophy]?)"

Another work plan shows that she had set herself tasks for every hour of the day and that although she wanted to do a frightful amount of work in the last year, she did not intend because of this to give up her courses at the rue Falguière.

I don't know whether she was able to do everything that she had intended to do, yet it is clear that this year she worked even more than usual.

Was it this excessive work that was the underlying cause of her headaches, which began this very year? It is difficult to know; she herself was never quite sure, nor were her parents, since the doctors could never discover the cause of the ailment. In 1939, shortly before the war, she had begun to think that it could be caused by a larval form of sinusitis. Her father had shown her an article on larval sinusitis in a medical journal and the symptoms described seemed to be the same as those she had. She did not have the time to try a treatment based on this hypothesis; perhaps such a treatment might have been effective; it could also have been useless, like all those she had tried up until then.

Mme. Weil claimed that while doing gymnastics and track at the Elizabeth Stadium, Simone had caught a very bad cold in the winter during her last year at the Ecole Normale. (This was most likely at the start of the winter, for Simone seems to have said several times that her headaches began in 1930.) Sweating after her athletic exertions, she would often sit on the grass without covering herself. That is how she had caught this rhinitis and, in Mme. Weil's opinion, it was this illness that could have left her with a case of larval sinusitis.

Simone may have also had a congenital predisposition to headaches. I recall that her father, whom she resembled, suffered from migraines and when he was having an attack, he didn't eat, like Simone. But her headaches seem to have been much more serious and more painful than his.

In any event, from then on she always suffered from headaches—at times more, at times less so. No doubt because of this her life was secretly darkened by a sense of misfortune. (This was perhaps the only misfortune she had not deliberately chosen and in which her will played no part.) Possibly it oriented her activity in a different direction from what it would have been without this disability. Simone later said to her mother, "You oughtn't be sorry that I have had headaches, for without them there are many things I would not have done." According to Mme. Weil, she meant to say perhaps that, for example, she would not have written so much because she would have been able to do many other things; or she would have done dangerous things—more dangerous, since she did do dangerous things—and would have died very young.

During this year an unfortunate incident altered my relations with Simone for some time. I would prefer not to speak about it, not so much because I was ridiculous but because I dislike telling the story from my point of view when she can no longer tell it from hers. But since I was ridiculous, I must undoubtedly tell the story. It would have been a trifling matter if I had been able to take it lightly, but I was overly sensitive. What still fills me with shame is not the affair itself, but that I wasn't able to hide the pain it caused me and that I didn't react to it as I should have. I should have reacted forcefully and then not have thought about it further; instead, I reacted by going off by myself and thought about it for much longer than it deserved.

At the Cité Universitaire, the students' hostel where I then lived, soon after the start of the school year the wife of the hostel's director asked me, as well as others, to take up a collection on the streets one Sunday for the "orphans of the sea." (This was a collection for fishermen's children, which must have taken place all over France.) I didn't know how I could refuse. When I went to get my collection can at the city hall, I saw that we also had to distribute insignias, small tricolor fleurettes such as are still given out in collections of this kind. I thought this was natural in an official collection, but this shocked the antimilitarism and antinationalism of some of my comrades at the Ecole. A few days later, to mock me, several of them, including Simone, gave me the surprise of welcoming me in a den covered with tricolor decorations.

It was just a prank, but this prank implied a criticism—the idea that I had not behaved as someone who seemed to share their opinions should. Of course, I thought that I shared their opinions, though I attached less importance to politics than they did, but I had not understood that one had to have an unconditional horror of the tricolor flag. More serious than their judgment of what I had done was the fact that they seemed to think I had done it to please the director of the student hostel and his wife. Now I never went to see them, nor did I try in any way to curry favor with them. I don't even know why I should have sought them out. (Since I had already been accepted at the hostel, what could they do for or against me?) I was indignant at their suspicions and above all at Simone, who had sided with the others against me. I could have no doubt that if she had, it was because she thought that I deserved it and that it would do me good. Actually, I no doubt deserved it in some sense. But the fact that she had participated in this condemnation astonished me, even when I told myself that I probably did deserve it. I thought that I had been wrong to consider her a friend. I thought this for some time, perhaps a month, and even through the following months I thought that she was less my friend than I had believed.

She realized that I had been hurt—I was much more so than was reasonable—and she knew I was angry with her. She tried to win me over again and regain my friendship and gradually succeeded. She pursued me generously, insisted on pulling me out of my silence, for I had stopped talking. Not being too skillful at defending myself with words, I nevertheless didn't want to approve of the others or associate with them, so I kept silent. But with her at least I resumed little by little our former relations as good comrades—and yet I had been hurt more by her attitude than that of the others.

For a long time I was convinced that she was no more interested in me than she was generally interested in other people. That was already a great deal, so why should I have asked for more? She had never told me that she felt a great friendship for me; besides, I knew that I didn't deserve her friendship. I continued to admire everything that was good and fine in her, yet despite myself I felt isolated, less close to her, and no longer considered myself obliged to become associated with her enterprises.

She had already formed the plan of going to work in a factory. She had thought about this for some time now and wanted to put the plan into effect at the end of the vacation period, after the final exam for the *agrégation* diploma. She spoke to me about it and proposed that I become a worker with her. I didn't refuse, but also didn't accept definitely. The thought of being a worker did not displease me—I had always liked to work with my hands, and no doubt this was the work I was destined for—but I was frightened at the thought of my parents' chagrin and disappointment. After the unpleasant incident and when we were already somewhat reconciled, I told her that I would not follow her on the path she wished to take, and, in particular, that I would not become a worker with her. I didn't feel, like her, that this step was a necessity for me, and I had decided never again to do, out of a mere feeling of being obliging toward her, anything I regarded as painful (for others and for myself) and useless.

I began this year to think about the relationship between human freedom and the grace of God in the light of certain Christian doctrines, and it seemed to me that there was some truth in the Jansenist doctrine. Now and then I tried to tell Simone something about these reflections of mine, but she resolutely resisted my arguments. She would answer me in line with Alain's ideas, and I saw that my ideas were so distant from hers that there was no point in insisting.

She continued, however, to be not at all hostile to Christianity—just the opposite. One day when she was returning from a class with the group of last-year students at the Ecole, they began making rather pointed antireligious remarks. (I certainly was not present, since I don't remember the incident.) Clémence Ramnoux, rather shocked, for she was very attached to her religion, drew a little behind the others. Simone also fell back and said to her, "You know, I'm perhaps the one who will become a nun."

On May 22 there was a demonstration of pacifists in honor of Briand. He was returning from Geneva that evening, and some groups of pacifists had told their members to go and wait for him at the Lyon station and welcome him. In the opposite camp, Action Française, the ultranationalist organization, had announced that its followers would also be at the Lyons station to stage a counter-demonstration. Very excited in anticipation of this battle, Simone wanted to go and asked me to accompany her. We went together. There were many pacifists along the approaches to the station, but we didn't see any of the Action Française people. After greeting Briand with cheers, the demonstrators divided themselves in several columns, some of which headed for the Quai d'Orsay by following the streets along the Seine while another got there by way of the main boulevards, in order to greet Briand again. Simone and I went with the column that marched down the boulevards. Simone would have liked to be in the first rank, but the men who were at the head of the column would not permit it. We had to be satisfied with the second rank. The police wanted to stop our procession. They did so at first with simple, peaceful barriers that were easily overturned and bypassed. At the third or fourth barrier, the policemen charged. Since we were in the second rank, we saw them quite clearly, rushing toward us with their clubs raised. We did not retreat, but the men of the first rank crowded back against us and Simone was knocked down. No doubt the policemen disdained us. When she had gotten up, each policeman was grappling with one or several demonstrators, so we could easily slip between the groups of combatants and get past the barrier. Others did the same and the column reformed, though now less numerous than before. After this we arrived without further difficulty at the Quai d'Orsay. Some people from the other columns had already arrived. A young man next to us was rubbing his aching head; he had been hit by a policeman's club. Briand appeared for an instant at the window, we cheered him, then we dispersed and went home.

I remember two of the three subjects assigned for the final written exam for the *agrégation.* For the history of philosophy we had to discuss "Causality in Hume"; for morals the question "Must moral judgment deal with act, intention, or character?" I have forgotten the subject for general philosophy. Bréhier was our examiner for the composition on the history of philosophy. Simone admired his noble Stoic's comportment and said, "In any case one should try to do something good for this fellow." Afterward, when she learned what her marks were, she was amazed to discover that this dissertation had received the lowest marks of all three; she didn't think that it had been so lacking in merit.

(Perhaps she was tired when she did it, for this was the third day of the exams. And perhaps Bréhier had been mistaken in the mark he gave her.)

Simone's subject at the oral examination was, I believe, "The beautiful in nature and art." Several of our classmates wanted to attend this session.

Before the final tests, the story had gotten about that Bouglé had predicted, "So-and-so, so-and-so, and so-and-so will pass. As for the Red Virgin, we shall leave her in peace to make bombs for the coming grand social upheaval." But Simone passed, though only in the middle rank (seventh). When she learned what her marks were, she thought that she might have even failed. She said that she felt like the man who had crossed Lake Constance on the ice and was terribly frightened after he reached the other side.

On the evening of the day that we heard the results we celebrated our success at the Weils. We drank wine and sang songs. Simone asked me to sing certain student songs; I didn't refuse, though these songs were not very respectable. Her parents seemed to be very amused by them, though they may have been a bit shocked. I wasn't entirely in my normal frame of mind. It was that evening that we began, Simone and I, to give each other the informal "*tu.*" At first it was just one pleasantry among others.

A few days later, on the first of August, an inspector of the educational system, perhaps Roustan, summoned us to his office. He wanted to talk to us about vacant posts, ask us what we hoped to do, and in what region we wanted to work as teachers. The procedure was to enter his office one by one. Simone and I entered together. He was surprised and told us that in principle he received the new teachers separately. Simone said, "We have no secrets from each other."

I don't recall much about the interview. But according to Cabaud, who has seen Simone's dossier at the Ministry of National Education,[15] she had not yet definitely decided to ask for a post for the school year of 1931–1932. No doubt she had not yet given up the idea of working in a factory after her *agrégation.* It was only ten days later that she wrote to the ministry requesting a post "preferably in a port (Le Havre, if possible) or in an industrial town in the north or center of France."[16] Due to the economic crisis, which was then quite severe, she had provisorily given up the plan to become a factory worker; she wrote to me in September: "My great project has been temporarily abandoned because of the crisis." Finally she was appointed to Le Puy, which did not at all correspond with her wishes.

Rumor has it that after the final exams, Bouglé said, "We shall send the Red Virgin as far away as possible so that we shall never hear of her again." And in fact she was sent far away, but Bouglé was mistaken if he thought he had heard the last of her, as we shall see.

5

Le Puy
(1931-1932)

After receiving her *agrégation* diploma, Simone left for Réville, which is north of the Cotentin peninsula and close to Valognes. She at first stayed there with her parents and then by herself. They all lived with the Henri Passily family. As soon as she had arrived at this coastal town, Simone wanted to share in the work of the fishermen. She asked several of them to take her out to sea. Most of them refused; the only ones who agreed to it were the Lecarpentier brothers. They had been told that she was a communist and had said, "It doesn't matter to us whether she's a communist or not." These two brothers fished from their own boat and had only one man in their crew.

Simone tried to make herself useful on the boat, but it was rather difficult to find work for her. She was really in the way. To keep her occupied, they gave her the task of winding up the fishing lines. She would often go out with them at night, and the people thereabouts were scandalized by this.

One night there was a big storm at sea. Simone was out in the boat with the Lecarpentier brothers. Very tense and anxious, her parents and the Lecarpentier family waited up for them together. Finally the fishermen and their new crew member returned, soaked to the skin. Simone had not shown any fear during the storm.

When she returned to Paris, Simone attended, from September 15 to 18, the twenty-seventh national congress of the C.G.T. (la Confédération générale du Travail [General Confederation of Labor]), to which she accompanied Cancouët. This congress devoted most of its time to discussing the problem of trade union unity. At that period, there were two large trade union movements, the General Confederation of Labor, or C.G.T., and the United General Confederation of Labor, or C.G.T.U. There was even a third organization, the Independent Federation of Functionaries, or F.A. [Fédération autonome]. This division weakened the working class. Some militants who belonged to the three different organizations had met on November 9, 1930, and had issued an appeal for unity. They advocated the reconstitution of trade union unity on the basis of the Amiens charter. The signatories of the manifesto numbered twenty-two (seven C.G.T., seven F.A., and eight C.G.T.U. militants). At the 1931 C.G.T. congress, which was held in Japy Hall and which Simone attended, the motion for unity presented by the "Twenty-Two" was supported by Dumoulin. But since the bureaucrats who controlled the C.G.T. opposed it, the motion was voted down by a crushing majority. However, on the last day of the congress, Jouhaux, the secretary general, who had sensed a deep desire for unity among the militants, decided in his turn to come out for unity but through a meager "at the base," that is, of the rank and file, and without any prior agreement between the organizations, and accepted the idea of a special congress to effectuate the merger. One member had demanded the addition of this last condition to the final resolution, and this had been accepted. So, although the method of unification proposed by the "Twenty-Two" had been rejected, the idea of unity, which they had reawakened, had gained ground. To tell the truth, in Jouhaux's mind merger at the base simply meant the return of all the members, as individuals, to the C.G.T.; nevertheless, some real concessions had been granted. The Japy motion stated that there would not be "any conditions set for a return to the C.G.T.," and gave the trade union groups and federations "full latitude as regards the application of the statutes." In the *Libres Propos* of October 1931 can be found a fine report on this congress by Simone.

·She had also made contact, thanks perhaps to the Alexandres, with the revolutionary syndicalists belonging to the groups connected with the *Révolution prolétarienne* and the *Cri du peuple,* particularly with Monatte, Chambelland, and Daniel Guérin. She asked them for the addresses of militant trade unionists in Le Puy and its environs. They told her chiefly about Claudius Vidal, the secretary of the Confederated Union of Teachers in the Haute-Loire, and advised her to go to Saint-Etienne and see Urbain Thévenon, a teacher and member of the administrative council of the Labor Exchange and assistant secretary of Confederated Union's Loire section.

Simone put her hopes in the activity of the unions rather than that of the political parties. She still believed, so it seems, in the possibility of a revolution, but thought that only a revolution prepared and carried out by the trade union organizations could be a genuine revolution. In an article she wrote three months later she contrasts time and again the groups based on opinion, that is, the parties, whose effect on society, she claims, is only imaginary, with the groups based on occupations, which are the only ones that could really change society. "Experience has shown that a revolutionary party can effectively, according to Marx's formula, take possession of the bureaucratic and military machinery, but not in order to smash it. For power really to pass into the hands of the workers they would have to unite, not through the imaginary ties created by the community of opinion but through the real ties created by the community of their productive function."[1] Consequently, she had to contact the revolutionary trade unionists, who must wage the revolutionary struggle inside the factories and on the corporate level.

The time to leave for Le Puy finally came. Mme. Weil went with Simone to help her find a place to live and to get her settled. They reached Le Puy on September 30, near the end of the morning. The town seemed to them livelier, prettier, and more interesting than they had expected, and Simone was no longer sorry that she had been sent there. While roaming through the streets one of the first things she discovered was a postcard that showed "the Red Virgin of Le Puy" (a bronze statue set on a huge cliff of rock). Delighted, she bought it and sent it to Bouglé.

When she went to the lycée accompanied by her mother, the custodian, taking her for a student, asked her in which class she wanted to enroll. For this first visit to the headmistress of the school, she had consented to wear gloves. She was ill at ease and kept staring at her swathed spread-out hands. She vowed after that that never again would she wear gloves, and doubtless never did. During the course of this interview she learned that another young woman had been appointed to teach philosophy at Le Puy. Embarrassed, the headmistress didn't know what to do. Disappointed and angry at having been sent so far perhaps for no reason, Simone told her mother afterward that since they had sent her to Le Puy, she intended not to budge.

The next day she met this other young woman at the lycée. It was Simone Anthériou, also one of Alain's students (she, too, had taken his courses at the Sévigné), who also knew the Alexandres. Since she had received her female *agrégation,* she could teach either philosophy or literature. She agreed to teach literature so that both she and Simone could remain at Le Puy.

On the very first day Mme. Weil and Simone had found a small apartment that seemed suitable for Simone. It was on the rue Pannesac, on the fourth floor of the house of an architect (M. Proix, the town architect). There was a large room with a slightly sloping ceiling and a fine view, and another large room that served as both bathroom and kitchen. Simone lived there for about twelve days, while her mother stayed at a hotel. Simone was absolutely delighted to have her own apartment, which she would pay for herself.

Classes began on Friday, October 2. Mme. Weil felt that Simone was a bit nervous about her first days as a teacher; she hadn't slept too well. The first day she went to school she wore a hat, which she rarely did and most likely never did again. Later on, four of her students in the philosophy class wrote:

"Her natural inelegance, the hat she wore that first day of class for the first and last time and which she would replace with a beret, caused some smiles that soon disappeared after the first few lectures.

"Her carelessless in dress did not shock us; she was neither affected nor tomboyish; we paid less and less attention to these things, already sensing that Simone Weil's time and thoughts were devoted to occupations of another order.

"The clumsiness of her gestures, above all of her hands, the special expression on her face when she would concentrate on her thought, her piercing look through her thick glasses, her smile—everything about her emanated a feeling of total frankness and forgetfulness of self, revealing a nobility of soul that was certainly at the root of the emotions she inspired in us, but that at first we were not aware of."[2]

At the start there were only eight students in the philosophy class. But some of the students were late returning to school and so in the end there were fifteen in the class. Simone also gave a course in Greek to some students in the third form—not too many, only four at the beginning. And she taught the history of art for a half-hour each week to students in the sixth form. Her daily schedule was not too heavy, but she prepared each lecture carefully in advance, so she worked very hard and suffered from headaches from her first days at Le Puy.

Her pupils realized that her teaching was based on a strong, solidly connected, and rigorous system of thought. They admired her profoundly. At the same time they tried to protect her, for they could see that she was utterly inept when it came to practical matters. Even the youngest students, who studied Greek with her, were maternal toward her. Once she came to their class with her sweater on backward. The little girls told her and arranged things so that she could hide behind the blackboard, take the sweater off, and put it on right. One of the girls stood guard at the door to warn her in case the headmistress should appear while all this was going on.

According to Mme. Weil, the headmistress, on the first day of school, had not responded in a friendly manner to Simone's requests for an adjustment in her schedule. But Simone had been quick to let her understand that she wasn't going to be intimidated.

On October 7, after breakfast, she left for Saint-Etienne. (She didn't have classes on Wednesday or Saturday afternoons.) She told her mother that she would surely return that evening, but not to worry if she stayed away longer. In fact she didn't return until the following afternoon. She had gone to visit the Thévenons.

Urbain and Albertine Thévenon were both teachers. Urbain played an important role in the trade union movement, both in Saint-Etienne and the region; he was not only a particularly courageous and devoted militant but also a wise and thoughtful man. Albertine was not active in the movement, for she had too much to do in her home—they had children—and her profession; but having been born in a working-class family, she sympathized fully with her husband's activities. Since the conversation with Simone went on till very late, they put her up for the night on a bed in their dining room. The next day they introduced her to some of their comrades, among them Pierre Arnaud, the secretary of the Miners' Union of C.G.T.U., about whom Simone spoke enthusiastically to her mother on her return.

Albertine Thévenon has more than once told the amazing story of how her first meeting with Simone took place. Jean Duperray describes it as follows in his account: "The Thévenons then lived at Saint-Etienne on a busy, populous street in an apartment whose vestibule was one of those long, dark hallways customary in houses in the old working-class districts. Simone rang the bell. Albertine went to open the door, one hand wrapped in a sock she was darning. Simone asked, 'Is Monsieur Thévenon in?' When Albertine said he was, Simone shoved her aside with a thrust of her shoulder and before Albertine had time to close the door and turn around, she had already rushed down the hallway and stepped into Thévenon's room, where he was surprised to see her suddenly appear."[3]

Simone's strange act, pushing Albertine rudely aside so as to rush to Thévenon's room, can be explained by some previous experiences. The wives of trade union comrades often disliked or distrusted her and would try to prevent her from seeing their husbands.

On coming back from Saint-Etienne on Thursday, Simone met a trade unionist in Le Puy with whom she had already been in contact. (He had been pointed out to her by the *Cri du peuple,* that is, most likely Daniel Guérin.) That same day he in turn introduced her to Claudius Vidal, the secretary of the Haute-Loire section of the National Teachers' Union.

From then on, she was deeply involved in the trade union movement of the Haute-Loire and Loire regions. She somehow managed to become a member of the National Teachers' Union (C.G.T.), either because there was no local for the secondary schools or because she preferred the society of teachers to that of professors and succeeded in getting her way.

Simone was a resolute advocate of trade union unity. From the start, she tried to organize meetings at Le Puy between militants of the C.G.T. and the C.G.T.U., and to set up a group that would gather together trade unionists of all the different tendencies.

Mme. Weil, meanwhile, was somewhat concerned at the idea that her daughter would be living alone. She doubted that she would arrange for the proper heating or that she would pay much attention to her material needs. Besides, Simone had already made up her mind to use only that part of her pay equal to the pay of a new teacher (six hundred francs a month), and not of a new full professor, which is what she was. This seemed to promise a very Spartan, uncomfortable life. Mme. Weil hoped that Simone could live with a family, but she could not find a satisfactory arrangement of this kind. She even began to think that she should live with Simone Anthériou; and she wanted this even more when she discovered a fine apartment, one of the most comfortable available in Le Puy, but too large for one person. The two Simones, though quite friendly, had not thought of living together, but Mme. Weil arranged everything and they soon found themselves launched.

The apartment was on the second floor of a house located just outside the town, about a quarter of an hour's walk from the lycée (the Fabre house, on the Saugues highway). It was one of the rare apartments in Le Puy that could boast a bathroom. Mme. Weil rented it unfurnished for a moderate sum and then somehow convinced the owner to furnish it adequately. It contained a living room, dining room, two bedrooms, a study, a bathroom, and a large completely tiled kitchen. From the front rooms there was a beautiful view of the town, and the back rooms overlooked a large garden that the tenants could also use. Simone didn't readily consent to being housed so comfortably and in such a bourgeois manner; Mme. Weil had to muster all her diplomatic skills and managed to convince her. Detesting the idea of having a living room, Simone decided to fill the room with ropes and use it to hang up their clothes. So they converted it into a kind of large wardrobe closet. The walls of Simone's bedroom were covered with a figured wallpaper, and either because this was bourgeois or the pattern appeared to her in bad taste, she had the room recovered with a solid-color wallpaper. She wanted only a few furnishings—a couch, a large work table, some book shelves, and a small, very pretty antique chest for her linen. From then on, it was forbidden to enter her room to sweep it, since the floor was covered with books and papers.

Mme. Weil also found them a maid. Simone Anthériou soon noticed that she was stealing food and even linen. She didn't say anything about it to Simone, who found it hard to believe anything bad of a proletarian, or perhaps would have considered it quite right that she should take what she needed. But Simone noticed that she was going through her papers and especially her correspondence. She thought that the woman could be working for the police and dismissed her immediately.

When Mme. Weil returned to Le Puy (during this school year she frequently traveled back and forth between Paris and Le Puy; it was long and tiring, and she used to say that she was the one Bouglé had played the nasty trick on), she again found a maid for them. Simone insisted that she be paid at the going trade union rates. This was the skilled workers' rate, two or three times more than what maids were usually paid. The poor woman argued about this as much as she could, having the feeling that she was agreeing to something dishonest. She herself

was honest and a good worker and remained with the two Simones until
the end of the school year. To make up for her unusually high wages,
she would bring them bags of pine cones to light the fire. These big bags
would often be used by the girls as chairs.

Mme. Weil asked Simone Anthériou not to ride a bicycle, since that
might give Simone the idea of doing so; Mme. Weil said that it was
dangerous for her because her reflexes were too slow. Simone Anthériou promised and kept her word; nonetheless, soon after Simone
wanted a bicycle to go and visit some trade union comrades who lived
on the outskirts of Le Puy. In one of her letters she asked her parents
to send her her bicycle and, foreseeing their objections, told them that
if she didn't get it, Vidal would come and fetch her on his motorcycle,
which he drove very fast. Yet a little later she wrote to tell them that she
no longer needed her bicycle; she did ask for it again near the end of
the school year, but, finally, it seemed the bicycle was never sent.

Mme. Weil also convinced Simone Anthériou that she should buy the
best cuts of meat for Simone, because she could not tolerate anything
else. In fact, according to Simone Anthériou (who later married and
became Mme. Canguilhem), Simone could only eat absolutely fresh
food of the highest quality. For her, eating was more of a chore than a
pleasure; she was not greedy and was disgusted by anything that was not
absolutely flawless. Just a spot on a piece of fruit was enough to make
her lay it aside. She tried not to show these feelings of disgust that she
evidently could not overcome, but Simone Anthériou had become aware
of them. So she promised to buy the best cuts of meat. Simone did not
realize that these were relatively expensive cuts and thought she was
eating ordinary meat.

Simone Canguilhem says that Mme. Weil secretly protected Simone
and sometimes would deceive her a bit in order to protect her. When
she came to Le Puy, she would often bring a skirt, stockings, or some
other clothes and slip them on the sly among Simone's things. Simone's
disinterest in such matters and her lack of time to deal with them made
it rather easy to deceive her. When they had first moved in, Mme. Weil
had bought a large supply of coal. Simone did not think to ask who had
paid for it. It is true that she didn't use it for herself. Believing that the
unemployed could not afford coal for heating, she had decided not to
heat her room. She slept with the window open and worked without a
fire, swathed in shawls. And she did not light a fire in her room except
when friends came to visit her. (One day she learned to her great
surprise that the unemployed generally found some way of heating their
houses.) The coal they had bought was used to feed a slow-combustion
stove that stood in the apartment's entrance hall.

During the course of the year Mme. Weil often sent big packages of
foodstuffs, filled with large rounds of Dutch cheese, Heudebert patés,
and so on. Simone would have been very well nourished if she had been

able to eat every day. According to Simone Canguilhem, she ate well and normally when she was not suffering from headaches. Indeed, she and her roommate would now and then hold what they jokingly called "little celebrations."

But when she had her headaches Simone would at times go for five or six days without being able to eat. She could only bear to eat raw, grated potatoes. These headaches would sometimes make her vomit; indeed, any effort, such as trying to masticate, could cause this. To avoid all movement, she would wedge her head in a pile of pillows.

Even when sick like this, she still continued to give her classes. Several times she had Simone Anthériou take her to the lycée, leaning on her arm all the way. Just stepping up on the sidewalk was a painful effort for her, yet she did not want to miss her class. Nevertheless she still had to take two short leaves of absence, one of them toward the end of the school year.

After having had some further repairs and changes made in the apartment, Mme. Weil left Le Puy around October 16. On the twentieth of that month Simone wrote to her family:

"Dear family:

"Everything is going very well. Just back from the Unity Committee (simply thinking about Cancouët makes my hair stand on end), where the minority attacked the leaders of the Twenty-Two with unusual and perfectly appropriate violence. I saw the Thévenons's children and they are marvelous kids, and also his in-laws, who are very interesting. I met Vidal again. Tomorrow he'll get me into his union. This coming week I'll be stuck with four hours of Latin classes (the teacher is sick). Which will allow us to have some supplementary celebrations. The 'boss' [her nickname for the headmistress] has conveyed my schedule for those four hours through S. Ath, and with, it appears, a thousand oratorical pardons and excuses. Could she be afraid of me?

"I haven't received Olida's package. I'll drop by the post office tomorrow. Send me as soon as possible the paper I wrote for the Ecole. I also need Hegel's *Philosophy of the Spirit,* the volume in which he has a chapter on habit. Maybe you can get it through Charron?* I'll return it immediately. My trade union greetings to Pot.† I've learned by chance that Cancouët recommended me to the secretary of the C.G.T. railway men. I had lunch with him. Very nice. Thank Cancouët for me. For the rest, it seems really that there is nothing to do at Le Puy. Bouglé has chosen well. Embrace Biri for me and regards to all my friends.

"P.S. I just got the package. It looks like a package for a soldier on campaign!"

*A functionary at the Ecole Normale library.
†The treasurer at the Ecole Normale.

The Committee for Unity mentioned in this letter was the group at Saint-Etienne. Its first meeting had taken place on October 17, and Simone had attended it. Although generally in agreement with the Twenty-Two group, Simone understood the objections that certain trade unionists, whether in the C.G.T. or the C.G.T.U., brought against them. Between the C.G.T. and the C.G.T.U. there existed not only a factual division but also a divergence of principles, in that the C.G.T. defended trade union independence as regards the political parties while the C.G.T.U. was in favor of a close connection between trade unionism and politics—in fact, its trade union activity was closely tied to the program of the Communist party. However, the C.G.T.U. waged the class struggle more energetically than the C.G.T., which was rather reformist. Some trade unionists also had their doubts as to the possibility of a merger that was not actually a capitulation of one doctrine to the other and an absorption of one of the central movements by the other. Simone at one and the same time supported trade union independence (C.G.T.) and the class struggle (C.G.T.U.). She could simultaneously approve of those who spoke in favor of unity and understand those who, in the name of principles she partly agreed with, fought against it.

Thévenon asked her to write a report of the Committee's meeting and send it to the *Cri du peuple*. She wrote it and sent it, but subsequently realized that it could not arrive in time to be published in the next issue of *Cri* (which appeared on Tuesdays). She then telephoned Daniel Guérin and gave him a summary of the essential events. She wrote a letter of apology to Thévenon:

"Dear comrade:

"You may have been surprised by the last issue of the *Cri*. I wouldn't want to incur your and Arnaud's reproaches. This is what happened: I was convinced, I don't know why, that there was a train leaving Le Puy about eight o'clock in the evening, which led to my sending my report at a time that did not permit the *Cri* people to receive it before Wednesday evening. As I didn't know to what extent Arnaud had to base his propaganda on published texts, I telephoned D. Guérin Wednesday morning to tell him the essentials of what had happened at the meeting. I don't know what he will do with the detailed account (too detailed, I am afraid) that I sent him. Anyway, you have my apologies. I am terribly unhappy that I failed to do the first job that you entrusted to me.

"Vidal has gotten me admitted to the Teachers' Union. I've met Delhermet—very, very nice. I also made the acquaintance of the secretary of the C.G.T. railwaymen, to whom Cancouët had recommended me. He is in complete sympathy with the Twenty-Two group.

"I will soon send you your Committee notebook, in which I have not yet written out the minutes of the meeting. I work all the time. Moreover, Vidal and Delhermet have insisted that I give them an article for their bulletins. . . .

"I shall certainly come to see you on All Saints' Day. I can't come before that. In the meantime, my best regards to your in-laws . . . and my warmest best wishes to your wife.

"Fraternally"

About the same time she wrote to her family:

"Dear family:

"Everything is still going along well. I have been admitted to the Teachers' Union. As for the railroad man, it was actually he who had come to the lycée. I am dying to get some news about Cancouët, who seems to me to be behaving quite well on the question of unity.

"The class is going fine. Tomorrow I will do my last supplementary hour of class work. . . .

"We are eating like kings. S. is an excellent cook. We even eat meat! The Dutch cheese is first-rate, and the bacon is very good too. Received the Heudebert and the papers. Thanks.

"I absolutely need my bike as soon as possible. I can go and see Vidal and Delhermet (whom I have just met—no one could be more pleasant) on a bike and along roads that are absolutely safe; and this is good from the sports point of view, until we can go skiing. If you don't want to send it to me, I have a decisive argument until I get my bicycle: when I want to go and see Vidal, he will come to fetch me on his motorcycle and I shall sit behind him. Now I can't guarantee that he drives slowly and cautiously. . . .

"Vidal and Delhermet are already my comrades in the full sense of the word. Their wives are very sweet. . . . The United railroad men here seem quite nice. Tell Cancouët that I am trying to get them to merge (United and Confederated railroad men), and that the terrain seems favorable. . . .

"What is the news from Paris? Is there still a lot of misery? What is my friend Chiappe doing?‡ What is happening to the bourgeois panic? Is it increasing or diminishing?"

She wrote again to her family at the end of October:

"Dear family:

"I reply by return mail. Delighted at the prospect of Cancouët's arrival. [Cancouët was not able to realize this plan.] I deduce that he's not too furious with me. Did he contact the Twenty-Two? Tell him that I will introduce him to some really worthwhile comrades here. Tell him that we are in the process of organizing a unity group of all tendencies in the trade unions, so as to give a little push to the militants here in town.

‡In calling the prefect of police, Chiappe, her friend, Simone is obviously being ironic.

"I need Proudhon's *What Is Property?*—if possible in a friendly edition, i.e., not annotated by Bouglé. Could I get it? Thanks for the paper, the Heudebert products, and the Hegel. If the Proudhon is too much trouble, forget it. I'll write to the Library of Labor.

"I need several pieces of information. 1. How do you cook rice? 2 . How do you eat bacon—raw or cooked? If you want to eat it with eggs on a plate, do you have to cook it first?

"I demand details about your life. . . .

"In case you don't know what to do with your money, I might point out that *La Révolution prolétarienne* and *Le Cri du peuple* are both very hard up. The usefulness of the *Cri du peuple* could be argued about, for it is an organ of combat (but obviously I think it's useful, since I give them my support . . .). But as for *La Révolution prolétarienne,* the only magazine that publishes first-rate historical studies on social problems and the only independent revolutionary magazine, its disappearance would be a disaster. I think that it would be really a good idea to climb the four flights at 54 rue du Château-d'Eau and bring some money to charming Barat (telling him that it is on my advice). . . .

"I must point out that I have to carry the packages from the station by myself. So don't go overboard."

Simone did not go to Paris for All Saints' Day nor for the holiday on November 11; she had too much to do at Le Puy. She had thought she might go to Saint-Etienne for All Saints', but most likely didn't because it was clearly on the eve of All Saints' that she wrote to Thévenon:
"Dear comrade:
"It finally appears impossible for me to come tomorrow. I need these two days to make a detailed outline for my course for the rest of the trimester, find certain texts that have to be read, etc. I would have come in any case if I had thought that right now there was something positive to be done in regard to the workers' course, but since I haven't heard from you, I presume that there is nothing. But I will try to come Wednesday.

"I'm sending you your book of minutes. I'm ashamed to have kept them so long. My excuse is that besides my work at the lycée I have begun to organize on your and Arnaud's advice and in agreement with Vidal and Delhermet, an intertrade union group of the different political tendencies. Hence people I have to see, etc., and since there is only me here at Le Puy, I must do all this work alone. Anyway I have the feeling that it should succeed.

"I fear that you're angry with me because of the report on the Committee. Besides, I'm angry at myself, and all the more since I'm not quite sure how important it could have been. If you feel strongly about it, don't spare me, but all the same don't lose confidence in me because of it. . . ."

So she had set about organizing an intertrade union group at Le Puy. In a letter that her parents must have received on November 4 or 5, she says: "We are in the process of bringing together all the working-class elements in the town, without distinction, including the Communists. Moreover, a relationship has been established between the Confederated and United railroad men, both secretaries being partisans of unity and sympathizing with the Twenty-Two. The funniest thing about it is that neither of them knows the other man's name. I had to come from Paris for them to get into contact with each other and with Vidal."[4]

But in Paris the movement for unity was having its difficulties. From November 8 to 11 the national congress of the C.G.T.U. was held in the Magic-City Hall. If the congress of the C.G.T. had already largely rejected the proposals of the Twenty-Two, the C.G.T.U.'s congress was even harsher toward them and held out no hope at all. The supporters of unity were to write a few months later: "After Magic-City, we had better give up the idea of a merger congress. . . . The C.G.T. accepts the merger with the rank and file. The C.G.T.U. does not want to hear of merger, either through the rank and file or at the top. . . . It advocates only a congress of unity directed by itself, which moreover could not even discuss its international affiliation."[5]

However, the inter-union meeting still took place at Le Puy, as planned, on November 11. Simone had written to her family two days earlier: "I begin to breathe a bit now that the preparatory work for the inter-union meeting, which will be held the day after tomorrow, has been done. I don't know whether it will produce anything. Right now I look upon it as a spectacle, with just a feeling of curiosity. If it doesn't produce anything, it will still give me the chance to meet two or three likable fellows and become acquainted with Vidal, who is the best one can hope for in a pal (as for Delhermet, I haven't yet been able to see him as much)."

The meeting was a success; they decided to form an inter-union group and established certain rules whose observation could in the future favor unity. They promised above all to fight any attempt to form a new trade union where there already was a union, whatever its tendency—Confederated, United, or Independent; and where there was none, they advocated the formation of a single union that would freely decide upon its orientation.

Simone wrote a full account of this meeting.[6] It was published on November 21 in *L'Effort,* the newspaper of the Independent Alliance of the Building Trades of Lyons, which Thévenon had launched. In this article, when describing how the initiative for this meeting had been taken by militants from three different trade union groups, Simone does not mention her own role in this, which undoubtedly was decisive.

The end of this article makes it evident that she was aware of the difficulties that the inter-union group would have to overcome. She foresaw them even more clearly since she already knew when she wrote the article of the decisions at Magic-City. But it is obvious that she was determined to continue the fight for unity, despite the opposition of the trade union bureaucrats. "Unity at the top having proved unrealizable, the members of the rank and file are now compelled to take the job into their own hands." Of course she does not want to weaken the existing organizations. "One must respect the existing trade union organizations, which are the most precious conquest of the working-class movement; and one must realize unity without the support of these organizations or even, in many instances, in spite of them. This seemingly insoluble problem must be solved by the working class, or else it will be condemned to disappear as a revolutionary force."

In her letter of November 9, Simone wrote: "On Wednesday the eighteenth, Thévenon must present the question of courses to the Committee for Unity at Saint-Etienne; he is sending out a circular on this subject at the same time as the call for the meeting. He thinks that it will be accepted, and in any case is inclined to go all out in support of the project." This was a project to organize some courses for miners at the Saint-Etienne Labor Exchange.

Courses for workers had already been held at Saint-Etienne. In 1928, Workers' Colleges had been created by the Regional Union and the local C.G.T. In 1931, Thévenon, with another teacher, Claveyrolas, had been in charge of these courses. So Simone found an already functioning organization into which she could pour her devotion. But no doubt she insisted that they should develop these courses as much as possible. Mme. Weil wrote to André on November 12: "She has persuaded a teacher at Saint-Etienne to create a working-class university of which she will be one of the mainstays. (Saint-Etienne is about three hours from Le Puy—*Klienigkeit!*)."

As we have already seen, Simone, thinking of the conditions for a real revolution, regarded the ability of the workers to attain knowledge and culture as of prime importance. She presented her ideas on this subject in an article published by *L'Effort* on December 19 and entitled *"La vie syndicale: en marge du Comité d'études."* ["Trade Union Life: Notes on the Committee for Instruction."]

Recalling the failure of the peoples' universities before the First World War, she writes: "Is this a reason to condemn all work of this kind? On the contrary, the important thing is to distinguish, among the attempts at working-class culture, those that are conducted in such a way as to strengthen the ascendancy of the intellectuals over the workers, and those conducted in such a way as to free the workers from this domination."

In this article certain observations can be found on the role of religion in the origins of human culture that will recall those found in her diploma dissertation. "At all times the ability to handle words has seemed to men something miraculous. In primitive societies the run of men, those who know how to hunt, fish, handle tools and weapons with admirable ingenuity, docilely obey certain privileged beings whose only knowledge consists in being able to express certain formulas. These privileged beings are priests; and the fact that their formulas are absolutely bereft of effectiveness does not prevent them from being regarded as possessing an essence superior to those who know how to act. This domination of those who know how to handle words over those who know how to handle things is rediscovered at every stage of human history. It is necessary to add that, as a group, these manipulators of words, whether priests or intellectuals, have always been on the side of the ruling class, on the side of the exploiters against the producers."

Alain had defined the bourgeois as the man who earns his living by persuading—the man who has dealings with men, not with things—and how can one persuade men if not by language? Simone defined the class of men who could handle language and not things (the bourgeois class in Alain's terms) as being essentially the class of the priests and intellectuals.

But to the extent that religion and science signify respect for language and the knowledge of language, she believed that the proletariat should not have contempt for them but rather appropriate them. For her, this is the true revolution.

"This respect accorded language and the men who are best able to use it has been indispensable to human progress. Without it, men would have remained blind and routine when doing the necessary work of life. It is out of religion that all human thought has developed, including the most positive form of science. So it is not by inspiring them with contempt for culture, described here as bourgeois, that the workers can be freed from the intellectuals' domination. Certainly this superiority accorded up until now to intellectuals over producers, through a convention that has been indispensable to human development, must now be absolutely rejected by the workers. Yet this does not mean that the workers must reject the heritage of human culture; it means that they must prepare to take possession of it, as they must prepare themselves to take possession of the entire heritage from previous generations. Indeed, this act of taking possession is the revolution.

"In Marx's eyes, perhaps the most important conquest of the proletarian revolution should be the abolition of what he calls 'the degrading division of work into intellectual and manual work.' The abolition of this degrading division can and must be achieved, and we must prepare for it now. To this end we must, first of all, give the workers the ability to handle language and especially the written language."

On Wednesday, November 18, the organization of the courses had to be decided upon, and the methods that would be followed were to be decided upon eight days later. So Simone went to Saint-Etienne on Wednesday. In a letter that was probably written on November 19 she wrote that all week until Wednesday she had eagerly awaited the day she would spend there. Her meetings with her comrades at Saint-Etienne were among her greatest joys.

It was decided that they would have a course in French given by Simone and a course in political economy to be given jointly by Simone and Thévenon. These were to begin on Saturday, most likely on December 5. From December on, therefore, Simone would be in Saint-Etienne on Saturday afternoons and Sundays.

It is understandable that in her letter to André Mme. Weil said that Simone was killing herself with overwork. Not only was Simone teaching her courses at the lycée, doing the preparatory work for the miners' courses, carrying on her trade union activities at Le Puy, taking her trips to Saint-Etienne and sending in articles to *L'Effort,* but she had also found the time to write an article for the November bulletin of the National Union of Public School Teachers in France and the Colonies, section of the Haute-Loire. This is the article entitled "Reflections on the Economic Crisis."[7]

In this article she maintained that even in a period of economic crisis the proletariat should continue the class struggle and not be swayed by arguments according to which, under these circumstances, one must stop making demands and institute a policy of collaboration with the bosses. She thought that even in a time of crisis, the interests of the workers and those of the bosses were still at opposite poles. To collaborate with the owning class would prolong the life of capitalism, in which economic crises are an inevitable result; thus it would only help to prepare another economic crisis. Hence this bold conclusion: "There is no point in trying to find a remedy for the crisis, something that could only be done with the assent and under the domination of the ruling class. The only thing that should be done is to organize the struggle immediately. Considering its present degree of decomposition, the regime can only subsist because the lack of unity, good organization, and clear ideas keep the working class in its present state of weakness."

In November, Mme. Anthériou had come to spend some time with her daughter. She was rather shocked by Simone's ideas and activities and could not conceal her anxiety at seeing her daughter in such company. Simone was amused by her indignation and did nothing to reassure her; just the opposite, she increased her anxiety by discussing Christianity. Mme. Anthériou was a fervent Protestant. Simone reminded her that the early Christians had at first scandalized people and had been persecuted, and that the Protestants had originally been an opposition party and had also been persecuted. She then set about proving to her that at the time of Christ she, Mme. Anthériou, would undoubtedly have been on the side of the Pharisees. Poor Mme. Anthériou couldn't sleep. Yet she was forced to admire Simone's knowledge of the Bible ("she could advise a minister," she said), and lost all of her assurance and all moral tranquillity. She returned home "stunned," predicting serious trouble for her daughter and vowing that she would never visit her again.[8]

After the Japy Congress, the Twenty-Two were racked by dissension. In fact their differences had always been a threat, owing to the different loyalties within the group. Moreover, some members of the Committee (especially the independents), reproached the C.G.T. members for having supported the Japy motion, which in their opinion simply meant that the C.G.T. was maneuvering to absorb all the trade unionists. They wanted a return to the original program: a merger congress convoked on the basis of the Amiens charter. After Magic-City, the divisions were accentuated and it became clear that the Committee of Twenty-Two was doomed to disappear. In a letter to her parents that must have been written about November 19, Simone wrote: "The congress of the C.G.T.U. seems to have succeeded in sowing dissension among the Twenty-Two. No doubt some of them want to split from the group, though the Committee hasn't broken up as yet."

In fact the Committee soon did break up. At a meeting held on November 20, the C.G.T. and C.G.T.U. members both refused to support the original position taken by the Twenty-Two, and each resumed its freedom of action.[9] Yet there was still another meeting of the Committee on Sunday the twenty-second, because Simone, on a postcard she must have written about November 28, anxiously asks her mother for news of what is happening in Paris, and especially what course was adopted by the Twenty-Two on the previous Sunday.

"Just got your letter. You say that things are not going well for the Twenty-Two. You cannot imagine what it means to be thirteen hours from Paris at such moments and not know exactly what's going on. At least try to find out from Barat (whom you should give my fraternal greetings) certain precise things: 1. what Cancouët has done (if he knows); 2. the precise resolution adopted by the Twenty-Two on Sunday; 3. the attitudes of Engler, Boville, Chambelland, and Monatte; 4. the future fate of the *Cri* in general and of D. Guérin in particular. You can tell him that he need not fear my betraying the secrets of the Twenty-Two, because Thévenon will not hide anything from me—I am sure of that. But I won't see him until Saturday (first course for the miners). I beg you to write me immediately and send it by express letter to the lycée. If necessary, get him to write a few lines himself, if you can't transcribe what he says with sufficient precision."

In a postscript she again asks: "Send me the important news about the unions by express letter. It can be important for us to have this a day sooner."

In this postcard she mentions an accident that Simone Anthériou has had. While she was with Simone and a friend of hers (the comrade from the railroad union), she had fallen down the stairway in their house and had broken her wrist. She had been treated for a day in a hospital, then sent to her home in Nîmes to convalesce.

Simone's concern for the *Cri du peuple* in general and Daniel Guérin in particular was due to the fact that the *Cri du peuple* had been launched by the Committee of the Twenty-Two. The end of the Committee meant the end of the *Cri.*

The disappearance of the Twenty-Two did not mean for Simone, Monatte, or Thévenon—nor in general for the supporters of unity—the end of their struggle for trade union unification. They thought that the efforts to realize unity among the rank and file should now be intensified more than ever.[10]

Mme. Weil left for Le Puy on December 10. She found the apartment in great disorder and without any heat, just when the weather was freezing cold. In a letter to André dated the sixteenth of December, she wrote:

"Many, many silly pranks here. To begin with, on my arrival. After having traveled (very uncomfortably) from nine o'clock in the morning until ten o'clock at night, I found the trolless* at the station, with the son of the lycée's custodian. They had just come from a meeting of the C.G.T.U. at the Labor Exchange. Simone expected me to go back there with them, but I told her to count me out and took a taxi to the apartment. A glacier, no heat anywhere—and for several days the temperature has been three or four below. The bed wasn't made—after great difficulty I found the sheets. No provisions; and I had just enough to pay for a glass of water. And I couldn't even get angry with the poor trolless, who is so good and affectionate to me; but she hasn't the slightest idea of anything, and since S. Anthériou's departure a dozen days before my arrival, she has been living like this, without a maid, without heat, eating at noon at a restaurant and in the evening making herself potatoes or cocoa with water. And the disorder! For the last eight days of my stay here I've been slaving from morning to night to get things into a halfway decent state!

"Two days before I got here the trolless, when she came home in the evening at six o'clock, noticed that she had shut the door behind her and left the keys inside. No locksmith at that hour. Some obliging neighbors

---

*This was the nickname André had given Simone, no doubt because trolls in Scandinavian mythology were mischievous spirits. Simone, with her incessant questions, her arguments, her scruples, her unusual enterprises, could resemble an imp who torments people or at least plays tricks.

brought over a ladder (luckily, she had left a window open), and she climbed up at least one story and then, since the ladder was a bit short, she straddled the balcony and fell into the room on her back—and got a pretty bad bump. This week she forgot her purse at the Labor Exchange in Saint-Etienne when she was there on Sunday, and in it there was an urgent letter to the Alexandres she had brought there just so it would reach them more quickly."

From Mme. Weil's letters to her husband we learn that Simone had had terrific headaches the week before her arrival. "And just think, she was all alone! But she insists that it was perfectly fine that way and that she much prefers not having anyone near her in such circumstances. Now she says that she feels better, though she still has some sort of headache. . . . But finally she looks better and is in good spirits, which is the main thing."[11]

Simone had been asked to give a course in Latin again to the students of the sixth form. The Latin teacher's children had scarlet fever and Simone was the only member of the staff who could take her place. So she had more work than usual and stayed up every night, to one o'clock. These sixth-form students told her one day that they liked her better as a teacher than the woman she had replaced. "Simone was very embarrassed and didn't know what to say."[12]

Mme. Weil thought the pay was rather poor for these supplementary hours of work. But Simone declared that she would never make a protest over questions of money. "Yet she intends to challenge the headmistress at the next teachers' meeting. The headmistress came into the classes to distribute to the students some antituberculosis campaign stamps for them to sell. So Simone wants to ask her why she should not be authorized to distribute lottery tickets for the C.G.T.U. miners' relief fund. Her pupils had already seen her holding them the other day and had asked her if they could buy some."[13]

Mme. Weil lit the stove, got firewood to heat the rooms, and gradually put the kitchen and the rest of the apartment in order, except for Simone's room, where it was forbidden to set foot and where Simone didn't want a fire. Simone could not help but be pleased with this transformation. "It's obvious that she finds the apartment much more pleasant now, but she's afraid that she will become too soft."[14] When her mother had prepared a good meal, Simone couldn't help exclaiming, "This makes me feel much different, eating good food again!"[15]

On December 12, Mme. Weil went to see Simone off for Saint-Etienne. "I accompanied the trolless to the station at two o'clock; she was carrying a load of books weighing at least forty pounds, which she had dragged from her house to the station. Since it was for the miners' course (or to loan them out, I'm not quite sure), she insisted that it wasn't at all heavy! So as you can see, she hasn't changed."[16]

The following day, Sunday, Simone returned from Saint-Etienne at ten-thirty at night. "She only spoke in monosyllables and immediately started correcting some compositions until God knows what hour! I found out later that there had been two miners in her French course and eight in the course of political economy that she gives with Thévenon! Well, after all, if that's enough for her. . . ."[17]

At the same time Simone undoubtedly was working to prepare for the second inter-union meeting, which was to take place in Le Puy on December 20. "Just imagine," Mme. Weil wrote to her husband, "she was the one who did everything to arrange this meeting: contacted the trade unions, the editors of the various newspapers, etc. They wanted to appoint her secretary, but she refused to accept the title, content just to do the work."[18]

André must have told his mother that he had made certain discoveries in mathematics. Mme. Weil wrote to her husband that she had cried with joy; and she added: "By a kind of seesaw action that is no doubt quite natural, I am less enchanted with the trolless at this moment. Not that she isn't always the same loyal and affectionate creature, but she really is too unreasonable when it comes to the necessities of everyday life. . . . She stays up every night without exception and she still has the same absurd ideas on what a maid should be paid. Her comrade from the railroad union, who ate lunch with us today (he brought us the package from the wholesalers; even when you pay on delivery they do not bring it to your house), and to whom I spoke alone for a moment, for I can't get over this ridiculous business of five francs an hour to the maid, told me that in this time of unemployment one could certainly find many women who would be happy to come and work all day for the usual salary of two hundred francs a month."[19] In another letter she said: "Of the two dozen handkerchiefs I had given Simone to take with her, there are eight left! And the trolless greets this information with a broad smile, since she seems to think that that's quite in the order of things. No, really and truly, I don't think she is marriageable! Can you see her as a mother of a family?"[20]

The "events at Le Puy," as they are called, began on December 17, 1931. These events are now well known in their main outlines, but it would be valuable to gather together here certain documents that give a more detailed picture of them. A summary of what happened on December 17 was presented in an article by Vidal, published in the bulletin of the Haute-Loire section of the National Teachers' Union at the beginning of 1932 and no doubt written on the basis of information supplied by Simone herself.

"On December 17, a group of unemployed meeting at the Labor Exchange decided to send a delegation to the mayor of Puy to present him with a list of demands. S. Weil, a teacher at the girls' Lycée, participated in this delegation. The mayor refused to consider the demands that were addressed to him. Confronted by this setback, the unemployed decided to go that very evening and attend a meeting of the city council. At the moment when the mayor ended the meeting, the unemployed came forward to present their demands. S. Weil was among them."[21]

According to a report the mayor presented to the meeting of the city council on February 18, 1932,[22] the visit of the unemployed to the mayor's home should have taken place on December 16. But a letter Mme. Weil wrote to her husband on December 21 confirms that this visit actually took place the same day as the appearance of the unemployed at the city council, that is to say on the seventeenth. Furthermore, she explains the reasons that led to the protest of the unemployed:

"The unemployed of Le Puy don't get any assistance. Those who wish are employed at breaking stones (on the place Michelet, in front of the girls' lycée). Since they are paid by the cubic meter and since they don't know the trade, if they work all day they manage to earn six francs, and besides, since they don't have the knack, they end up thoroughly exhausted. They held a meeting that Simone attended. They asked her to join a delegation that was to go and see the mayor. She went with them, and at a certain moment, when she realized that the unemployed were letting themselves be intimidated, she spoke out. That evening, she returned with them to a meeting of the city council; there too, at a given moment, she spoke again."

Simone had therefore accompanied the unemployed first to the mayor and afterward to the city council. Each time she had at a certain point spoken. Here is the report by *Le Mémorial*,[23] the conservative newspaper of the Haute-Loire, of the meeting of the city council:

"The city council of Le Puy met on Thursday, December 17, in an extraordinary session at eight-thirty in the evening. . . . The hall, usually deserted, particularly at such an hour at this time of the year, was suddenly packed with workers in their work clothes, led in a squad by a suffragette, a person who was still quite young, and who marshaled her ranks with amiable authority. And it must be said right off that this audience behaved very well as long as the meeting lasted. This unusual crowd had the effect of making our surprised city councilors somewhat nervous for a few moments. The discussion dealt with the following questions that were on the agenda: (There follows a series of questions concerning the city's administration, with the decisions taken by the council on these matters. Certain work projects were adopted.)

"It was at this moment, the very moment when the city council had not hesitated to reach a painful decision, however hard it will be on the taxpayers, with the aim of coming effectively to the assistance of the unemployed, it was this moment that was chosen by the bespectacled intellectual lady, with her legs sheathed in sheer silk, to unleash her little demonstration. She herded her hundred or so workless people before the table of the council. To tell the truth, the demands of the workers have merit. But this is no excuse for an individual to act in a vulgar manner toward the mayor and attack him in his professional capacity. The mayor was very firm. Perhaps he has the right, considering the responsibility he was about to take on. He told the demonstrators that their demands could not be discussed; municipal law is formally opposed to it. An extraordinary meeting could only discuss questions that had been previously placed on the agenda. . . . The demonstrators withdrew and, after having shouted for a while in the corridors, they went to hold a meeting at the Labor Exchange."

Reflecting on this event, the author of the article admits that the "problem of unemployment has become very distressing." "When one hears someone ask for bread, it is always painful."

"And yet," he continues, "there is something surprising in all this. That is to see a person who, on the basis of her diplomas, one must believe to be very well educated, who teaches philosophy at Le Puy and who must not be unaware, which makes it unforgivable, that municipal law requires that the mayor not recieve at a public meeting unemployed workers' protests, however legitimate they may be. Knowing this and having done what she has done, she intended, and in a very premeditated fashion—after all, she is a professor of philosophy!—to organize a demonstration, that is, incite agitation.

"Yet this is a young person who, paid according to her merit, I do not doubt, has an agreeably heavy purse at the end of each month and no fear of unemployment herself. That she bends over the miseries of others with solicitude, with altruism—I dare not say with charity; that would anger her and I would not want to do that—shows her kind female heart. But that she drags along, as she did yesterday evening, those who have put their trust in her, organizing a demonstration out of which she knows that no practical result could be expected other than that of embittering the poor devils who have enough bitterness from their present misery, is quite another matter. Once again it must be said that this really amounts to inciting agitation. When a person has agreed, in return for adequate—if not more than adequate—compensation, to fill a certain position, she has thereby assumed certain obligations toward the society that pays her. At least the obligation not to start a riot. Oh yes! There is such a thing as individual freedom; it is sacred, but when one has given it up, one has only to take it back.

"There is also the inviolability of contracts. Is this person certain that her attitude does [not], in the minds of the students' families, damage the establishment in which she has a mission to teach? Since she knows so much more than I do about philosophy, she has undoubtedly resolved this problem of professional conscience. . . .

"One can never have enough solicitude for the miserable, unemployed worker. It is for him that such feelings should be reserved and not for those intellectuals who want 'to make a splash' and who flourish on the misery of the poor like mushrooms on humus.''

It is clear that the author of this article has tried to be moderate in his attack. He does not mention Simone by name, and his tone is ceremonious and prudent. However, he hints that she could harm the lycée, which is tantamount to making a discreet appeal for the intervention of the educational authorities. He suspects that Simone wants to "make a splash," most likely in preparation for an election. The idea of the salary that she must receive preoccupies him; it does not even pass through his mind that she does not take it entirely for herself.

La Haute-Loire, another local newspaper, had a briefer report of these events. While describing how on December 19 the unemployed appeared at the city council, this account makes only a passing mention of Simone's presence. "People were a bit surprised to see at the head of the group of unemployed a female personality who enjoys a situation that puts her out of the reach of the economic crisis.''

The next day or the day after that (the day after, according to Mme. Weil's letter, but December 19 in Vidal's account), Simone was summoned to the academic inspection of Le Puy. Mme. Weil writes: "The next day the school inspector summoned her to his office to ask her for an explanation. He was very friendly, told her that they were very happy with her as a teacher, and in any event he found her ideas extremely noble, etc., etc., yet nonetheless he saw himself compelled to make a report, and such a matter, which could go unnoticed in a big city, would certainly cause a scandal at Le Puy. Simone replied that they knew what they were doing when they had sent her here, and that it wasn't her fault that she had not been sent to Valenciennes or Saint-Etienne. The next day she happened to see the headmistress, who told her that she would regret it very much if there was a scandal, that she liked Simone a great deal and appreciated her uprightness and her loyalty, etc."[24]

Vidal wrote: "On December 19, S. Weil was summoned to the academic inspection to reply to a police report. She had to answer the following questions:

"Did she lead the unemployed?

"It is true that after leaving the city council she went to a café with a group of the unemployed and paid for their drinks there?

"Is it true that the next day she was seen crossing the place Michelet, holding a copy of *L'Humanité,* and that she shook hands with an unemployed man, a stone-breaker?"[25]

It is obvious that what, among other things, shocked people was the fact that she had gone to a café with some workers. A woman who went with men to a café in Le Puy lost her good reputation. Soon afterward, the police superintendent also questioned her on this point. She told him, "I refuse to answer questions about my private life.''

People were also shocked that she had shaken the hand of one of the stone-breakers on coming out of the lycée. More amused than indignant over the question that was put to her about this, Simone wrote an article that was published in the bulletin of the National Teachers' Union of the Haute-Loire,[26] with the title "A Survival of the Caste System."

"The national university administration lags several thousand years behind human civilization. It still lives under the caste system. It regards certain people as untouchables, just as the backward populations of India do. There are people with whom a teacher at a lycée can, in a pinch, associate with in the secrecy of a well-locked room, but on no account should the parents of her students see that teacher shaking hands with them on place Michelet.

"Of course, these people are not crooked bankers, corrupt politicians, or old statesmen guilty of having sacrificed human lives for no reason. They are workers whom the industrial crisis prevents from practicing their trades and who are reduced to breaking stones for the municipality in return for a derisory wage. . . .

"It is known that an officer in the navy is forbidden to drink with an ordinary sailor. One is forced to believe that similar regulations have been applied to the social contacts of members of the teaching profession. . . . We demand from the administration a precise ruling, indicating exactly under what conditions each category of the teaching profession has the right to associate with the members of the various social classes."

Vidal's article points out that on December 21 Simone, accompanied by two unemployed workers, presented the mayor with a resolution that the Committee for Trade Union Unity had asked her to deliver.

Mme. Weil was somewhat worried by these events. But she was more worried about the overexertion all this meant for her daughter. In a letter she wrote to her husband on the same day, December 21, she said: "For my part, what upsets me is that this child is absolutely wearing herself out. As is right, she makes it a point of honor that her work in class should not suffer from all the things she does outside of it, and throughout this week she has gone to bed at hours that varied from half past twelve to two in the morning. If she could have stayed in bed for part of the morning, there would be nothing wrong in this, but she gets up between seven and seven-thirty. Combine that with the cold apartment and the disorderly way she lives, and I can't see how she can possibly stand up under all this. . . . So I feel that you must absolutely go and see M. Thévenon at Saint-Etienne and talk to him—insisting that he keep it secret, of course. Tell him about the unheated apartment, the meals of boiled potatoes, the maid (nonexistent) at five francs an hour, and above all this ridiculous business of staying up to all hours. And when it becomes very cold, how can one stop her from taking the trip to Saint-Etienne in trains that are often unheated?"

Mme. Weil sent the article published in *Le Mémorial* to André, who, very amused, wrote to Simone from Aligarh and called her a "mushroom on the humus." His sister's activity astonished him, but he approved of it and encouraged her.

On December 23 Simone was summoned to the rectorate at Clermont-Ferrand and had to make the trip. When he met her, the rector could not help but try to see the sheer silk stockings mentioned by the reporter for *Le Mémorial*. He didn't see them, because Simone never wore anything but very ordinary woolen or cotton stockings.

The rector informed her that the authorities were displeased and had demanded her dismissal. Like the school inspector and the lycée's headmistress, he recognized her value and her conscientiousness as a teacher; and he even declared that as regards her teaching she was irreproachable.

Discovering just before the Christmas vacation that their teacher was being threatened with dismissal, the students of the philosophy class urged their parents to do something to help her. Unanimously, the parents signed the following petition: "The parents of the students of philosophy in the girls' lycée at Le Puy, having learned that Mlle. Weil, the philosophy teacher, could be dismissed, earnestly request the Minister of Public Education to keep this young teacher in her present position.

"Due to the interest of her courses and her conscientiousness as a teacher, Mlle. Weil has won the sympathy and esteem of her students; her teaching has always been distinguished by its impartial character, as the classes' notebooks will testify, and she has had an excellent effect upon all the girls in her class. . . ."[27]

Simone was greatly loved by all of her students. What's more, she herself had an unusual devotion to these youngsters.

"She was not the usual kind of teacher. She would go out of her way for her students, putting both her knowledge and her time at their disposal. For example, when one of us could not pass the *bachot* due to not knowing Latin, she immediately proposed teaching it to that student, and free of charge, it goes without saying.

"Thinking that the history of mathematics interested us, she gave a supplementary course in it, optional and free, on Tuesdays; and all her students attended it assiduously.

"She was even concerned about our material needs. Did we need a book, for instance in French? We would see her arrive one day, carrying with great difficulty about twenty books that she had ordered and paid for in advance, so that we could benefit from the discount bookstores granted to all teachers.

"On Tuesdays she would often bring students who boarded at the school the books she had promised them. What a pleasure it was to see Simone Weil arrive in the courtyard of the building for the boarding students, where the teachers rarely came, especially on their day off!

"She even went so far as to put us ahead of her own peace and personal interests. Indeed, one afternoon, during the second trimester, she approached our group and asked us if we were still satisfied with her. A bit surprised, we answered in the affirmative. She then explained that the administration, wanting to rid Le Puy of her, had offered her a post near Paris, where her family lived, but since we felt strongly about it, she intended to stay on. Our protests and our sincere concern at seeing her turn down a proposal that from every point of view was to her advantage, did not change her mind. She was adamant, and in such cases we knew that it was futile to insist, just as futile as trying during a hike to pull off her shoulders the Troilean knapsack that contained the provisions for the entire group."[28]

According to Vidal's account, the rumor had begun to circulate, before the statement made by the parents of Simone's students, that the president of the Parents' Association, in the name of the association, had brought a complaint against Simone. But if this were true, the president had brought the complaint without consulting the association's committee.

Simone had decided not to go to Paris for the Christmas holidays, though she wanted to very much. She felt that she needed these free days to prepare her philosophy course for the second trimester. Her mother urged her to go to Paris or to a place where she could rest, but could not convince her. Thévenon, "always a swell guy," had proposed that she live in his apartment during this period, for he was leaving on a trip with his family. Simone was strongly tempted, above all by the joy of being able to go to the Saint-Etienne Labor Exchange every day, but for her work she needed the books she kept at Le Puy. So she probably spent most of her holiday at Le Puy, and then perhaps a few days at Saint-Etienne with her mother and father, who had traveled down from Paris.

On December 30, the unemployed at Le Puy again appeared at a meeting of the city council. Simone accompanied them, but this time she did not speak. *Le Mémorial* of January 2 described "this small demonstration, again stage-managed by the same woman, who spoke this time from the wings," and it concluded with: "The unemployed have the public's entire sympathy; these leaders should be careful not to do anything to make them lose it."

Dr. and Mme. Weil returned to Paris on January 3. Mme. Weil wrote to her son on the seventh:

"We returned from Le Puy on Sunday, after having copiously filled Simone's pantry with provisions, so from now on she will no longer have —or at least not immediately—meals made up of boiled potatoes and tea. Then we got into surreptitious contact at Saint-Etienne with a fellow teacher who organizes the miners' courses, so that he might keep a bit of an eye on the trolless. After learning about the kind of life she subjects herself to, he spontaneously declared that he will no longer accept her sumptuous gifts for the trade union welfare funds, her contributions to the newspapers, etc. But I haven't the slightest doubt—she'll find some way to play the usual silly pranks. Of course we've had no news from her since our departure. Just the day before we left she received a deputation of her students; they told her that the great majority of her students and their parents (except for one father, an avowed reactionary) had sent a petition to the ministry asking that she not be transferred."

Simone wrote to her parents on January 4 and 5, but the letter was not mailed until the sixth:

"Monday.

"Dear family:

"All goes well. S. A. [Simone Anthériou] has arrived in good shape. Two of my kids have come to see me again, just before class, showing me a petition signed by the *majority* of the parents of my children in 'philo,' saying that I have had a good effect on them(!), etc., etc. I was far from expecting this. You might tell this to Cancouët, who seems to be saying that I behaved in such a way as to turn everyone against me. The girls in the Greek class have said nothing, but they've been particularly well-behaved, which is evidently their way of showing their sympathy. . . . After having asked the Alexandres, S. A. confirmed the fact that suspension *with salary paid* is one of the sanctions!!!

"This afternoon, a demonstration of the unemployed at the main police station, to which I didn't go. . . .

"*At once* beg Cancouët to inform me of the results (no doubt known by now) of the merger on the state railroads.* What is the exact percentage of those who returned to the C.G.T. and of those who remained in the C.G.T.U.; and whether any non-Communists have remained in the C.G.T.U.

"Tuesday. Nothing new. I suppose that things are going to work out. No demonstrations by unemployed here. They say that it will take place tomorrow. My colleagues are cordial, which surprises me greatly.

"Affectionately."

On January 12 there was a demonstration by the unemployed at Le Puy. Simone had gone to the meeting in the course of which the demonstration had been decided upon, but she had abstained from giving any advice. The unemployed considered the salary of sixteen francs a day that had been promised them insufficient. *Le Mémorial* on January 13

*The two unions on the state-run railroads—the C.G.T. and C.G.T.U.—had decided to merge.

described the demonstration in an article that is dated the twelfth in these words:

"This afternoon, about six o'clock, a procession of the unemployed —or those so-called—staged a demonstration on place Michelet.

"For those of our readers who do not live in Le Puy, we should explain that there has been opened on the place Michelet a city works project, where, by breaking stones, those without work can earn their daily bread—oh, surely, with not too much butter on it, that is understood. Just as it is also understood that this works project is clearly inadequate. But it is an interim organization. . . .

"In any event, this evening a band of unemployed burst onto the place Michelet in order to persuade the unemployed working there to go on strike. Very courageously, the police superintendent intervened, and it must be believed that he didn't heed the suggestions flung at him by an unemployed man perched on a pile of stones that he had not broken!

"The event in itself should not be given more importance than it merits. But what should be said of a young woman who, this time, must be named—we refer to Mlle. Weill [sic], teacher of philosophy at the girls' lycée at Le Puy, who came all the way to the place Michelet to indoctrinate her band and who, on the approach of the police superintendent, ran away as fast as her thin legs luxuriously swathed in silk stockings could carry her."

It is necessary to explain this last accusation. In a letter written to her parents about January 25, Simone tells what happened on the twelfth: "I had a class from two to four. Strike at the public works at three-thirty. The strike committee arrived in front of the lycée at four, to persuade the stone-breakers to go out on the strike. The headmistress went into a panic and wanted to barricade the lycée. As for myself, I had been urgently summoned to the office of school inspector of the region, so I came out of the lycée at four, saw and spoke to the strikers for about five minutes, then set off quickly for the office of the inspector. Just at that moment the police arrived; hence the accusation of my running away. When I got out of the inspector's office, I went to the Labor Exchange. Coming out again to run an errand, I was greeted by a cop, who grabbed me by the arm and led me to the police superintendent, who, with the graciousness typical of his kind, asked me when I intended to quit agitating in Le Puy. He then informed me that he was fed up with it; accused me of being a ringleader; and announced that five or six of my friends would be sent to summary police court, and perhaps me too. That was all. Of course I answered him as he deserved. In fact, three fellows will undoubtedly appear before summary court this coming Monday. As for the demonstration, this afternoon there was a procession in the streets, people singing the "Internationale" and "Carmagnole" and shouting in front of the houses of the mayor and town architect. The fellows advised me to stay out of it. I took their advice, but since I feared serious events, clashes with the police, etc., I followed them . . . on the sidewalk. . . ."

In fact there was a second procession of the unemployed, after five o'clock, but Simone took no part in it; she simply watched it pass by.

Let us return to the article in *Le Mémorial.* The reflections with which it ends express great anger this time.

"There are at Le Puy unemployed, authentic unemployed; and, unfortunately, there are too many of them. But there are also too many chronically unemployed who do not try to get work and do not want others to work when they can. These are the dubious elements whom a very well paid civil servant has mobilized to induce the workers to go on strike, in order to stir up trouble in our city, at the very moment when the municipality is adopting effective measures that will procure bread for all the unemployed of good will. . . .

"Bread! that is what the demonstrators demanded this afternoon. Several of them even wanted to demand a supplement of wine, and again because of the prodding of a woman whom we no longer scruple to denounce: Mlle. Weill [sic], teacher of philosophy at the girls' lycée.

"For the true, the hard-working unemployed, enough can never be done. . . . But we take our stand with the Le Puy population in condemning demonstrations that have no other defined goal than that of creating a Communist agitation in our city, at the instigation of a woman who is recompensed on a princely scale by the government of the Republic, as they put it in official speeches.

"This same personage, in a communiqué that *La Tribune* has published, haughtily rejects charity for her assault troops. Furthermore, she does not want work for them, since she leads them in an attack on the municipal public works. So what does she want? As she herself has said, again in *La Tribune:* a good day's pay, without work; ration tickets for milk and foodstuffs; a reading room; and showers. All of this free of charge and without any actual work.

"Who will pay? The businessmen and factory owners who have also been hard-pressed by the crisis? Or the farmers, who have been even more severely hit?

"Bread in exchange for work—this, as for all of us, is the formula. This is what the municipality has adopted. It is the best way.

"And now . . . what about our female agitator?

"This question cannot remain unanswered. We shall not permit it."

La Haute-Loire on January 13 described the demonstration more briefly and added: "Nobody denies that the cause of the unemployed is worthy of the interest of the population and the governmental powers. But one cannot help but say that their methods and their spokesmen have been quite badly chosen. The presence among them on the place

Michelet of a teacher at the girls' lycée, her briefcase under her arm, has given rise to some particularly harsh comments on the part of the public."

The threatening article in *Le Mémorial* foreshadowed administrative sanctions. In fact, on January 14, Simone was again summoned to Clermont-Ferrand, to the rectorate. The rector asked her to sign a request for a transfer, saying that if she signed it she would be sent to an industrial town (no doubt Saint-Quentin), as she had wished, but that if she did not she could be given an administrative transfer and then perhaps would not be sent there. Simone refused to sign, pleading her students' interest in her course. "I began the year at Le Puy and I want to go to the end." Finally, the rector made a gesture of despair: "I was sure that I would not be able to persuade you."

He had perhaps given her to understand that she could be dismissed, since it was perhaps to him that she replied, "I have always considered dismissal as the crowning of my career." This was not bravado; this is how she really thought.

The C.G.T. Teachers' Union, which Simone had joined, worked actively to defend her. Already, at a meeting on December 24, 1931 the trade union council had unanimously decided to send a protest to the school inspector and the prefect of the Haute-Loire: "The trade union council, having heard of the threats of sanctions that hang over our comrade Simone Weil. . . . protests these threats energetically and demands the end of all such proceedings; we solidarize completely with our comrade and assure her of our union's full support."

On January 14, 1932, the trade union council met again. Vidal reported on "the Simone Weil affair"—this is the report from which we have already quoted—and concluded:

"For what can Simone Weil be reproached? *Nothing.*

"She has the right to do what she has done.

"Once her work is performed, and she performs it scrupulously in the opinion of her superiors, her activity is no longer under the control of the administration. Only common law has the right to intervene. There is no special legislation that regulates the extraprofessional activities of civil servants.

"S. Weil could have led the movement of unemployed, but we must in truth say that she has not even tried to influence it. She wanted to help the unemployed, to 'serve.' . . .

"What has S. Weil done?

"What we all should do."

Vidal presented a resolution that was unanimously adopted: "In the face of the violence of the campaign unleashed against her by the reactionary forces in Le Puy, the trade union council assures Simone Weil of its complete solidarity and fraternal sympathy."

He also read a note to be sent to the local press, which actually was published on January 18 by *La Tribune républicaine* and on January 24 by *Le Rappel de la Haute-Loire:*

"For freedom of opinion.

"The reactionary forces in Le Puy have launched a violently tendentious campaign, based chiefly on vicious gossip, against one of our comrades, a teacher at the girls' lycée. . . .

"Faced by the hypocrisy of this campaign, it is necessary to reestablish the simple reality.

"Our comrade felt that it would be useful to become active in support of the local movement of the unemployed. Her thoroughly disinterested aim was to help the unemployed to express their thoughts. She wanted to serve working-class comrades whose distress had struck her profoundly.

"The campaign has pictured her as a 'ringleader,' an 'agitator.' And on top of this—imagination and perfidy rarely being idle—they piled the most blatant stupidities. . . .

"Let us say, in passing, that if the agitation of the unemployed were to overcome the inertia of the public powers, it would be difficult to condemn her.

"But on this terrain our comrade does not bear any responsibility. She has never tried to impose herself or influence anyone. She has a completely different conception of the working-class movement. . . .

"A piece in a newspaper has spoken of an 'agent provocateur.' We reject with disgust such a base accusation. . . .

[Signed] "The C.G.T. section of the teachers of the Haute-Loire."

The council charged Vidal with the task of informing the League of the Rights of Man and other groups. It was a matter of organizing a public meeting to defend Simone. Vidal had already given a report of the affair to Mérat, secretary of the General Federation of Teachers, who, in Paris, had contacted Vial, the director of secondary education. Moreover, fearing a swift sanction, Vidal sent the following telegram to the Ministry of Public Education: "We protest the threatened official transfer of Mlle. Weil, teacher of the lycée in Le Puy.

"We declare that she has not played a leading role in the local movement of the unemployed.

"Local reactionary campaign based on gossip revolts honest people who know the facts.

[Signed] "Teachers' section of the National Trade Union (Haute-Loire), Secretary Vidal, teacher at Saint-Germain-Laprade."

And finally Vidal sent another protest to the mayor of Le Puy and its prefect: "In the name of our group, I have the honor of addressing to you a categorical protest against the police measures employed in regard to Mlle. Weil, teacher at the girls' lycée at Le Puy.

"On January 12, at five o'clock, our comrade was arrested by a policeman on coming out of the Labor Exchange and then brought before the police superintendent, where she was threatened with summary court proceedings under the accusation—in any event, false—of 'leading' the unemployed. In our opinion, this fact constitutes a clear and serious violation of individual liberty.

"Furthermore, it would be easy for you to find out that Mlle. Weil did not participate in the demonstration, since she was working from two to four o'clock at the lycée; and that she did not 'run away from the police' on the place Michelet, but had been summoned to the school inspector's office, at which she appeared. . . ."[29]

When Simone had been taken to the police station, it is interesting to note, some comrades—no doubt members of the unemployed—followed her. They waited at the door and were ready to intervene if at the end of a certain time they did not see her come out.

In Paris, the Alexandres, informed of the events by Simone Anthériou, had discussed them with Alain and Cancouët. The latter disapproved of Simone's behavior. According to a letter by Mme. Alexandre, dated January 15, he said roughly as follows, "The proletarians don't need a Joan of Arc. Let her do her job and stay in her place." But the Alexandres rather approved of Simone: "We supported her to some extent and explained her excesses by the fire of youth that rarely is fed by such aliments. Alain, as the arbiter, hesitates, leaning most often to Cancouët's side. . . ."

If he did not entirely approve of her, Alain was no less ready to defend her. He wrote the following letter to Villard, a teacher at the boys' lycée at Le Puy:

"Paris, January 15, 1931

"My dear colleague: I am very happy with Guillou. I am also very happy with the child Simone Weil. These are the things one does when young, and they are beautiful more than useful. In this case one must repeat: 'The freeing of the workers will be the job of the workers themselves.' I should add that if I were Jupiter, I would let the consequences go hang; for they form part of experience. One should profit from the time when one can flit about easily and mock the administration. That said, I would on principle always defend her as much as I could—it is not very much—since it is obvious that they will hold me responsible for these generous deeds; at least I hope so, and I even deserve it in a sense, although I have yielded more than once, since the war, to the desire to be comfortable and not have any more troubles. That is permitted to an old man; and yet one must not count on great concessions. Please send my regards and compliments to this fine child and beg her not to stop laughing at the administration, which is just an old lady.

"My cordial wishes to you; very happy with your excellent letter."

In spite of his disapproval, Cancouët himself was to defend Simone in an article that was published in *Le Populaire* on February 8.

Alain could not help but laugh over certain aspects of the affair. He said of Simone, "Who else but she could succeed in starting a strike among the unemployed!"

On January 16, *L'Oeuvre* supported Simone. Maria Vérone, president of the French League for the Rights of Women, published an article in it entitled: "Is a Graduate of the Ecole Normale a Citizen?"

Without mentioning Simone by name or the town of Le Puy, she told the story of a young woman graduate of the Ecole Normale, assigned to a town in the center of France, who had agreed to accompany a group of unemployed first to the mayor and later to a meeting of the city council, and at the end of the meeting had presented the demands of the unemployed. This public action, she claimed, had met with complete success. "So everything would have been fine if the mayor, furious at being forced to come out of the pleasant torpor in which he lolled, had not brought a complaint against the young woman who had pulled him out of his somnolence. And behold, immediately the administration began to move; inquiries and counter-inquiries followed. How far will it go? . . ."

The comrades at Saint-Etienne did not remain inactive. The Committee for Trade Union Independence met on January 16, and the Regional Congress of United Miners on the seventeenth. The secretary of the Committee was Thévenon; the secretary of the United Federation of Miners of the Loire was Pierre Arnaud. They both signed the following text, which was published by *L'Effort* and by *La Tribune républicaine* on January 23:

"On December 17, our comrade Simone Weil accompanied the unemployed of Le Puy, who had gone to the city council to draw the attention of this body to their just demands.

"She did not have the good fortune of pleasing Monsieur the Mayor of Puy, who immediately sent a report to the prefect demanding our comrade's dismissal.

"To justify this dismissal, they have even gone so far as to bring complaints against S. Weil, in certain police reports, for having shaken hands with stone-breakers in front of the lycée, for having held in her hand a left-wing newspaper and having gone to a café in the company of workers.

"The working class of our region will not tolerate that owing to the mere intervention of a mayor, members of the teaching staff can be arbitrarily dismissed.

"The trade union organizations of Saint-Etienne and the Building Trades Alliance of Lyons have decided to carry out an active campaign for our comrade, to make sure that she is kept in the post that she presently occupies to the complete satisfaction of the students' parents.

"The following resolution was adopted unanimously by the Committee for Trade Union Independence on December 16 [sic, for January 16] and by the Regional Congress of the United Union of Miners in the Loire on the seventeenth.

"Considering:

"1. That a functionary of the state can, outside of her work, defend political or social ideas as freely as any other citizen;

"2. That the fact of participating in a demonstration cannot constitute a professional crime;

"The Committee energetically protests the threat of sanctions that weigh on our comrade Weil. . . .

"Threats that are even more shocking since it has been recognized officially that our comrade is above reproach from a professional standpoint and that her pupils and their parents have unanimously expressed their complete confidence in her after these events. . . ."

La Tribune républicaine also continued to defend Simone; on January 18 it published a letter by the president of the Haute-Loire Federation of the League of the Rights of Man that promised the support of the League.

What did Simone think about this uproar?

On January 19 she wrote to her parents:

"Dear family:

"No time for a long letter.

"1. Summoned on Tuesday to Clermont. Refused to sign a request for a transfer. Reason: my class's interest. The rector found my scruples 'honorable but exaggerated.'

"2. Wednesday, January 12, day of the national demonstration of the unemployed. Revolutionary events at Le Puy. Strike of the unemployed working for the municipality. Paraded through the streets. Sang the "Internationale" and "Carmagnole." All this without my doing anything. But I wasn't too far away. . . . They accused me of being an agitator. I was taken to the police station, without consequences. Campaigns in the press, etc. . . .

"Villard, a swell fellow, has launched a campaign for me. Has gotten eight or nine colleagues to sign a letter of solidarity concerning me. Has written an article in my favor for *La Tribune*.

"They have not yet officially asked me for an accounting of my behavior on Wednesday. Vidal is going to send an objective report to the Ministry. I imagine that they won't notice that, since there has not been an inquiry.

"The rector told me that if I am officially transferred, they probably won't send me to Saint-Quentin. Ignoble blackmail.

"Inspected today (school inspector). Some indirect insults, to the great joy of the kids. . . .

"Affectionately,

"P.S. And what about the four copies of *Aesop's Fables?*

"Beg you to send fourteen copies of Plato's *Republic* (to the lycée), in a translation.

"Beg you to send me my *New Testament* in Greek (no doubt in my library)."

Her parents asked her for details; she wrote to them a few days later, on the twenty-fifth or twenty-sixth:

"Dear family,

"Received your letter. Didn't give you details because I'm fed up with the whole business, to a point. . . . Now it's subsiding. Mérat has written me that Vial told him that nothing in my activity up to this point would justify a disciplinary measure." [She then tells the story of the demonstration on the twelfth which we have quoted before.] She concludes: "The mayor must be furious that he can't get me, especially since I've written an extremely brutal article against him.

"Practical matters: the maid is coming. We eat decently. Magnificent weather. We take walks.

"Received the *New Testament* and the chocolate. Two packages are waiting for me at the station, no doubt the ones you promised.

"This rascally brother of mine is much too lucky. I will not forgive him if he visits the U.S.S.R. before I do.[30]

"And finally, I'm staying here! I wouldn't have been able to leave Vidal, Delhermet, Thévenon, and the miners who (I've had the pleasure of seeing for myself at Saint-Etienne) really want me to stay on. It's a joy nonetheless.

"Affectionately."

Simone's students, who were worried about her, sometimes spoke to her about the affair. But "she seemed only to have been struck by its comic aspects."[31]

Not only did she intrepidly pursue her activity, but she became even more adamant. On January 14 *La Tribune* published, in its Haute-Loire edition, a communiqué from the Committee of the Unemployed of Le Puy written by Simone. She explained the reasons for the strike on the twelfth, drew up a balance sheet of the advantages already obtained by the unemployed due to their energetic action, and exhorted them to continue this action:

"*Communiqué of the Committee of the Unemployed.*

"Those who hoped that the movement of the unemployed would fade away were deceiving themselves. It continues with ever-growing strength; it has taken the path not of violence, as a good many people would like to think, but of direct action; it has gained some new concessions.

"The unemployed can at present reflect on their action, draw up a balance sheet, and deduce from it the lessons that it offers. Before they organized, what assistance had they obtained from the municipality? All they could do was break stones throughout the day, and they earned about six francs a day for this exhausting work for which inexperience had rendered them inept. One fine day they organized as a group, they sent a delegation to the mayor; and with what a tone of contempt was this delegation greeted! These workers, reduced to misery for having, under duress, worked too hard—for is not the present unemployment regarded by everyone as a result of overproduction?—were treated like idlers.

"Faced by this haughty reception, the unemployed did not give in; once, twice, they attended meetings of the city council, where they maintained an attitude as firm as it was correct. Results soon came. A soup kitchen was created; a municipal works was opened. The mayor at first had only spoken of engaging thirty unemployed in this new works project, but confronted by the solidarity of the unemployed, he did not dare stick to this number; he yielded once more; all the unemployed who sign up are engaged.

"They are engaged, but they are only paid two francs an hour. The reason given is that the unemployed are not trained to work as ordinary laborers. But have the unemployed asked to leave their trades? They did not agree to do work that, because of lack of habit, is exhausting to them, and into which they were forcibly thrown, for a derisory wage.

"They unanimously stopped work; they paraded through the streets of Le Puy; they sang the "Internationale." People have seized on this to misrepresent their movement as political agitation. But the "Internationale" is not a political song; it is the song of those workers who refuse to be the slaves of the profiteers. Has this refusal a political character? The ruling class would like to think it has. It is a class movement with an entirely different significance from the usual political disputes.

"The mayor has made a new concession. He has promised to raise the wage, perhaps even to grant the salary of 25 francs a day demanded by the unemployed. The unemployed have taken official note of this promise; they will insist on its being fulfilled.

"Another concession wrested by the magnificent solidarity of the unemployed was the formal promise of engaging foreign unemployed at the municipal works. National distinctions do not exist for the workers; their action has proven that the oppressors of the working class vainly try to disrupt the fraternity of all the oppressed.

"Let us hope that the unemployed continue to maintain the firmness that they have shown until now. They must continue to be alert, so that the promises they have wrested from the city will be carried out. They must force the municipality to take measures on behalf of women, old people and children, and measures that are not reduced to mere announcements.

[Signed] "The Committee of the Unemployed."

Once again, on January 22, *La Tribune* published a communiqué from the Committee of the Unemployed of Le Puy, written by Simone and even harsher in its tone and demands. This is the "extremely brutal article" she mentioned in the letter to her parents that we quoted before.

"*An Instructive Story.*

"We have received the following note with the request to print it:

"Once upon a time there were some unemployed who, tired of being exploited, on the very day that the municipality deigned to permit them to engage in exhausting work for a derisory salary, unanimously stopped work and demonstrated in the streets.

"They sent a delegation to the mayor. The mayor promised them an increase that could even go as high as the twenty-five francs they had demanded.

"The unemployed kept quiet. Yet, ten days later, since nothing had happened, they sent another delegation to the mayor.

"On that day there was neither a strike nor a demonstration. So the mayor denied having promised them anything and rejected all their demands.

"What should be concluded from this story? If he were not a mayor, an eminent member of the local high bourgeoisie, one might almost think that on the day of the demonstration he was frightened and that afterward he failed to keep his word.

"A worker would be ashamed to have deserved these two accusations. But the morality of the elite is undoubtedly very different from the morality of the workers, who are naive enough to regard courage and loyalty as two virtues that can be transgressed only at the cost of dishonor.

"In any case, if the mayor is reassured by the present calm of the unemployed, he is greatly mistaken. The calm after an action is not a sign of weakness but of strength. If the unemployed are forced to recognize that they can only obtain something insofar as they make people tremble, they will learn this lesson well.

"Perhaps it is better this way. Between the unemployed and the ruling class there are only relations of force. These relations of force are sometimes disguised by the public powers with fine appearances; sometimes, they are left naked, and then they educate the working class more effectively than anyone ever can. Perhaps someday the working class will thank them by showing them that it has learned its lesson.

[Signed] "The Committee of the Unemployed."

When Simone wrote these communiqués in the name of the Committee of the Unemployed, she stayed up almost all night, working harder than she would have on a philosophy article, weighing each word, waking up Simone Anthériou at two in the morning to show her what she had done and to ask her for advice. She wanted to be at the service of the workers and to serve them effectively.

Naive in certain respects, she was astonished that the police and others had immediately guessed that she was the author of these communiqués.

In the same issue of *La Tribune* there appeared the letter of solidarity Simone had mentioned in the first of the two letters quoted before. It was a message of sympathy signed by nine teachers in the girls' and boys' lycées at Le Puy. Villard had collected the signatures; he had probably also drafted the letter:

"To Mademoiselle Weil, *Normalien*, professor of philosophy at the girls' lycée:

"The teachers of the girls' and boys' lycées who have signed this, faced by the general abrogation of our most evident rights and our most cherished liberties, feel it their duty to inform you that they indignantly decry the scandalous attack against our freedom of thought and action on the part of the authorities. They are anxious to let you know, since their small number reduces them to impotence, that at the least they regard the police methods that have been used against you and the threats to which you have been subjected as an affront to their dignity as university graduates.

"It is not for them to judge your acts. But they consider them with the respect that should be given all sincere convictions, which you have manifested through the full exercise of your rights.

"They offer you the homage of fraternal sympathy and authorize you to do whatever you wish with the present message.

[Signed] "Mme. Villard, professor at the girls' lycée; Mme. Latour, professor at the girls lycée; Mlle. Anthériou, professor at the girls' lycée; Mlle. Chirol, professor at the girls' lycée; Mlle. Borel, teacher at the girls' lycée; M. Villard, professor at the boys' lycée; M. Cachard, professor at the boys' lycée; M. Paulin, professor at the boys' lycée; and M. Mathieu, teacher at the boys' lycée."

These two documents—the message of sympathy and the communiqué of the unemployed entitled "An Instructive Story"—brought *Le Mémorial*'s indignation to its highest pitch, and it reprinted them in full in the January 23 issue under the headline "A Good Report and an Incitement to Violence."

In the communiqué of the unemployed, the paper underlined the passages relating to the mayor: *he was frightened, he failed to keep his word,* and two other sentences: *If the unemployed are forced to recognize that they can only obtain something insofar as they make people tremble, they will learn this lesson well. Perhaps it is better this way.*

On the same day *Le Charivari,* a Parisian weekly, published the following note:

"*Let Us Be Logical.*

"We have been asked how the Jewess Mlle. Weill [sic], professor of philosophy at the girls' lycée in Le Puy, can lead demonstrations of the unemployed of this town. It is quite simple. Mlle. Weill [sic] is a militant of Moscow.

"Why doesn't she begin by sharing her salary, said to be quite comfortable, with Le Puy's forty unemployed?"

A Catholic friend of Mme. Anthériou heard a priest in a cathedral at Le Puy preach against Simone. While on a train Mme. Anthériou also heard someone say, "It seems that the Anti-Christ is at Le Puy. She's a woman, but she is dressed like a man."

At the beginning of February, on the second and fourth, there were more demonstrations of the unemployed at Le Puy. Simone wrote to her parents on the third and fourth of February.

"Feb. 3

"Dear family:

"Thank you for your good wishes. Without you I would have forgotten my 23 years. . . .

"Nothing new for me except that yesterday I was at the Labor Exchange for a meeting at the end of which it was suddenly decided to stage a demonstration immediately, and in such a manner that I could not avoid taking part, despite my desire not to introduce new complications. I don't know what the result will be. What Vial said to Mérat, which you know no doubt through Alexandre, makes me think that perhaps nothing will come of it.

"I received a charming letter from a C.G.T.U. professor, who was informed by the newspapers, and who sent me the congratulations of his federation and the promise of their energetic support.

"The general situation seems pretty somber. China, the conference for disarmament—all this looks bad. The miners are more and more poverty-stricken. And now 10 percent reduction of salaries that are already insufficient to live on. And the struggle between the political tendencies is more violent than ever just when action should be undertaken. This way, they will certainly never accomplish anything. . . .

"As for the police methods that you find so shocking, I haven't had any difficulty in keeping my temper. I had prepared myself in advance for the worst and had resolved, even in the case of much more shocking treatment, to abstain from all violence of gesture or speech. I don't think that I run the risk of losing my composure so long as their persecutions are only directed at me.

"As for our life here, it's going along very well. The maid comes regularly. We sleep well and eat well. Today I took a magnificent walk up around the Polignac Castle. I go to Saint-Etienne only every fifteen days, which leaves me more free time. The miners have definitely adopted me as a comrade. The courses seem to be going well.

"I see by *Le Charivari* that I am classified as an agent of Moscow. Unfortunately, the true and the pure still look at me with a distrustful eye! And for my part, I am less and less communist, for I see how much they fall below what is demanded in such a critical period, especially in Germany....

"You could perhaps, if you still see S., ask him to inform himself unofficially so as to find out whether I would have some chance of being appointed to Saint-Etienne for the coming year. If the course really goes well with the miners, I would prefer not to leave the region. On the other hand, I would like very much to leave Le Puy, despite my wonderful pals hereabouts and my attachment to the Teachers' Union. (Vidal has put me on the roster of the trade union council, as a sign of their complete solidarity.)"

"February 4

"Today, February 4, the day of the national demonstration ordered by the C.G.T.U.... A battalion of mobile guards stationed around the Labor Exchange ... Vidal has made me promise to stay away and I did, but not willingly. We'll see what will happen. Perhaps nothing ...

"Adieu, very affectionately."

Concerning the demonstration planned for February 4, *Le Mémorial* had written on the third:

"*Le Puy.*

"*In Our House, Too?*

"A Communist demonstration has been ordered—from Moscow via Paris—for February 4. We know all this.

"The last demonstration had also been led by Moscow. Moscow has a correspondent at Le Puy. We know her. It is necessary to make things very clear and to dot all the i's.

"There is no one, unless he is a person utterly without feelings, who does not have compassion for the cause of the unemployed. On the other hand, there are very few people who do not object to the political exploitation of the misery of the unemployed. We do not speak of the so-called unemployed who are the chosen prey of male and female agitators.

"Let these workers think it over. The various collective bodies—to begin with, and to be completely fair, the municipality and also the bosses—are making sacrifices at the present time ... in order to provide employment for the maximum number of workers. The real workers will know how to defend themselves against the enterprises of Communism, and it is for them that we say, with proof in hand, that the demonstration on February 4—which perhaps at the moment has been aborted, but certainly was ordered and prepared—is a demonstration desired by Moscow, which has its special female agent at Le Puy."

In its issue the next day, February 4, *Le Mémorial* reported on the demonstration of the second. The article was dated the third:

"*Le Puy Is Moving.*

"On Candlemas Day, the registered unemployed have had their little demonstration, a dress rehearsal before the announced premiere, which, in line with the program established in Moscow, will take place tomorrow in the early hours of the afternoon, that is, at the moment when many readers will be reading these lines.

"The demonstration was preceded by a meeting at the Labor Exchange. Mlle. Weill [sic], red virgin of the tribe of Levi, bearer of the Muscovite gospels, indoctrinated the wretches whom she has led astray. Then, after having formed them in ranks for the procession, she assigned them as their objective the house of the mayor, who had the good fortune to be serenaded. In the musical part of the program, the "Internationale" and the "Carmagnole"; such a program gives the political keynote of this movement; for it can now be seen quite clearly that it is only a political movement—Communist, to be precise.

"In truth, the demonstrators were not more numerous than before —about sixty persons. We shall see them traverse the streets of Le Puy again tomorrow, under Moscow's orders.

"In a word, this is agitation, when what is needed is the collaboration of classes . . . in order to palliate a crisis that is only too certain. . . . Now if Communism has made a paradise out of the countries subjected to its laws, let us remember that there is plenty of room in vast Russia . . . and that civil servants who are dissatisfied here need only apply for a passport. There also is Zion, where the settlers do not appear to be rushing. France intends to remain the country of measure and order."

An account of the demonstration on the fourth appeared in the newspaper *La Haute-Loire.* The beginning of this account was published in the February 5 issue (the article, dated the fourth, was written before the end of the demonstration):

"The Unemployed Demonstrate.

"This afternoon, at four o'clock, responding to the Communist watchword, the unemployed have left their works projects and gone in small groups or one by one to the Labor Exchange. One was surprised at noticing among them many young boys who did not look very well qualified to give expression to serious demands.

"A detachment of twenty-five gendarmes and police were ready to intervene to insure the maintenance of order.

"From four o'clock on, many curious onlookers had stationed themselves on the square in front of the Hôtel de Ville, waiting for events that would most likely not be serious.

"At five-thirty, the unemployed began coming out of the Labor Exchange one by one.

"They were immediately rounded up by the police, who searched and questioned them and then set them free. . . .

"Until this moment, there have been no incidents."

On February 6, *La Haute-Loire* returned to the demonstration of the fourth, finishing its report:

"The Demonstration of the Unemployed.

"The energetic intervention of the police and the gendarmes brought about the failure of the Communist demonstration organized Tuesday afternoon by the unemployed.

"These people, after their pitiful exit from the police station, effected beneath the ironic gaze of the crowd, tried to regroup at Pouzarot. Not too many of them began marching again, preceded by a red flag carried by a woman. When they reached boulevard Maréchal-Fayolle, the demonstrators saw a patrol of gendarmes. They immediately took flight.

"Soon afterward they were seen again on rue de Collège, but they definitely disappeared at the sight of a policeman's cap.

"The red flag floated down our streets, but this is no reason to get excited. The 'Great Evening' did not take place yesterday and it will not take place tomorrow. But this demonstration clearly confirmed the Communist character of the agitation among the unemployed.

"What do they want exactly? They do not tell us in a very precise fashion in the injurious and ridiculous tracts that they have distributed in the town. . . .

"Be that as it may, the energetic attitude of Dr. Durand [the mayor] and the municipal authorities, the ability with which the preventive operation of the police and gendarmes was performed, the loudly expressed disapproval of public opinion, will perhaps result in putting the unemployed on guard against the bad advice of which they will be the sole victims; because those who indoctrinate them have already taken their precautions. . . ."

It may be wondered whether the woman who carried the red flag was not by chance Simone. It is not impossible, for she did so soon after, on May 1 at Saint-Etienne. True, Vidal had gotten her to abstain from all action on February 4. But, as we have seen, she did not agree willingly, and some unforeseen circumstance could have led her to change her mind.

In the opposite camp, Simone's defenders continued to publish articles. Some new groups had gradually entered into the fray. On February 7, *Le Rappel de la Haute-Loire,* the weekly organ of the Union of Leftists, published a communiqué from the Masonic Lodge of Le Puy:

"Le Puy. The Masonic Lodge. 'The Old Alarm'

"Deeply alarmed by the attitude taken by the official powers in regard to various civil servants in education and notably Mlle. Weill [sic], professor at the girls' lycée at Le Puy. . . .

"Demand from the constituted powers, the government of the Republic and its local and regional representatives respect for the individual liberties of citizens, notably in the domain of thought, and protest indignantly the police maneuvers of delation and persecution in regard to civil servants whose independence of mind has singled them out for the capricious vindictiveness of governmental and administrative authoritarianism."

On February 8, *Le Populaire* published Cancouët's article "Confronting the Crisis. The Generous Initiative of a Graduate of the Ecole Normale."

Cancouët told the story of Simone's speech in support of the unemployed and its success. He said that in order to induce Simone to leave Le Puy, the authorities had offered her a post at Saint-Quentin.

"Our friend wouldn't hear of it. The organizers of proletarian misery and all the Tartuffes who protect the powerful are involved in this affair. She was right not to give in.

"... For our part, being quite familiar with the social organization, we know that a gesture, no matter how generous it might be, cannot solve very much. ... The workers must be taught to defend themselves by organizing both in trade unions and cooperatives. ... They must come to understand the political value of their rights as citizens.

"We hope that our young Ecole Normale graduate has told them all this, for if not, she has accomplished only a very small part of her task.

"Whatever the case may be, we salute her with great respect, hoping to obliterate the blows that all of the reactionaries have so generously directed at her.

"As for us, we railroad men cannot forget the instruction she gave us without pay for three years, and we are happy to take this occasion to express our feelings of gratitude and friendship."

Finally, on February 9, *Le Populaire* published a forceful protest by the Socialist Federation of the Haute-Loire:

"For Freedom of Opinion.

"The Federation of the Haute-Loire has sent the central bodies of its party and parliamentary group a resolution demanding energetic action in support of freedom of opinion for civil servants. The text then refers to a definite instance:

" 'The Federation denounces a particularly characteristic case, that of a professor of philosophy at the girls' lycée at Le Puy, Mlle. Simone Weill [sic], who, because she helped the unemployed in a social conflict, was threatened with an official transfer from her post by the university administration, although there had never been a complaint about her work, and, what is more, her students' parents had signed a petition in her favor.

" 'The Federation of the Haute-Loire believes that, without having to judge the position taken by Mlle. Weill [sic], the party must guarantee freedom of opinion for civil servants, not permitting them to be harassed for opinions expressed outside their work.

" 'It demands that this affair be denounced to the public and that the parliamentary group envisage, should the occasion arise, a formal question to the minister.'

"Meanwhile we protest vigorously and cannot tolerate it, no matter how clerical the town of Le Puy may be, that a professor can be harassed on the false pretext that she must bring her public behavior into accord with its convictions."

Was the formal question mentioned here ever asked? Mme. Weil thinks she recalls that there actually was a formal question in the Chamber of Deputies, but she thinks that it was a question hostile to Simone.

Was it the fear of seeing the affair take on greater and greater proportions that made the administration back down? Was it Simone's firm and audacious stand? Because of her stand, she forced the administration either to take real sanctions against her or to yield. Now, as is well known, the administration does not like trouble; as much as possible it avoids resorting to open force and engaging in a struggle with unpredictable consequences.

In any event, by the second week of February, the whole affair suddenly seemed to calm down. The right-wing press no longer attacked Simone. The local authorities had undoubtedly lost hope of obtaining an administrative sanction through a campaign in the press and had by now become resigned. A strange thing—it was the police superintendent who was to be transferred. On February 10, it was announced that he was being appointed to Anzin, in the north of France. It is true that this transfer was accompanied by a promotion, but did they really want to reward him or get rid of him? At any rate, he certainly did not want to leave Le Puy; he refused to accept the change and succeeded in remaining there while still benefitting from the prearranged promotion.[32]

On January 12, this police superintendent had said that he was sending five or six of the unemployed to summary court. In the end, only two of the unemployed were made to appear in summary court on February 15, charged with impeding the freedom to work. The accused didn't appear and were each sentenced to a month in prison with a suspended sentence. The C.G.T. Teachers' Union of the Haute-Loire, to which Simone belonged, protested this sentence vehemently in a communiqué that was published by *Le Rappel de la Haute-Loire* on February 28.

But the unemployed still kept all the gains that had been granted them. They had obtained work for all, improved general work conditions, better wages, and a soup kitchen from which, however, very few of them wished to benefit.[33]

At a meeting of the city council that *La Haute-Loire* reported on February 20, the mayor defended himself against the charge of having granted all these improvements under the pressure of the demonstrations. He assured the council that the social measures had been foreseen and prepared for even before the first demonstrations. It seems, however, that the "agitation" had at least induced him to hasten, and no doubt also to carry generosity further than he had at first thought necessary. Simone's activity had not been in vain.

Before concluding this account of the unemployment at Le Puy, one should also quote from a declaration that Simone herself later wrote on the subject. She undoubtedly wrote it in the early days of the war, at a time when, desiring to participate in the defense of the country and meeting with distrust on the part of the organizers to whom she offered her services, she tried to make them understand that she had never had ties with the Communist party.

"I have always," she declares, "wanted a social transformation to the advantage of the less fortunate, but I was never favorably inclined toward the Communist party, even during my adolescence. When I was eighteen, only the trade union movement attracted me. Since then I have never stopped going farther and farther away from the Communists, even to the point of regarding them as the principal enemy at a period when they still deceived many politicians who today hold high positions.

"When I attended the Ecole Normale from 1928 to 1931 I readily manifested my nonconformist feelings, and perhaps with some exaggeration, as often happens when one is twenty years old. That is why Bouglé nicknamed me "the Red Virgin." Unfortunately this nickname has always stuck to me, especially in National Education circles.

"During my first months of teaching in the autumn of 1931 at Le Puy, there had been some rumors about me. The Communists of Le Puy had decided to demand a city welfare fund for unemployment. For my part, since I thought it right that an unemployed person should have something to eat and believed it my duty to help unfortunates unable to defend themselves, I accompanied the unemployed several times to the city council and the mayor. It was thought in the town that I was a Communist; there was some question of giving me an official transfer; finally, since the administration officials could not prove anything against me, in order to get me to leave the town they offered me a promotion, which I refused. During all this, the local Communists kept telling me that they considered me to be on the other side of the barricades in relation to them and treated me on occasion as such; at the same time, they were very happy to see me exposed to repression instead of them, since I was suspected of being one of their followers."

It can be seen from this declaration that it was Le Puy's Communists who had demanded a welfare fund for the unemployed. On this score Simone was certainly in agreement with them. Moreover, she was close to them because of her conviction that for proletarians only the class struggle could procure an improvement of their conditions. During her stay at Le Puy she had many contacts with Communists, since several of the unemployed were members of the party. She went many times to their cell meetings. At these meetings a dozen people would gather in the back room of a store; they would go to the meetings hugging the walls along the streets, so as not to be noticed, and, of course, the result was that everyone noticed them.

A certain professor was active in the party under an assumed name. Simone met him at one of these meetings. He was very upset that she had by chance discovered his double identity.

More than once she went to see the secretary of the cell, a very old tailor with rather confused ideas but a kind and pleasant character. She had a warm feeling for him. He had confided in her that although he loved his daughter very much, he had nonetheless separated from her to send her to live with an aunt, who he hoped would leave her money. Simone found this Communist's concern about an inheritance extremely amusing.

According to Simone Canguilhem, during the Le Puy period Simone was not yet entirely hostile to joining a political party; she wondered whether it wasn't necessary to join not only a union but also a party, and this party would have been the Communist party. She had discussed the matter with Vidal and Delhermet, and it was most likely they who had convinced her that the revolution must be made only through the trade unions. However, the declaration we have quoted shows that later on she remembered things much differently. And even if one thinks that her memory may have played tricks on her, the article she published in *L'Effort* on January 2, 1932 ("After the Death of the Committee of Twenty-Two") seems to demonstrate quite clearly that from the month of December 1931 on she had only contempt for the activities of the political parties.

She certainly had many friends among the members of the C.G.T.U. —especially those miners of Saint-Etienne who had become her comrades by joining the C.G.T.U. Miners' section. She herself would join the United Federation of Teachers. (She most likely was already a member when she was at Le Puy, toward the end of the school year, while belonging at the same time to the C.G.T. Teachers' Union, since if one taught in the lower schools a double affiliation was possible.) But the majority of the C.G.T.U. Teachers Federation was independent of the Communist party. The Communists were only a minority, organized under the name of M.O.R. (Minorité Oppositionelle revolutionnaire— Revolutionary Oppositional Minority). Therefore in the Teachers' Union one could be a member of the C.G.T.U. without following the Communist line. Simone considered it rather unimportant whether as a teacher she joined the C.G.T. or the C.G.T.U. union.

The United Federation of Miners at Saint-Etienne, for whom Pierre Arnaud was the secretary, also belonged to the minority group in the C.G.T.U., that is, those members who did not follow the Communist party line. What's more, the Miners Federation had to leave the C.G.T.U. at the end of 1932 and join the C.G.T.

Yet Simone did nothing to avoid the appearance of being a Communist. She would buy and openly read *L'Humanité* in public. She even went so far as to draw the hammer and sickle on one of her pupil's compositions. At a certain period two policemen would wait for the two Simones near their house and, when they came out, would follow them all the way to the lycée. Simone would then amuse herself by talking at the top of her voice about the gold she was getting from Moscow. She never passed up a chance to mock her adversaries and give them something to gossip about.

It is understandable that under these conditions the people in Le Puy thought she was a Communist. From the month of December on some truly fantastic notions about her were in circulation. A student's mother (but certainly not one of Simone's students) had confided to the headmistress of the lycée: 1. that Simone had a sister married to a notorious Communist; 2. that she had a brother who was agitating in India with Gandhi; 3. that she had another brother who was a hoodlum; and 4. that her mother was well known as a revolutionist and had taken Simone since her childhood to Communist meetings.[34]

Simone's quoted declaration also alludes to her reputation in National Education circles. Her parents knew a functionary at the ministry (one of the doctor's patients), who gave them some information on her dossier and what was thought of her there. He told them, "She has a big dossier!" The people working at the ministry could not help but laugh at the reports they had received. They had never seen Simone and knew her only through these reports; they imagined her to be dreadful and called her the "virago."

Mme. Weil returned to Le Puy on February 23 or 24. On the twenty-sixth she wrote to her husband: "Simone seems completely happy with her class; her students are absolutely first-rate, and it appears that some are even quite remarkable."

Simone had not given up her trade union activities, but she was tired of the "affair" and didn't want to talk about it anymore. Moreover, the time that separated her students from their exams was growing shorter and so she was more and more concerned about her class and devoted almost all of her work to it.

Vidal proposed that she be made a member of the trade union teachers' council, and in fact she was elected a member toward the end of February. Mme. Weil wrote: "She means to start things humming. They don't know what they've gotten into!" Actually, a meeting of the council took place on March 3, and Mme. Weil, who had been allowed to sit in on it, wrote to her husband: "I guarantee that she will shake them out of their inertia."[35]

Two workers from Le Puy, Simone's comrades, came to ask her to give a course on Karl Marx, as she was doing at Saint-Etienne. Despite all of her work, she did not refuse. Mme. Weil wrote: "It is amazing to see the authority that this youngster assumes quite naturally over workers, teachers, etc., who are not always necessarily easy to win over, and the confidence that one feels she inspires in them."[36]

When she went to Saint-Etienne at this time, instead of leaving on Saturday afternoon, she would sometimes leave on Sunday at five in the morning and so have to get up at four. She found that she was less tired that way, but in truth she was overfatigued and often suffered from headaches. She looked forward to a rest, but would not agree to stop working at this time.

But she did agree to go all the way to Paris for the Easter holidays. She had at first made other plans, but she wanted to give this pleasure to her parents and besides had no more money to pay for her holiday. She had borrowed two hundred francs from her mother to contribute to a welfare fund for the children of the unemployed.

Mme. Weil departed for Paris on Wednesday, March 9. She passed through Saint-Etienne, where she was to see Simone once more on Thursday morning before taking the train to Paris.

Simone obtained the authorization to visit a mine. (In general, women did not have the right to go down into the mines.) At Sardou near Rive-de-Gier, there was a small artisan-type mine into which one descended by an inclined ramp instead of an elevator cage. This mine was worked by "Papa" Guillot, a former shop steward whom Thévenon knew. He permitted Simone to go down into the mine. This was undoubtedly on March 10. So after putting on miner's overalls and a hard hat, she went down. They let her use a pickax and a compressed-air drill (the tool that is held against one's chest and shakes one's entire body). According to Thévenon, if they had not stopped her, she would have kept on using the air drill until she had collapsed. She asked if the boss would agree to hire her; she was given to understand that this was impossible.

She published an article in *L'Effort* on March 19 that described her visit to the mine. (It may also have been published in *La Tribune syndicaliste des mineurs de Saint-Etienne.*) She described the miner's condition in terms of the tool that he uses (or rather the tool that he serves):

"At present the drama is no longer played out between the coal and the man but between the coal and the compressed air. It is the compressed air that, at the accelerated tempo that is its proper tempo, drives the point of the pickax into the wall of coal, and stops, and then drives again. Forced to intervene in this struggle between gigantic forces, man is crushed. Clinging to the pickax or drill, his entire body being shaken, like the machine, by the rapid vibrations of compressed air, he confines himself to keeping the machine applied at each instant to the wall of coal, in the required position. Before this he adapted the form and functioning of the tool to the form and natural duration of his movements; the pick was for him akin to a supplementary limb that was an extension of his body and amplified the movements of his arms. At present, he forms a single body with the machine and is added to it like a supplementary gear, vibrating in time with its incessant shaking. This machine is not modeled on human nature but rather on the nature of coal and compressed air, and its movements follow a rhythm profoundly alien to the rhythm of life's movements, violently bending the human body to its service. . . ."

And she concluded: "It will not be enough for a miner to expropriate the companies in order to become the master of the mine. The political and economic revolutions will become real only if they are extended into a technical revolution that will re-establish, within the mine and the factory, the domination that it is the worker's function to exercise over the conditions of work."

Here again we encounter the problem that concerned her more than any other: under what conditions could a revolution really be effective? She saw that political changes are a trifling matter, that they have never done more than replace one oppression with another, while it is technique that commands politics and certain machines by themselves imply oppression. Certain machines, and perhaps even the majority of the machines employed in industry. In an article published by *L'Effort* on March 12, "Capital and the Worker," she criticized technology in general—not only certain machines. She described technology as the most truly oppressive feature of capitalism: "Capitalism is defined by the apparent fact that the worker is subjected to the capitalist; in reality, by the fact that the worker is subjected to a material capital made up of tools and raw materials, which the capitalist simply represents. The capitalist regime consists in the fact that the relationship between the worker and the means of work has been reversed; the worker, instead of dominating them, is dominated by them." She quotes Marx: "The machine, Marx says, does not leave anything more to man than the purely mechanical role of a motive force, at the same time that it imparts to him the new task of supervising the machine. . . . In manufacture and handicrafts, the worker makes use of his tools; in the factory, he serves the machine."

Thus she demonstrates that one must number, among the conditions of a true revolution, a profound transformation of technology. But in the same article of March 12, she also recalls that technology is connected with a collective mode of production that formidably augments the productivity of human labor. It is therefore necessary "to re-establish the worker's domination over the conditions of work without destroying the collective form that capitalism has stamped on production." "The solution of this problem," she adds, "is the complete revolution."

The revolution must therefore be prepared for not only by raising the level of the proletariat's culture and knowledge but also by a theoretical inquiry into the problem that, if it is not solved, will be posed again after the revolution and render it vain. Furthermore, the revolution is in fact this—finding a means of coordinating work without subordinating the people who do it. The question that the revolutionary is faced with is not how to overturn the government, but rather how to find a form of organization so that the revolution does not finally prove to be futile. During this year at Le Puy, Simone's reflections always returned to this: one must first of all analyze the real causes of oppression, so as to be able to judge how and by what method oppression can be eliminated or reduced in other ways than mere appearances. So long as this work of analysis was not done, it seemed to her criminal to work for an overturn that would entail inevitable evils as against advantages that were far from certain. On January 30, 1932, she wrote in an article that is tantamount to an introduction to the last two articles we have mentioned: "Since there are exploited people, there are people who revolt. These rebels have killed and have been killed; yet they have neither destroyed exploitation nor did they even generally mitigate it. It is not enough to rise up against a social order based on oppression; one must change it, and one cannot change it without knowing it."[37]

From a postcard that Simone sent her parents after the visit to the mine, it is clear that on the occasion of the death of Briand some professors had been assigned the task of explaining France's efforts toward peace to their pupils and that they had avoided conferring this task on her. In fact, it was known that she did not approve of France's foreign policy. She had expressed her opinion on this in an article published in *L'Effort* on February 20, 1932, "The Conference for Disarmament." In the article she had criticized both the French memorandum to the Conference for Disarmament and Litvinov's speech at this same conference. France had proposed the creation of an international force at the service of the League of Nations. This proposal, according to Simone, had no chance of being adopted and consequently was not serious. Another French proposal seemed to her more serious, that of establishing rules to protect the civilian populations in case of war. But, in her view, this proposal only helped to increase the probability of war by guaranteeing the safety of governments and general staffs. She felt that everyone should be in danger if any one person was; the equality of danger was to some extent an assurance against the war. As for Litvinov's speech, she regarded it as reformist in spirit. By proclaiming its desire to collaborate with the capitalist states (at least for the maintenance of peace), and by proposing nonaggression pacts, the U.S.S.R. had cut its ties of solidarity with the revolutionary movements of the entire world. Certainly Simone wanted peace above all; she did not look forward to a revolution that had been brought on by the war. But she undoubtedly thought that a truly socialist state, without going to war, should not have involved itself in pacts with the capitalists.

Simone spent fifteen days in Paris during the Easter holiday. It was a rest for her. (But she took advantage of it to see her trade union friends in the Paris region.) On March 24, she attended the funeral of an unemployed man, Fritsch, an old cabinetmaker from the suburb Saint-Antoine, killed by a policeman on March 17 on a construction site that he had entered with other unemployed men to upbraid the workers there for working overtime during a period of unemployment. According to the police communiqué, the policemen, who wanted to drive the demonstrators off the construction site, had been greeted by a fusillade of bricks; according to the workers, the bricks had been thrown only after the police had started shooting. Convinced that this last version was the true one, Simone wrote two indignant articles—one article with Busseuil for *La Révolution prolétarienne* ("The King Cop: The Murder and Burial of Fritsch"; the other for *L'Effort* ("Concerning the Death of Fritsch"). She not only attacked the police but also the trade union organizations, which had not reacted energetically enough. On the other hand, she observed that if the twenty thousand workers who had followed Fritsch's funeral hearse had gone to the cemetery singing revolutionary songs and hooting at the police (who did not yet dare show themselves), they had returned silent and seemingly defeated between two thick rows of policemen, who in the meantime had taken over the streets. It was with bitterness that she said, speaking of the procession that had gone out to the cemetery: "We were almost tempted to believe in our strength." Contrary to the declarations of the left-wing press, she was struck by the real weakness of the working class.

She also devoted part of her free time to teaching geometry to a young worker. A letter has been found that the worker wrote to her on March 31, in which, amid some naive reflections, one can see both the friendship and respect that Simone inspired in him. As for the instruction she had given him, he says: "I have reviewed the circles on the basis of the demonstrations you have given me. . . . In the three lessons I had with you, you have given me almost all the elementary facts of geometry; it is a pity that I cannot see you more often, for I would have ended by becoming a truly learned person. What was really marvelous about it is that I remember almost everything you taught me, even though I could only grasp about half of it; and that with you as the teacher I was never bored for a second; and these few instants exalt all the noble thoughts that inhabit me. If I could see you more often, I would make double progress, intellectual as well as moral. . . ."[38]

This feeling of being lifted above oneself by her presence was experienced by many others.

No doubt it was during her holiday that she wrote to Louzon on the advice of Busseuil, a letter whose first draft has been found and a fragment of which was published in *La Révolution prolétarienne* of April 1932.[39] This is the rough draft:

"Dear comrade:

"Busseuil has advised me to write to you after a conversation I had with him about 'socialism in a single country.'

"I had told him that the problem seemed to be insufficiently clarified, even by Trotsky, at least in what I have read of his (*The Third International after Lenin, The Permanent Revolution*). He does not demonstrate clearly enough, at least for me, that Russia (presuming that she has on her territory all the necessary raw materials) cannot, once completely equipped, close its frontiers, form a small world apart, a slice of the world, and build socialism in a test tube.

"Now this is a capital question. In the preface to *The Permanent Revolution* Trotsky, in a luminous fashion, connects the theory of socialism in one country with all the mistakes of the Third International. I believe that one can connect it with everything for which the Communists can be reproached. If the U.S.S.R. could build socialism all by itself, the world proletariat could spare itself the trouble of making a revolution, provided that the U.S.S.R. is preserved until its technical setup is complete. It would then matter little that the Third International failed in all of its revolutionary movements; it would not be an organization of revolutionary action but simply a propaganda organization for the Russian state. It would matter little that the International barely lived, provided that it was strictly subordinated to this state. It would matter little that it might have no contact with the masses, provided that it had the leading positions in the skeletal trade unions, which would, however, have the revolutionary workers behind them in case of a threat of aggression against the U.S.S.R., and which would direct, once socialist Russia was constituted, the transition from capitalism to socialism in the other countries. In the same way, a foreign policy modeled on the most banal pacifism is imposed absolutely on the U.S.S.R. and the Third International (see Litvinov's speech). All the concessions to the capitalist states are legitimate if they hasten the construction of industry. Everything that can bring closer the moment when this construction will be complete is legitimate: speed-up at work and the undernourishment of a generation, the ever-increasing inequality of wages, progressive bonuses, work rewards, forced labor, the oppressive power of the state, etc. On the contrary, if socialism cannot be built in a single country, these are then simply crimes against the proletariat.

"If I could be shown that socialism can be built in a single country, I would join the party immediately and would never leave it. If the opposite was proven to me, I would fight against it without stint. The intermediate position seems to me impossible. Either the party is betraying the proletariat, or those who are not with the party are traitors. All this depends solely, in my opinion, on the problem of socialism in a single country.

"Now such a problem, on the solution of which would depend whether in my eyes I am or am not in the process of betraying the proletariat, I would like to see settled as clearly as $2 + 2 = 4$. Probable solutions are not enough for me, nor are the authorities, even those as respectable as Marx, Lenin and Trotsky. As for saying that there is no uncertainty possible on the problem and that Trotsky is obviously right before any examination, that does not seem to me to be serious.

"I think you are the only person in France who can study this problem in the proper way. That is why I have taken it on myself to follow Busseuil's advice, although I know you only through *La Révolution prolétarienne* and the conversations with Thévenon, Busseuil, etc.

"Since I have begun to bother you, I would also like to ask you what serious attempts have been made since Marx to apply the Marxist analysis to the study of the new economy (large banks, credit, paper money, finance capital, etc.). . . .

"Your theory on the economic crisis[40] throws me into endless perplexities. Its mathematical precision seduces me. I believe that you would be doing a great thing if you put it to the test of the facts, examining minutely, in the light of this theory, the entire history of the crisis, on the basis of precise statistics. A history of the beginning and development of the crisis seems to me the most important work at this moment, and even something that you alone could do. . . .

"Forgive me for having bothered you by telling you my ideas in this way, especially since I have no right to do so.

"Very cordially."

I have quoted almost all of this draft for a letter because it helps to clarify Simone's position in regard to the Communist party. Perhaps in order to get a reply from Louzon and the rigorous demonstration that she requested, she exaggerated a bit her readiness to join the Communist party if he could prove that socialism could be built in a single country. It is doubtful that she could have tolerated not saying everything that seemed to her true, as one must do when one is under the orders of an organization that imposes both dogmas and tactics. Nonetheless, what she says here gives a certain weight to Simone Canguilhem's conviction that Simone was not yet completely certain that one didn't have to join the Communist party.

The fragment of this letter published in *La Révolution prolétarienne* consisted of the paragraph about the crisis. It has some differences in form compared to the same passage in the draft—which proves that the letter that was finally sent was not identical with the draft. Perhaps the differences were minimal; but it might also be that the letter contained almost nothing but the passage that was quoted. Perhaps Simone had set aside till later her questions on "socialism in a single country."

On her return to Le Puy she learned that her friends Vidal and Delhermet had been defeated in the trade union elections. She wrote to her family on April 8:

"Saw Vidal today. Catastrophe. The departmental councilors chosen by the union have been defeated by the outgoing councilors (those with whom Vidal and Delhermet disputed in the trade union council), who are also trade unionists but presented themselves in spite of the union. As a result, the trade union council is going to resign. And it is due in part to my affair with the Red Relief! A heavy responsibility!"

Simone's parents decided to go to Naples and wait for André, whose ship was due on May 21. Mme. Weil had at first thought of meeting her daughter at Saint-Etienne and then joining her husband later. But the meeting with Simone did not take place. Her parents went directly to Italy. Simone spent the days of the Pentecost vacation at Toulon with her friend Suzanne Gauchon.

Suzanne, who had prepared for her teaching license at the Sorbonne and had passed her examination in 1930, lived with her parents. Her father had been an engineer in the Navy. Simone wanted to know what life was like in the Navy. Suzanne Gauchon got permission for her to visit the battleship *Bretagne,* escorted by a young officer. Before her visit, Suzanne said to Simone, "Try not to make any disagreeable remarks." Simone replied, "You don't know me. When one is with the enemy, one keeps one's mouth shut."

She did not speak to anyone about this trip to Suzanne. Either because she made a mystery of her friendships or for some other reason, she said one day to Simone Anthériou, while showing her the envelope of a letter from Suzanne Gauchon, "You see, letters that come from there [Toulon] and that have this handwriting, promise me that you'll never try to find out from whom they come."

The exams for the *bachot* were near at hand. Lessons were cut to a minimum; the students were reviewing their subjects and worked mainly at home. Simone, who for a long time had been overworked, took advantage of the fact that she could no longer be very useful to her students by asking for a leave of absence. She wrote to the ministry on June 11, requesting a leave in order to undergo medical treatment in Paris. This leave was granted her from June 16 to July 7.

It was no doubt during her stay in Paris that she wrote the article "The U.S.S.R. and America," which was published in *L'Effort* on July 2. In an interview, Stalin had expressed admiration for American "efficiency," especially efficiency in industry and technique. Simone affirmed that nowhere else had the "subordination of the worker to the conditions of work" been pushed so far as in America. She concluded that Stalin had abandoned Marx's point of view and had let himself be seduced by the capitalist system in its most perfect form.

It was also in Paris that she was to learn the results of the *bachot* exams. According to Cabaud, only three of her students had qualified and only two had passed. She wrote to me from Paris on July 6, telling me that only two of her students were qualified (it may be that she said "qualified" for "passed," or that she had been informed somewhat inexactly, or that Cabaud's information may be somewhat inexact).

"Only two of my kids qualified for the *bachot*. It seems that the philo examiner is an administrator and has given ridiculous marks. What a shame that I'm not Lagneau." (Lagneau had made them change a manifestly absurd mark given to one of his students in the *bachot* exam. Alain tells this story in his *Memoirs of Jules Lagneau.*)

She left Paris on the afternoon of July 6 and spent eight days at Le Puy, saying goodbye to her students and comrades in case she actually did obtain a transfer.

6

Trip to Germany. Auxerre
(1932-1933)

A congress of the National Confederated Teachers' Union was held in Clermont-Ferrand on August 3, 4, and 5, 1932. At almost the same time, a congress of the United Federation of Teachers, which Simone had probably joined during the course of the school year of 1931–1932, was held at Bordeaux on August 4, 5, and 6. But Simone did not attend either congress. She had decided to go to Germany to try to understand on what the strength of Nazism rested.

She wrote to the Thévenons, no doubt in the second half of July.

"Dear comrades,

"A hasty note to tell you: 1. that I will undoubtedly be appointed to Saint-Quentin. I regret it somewhat because of you, the miners, Vidal, and Delhermet—never again shall I find such pals. But I'm happy to be only an hour and three quarters from the Paris libraries—and besides that, my parents. In any event, Monatte has an old, very interesting comrade there from the building trades.

"2. I'm definitely going to Germany. Monatte has given me a recommendation to a pal in Zurich, B. He is a party member, although he doesn't completely follow the line. So I have no more need of Vaillant-Couturier! I might even help with the illegal work. You will learn with pleasure that my admiration for Monatte grows with each of my talks with him.

"Saw Louzon and Péra. Unfortunately, I haven't talked with Louzon as much as I would have liked.

"As for Péra, I've especially fraternized with him.

"I attended a meeting of the 'Core'*—stormy discussion. On the question of "Stalinist methods" everyone kept to his original position (I approve completely of Louzon on this point). Nonetheless, comradely relations seem to be re-established, at least as far as Monatte is concerned.

*The small group that published *La Révolution prolétarienne*.

"I am still counting on your visit in September.

"Fraternally.

". . . Send all my friendly greetings to the miners (especially La Sablière) and tell them that I miss them."

Simone had become acquainted with Raymond Molinier, a Trotsky-ist. When he found out that she was leaving for Germany, he begged her to get into contact with Trotsky's son, Léon Sédov. He said Léon was in great danger in Berlin and needed help.

Hitler was not yet in power, but it already seemed that he would be in power soon. In Germany there were often assassinations and street fights. Simone's parents were unhappy at the thought that she was going to travel through a country in turmoil, already almost under the rule of a violently anti-Semitic party. They hoped that Dr. Bercher, who wrote in *La Révolution prolétarienne* under the name of Péra, could accompany her. But Péra was not sure that he could, and Simone left before him.

Before leaving she wrote an article on Trotsky's essay, "What Next?" for *Libres Propos.* Certain parts of this essay dealt with the internal situation in Germany. So Simone prepared for her trip by this sort of research. The article is dated July 25, 1932, and was published in the August issue of *Libres Propos.* [1] It shows that Simone at that time had very great esteem for Trotsky, whose strength of character and lucidity she praised. Nevertheless, she criticized his "superstitious" attachment to the Communist party and his conviction that a revolution could not triumph save under the leadership of this party.

She first went to Zurich, where she spent a few days. When she reached Berlin, she wrote to her parents:

"Saturday.

"Dear family:

"My telegram must have already reassured you. Everything has gone wonderfully. I immediately found the French woman I had to see, and after that I went directly to the friends of Nicolas,[†] where I am living right now. He at present is in a rest home, because he just had a very serious operation. He will return on Wednesday. I will leave then, because there are two rooms and a kitchen and three children, and I sleep in the parents' bedroom, so that I'm afraid of upsetting things when he returns. But in the meantime the French comrade will have found me a room. The three youngsters are girls, two thirteen and one nineteen, all burned brown by the sun, with blond hair such as can only be seen here, and all belonging to left-wing sports organizations. They are all as sweet as can be and I'm in the process of falling in love with the German people. Contrary to what André may think, I have even

---

[†]Probably Nicolas Lazarévitch, whom Simone must have met at *La Révolution prolétar-ienne* and who was one of her friends. In the following sentence, it is not he who is the person referred to, but rather a worker in whose house Simone was staying.

managed to talk with them. As for Berlin, it is at the moment the calmest city in the world. Everyone is in a state of expectancy and no one foresees any serious events before the autumn (October–November). Absolutely no feeling against foreigners; everyone (on the trains, in the street, stores, and streetcars, etc.) has been very polite to me. I inspire much sympathy, especially among the people working on the streetcars! Very few Nazis are seen in uniform, and those one sees keep quite calm.

"Don't forget to send me information on those famous little places where one eats well and cheaply in Berlin, and tell me which are the two or three most beautiful museums.

"I kiss you all."

Simone's parents, seeing that Péra was not going to join their daughter, decided to go and meet her themselves. Their son was leaving on a trip to attend a congress, so they were free. They wrote to Simone and told her of their plan. She again made an effort to reassure them, writing a long letter in which she described the political situation in Germany.

"Dear family:

"Received your letter. The address is good (only it is written Neu-kölln). . . .

"Until now I've managed quite well. Going about Berlin has ceased being an adventure for me. . . . The very first hour I was in Berlin I had an appointment at the zoo; a German woman asked me on the subway train whether the train went directly to the zoo. Naturally I told her it did, and naturally I was wrong. Now I understand the Berlin subway system. But even at the beginning I never got lost.

"Politically, everything is still quiet. I beg you to reassure my various adoptive fathers, Cancouët, Busseuil, etc.[2] People are less excited here about German events than in Paris. One sees only a few Nazis in uniform on the street, and they behave like everyone else. In the morning one reads in the newspapers that there have been some attacks here and there, somewhat in the same state of mind that one reads that there have been so many automobile accidents. . . . The adversary newspapers don't confront each other on the subways and streetcars, people don't discuss politics. There are no more clashes in the streets. Nothing denotes a particular situation, except for the calm itself, which is in a sense tragic. For the workers the question that is in suspense is the *Arbeitsdienst* (these concentration camps for the unemployed), which exist in the form of *Freiwilliger Arbeitsdienst*[‡] (10 pfennigs a week), but would become obligatory under a Hitlerian government. At the present time only the most desperate go to them. It is hard to imagine this magnificent German working-class youth, who are active in sports, go on camping trips, sing, read, and play with children, reduced to a military regime. Another question is not only that of the prohibition of the

‡Voluntary Labor Service.

Communist party, but the systematic massacre of the best elements. The Nazi papers are full of calls for murder (or, more precisely, for vengeance of the S.A. Männer victims of the 'Red Terror'), and they say openly: "One must not become restless now (that is, don't make any attacks), for we shall soon be in power." Of course, this will not happen immediately after Hitler's victory. Passions are not overstimulated and discipline is still strong. The workers are simply waiting for the time when all this will crash down on them. The very slowness of the process increases the demoralization. Courage is not lacking, yet the occasions for struggle don't present themselves.

"The Nazi ideology is astonishingly contagious, notably in the Communist party. Most recently the Nazis thundered against the fact that a *"jüdisch-marxistisches Weib"* (Clara Zetkin) inaugurated the opening session of the Reichstag. To which *Welt am Abend* (official newspaper of the party) replied: "First of all Clara Zetkin is not a Jew. And even if she were, that would not mean anything. Rosa Luxembourg, *although a Jew*, was an *'ehrliche Person.'*. . . !* As for nationalism, the Communist party (it seems) is unbelievably impregnated with it, calls the Social Democrats *"Landesverräter,"*† etc.

"But once again anti-Semitic and nationalist feelings don't appear at all in personal relations.

"My impression, up till now, is that the German workers are not at all disposed to capitulate but that they are incapable of fighting. The Communists and Social Democrats each accuse the other party (and quite rightly) of not deserving any confidence—and this also among the most honest militants in the rank and file (example: the Communist worker with whom I live and who is opposed to a united front). A division that is all the more serious since the Communists are unemployed, while the Social Democrats are working. To this should be added the fact that those who have been unemployed for two, three, four, and five years no longer have the energy that a revolution demands. The young people who have never worked, weary of their parents' reproaches, kill themselves, become vagabonds, or are demoralized completely. You can see frightfully thin children, people who sing lamentably in the courtyards, etc. On the other hand, this terrible question of the *Arbeitsdienst* does not involve the workers who are working—and even among the unemployed, this regime of military slavery is no doubt the only one that the most demoralized can bear. . . . On the contrary, those who go in for sports and political propaganda, etc., could not bear it. But it is to be feared that they struggle all alone and may be exterminated.

*Fine person.
†Traitors.

"I haven't yet seen many people, politically speaking. The Communist family I mentioned, the Trotskyist group (interesting here, unlike the French group), an old Brandlerite. I've taken quite a few futile trips around town (wrong addresses, etc.), but they have shown me the city. The modern workers' districts are truly splendid (but it seems that the houses are often very damp). I'm gradually getting accustomed to the oppressive ugliness of the sections in the center of town.

"As for swimming, today was the first good weather we have had! If this continues, I'll surely go swimming.

"I beg you, don't go into a panic reading the newspapers! When I think how ridiculous the recommendations given to me in Paris seem here, even from experienced people! Truly, I feel completely safe, and that would be so even if by chance Hitler would take power. The Germans are too disciplined to wage a sporadic struggle and *nothing* here reveals preparations this month for a serious political struggle. From my point of view, I have even—given the complete calm—come at a bad time. No chance of observing very much.

"It goes without saying that this letter can be communicated to my political friends.

"I won't always write at such length. As for the telegrams, I earnestly beseech you to let me dispense with them as long as the situation remains so calm. . . .

"I've just received your second letter. I see that you are being more reasonable. I haven't had any news from Péra and don't know whether he has received my address. I don't know where he is at this moment. . . .

"As to whether you should come to Berlin, I really don't know what to say. . . . I've paid for my room here until the end of the month. And of course I'm very busy; getting around Berlin takes an awfully long time. But if you can find a pleasant place near Berlin, it would of course be a pleasure for me to have you nearby.

"As for my going to the seashore in September, don't count on it. Either I'll prolong my stay here or I'll go to Briançon, or directly to Paris.

"I kiss you both."

Simone's parents communicated the contents of this letter to her political friends, as she had authorized them to do. *La Révolution prolétarienne* published an extract from it in its August 25, 1932, issue.[3]

Dr. and Mme. Weil first went to Hamburg, no doubt both to visit the city and because this visit gave them an excuse for getting close to Simone without seeming to do it just to protect her. (They knew that she didn't like to be protected. They themselves wanted to leave her free as much as possible. They had always given her a great deal of freedom, even when she was a child, not only because it would have been difficult to make her obey against her will but also because they really wanted to let her develop her own character and give her the joy of doing what she wanted to do. So they tried to protect her, but timidly, sometimes hiding their intention or creating pretexts.)

They were at Hamburg when she wrote them again:

"Dear family:

"All still goes well. Still calm. (A battle between Communists and Nazis yesterday, but I wasn't there! No chance of my ever participating in these battles.)

"I continue to run about Berlin in diverse directions. One of these days I shall go to the opera. I haven't seen many people until now (too many incorrect addresses!), but all the same it is instructive to be here.

"Magnificent excursion the other day, on a boat from which I wrote to you. With a bunch of kids from twelve to thirteen, up to their necks in politics.

"You really have nothing to boast about with your place where one eats for a mark! I have a principle never to eat for more, and until now I have respected this principle. Today I ate for sixty-five pfennigs in all (soup; a pork cutlet, well prepared and respectable in size; boiled potatoes in an even more respectable quantity; compote in an infinitesimal quantity; and water.) About two minutes from my house one can eat two delicious sausages, a slice of bread, and a slice of cucumber for ten pfennigs! Made quite agreeable by the company of many workers. And one can eat outside in the open air.

"To even matters, I am going bankrupt paying for transportation and newspapers.

"I've bought two sleeveless sports blouses, washable, bluish-gray, two marks each. I want to carry off a real cargo!

"I manage to find my way around quite expertly now. It's much better than at Zurich, where despite the false hopes you gave me, they speak almost only German and I didn't know what *'aussteigen'* meant.

"Still nothing from Péra. It seems certain that he is not coming.

"No letter for several days now. Why?

"I kiss you.

"P.S. Just got your postcard. Happy stay at Hamburg! I look forward to making a trip there one of these days.

"Did you get my last letter to Paris? If you did, send me immediately by special post what I asked you for (the maps).

"And what about the homework of the kids?

"I'm afraid that you haven't received this letter at all. That would be disastrous for me."

(I don't know what maps Simone had asked for.)

Simone had lived at first, as we have seen, with a working-class family that had children. Since they did not have too much to eat (the father was undoubtedly unemployed), Simone ate even less than her share, so as to leave as much nourishment as possible for the two small children. When the Weil parents were in Berlin, the mother said to Mme. Weil, *"Ihre Tochter isst wie ein Spatz"* ("Your daughter eats like a sparrow").

The older daughter belonged to a nudist organization. She had tried to convert her mother to nudism, but her mother thought that in view of her age and corpulence, nudism wasn't quite right for her. One day this young girl asked Simone, *"Hast du auch einen Freund?"* ("Do you have a friend, too?") Not understanding the sense in which the word friend had been used, Simone told her that she had many friends. The young German seemed to admire such generosity.

Simone made an effort to get in touch with Léon Sédov. She found him calmly seated in a café, very surprised that people were anxious about his safety. They talked; Simone found him quite nice. He asked her to take to Paris a suitcase filled with documents and papers that he wanted to get out of Germany. It contained, among other things, a notebook in which, for each of the main German cities, he had written the list of Trotskyists who lived there, along with their addresses.

Dr. Weil could not stay in Germany for long; he returned to Paris. Simone visited Hamburg with her mother. She put Léon Sédov's suitcase in with her luggage.

While traveling with her mother in the train that was taking them back to Paris, she had some apprehensions as they were about to cross the border, not for herself but for the documents entrusted to her that could compromise a great number of people. She said to her mother, "People distrust me as soon as they lay eyes on me. If the customs people see me in the compartment, they'll make me open the suitcase. As for you, they'd trust you with the bank of England. I'm going to leave you here with the suitcase and get into another compartment with my luggage." The plan worked beautifully. The customs officials simply asked Mme. Weil whether she had anything to declare, and they did not make her open the suitcase.

Léon Sédov had given Simone the address of an old miner in Charleroi, a Trotskyist. She stopped off at Charleroi to see him. This was on September 6, the next-to-the-last day of a Belgian miners' strike whose dramatic ups and downs had been going on since July 6. An incomplete article that she wrote about it has been found. It was probably the beginning of an article destined for *L'Effort* that she never finished.

"*Memories of Belgium.*

"It is September 6, the next-to-last day of the strike of Belgian miners, which I have had the chance to discuss at length with one of the foremost militants in Charleroi.

"An old miner, who has never stopped working. One feels immediately that he is an authentic worker, who never in his life has had the attitude or thoughts of a bureaucrat. A man made out of rock, who has battled every day with the coal and has spent his evenings and Sundays battling with the regime. The struggles of political factions and intimacy with intellectuals and professional revolutionaries, who so often corrupt militants, have never affected him. In his every word and every attitude one feels the crudity, strength, and simplicity of the working class.

"He is one of the Trotskyists who lead the organization of the 'Knights of Labor,' a red trade union that at the start organized all the militants expelled from the reformist organization. It numbers among its members only those who do not live in the wake of the Third International, since the Stalinists, here as everywhere, have split away. The 'Knights of Labor' is a red trade union the like of which we have not known in France or America, for it does not recruit. The Trotskyist leaders have always tried to keep in the reformist unions those who wanted to leave.

"The miner told me about the strike. . . ."

(The article stops here.)

When she was installed in Auxerre, to which she had been appointed as a teacher, Simone wrote to the Thévenons. The letter she sent gave them a summary of the lessons she had brought back with her from Germany and the position she then took in regard to the principal political and social movements.

"Dear comrades:

"So I am at Auxerre (and not Saint-Quentin, as they had promised me—no doubt Saint-Quentin is too working class!). A small, charming town, with churches, a factory (1,500 workers before the crisis, 500 now), and a large barracks that houses the first regiments of infantry that will leave at mobilization. Grape growers, anticlerical and antimilitarist, so they tell me. No mines in the vicinity, unfortunately! What do you think of the proximity of the barracks? Do you think there would be something to do there? While awaiting something better, I'm always willing to work in the grape harvests. I've gotten to know a remarkably enlightened, almost revolutionary, vineyard worker.

"Work on an article for *R.P.* (so long that, I fear, it will dismay Louzon) has prevented me from writing to you until now. It's on Germany, of course. I haven't been able to do anything for *L'Effort.* It's much too complicated for a short piece. Nevertheless I shall try. In this connection, C. is a charming little fellow, but his stories about the German trade unions, the only force capable of making the revolution, don't stand up. Nothing is more reformist, more organically reformist, than the German unions (although the workers may be in the process of dragging them into action by force; but a scattered action, which the organizations will endeavor to keep that way). I must confess that I've returned from Germany with the feeling that our revolutionary syndicalism has no international significance (D. Guérin, who also has been there, has come back with the same conclusion). The German unions are *above all* associations for mutual welfare. They could be dragged along by the masses like dead weights, but that is all.

"Conversely, in Germany I lost all the respect that in spite of myself I still felt for the Communist party. The contrast between its revolutionary phrases and its total passivity is much too scandalous. Actually it seems to me as culpable as the Social Democracy. I think that at the present moment all compromise with the party or any reticence in criticizing it is criminal. Trotsky himself seems to me to still retain a kind of timidity toward it that gives him some share of the responsibility for the Third International's crimes in Germany. It is true that a different position would be very difficult for him.

"In Germany I saw Trotsky's son (Liova, the son who accompanied him in his deportation and exile). Intelligent, he seems, and quite nice, although a one-hundred-percent Trotskyist. He told me some stories about Russia (for example: a good part of the last harvest was lost, simply due to a *lack of grain silos!*) . . .

"He gave me the address of an old miner at Charleroi (the Knights of Labor, a red organization that played a big part in the strike, is led by a purely *working-class* group of Belgian Trotskyists, who in reality have a rather syndicalist spirit), with whom I stayed one night while passing through. It was the last day of the strike. He told me about the beginning and spontaneous development of the strike. He greatly feared a large movement among the miners for leaving the reformist unions and joining the red unions, and was determined to oppose it with all his strength. This seems to me an excellent way of approaching trade union splits: bringing together the best militants, expelled by the reformists, in very small organizations, which do not recruit but exert an influence from the outside. What do you think of it?

"Have they written about this strike in *L'Effort?* Do you want a short article in which I would sum up this conversation?

"I could also try, despite everything, to write a page on Germany.

"I accepted Auxerre because of the possibilities of work offered by the proximity of Paris—and because Saint-Etienne and Roanne were impossible. But you can take me at my word when I say that I miss your little apartment in Saint-Etienne and the Labor Exchange and Victor's pub—and Papa Guillot's mine. If I get the chance, I'll come out to see you (perhaps on All Saints' Day? I'm not so very far away). . . .

"Here, what I miss until now are comrades. I haven't yet contacted the trade unions. I hesitate between a United M.O.R. union and a Confederated majority union. Just my luck! No workers' unions. (But surely there must be a Communist party cell.) Send me the news as soon as you can, so that I can at least savor by letter some of your region's comradely atmosphere.

"I hope that you aren't angry with me for coming here. If I've done so, it was because I thought that if I stayed on at Le Puy I could not truly be useful for anything very much and could no longer continue my personal learning. Apart from all that, I miss the Haute-Loire and Loire regions.

"I see I have nothing more to tell you. Except that one can't imagine anything more fraternal, more courageous, and more lucid in the midst of a crushing situation than the young workers of Berlin. The cultural level of the German workers is also something unbelievable. If I were free to go where I wished, I would fly there as fast as I could. One has the feeling that in comparison, the French are all sleeping. And, just between us, if I can speak quite frankly, Monatte, etc., although they are without a doubt the best comrades hereabouts, seem to be considerably below the level of the world situation. . . .

"So I await news from you two, about the children, the present situation in Saint-Etienne, the miners' union, and all my pals.

"Very friendly greetings to the miners, especially La Sablière, Nicolas, Papa Blanc, and all the young people who are taking the courses—not forgetting Arnaud himself.

"Fraternally.

"P.S. I have some officers' daughters in my class. This promises some fun when the question of patriotism comes up! In the meantime, I have the best relations with my class . . ."[4]

Simone rented an unfurnished apartment in Auxerre at the edge of town, in the factory district. It was at 34 rue de Preuilly, at the junction of rue de Preuilly and the Vaux highway, above a café and near the railroad bridge. Quite close by there was a small restaurant where she ate now and then.

Generally she cooked her own meals. She was often seen going home with a large loaf of bread under her arm. This was obviously her provision of bread for several days. Devoting as little time as possible to her nourishment, she ate little and badly. When she ate at the restaurant, she didn't eat much better, since she was concerned about not spending too much money on herself. During one of her stays at Auxerre, Mme. Weil, seeing that Simone was absolutely famished, gave the restaurant owner money on the sly so that at least when she ate at the restaurant Simone would get a decent meal. He promised to keep an eye on her. Mme. Weil later admitted this to Simone, who told her that the maneuver had not helped at all, since the restaurant owner perhaps had forgotten his promise or had soon given up trying to influence his customer.

Mme. Weil had gone with her to Auxerre, just as she had gone with her to Le Puy. She helped her find an apartment and furnish it. According to Cabaud, as soon as her mother left, Simone rid the apartment of all the furnishings that she considered unnecessary.[5]

Her mother also accompanied Simone when she paid her first visit to the school's headmistress. What happened at this first meeting is not known, but afterward Simone's relations with the administration were even worse than at Le Puy. The way the headmistress spoke of Simone to Cabaud shows that after more than twenty years she could not forget Simone's rudeness or overcome the irritation she had felt because of it. She said that when she spoke to her, Simone would turn her back, and when she visited the classroom, the students would stand up but Simone remained seated, turning away her face "in which two bulging black eyes flashed fire."[6]

Simone's relations with her colleagues were just as bad, or, to put it more precisely, they were nearly nonexistent because of mutual antipathy. According to the story the headmistress told Cabaud, the other teachers found it hard to take Simone. And she avoided them as much as possible. She was never seen in the teachers' room; after her lessons, she would quickly leave the school. At the teachers' periodic, obligatory meeting, she would sit there without speaking or listening, her head plunged in a newspaper, smoking, alien to everything around her. Moreover, in a draft of a letter she wrote from Auxerre to one of her former students at Le Puy, this brief judgment can be found: "My relations with the administration are even worse than at Le Puy and my colleagues' level is incredibly beneath anything imaginable."

As for her class, in the same letter she says: "Do you want me to tell you about my class at Auxerre? Some nice young girls. The parents are infinitely more bourgeois (three officers!), more unresponsive, and narrower than at Le Puy (except of course for M. Ch. . . .), which is all reflected in the class. They are polite, listen attentively, even understand quite well, but it all slides away. Ideas don't get any grip on them. A single exception, the only one who gives me as much satisfaction as the best students of last year; I've had the pleasure of converting her to mathematics, although in this field she is the most hopeless in the lycée."

Outside of her class, Simone's main activity at first consisted in writing articles about Germany. On October 25, *La Révolution prolétarienne* published the long article she had mentioned in her letter to the Thévenons, "L'Allemagne en attente" ("Germany Waits"). The conclusion of this article voices a doubt and a fear. After having enthusiastically praised the German proletariat and having declared: "When the moment comes in which all of them together, the workers in the factories and the unemployed, will decide to rise up, the working class will appear in its full strength and with much more brilliance and dash than in the Paris of 1871 or the Saint Petersburg of 1905," Simone added: "But who can say whether this struggle will not end with the defeat that up till now has crushed all such spontaneous uprisings?"[7]

The editors of *La Révolution prolétarienne*, feeling that this last sentence was too disheartening, cut it out. So the article ended with a sentence that seemed to predict the triumph of the German proletarian revolution. Simone was very indignant when she saw how they had changed her article.

This article also appeared in *Libres Propos,* which printed it as written without any changes but in two parts, on October 25 and November 25.

After this she wrote two short articles about the events that had taken place in Germany at the beginning of November: the transportation strike in Berlin, which was started by the Communists and Nazis on November 4 and lasted until the eighth, and the German elections, which had taken place at the same time, on November 6. These articles appeared simultaneously in *Libres Propos* and *La Révolution prolétarienne* on November 25. Contrary to the evaluations of the Communists, Simone did not see any reason for much hope in the success of the transport workers' strike. The German Communists had not been able to prevent the resumption of work when the Nazis had ordered it. "The power of the Communist party, when reduced to its own forces, is in terms of any real action exactly nil."[8] As for the elections, which marked a setback for the National Socialists at the same time that the Communists registered some gains, she also took care not to draw from this conclusions that were too optimistic. She said that the Nazi party, which still remained much the stronger, was far from disintegrating, and concluded: "Although the Fascist danger is perhaps not immediate, it is more menacing than ever."[9]

Finally, she wrote a more detailed series of articles on Germany for *L'Ecole émancipée,* the publication of the "federal majority" of the United Federation of Teachers.[10] As we have said before, this Federation belonged to the C.G.T.U., but the majority of its members did not follow the Communist line. In *L'Ecole émancipée* Simone published articles in which she severely criticized the German Communist party, which refused in practice to ally itself with Social Democracy against the Nazis and maintained this position right up until the moment Hitler's victory was complete, that is to say, until March 1933. Moreover, Simone's criticisms of the Social Democratic party were just as severe. Her predictions as to Germany's future were dark and, unfortunately, all too lucid. Even before the last of her articles appeared—they were published in the period between December 4, 1932, and March 5, 1933—Hitler had become the Reich chancellor, and the Reichstag fire had put him in a position to obtain full powers.

During the All Saints' holiday, Simone probably took a short trip to see her friends at Saint-Etienne. A story of Duperray's and a report from Albertine Thévenon saying that she had seen Simone cry on her return from Germany seem to imply this.

A little later, probably in November or December, she made the acquaintance of Boris Souvarine. He had heard Nicolas Lazarévitch talk about her several months before, while she was in Germany. Meeting

Lazarévitch in a café in Montparnasse, he told him, "I am preparing a magazine and I'm looking for people who can write for it." Lazarévitch asked him, "Do you know Simone Weil? She's just what you need." Since then he had tried to meet her. But this did not take place until after he had read an article she wrote on Germany (either the article in *La Révolution prolétarienne* or the first one in *L'Ecole émancipée*), whose masterly style impressed him and, more anxious than ever to know her, he finally managed to meet her.

He was to become one of her best friends, perhaps the closest person to her at a certain period, one of those for whom she had the deepest affection. She spoke to me later about him, expressing great admiration for his abilities as an organizer and for his honesty and courage. She hoped that together they might undertake some important work. She was to write to Albertine Thévenon in 1935: "It does me good to hear what you say of Souvarine. It is true that he's a great guy, you can be sure of that. And he's alone—almost everybody misjudges him."

I had been appointed to a teaching post at Caen in October 1931. But having fallen ill at the beginning of 1932, on doctor's orders I had been sent to the mountains, at Briançon. As Christmas was approaching, Simone wrote to tell me that she wanted to come to Briançon for the holidays:

"My dear Simone:

"Forgive me for not having written to you for so long, and for writing now only to ask you if I can come to visit you.

"I would be happy to see you after more than a year's absence, if you're well enough to enjoy it.

"I'll be in Paris on Tuesday the twenty-second. I have to return on the fourth. Almost fifteen days!

"Perhaps, before or after having seen you (after, preferably), I might take a little trip to the South. Especially since on the thirty-first there will be a meeting of the federal council of the United Federation of Teachers at Avignon. But all this is subordinated to your arrangements. For example, are your parents coming to see you? And when? I think it would be best that I be there before or after them . . .

"Fraternally."

My health had improved somewhat since the beginning of December. I reserved a room for Simone near the Hôtel des Neiges, where I was being treated. She took her meals with me. We talked about philosophy and politics. In philosophy, I still had the same ideas I had during my last year at the Ecole Normale—indeed I was even more committed to them—and she continued to disapprove of them. I recall that I quoted to her some sentences from Céline's *Journey to the End of the Night:* "You have to choose, to die or to lie. I have never been able to kill myself." I wanted to show her that love of the truth, when it is a matter of the truth about oneself, is beyond and above nature.

In politics, there was nothing I could argue with her about, but indeed there was everything to learn. (My only ideas in politics were summed up by a great admiration for Jean-Jacques Rousseau, which in turn meant great distrust for what he criticized under the name of society, or progress, and which is in fact the growing interdependence of individuals in the large states.) She told me about her trip to Germany, her anxieties about the German workers, her doubts as to the possibility of a real revolution, and the difficulty of understanding the crisis. Louzon's theory on crises seemed logical to her, but she did not say that it was true. She was much less certain about all the other theories. Contrary to the predictions made by the left, she thought that the adoption of a forty-hour week would not solve anything in the crisis but only aggravate it.

She was very severe with Stalinism. Yet she felt that, if one must condemn it when among one's own people, that is, trade unionists or leftists, one should avoid doing it too publicly so as not to give weapons to the bourgeois parties. I remember that we talked about Panaït Istrati, the Rumanian writer who had recently defected. I had just read, I believe around this time, a statement of his that had struck me: "No organization can help or will ever help anyone but the organizers themselves." She told me that she fully agreed with him on the subject of the Russian regime, but she seemed to regret that he had not found a way to make his criticisms known only inside the workers' movements. In her opinion, one certainly had to tell the truth to the workers, but when doing so, one should not play the capitalists' game.

She spoke to me about Cardinal de Retz's *Memoirs*, which had aroused her enthusiasm. She admired not only the profundity of his views on the political struggles but also his character, the feelings of a man who above all esteemed will, resolution, and lucidity.

I introduced her to another patient being treated at the Hôtel des Neiges, Mme. Nina Bernadas, who, like us, was a philosophy professor at a lycée. Simone enjoyed talking with her. Mme. Bernadas had written a novel whose manuscript she had brought with her to the Hôtel des Neiges and that had not yet been published; I don't know if it ever was. Simone used to call her "the novelist."

On a day of fine weather the Hôtel des Neiges had organized a trip by cable car up to the saddle of Mount Genèvre for the patients. Simone, who had brought ski clothes in her luggage, took advantage of this excursion to practice skiing. I was not permitted to ski; so I sat with another patient, Mme. A., the wife of a Parisian doctor, on the terrace of a café or hotel that was right across from the ski run. All afternoon we watched Simone go up and down the slope. She would climb up in a straight line, tackling the hill at its steepest point, not obliquely and in a zigzag path like the others. She used the fatiguing procedure that consists in placing, at each step, the upper ski perpendicular to the lower ski. When she reached the top, she would try to ski down and each time she would fall. She would immediately get up and start all over again. Watching her, Mme. A. kept saying, "What will power! What will power!"

After these few days spent at Briançon, Simone left for Avignon. We had sent a joint New Year's greeting card to Alain. In reply he sent a very affectionate letter, which arrived just after Simone's departure.

"Paris, December 30, 1932.

"My dear girls,

"Although I'm not quite sure of the address, I reply to your greetings, which have deeply touched me. Your students' days marked a fine moment in my teaching career that will never return, since everything changes. There has been a decline among the girls, and now a resurgence, but of another kind, of a lighter, more mathematical species. You are part of the mystical age. Have I myself passed the mystical age? Perhaps. Plato, being more frivolous than Descartes, is also more severe. You are in the style of Louis XIII. Be happy with your natures; you have something to work on. My fondest greetings to my two girls.

"Alain."

In speaking of the Louis XIII style, he was obviously thinking of Simone. He loved this style. He had said one day that in the most insignificant house in the Louis XIII style there was something more beautiful than in the Versailles palace.

I sent this letter to Simone at Auxerre, asking her to send it back to me. I told her that if she kept it, she would lose it. She answered me on the stub of a postal money order with which she reimbursed me for a small sum that after her departure I had paid to send her some of her luggage:

"Dear Simone,

"Lost the number of the check. Forgot the amount of my debt; is this right? (There should have been another suitcase.) Sent nothing for you to the longshoremen, the comrades (very nice), having no way of getting it to them directly. . . . I will return Chartier's letter to you (though I would not have lost it). Happy about the 'Louis XIII style,' because of my dear friend Retz. As for mysticism and the lack of the mathematical mind. . . . You yourself must write to your Federation in order to join (for example—in my region—to Mussigmann, Boys' Lycée, Tournon). Didn't order anything yet for you from Hasfeld; haven't been able to get to Paris.

"*Very* happy to have seen you. Be good.

"My best regards to the novelist."

The unfinished sentence about mysticism shows that Simone at this period was not very pleased to be considered a mystic.

She forgot to send me Alain's letter, and although she thought she would not lose it, she soon didn't know where she had put it. Long after her death, her mother found it between the pages of a book.

A good part of Simone's activity during the year at Auxerre was devoted to the debates and struggles inside the United Federation of Teachers. At the beginning of the school year, when she wanted to choose a union, she hesitated as we have seen, between joining a United M.O.R. union or a Confederated majority union. Both of them had something she did not like, the former because it followed the Communist party line, the latter because it was part of the majority group in the C.G.T., that is, Jouhaux's reformist tendency. (That is why in her letter she had added: "No luck!") Finally she opted for the United union, or rather found out that she was automatically a member since she belonged to the United Federation of Teachers. She wrote to the Thévenons in January:

"I've joined a United union (or rather, as a member of the Federation, I automatically became a member). Thirty members. M.O.R., but not 100 percent; the purest amount to about 90 percent. I try to demolish them, but they resist. . . . I have entered unfurling the banner of the opposition. Nevertheless the atmosphere is good. There are fine people here. There never has been an expulsion in this region because of political beliefs. The union unanimously criticized B. (for insulting those who have other political opinions)."

Joining a United union did not prevent her from supporting her friends, the miners of Saint-Etienne, who for the most part were leaving the C.G.T.U. to rejoin the C.G.T. They had decided to do this at the end of December 1932, no doubt because a Stalinist group had been organized which made life impossible for them. In the same letter, Simone said:

"According to what you wrote to me, I entirely agree with Arnaud —provided that the former members of the United union don't fall asleep as a result of the easing of their situation caused by their return to the C.G.T., don't let up a bit on their polemic against the pure, and never cease denouncing the role played by the C.G.T. since the split! And provided that they don't develop—like the railroad workers at Rambaud—patriotism toward the old home. For my part, I have confidence in them."

Yet she had scant hopes of reforming the C.G.T.:

"As for the prospects of reforming the C.G.T., I am not as optimistic as you. France is not an independent or decisive factor in the world situation; on the contrary, it follows (Hasfeld said that it would have its revolution when the republic of Andorra had its). The movement among the civil servants gives me more pain than pleasure, owing to the petty character of its purely selfish demands, which lack all social content.

"Yet one can always work."

She was troubled to see her friends among the teachers in the Haute-Loire "drowned in this amorphous and gelatinous mass of old reformist teachers," and wondered whether it wouldn't be better for Vidal to leave the National Union in order to join a United union.

Not content with having joined a United union, she also made contact with the leaders of the United Federation of Teachers, particularly with Gilbert Serret, a teacher at Saint-Montant in the Ardèche. It was perhaps at the federal council meeting of December 30, 1932,[11] in Avignon, that she met him for the first time. Still in her January letter to the Thévenons, she says:

"I have contacted the federal majority in the Federation and I'm quite happy about it. Serret is *very* nice. Ideologically they are—at least Serret is—very close to us, contrary to what Barrué wrote in the *R.P.*—Of course, they are angry with Cornec, but that's something else. . . . Someday I'll tell you about it."

(Cornec had left the United Federation to join the C.G.T.)

Also at this federal council meeting in Avignon, Simone met Mussigmann, bursar of the lycée at Tournon, who represented the federal majority in the Committee of Professors. This committee had organized, within the United Federation of Teachers, the teachers in the secondary schools and universities.

When Mussigmann got sick, probably in January 1933, he gave her his task of editing a circular addressed to those professors in the United Federation of Teachers who belonged to the federal majority group. These professors were not very numerous; most of the professors in the United union, unlike the grade-school teachers, belonged to the M.O.R. group, that is, in practice they subordinated their trade union activity to the Communist party line. In the circular that she edited, Simone asked the professors of the "federal majority" to manifest their existence and opinions in opposition to the M.O.R.

"Dear comrade:

"Since the Committee of Professors has achieved unity, the M.O.R. has been alone, due to our shortcomings, in manifesting its existence.

"Before Bordeaux,* we were united against the M.O.R. on the question of discipline with respect to the Federation.

"This question seems for the moment at least provisorily eliminated. The question now being posed is that of the activity of the Committee of Professors. We want to know whether, on this new terrain, we should continue to fight the M.O.R., and whether we will remain united in this struggle (a struggle that, be it well understood, would not in any case exclude normal collaboration between comrades of the same organization).

"In particular, are you satisfied with *L'Université syndicaliste?* If you

---

*The Bordeaux congress in August 1932.

are not, what precisely do you disapprove of? And what do you propose to rectify it?

"On this subject, here, simply as straws in the wind, are a few personal ideas:

"1. We must not bear in silence Bruhat's twaddle about the 'class struggle' position of the professors of the General Federation of Teachers. . . . Nobody can seriously believe that in all this grumbling about salaries there is the slightest sign of real class struggle. This sort of demagogy is dishonorable.

"2. *L'Université syndicaliste* could only fulfill all of its duties if it helped to provide an honest, more profound study of the questions that are posed by the idea of a revolutionary culture. (Perhaps we should call it instead socialist culture?) These questions are wrapped in mist, in commonplaces that should be gotten rid of, without being concerned about orthodoxy or frightened by any authority, including that of Engels. In particular, there is good reason to discuss the legitimacy of the connection, usually admitted without examination, between historical materialism and philosophical materialism.

"In the same way (since all these questions are connected), it would be appropriate to examine the peculiar predeliction of many revolutionary theoreticians in regard to that which, in modern science, seems most shocking to the mind (curved space, etc.). This predeliction of theirs, in any case, they have in common with the most stuffily bourgeois theoreticians, Brunschvicg . . . There is good reason to ask oneself whether this is not an example of the contamination of revolutionary thought by bourgeois thought.

"3. In a general way, we should never forget that our task is the preparation of a society "in which the degrading division of work into manual work and intellectual work will be abolished" (Marx). Among all the particular tasks implied by this general task, one of the most important is to create, in the different branches of culture, the basis for a true diffusion of knowledge.

"4. We must imitate our teacher comrades by studying educational problems more closely.

"We ask you not only to send in your opinions about these ideas but also to give us your personal suggestions. We cannot try to do anything useful about *L'Université syndicaliste* before having confronted our own ideas among ourselves."

Bruhat, secretary of the professors' section and one of the leaders of the M.O.R., heard of the existence of this circular and became very indignant. He published it in its entirety, as an example of a revolting maneuver, in *Le Travailleur de l'Enseignement*,[12] monthly organ of the supporters of the "Confederated majority" in the United Federation of Teachers. (The "confederated majority" was the majority group in the C.G.T.U., that is, the orthodox Communist group, or, if one wishes, the

M.O.R. It was opposed to the "federal majority" which was a majority group only in the Federation.) Bruhat accused Simone and the federal majority of wanting to split the professors in the Federation, contrary to the spirit of conciliation and unity that had been expressed at the Bordeaux congress.

In the same issue of *Le Travailleur de l'Enseignement* there appeared a fragment of J. Berlioz's reportage on Germany under the title "In the Form of a Reply to Mlle. S. Weill" [sic]. This title was added by the editors of the magazine, who presented Berlioz's reportage with these words: "Our brothers in Germany are making superhuman efforts to align the German proletariat against fascism. They fall by the dozens on the battlefront. This is the moment chosen by our federal leaders to insert in *L'Ecole émancipée* a series of articles by S. Weil in which the activity of the German Communist party is odiously distorted.

"We cannot reply better to this than by publishing here part of our comrade Berlioz's reportage. ...."

This was perhaps the first protest against Simone's articles on Germany; it was to be followed by several others.

Simone anxiously followed the events in Germany. It was most likely toward the end of January that she wrote—we don't know to whom—this fragment of a letter:

"Péri in *L'Huma* continues his sad role, which consists in camouflaging German defeats as victories.

"Each time that there is the prospect of a battle over there, I cannot help having the feeling that I am deserting them by staying here. A feeling, moreover, which is hardly reasonable since I have no great illusions on the probable outcome, and on the other hand I am intensely aware that they are fighting (when they fight) blindly. For insurrections on the order of the Commune are admirable, but they fail (true, the proletariat is much stronger than it was then; but so is the bourgeoisie). Insurrections of the October 1917 type succeed, but all they do is reinforce the bureaucratic, military, and police apparatus. And at this moment nonviolence à la Gandhi seems simply a rather hypocritical species of reformism. And we do not yet know any fourth type of action. I cannot understand why militants don't pose the question clearly, now that we can see the October Revolution from a certain distance. It is posed for all those who do not approve of the Stalinist course and who, being materialists, consider it not as having fallen from the heavens but as a natural development of the October Revolution. The fact that nobody has systematically tried to draw the lessons from a comparison of the two experiences we have had until now (1871 and October 1917) shows the inadequacy of revolutionary thought. It could be said that the militants fear demoralizing thoughts. For my part, I have decided for some time now that, the 'above-the-fray' position being in fact practically impossible, I would always choose, even in the eventuality of certain defeat, to share the defeat of the workers rather than the victory of their oppressors; but as for shutting one's eyes because of the fear of weakening one's belief in victory, I do not want to do this at any price. And I cannot help but be struck by the ease with which we all—even the militants most deserving of admiration—agree to repeat formulas to which we are unable to attribute any real significance.

"There is an obvious fact whose significance nobody wants to recognize: *State and Revolution,* Lenin's most important book, establishes the principles of a revolution that failed and was followed immediately by a victorious revolution, but that, almost from the start, was in complete contradiction with those principles, a contradiction that has only become sharper."

The beginning of this excellent piece of writing refers to some articles by Gabriel Péri published in *L'Humanité* on January 23 and 24, 1933, following the Nazi demonstration on the Bülow Platz in the working-class section of Berlin, directly in front of the central headquarters of the German Communist party.

In February (apparently) Simone was irritated by an article that she thought was written by Thévenon and that in fact was by one of his C.G.T. comrades. This article said that the federal executive of the United Federation of Teachers regretted not being able decently to back down when an action was proposed by the National Union. Simone energetically defended the Federation; she wrote to Thévenon:

"Dear comrade:

"It's a shame—but I must bawl you out a bit!

"How could you have so far forgotten yourself—blinded by anti-Communist passion—as to speak as you have of the Federation of Teachers, which is being basely slandered by the M.O.R.?

"So not engaging its 3,000 members in an action, in order not to expose them without defense to repression, is 'backing down'?

"If I read that from the pen of a one-hundred-percenter [that is, an orthodox Communist], I would call it provocation. . . .

"Things are going badly in Germany. The C.I. [Communist International] has practically ceased to exist, it seems to me.

"This is not the moment to attack honest revolutionists, nor to confine oneself to 100 percent syndicalism.

"This is the moment for everyone to come to an agreement: syndicalists, opposition Communists—even sincere orthodox, rank-and-file Communists. (I don't think that this creature exists to any extent at Saint-Etienne. For my part, until now I have had idyllic relations with my M.O.R. union and the local cell, although I don't pass up a single opportunity to take a poke at the C.I. and, as a result, *Le Travailleur de l'Enseignement,* organ of the M.O.R., has begun attacking me seriously.)

"This is the moment above all—above all for all of the young—to start seriously reviewing all ideas, instead of adopting 100 percent any program from before the war (prewar C.G.T. or Bolshevik party), at the present time when *all* workers' organizations have *completely failed.*

"You must see that—to the degree that 'revolutionary syndicalism' is a dogma for you, as the 'party' is for Communists who follow the line or belong to the opposition—I decidedly cease being with you. . . .

"This is not to say that I am more attracted to the Communist movement—*on the contrary!*—but I no longer want to admit any of those prewar ideas to the status of articles of faith, and especially since they have *never* been seriously examined and have been disproven by all of subsequent history. I wish that we could make a clean sweep of all political tendencies, and that we could finally learn how to pose problems honestly—which the militants rarely venture to do.

"I am stifled by this revolutionary movement with its blindfolded eyes . . .

"As for you, I beg you to pay attention to this anti-Communist trend that has already engulfed so many good comrades and that, by its own logic, leads one where one does not wish to go. I don't mean to say to reformism but to rather blurred attitudes. . . . That would make me feel very bad.

"Fraternally, to both of you. Try to write to me."

Thévenon sent her a letter explaining what he had done. Simone wrote to him again:

"Dear comrade:

"You have not read X.'s stuff carefully. He accused the F.E. [federal executive] of being sorry that it could not decently back down when an action was proposed by the National Union.

"If he had only written what you say he wrote and had given his reasons, I would not have protested, although it might seem to me to be a little too harsh.

"I don't want to offer an apology for the Federation. What revolted me was the hate-filled, contemptuous tone. . . . It is one thing to point out as a comrade the mistakes made by comrades, which one deplores and one is forced to point out because of a concern for the truth, yet it is quite another to point them out as if they were the acts of enemies, and in a tone full of insulting implications.

"By 'the position that the march of events condemns,' do you mean that the Federation remains outside the C.G.T.? If it is that, I don't agree. I would agree perhaps if it were a completely different corporate body. Perhaps in fact the militants of the Federation would have more influence on corporate action in the National Union. But for it, that is not the essential question. The Federation has something precious to preserve: its revolutionary traditions (to which, alone in the C.G.T., it remained faithful throughout the war), its independent spirit thanks to which it alone stands up to the Stalinists, its theoretical level—not very high, but much higher than that of the National Union! In pedagogy, the educational task takes precedence over the improvement of working conditions. The Federation doesn't acquit itself too badly; it could do much better; but to do so it must remain independent.

"As for syndicalism, what you say comes to this: nothing can be done —at least let us go where there are workers, i.e., in the unions. But everyone agrees on that point. If your syndicalism leads to that, and to the struggle against the political parties as the disrupters of the unions, we are still in agreement.

"For the rest, 1. it is false that the failure of the C.I. proves the failure of political parties in general; the C.P.'s [Communist parties] have always been parties apart, dependent not on the revolutionary proletariat but on a state apparatus. And besides, what is a 'party'? This word can designate essentially different organizations (Trotsky calls the Jacobins a 'party').

"As for the elite:

"1. Everyone agrees that socialism is government by the working class itself.

"2. That does not at all solve the problem, which is: by what *stages* can the masses be made conscious enough to govern? Through a syndicalist organization inside the regime? (But what will happen to your trade unions when confronted by Fascism? Besides, the trade unions, organized as they are, do not prepare the proletariat *in any way* for power; they organize an almost passive resistance. As for education, they are not set up to do it.) Or through the taking of power by a conscious 'elite,' which will govern while waiting for new generations to mature? The second solution is defective. The first solution perhaps even a little more so. Well then? Then, once more, it is necessary to think.

"And above all, *if* the trade unions could take power—but then that would amount to the rule of an 'elite,' just as in the case of a party! Even under a capitalist regime, are not trade unionists in the unions subjected ot the dictatorship of the bureaucracy? Less so in France than elsewhere —but nevertheless a considerable amount! And in this sense the situation is getting steadily worse.

"That is why my pal Prudhommeaux employs precisely the same phrases as you do (on the workers, etc.) to preach the *destruction* of the union movement.

"As for the struggle against the C.I., I am as much for it as you are. But on the condition that one appears in the wrong as little as possible in the eyes of the Communist *workers* and militants of the second or third level (the honest ones). They want a united front. (Besides, there is nothing to prove that the C.I. could not sincerely want a united front, in specific circumstances.)

"The problem is: to find some way of forming an organization that does not engender a bureaucracy. For the bureaucracy *always* betrays. And an unorganized action remains pure, but fails.

"The 'revolutionary syndicalists' are against bureaucracy, I know. But syndicalism is itself bureaucratic! And even the revolutionary syndicalists, discouraged, have wound up by coming to terms with the bureaucracy. Wasn't the Twenty-Two group a movement of bureaucrats, after all? (And in good part corrupted!) . . .

" 'There are some principles that have not failed,' you say. —None! Or they are principles too far removed from reality to be 'disproven by it.'

"Conclusion: should one be with the working class? should one struggle, think, build with it? Yes! But the third is at present impossible. The first is possible only to a feeble degree.

"The revolution is a *job,* a methodical task that the blind or people with blindfolded eyes cannot perform. And that is what we are at this moment . . . We must open our eyes. In any case, I fully recognize the value of your work. . . .

"Fraternally to both of you . . ."

Prudhommeaux, who is mentioned in this letter, wrote for *La Correspondance internationale ouvrière.* In her January letter to the Thévenons, Simone had called Urbain Thévenon's attention to the interesting documentation contained in this bulletin. She asked him to support it, though warning him that the people who published it were *antisyndicalist* anarchists opposed to all forms of bureaucratic organization. (They thought that the organization always betrays and wanted only committees for action.) "It's up to you to decide," she said, "what matters most: the interest of their documentation or the dangerous character of their tendency. I would say the first, from my personal point of view. But make up your own minds." She had also tried to recommend this bulletin to Monatte, who, naturally enough, as a syndicalist, had his reservations. She tried as much as she could to bring into closer contact and gather together all these revolutionists whom she judged to be honest, and persuade them to surmount their differences.

The forcefulness of her arguments in the two letters I have just quoted could no doubt be laid to the fact that she was extremely unhappy over what was happening in Germany.

On January 30 Hitler had become Chancellor of the Reich. But this had not given him full power. With good reason, Simone had written in an article published by *Libres propos* on February 25 ("The Situation in Germany"), that he still did not have the reality of power because military power (the Reichswehr) and economic power were still in the hands of the bourgeoisie. But she had added that one must take into account "the continuous progress achieved by the Nazi party . . . as regards the relationship of forces within the bourgeoisie." "So long as

Hitler holds the trump card in his hands that has permitted him to obtain the post of chancellor, the German bourgeoisie must grant him an ever-increasing degree of power and finally, perhaps, complete power."

Actually, two days later, Hitler found himself in a position to take complete power. On February 27 the Reichstag fire occurred, permitting him to overcome the bourgeoisie's fear of him by an even greater fear. A great number of Communists were arrested, and personal freedom was abolished. On March 5 new elections took place; the number of Nazi deputies rose from 195 to 288. Finally, on March 23, Hitler received full powers from the Reichstag and the Reichstag itself was adjourned *sine die.*

Terror struck the militants of the working-class movements. Many of them went into exile to escape prison or the concentration camp, torture, and perhaps death. There was an exodus of republicans, leftists, trade unionists, and Jews. From this moment on, a great part of Simone's activity was devoted to helping German refugees.

She made special efforts to help those who did not belong to either of the two main Internationals and so could not obtain assistance.[13] One of the first persons whom she put up at her parents' house in Paris was Jakob W., one of the leaders of the S.A.P. (Sozialistische Arbeiter-Partei), a dissident group of the Social Democracy, though more to the left than the latter. An old metal worker, he was, it appears, a jolly man who liked to joke, was concerned about his comfort, and was not burdened by too many scruples. Mme. Weil thought that he did not inconvenience himself very much. His girl friend, with whom he lived, told the Weils, "*Er braucht ein kräftiges Essen* ("He needs very strong nourishment") to explain his astonishing alimentary demands. He gave Mme. Weil his socks and linen to be mended; yet his girlfriend felt that the mending job had not been done well enough. When he finally had to leave for good, the Weils, relieved, offered to wake him up in time, since he had to catch a train at five in the morning. "Oh, yes," he said to them, "for middle-class people like yourselves it costs nothing at all to get up early in the morning!"

But Simone had much more serious criticisms of him. A young man named Emil who belonged to the S.A.P. had been arrested and sentenced to death in Germany. He wasn't even twenty. He had been helped to escape. He had stayed for a while in Lyon and subsequently had been brought to Paris and was also put up in the Weils' apartment. Soon after he arrived he fell into a deep depression. Simone questioned him; he told her that his friends in the S.A.P. wanted to send him back to Germany and that he was sure he would die there, for he was a marked man and easy to recognize. Simone had a violent argument with W. about this, protesting against the plan of sending this "little fellow," as she called him, back to Germany. Some time later, since Germany demanded his extradition and he ran the risk of being expelled from

France, she gave him the money to go to Norway. After this incident, she lost almost all interest in W. In 1942, according to Mme. Weil, she knew that he was in the United States when she was there, but didn't wish to see him.

Simone had met W. through one young woman among her friends who had taken him in for some time. It was through this same friend that she met Hans R., a young man from Frankfort. He too came to live with the Weils. He said that he had been given some important sums of money and was going to leave for England, where all doors would be opened to him. They thought he was a rather shady character. Finally he left for Ibiza, one of the Balearic Islands. There, a woman who belonged to the S.A.P. executed him because it had been discovered—or they thought it had been discovered—that he had sold documents to the Gestapo. Dr. Weil had to tell the young man's parents about his death, and he was their only child.

The Weils also had Kurt Landau, a Trotskyist, and his wife as guests. One day Simone arrived at noon and told her parents, "You must give them lunch and a place to stay, because it's my fault that they've been thrown out on the street." She had gone to visit them at N.'s house. N., the son of a banker, lived on the second floor of his parents' town house. He had secretly taken in Kurt Landau and his wife. Simone, who did not know the special conditions under which they lived there, rang the bell and told the maid who opened the door, "I've come to see Comrade Kurt Landau." "There is no comrade here," the woman snapped, and shut the door in her face. As a result, N.'s parents suspected the presence of comrades in their son's part of the house; they discovered the Landaus and showed them the door. The Weils put them in their apartment on the ground floor. The Landaus ate with them. Kurt Landau never grew weary of talking about politics; he would pursue Mme. Weil into the kitchen to expound his theories. He had played a role among the Trotskyists, but then had had a falling out with them. One day Mme. Weil told him that young Sédov was dropping by. Landau said, "He must not know that I am here," and hid in a bedroom. They had to make sure that Sédov didn't see him.

In Berlin, Simone had met Fröhlich, the author of a book entitled *Illustrierte Geschichte der deutschen Revolution,* who had also edited the works of Rosa Luxembourg. He was an old Brandlerite [of the so-called "right" opposition that followed Bucharin] who had gone over to the S.A.P. When she returned to Paris, Simone had recommended him to Marcel Martinet, so that he might try to get him a regular job with the magazine *Europe,* and also so that Martinet might assign him the task of writing a book on Rosa Luxembourg that he wanted written. When Hitler became dictator, Fröhlich was put in jail. Simone was in torment over him, concocted plans to free him, and even thought of going there herself to take his place in jail.[14] She finally had given up these romantic plans, but she did send money to get him a lawyer. Fröhlich was finally freed and came to Paris at the beginning of 1934. He too lived with the Weils. He told them how, in prison, the conversation of the prisoners was chiefly about all the tortures they would inflict on the Nazis if and when they took power. This is how they kept up their morale.

Simone's articles on Germany provoked strong reactions, particularly among the orthodox Communists. In the United Federation of Teachers, some people criticized the editors of *L'Ecole émancipée* for having published them. The editors, who were impartial, also published, after the appearance of the offending articles, the protests and the answers to them.

On March 19, two graduates of the Ecole Normale, J. Daudin and P. Lussiaa-Berdou, protested as students of the same school as Simone: "We consider excessive the place given in your journal to an article of pure impressions. Moreover, this article, in which there are quite a few omissions and even inaccuracies, especially on the role of the Communist party in the strikes since the autumn of 1932 and on the position taken by revolutionary workers toward the Versailles Treaty, tends to justify the most pusillanimous spirit of panic. A certain number of middle-class persons . . . are demoralized by Hitler's temporary success. . . . We must therefore, as students of the same school as S. Weil, energetically protest the spirit of this article, while quite happy that S. Weil asks the Federation to take over the support of the German proletariat."

Simone addressed only a few words to "young Daudin" and "her friends of the rue d'Ulm" when a little later she answered the M.O.R.'s attack.[15]

On March 26 and April 2, *L'Ecole émancipée* published an article in two installments by R. Ranc, a typographical proofreader, "The German Communist Movement: A Reply to Our Comrade Weil." At the start, the author made his apologies for being only a "guest correspondent," not belonging either to the Federation or the C.G.T.U. (he was a member of the only trade union for print-shop proofreaders in Paris, which was affiliated with the C.G.T.). He defended the German Communist party and attacked the reformists. Furthermore, he was well informed about the workers' movements and perhaps scored a few points against Simone, though he did not refute her on the essential questions. His article had a moderate tone; he tried to prove that the German Communist party could scarcely have acted in any other way than it did. He concluded by saying that Simone didn't offer a solution.

Simone would answer him briefly when she answered the M.O.R. She said that Comrade Ranc's article brought up neigher facts nor arguments that could change the fundamental aspects of the problem. "He simply informs us that the recent mistakes have their roots in a more distant past."[16]

On April 9 *L'Ecole émancipée* published an article by Pierre Naville, a Trotskyist, that this time expressed approbation. Naville only wanted to complete Simone's articles by presenting the Trotskyist thesis, and also demanding that the federal majority take a clear position toward the policy of the Communist International.

Simone felt that Naville had to be answered, even though he had not attacked her. She replied with a short article that appeared in the same issue (April 9).[17] While praising Trotsky's lucidity, she criticized his hesitant, uncertain attitude toward the Communist International and observed that he too could be asked to take a clear position. Naville having written: "The Communist International, dominated by the Stalinist faction, has renounced its role of leadership of the proletarian revolution in Germany," Simone felt that this affirmation did not have to be qualified by the two last words "in Germany." "We would like to know *in what* country," she said, "the Communist International has retained this role." She also said that a militant like Trotsky didn't have the right "to take an ambiguous position." This criticism of and appeal to Trotsky may perhaps have contributed to his decision soon after to break definitively with the Communist International and found the Fourth International.

And finally, on April 30, the M.O.R. answered Simone through the voice of "the Confederated majority of the union of l'Herault." They arranged for *L'Ecole émancipée* to publish an article entitled "On the Situation in Germany—a Few Corrections." It began with these words: "At last this great, very great analysis of S. Weil on Germany is finished —great because of the number of pages it contains, great because of the accumulation of mistakes and lies, great because of the author's claim of drawing up a crushing indictment against the German section of the Communist International, and great finally because of its sadistic pleasure in burying the revolutionary organizations once and for all. . . . The revolutionary comrades are indignant and their distrust of *L'Ecole émancipée* grows. . . ."

After having contradicted Simone's accusations with some declarations of a general character instead of a detailed and precise discussion of the facts, the authors of the article concluded: "The time has come not for defeatist newspaper articles but for action."

Simone replied in the next issue of *L'Ecole émancipée,* on May 7, in an article entitled "Some Remarks on the Reply of the M.O.R."[18] She said, in particular: "Although the M.O.R. speaks of an 'accumulation of mistakes and lies,' it does not point out even the smallest inaccuracy in the articles that it wishes to refute. . . . As for the comrades who want to know the truth . . . they can find, in this vain attempt at a reply, clear proof that the description of events published by *L'Ecole émancipée* was rigorously exact.

"Let us hope that these comrades fully understand the mortal danger that hangs over the revolutionary movement due to the fact that it is in the hands of men, some of whom much prefer to be guided in their thoughts and actions by myths instead of a clear view of reality, while others believe it is not good for all truths to be uttered. . . . Today, on all the important questions, the workers' movement is entirely given over to illusions and lies. . . .

" 'The time has come,' the M.O.R. says in its conclusion, 'not for defeatist newspaper articles but for action. . . .' From this it might be concluded that while we are anxiously searching for some effective action that is still possible for us to undertake, our comrades of the M.O.R. have already solved the problem. We beg them to let us profit from their knowledge. . . .

"It is futile and dishonorable to shut one's eyes. For the second time in less than twenty years the best organized, most powerful, and most advanced proletariat in the world, the proletariat of Germany, has capitulated without a fight. . . . The significance of this collapse goes far beyond the confines of GermanyYs borders. . . ."

In fact, not only Germany was at stake; because of its consequences, the German drama would involve the entire world—this was seen afterward—but it was also the decisive proof that there were serious mistakes in revolutionary theory. The way in which this catastrophe had come about not only helped to clarify Simone's mind on the question of Stalinism—it also convinced her that all the dogmas had to be re-examined. Simone was concerned about the failure of theories, a failure not merely or organizations but also of doctrines.

The essay entitled "Reflections on Technocracy, National Socialism, the U.S.S.R., and Certain Other Matters," later published in the volume entitled *Oppression and Liberty,* was evidently written during the period in which fascism had won in Germany. The same is true of the first fragment published in the same collection after "Reflections Concerning the Causes of Liberty and Social Oppression." These two texts were a prelude to the important article, "Prospects," which was to be published a few months later. They show that Simone was no longer satisfied with Marxism. "We are living on a doctrine worked out by a great man certainly, but a great man who died fifty years ago."[19] It was not the Marxist method she questioned; on the contrary, she would like to see it applied to the study of the phenomena of our time. But Marx was understandably not able to do this; he could only apply it to the study of his own time, and it is our job to use it to understand our own times. We are living without seeing "this prodigiously new period, which belies all previous forecasts."[20] It seems that only our bodies are alive in it; our minds "are still moving in the prewar world that has disappeared."[21] The new fact is the power of the bureaucracy, which has taken the place of capital. The new problem is: "Is it possible to organize the workers in a given country without this organization secreting, as it were, a bureaucracy that immediately subordinates it to the rule of the state apparatus?"[22]

Since the end of 1932, a small independent Communist group that had split from the party, the "Autonomous Group of the Western Parisian Suburb,"[23] had been proposing the holding of meetings in common with other, similar groups, with a view to thrashing out their various positions and, if possible, arriving at a common political policy. In the spring of 1933, these efforts finally led to what was called the Conference for Unification. Not only were groups invited, but also individuals who did not belong to any political group—Simone among others. The first meeting was held in a café on the rue des Archives (Café Augé, 6 rue des Archives), no doubt before April 9, perhaps on the eighth. (In fact, if I understand correctly what was said in the Trotskyist newspaper *La Vérité*, in its issues of April 14 and 28, 1933, the meeting on April 9 appears to have been the second one.) Invited to this meeting, the Trotskyists sent a delegation. But their spokesman immediately demanded that some of those present be barred from the discussion, and when they were unable to obtain this, they withdrew. Those whom the Trotskyists wanted to exclude in this fashion were the people who declared that Russia was no longer a real workers' state, that a break must be made with the Third International directed by Moscow, and that preparations must be made to form a new organization, a Fourth International. Simone was one of those who supported this position.

As is known, Trotsky himself was to break with the Communist International during the summer of 1933, sending out a call for a Fourth International. But at the time of this meeting, his political perspective was based solely on reforming the Third International. He certainly did not envision withdrawing from it, and *La Vérité* had only sarcastic comments for supporters of a Fourth International. As for the nature of the Russian state, Trotsky believed—and believed for a long time, even after he had founded a new International—that, despite its "bureaucratic deformations," Russia was essentially a workers' state.

After the departure of the Trotskyists, the meeting continued. Two currents soon became evident among the participants: on one side, those with whom the Trotskyists had not wanted to discuss an eventual unification, that is, the partisans of a break with the Third International; and on the other side, those who, though not being entirely in agreement with the Trotskyist position, were less distant from it. This division into two groups would become even sharper and deeper in the course of the next meeting.

The next meeting was undoubtedly held on April 9, as I have said, and most likely in the same place as the first. I don't know whether it was at the first or the second meeting that Simone took the floor to argue that the events in Germany forced them to re-examine all of their theories, In fact Collinet recalls a speech she gave in the café at the rue des Archives. She said, approximately, speaking of the victory of fascism in Germany: "This is the failure of the hopes that we have placed in the historic mission of the proletariat." She also said that the "historic mission of the proletariat" was simply a Marxist fiction without any precise meaning. According to Collinet, some of those who heard this speech were deeply shocked; they could not accept this negation of their dogmas and hopes.

The April 9 meeting ended with a split. Those who most decisively rejected the Trotskyist position—Simone, Patri, Prader, Rabaut, Treint, etc.—afterward held a separate meeting on April 22. At the end of this meeting, they adopted and signed a declaration that, it appears, was drawn up by Simone. She had aksed to write it, "saying—which was very much like her—that only this way could she be sure of agreeing with the text."[24] Of particular interest in it is the following:

"We believe that, despite all the maneuvers engaged in to keep alive a deplorable confusion, the first day of the so-called conference for Unification, to which we had wanted to give the significance of a conference of clarification, has had a result. The stand we have taken has not permitted the conference to avoid the essential problems. . . .

"Nevertheless, two currents have been sharply delineated. One current is composed of comrades who have only separated from the Communist League [that is, the Trotskyists] over questions of the group's leaders and internal regime, and who have remained attached in principle to the positions of orthodox Trotskyism on such matters as the reform of the Soviet state regarded as essentially a workers' state despite its bureaucratic deformations, and the reform of the Communist International regarded as essentially revolutionary despite its mistakes. The other current is represented by those comrades who have no formal ties with any organization and who have arrived by independent paths at the following concepts:

"They do not underestimate the importance of questions of leadership or internal regime—indeed, on the latter point one is forced to recognize a marked resemblance between the Trotskyist faction and the Stalinist party. But they put such questions in a subordinate category. . . .

"They separate themselves sharply from Trotskyist orthodoxy on the following points:

"They feel it is impossible to regard the present Russian state, in which there do not subsist, except on paper, any of the political or economic forms of workers' control, as a workers' state going forward on the road to socialist emancipation. . . . The necessarily provisory rule of the Bolshevik party has been followed by the rule of an heir that is not the Russian proletariat but the state bureaucracy. This bureaucracy . . . orients the U.S.S.R. not toward the disappearance but instead toward the continued growth of the power of the state; it subordinates the workers to the material means of work, that is to say, to the capital that it controls as its private property; therefore it institutes not a march to socialism, but a regime in which the state apparatus . . . although it does not wield political power for the profit of the owners of the means of production, as in the capitalist countries, still possesses these means of production, and as a result directly represents the domination of the means of work over the worker.

"They believe that the Third International, despite the proletarian character and confusedly revolutionary orientation of its rank and file, has ceased to represent communism according to Marx's definition, that is to say, in terms of the general and historic interests of the proletariat. . . . For them, the present duty of alert militants is to break morally with the bureaucratic Third International as they have broken with the bourgeoisified Second International; they think that from now on one must work for a reorganization of alert revolutionaries, which should be done without any ties to the bureaucracy of the Russian state. . . .

". . . The formation of a new revolutionary organization on the national and international plane represents for them not an immediate, actual orientation but a historic orientation toward which from now on all efforts of enlightenment, education and propaganda should be directed.

". . . The ideas that have been presented here constitute simply the points on which they have agreed as the result of a personal effort of reflection accomplished independently of each other. . . . They therefore wish expressly to observe that, up to this point, they are agreed and united only upon the contents of the present statement."[25]

The Fourth International was not openly named in this statement, but it was indeed the foundation of a Fourth International that was being advocated, not as an immediate prospect but as a goal toward which efforts should be directed. The idea of founding a Fourth International had been proposed since the end of 1932 by the Independent Communist Federation of the East, a group organized by teachers and professors of the elementary schools and lycées of Belfort and Doubs. These teachers had broken with the Communist party; one of them had written in November 1932, speaking of the day when many others would follow their example and when all dissidents would unite: "We can then resolutely and proudly assume our true name: French Communist party, section of the Fourth International."[26] Since then, this slogan had been adopted by several small groups of young revolutionists, and also by the militants who led the United Federation of Teachers. Simone was more or less in agreement with all of them on this point.

The groups that were less opposed to the Trotskyist thesis (the Autonomous Group of the Western Parisian Suburb and several others) in turn held a meeting in which the Trotskyists also participated. But once again the Trotskyists and non-Trotskyists could not come to an agreement. The "Conference of Unification" only ended with new schisms and the confirmation of their differences. "Heresy," says Alain, "does not found a Church; it founds a thousand of them, because what heresy postulates is the right to heresy."

Simone felt that her ideas were "heretical as compared with all orthodoxies."[27] She tried, often in vain, to induce her comrades to shatter the dogmas in order to see the things that the dogmas concealed from them.

She also debated with her comrades among the teachers in the United Federation of Teachers. She wanted to induce them to rethink all problems. In a letter she wrote to Gilbert Serret at the end of April or the beginning of May, she discussed the reduction of the workday. Serret had advocated the forty-hour week in *L'Ecole émancipée* (December 25, 1932); he saw it, as did most authorities on the left, as the remedy for the economic crisis. As we have seen, Simone did not at all believe that the reduction of the workday could have an effect on the crisis, and even thought opposite. She explained her reasons to her correspondent, who evidently was astonished by her position. She said that she had met only one comrade who agreed with her on this matter: Péra, of *La Révolution prolétarienne.* Of course, she wanted the reduction of the workday and believed that one should fight to get it; but one must fight with the awareness that there could not be any reformist action in a period of economic crisis; one must understand that this demand necessarily assumes, in such a period, a revolutionary character, since it is tantamount to demanding a profound transformation of the regime.

In the same letter it is clear that she is trying to reunite two of the factions of the Federation into one: the "federal majority" group and that of the pure syndicalists (for example, Barruè and Jacquet) did indeed form a group distinct from the federal majority (Serret, Bouët, Salducci, Dommanget, etc.). Though in agreement on most questions, they were divided by their attitude to political parties. The members of the federal majority believed that the organization of the proletariat into a party could be useful, provided that the party was good; the members of the "Syndicalist League" only put their trust in unions.

There has also been discovered a piece of writing in which Simone argues against the separation of these two groups and advocates their merger. This text shows that Simone had even begun to move away from the pure syndicalists (this can also be seen in a letter to Thévenon). She attempts to prove that one can no longer put much more trust in a union than in a party, even if the union is the only one, and is independent and revolutionary. She recalls the fact that the prewar C.G.T. capitulated in 1914 to the war hysteria, although it was alone in the field, was independent, and had a revolutionary spirit. She admits that the proletariat needs a centralized organization, but she asks: "How can one make sure that the leaders of this organization will not turn into oppressors?" Certain people, she declares, propose a "good party," but they forget to tell us how such a good party can be constituted and can be prevented from becoming corrupt. Others want to give the chief role to the unions, yet they do not tell us why the trade union apparatus, after it has overturned the capitalist state and begins to wield power, would not run the risk of becoming as oppressive as a party apparatus. While awaiting the solution of this problem—perhaps insoluble, but it must be posed in order to be solved—nothing justifies the pure syndicalists in remaining separate and apart from the federal majority.

It was probably about the same time (end of April or the beginning of May) that she wrote a letter to one of our old comrades from the Ecole Normale in which she explains at length and very clearly her position on trade unions and political parties. She also discussed the Russian Revolution, and here one can see what her position was in regard to the Trotskyists and the pure syndicalists. A draft of this letter has been discovered:

"My dear B.,

"A brief reply:

"1. The C.G.T.U. is run by the Communist party, but, contrary to what happens in the party, one is not, up until now, excluded for reasons of political tendency (although they sometimes have managed to make life impossible for non-Communists).

"For my part, a union is not a party, and there should be only one central trade union organization. Actually, there are two. The ideal thing would be to join both of them, as the comrades in the Teachers' Union have quite rightly done, if one can do so without becoming suspect to the two sides (but I believe that this is only possible in the elementary school section of the union). If one cannot do so, one must go where there are the most interesting working-class elements and one can more effectively help the workers, which depends mainly on local conditions.

"Furthermore, I myself have (but this is a purely emotional consideration) a strong attachment, not to the C.G.T.U., which is collapsing, but to our United Federation of Teachers, which has a glorious past, which is almost the only group at present in the C.G.T.U. that struggles against the ascendancy of the party, and which is led by teachers who quit the party or were expelled, comrades for whose character and intelligence I have great esteem. This reason (which is not a reason of principle) will prevent me, so long as our Federation exists, from leaving the C.G.T.U. . . .

"So I would advise you, if you can, to join the C.G.T. and also to join the United Federation. . . .

"2. As for the Russian Revolution, I think that its present leaders are not simply maneuvering but are defending interests other than those of the workers—therefore they are betraying them.

"The signs are: 1. Lenin, when he retreated, said, 'We are retreating.' Stalin always says that he is going forward. Lying to the workers is *never* excusable. 2. When a Russian factory does not achieve the 'tempo' foreseen by the plan, they do not ask whether this 'tempo' is not too fast, or whether the organization is bad; no, they begin by demanding that the workers buckle down and do better. Exactly as it was among us with soldiers in time of war. This can be seen even in the Communist press.

"There are other things to be said, though that should suffice. There is also the disastrous policy of the International, for which the Russians are responsible.

"Lenin himself and the Bolsheviks of October; do they bear a responsibility for the Revolution's present decadence? Or did they do what they could do? A question that is not clear to me.

"3. Is the C.G.T.U. 'purer' than the party? What do you mean to say? That there are fewer informers, or what? I know nothing about this. I believe that the answer is yes for several reasons. But in any case, there one can try to correct things, since one can disagree with the 'line' without being flung out the door—and above all in our Federation, where the atmosphere is truly more friendly than anywhere else.

"4. Do reforms soften the revolutionary will of the proletariat? Or do they give it courage? I don't know. One can support both ideas. No doubt both are true depending on the circumstances. In any event, *that is all the same to me.* If the proletarians are satisfied with the reforms, they are welcome to them. They are the ones who bear the risks and above all the responsibilities of a revolution; it is up to them to make the revolution or not. I wish to *help* them with it, if I can, not to *push* them into it. The idea, held by certain Communists, of driving the workers into a revolution by making them miserable fills me with horror, even if I did not consider it absurd.

"Besides, the workers don't organize except in the struggle and don't struggle except for the satisfactions of 'immediate demands' as you say, so long as they don't bring down the regime. . . .

"Finally, the workers would not want to make the revolution except when they considered the satisfactions of the 'immediate demand' insufficient or impossible owing to the very structure of the regime.

"But it is absurd to believe that workers too badly organized to obtain reforms compatible with the regime would feel capable of overturning the regime itself."

(It can be observed that, in these last paragraphs, Simone, contrary to her wont and perhaps for the first time, to a certain extent justifies reform.)

After having recommended certain magazines to B.—*La Révolution prolétarienne,* organ of the syndicalists, and *La Lutte de classe,* organ of the

Trotskyists ("You see," she told him, "I get along with everyone")—she wrote:

"When you will have examined all these questions, if you are *very firmly* decided to have nothing to do with the party and *only in this case,* you should write, mentioning my name, to Mussigmann, representative of the federal executive of the Teachers' Union in the Committee of Professors (which brings together, inside the Federation, the secondary and upper school teachers and is Stalinist in its majority, while Mussigmann belongs to the Federation group).

"I say *only in this case*—and I count on your good faith and firmness of character—for, due to the methods employed by the pure Communists (who often are not repelled by anything in the struggle of political tendencies—in Russia they force the oppositionists to die slowly in Siberia, and elsewhere they sometimes systematically beat them up at meetings), we must know who are the reliable comrades, on whom we can count in a political struggle, and who are those who sympathize with us but still are hesitant and continue to be overawed by the presige of the Communist International. . . .

"In short, the tendency of the majority of the Federation of Teachers can be summed up (it is also very confused) as follows: one must have a party to lead the proletariat to victory. But a *good* party. The Communist party is very bad; so we must fight against its claim to control the unions. We should no longer try to reform it (here they part company with the Trotskyists, and I approve of this). We should think about a Fourth International. On the other side there are the pure syndicalists, who look upon the trade union ('good' unions, just as nonexistent as the federal majority's 'good' party!) as capable of leading the proletariat in all of its revolutionary tasks. I had at first been with them, but at the moment I realize that they leave many problems unsolved. In my opinion, instead of taking such a position and becoming a partisan in this fashion, in the light of recent experiences we must pose anew and examine without prejudice the question of the organization of the proletariat. Finally, the third faction is the Stalinist faction. . . ."

Serret represented the Federation in the Committee for the Struggle against Imperialist War, created as a result of the Anti-War Congress, which had met in Amsterdam from August 27 to 29, 1932. He no doubt had put before his comrades in the Federation the problem of the Sino-Japanese War. Simone had replied to him with a letter whose draft has been discovered:

"Dear comrade:

"Your question reawakened in me some questions that I in fact had the intention of trying to elucidate in an open discussion.

"The Amsterdam movement is against the *imperialist* war. But it has never said what sort of war it was *for.*

"One can distinguish:

"1. the war of proletarians of a country against the capitalists of the same country (civil war);

"2. the war of a colony against the colonizing power;

"3. the war of a semicolonial country (China) against the countries that want to colonize it;

"4. the war of the U.S.S.R. against a possible attack;

"5. the war of an imperialist country.

"Each case must be seriously studied. The first is clear. The second could be bracketed with the first, because of the leading role taken by the exploited classes in a colonial uprising. The third is the one that you want to examine.

"What can one say for this war? That China is not, or barely, a capitalist country. That it is a country without true state power and that the Japanese conquest brings even larger sections of exploited Chinese under the domination of the marvelously organized Japanese state (for the machinery of the state is an even heavier burden on the proletariat than a reactionary, bloody, but anarchic regime). That the Chinese war is an obviously defensive war. That in 1871 Engels wanted to offer his military collaboration to Gambetta. That Lenin recognized 'national' wars. . . .

"Yet all this seems to me insufficient. This is the situation: the Chinese proletariat will in any event be subjected to the power of a state. The Japanese state, if Japan is the victor; the Chinese state, if China resists—because it can resist only on the condition that it sets up a strong state power. Is it possible? That is another question. In any case, it is much better that the workers be the slaves of foreign imperialism than of their own nationalist state, for their own state deflects the hatred of imperialism to the foreigner and so establishes its domination not only over bodies but also minds."

As one can see, Simone, with her usual boldness, pushes pacifism quite far. She thinks that the class struggle must take precedence over the concern for national independence.

It is difficult to say whether this letter was written before or after the letter, also addressed to Serret, that we have already mentioned. It seems to have been written more or less at the same time, that is, at the end of April or the beginning of May.

Serret had been chosen as the reporter on the question of the war for the annual congress of the United Federation of Teachers which was to be held that summer at Rheims. Moreover, some organizations affiliated with Moscow's Trade Union International were preparing a large anti-Fascist congress. (This is the congress that was held in Pleyel Hall on June 4, 5, and 6, 1933.) Simone persuaded her union at Yonne to vote for a resolution to be presented at the anti-Fascist congress, a resolution that dealt with the united front, trade union unity, and the policy to be pursued in the struggle with Fascist movements. At the same time she also got the union to vote on a resolution for the Rheims congress that outlined a position to be adopted in case of war. She wrote about this to Serret, either during the last days of May or the first days of June, in a letter of which two drafts have been found. Here is the beginning of the longer draft:

"Dear comrade:

"Enclosed my union's resolution for the anti-Fascist congress—which I wrote myself, as you will recognize easily from the contents. Fortunately, outside of this, the union is completely M.O.R.!

"On the other hand, a proposal for a simple *request of information* from the Russian embassy concerning Victor Serge has split us, seven votes against seven (and seven abstentions). . . .

"As for the different kinds of war, I posed a question that you made the mistake, I believe, of overlooking in your questionnaire: that of a war between imperialist countries, one of which will be allied either with China or the U.S.Ș.R. We are in agreement that revolutionary defeatism is *also* appropriate for this country. (Parenthetically, on this point, my fine M.O.R.'s at Yonne go much farther than the Trotskyists!)

"The question evidently is: does a war in which the U.S.S.R. intervenes have perforce a class-struggle character? On this point, until now the Stalinists and Trotskyists have in common accord always replied in the affirmative. According to this view, the slogan of defense of the U.S.S.R. must take precedence over that of revolutionary defeatism.

"Now it is clear at present that the U.S.S.R., in its relations with the imperialist states, plays the role of a state and *not* that of a representative of the proletariat. The proofs: the Franco-Russian nonaggression pact. The monstrous letter Litvinov sent to Herriot, on May 20, published by *l'Humanité.* (You undoubtedly have it; if you don't, I'll send it to you. It *absolutely* must be reproduced.) Its relations with Hitler's Germany. A very curious article in the *Deutsche allgemeine Zeitung* (the newspaper of German heavy industry) on German-Russian relations (D.A.Z. of May 27). . . ."

Simone was to insist that the U.S.S.R. was by now a state like the others and did not represent the world proletariat in two articles that were published in July, but of which the second at least was certainly written in June: "The International Country of the Workers"[28] and "The Role of the U.S.S.R. in World Politics."[29] In concluding the second of these articles, she wrote: "Let us not shut our eyes. Let us prepare ourselves not to count on anyone but ourselves. Our power is quite small; at least let not this little we can do fall into the hands of those whose interests are alien to the ideal we defend. Let us take thought to preserve our honor at least."

At the anti-Fascist congress at Pleyel Hall, Aulas, the delegate of the United Federation of Teachers, was quickly interrupted and denied the floor when he tried to present ideas different from those of the Stalinists. As a result of this congress a Committee of Action against Fascism was created which merged with the Committee for the Struggle against Imperialist War, created after Amsterdam. Serret, who represented the Federation in the latter organization, was therefore also seated in the Committee of Action against War and Fascism, which was formed by a fusion of the two previous organizations. Since he could not easily get to Paris, he delegated Simone to attend a meeting of the committee in his place and to protest the chair's treatment of Aulas at the congress in Pleyel Hall. From Serret's note in *L'Ecole émancipée* of July 23 we learn that she was heckled so much by the Communists that she could barely speak. "I had asked," he said, "Simone Weill [sic] to represent me at the last meeting of the French committee. I had especially asked her to protest the chair's incredible treatment of Aulas at the anti-Fascist congress. Not only did the committee defend the Pleyel Hall chair, but once again S. Weill [sic] was prevented from expressing any opinion that was damaging to the Stalinists. With their systematic interruptions and heckling, the Stalinists at times even managed to stop our comrade from speaking."

Serret sent a written protest to the committee. All that came of this was that in practice he was excluded from the committee. Nothing intimidating was said to him, no attacks were made on him, they simply stopped notifying him of the committee's meetings. . . . As J. Malaubre put it, he was "conjured away."[30]

It was a frequent occurrence at C.G.T.U. meetings for speakers to be prevented from speaking when they did not agree with the majority or the presiding authority. People who wanted to express opinions different from those of the orthodox Communists were drowned out by a storm of interruptions; at times they were even roughed up or thrown out of the meeting. About the same time that she tried to protest the intolerance exhibited at Pleyel Hall in a speech from the floor, Simone with two other trade unionist also protested in writing a number of violations of trade union democracy. With Charbit, a member of the typographers' union, and Craipeau, a member of the Federation of Teachers, she signed an article that was first published on June 30 in *La Vérité*, the Trotskyist newspaper, under the title "For respect for trade union democracy inside the C.G.T.U.: Against expulsions for crimes of political opinion, an appeal addressed to all trade unionists, all trade union factions, all unions, and all the trade union leaders in the C.G.T.U." Afterward it appeared on July 10 in *La Révolution prolétarienne* under the title "An appeal to trade union members of C.G.T.U.: For trade union democracy! Against expulsions for political opinions!" In *La Révolution prolétarienne,* the article was somewhat shortened, since the quotation of certain texts relating to condemnations and expulsions was cut out.

On June 21, the prefect of the Alpes-Maritimes district sent a note to a schoolteacher, Freinet, informing him that he was being given an administrative transfer. In the *Libres Propos* of June 25, Simone wrote an article in which she described the campaign that had been conducted against Freinet by the mayor and parish priest of Saint-Paul-de-Vence and concluded by saying: "We take . . . this opportunity to tell Freinet of our admiration and our solidarity in the face of the persecutions that the coalition formed by the fascist press, the fascist mayor, and the parish priest of Saint-Paul, hand in hand with the educational administration, have inflicted on him."

Obviously, it was not without the approval of the Minister of Public Education that the prefect had transferred Freinet. Moreover, this same minister had demanded an explanation from a professor named Alessandri in a lycée at Nice as to some statements he had made during a conference that was totally unconnected with his work. Alessandri, like Freinet, was a member of the Communist group and most likely a Stalinist, but this did not prevent Simone from wanting to defend them. In an article she probably wrote in the second half of June (for it seems to be an answer to an article by E. Blaise published in *L'Ecole émancipée* of June 18), she presents the question: "To what extent are we members of the teaching profession in the secondary schools being exploited?" Her answer is that for teachers the essential oppression is intellectual and moral, rather than questions as to the rate of pay. The teachers' struggle, she affirms, must be: "A struggle for freedom of opinion outside our professional duties (Alessandri); against brainwashing on the job (Freinet); against the administrative authority; for pedagogic reforms; for a decrease of differences in salaries; and a fight on behalf of the most exploited categories." She ends her article with these words: "We need a united front on this basis. . . . If we take any other path we can arrive only at this string of absurdities: 'Class struggle,' solidarity and demands for improvements and increases in pay (disgusting!)."

It was about this time that she told Bercher that she wanted to organize a trade union among the graduates of the Ecole Normale whose aim would be to fight against the privileges they were granted and to demand that their salaries should not be higher than those of other teachers. I don't know whether she ever really tried to organize this union; certainly it did not have a great chance of succeeding. Bercher talked about this project to an Ecole Normale graduate, who exclaimed, "My goodness, she really is stupid!"

The fact that the C.G.T.U. branch of the Teachers' Union at Yonne had voted in favor of a resolution that Simone had written for the anti-Fascist congress and had also agreed with her on the question of war shows that she had maintained good relations with these M.O.R. teachers almost to the end of her stay in their region, perhaps even to the very end. And yet, as we have seen, two thirds of them refused to follow her when she proposed that they present a request for information from the Soviet embassy in Paris concerning Victor Serge's status in Russia. Despite her good relations with them, it would indeed appear that she did not have with any of them the warm, trustful relations she had had with Vidal and Delhermet at Le Puy.

She was also, at least at the start and up until February, on good terms with the local Communist cell, though she never passed up an opportunity to "take a smack at the Communist International," As she had said in her letter to Thévenon. In another letter Thévenon got from her in February, she said: "The cell here has organized a course on Marx, given by me. They were the ones who asked me to give it. So you see, the spirit is better here than at Le Puy."

So she undoubtedly gave a course in Marxism that the cell had set up. However, Albertine Thévenon believes that she recalls that the Communists in Auxerre, who at first did not distrust Simone and then asked her to give a course, did end by attacking her. For her part, Mme. Weil said that a certain Communist at Auxerre, whom Simone called Chlorinated Water because he sold the stuff, played terrible tricks on her.

Another communist, whom Simone had nicknamed Faucet because he had taught himself how to make faucets, lived not far from house. He had been a worker and had set himself up as an artisan with his brother; he could do plumbing and also repaired cars. He was a very skillful craftsman; Simone thought that he had a kind of genius because of the intelligence he displayed with machines and mechanics of all sorts. He would make fun of Simone's awkwardness, in this way revenging himself on her for the torments she caused him when she discussed politics with him. He said that after he had argued with her in the evening, he would not be able to fall asleep for a good part of the night.

Simone had friendly relations with farmers and workers at Auxerre, as she had had at Le Puy, and tried to work with them. As we have seen, she took part in the grape harvests. She also helped, it seems, to dig up potatoes grown in the workers' truck gardens surrounding her café. And she probably worked now and then in a factory near her house that manufactured ocher paint.[31] One day she even began to work with a crew that was making repairs in the courtyard of the boys' lycée, and they taught her how to solder a joint. Passing through the courtyard, the headmaster saw her working in this way.

Had she told her working-class comrades to come and wait for her at the girls' lycée, or had they done so of their own accord? One day a group of workers who appeared to be waiting for someone was seen in the lycée's courtyard. When asked what they were doing there, they answered, "We're waiting for Simone." They were told that they had to wait outside; they were then ushered out and the courtyard gate was carefully locked behind them.

On another occasion a poor man presented himself at the girls' lycée, his eating utensils in hand. "Mlle. Weil told me to come to eat here today," he announced. "She said that if there was enough food for three hundred and fifty, there would be quite enough for three hundred and fifty-one." Cabaud reports these last two episodes.[32]

During the course of the year, the school inspectors' reports had not been very favorable to Simone, even from a professional standpoint. On November 22, 1932, the academic inspector had observed her class. In his written report he said that her class "did not seem to be sufficiently prepared to be suited to the students," that some of them had difficulty following it, and that the compositions, though carefully corrected, were in general poor.

On December 15, Mme. Lesne, the headmistress, wrote: "Mlle. Weil at first sight impresses because of the high quality of her university degrees. Moreover, she does not count the time she devotes to her students." But she added that this professor's teaching was confused and the discipline in one of her classes left much to be desired. She also mentioned in passing Simone's extremely advanced political opinions and let it be understood that she was occupied with too many different things. "Mlle. Weil should dole out and husband her activity, for the bad state of her health often forces [her] to stop working."

(In fact, Simone suffered as much from headaches at Auxerre as at Le Puy. When these headaches became too violent, she could not give her class. Nevertheless, she would come to the lycée but have the students read some texts aloud as she listened, her head clutched in her hands.)

On March 13, 1933, the rector, after having heard Simone's class, wrote: "Certainly a distinguished mind but as a teacher she has no pedagogic sense. Extremely disjointed lesson in which she reviewed the ideas on error that can be found in Plato, Descartes, Spinoza, Kant, and Hegel ... without any plan and without any conclusion. There is a constant scattering of thought. ... Her students ... strain to take notes about which they understand nothing. Since Mlle. Weil does not confine herself to a program, it is to be feared that the class in philosophy will gradually be deserted."

Finally Parodi, an inspector general and a specialist in philosophy, came to observe Simone's class on May 13. He sent the ministry a report that, according to the rules, was shown to Simone and countersigned by her.

The lesson he heard dealt with sociology and its methods. He felt that Simone's exposition, though "very abundant and very rich in details," lacked firmness and concision, that it was "diffuse and even quite confused." "Moreover, the professor has the bad habit of speaking without looking at her pupils, her face bent over her papers, and she does not articulate clearly enough. Yet her teaching seemed to me based on substantial knowledge; and one feels an effort both to impart information and to express the results of personal reflection, even if this effort does not produce a very clear or solidly constructed lesson.

"Unfortunately, her teaching is also extremely tendentious, respectable no doubt, and even attractive due to the sincere conviction it reveals, yet full of violent or simplistic statements and allusions to events and personalities of the present or recent past that all too often give the aspect and tone of a political pamphlet.... Unquestionably, this can jeopardize the school in which she teaches. It is obvious that Mlle. Weil has completely failed to take into account the reserve her position demands or the respect she owes to the opinions of her students and their families. I ask her, in all earnestness, not to renounce her ideas or give up her rights, but to recognize that it is not in class that she ought to explain or defend these ideas.

"Yet Mlle. Weil's conviction and disinterestedness are, I must repeat, of the most honorable sort."[33]

(Obviously, Simone has abstained even less than usual from revolutionary statements just because she was speaking in front of the inspector.)

The results of the *bachot* would seem to confirm the judgments of the academic authorities. Out of the dozen students who took Simone's course in philosophy only three or four, so Cabaud claims, were accepted.

This permitted the headmistress to employ a heroic remedy to rid herself of Simone: she abolished the lycée's philosophy class. It was decided that if the next-year students wanted to prepare for the baccalaureate examination in philosophy, they would take the course at the boys' lycée. This measure had probably been envisaged for the last several months. The rector's report, which was written in March, seems to indicate this.

So Simone was forced to request a new post for the coming year. This must not have been too painful for her, since she wanted to be closer to her friends in Saint-Etienne.

7

Roanne
(1933-1934)

As soon as she was free of her teaching obligations, Simone left for Saint-Etienne. She was there in July 1933 and perhaps again during the first days of August. She gave a number of lectures in this region on the events in Germany to small meetings of working-class militants.

She gave one lecture at Firminy, and another at Saint-Etienne. This last lecture was organized by the local unions of the C.G.T.U. Simone, who intended to criticize the German Communist party, had warned the leaders of the Communist group at Saint-Etienne of her intention the day before the lecture, inviting them to come to the lecture to reply, if necessary, to her criticisms. They did not attend, but one of them wrote a sarcastic article about this lecture. The working-class militants at this lecture numbered about seventy.[1]

It was no doubt during her stay at Saint-Etienne that Simone put the final touches to the essay "Prospects," which was to appear in *La Révolution prolétarienne* of August 25, for she discussed it with Urbain Thévenon and submitted it to him before publishing it.

She left Saint-Etienne to attend a congress of the United Federation of Teachers that took place at Rheims on the fifth, sixth, and seventh of August. The debates at this congress were stormy and impassioned. The opposing political tendencies clashed on nearly all the important issues. The groups confronting each other were essentially the federal majority (Serret, Dommanget, Bouët, Salducci, etc.) and the M.O.R. (Bouthonnier, Bruhat, etc.).

The M.O.R. had brought along a Soviet delegation. As a result, the representatives of the federal majority had a chance to ask the delegation embarrassing questions, especially in regard to Victor Serge. Dommanget presented and got a vote on a resolution supporting Victor Serge, Trotsky, Riazanov, and Rakovsky. "Bouët, in the presence of the Russian delegation, told of his anguish as an old militant faced by the growing misery in the U.S.S.R. and the suppression there of all workers' control, and, though refraining from any final judgment, demanded an explanation. Put formally on the spot by this handful of militants, who had in fact belonged to the first Federation to hail the October Revolution and defend it, the Soviet delegation could only reply by pointing to the beauties of the Five Year Plan and admitting its ignorance of the charges brought against Victor Serge."[2]

On the last day of the congress and very late at night the M.O.R. provoked the chief debate on the German question. It had only been mentioned in passing on the previous days. Despite the lateness of the hour, Bouthonnier insisted that the congress should hear Maria Reese, Communist deputy to the Reichstag. After the chairman gave her the floor, Maria Reese made a speech in which she angrily rejected all the criticisms directed at the policy of the Third International on the previous days. "Her voice was loud and her delivery was rapid. Turning toward Dommanget, Bouët, Rollo, and Serret, the leaders of the anti-Stalinist federal majority, who were clustered at the foot of the speakers' platform, she shook her right arm, at the end of which the clenched fist seemed to want to reduce her political adversaries to abject surrender. And what came out of her mouth were certainly not amenities and compliments."[3]

Simone was then given the floor and stepped up to the speakers' platform. She asked a series of precise questions regarding the U.S.S.R.'s attitude to Hitler. She read an article from the *Neue Weltbühne* in which a German Communist complained that the U.S.S.R. had closed its borders to persecuted German Communists who had been forced to flee. And she finally read the reply of *Gegenangriff,* organ of the German Communist émigrés and sympathizers. This reply contained an admission that Russia's borders had been closed to the German emigration and justified this by the argument that "problems of strategy cannot in any case be solved by humanitarian sentimentality."[4]

According to Mme. Weil, the Stalinists made a concerted effort to interrupt her and drown out her voice. She had to shout to make herself heard, so that when she came back from Rheims she could speak only in a whisper. Jean Rabaut wrote: "I can still hear a young Stalinist shouting: 'Viper!' "[5] Mme. Weil also said that at one point the Communists climbed up on the platform and moved toward her in a body, as though they wanted to beat her up, but her comrades formed a ring around her and protected her.

After Simone's speech, the chairman consulted the congress and declared the debate closed. It was four-thirty in the morning.

Poor Maria Reese, who had put so much energy into defending the orthodox Communist position, was expelled from the party soon after this. Simone would write to her mother a few months later, probably in November: "Maria Reese, the Reichstag deputy with whom I had a bit of a quarrel, starting at Rheims, has just written a letter to the Communist International that, I swear, is quite dignified and full of severe criticisms—and the upshot is that she has been expelled! I propose that she be invited to our next congress and that we give her a standing ovation!"

After this last, stormy session, just as day began to break, a group of the people who were at the congress, among them Simone, suddenly got the whim to visit the cathedral. Jean Rabaut has described this walk and the discussion that subsequently took place: "The congress held its last meeting at night, and it lasted to the early hours of the morning. What inspiration suddenly seized us to go to the cathedral, which was open and completely empty? We were carrying pamphlets of the extreme left, notably the *Communist Bulletin,* which Souvarine had just republished on the occasion of Trotsky's arrival in France, in order to emphasize his disagreements with him. We got the idea of slipping these *Communist Bulletin*s on the table covered with pious booklets, so as to shock the devout. Simone was there and did not say a word. But afterward we went to a café, and after we had ordered our drinks, we began a discussion on religion and related matters. Before these anticlerical teachers, I can still hear Simone Weil praising the nuns. Some of them, she said, were the best people she had ever known! You can imagine the looks on their faces! . . . Then, I don't quite know how, the discussion got on to Jean-Jacques Rousseau and Simone spoke in his favor. And I can still hear a pretty young brunette with a marked south-of-France accent answer her. This was Colette Audry. . . . Colette told Simone that there was nothing falser and more against nature than Rousseau's philosophy. After that we went off to bed; it was about time."[6]

Jean Rabaut also tells us that at this congress, alongside the plenary sessions, there was a smaller meeting of the Committee of Professors, and he reports an exchange Simone had with Bruhat.

"I recall . . . a smaller meeting of the Committee of Professors, the technical section of the Federation, where she had a bone to pick with Jean Bruhat. We were discussing votes; the provincial groups of the Federation in secondary education were so small that Simone constituted a regional committee all by herself! She jokingly remarked that at least it had unanimity. At which Bruhat . . . replied that we were not so sure of that. . . . He had put his finger on the torturing inner contradictions that racked Simone Weil."[7]

According to Rabaut, Simone's articles had caught the attention of militants in the Federation, and a number of them were very anxious to meet her. "Simone's articles in *La Révolution prolétarienne* and *L'Ecole émancipée* had made a stir among militants in the provinces. Several of them said to me, 'I'm dying to meet Simone Weil.' When they did meet her in the flesh, some of them felt let down. They thought she was too much of a busybody and too inquisitive. She seemed to know all the big and little gossip of the movement. She must have seen quite a few people and somehow got them to confess."[8] She was curious, true enough, and had the art of getting people to tell her their secrets. But this curiosity was so mixed up with her desire to help others, to know what they might be suffering from in order to help them, that it is very hard to separate the two things.[9]

Rabaut also testifies to the unreserved veneration that certain people felt for her: "Claude Jamet, who later on wrote for the *Feuilles libres* and corresponded with her, called her 'the saint.' And it is true that she had every kind of courage—physical, moral, and intellectual."[10]

When the congress ended, Simone returned to Paris in the company of several schoolteachers. They lunched at the Weils' and told her parents what had happened at Rheims.

Soon after, Simone left for Spain, to spend the holidays. She went with her parents and Aimé Patri, who had also participated in the congress at Rheims. They spent about eight days in Barcelona. Then, while her parents remained in Barcelona, Simone and Patri traveled to Villaneuva, where Patri knew some people, and after that to Valencia. They stayed for almost three weeks in Villaneuva and for about eight days in Valencia.

In Barcelona, Simone had contacted the militants of the Iberian Communist Federation, dissidents from the Spanish Communist party. This was the so-called right opposition and hostile to Bolshevism, similar to the opposition of Brandler and Thalheimer in Germany. (Later on, owing to a merger with other groups, they formed the P.O.U.M., Partido Obrero de Unificación Marxista—the Workers' Party of Marxist Unity.) Most of the militants in this Federation were old anarchists who wanted to find a more realistic road to socialism than could be found in the Iberian Anarchist Federation (the F.A.I.). Simone met and talked with Maurin and Miravitlès.

She went to a bullfight once. She went with Patri despite the advice of their Spanish comrades, who, although the veterans of many social battles, real *pistoleros,* and quite willing to throw bombs, condemned the bloody spectacles. Simone thought the spectacle very beautiful. Mme. Weil, who also attended this bullfight, claimed that on that particular day there were not too many "cruelties"; and, furthermore, they were sitting very far from the arena and couldn't see too well. She thought that if her daughter had witnessed some of the bullfights she saw later on, she certainly would have disliked them.

(Patri thinks that if there had been revolting spectacles, Simone might have found the work of the bullfighters badly done, but that she would have overcome her disgust by an effort of will; she wanted to be able to stand cruel spectacles. He says that what aroused her enthusiasm for the bullfight was the sight of man dominating the brute, and besides, the entire atmosphere of the ritual.)

With Patri and some friends of his, Simone spent a night at the

Criolla, a cabaret where boys dressed up like girls danced and sang. The chief attraction, though, was an extraordinary male singer who was dressed like a woman. After seeing this show, Simone said, "I wish I were Balzac." Her Spanish friends were amazed to see her there. She left the nightclub about five or six in the morning, and she and Patri then took a sail in a boat. The boatman told them stories about the 1909 insurrection (against the war in Morocco), when they had set fire to the churches. He described the monks scampering away like rats. Just at that moment rats were actually running along the jetty, and the boatman pointed to them to show how the monks had run.

"But why?" Simone asked him. "What do you have against these monks?" He answered, "They did not teach us how to read."

At Villaneuva, Simone went swimming in the sea and took sunbaths. Patri thinks that never was she so close to the simple pleasures of life. And Mme. Weil said that when she returned home she had an extraordinary color and looked better and healthier than ever before. They would go to sleep late and rise at noon. She lived in her bathing suit, not even dressing for meals. (The owner or manager of the Marina Hotel reprimanded her for this and insisted that she at least wear a bathrobe.) Since she had removed the outfit that made her look ugly, one could see that she was far from ugly. One day someone stuck a flower in her hair. (Patri seems still to have a vivid remembrance of this, for the simple ornament revealed an unsuspected beauty.)

Some nights, when they were unable to sleep because of the heat, they would go up on the hotel's terrace and Simone would tell him fairy tales.

But even in these circumstances she did not forget men's misfortunes and her desire to share them. On the beach at Villaneuva she said to Patri, "It is quite possible that one day we will be tortured; so we should prepare ourselves for it. Do you want to drive some pins under my nails?" Patri threatened to slap her.

There was a fishermen's guild at Villaneuva—the Posit de pescadores—which owned a library that contained only classic works. Simone met a fisherman who had read the second part of Goethe's *Faust*. This delighted her and she gave him a gift of a copy of Rousseau's *Confessions*. These fishermen lived in an atmosphere of noble, unconcerned, and cheerful poverty.

There was a longshoremen's union at Valencia that had many services (social welfare or insurance, a hospital, a school, and an old-age pension fund), all of which functioned without being administered by the union's "big shots." The secretary or president of the union worked on the docks like all the other workers. Only the treasurer was a permanent elected official. Simone found this very close to her ideal: trade unionism without a bureaucracy.

They returned to Barcelona. According to Mme. Weil, they once went to a café on the Paralelo where they saw a marvelous female dancer.

While Simone was resting in Spain, the *Révolution prolétarienne* published, in its August 25 issue, her article entitled "Prospects."[11] (The magazine added the subtitle: "Are We Going Toward the Proletarian Revolution?") This article was the crystallization of her reflections on the failure of the Russian Revolution (a failure, in her eyes, since it had not brought about the liberation of the proletariat), the defeat of the German working-class movement, and the experience that she had already had with the working-class movements in France, an experience that revealed an immense divergence between the hopes aroused by the imagined revolution and what could be expected from a real revolution.

Some people think that this article is the most forceful writing she ever did on a political subject. In any case it did present a new analysis of the social situation, the clear-sighted view of a new and fundamental fact, revealed in our epoch and certainly not foreseen by Marxism: the fact that capitalistic oppression is not, as Marx believed, the final form of oppression; that a new form was taking shape in our time, that is, oppression in the name of administrative *function* and *managerial organization.* Simone shows that the principle, always presupposed by revolutionists, according to which there can only be two forms of the state, the capitalist state and workers' state, is false, because the modern state is neither capitalist nor working class but a third type; that Fascism is not, as the parties of the left maintain, "capitalism's last card" but rather a new social form; that the Russian regime is not, as the Trotskyists believed, a mere bureaucratic deformation of the proletarian dictatorship but a new social form, which, moreover, is the same as Fascism, or pretty much the same; that the revolution of the twentieth century, the revolution that succeeds is a revolution of the managers rather than a proletarian revolution.

This article was much admired and much criticized. Monatte liked it a great deal. Marcel Martinet told Urbain Thévenon that it was a work of genius and that nothing so incisive had been written since Rosa Luxembourg. Boris Souvarine said of Simone: "She is the only brain that the working-class movement has produced in many years."[12] But others were mostly revolted by her pessimism. They could not understand how she could fight so energetically in defense of the oppressed when she had so little hope. Simone expresses her spiritual strength when she writes in this article: "There is no difficulty whatever, once one has decided to act, in maintaining intact on the plane of action those very hopes that a critical examination has shown to be well-nigh unfounded; in that lies the very essence of courage." But for some people it was not so easy. Jean Rabaut wrote: "She fought for something that she herself considered unrealizable and definitely compromised. Her pessimism about an activity that she carried out without ever retreating proved quite disconcerting to her comrades."[13]

In *La Révolution prolétarienne* of September 25, a letter from Roger Hagnauer was published under the heading "Not So Much Pessimism!" He wrote: "Simone Weil inspects the world as viewed from on high and, among the many reasons to be frightened, she also gives us a few reasons for hope, the clearest of which is 'to understand the force that crushes us.' This reminds us of Pascal's 'thinking reed.' Simone Weil would at the worst resign herself to defeat if she were able to identify its causes. Has this lofty intellectual resignation anything in common with our revolutionary syndicalism? . . . Will not Simone Weil's 'lucid' pessimism weaken even the most resolute?" He also objected to the identification of Bolshevism with Fascism. In conclusion, speaking of the 'reasons for fear' enumerated by Simone, he said: "Simone Weil could have added to these numerous reasons for fear . . . another one. It is the role played in the workers' movements by adventurous intellectuals who do not respect organization.

"These adventurous intellectuals—with their generous inspiration and their doctrinal vigor—should stop brooding over the proletariat's weakness! Instead, they should try to become aware of their own ineptness at leading it!

" 'Shall we perish powerless both to win and to understand?' Simone Weil asks. I must confess that I can say nothing about all this. . . . I cannot predict such distant events. Yet there are a few of us who understand why we have not won up until now. It is because we have been the easy prey of these leaders of the 'political factions,' these concocters of theses, these prophets for the small cliques or sects; because we have given in to their ideological mania, this 'intoxication with abstractions' that Monatte denounced in 1924. . . . Simone Weil has enough revolutionary determination to accept this lesson of optimism."

This attack was one of those to which Simone could be quite sensitive, and it was unfair, at least in part. For Simone had never made any claim to lead the workers' movement; she was on her guard against this very temptation, and on the contrary warned the workers not to let themselves be led by the intellectuals. She had only wanted to serve the workers' organizations and, by helping the workers acquire a general knowledge of things, put them in a position to run their own affairs. What's more, it was doubly unfair to mock her as an intellectual and to doubt that as such her opinions could help the proletariat. For, if anything, she was even too conscious of what she felt as an inferiority and a great defect: not to be one of those who work with their hands. From that time on, and even some time before that, she wanted to change her position in life and in fact soon afterward she did.

In its December 10 issue *La Révolution prolétarienne* published an article in which Simone's analysis was discussed in greater detail and much less severely. This article was entitled "Clarifications: Are We Going Toward the Proletarian Revolution?" and was signed "A Prisoner." It contained a good deal of praise and approbation, but then the author indicated in passing those places where the picture painted by Simone seemed too black to him. Alluding to her courage and generosity and recognizing that from this standpoint she had nothing to learn, he wrote: "It is rather her tendency to pessimism that she should try to guard against."

Trotsky himself reacted to this article. In a pamphlet that appeared on October 13, 1933, "The Fourth International and the U.S.S.R.," he said: "The Left Opposition [that is, the Trotskyists] did not have to wait for the discoveries of Urbahns, Laurat, Souvarine, Simone Weil, and others before declaring that bureaucratism, in all of its manifestations, corrodes the moral texture of Soviet society, engendering a sharpened, legitimate discontent among the masses and entailing great dangers . . ." And he added, in a note: "Despairing over the unfortunate 'experience' of 'the dictatorship of the proletariat,' Simone Weil has found consolation in a new mission: to defend her personality against society. A formula of the old liberalism, refurbished by a cheaply bought anarchist exaltation. And to think that Simone Weil speaks majestically of our 'illusions'! Many years will have to pass for her and her like before they free themselves of the most reactionary petty bourgeois prejudices. . . ." An extract from this pamphlet that included this passage and note was published in *La Vérité* on October 13.

"To defend her personality," Trotsky had said. It was a remarkably acute observation. Not to be dishonored was certainly one of the chief concerns that guided Simone (and a concern, in her eyes, by which everyone should be guided). Not to die without having existed, "to traverse this somber age in manly fashion," "to perish with a clear vision of the world we shall be leaving behind," "to work toward a clear comprehension of the object of our efforts, so that, if we cannot accomplish it, we may at least have willed it, and not just have desired it blindly,"—these formulations that can be found in the article "Prospects" show that she regarded the duty to oneself as one of her first duties, perhaps the very first. Patri wrote quite rightly: "I doubt that anyone has ever pushed so far the respect for the superior part of oneself."[14] Alain had tried to make us understand that in doing one's duty to oneself one could not fail to do it to others, and Simone's example demonstrates the truth of this idea. It could be said that for Alain it was first of all a question, under all circumstances, of saving one's soul, provided that one meant by this an ongoing, actual salvation and not a future one.

Trotsky nevertheless seems to have been influenced by the political current represented by Simone and her friends. There was a sharp turn in Trotskyist policy in the summer of 1933, and the decision to found

Mme. Reinherz, Simone Weil's maternal grandmother.

Dr. Bernard Weil (1872–1955).

Mme. Selma Weil (1879–1965), from a photograph taken in 1965. *(Photo Mrs. Else Fischer.)*

Simone, two years old,
and her brother André,
Paris, 1911.

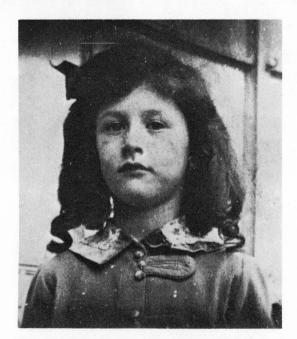

Simone Weil, Mayenne,
1915–1916.

Simone sitting on her father's lap at Mayenne.

Simone and her brother at Mayenne.

Simone Weil, Penthièvre, 1918 or 1919.

Simone and her brother at Penthièvre, 1918 or 1919.

Three photographs of Simone Weil at Baden-Baden, 1921.

Simone and her brother at Knokke-le-Zoute, 1922.

Simone at the Lycée Féne-lon with her classmates, 1922–1923.

Simone Weil at Henri IV in 1926. René Château is on her right.

Alain and his *cagne* class at Henri IV, 1928.

Two photographs of Simone Weil surrounded by her students at Le Puy, spring, 1932.

Simone in Indian dress, on the occasion of a visit to her parents
by an Indian family who knew her brother, c. 1933.

Simone Weil with her students at Roanne, winter, 1933–1934.

Simone teaching her class in the park at Roanne.

Gilbert Serret (1902–1943), General Secretary of the United Federation of Teachers. *(Photo Machabert.)*

the Fourth International was the external proof. Until then, Trotsky had maintained that the Communist International and the parties associated with it could be reformed, and that one must remain faithful to it while attempting to influence its policies. We have seen before* that at the unity conference of the various Communist opposition groups, the Trotskyists at the very start had taken the floor to combat the idea of a Fourth International.[15] The Trotskyist newspaper, *La Vérité*, in its April 14, 1933, issue, made sardonic comments on those groups that advocated this slogan, only to adopt it itself a few months later.

Having returned to Paris in September, Simone set to work. Two short critical articles she wrote appeared in the September issue of *La Critique sociale*, a magazine founded and edited by Souvarine. One article dealt with E. O. Volkmann's book *The German Revolution*, and the other with E. Gunther-Grundel's book *The Mission of the Young Generation*. This last book also concerned Germany.

In the same issue of *La Critique sociale* there appeared an article by Julius Dickmann, "The True Limits of Capitalist Production," which Simone greatly admired. In it she found support for certain opinions she would develop later in her "Reflections on the Causes of Freedom and Social Oppression." Dickmann demonstrated that the advantages of technical progress are subject to certain limitations, and that from a certain moment on and in certain domains they increase only in ever smaller proportions.

Simone also attended the national congress of the C.G.T.U. that was held in Paris from September 23 to 29 in the Huyghens Stadium. On the subject of this congress, F. Charbit wrote in the October 10 issue of *La Révolution prolétarienne:* "The seventh congress of the C.G.T.U. has given us the spectacle of a hatred that reached the point of paroxysm as regards the minority groups. Never at any congress has a minority been harassed so thoroughly as at this one. . . . At least they would let us speak. . . . This time, we only had the right to be jeered at, insulted, threatened, and physically attacked. All efforts were directed at giving us the impression that in fact we are nothing but an 'alien body' in the C.G.T.U. and that anyone who is not a member of the Communist party or does not sympathize with its political policy no longer has a place in these United unions. . . .

"Comrade Simone Weil, who wanted to speak on the German events, could not get the floor; nor for that matter could I, even though we had both put our names on the speakers' list on the second day of the congress.

"But the hostility of the majority in our regard and its fanatical intolerance were manifested in a much more serious fashion. Our readers know that on the appeal of the Socialist Workers Party of Germany

*See p. 157.

(and today of the bulk of the German revolutionary groups outside the Second and Third Internationals), a Relief Committee was formed in Paris. We wanted to tell the people attending the congress about the appeal of this committee, which was effectively helping hundreds of imprisoned workers and their families. First of all, the distribution of this appeal was prohibited inside the congress by a directive from the chair. 'You can only distribute them outside, when the people leave,' Racamond finally told us, after we had asked permission to do it in the hall. But when we stood outside we were the target for attacks organized by the trade union bureaucrats, with toughs jumping on us to tear the leaflets out of our hands and prevent them from being handed out. . . ."

Simone and Charbit were the ones who were prevented from handing out the leaflets of the Relief Committee.

Simone wrote an article about the congress that was published in *L'Effort* of October 28. In it she said: "This congress was as boring as a congress of the party. There were empty speeches and the usual singing of the 'Internationale' and 'Rot Front.' The opposition's only participation in the congress was through the insults to which it was subjected. . . .

"Serret and Bouët gave remarkable speeches in the name of the Federation of Teachers. Bouët, notably, described the deep distress of an old sincere militant confronted by the degeneration of the Russian state. . . . Salducci also defended the Federation of Teachers. As for Charbit, he was purely and simply refused the floor. The same thing happened to Simone Weil, who wanted, in reply to Racamond's direct provocation, to justify the attacks on the German Communist party that were made at the congress of the Federation of Teachers. Engler was allowed to speak and did so with his customary energy and sincerity. In return, the chairman splattered him with the most ignoble calumnies. . . .

"The true character of the congress was fully revealed when, after the session ended, Charbit and Simone Weil were brutally and physically prevented from distributing appeals in the street for solidarity with German comrades, victims of Fascist terror, who did not belong to either of the two main Internationals. Such things would be impossible in a real trade union organization. But the C.G.T.U. is an outright appendage of the Russian state apparatus. . . .

"The small opposition in the C.G.T.U., though persecuted and calumnied, did not lose heart. The last congress of the C.G.T.U. has brought us closer together. For the first time an agreement was reached between the militants of the Federation and the syndicalists. Let us hope that this is the initial stage toward the rallying of the revolutionary forces that have remained healthy."

Simone had been appointed to teach at Roanne, a post she herself had applied for, so that she could be closer to her friends in Saint-Etienne. As long ago as August she had announced the news to the Thévenons on a postcard sent from Spain. So she went there to take up her duties. She rented a room on the fourth floor of an apartment house on the avenue Gambetta. Mme. Weil had accompanied her to help her settle in and she stayed with her for a few days.

In the lycée in Roanne, Simone's relations with the administration were for the first time very good. It is true that the headmistress sometimes appeared in her class to insist that she give the students marks and grades, which Simone generally refused to assign. The students also were ordered to remove the Platonic inscription that they had traced in block letters over the door to the classroom: "Nothing can enter here that is not geometry." But it seems there were no serious disagreements. The class was quite small, probably four or five students in all.[16]

Anne Reynaud, one of her students, later published the notes she had taken in Simone's class in a book entitled *Leçons de philosophie de Simone Weil* (1959). In the introduction to her book, Anne Reynaud writes: "Our class, quite small, had a wholly familylike character; at the side of the lycée's great walls, in a small pavilion almost hidden at the back of the park, we were introduced to great ideas in an atmosphere of perfect independence. When the weather was mild, classes were held under a beautiful cedar that cast its shadow over us. These lessons were sometimes transfomed into an inquiry into a problem in geometry or simply a friendly conversation."

For seven hours each week Simone also gave a course in literature to the fifth form students.

Since Roanne was close to Saint-Etienne, Simone resumed her activities at the Labor Exchange. During this year, the Thévenons no longer lived at Saint-Etienne; they had both been appointed to posts at Cellieu, in a school on its outskirts. When Simone had to spend the night at Saint-Etienne, she would stay with various comrades, or even, after having worked till very late "in a room in the bar with the last light still lit, a place opposite the Labor Exchange that the owner let her use. She would sleep there for a few hours, right on the leather-covered bench, so as to be ready to catch an early morning train that would transport her to her other tasks, thus avoiding the objections of her friends, who would try to convince her to rest longer in the morning when she accepted their hospitality."[17]

These sentences were written by Duperray. It was chiefly to this year of 1933–1934 that his memories of her returned, memories that he published under the title "When Simone Weil Passed Among Us."[18] A schoolteacher at La Talaudière, a mining town in the Loire, he was a friend of the Thévenons and also frequented the Labor Exchange.

On October 22, 1933, Albert Lebrun, the president of the French Republic, came to Saint-Etienne to unveil a monument to the war dead. He was a native of Lorraine who people claimed was unduly influenced by the trust of French arms manufacturers, the Comité des Forges. The local of the United trade union decided to organize a protest meeting on the eve of his arrival, on Saturday, October 21. They invited the Confederated unions to join them, but the latter, annoyed by the way the United unions had treated them in their previous attempts at a "united front," decided to hold their own meeting on the day Lebrun came to town. When the people who attended the United meeting came out, the special police sent from Paris intervened; many militants were clubbed and a great number were arrested. The Labor Exchange was closed. The next morning when the Confederated members, to whom were added members of the independent unions and a group of pacifists, arrived at the Labor Exchange, they could not go in and were forced to hold their meeting on the sidewalk. However, the secretary of the Labor Exchange spoke quite effectively from the second floor of the Labor Exchange, which he had somehow managed to enter. Then Simone Weil was lifted by some comrades onto a window ledge of the Exchange and gave a short speech that the people there could barely hear. According to the report in *L'Effort,* she denounced "the provocation to the proletariat of Saint-Etienne constituted by this visit of a servant of the arms merchants, of the man who would let the elite of the intellectual youth and the workers of Indochina perish."[19] The people gathered on the square and sang the "Internationale." The police, who did not have a large force on hand—almost all the available police were busy protecting the official ceremony on a nearby street—could not stop the two brief speeches or the singing.

After these events, the polemic between the United and Confederated unions at Saint-Etienne was kept alive by further disagreements. The United union reproached the Confederated union for having refused the united front and mocked it by pointing to the small number of demonstrators who were present at their Sunday meeting. As for the Confederated union, these attacks and mocking criticisms from the United union did not deter it from protesting, in a motion adopted on Monday, the police brutality and the arrests of United members. It then agreed to participate in a new United union meeting organized for the following Thursday to obtain the release of the people who had been put in jail. But once again Confederated members were disappointed by the way in which the orthodox Communists understood the united front. They had promised to abstain from all attacks on the Confederated union members; yet from the very start of the meeting, the attacks against them began. Thévenon asked for the floor; they refused to let him speak. An article in *L'Effort* of November 4, "After All This, Don't

Talk To Us about the United Front!" expressed the bitterness that the members of the Confederated union felt about all this.

As for Simone, she was singled out for an attack by *Le Travailleur de l'Enseignement,* for having helped a Confederated demonstration, since, through the Federation of Teachers, she was a member of the C.G.T.U.

Simone knew René Lefeuvre, who published the magazine *Masses.* Perhaps in September she had written an article entitled "A Socialist Appeal to War" for this magazine. And in the September issue of *Masses,* this article was announced for its next issue; but it did not appear. Lefeuvre, it seems, turned it down,[20] something in it having perhaps shocked him. Simone then worked on it further and printed it in the November issue of *La Critique sociale* as "Reflections on War."[21]

In the article she reviews the various positions taken on war by revolutionary leaders and thinkers; and she shows how the opinion was formed that there is a "revolutionary war," that is, that certain wars could serve the revolution. Against this opinion, she maintains that a revolutionary country cannot wage war without renouncing the revolution; that even if the *goal* is the liberation of the people, the *means* set in motion by the war must necessarily lead to the opposite result. "The materialist method consists above all in examining every human event by taking into account the ends pursued much less than the consequences necessarily implied by the effect of the means employed."[22] "The revolutionary war is the grave of the revolution and will remain this as long as the soldiers themselves, or rather the armed citizens, are not given the possibility of waging war without the ruling apparatus, without police pressure, without exceptional laws and without legal punishment for deserters. Only once in modern history was a war fought in this way—during the Paris Commune; and we know very well how this war ended. It appears that a revolution involved in a war has the choice either of succumbing to the deadly blows of the counter-revolution or of transforming itself into a counter-revolution. . . ."[23]

In the same issue of *La Critique sociale* there appeared two of Simone's book reviews, one of Rosa Luxembourg's *Letters from Prison* and the other of Lenin's *Materialism and Empirio-Criticism.*[24]

Her criticism of Lenin's philosophy, and above all of his method, is harsh. "It is a typical method that consists in thinking only with the purpose of refuting, the solution already being given before the research into the problem. And by what, then, could this solution be given? By the party, just as it is given for Catholics by the Church. . . . Such a method of thought is not that of a free man. . . . Long before it robbed the whole of Russia of freedom of thought, the Bolshevik party had already taken it away from its own leader."

As for Lenin's philosophy, that is, the materialist theory of knowledge, she emphasizes its inherent absurdity in that "it represents thought as one of the products of the world, a product that by some inexplicable coincidence also constitutes its image or reflection." And she tries to prove that unlike Lenin and Engels, Marx was not really a materialist. "Marx's entire work is permeated with a spirit incompatible with the vulgar materialism of Engels and Lenin."

The other article, however, expresses sympathy and unqualified admiration for Rosa Luxembourg. Her political and social ideas are not in question but rather her attitude toward life, her love of life and the world. This gives Simone an opportunity to express her own love of life and the world. It is clear that she does not greatly prize sadness and aspiration to sacrifice. She writes: "It is difficult to understand why the editor has used as an epigraph a sentence that undoubtedly escaped by chance from Rosa's pen: 'I hope to die at my post: in a street fight or in prison.' If this statement expressed a profound emotion, it would not greatly do honor to its author; but the reading of this collection of her writings leaves us in no uncertainty in this regard. Rosa's life, her work, and especially her letters bear witness to an aspiration to life and not to death, to effective action and not to sacrifice.

"In this sense, there is nothing Christian in Rosa's temperament. She is profoundly pagan. Every sentence in this collection emanates a feeling for the Stoic conception of life, with the sense that this word had for the Greeks, not the narrow sense it has assumed in our day. In truth, the virile attitude toward misfortune, which is what is ordinarily meant by the term Stoicism, often appears in these letters. . . . But what mainly appears here is the truly Stoic feeling, so rare among moderns and above all in our day, of being at home in the universe, whatever event it may produce. Hence Rosa's love for Goethe. Certainly she would have marked out the famous verses: 'My happy eyes, everything that you have seen, whatever it may be, was yet so beautiful!' For her, sadness was only a momentary weakness that one had to submit to in silence and rid oneself of as quickly as possible."

L'Effort of December 2 published a new article by Simone, "The Problem of the U.S.S.R." In it, she opposes the principle according to which it was permissible to sacrifice the individual to the collectivity. "This principle leads in the last analysis to the sacrifice of the people as a whole to the interests of some privileged individuals. . . . The collective interest always and without exception signifies the interests of those in power." Answering an article published previously in *L'Effort,* in which it was stated that Fascism and Stalinism, far from resembling each other, were at opposite poles, she shows that the differences between them are more apparent than real. She shows above all that in one sense the capitalist can also be considered to be working for the collectivity. His profit is not used for personal luxury, save to a very small degree. "The capitalist system essentially signifies the sacrifice of the workers, not to the well-being or luxury of the boss but to the growth of enterprise, that is, the growth of the productive apparatus, the mines, machines, and factories, in short those forms of work of which one can say, and not only for Russia, that 'the community will reap the profit later on.' The only drawback of the system is that, since the worker is simply the slave of the machine, no one reaps the profits in question save the new machines; the work extorted from the worker is always used to develop the productive apparatus, and, due to competition, this process never ends. But it is precisely the same in Russia. Russia is also threatened by the competition of other countries. To defend itself, it must ceaselessly enlarge its productive apparatus. . . . There is no difference . . . except that the Russian state possesses not only the means of production and exchange but also a police and an army, and by force can prevent its workers from selling their labor to another boss. . . ."

On the third and fourth of December there was a march of miners from La Ricamarie to Saint-Etienne and a miners' festival. To protest the cut in wages and unemployment, the Confederated Miners' Unions had decided to organize marches on all the prefectures and subprefectures. These would be peaceful though large and forceful demonstrations. They took place in the Carmaux Basin on November 19, in the north on November 26, and in the Loire on December 3.

So the miners of La Ricamarie formed ranks on Sunday, December 3, and marched to Saint-Etienne. Simone, with some other comrades, waited for them at the entrance to the town. She joined the procession and asked to carry the red flag. She carried it for quite a while, not letting anyone take it from her; and she carried it well, though she did not have a leather flag rest.

The next day, on December 4, the Feast of Saint Barbara, the miners' festival was held. Simone had gone back to Roanne. Pierre Arnaud asked Duperray to go and fetch her in a taxi so that she could "give a talk on Fascism" at the close of the amusement session that the C.G.T.U. was offering the miners in the large hall of the Labor Exchange.

"I reached Roanne," Duperray writes, "just when the lycée was letting out. She came out with great strides, her scarf floating in the December wind, her *toque* pulled down over her ears, her bulging briefcase under her arm. I had hidden in a corner of the street and when she walked through the gate, I called to her. I told her who had invited her and she was so happy that she began trotting, pulling me after her, to rush to her apartment and get rid of some of the heavy books.

"When we reached the Labor Exchange at Saint-Etienne, quite late, she stepped up on the speakers' stand and shouted in a shrill, heartrending voice a series of slogans that were applauded with a frenzy she had not expected:

" 'We must arm against Fascism! We must arm ourselves, but in the real sense! not figuratively!'

"After the banquet that evening, there was a ball in the large hall of a municipal building, the bare walls of the shower rooms of the public baths having been decorated with garlands for the occasion. One of the miners called Le Boul Chapuis asked Simone to dance. His cap cocked on his head, he held her at a respectful distance. He was very attentive, full of pride and delicacy. He was also amazed that he could not get this young girl to follow him in time, since she did not know the ritual of popular dances or the most elementary steps of the simplest dances. . . ."

From Roanne, Simone traveled from time to time to Lyons. She wrote in December to one of her former students at Le Puy, now studying at Lyons. This letter shows that she had had the intention of going to the congress at the Bâtiment, the congress of her friends of *L'Effort*, but in the end she did not go.

"My dear girl:

"I'm sorry that I couldn't go to the congress at the Bâtiment, after your letter even more than before. The truth is that I missed the train, not through negligence, obviously, but because that morning I was in a bad physical state and didn't have the courage to get up in time. But don't be upset by this; it was nothing. Simply a headache that afterward went away.

"I'm happy that you felt friendly to the kids at the Bâtiment. You should read *L'Effort* now and then so as not to lose sight of them."

This letter also shows the concern she had for her students, her affectionate, maternal devotion to them:

"What you tell me about your headaches, your lack of enthusiasm for work, etc., troubles me. I think that you should quit all this as soon as possible for some productive work. I am thinking of something for you, something that would be marvelous, but I don't want to tell you about it yet, for it is too vague and I would not want you to be disappointed. After the new year, perhaps I'll be able to tell you something more precise.

"Did you know that among the teachers at Rhône there are very nice people who could become friends of yours? I am telling you this because you seem very lonely. You could see, with my recommendation, F.B. . . . who is a fine old man and would put you in contact with a group of very interesting young people. . . .

"You haven't told me anything about the way you live, and, according to what you say about your health, I am very much afraid that you are doing something foolish (not sleeping, not eating, etc.). . . ."

The study circle at Saint-Etienne's Labor Exchange had to be reorganized. A meeting was held on Wednesday, November 15, with a view to reorganization, and some courses had been announced by *L'Effort* on November 25: a course in French, another in orthography, and a course intended to give the trade unionists "an insight into Marxism." This last course would be given every fifteen days on Wednesdays at eight o'clock in the evening, and would begin on December 6.

This course in Marxism was just made for Simone. The first lecture was shifted from the sixth to twentieth of December. Duperray gives the outline of Simone's lecture on Marxism, which he seemed to think was the first lecture, and this outline corresponds to the chief divisions of an outline that *L'Effort* of December 16 published as that of a lecture Simone was to give on the twentieth at the Labor Exchanges of Firminy and of Saint-Etienne. This very detailed outline had certainly been sent to the newspaper by Simone herself. She evidently wanted to permit the workers to familiarize themselves in advance with the subject of the lecture, which was to be "The Idea of Scientific Socialism."

In this outline, or rather article, one can see that Simone had progressed toward the kind of research that would form the basis for her "Reflections on the Causes of Liberty and Social Oppression." She presented a brief sketch of the history of science and a history of the struggles against oppression, and then declared that these two human efforts, the effort to build up science and the struggle against oppression, which for a long time had run parallel to and independent of each other, had finally been united in Marxism. She concluded that one must above all "endeavor to define the causes of the different forms that social organization assumes."

Simone returned to Paris for the Christmas holidays. It was during these days that her encounter with Trotsky took place. He had been authorized by the Daladier government to stay in France under certain conditions. He had arrived on July 24, 1933. He resided at Barbizon and did not have the right to participate in political meetings.

Simone was not a Trotskyist, but for a long time she had wanted to get an opportunity to meet and talk with Trotsky. The way in which he had dealt with her article "Prospects" had amused her more than it had roused her indignation. In October, she had written a letter to her mother:

"Not astonishing that Raymond was monosyllabic: Papa [Trotsky was called Papa and his son the Crown Prince] has done me the honor of attacking me on the subject of my article, with a great array of insults, in a pamphlet of which *La Vérité* has published a fragment. 'Vulgar liberalism,' 'cheap anarchist exaltation,' 'the most reactionary petty-bourgeois prejudices,' etc., etc. It was to be expected. But, alas! I will no longer get a chance to meet him. Curious to know what the youngster's attitude to me will be, he's been so polite up until now."

Léon Sédov, the "youngster," had written to her soon after, no doubt in November, and Simone had answered him. Mme. Weil, who had seen her reply, wrote to her daughter that he must be furious with her. Simone replied to her mother: "I don't see why Liova should be furious. Nevertheless, I can hardly say that I approve of a pamphlet in which I am insulted. L. D. [Léon Davidovitch Trotsky] himself would not expect that much."

Despite these differences, she still wanted to talk with Trotsky. Besides, she was always ready to help those with whom she disagreed if they were being persecuted. During the first days of the Christmas holidays, she said to her parents somewhat as follows, "The apartment on the seventh floor is empty at the moment. Trotsky would like to hold a small meeting with some of his political friends and representatives of political parties close to him. Couldn't he hold it in this apartment?" The Weils could never refuse their daughter anything. They gave their consent.

The meeting was to take place on December 31, 1933. Trotsky arrived on the twenty-ninth or thirtieth, with his wife Natalia Sédov and two bodyguards. He had shaved off his goatee and mustache and had used pomade to flatten his thick mane of hair. Thus transformed and dressed like a bourgeois, he was quite well disguised. He asked the Weils to add an armchair to the furniture at his disposal in the apartment on the seventh floor. This was for his bodyguards. During the night one of them had the right to take a nap in the armchair while the other stayed awake, seated on a chair, revolver in hand.

Trotsky wanted to see a film of Eisenstein's which was being shown in the neighborhood. He and his family, his guards, and some friends left at night, their hats pulled down over their eyes and their coat collars raised to their noses; they looked just like conspirators, and everything they did made them even more noticeable. When they returned after midnight, they all piled into the service elevator, which, overloaded, stalled between floors. To get out they had to wake up the whole apartment house. It was not the best way to be inconspicuous.

Simone took advantage of Trotsky's presence to have a discussion with him. The discussion quickly turned into a quarrel; in the adjoining room, where they were seated, the Weils heard a series of loud shouts. (The shouting was most likely done by Trotsky. Simone always spoke calmly; she never got excited during a discussion.) Natalia Sédov, who was sitting with her parents, exclaimed in astonishment, "This child is holding her own with Trotsky!"

Simone reproached Trotsky in particular for his conduct toward the Kronstadt sailors. Trotsky told her, "If that's how you think, why did you put us up? Do you belong to the Salvation Army?"

A page of notes taken by Simone after this conversation has been found. She wrote down chiefly what Trotsky had said to her and more rarely her own replies:

"You are completely reactionary. . . ."

"Individuals (democrats, anarchists) never fully defend the individual (it is impossible), but [combat] only that which troubles *their* individuality."

"The Russian worker controls the government to the extent that he tolerates it, because he prefers this government to the return of the capitalists. That is what the government's domination amounts to!"

"—But the workers also tolerate . . ."

"—We know more than Marx in 1871, [than] Lenin before October 1917. Russia found itself isolated. History moves slowly. . . . To fight the enemy, you need an army."

"—If you were in Russia, the government still being isolated! . . ."

"—That is precisely why I am not in Russia."

"You have a juridical, logical, idealist mind."

"—You're the idealist, you who call the dominant class a subjugated class!"

"—Domination is not what you imagine it to be, perched on some Olympus . . ."

"A great deal has been done for the workers (women, children . . .)."

"—What can you give this young generation subjected to brainwashing?"

"—(An evasive, disheartened reply.)

"To the degree that production will progress . . ."

"The Russian proletariat is still at the service of the productive apparatus—inevitable until Russia has caught up with the capitalist countries. The October Revolution analogous to a bourgeois revolution . . ."

"I have nothing to reproach Stalin for (save for the mistakes in the framework of his political policy); the objective conditions. . . . But at the time of the struggle against the Narodniks, we also used to say that capitalism in Russia would be progressive; but that we would not do that work, but instead would prepare for the future. In the same way I, at this moment . . ."

"(At bottom, L.D. and Lenin have played a role similar to that of the big capitalists when capitalism was still 'progressive'—at the price of crushing thousands of human lives.)"

"The final balance sheet of the Russian Revolution: it produced the Left Opposition (!). I don't believe, I'm sure that it will make the revolution."

"Why do you have doubts about everything?"

"The Russian proletariat: a situation analogous to that of the middle class that, at the beginning of capitalist accumulation, deprived themselves of everything in order . . ." (The notes break off here.)

So the conversation between Simone and Trotsky revolved chiefly around the problem of whether Russia was a workers' state. Trotsky maintained that it was. Simone had expressed her opinion on this in her article "Prospects": "Descartes used to say that a broken clock is not an exception to the laws governing clocks, but a different mechanism obeying its own laws; in the same way, we should regard the Stalin regime not as a workers' state out of order, but as a different social mechanism, whose definition is to be found in the gears from which it is composed and that functions according to the nature of those gears."[25]

The meeting organized by Trotsky took place, as foreseen, on the evening of Saint Sylvester's Day. Trotsky wanted to induce certain parties, notably the S.A.P., to merge with his group. He did not succeed in getting the representatives of the S.A.P. to support the motion that he proposed, but he did obtain some results, for when saying goodbye to the Weils, he told them, "You will be able to say that it is in your house that the Fourth International was founded."

Jacques de Kadt, who participated in this meeting, has told the story of Trotsky's departure and his own:

"When we entered the hallway to get our overcoats, a young girl or young woman came to help us. Trotsky asked her, in a bantering tone, whether she was still clinging to her counter-revolutionary ideas. She replied, as though she did not notice the light tone, with a definition that established a sort of identity between the terms 'revolutionary' and 'counter-revolutionary,' maintaining that when searching for the truth, one must restrict the use of this terminology. I knew this serious way of reasoning from some articles that I had read in *La Révolution prolétarienne* . . . articles that had made an impression on me.

"This young woman was Simone Weil. At that moment her spiritual evolution had just begun. Her intelligence had been revealed to me by her articles, but with something more: a moral courage that was not checked by the conventions and that sometimes dared to accept generally disapproved conventions when they seemed right to her. Above all, a moral purity and disinterestedness carried to the highest level.

"All this had moved me and I had had translated and published one of her articles in *De Fakkel* ("The Torch"), the biweekly newspaper of the O.S.P. [the Dutch Independent Socialist party]. However, I did not share any of her ideas. She was not traveling in my direction but in Gandhi's, which explains why De Ligt's monthly organ *Liberation*, had also translated some of her articles and later even published them in pamphlet form. But although I did not take seriously the value of a De Ligt or his followers, Simone Weil's value was so striking and based on such strong arguments that one had to reply to them before continuing on the road leading to the renovation of socialism. . . .

"Meanwhile Trotsky departed with his secretaries; we had to wait so as not to leave at the same time as he. I took advantage of this to introduce myself to Simone and to tell her that I had published one of her articles in my newspaper, not because I agreed with it but because it seemed to me necessary that one should reflect calmly on the problems of socialism, instead of speaking in clichés, as did Trotsky and other Marxists who never cease repeating the same worn-out, stale formulas. She thanked me for my sympathy, but told me that right now she wanted to take part in the 'comrades'' argument. So I let her continue her discussion with the 'comrades' but was glad to be able to say goodbye to them and to be the first to leave the house after Trotsky."[26]

Simone seemed rather proud about having talked with Trotsky. A few days later, receiving a comrade (Lefeuvre), she said to him, "Do you see that chair? Do you know who was sitting in it a few days ago? Trotsky."

L'Effort of February 3 announced a lecture of Simone's at Saint-Etienne on Wednesday, February 7, and, as had been done for the lecture on December 20, published a detailed outline. This time the lecture was to deal with historical materialism, and the outline, like the previous one, was obviously written by Simone herself.

Even more than in the December 20 lecture, one feels in the February 7 lecture that an approach is being made to "Reflections on the Causes of Freedom and Social Oppression." At the start Simone says: "We will not have a method for overturning oppression except on the day when we will have understood the causes of oppression as clearly as we conceive of the conditions that produce the equilibrium of a stone. Hence the first question that is posed is: what sort of conditions produce, in a general way, the structure of a human society?" So she thought more than ever that before attempting a revolution, one must renew the theoretical work and construct a science of society. She sketched an analysis of the fundamental conditions that are imposed on all kinds of societies, an analysis that will be much more fully worked out in "Reflections."

Duperray tells us that after these lectures they would usually gather at a comrade's house and Simone would sometimes sing or recite poetry. "The comrade's house to which we would go after the lectures had a pile of newspapers in a corner instead of a sofa. In this bare room, the most fortunate occupied the few chairs. The others settled down on the mattress of newspapers. We smoked. The host served us drinks in all sorts of receptacles. Le Boul, to whom the most disastrous doses of alcohol were innocuous, would use a milk bottle or a bowl. On her days of euphoria, Simone would sing students' songs; it was impossible to sing more out of tune than she did, even if one tried. This amused her, but at other times she would only listen, murmuring: 'I don't know,' with a sad air. She told us how she wandered through the streets of Paris on the days of the July 14 celebration, from one popular dance to another. But she did not dance. 'I don't know how.'

"As the night wore on, she would begin to recite poems, whole pages from the Greek tragedies that she seemed to dredge up from her inexhaustible memory. . . .

"One of these evenings, we had sung our revolutionary songs for quite a while, recited our poems, read pages of books, and felt very good, stretched out on our host's newspaper-sofa. I was smoking, gazing up at the ceiling. I couldn't make up my mind to take my leave, to go down into the street. . . . Simone Weil was gay. She left her chair and came over to me with a smile on her face. She settled herself comfortably on the papers next to me, propped on her elbow. That evening she was holding her cigarette between two stiff fingers, like a novice smoker who, after the family meal, just as it happens at Saint-Etienne, cautiously takes her first puffs before her father bawls her out and slaps her fingers.

"Simone looked at me, took her time, then suddenly, as the others would have said, "Say you! sing something!" she murmured, temptingly, 'Little one, wouldn't you like to do some math?'

"When some of our friends who were there started to laugh, she protested. She thought that they considered it preposterous that one could be interested in mathematics. She could not understand that what was preposterous was that she was offering math to me personally as a kind of intellectual tidbit and was proposing this delight at that hour and under those particular circumstances."[27]

After this, Duperray tells an astonishing story:

"One morning when our staying up after the lecture had lasted until dawn, we organized a kind of encampment in our comrade's accommodating quarters, so as to doze off for a while while waiting for daylight and the coffee he had promised to prepare for us as soon as he awoke. Simone had retired to stretch out on the bed in the next room with another girl comrade. There were three of us men sleeping with our host on the piled-up newspapers.

"Less than an hour later Simone Weil was already up, her briefcase under her arm, and, walking on tiptoe, had reached the door to the apartment. I knew that she had a train to catch for a trade union meeting at Lyons. But she could have left later. I got quickly to my feet and opened my arms wide to stop her. Before I could say a word, I was flung away from the door and, as she shoved me, she struck me with the side of her hand under the chin, in a gesture that was both brutal and maladroit.

"This episode always amazed me. I mentioned it to her afterward. She would avoid it by saying, 'I don't know,' or 'I was in a hurry.' Nothing that would explain this strange act.

"Much later in her book *Gravity and Grace,* while describing her subsequent mystical experiences, I came across a kind of confession in three lines, in which Simone explains that while suffering from violent headaches, she sometimes had an intense desire to strike someone violently on the forehead. She offered this incident, whose singularity she does not seem to grasp, as an example of more general human instincts—whereas it actually seems to me to resemble the blow she gave me."[28]

I don't know whether the explanation Duperray offers is true. Perhaps Simone had simply thought, since he had stretched out his arms to bar her path, that he wanted to kiss her or become fresh with her. She was alert to this sort of danger and was very well prepared to defend herself from it. She had most likely studied a form of jiujitsu. (I recall that when we were students we had started horsing around for the fun of it and I could see then that she was quite familiar with certain very effective blows—even too effective—which I did not know. I also observed that she hit out with nervous, maladroit movements and could possibly hurt you without wishing to.)

Nothing seemed more detestable to her than to force upon a woman physical attentions that she did not desire. To speak of extreme instances, nothing filled her with more horror than rape. Mme. Weil said that she would have killed in no other situation, but perhaps she might have killed to prevent a rape or defend herself from it. This crime seemed to her even more frightful than murder.

She was very careful not to give any occasion for such advances. Her very style of dress was a precaution against this. And if by chance, despite her dress and her tomboy manners, a comrade seemed to become interested in her as a woman, she did everything to discourage this as quickly as possible. Another story that Duperray tells can serve to clarify the previous one. "If the jokes that she considered people's jokes often confused ordinary people, she herself was confused by the only joke about her that Le Boul permitted himself. Le Boul used to sing songs that he had learned in the African battalions, such as:

> " 'I shall always remember
> Theresa, my little French girl.

One day Le Boul sang it with a new ending and a little bow:

> " 'I shall always remember
> Simone, my little French girl.'

"Simone Weil stood up abruptly. She looked at each of us in turn and then gave Le Boul Chapuis a very cold stare. She had brought the evening to an end. She seemed to be constantly afraid to see anyone, even the most humble friend, attach himself to her. Had she perceived behind Le Boul's gracious words a kind of crude tenderness whose homage she feared? Le Boul must not be permitted to see in her an object of adoration . . ."[29]

Nevertheless, Duperray says that she did not see men and women as abstract beings. She was attentive to and indulgent of each person's personality: "A girlfriend told her of her inability to live for the future and asked her if this was what she called 'To live in such a way as not to exist.' And Simone Weil replied, more or less, 'Not at all! I love you as you are, living in the present as I don't know how to do. It is for those who live in the present that the present exists, and for whom the chain of days is something more than just a series of days without human content.'

"Another friend complained about being nothing and not doing anything with his life. 'There are those,' she replied, 'who, because others love them, should be just content to exist.'[30]

She could be tender in friendship, not only with words but sometimes even with gestures, though this was quite unusual. Albertine Thévenon says that one day at the movies Simone put her arm around her shoulder; but she also says that such demonstrations were extremely rare for her.

(She also made this gesture with me one day and leaned for a moment on my shoulder; but it was late in our relationship, just before the war, and it was the only time. I remember that I thought then that I would remember this forever.)

She was not a prude or severe with other people, at least in certain areas. Lovers' weaknesses were those toward which she was the most indulgent. When she told me about the question the young German girl had asked her, "Do you have a friend, too?" she added, in her mother's presence, that she saw nothing wrong with it and she herself would certainly have a friend if that gave her pleasure, but for the moment this did not tempt her. She told me on another occasion the story of a young girl who wanted to have a child to raise and who had said, "It would be even better if the child was mine." So she had arranged to have a child without anyone knowing about it and subsequently managed to adopt it. Simone seemed to approve fully of this behavior. Among the writers for whom she had the greatest sympathy there were, for example, Villon and Cardinal de Retz, neither of whom can be considered very respectable. Alain admired Cardinal de Retz's *Memoirs* but severely criticized his behavior toward women. Simone spoke to me more than once about Cardinal de Retz without even thinking to reproach him on this score.

She had a deep feeling of pity for prostitutes and wanted to get to know their milieu, just as she wanted to know all forms of misery in order to try to understand what could be done to change them. When Duperray writes: "Simone could not imagine that the nocturnal feats of her comrades could differ from the students' rowdy pranks she had known, and Thévenon, like a brother, had to lead away 'the professor,' who would have so much liked to follow her big boisterous brothers in their joys as well as their hardships,"[31] he is undoubtedly mistaken as to Simone's intentions. She knew very well what those nocturnal feats of her comrades were, and if she wanted to go with them, it was with full knowledge of what was going to happen. Thévenon told me that she wanted to go with them to the brothel, but they didn't take her and besides she would not have been allowed to go in. An attempt she later made that has been recounted,[32] as well as the answer she gave the police superintendent at Marseilles who threatened to put her in jail with prostitutes, confirm Thévenon's story.

She lectured not only at Saint-Etienne but also at Firminy. Duperray recalls an incident that occurred during one of her lectures: "Jean Giry, a militant in the Teachers' Union, started a study circle here at Firminy, a kind of appendage to the one Thévenon and Claveyrolas had organized at Saint-Etienne. Simone Weil had also taken over the course 'Insights into Marxism.' One day a big fight broke out. A young technician from a nearby metallurgical factory, whom nobody knew at the time, was taking copious notes. This exasperated a metal worker, a student in the circle.

" 'He's a fink!' he shouted. 'He's going to report everything to the boss.'

"Navant, the secretary of the Labor Exchange in that small industrial city, stepped in to calm the exasperated comrade. . . .

"Simone Weil listened, flabbergasted. And she kept asking for an explanation long after the incident.

"In fact the young technician became an assiduous auditor at the lectures, a knowledgeable trade unionist, and later on himself a teacher at the Labor Colleges in the Loire. The boys no longer considered him a stool pigeon. . . . And Simone, dressed in her new zipper-fastened work-blouse, which was a bit too large for her, continued her lectures week after week. Jean Giry had preoccupations of another order. 'This Simone,' he said to me, privately, 'just look, five times she lights her cigarette and throws the matches and sparks on her blouse. She'll end up by setting herself on fire.'

"These jokes about Simone's clumsiness were for many comrades a way of resisting the magical power that was conferred on her by her relentless arguments, her scorn for material contingencies, and her great capacity for work, which defied fatigue, illness, the need to eat or sleep. . . ."[33]

One cannot find in Simone's letters to her family any remarks about the riots on February 6 or the general strike on the twelfth, which was, in all of France, the reaction of the workers' organizations and the leftist parties to these riots. (It is not because the events left her indifferent. If she must have rejoiced at the success of the anti-Fascist demonstrations on February 12—which were particularly important in Saint-Etienne[34]—the Fascist, or Fascist-tinged, riots must have seemed to her a disquieting sign and most likely reinforced her political pessimism.)

On the other hand, she speaks in her letters of the Socialist insurrection that took place in Vienna and was crushed on the twelfth, thirteenth, and fourteenth of February. She is indignant, not only because of the repression but also at the imprudence of the Socialists, who had unleashed this "senseless uprising." In her first letter, she says: "Boris has sent me Dickmann's letter. And besides I received one directly from him. The elite of the Socialist youth—the Schutzbund—fought without any help from the population; and all was lost in advance. And the 'Red Vienna,' which they were trying to defend, comes down in the last analysis, he claims, to a bureaucratic system that managed, during the period of prosperity, to benefit a fraction of the working class with great material advantages at the price of the misery of the workers and peasants in the rest of Austria, and which could not function in a period of crisis.

"The articles in *Popu* on the defeat perfectly reproduce the tone of the proclamations issued after a calamity by a general staff. And eighty-five children were killed in the battle. . . .

"I feel less and less ready to die for the military bulletins of all these bastards, whether they be Socialist or Communist leaders. They are all the same."

The other letter in which she mentions it is a long letter that deals chiefly with Fröhlich, who had finally arrived in Paris:

"My dear Mime:

"Thanks for your letter and Fröhlich's. Tell him that it gave me great pleasure. Above all it makes me feel good to hear that he is so happy. He believes incorrectly that my *Weltanschauung* is sad; only my historical perspectives are. Tell him one or two things for me, until I get the time to write him at length (which I shall do as soon as I can), or until I can see him, which would be better. (Won't he be there at Easter?) I would love to be able to shake his hand, after having thought for so long that this would never happen! (Which does not stop me from realizing very well that if ever the S.A.P. retakes power in Germany as the result of a revolution, and I happen to be there, Fröhlich would not hesitate to have me shot. . . . At least that is what I conclude from the passage in his letter that deals with 'dictatorship.' You can tell him that. . . . It is quite serious, of course. But that doesn't stop me, while waiting for that day, from having a strong emotion of comradeship. . . .)

"As for the arguments he presents against my article,* I don't have the time to answer them at length; for the moment it suffices to say that I have taken *everything* into consideration and pondered it for a long time before writing that article. Which is to say that they were not enough to persuade me.

"As for the U.S.S.R., one must: 1. show him Victor Serge's great letter (it is in my room, I think); 2. he should go and see G. I would also

*This is undoubtedly the article entitled "Prospects."

like him to talk with X., who was there from 1912 to 1933. . . . She is emotionally a revolutionary, although estranged from politics; she knows many Communists; they have asked her several times to make an application for party membership; she has never had anything to do with the opposition. Through her I found out, once her morbid terror vanished, that everybody is so fed up with the regime that the peasant masses and a good part of the workers look forward to a war to get rid of Stalin. (Only the Komsomols are happy and full of faith, but this is due to intensive brainwashing, total ignorance, and crushing work that leaves them no time for reflection.) That one can see at S. (a town without any unemployed!) people scouring the fields and eating raw, rotten potatoes. That the workers go to sleep in 40-degree weather in unheated huts. That in the Ukraine whole villages have died of hunger. That they had to pass a law prohibiting cannibalism, with the punishment of immediate execution. That the misery has destroyed the communal feeling that is so profound among the Russians and that people no longer help each other. G. also says that, in a family of specialized workers, the bread is no longer put in common but that each person eats his legal ration: 800 grams for the man, 600 grams for the woman, and 200 for each child (the *sole* nourishment). That, on the other hand, everyone steals products of prime necessity. That nobody dares say anything to anyone, because of their terror of the G.P.U. . . . Is he unconcerned about all this?

"Like him, I believe that one must 'educate an elite class' (except that we surely don't see the word 'education' in the same way), but the best way to do this is not to massacre it. I shake with indignation when I see the *Neue Front* approve the senseless insurrection that has annihilated the flower of the Viennese working-class youth (and eighty-five children on top of that!). . . .

"Did you get him to read my article on war? That will really shock him. . . .

"But the most urgent thing is to find him a publisher. Tell him to go and see Marcel Martinet . . . who has great sympathy for him and would gladly take him to Gallimard. . . .

"I embrace you and shake Fröhlich warmly by the hand—I would be terribly happy to do this in reality."

In a postscript, she added:

"As for the headaches, they have certainly diminished—but not disappeared.

"For Easter, I have decided to stay in Paris.

"Yesterday's *Le Travailleur* carries a horrible piece of news: four young people of the S.A.P. were delivered by the Dutch to the Nazis. I would like to burn down the Dutch legation in Paris! Was Ebeling one of them? Answer *immediately* about this. Until then I will live in mortal anxiety, so as not to get out of practice. And tell me the truth, you understand. I hope that his work prevented him from taking the trip. But who was it?"

It was probably between March 1 and March 19 that Simone had an abscess in her throat. Her father insisted that she come to Paris to be treated. She took advantage of this forced vacation to translate Machiavelli's text, which she published in the March issue of *La Critique sociale* under the title "A Proletarian Uprising in Florence in the Fourteenth Century."[35] She must also have read Otto Rühle's biography of Karl Marx, which she reviewed in the same issue.

It took some time before Simone recovered completely. Her illness had weakened her. She was forced to remain in Paris to the end of the Easter holidays, that is, until April 8. (That year Easter fell on the first of April.)

She wrote to me a little before Easter, about March 20. At the time I was at Leysin, in Switzerland.

"My dear Simone:

"I must once again begin, as usual, by making my excuses to you. . . . I didn't reply to your invitation at Christmas (I know that my mother had written to you) because until the end of the holidays I didn't know if I could despite everything take the trip to see you; and afterward I had planned to come to Leysin for Easter, and I wanted to wait to be sure in order to write to you. But I have been quite wrong. . . . I write to you now from Paris, where I have had to go due to a stupid abscess in my throat, which began about fifteen days ago. . . . It is practically cured, but I still have little strength. . . .

"Nothing new here, save that the country goes straight to Fascism, or at least to a very reactionary dictatorship; but you must know all that. All the news from Russia is dreadful and hopeless. As for Germany, best not to talk about it. Well, no point in dwelling on all this.

"Chartier is pretty sick. He reads, writes, but he doesn't see anyone. He has dizzy spells—some trouble with his ear, it seems. As for the N.'s, they seem very excited and are preparing to bar the road to Fascism with their chests.

"As for myself, it is just the opposite: I have decided to withdraw entirely from any kind of political activity, except for theoretical work. That does not absolutely exclude possible participation in a great spontaneous movement of the masses (in the ranks, as a soldier), but I don't want any responsibility, no matter how slight, or even indirect, because I am certain that all the blood that will be shed will be shed in vain, and that we are beaten in advance. . . ."

This letter makes it clear why there is no question of Simone participating in the great movement of mobilization and organization of the democratic and anti-Fascist forces that had sprung up after the sixth of February. Her comrades of the United Federation of Teachers, such as Serret and Salducci, summoned the workers to the struggle with articles entitled "On Guard against Fascism!" "Stand Up against the Fascist Threats!"[36] Appeals of the same sort were being made in most of the unions and parties on the left. An anti-Fascist front was being formed. Though sick and though he did not like to associate himself with any group, Alain himself had since February agreed to support, with Langevin and Rivet, the Committee of Vigilance of Anti-Fascist Intellectuals. Since his state of health made it impossible for him to attend the meetings of this committee, he got Michel and Jeanne Alexandre to represent him.

Simone seemed to have kept away from all this and to have remained silent—or at least not to have published anything that could urge on or excite anyone. Perhaps she had already begun to write what at first was only an article and eventually became her long essay "Reflections on the Causes of Liberty and Social Oppression." In any case, she was tormented by the ideas that she would express in this essay. She had now come to believe that present-day industrial society seems to evolve toward a totalitarian regime rather than toward greater freedom. This pessimism—or this lucidity—isolated her, separated her more and more from her political friends, although she was always ready to join them in a specific action and to expose herself personally in any struggle that had some chance of being useful.

After returning to Roanne, she still felt tired and worn-out for some time. One Sunday in April she wrote to her mother:

"My dear Mime:

"I reply, as you see. I am still 'crawling between heaven and earth' [English in original], but this begins to subside, and some flashes of energy show up now and then. It is the sign that I will soon be in good shape. . . ."

She continued to be concerned about the German refugees. It was most likely in April that she wrote to her parents:

"Would you please get busy fraternally with this pal—a real German worker, a qualified metal worker, S.A.P., *very* nice and interesting, who escaped from a concentration camp, etc., etc.? He will tell you his story. See if there are possibilities of getting him a place to stay. If Fröhlich has already left, you could perhaps put him up in his place (despite the vows Biri has made). . . ."

(Biri's vows refer undoubtedly to the fact that Dr. Weil, irritated by certain experiences, had sworn not to put up any more German refugees. He was much too kind, as his daughter knew, to keep this vow.)

Mme. Weil advised her daughter to ask permission to leave on the first of May. Simone replied:

"You don't want me to ask for a leave of absence on the first of May? No, on that day one either works or strikes, and alas! the teachers won't strike."

Nonetheless, she did strike. On the first of May her students waited for her in class, but she never came. When they left the lycée at noon, they saw her at the head of the procession, under the red flags, her fist raised, singing the "Internationale" along with the other demonstrators.[37]

At the beginning of May, Simone felt that she was being reborn:

"My dear Mime:

"All goes well, May is here, nature is coming to birth again and me too.

"I was at Le Puy yesterday. Spent the afternoon on one of the nearby hills with Vidal and the two sisters, my old pupils. Charming kids. Vidal is still a swell fellow. . . ."

One of her former students at Le Puy, one of those who had taken her course in Greek in the third form, had written to tell her, perhaps in April or at the beginning of May, that she had left a profound imprint on her former students, that their entire class, because of her, had been "radicalized," and that all the students of this class were "malcontents." Simone seems to have been both amused and a bit worried by this. In a letter to her mother she said that she had written to the student in question and added, half-jokingly: "Do you realize what this means? What a responsibility!" Since this former student asked her what she thought of the political situation, she replied with a letter full of very somber predictions and warnings. She especially attacked the illusions these young girls might have on the subject of Russia.

"My dear child:

"It is quite hard to answer you: these days nobody knows what can happen in foreign policy. One thing is certain: war is always possible, at every instant. That the states don't have money does not matter at all; they have an unlimited ability to manufacture it, thanks to bank notes (monetary inflation is a disguised tax; through it, the state increases its funds at the expense of private individuals). . . .

"That having been said, I don't think war is imminent, although I'm not certain about this. The ruling French groups are afraid of it, since they are convinced that Germany is stronger. On the question of the Saar, France seems ready to yield. It has already yielded to a large extent, since it lets the terrorist bands sent by Hitler sow panic among the Saar population. The freedom to vote will not be respected. The question of the Saar is one of those in which all solutions are bad: to be re-attached to France would be a triumph for French imperialism and war; the re-attachment to Germany would amount to the working-class population being handed over to a horrible regime of terror and oppression.

"The second solution is at the moment almost certain and, alas, one is forced to be happy about it, since it will momentarily avoid the even crueler horrors of war. . . .

"A general piece of advice: distrust all newspapers equally. Notably

L'Humanité, which tells just as many lies as Coty's *L'Ami du peuple*—which is not a little. How does this happen? It can be connected with events in Russia. The Russian Revolution has evolved rather like the French Revolution: the necessity to struggle with arms against an inner and outer enemy (there was a war in Russia, roughly from 1918 to 1923), resulted in the death of the best elements and forced the country to hand itself over to a bureaucratic, military, and police dictatorship that has nothing socialist or communist about it but the name. ... In no country, not even in Japan, are the working masses more miserable, more oppressed, more humiliated than in Russia. If I tell you this categorically, it is, as you can imagine, because I am sure of it. My sources of information are either people who have lived there for years, whose stories agree and whom one cannot suspect of systematic bad faith (some of them went to Russia out of enthusiasm for the revolution and had responsible positions in the Communist International; others are workers without a party but with a revolutionary outlook); plus the official Russian documents, the Russian press, and even *L'Humanité,* for if one reads it with a critical mind, one can find proofs of barbarity and oppression that are paraded proudly in the name of the Soviet regime. This should make it clear that all the Russian literary works that date from these last years are packed with lies (it was different during Lenin's time). The writers in Russia who refuse to lie are sent to Siberia where one leaves them—let us be clear about this—they and their families, without *any* resources to live on. In Ilya Ehrenburg's book, the only true thing is the picture of the enthusiastic youth eager to build, but this enthusiasm, nourished by ignorance and fanaticism and deeply tainted by nationalism, does not differ in essentials from that of the young Italian Fascists or the young Nazis. ...

"The corruption of the Russian regime has led to that of the Communist parties, which are entirely controlled by Moscow. The German Communist party bears a great responsibility for Hitler's victory. The French party continues to make the same criminal mistakes. ...

"As for the Socialists, they are more than three fourths bourgeoisified.

"My heart breaks to have to tell you these sad things. But I owe you the truth. On the entire earth's surface, oppression and nationalism are triumphing. This is no reason to renounce one's ideals; it is already something not to let oneself be brainwashed. That is why, at bottom, I'm quite happy that you are all 'malcontents.' ... And yet I'm rather frightened by the responsibilities that I have unconsciously assumed (unconsciously, because I never would have thought I had indirectly exerted so much influence on your class); because the present society can only heap misfortunes and disappointments on those who refuse to adapt to oppression and lies. Realize this fully, from now on. We don't live in one of those periods when rebels are stimulated and supported by large currents of opinions. The rebel is morally and materially alone—I speak of true rebels. For example, I don't consider the Communist leaders rebels who make a show of fighting against one form of oppression but in practice accept an even worse form of it, namely, Stalin's; nor the Socialists, who are always ready to bow before force—and will be more and more ready. Only those who are really strong, really pure, really courageous, really generous, will be able to meet the challenge. Although one has the right to some illusions at sixteen, it is best that you should know the whole truth immediately. I haven't the time to support everything I have said with proofs, but you know very well, don't you, that I would not lie either to you or myself. Particularly about Russia, I have grudgingly been forced to admit the sad reality.

"Affectionately yours."

Although Simone regarded her information on Russia as quite reliable, she wanted to be able to verify it herself. Mlle. Descamps, her colleague at Roanne, told Cabaud that Simone longed to take a trip to Russia but never could get the necessary papers, whereas she herself, Mlle. Descamps, obtained them without difficulty.[38]

Souvarine also recalls that she wanted to go to Russia at a certain period. He told her, "You will be seduced by Slavic charm; you won't want to leave."

(I don't know whether she would have been seduced by Slavic charm, but what is certain is that such a trip would have been very dangerous for her. Even supposing that she could have kept from saying what she thought, her curiosity, her desire to become informed about everything, would have easily led to her being taken for a spy.)

She returned to Paris for the Pentecostal holidays. She saw Souvarine, who was just completing his book on Stalin. He was experiencing difficulties in financing *La Critique sociale;* he didn't know whether he could continue to publish it, though he thought that he could get out one more issue, and Simone intended to write an article for it.

When she had returned to Roanne and wrote again to her mother, she had already begun writing this article, which would become "Reflections on the Causes of Liberty and Social Oppression." In a letter that may date from the end of May or the beginning of June, she says:

"Boris has written to me that he has given up the issue of *Critique.* But I go on working as if nothing had happened, for you know how it is when I have an article under way: life is intolerable to me until I put down the last period. . . ."

This "article," which soon took on the dimensions of a short book, kept her busy without a break not only during the entire end of the school year but for a good part of the summer and well into the fall. . . . Profoundly absorbed by this work, every diversion seemed to her to be at its expense.

At the start of the same letter she says to her mother:

"My dear Mime:

"You make some demands! Write every three days! It's not the writing that is difficult, it is to keep track of the time. But I'll try.

"I had a strange dream this morning. I dreamt that you were saying to me: I love you too much, I can no longer love anyone else. And it was dreadfully painful."

On the twelfth of June, the Croix-de-feu, the reactionary organization, was to hold a meeting in the afternoon at Saint-Etienne. The committee of Anti-Fascist Vigilance at Saint-Etienne and the Amsterdam-Pleyel Committee called upon their followers and the working-class population to hold a counter-demonstration. A large gathering formed in front of the headquarters of the Committee of Vigilance about the same time as the Croix-de-feu meeting was to begin. It was composed mainly of C.G.T. members, many of them Simone's friends, teachers, and miners. The demonstrators intended to march singing the "Internationale." At the very start, they encountered a police barrier, then Mobile Guards on horseback who rode them down and chased them. Driven off the main street, they regrouped in the adjacent streets and soon returned to it. They were then met by another charge, more violent than the first. Men rolled under the horses' hoofs, and several were struck by rifle butts. The workers became enraged; they turned over streetcars and then pulled back to the poor districts and built barricades. A good part of the night was taken up with pitched battles and pursuits. When a barricade was captured, the demonstrators would run away and regroup somewhere else. They had to run quickly; the stores were all closed, for the owners had locked their doors, and so they could not hide anywhere to escape the militiamen who were clubbing people and arresting them. The miners said, "Oh, if only Simone was here!" But soon after they said, "It's lucky she wasn't, because she doesn't know how to run."

Simone was at Roanne. When she found out what had happened at Saint-Etienne, she was very angry that she hadn't been told about it in advance and telephoned her friends to bawl them out. (Since the demonstration had taken place in the evening, she could have been present. Thévenon had purposely not told her beforehand; he knew that she would have wanted to come.) Thévenon also says that if she had been there, her comrades would not have let the police take her; three or four of them would have gone to prison if a policeman had raised a hand against her.

When exactly did she decide to take a sabbatical so as to work in a factory the following year? I don't know. In any event, her resolution was taken when she wrote to her mother, at the end of June:

"My dear Mime:

"A word only to tell you that I am well and that the article, just about to be finished (never has a delivery been so painful!), obsesses me so much that I am physically incapable of thinking of anything else, above all about the questions you have asked me. So telephone Alex for the scholarship. I had already asked for a leave, having learned by chance that from July 1 on one can no longer ask for it. (However, there will still be time in September to change my mind. But that obviously is not very likely. It may be the case if experience proves that I am absolutely incapable of working in a factory. But I doubt that that is so. . . .")

For a long time she had wanted to work in a factory, as we have seen. Yet she had already put off the realization of this dream, so she could put it off again. Why did she decide to do it in 1934? There are certainly several reasons. One of them must be that this plan was much too important to her to be deferred any longer and so run the risk of perhaps never being put into practice. But another reason must be the fact that she had reached an impasse in her theoretical thought. For a long time now she had tried to imagine how the organization that an industrial society demands could be reconciled with those conditions of work and life suitable to a free proletariat. How could one coordinate factory work without oppressing the workers? She had not found an answer to this question. She was forced to think that where theoretical thought could not find a solution, actual contact with the object might suggest a way out. The object was the misery for which remedies had to be found. If she herself plunged into this misery, she would be able to see more clearly what remedies were appropriate to it. And, after all, one must know all this in order to speak of it.

She felt a deep joy at the thought of realizing this dream. Yet at the same time she could not help but be apprehensive. She knew that she was clumsy; she foresaw, not without reason, the hardships and fatigue that she was not certain she could surmount. On the other hand, in view of what she thought she owed to herself, she knew that she would not allow herself to abandon the project or, once she had begun it, forgive herself if she did. She herself said to me sometime later, when she was already a worker, that she was determined to kill herself if "she couldn't take it." (A confidence that was quite terrifying, especially when one knew her almost inhuman energy and her lack of self-pity. No doubt she was determined to do this even before she began to undergo the test. That is why she wanted beforehand to write a summation of everything that had accumulated in her head, all the reflections she had had that could be useful to others. Her article grew longer and longer; she wanted to say everything. That is also why she soon called it (with a smile) her "Magnum Opus" or her "Testament."

Simone's request for a leave "for personal studies" is dated June 20, 1934. Of course she does not mention her plan to work in a factory.

In her request, she says: "I want to prepare a philosophy thesis concerning the relationship of modern technique, the basis of large industry, to the essential aspects of our civilization—that is, on one hand, our social organization and, on the other, our culture."

She did not feel obliged to inform the ministry of her real intentions. Yet the relationship she mentions, the relationship of modern technology to the social organization and culture, was actually what she intended to study. It was a question of study, not simply an "experience," as some people think. She wanted to discover what mechanism establishes the oppression of man by man and, above all, the oppression of man by the machine, so that one could know how to abolish it. The only doubtful thing is that she wanted to write a thesis on this subject.

Leave was granted her by a ministerial decree dated July 13.[39]

One of Simone's students applied for the *bachot* and was accepted. From a professional point of view the year of 1933–1934 seems to have been a happy one. There had indeed been some criticisms and complaints but nothing serious, so far as one can judge. Neither from a professional standpoint nor from that of her relations with her comrades at Saint-Etienne did Simone have any reason for wanting to leave Roanne. At Saint-Etienne not only had she been admitted into the milieu of the trade union militants but she was also surrounded with friendship, confidence, and respect. At Roanne, the administration had for the first time accepted her. Everywhere her students had loved her. Besides, work as a teacher did not bore her; on the contrary, she had a passion and a vocation for teaching. But the very absence of difficulties that had to be overcome could perhaps be counted among the circumstances that had led her to think of leaving. Difficulties would have kept her there.

She returned to Paris about July 20 or a little after that. Since the month of June I had been living with my parents in Enghien-les-Bains. I went to see her in Paris. It was the first time I had seen her since the beginning of the summer of 1933, perhaps even since the Christmas holidays of 1932. For I am not sure that I had seen her when I stayed for a short while in the Parisian suburbs at the beginning of the summer of 1933.

We talked about all sorts of things, among others about the political situation. She no longer believed in the liberating powers of the revolution; she thought that it would be a great deal if in France we could preserve the liberties we still enjoyed. Thinking to tease her, I told her that she had become a conservative. She said to me, "Certainly, at least about many things."

She objected to Marx not only because of his belief in a liberating revolution but even more because of his theory of the infinite development of the productive forces after the revolution. According to Marx, she said, roughly, capital is a means of power much more than a means of pleasure; the luxury in which capitalists live is a small matter compared to the profits they reinvest in production. Where then would one get the means, after the revolution, to develop the productive forces "to infinity"? Isn't capital already engaged almost entirely in production? She seemed to doubt the progress of industrial society not only toward liberty but even toward wealth, and in any case toward such wealth as would permit a notable decrease in human labor. She spoke to me about an article by Dickmann that demonstrated that there is a limit to the advantages obtained by the progress of the means of transportation, even if this progress, in itself, in terms of technical progress, is unlimited.

I recall that we spoke about the Reichstag fire and Van der Lubbe and discovered that we had the same opinion. At Leysin, where I had spent the winter of 1933–1934, I had wanted to read the *Brown Book,* thinking I might find in it the proof that the Nazis had set fire to the Reichstag. I had discovered, not without some amazement, that this book did not present any decisive proofs. However, certain statements made by Van der Lubbe, among the few he pronounced at his trial, seemed to be those of a sincere man. One day at a meeting of scholars, who had come together to discuss the Reichstag fire, I said that after having read the *Brown Book* I had not found it persuasive; that I was not sure that the fire had not been started by Van der Lubbe alone, as was maintained by him; that he seemed sincere to me and that it was hard to believe that he had been an accomplice of the Nazis. Everyone had stared at me with indignant amazement; then, after a silence, someone had spoken negligently about something else, as if my remarks were too shocking to be taken up. So I thought that few people had my opinion on the matter, even among those with whom I generally had ideas in common. I was glad to see that Simone judged it as I did. She said to me, even before I had said what I thought, "You know, I know some of Van der Lubbe's Dutch friends. They don't think that he was an accomplice of the Nazis."

On July 25 *La Révolution prolétarienne* published an extract from one of Simone's letters, no doubt addressed to one of the editors of the magazine. This extract began with approbation: "The *R.P.* as a whole manages successfully to stay apart from the mounting tide of stupidities and dirty deeds." But Simone adds: "For example, the manifesto of 'Power to the Unions' seems to me a huge joke. The workers do not have power in their own unions; they are in the hands of the big shots, who, moreover, have no other means of domination than their bureaucratic functions. What would become of the workers if these big shots also had the army, the police, and the whole apparatus of the state in their hands! Trade union Stalinism does not attract me any more than the other forms of the state. You will see—the first magazine to be prohibited will be *R.P.*!"

In fact, *La Révolution prolétarienne* had published on February 10, 1934, a manifesto entitled "Power to the Trade Union Movement," which began as follows:

"The march of events poses in a sharpened form the question: Parliamentarianism or Fascism?

"We reply: neither parliamentarianism nor Fascism.

"All power to the trade union movement!"

Already the Rhône section of the General Confederation of State Employees, in a manifesto adopted on February 1, had declared on the subject of the unions: "This is the only force that *remains intact* and in which we have faith. . . . Trade unionism is ready to take all power without sharing it."[40] In its February 24 issue, *L'Effort* had associated itself with the manifesto published in *La Révolution prolétarienne.*

However, *Le Combat syndicaliste,* organ of the General Confederation of Workers' Revolutionary Syndicalists (a group with an anarchist orientation), had in its March 9 issue proclaimed: *"All of the economy to the unions! All social administration to the communes!"* They continued to defend this slogan, while *La Révolution prolétarienne* continued to support its manifesto.

Now we have seen from Simone's letter to B. and from one of her letters to Thévenon, that she had broken with her revolutionary syndicalist friends for more than a year, at least from the standpoint of doctrine. She remained tied to them by affection and loyalty, but she had as little faith in the "good union" as in the "good political party." Duperray, in a part of his work not published in *Les Lettres nouvelles* but quoted by Cabaud, tells us that, sitting one day in a café at Saint-Etienne with her comrades, Simone laughed at the manifesto of *Le Combat syndicaliste* and said of this program, "A terribly premature slogan!" But she found this slogan even preferable to that of *La Révolution prolétarienne,* since the formula of the anarchistic revolutionary syndicalists pointed at least to the fact that the unions' taking control of the economy must not be confused with the seizure of power. "Power to the ideal trade union," Simone said, "is similar to power to the ideal party. Our unions are real unions. They are not capable of taking power—fortunately!"[41]

I don't know whether at this time she had also expressed her disagreement with the Communist Democratic Circle, which she had never explicitly joined. This was in any case before the disappearance of *La Critique sociale.* There has been found a draft of a "Letter to the Circle" on a torn, fretted sheet of paper; she advised the members of this circle to disband.

"I must be forgiven for expressing myself in so personal a manner. The Circle is a psychological phenomenon. It is made up of mutual affection, of obscure affinities, of repressions, and, above all, of contradictions that have not been clarified, among its members and even in each of its members. . . . I will give you a few examples:

"1. The question of the final goal. Bataille has written to me that he wants me to join the Circle, because many of the comrades have brought forward, he says, reservations as serious as mine and probably the same ones. Put in another way, he wishes me to join the Circle in order that I become active, with him and others, in what the Communists would call factional activity. . . . Now the revolution is for him the triumph of the irrational—for me, of the rational; for him, a catastrophe—for me, a methodical action in which one must endeavor to limit the harm done; for him, the liberation of the instincts, and above all those that are currently considered pathological—for me, a superior morality. What do we have in common? I know that Boris is in agreement with me on all this, and I hope that there are also others. Notably, I believe, Ch. and P.K. How can one coexist in the same revolutionary organization when on either side the revolution means two contrary things? If it is a matter of action, one would separate very quickly since that would pose certain real problems. If it is a matter of theoretical clarification, no common effort of clarification could be attempted starting from standpoints so totally opposed and with such entirely opposite methods. The confusion is increased even more by the fact that Bataille is surrounded by comrades about whom one does not know—including no doubt themselves —to what point they adopt his attitude. And no doubt Bataille himself is indeed much less coherent than I indicate.

"2. Question of organization. Officially the Circle is oriented toward a new party. However, except for Prader, etc., Boris is the only one, I believe, who still admits this idea of a party, and then only to a certain point. Neither Ch. nor P.K. admit it, even less Bataille and the others. But they do not declare themselves for any form of organization, for they are not syndicalists. D. is against all organization in general—if one puts aside the organizations that are born spontaneously from the struggle and die with it—but he claims nonetheless that he is not an anarchist. . . . As for Boris, he continues to speak of parties, but since he is against a general staff of professional revolutionaries, he obviously means by this a completely new form of organization, which one finds it hard to conceive of. Prader, etc., believe in a new party, somewhat like the people in the 'East' group.*

"On this point, the confusion derives above all from the coexistence in Boris of two Borises, one a survivor of the political struggles of the war and postwar period, and another who is our contemporary. . . .

"3. Question of the Circle's aims. Prader, etc., desire action but what they mean above all is discussions with a great number of small, unimportant groups. The rest of the Circle finds this useless—in my opinion,

*The Independent Communist Federation of the East, which published *Le Travailleur*.

for good reason. Action would demand armed groups, preparation for illegal struggles, etc.; but that presupposes a severe selection in the membership and all sorts of things alien to the Circle.

"As for theoretical clarification, one must know whether the best way to become aware of problems is*

"I conclude with a concrete proposal. It can be said that I do not have the right to make such proposals, since I am not a member of the Circle; but this proposal is of such a nature that it renders precisely all adherence on my part impossible. This proposal is for the dissolution of the Circle.

"This does not mean, obviously, that all ties are broken. If you continue to do something in common (*Critique,* P.U.†), you will even meet from time to time. If not, it will be dispersion. But you will continue to see each other and to have conversations that, though often sterile, are nevertheless more fruitful than all the meetings. Those who are not held except by reason of affection, habit, etc., will leave. The others will become retempered in solitude. If there is ever some advantage in taking a position publicly on some matter, you can always meet for this purpose and draft a statement. If there is concrete action, you can . . . ‡ And each member will become wiser in solitude and silence."

Georges Bataille, the writer and critic, whom Simone mentions in this letter, had published in *La Critique sociale* of November 1933 a review of Malraux's novel *Man's Fate.* He had remarked upon the "unusual negative aspect" of the revolution in this book and let it be understood that the value of the revolution, in the eyes of revolutionists, is indeed tied, in fact, to the values of catastrophe and death. Simone wished to protest this conception of the revolution. She wrote a statement that she undoubtedly addressed to *La Critique sociale,* though it was not published (this was perhaps the time when the magazine stopped appearing), in which she criticized both Malraux and Bataille:

"*Man's Fate* is a fine book, but it has its limitations. What creates the basis of the book and the unity of all of its characters . . . is the idea of diversion, in the sense that Pascal used this term, that is, the idea that man cannot become aware of himself without intolerable anguish . . . and so plunges into action in order to lose consciousness of himself. . . . For Malraux's heroes, the revolution is exactly what religion was for Pascal—a means of escaping the awareness of the nothingness of one's own existence.

"One must seriously ask oneself whether revolutionary action, when it derives from such a source, has any meaning. If it is a matter of fleeing

*Unfinished sentence.
†People's universities?
‡Unfinished sentence.

from oneself, it is much simpler to gamble or to drink. And it is even simpler to die. At any rate, all diversion, including revolutionary action of this kind, is a disguised form of suicide.

"One cannot be a revolutionary if one does not love life. . . . The revolution is a struggle against all that which forms an obstacle to life. It has no meaning except as a means; if the end pursued is vain, the means loses its value."

It is precisely because the revolution was for her nothing but a means that Simone reflected so seriously on the results that one might expect from it, and preferred to give up the idea of revolution if these results proved to be too uncertain.

I recall having spoken with her about *Man's Fate.* The only character she fully admired in the book and whom she would have liked to be was Katov, the one who decides to be burnt alive and die, not in order to be annihilated but to save two of his comrades from the same death.

During the month of August she vacationed with her parents and brother at Chambon-sur-Lignon in the Haute-Loire. She had invited me to join them and so I went and spent a few days there.

I don't remember very much about Simone from this stay, because we saw very little of her, except at mealtimes. Her brother went swimming in the Lignon River, but she didn't swim. I took some walks in the woods with Mme. Weil; and we went with baskets to gather blueberries, but Simone was not with us. She remained shut up in her room, writing the "Magnum Opus."

One day, however, she left her work to take a walk with some of her former students from Le Puy who had come to see her. It was on this day no doubt that when these young girls became rather tired and were glad when the path turned down, Simone said to them, "Personally, I don't like going down. I much prefer going up."

Her brother teased her sometimes. In the pension where we were staying we had found a brochure left behind by some girl scouts and entitled "The Sergeant-Major Angel." We started talking at table about someone who had said or written that Simone was an angel. Her brother laughed and exclaimed, "If she is an angel, she's surely a 'sergeant-major angel'!" Simone laughed at this with all of us.

When she returned from Chambon-sur-Lignon, she stopped over at Saint-Etienne. She spent an evening in a café with her parents. There was an old worker accompanied by his wife, who was also quite old. They were expecting to receive an indemnity for an accident on the job of which the wife had been the victim. Someone told Simone that the old man knew people's songs or work songs. She went to sit beside him and asked him to sing some songs. Flattered, he thought he had made a conquest. His wife was dozing off and, at a certain point, had completely fallen asleep. The old worker then put his arm on Simone's shoulder and said, "The old woman is sleeping, let's take advantage of it." Simone didn't budge but sat there straight, stiff, calm, staring at him. He realized that he had made a mistake and left, not even forcing her to repulse him.

After this, she went to Réville, while her parents traveled to Spain and Portugal. She stayed again with the Henri Passilly family, the same place she had been at the beginning of September. She swam in the sea and wrote to her parents that she felt reborn. I don't know whether she later went to the Martinière farm to visit the Letelliers.

She returned to Paris about September 23, roughly a week before her parents' return.

About this time she wrote to a student from Le Puy to whom she had already written in May:[42]

"My dear child:

"I am very glad to have news of you. I think, as you do, that we are headed for a dictatorship. Nevertheless, the Fascist effervescence in the Haute-Loire is a local phenomenon. In the country as a whole the groups of Fascist tendency are remarkably quiet, while on the other hand the government is singularly indulgent toward Socialist and Communist agitation. And this is the reason: The Socialist-Communist 'united front,' which coincided with Russia's entry into the League of Nations, is little more than the Russian state's propaganda in France and is the mainstay of the Franco-Russian military alliance.

"The Socialists have completely forgotten all those cases of state oppression in Russia which a few months ago they were still denouncing. And as for the struggle against French militarism, colonial oppression, etc., it is being conducted with ever-increasing gentleness by both Socialists and Communists, preparatory to bringing it definitely to an end. . . . (They will still go on issuing slogans of a demagogic kind, but nothing serious.) On the other hand, if war breaks out, Socialists and Communists will send us forth to die for 'the workers' fatherland,' and we shall see once more those famous days of the sacred union [that is, suspending political disagreements in order to combine against an external danger].

"The Fascist groups, on the contrary, would mostly be in favor of a military alliance with Germany against Russia. Every military alliance is odious, but an alliance with Germany would probably be a lesser evil; for in that case a war between Russia and Germany (with Japan participating too, no doubt) would remain comparatively localized; on the other hand, if France and Russia marched together against Germany and Japan, it would be another conflagration which would spread to the whole of Europe and beyond—an incredible catastrophe. As you can imagine, these considerations do not make me a Fascist. But I refuse to play the game of the Russian general staff on the pretext of opposing Fascism.

"What a lot of young fellows will shed their blood in the coming months, believing it is for the sake of liberty, the proletariat, etc., . . . when in reality it will be for the Franco-Russian military alliance, and consequently for war preparations.

"Such being the situation, it is my firm decision to take no further part in *any* political or social activities, with two exceptions: anticolonialism and the campaign against passive defense exercises.

"Briefly, I foresee the future like this: we are entering upon a period of more centralized and more oppressive dictatorship than any known to us in history. But the very excess of centralization weakens the central power. One fine day (perhaps we shall live to see it, perhaps not), everything will collapse in anarchy and there will be a return to almost primitive forms of the struggle for existence.

"At that moment, amidst the disorder, men who love liberty will be able to work for the foundation of a new and more humane order than our present one. We cannot foresee what it would be like (except that it must necessarily be decentralized, because centralization kills liberty), but we can do what lies in us towards preparing for that new civilization. So I think that although there is no possible action for us and although we are to a great extent reduced, as you say, to a negative ideal, we can and ought to do positive work.

"The most important from this point of view, in my opinion, is the *popularization of knowledge,* and especially of scientific knowledge. Culture is a privilege that, in these days, gives power to the class that possesses it.

"Let us try to undermine this privilege by relating complicated knowledge to the commonest knowledge. It is for this reason that you ought to study, and mathematics above all. Indeed, unless one has exercised one's mind seriously at the gymnastic of mathematics, one is incapable of precise thought, which amounts to saying that one is good for nothing. . . .

"You said in your letter that you were impatient to escape from this unreal life and to find yourself at grips with the material necessities of existence. But, alas, there are not many people nowadays, especially in your generation, for whom it is possible to confront those 'necessities.' Because, apart from those whose bread is already buttered, the majority are in thrall to the misery of unemployment or to a degrading dependence which has no appearance of 'necessity' but only of a crushing fatality which one no longer even tries to resist. . . .

"In my opinion, instead of wasting your time at the lycée (which leads precisely *nowhere,* believe me, even if you get the *bachot*), you would do better to work for the Ecole Normale. . . . Do you realize that it is good to be a teacher in some out-of-the-way hole? It is even one of the best ways you have of making real contact with the people. . . .

"For the rest, believe me that no one could understand better than I your aspiration for a real life, because I share it. . . .

"I have taken a year's leave, in order to do a little work of my own and also to make a little contact with the famous 'real life.' Anyway, you can be sure that if the Ministry of Education continues on its present lines, I shan't last long as a teacher. They have their eye on me. I shall almost certainly get fired within two or three years, perhaps sooner.

"Yours affectionately,

"S.W."

8

The Year of Factory Work
(1934-1935)

We are now entering a new period in Simone's life. In fact, it might seem to us—and others have thought this, too—that two periods in her life can be distinguished and that the year in the factory marks the beginning of the second period. Not that too sharp a distinction can be made; from many points of view, there is great continuity between these two periods, and the year in the factory does not mark as profound a break as some people think. For example, it was not the experience of factory work which led Simone to part company, as regards her political ideas, with her revolutionary syndicalist comrades. We have seen that in this sense she had been drifting away from them since at least 1933. "Reflections on the Causes of Liberty and Social Oppression" and even the article "Prospects" indicate that she no longer shared many of their hopes. Her letters in the spring and fall of 1934* expressed the almost complete determination to give up all political activity. Work in a factory was the consequence of this evolution much more than it was the cause.

Nor were there any great changes in her way of life. If one considers only her acts, it could be said that it is not quite legitimate to divide her life into two periods. After just as before the year spent in the factories, she devoted the major part of her energy to serving those who belonged to "the humiliated layers of the social hierarchy." She always struggled for them and with them, wanting to be on their side whatever happened. She never gave up the fight against the forces of oppression and, for this reason, she involved herself in dangerous and unusual undertakings. She always passionately and obstinately searched for the truth, and in the most diverse domains. She always loved beauty, both the beauty of nature and great art, and sought it out as much as the small amount of her free time permitted. She was always generous with her time, her money, her efforts, and her knowledge. Even after 1938, that is to say,

*See pp. 198 and 212.

from the moment she turned her attention, much more intensely than before, to the doctrines taught by the religions, her way of life was not very different from what it had been up until then. If during her last years she lived a more and more ascetic life, it was probably not because of her religious ideas but due to the war and the fact that, detesting her privileged position, she could not bear to live more comfortably than the soldiers, prisoners, and other unfortunates of that time of misery. As always, she took her place with those at the bottom.

Even as regards her philosophy, although there had unquestionably been a change in her ideas around 1938 or so, she continued to base them, to a large extent, on concepts formed before the year of factory work. She always retained a good part of Alain's philosophy. If she diverged from him at important points, what she kept of his ideas is perhaps at least as important.

If nonetheless one can speak of two periods in her life, the second period beginning with the year of factory work, it is because at that time, it seems to me, something changed in her character or in the feeling she had toward herself and her life; and this change seems to have prepared the ground for those ideas of hers that will appear some years later.

This change of character or emotion has been described by Simone herself in her autobiographical letter to Father Perrin, where she says: "After my year in the factory . . . I had been taken by my parents to Portugal. . . . I was, as it were, in pieces, body and soul. That contact with affliction had killed my youth. Until then I had not had any experience of affliction, unless we count my own, which, as it was my own, seemed to me to have little importance, and which moreover was only a partial affliction, being biological and not social. I knew quite well that there was a great deal of affliction in the world, I was obsessed with the idea, but I had not had prolonged and firsthand experience of it. As I worked in the factory . . . the affliction of others entered into my flesh and my soul. Nothing separated me from it, for I had really forgotten my past and I looked forward to no future, finding it difficult to imagine the possibility of surviving all the fatigue. What I went through there marked me in so lasting a manner that still today when any human being, whoever he may be and in whatever circumstances, speaks to me without brutality, I cannot help having the impression that there must be a mistake and that unfortunately the mistake will in all probability disappear. There I received forever the mark of slavery. . . . Since then I have always regarded myself as a slave."[1]

So it was during the year of factory work that she began to feel singled out by affliction and slavery. And it may well be true that this feeling made way for the thoughts she was to be occupied with from 1938 on. Besides, it was immediately after the year of factory work, during this trip to Portugal which she mentions in her letter, that she had the first of "the three contacts with Catholicism that really counted."[2] Having experienced slavery, from then on she could recognize the religion of the slaves.

The period of factory work was thus the beginning of a less happy, more somber period, and at the same time a period of intellectual or spiritual evolution. She did not find in this experience, so it seems, what she was looking for: the discovery of methods that would permit a real transformation of the condition of the working class. But the experience had a profound effect upon her and in a way she did not expect. There was a modification of her feelings and, gradually, of her ideas, a modification she had not expected.

Of this change very little was externally visible, at least for several years. That her interest in Catholicism had become much greater was not revealed very clearly, except in Marseilles. As for her feeling of being pledged, as it were, to slavery and affliction, this did not appear save in infrequent confidences. Simone's conversation was still gay, she still made jokes and was humorous. It could barely be noticed that her spirit of joyous revolt, defiance, insolence, and juvenile turbulence had somehow abated. In a certain way, she always remained very young, and it might even be said that she always was the very image of youth because of her intrepidity, her generosity, her sense of mischief, a certain, partly conscious naiveté (the obstinate naiveté of a child who does not want to give up her exigencies because they may be unreasonable). Nevertheless, after the year of factory work, she was no longer the angry child she had been. Something in her had been broken, perhaps, and her character had softened. She was no longer the "terror," as Cancouët had once called her. She continued to struggle against injustice but almost without becoming irritated. She became more and more grave, calm, and sweet. One thinks of the words of the Epistle to the Hebrews: "That which he hath suffered hath taught him obedience."

So those who make the second part of her life begin with the year of factory work are right, although in certain ways there had been no great change, and even the change that then took place was at first not very visible. As for her ideas on religion, the year of factory work was simply the beginning of a very slow evolution.

The writing of her "Testament," that is, "Reflections on the Causes of Liberty and Social Oppression," took much longer than Simone had expected. Not only did what was to be an article develop to the point of becoming almost a book, but continual headaches interrupted and retarded the work on it. Souvarine, anxious to get out the final issue of *La Critique sociale,* kept after Simone, but she continued to put him off, saying that she needed more time. And she spent all of her time working in her parents' apartment in Paris, from the end of September 1934 through the months of October and November.

She had returned from Réville in September, while her parents were still traveling in Portugal. They had expected to be back by September

29 or 30, but anxious to see their daughter again, they hastened their return a bit. Instead of the night train they had expected to take, they took a bad day train, the worst train Mme. Weil could remember, and arrived home about midnight. There was no one in the apartment. Dr. Weil went to the bathroom and returned, saying, "I don't understand; there are some things in the bathroom that are not ours." In their room, too, they found unfamiliar clothes and a mountain pack lying on the bed. Finally, toward morning, Simone came in, having returned from a meeting. She was astonished to find them there, for she hadn't expected them until the next morning. "You shouldn't spring such surprises," she exclaimed, laughing. She explained that she had met a German in the street, a refugee without a place to sleep; he had been living at the Salvation Army house, but he could no longer stay there because they had asked him to pay three francs. Simone didn't know him, but he happened to know another refugee with whom she was acquainted. So she had offered for the time being to put him up and had taken him with her to rue Auguste-Comte. Adèle was in the apartment. (Adèle Dubreuil had worked for the Weils since 1930, almost since the day they had first moved to rue Auguste Comte.) She was not reassured when she saw this stranger, who was not much to look at. Simone told her, "Go buy two prime cuts, one for you and another for this boy; as for me, I don't eat meat." The German had then fallen asleep. Simone waited for Adèle's return so that she wouldn't ring the bell and wake him. But finally they did wake him and gave him a meal. After this, Simone and the German both went out, each for their own reasons.

Since the bedroom on the seventh floor was empty, the Weils quickly prepared a bed for him; and the doctor stayed up until the German returned in order to take him to the seventh floor.

One can date from this autumn the draft of a letter in which Simone gives some advice to one of her former students at Le Puy, the same student to whom she had written two long letters a little earlier. In it she told her, above all: "I completely approve of your schedule, with but one reservation: it seems to me that you are not giving sleep its rightful place. Be careful. Overfatigue suffered at sixteen or seventeen does not generally produce a sensation of fatigue, but it often leaves profound traces in the organism whose effects one doesn't feel until years later, when one can no longer seriously remedy them. I know something about this. And I don't want you to have the same experience."

The events that took place in Spain that fall deeply moved Simone and confirmed her in her resolve to break with all political groups. She wrote to the Thévenons a few days before going into the factory:

"Everything that has happened since we parted—including the present events in Spain—has made me more and more determined to retire once and for all into my ivory tower, and not come out except for two reasons: the struggle against colonial oppression and the struggle against the maneuvers connected with the idea of passive defense in case of war. As for the anti-Fascist struggle, it is impossible to prosecute it without joining those who are preparing a fine little war side by side with Russia; so I abstain.

" . . . What are P. and the others saying about the bastards in the F.A.I. and C.N.T. who have joined the insurrectional movement only after Lerroux has definitely won the fight?"

The anarcho-syndicalists in Catalonia had indeed been late in their decision to support the insurrection.

In France, negotiations had been started in October between the C.G.T. and the C.G.T.U., with the prospect of achieving trade union unification. The leaders of the C.G.T.U. had reversed their policy. Simone was very happy that unity was in the making, but had only modest hopes as to its real effect.

"One must hope that trade union unification will bring in some fresh forces, although I don't put much hope in it. It is still the only thing that gives one a reason for not as yet expecting the worst."

Sanctions had been taken by the Ministry of National Education against certain teachers, because of statements they had made during a trade union congress. Simone wrote: "If things continue in the Ministry of Education as they have begun, I can see a huge farce in prospect. Fortunately, I am on leave. But when I shall return to the job, I don't think they will let me stay very long. I already consider my work as a lathe operator (I am definitely going to operate a lathe!) as my real career. I don't look forward, unfortunately, to any brilliant successes!

"In any event, there's no point is getting upset about it: the alliance with the U.S.S.R. is preparing for us the good, just war, but in the meantime preserves us from Fascism. Let us take advantage of it. Life is beautiful. . . ."

There is no doubt more than a touch of irony in that last sentence. Besides the anxieties which the political situation caused her, Simone had been deeply saddened for several months by painful, even dramatic events that had occurred in the private life of one of her friends. Under the influence of this sorrow, this friend had perhaps at times been impatient when Simone tried to help and advise him. It was in great part these events, and the state of nervous exhaustion she had reached because of them, to which she alludes in September when she wrote to her parents from Réville that she felt reborn. But on her return to Paris the sadness had gripped her again, since toward the end of November she referred to this to explain to the Thévenons why she had not written them sooner.

"You must be quite surprised at my long silence. The unfortunate thing is that I cannot explain the reason for it, at least not in writing.

But here it is, briefly: I have had some serious trouble—not personal trouble, I hasten to say, but, you know, what concerns the people I love concerns me, too—so serious that it made an impression on me that is not quickly erased, and from which I am just now recovering. If one day I can tell you something about what happened, you will understand. All this must seem very mysterious to you. . . . In the end, though, all this is no longer important, for I have entirely regained my freedom of mind. But I could not decide to write to you sooner, because I don't like writing to my friends except when I am in a serene and happy frame of mind. . . ."

It was no doubt about this time and still under the impression of this trouble that Simone wrote for herself a text in which, starting with some observations on the relationship between pleasure and power, she lists the chief temptations she must struggle against, and finally meditates on her own character and the friendships she has had. It is appropriate, I believe, to quote almost all of this important piece of writing here.

"Pleasure and power.

"Pleasure can be *pure*—when it is not stunning—bitter—etc.

"Are there among the pleasures that stun those that have no alloy of power?

"Certainly not love.

"And what about luxury? Certainly not—in itself luxury is not intoxicating. One merely has to itemize luxuries one by one. In clothes: the pleasure of power. In food, partly there, too. In lodgings, quite obvious. Luxury and feminine pride. . . .

"The intoxications of drink, opium, morphine, and solitary vice. . . .? Certainly there, too; only this is a fictive power. But certainly on men.

"At bottom *the pleasures of the senses,* as such, are everything that is innocent (contrary to what Saint-Cyran thinks). Pleasures of sight (colors, forms), of hearing (pleasant sounds), of smell (pleasant perfumes), of touch (pleasant contacts), of taste (savory food and drink). Pleasures of the entire body (well-being). Pleasures of the active muscles. All this is healthy so long as the soul does not try to lose itself by filling up a void. You cannot be a slave of all this. The sole temptation which might be contained in this is idleness. What exactly is idleness (my special temptation)?

"Outside of this . . . (remember S.P.'s *topo*)*

"Ought one to make a list of temptations?

"1. The temptation of idleness. Flight from real life with its limitations, and from time, the essential limitation. Not to attempt anything that makes one aware that one isn't God . . .

*This most likely refers to the paper I read in Brunschvicg's course in February 1931, or the one I presented the same year in Laubier's course.

"2. The temptation of the *inner life* (all emotions that are not absorbed *immediately* by methodical thought and effective action). Put aside all actions that do not attain the *object.*

"3. The temptation of *domination.* (Power has as its correlative fanatical obedience. Racine: extreme violence demanded by the adaptation of man to his function. You, on that day of threshing . . .†)

"4. Temptation of self-sacrifice (subordination to any object whatsoever, not only everything that is subjective but the subject itself; this comes from not being able beforehand to make the separation).

5. Temptation of *perversity* (reply [react] to evil by doing everything to increase it).

"I really think that this is all . . .

"If you want to be cured, you must first of all become conscious of them . . . Then, subject yourself to merciless control and correction . . .

"I am not really free of any of these five, but the only one I have not been able to overcome at all is idleness. And at twenty-five it is quite late: one should have begun at twenty-five months. For me idleness signifies in the first place panic at the thought of *time*—this particular obligation at this moment: unbearable. (What a relief—work in the factory!) And this idleness is the source of feelings of remorse and piercing despair. It is because *time* is the first limitation, the only one, in different forms. Ah well! accept these limitations. I must get to the point where I can test myself on all this.

"Liberation from these five temptations is the very purity for which you thirst.

"You have nothing to regret. You must conquer them *successively.* Now is precisely the moment. But *you must do it* now. At the cost, if you fail, of never reaching full maturity."

Beneath the words "in the factory" an arrow points to the following reflections, written at the bottom of the page:

"Can you be one of those who are destined to obey because they lack the courage to take on responsibilities? In that case, B. is right to have contempt for you. But this perpetual physical exhaustion must indeed be caused by something.

"You have never been able to be a leader, like him, or to occupy a responsible position anywhere, even in the family—due to those whole periods when you let yourself go completely . . .

"You must live at least for a long time punctually, in order to find out what you are capable of. For, without this, it would mean that you are not fit to be in the world—that you must die."

On another page of this double sheet on which this is written one reads:

---

†This most likely refers to a day when Simone had worked at threshing grain, either at Martinière, the Letelliers' farm, or at her aunt's farm at Marnoz.

"*Never* forget this 'temptation of idleness,' the worst for me—the only reason I have to despise myself—because with all the others I have been able to rise above myself enough to give me confidence that, in relation to them, I can effectively expect to be free. But I have never begun to overcome this temptation of idleness in a stable fashion. To make resolutions is useless. To keep in mind, simply but continually, that if I do not rise above it, I would fail in my only ambition; I would live in a dream. Because punctuality and constancy are demanded of us by the universe, only artificial conditions of life can dispense with them. Next year . . .

"Do not lose sight of the 'temptation of the inner life.' Suzanne . . . Pierre and the others . . . Boris . . . Emotions that do not attain their object are equivalent to not loving. And you, you have never known how to . . . Why? Not because of lack of interest. Partly because of a natural fault. Partly because . . .?

"Must you no longer love? Yes, that would be possible if it were truly a question of a shadow of love. Not to suffer when knowing them to be unhappy? No, that is not possible. But to stop reacting in imagination: yes. To think clearly of their misfortune, so long as they give me the possibility. To think clearly of the remedies. To tell them as much as I can to make them understand. To act, as much as I can. And that is all.

"With Suzanne, because of 'loyalty,' I do not look at anything squarely. This is not trust and fidelity. No longer be pained except on their behalf, not because of them. I have a responsibility in their fate. It is only by consciousness that I can fulfill it. Not to suppress *any* thought. (Even if it were something questionable . . .)

"I cannot help B. except if I can meet him on an equal footing. And for this purpose, although in certain respects I am much farther advanced than he, something is lacking in me . . . to be able to deal with little things. This is the virtue of the good worker. This cannot be beyond my powers. So long as I do not have it, he will not trust me, and rightly so—nor can I trust myself. So long as I do not have it, I will in fact be a child. And at twenty-five years old that is a bit too much.

"That other beings, special beings, exist without being dominating or dominating others. When there is a moral encounter, it is friendship. When there is a physical encounter, it is love. But only so long as there can be love without desire. It is that which, since that business in the Luxembourg Gardens,* produces in me a revulsion and a fortunately invincible feeling of humiliation at being the object of desire.

"To wait . . . Not to accept anything impure . . . rather nothing at all.

---

*I don't know what is being referred to here. André Weil thinks that it refers to an incident without great importance, perhaps the encounter with an exhibitionist in the Luxembourg Gardens. Whatever it may have been, this incident, which occurred when Simone was still an adolescent, made a lasting impression on her.

"Toward B., to be above all invulnerable—not to expect anything (besides, I have no need of anything . . .).

"B., I can only help him materially and intellectually; not morally.

"You could formulate this 'temptation of the inner life' this way: never to overcome anything but the difficulties you encounter—or: never begin struggling except with the difficulties you encounter."

The words "what a relief, work in the factory!" seem to indicate that Simone had already started working in a factory when she wrote these pages. Which means that she wrote them in December 1934 or January 1935, since she says that she was twenty-five. But it could also be that she wrote them a little earlier, picturing for herself what work in a factory would be like, work in which at each instant the task is imposed without one having to deliberate. (She thought then that it would be a relief for her; after the experience, it seems that she had a different view.) It should be noticed that on the second page she says: "Punctuality, the universe demands it of us. Only artificial conditions of life dispense with it. Next year . . ." It may be that by "next year" she meant the coming school year and that she wished to say that during this school year, that is, from about October 1934 to July 1935, since she would be working in a factory, she would no longer be living under artificial conditions. Thus this text could be dated at the end of the school year 1933–1934 or the summer of 1934. It could not be much after the last months of the school year 1933–1934, since it is clear that when she wrote it, she had already made up her mind to work in a factory. On the other hand, one hears the echo of her disappointments in her friendships, which she had experienced in the spring and summer of 1934.

The thoughts expressed in this piece of writing can also be found, though more dispersed, in the notebooks that were published for the first time in 1970.[3] In particular, one can find a list of temptations to be struggled with,[4] and they are the same ones, the five temptations she lists here. And many of the thoughts found in this notebook were obviously written at the time that Simone was working on her "Testament," that is, at the end of the spring or in the summer and autumn of 1934. If the autumn is excluded so far as this text is concerned, due to the words 'next year," that leaves us with the end of the spring or the summer.

One does not have to call attention to the importance and beauty of these pages. This is the self-examination of a lofty and pure spirit; base temptations are completely absent from this list of temptations. These pages exude energy, sincerity, the seriousness of a moral search stripped of all commonplaces. And one can see here Simone's supreme goal: it was not to live in a dream, to live in the truth, to be in the world. One can especially see the importance she attaches to the emotions that tie her to others and, in these emotions, to what is true and real, not marred by the admixture of illusion or dream. She did not want to love in imagination. One loves in imagination if one is content with an inner emotion that does not reach its object; loving in imagination is to fool oneself, even because of loyalty, about that which one loves. Thoughts of the same sort are to be found in the *Notebooks* published in 1970. For example: *"Temptation of the inner life* . . . Allow yourself only those feelings that are actually called upon for effective use . . . Cut away ruthlessly everything that is imaginary in your feelings."[5] "Above all, never allow oneself to dream of friendship . . ." [p. 41] "Learn to reject friendship, or rather the dream of friendship. . . . Friendship is not to be sought for, dreamed about, longed for, but exercised (it is a virtue). . . ." [p. 43] Here too one feels some disenchantment, or rather the will to be lucid in regard to the friendships she has had. "Definitely give up the idea that X. can be anything more than the shadow of a friend for you . . . Learn to be alone, if only so as to be worthy of true friendship. . . . And as for X., tell yourself the same as for G. Suffer if necessary on his behalf but not on his account. . . ." [p. 12] "If the day ever comes when a *real* friendship is bestowed on you . . ." [p. 18] "It is not by chance that you have never been loved." [p. 43] These observations must have been all the more painful since, as she also says in this *Notebook* [p. 37], she would have sold her soul for friendship.

She does not accuse others, or barely. Very discreetly, almost without naming them, she alludes to those who have disappointed, in a certain measure, her need for friendship. She above all accuses herself. "It is good that X. should not be a real friend for you." [p. 12] *"Every* dream of friendship deserves to be shattered." [p. 43] In the text we have quoted she accuses herself, so it seems, for not having been able to love with a love that attained its object. I don't clearly understand what she meant by this, for certainly her affections were always turned into deeds. Perhaps she meant to say that she didn't know how to manifest her friendship by words or outward signs of affection but only by positively useful acts.

This text shows how deeply she felt that the ties of friendship or love should be on a plane of perfect equality. In her view, love or friendship should be entirely free of the tendency to dominate or to let oneself be dominated. If some people have had the feeling that her friendship was a dominating one, it was certainly not what she wished.

She does not at all condemn the pleasures of the senses. But she seems to condemn desire. This can also be seen in her *Notebooks:* "But only if there is no desire. . . . [p. 9] [Love] is outraged as soon as *need* and *desire,* even when reciprocal, enter in." [p. 10] Some people would speak perhaps of inhibition and trace the cause of this inhibition to the mysterious incident in the Luxembourg Gardens. But whatever effect this incident may have had on Simone's psyche, it would not by itself explain this attitude. One must think instead of the profound love she had for purity ("this very purity for which you thirst"), and of the cult of self-mastery she had practiced since childhood. Such an incident as the one to which she seems to allude when mentioning the Luxembourg Gardens would perhaps have had small importance for a person of another character.

One cannot help but be astonished by the fact that she considered idleness as her chief temptation. (One finds the same conviction affirmed several times in her *Notebooks*.) When one thinks of everything she accomplished, everything with which she filled each year of her short life, it must be said that if idleness was really her great temptation, she had indeed heroically surmounted it!

Without a doubt this idleness, the chief weakness for which she reproached herself, was only the feeling of physical exhaustion and the difficulty of pushing an overtaxed body to submit to the demands of an overexigent mind. It is also probable that what she meant by the word "idleness" was the difficulty she encountered in submitting to time. She was very critical of her lack of precision and of not being able to do things in the time she had set for herself.

It was through Souvarine that Simone met Auguste Detœuf, the managing director of the Alsthom Company (a company that built electrical machinery and had been formed by the merger of the Alsatian and Thomson companies). This owner of a large enterprise was a man of thought as well as action. A graduate of the Polytechnic Institute, very cultivated, and with an open, generous mind, he was searching for new ways to organize industry and society too, in general. According to Louis Armand, "he preached syntheses: the synthesis of science and technique, of intellectual work and manual work, of industry and classic culture."[6] He could therefore understand Simone's project. But above all Souvarine was able to persuade him to make the realization of her plan possible. Souvarine insisted that in any event Simone was determined to work in a factory. He said to Detœuf, "It won't be possible to stop her. It is better that she do it with you; at least the experience could be kept under some sort of surveillance." It was in this way that Detœuf agreed to have her enter one of his factories as a worker, the factory on rue Lecourbe in Paris.

If not for this, Simone would have had great trouble getting hired in a factory. Most factories were not willing to accept anyone who did not have a work certificate. If later on she was hired by two other factories, it was due to the fact that, having already worked at rue Lecourbe, she could now present a work certificate.

A friendship was to spring up between her and Detœuf. Later on in one of her letters to Posternak, she described him as "a free spirit and a man of rare goodness" and also said: "I like him very much." Nevertheless, she does say that people in his factory were quite unhappy. "His goodness does not spread to his workers." In her course at Roanne, she declared: "The boss has the power to be selfish, but he does not have the power to be good."[7]

Simone rented a small room on the top floor of an apartment house on 228 rue Lecourbe. Not only did she want to live near her work but she also wanted to live independently from her family and only on what she herself could earn. She was hired as a power-press operator and began working on Tuesday, December 4. It had been agreed that nobody in the factory would know under what conditions and for what reasons she was there. She was most likely always unaware that Mouquet, the foreman of her shop, had been let into the secret by Detœuf, who had asked him to keep an eye on Simone, but to do it discreetly, and to tell him what happened to her. Aside from the foreman of the shop, nobody knew or suspected that she was a professor. Yet some of her fellow workers noticed that her hands were not those of a manual worker. They thought she was most likely a student who had failed in her exams and who, not wanting or not being able to be supported by her family, had decided to work for a time in a factory.

According to the man who in her "Factory Journal" she called Jacquot (his name was Jacques Redon, but all his fellow workers called him Jacquot, while only the owners called him Monsieur Redon), she was not as inept as she thought. She would have maimed herself, he said, and besides they would not have kept her on. He said that Mouquet would have had the right to fire her if she had not reached the base rate, on an average. But Mouquet had his own reasons for not firing her, which Jacquot did not know.[8] Nonetheless, Jacquot's opinion shows that she was not so inefficient that people noticed it. Other workers were much worse. This at times happened, he claimed, with workers who had never worked in a factory and who proved to be completely unsuited for this sort of work.

Both Jacquot and Mme. Forestier, whom I met at Mme. Weil's, had a very clear remembrance of Simone. They had noticed her from the very first day because she had come to work in a white blouse. After that she only wore blue blouses, with an apron often stained with oil spots.

Mme. Forestier would sometimes leave the factory with her after work. Simone would accompany her when she shopped and bought provisions; but Simone never bought anything. The workers used to bring a snack to the factory; Simone never brought anything. Her fellow workers, seeing her so thin, thought that she didn't eat enough (which was often true). They would offer her bread or chocolate. Generally, Simone would refuse these offers, but sometimes she would end up by accepting them.

According to Jacques Redon, Mouquet was outwardly very serious and bossy, but the workers realized that he was good-natured and kind. He was very concerned about their safety.[9] At home, according to what someone in his family has said, he was very playful and full of fun. But the moment he put on his work shirt he was the boss and stopped joking.

Simone thought him the most interesting person among the foremen and managers she had known at Alsthom. She described him as follows: "A carved head, tormented—all twisted and torn—something monastic—always straining."[10] When faced by a problem, he would say, "I'll think it over tonight." She saw him happy only once. In the second factory she worked in, noticing that there was wastage, she will say, "No boss I have seen here compares with Mouquet."[11]

In the "Factory Journal," one can see what difficulties and disappointments she experienced, day after day, trying to reach the norms of speed that were demanded of the worker. It was torture for her. In fact, she never attained them and if nonetheless they kept her on the job, in return her salary was excessively low, the workers being paid at piece rates. She did not even earn enough to fill her stomach properly.

The work tempo was certainly too fast. On the other hand, Simone had always been slow at manual work, and perhaps in general had slow reflexes. Perhaps she also did not know how, or not sufficiently, to work without thinking, that is, mechanically. She herself said in a letter to a former student that was published at the beginning of *La Condition ouvrière:* "If you think, you work more slowly; and there are norms of speed, laid down by pitiless bureaucrats, that must be observed—both to avoid getting fired and in order to earn enough (payment being by piecework). I am still unable to achieve the required speeds, for many reasons: my unfamiliarity with the work, my inborn awkwardness, which is considerable, a certain natural slowness of movement, headaches, and a peculiar inveterate habit of thinking, which I can't shake off."[12] Certainly it is cruel that there are jobs on which one must force oneself not to think.

From the very first days she was even more tired than she had expected. She had invited me to dine with her in her small room on the rue Lacourbe; we had made an appointment, no doubt for an evening during her second week of work. On December 6 she wrote a note to ask me to put off this meeting.

"Tuesday.

"My dear Simone,

"I started work in the factory Wednesday morning. Things are going well, but in the evening I am rather worn out ... So I would like to postpone your visit and our little banquet for about fifteen days. Is that all right with you?

"Tell me what's happening to you. I am worried about you.

"Cordially.

"If you want to read my article without waiting for publication, which may be rather late, you only have to visit my parents some day when you are in the neighborhood and read it from a typewritten copy. If you read it before coming to see me, you can give me your considered opinion . . .

"Bring the 'notebook of ideas,' you bad girl! If it is idiotic, that will go right along with eight and a half hours of consecutive degradation in the factory."[13]

About December 11, she wrote to Thévenon:

"Dear Urbain,

"I haven't written sooner because, just imagine, I've been working in a factory for only about a week now. The writing of my 'Testament' has been fantastically prolonged, partly because of the turn it has taken (typed out it runs to one hundred and twenty pages, and it is so condensed that it could have easily been three times longer), but above all because I have gone through a period of very violent and completely uninterrupted headaches that lasted for several months and shackled me terribly.

"I shall write at greater length when my experience will have lasted longer—if in any case it does last. For I live in the fear of not being able to meet the work quotas that one must attain to stay in the factory.

"The women, assigned to unskilled labor, are quite miserable. There's nothing to be done with them, or very little. They are absolutely uninterested in the machines and the work. They are resigned, with a few flashes of impotent revolt; but if they dream of something better, it is usually in terms of personal luck (winning the lottery, etc.).

"The skilled workers are nice and interesting.

"I am not disappointed. I'm very happy to have done this after having dreamed of it for so long. I think more and more that the liberation (relative) of the workers must be brought about before all else in the workshop, and it seems to me that I will manage to perceive something of what that depends on. I have the impression that not very considerable changes must occur to make the factory into a joyful place.

"As for the atmosphere, I fit into the environment like a fish in water, as you can imagine.

" . . . You must forgive me if I don't write at length; I'm quite tired in the evening, when I come back from the job, and the Sundays go by quickly."

She ended by asking Urbain to try to gather subscriptions for Boris Souvarine's book on Stalin. She reminded him how strongly she felt that this book should be published.

On December 17 Simone noted in her "Journal" that she had dined at her parents'.[14] When this would occur during her year in the factory, at the end of the meal she would put the price she would have paid in a restaurant on the table and force her parents to accept it, which would send a chill through their hearts.

To make up for this, when her parents went to visit her, Mme. Weil would sometimes manage to hide a little money (very little, two or three francs, for if there had been more, Simone would have guessed where it came from) in some corner. Since Simone left her money all over her room, she was not astonished to find some coins here and there, and she joyously told her parents that once, not having a sou, she had the pleasant surprise of finding a a little money that she didn't know she had.

Finidori recalls that during the year of factory work Dr. Weil came to visit him and said, "I know that you have some influence over Simone. Tell her to get some rest. She's killing herself, and she doesn't listen to me."

On December 19, all the time she worked she cried almost without stopping; and when she got home she had a fit of interminable sobbing.[15]

I think we met on December 20. I went to meet her at quitting time outside the factory. When she saw me, she ran to me and kissed me. She didn't usually kiss me. The last time I had seen her I had told her about something that I had done of which I had no reason to be proud. I thought that if she had kissed me, it was to show me that this confidence had not altered her feelings of camaraderie toward me. Later on, when I realized how much she had suffered in the factory, I thought that it was perhaps also because after leaving this inhuman universe, she had suddenly been carried away with joy at rediscovering the world of human relations.

I ate with her in her room after a long walk (I recall that we walked for a long time on rue de la Convention). She made me a little meal, simple and quickly prepared but very good. I didn't dream that in order to offer me this meal, she had most likely had to eat even less than usual on the other days. I didn't yet know the strict rules she had imposed on herself.

Speaking of her life in the factory, she told me, among other things, that she had had to make a pile of iron bars that workers would then carry somewhere else.[16] She was doing this work with another worker. After a moment she thought that it would be a good idea to make distinct, very small piles so that the men who carried each of them were not overburdened. She told this to her fellow worker, who said, "If you worry about such things, you won't live very long." Perhaps Simone didn't know that this is a common expression that is said to anyone who is prone to worry too much. She obviously thought that this expression was directed at her personally and was a kind of prediction, and she also thought, quite clearly, that the prediction would come true. (Mme. Weil said that long before the age of twenty she thought that she would not live for very long.)

When we parted, she told me that if she could not stand up under the work, she was determined to kill herself. I said what I could against this new folly (I had already, like most of her friends, argued against her decision to work in a factory). But I knew that no one, not even her parents, could stop her from doing something crazy after she had decided to do it. To tell the truth, I thought that she would manage to do the job, not yet realizing all the difficulties she would encounter. But one could expect anything if she failed to do it.

While I thought that there was some element of madness in her projects, I recall that after having seen her I was even more convinced than before that she was some sort of saint. Moreover, since I was still feeling very shaky and had had certain troubles in the weeks and days that preceded our meeting, when these troubles suddenly disappeared, the idea crossed my mind that a miracle had occurred and that Simone's saintliness had caused it. I dismissed this idea as absurd; but I remember quite clearly having had it, and it shows the sort of impression Simone left with me after this meeting.

Some days later I also had the certainty that there was in her another kind of greatness. Having gone to see her parents and having read what she called her article ("Reflections on the Causes of Liberty and Social Oppression," which did not as yet bear this title),[17] I had the revelation of her genius, which until then I had only sensed. Her mother, who had typed the essay, gave me a copy that I took with me to the mountains at Leysin, to which I returned soon after. I got several of my fellow colleagues at the University Sanitarium to read it. They found it interesting but too pessimistic and did not seem to see all that was new and profound in her analysis. I recollect that one of them said to me, "You have the feeling that this is someone who no longer believes in anything." For him, having scant hope in the near future and especially not believing in the imminent possibility of a truly liberating revolution was tantamount to not believing in anything.

My colleagues' tepidity did not at all diminish my enthusiasm. Mme. Weil remembers that on my return from Leysin at the end of spring I told Simone that I would search for and surely find a way to get this essay published. But I was mistaken when I thought that only the difficulty of paying for the printing had prevented its publication. Souvarine was ready to publish it, but in the end Simone did not allow him to do it, for she wanted to improve its form. One of the people to whom she had shown it had criticized the style and she then had considered rewriting it entirely.

From Christmas to New Year's Day, Simone was temporarily laid off. (No doubt they could not keep all the workers on the job constantly due to the economic crisis that still was severe.) This was not much of a rest for her; she caught a cold and moreover had terrible headaches. When she resumed work on January 2, 1935, she was still suffering from the cold and above all was worn out by fatigue.[18]

When she returned to the factory, she was put to work on the afternoon of January 2 and the next morning at a particularly hard job, but for the first time in a workshop where the atmosphere was free and fraternal. She has described this work and shop in a letter to Albertine Thévenon.[19] She had to place large copper bobbins in a furnace pierced with holes so that the fire could pass through it, and then take them out a few moments later. The first day she worked there she did not yet know how to avoid the flames, which sometimes would lick her hands and arms, and for several months after she still bore the marks of these burns. Nevertheless, in this letter to Albertine, written after the end of the year in the factory, she says that if she could return to this little corner of the workshop, she would go back immediately. It was a corner where the manager and foremen almost never came. The workers, for the most part copper workers, did highly skilled work, which demanded much knowledge and adeptness, and they worked together "as a team, like brothers, carefully and without haste." On the first day, when Simone was scorched while putting the bobbins in or taking them out of the furnace, a welder working opposite her would look at her each time with a "sad smile of fraternal sympathy," which did her "untold good." And when, at the end of an hour and a half of this work, the heat, fatigue, and pain made her lose control of her movements and she could not pull down the furnace's shutter, a copper worker had jumped up and done it for her. ("What gratitude one feels at such moments!")[20] She was to work only four times in this workshop, but the times she spent there, despite the difficulty of the work, warmed her heart. By now she was feeling more at her ease, at least morally, in this factory. "I feel much better in the factory since I have been in the workshop at the back, even when I am not there anymore."[21]

But during the course of the seventh week of her life as a worker she felt so worn out and exhausted that she almost succumbed to the temptation not to think anymore. After the day's work on January 15 she wrote: "Exhaustion ends by making me forget the real reasons for my working in the factory, renders almost invincible the strongest temptation which this life brings with it: that of no longer thinking, the only and sole means of not suffering from it. It is only on Saturday afternoon and Sunday that I am visited by some memories, shreds of ideas. . . . The terror that seizes me when I realize my dependence on external circumstances: it would be enough if one day I were forced to work without a weekly rest . . . and I would immediately become a beast of burden . . ."[22]

When she awoke on January 10, she felt a sharp pain in her ear. On the fifteenth she was forced to go to a doctor, who diagnosed it as otitis. She moved into rue Auguste-Comte, with her parents, to get it cured. She would stay there for more than a month without returning to the factory.

Through the Alexandres she had sent Alain her "Reflections on the Causes of Liberty and Social Oppression." She wanted to know his opinion. She also asked him to try to approach Gallimard to urge them to publish Souvarine's book on Stalin. Alain wrote to her on January 14 and told her that Souvarine's book had not been accepted. On the "Reflections" he wrote:

"Your work is of the first magnitude; one would like to see a sequel. All concepts must be re-examined, and the entire social analysis must be redone. Your example will give courage to the generations disappointed by ontology or ideology. Criticism awaits its workers. Could you outline a plan of work? Or simply sketch it? . . .

"I regard it as very important that the attacks on the U.S.S.R. should be put aside in a work of *pure* criticism. The analysis (for example) of the bureaucracy must not rest on an inquiry concerning Stalin's government. . . .

"A work so new (Kant continued) ought to be careful to avoid all appearance of polemic. I tell you what I think. But, of course, if *Libres Propos* should print it, your text will be absolutely as you wish it. And I even believe that political passions would not much diminish the scope of your analysis of oppression or your doctrine on work. I am certain that essays of this kind, in the form that is natural to you, serious and rigorous, armed with continuity and mass, are the only ones that will open the near future and the true Revolution, infinitely close through the curve of present disorder (or present order). . . . But in my eyes it is also true that indignation alone would be capable of turning you away from your mission. Remember what I say: (the) misanthropic is false.

"Fraternally."[23]

Simone also profited from her rest to write to Albertine Thévenon:[24]

"Dear Albertine:

"I am obliged to rest because of a slight illness (a touch of inflammation of the ear—nothing serious), so I seize the opportunity for a little talk with you. In a normal working week it is difficult to make any effort beyond what I am compelled to make. But that's not the only reason I haven't written; it's also the number of things there are to tell and the impossibility of telling the essential. . . . Although this experience is in many ways what I expected it to be, there is also an abysmal difference: it is reality and no longer imagination. It is not that it has changed one or the other of my ideas (on the contrary, it has confirmed many of them), but infinitely more—it has changed my whole view of things, even my very feeling about life. I shall know joy again in the future, but there is a certain lightness of heart that, it seems to me, will never again be possible."

As to expressible things, Simone summed up her feelings on the workers' work by saying: "It is inhuman." "One's attention has nothing worthy to engage it, but on the contrary is constrained to fix itself, second by second, upon the same trivial problem, with only such variants as speeding up your output from 6 minutes to 5 for 50 pieces, or something of that sort." She then adds: "But what I ask myself is how all this can be humanized; because if the separate processes were not paid by the piece, the boredom they engender would inhibit attention and slow down the work considerably, and produce a lot of spoiled pieces. . . . Only when I think that the great Bolshevik leaders proposed to *create* a free working class and that doubtless none of them—certainly not Trotsky, and I don't think Lenin either—had ever set foot inside a factory, so that they hadn't the faintest idea of the real conditions that make for servitude or freedom for the workers—well, politics appears to me a sinister farce."

She admitted her fatigue. "To speak frankly, for me this life is pretty hard. And the more so because my headaches have not been obliging enough to go away so as to make things easier. . . .

"I am hanging on, in spite of everything. And I don't for one moment regret having embarked on the experience. Quite the contrary, I am infinitely thankful whenever I think of it. But curiously enough I don't often think of it. My capacity for adaptation is almost unlimited, so that I am able to forget that I am a 'qualified lecturer' on tour in the working class, and to live my present life . . . as though it would last forever and was imposed on me by ineluctable necessity instead of my own free choice."

She talks a bit of her fellow workers, among whom she found, doubtless to her great astonishment, very little real fraternity.

"But this too is hard to express. . . . They are nice, very nice. But as for real fraternity, I have hardly felt any. With one exception: the store-keeper in the tool shop, a skilled and extremely competent worker, whom I appeal to whenever I am in despair over a job that I cannot manage properly, because he is a hundred times nicer and more intelligent than the machine-setters (who are not skilled workers) . . ."

It is doubtless when thinking of workers like him that she was prompted a little later to write that among the workers she had known good-heartedness always went hand in hand with the development of thought and intelligence. "I have always found, among these rough, simple creatures, that generosity of heart and a skill with general ideas were directly proportional to each other."[25] She will conclude that what lowers the intelligence degrades the entire man.[26]

Worn out by the inflammation of her ear and also suffering from anemia, at the end of January Simone was not yet able to go back to work. Her parents managed to convince her to go rest a bit at Montana, in Switzerland. She left with her mother, and they reached Switzerland on February 3.

They stayed with friends, the Rosins, German refugees who had come to France in 1933 and had rented a chalet in Montana. With the Rosins was a friend of theirs, Fehling, whose conversation must have interested Simone a great deal since one can find in her "Factory Journal" a page with his name at the top and after that several listed headings, separated by white spaces: "His character— What he has said: about his profession—about the organization of companies—about mathematics." Simone obviously intended to write in these spaces, but she did not find the time to do it.

Alida de Jager, a German Socialist, was also staying at Montana-Vermala with her two daughters. They were living in an old wash shed they had transformed into a charming home. Some time before, Mme. de Jager had read one of Simone's articles translated into Dutch; the original text had appeared in *La Révolution prolétarienne.* She was struck not only by the loftiness of its judgments but also by the profound knowledge of the workers' movements. She had wondered: "Who is this old trade unionist, so widely experienced, whom I don't know?" She wrote to Simone, addressing her letter to *La Révolution prolétarienne;* the letter was forwarded by the magazine to Simone's usual address on rue Auguste-Comte. Now this happened while Simone was at Montana, and so finally the letter reached her there. She was delighted by the coincidence—in fact a quite astonishing one—that had brought it about that someone who thought she was in France had written to her from Montana just when she happened to be there. She went to visit Mme. de Jager, who was surprised to see that she was so young.

A great affection was to tie the Weil family to Mme. de Jager and her daughters. A little later, the Weils offered Mme. de Jager the chance to move to their house in Chevreuse. She accepted and lived there with her daughters during the two or three years that preceded the war.

Simone returned to France with Mme. Weil on February 22. On Saturday the twenty-third she moved back to her room on rue Lecourbe and on the twenty-fifth she returned to the factory.

Once again the obsession with the speeding up of the work fills her horizon. Once again the pages of the "Journal" are full of minute calculations: for each new type of work (Simone often changed work and machines), she notes down how many pieces she has made, in how much time, how many she should have made, and how much she has earned. Almost always she fell below the fixed rate, and the salary she earned was a derisory pittance.

However, she was not as tired, right at the start, as before the period of rest. She now could work without becoming overtired. On the first day (February 25) she notes: "If every day I could be only this nervous and tired, I would not be so unhappy in the factory."[27] At the end of the first week: "Much less tired than I had feared I would be. Even moments of euphoria at my machines, such as I had not had even at Montana (delayed effect!). But the question of food still remains an anguishing one."[28]

This week and the next the most irritable foreman and machine-setter, from whose reprimands she had suffered in January, was not there, and Jacquot had replaced him. (Jacquot was ordinarily a worker, but on occasion a foreman and machine-setter.) This proved to be an "indescribable relief" for Simone. She speaks more than once of Jacquot's kindness; he would give her advice quietly and fix the machine, as much as he could, when something went wrong.

However, after the first week, the headaches began again. On Wednesday of the second week (March 6), for the first time since she had resumed work, she felt "really crushed by fatigue, just as I was before leaving for Montana"; she had the feeling "of again beginning to slide into the state of a beast of burden."[29] The next day her fatigue caused her to make some mistakes in her work and even "dear little Jacquot" became impatient, though only for a short time.[30] Afterward, she was terribly afraid of making mistakes. At the end of this second week she was glad to learn that she was being laid off for about two weeks.

It was certainly during these days of leisure that she wrote to her friend Nicolas Lazarévitch. A draft of this letter (or a copy made by her) has been found.

"Dear Nicolas,

"It's been a long time since I gave you a sign of life. The reason is that I have been able, thanks to Boris, to realize a plan that has preoccupied me for years and that you would certainly understand: to work in a factory. I have been hired as a shearing-machine operator (that is, a worker on the power presses) in a factory that manufactures electrical equipment and is owned by a company whose managing director, a man with a broad and very understanding attitude, has good relations with Boris. I must admit that I have not been up to it; I caught cold, I had anemia, and I had to take a rest; but I have been back for three weeks. I have understood a lot of things which before this I could only guess at, I have corrected some false ideas, I have made many observations, some discouraging and others quite comforting. But I have not yet done more than catch a glimpse of what I am particularly interested in, that is, getting a clearer idea of a factory's organization.

"I have wanted many times to write to you, all the more since you are one of the few comrades capable of understanding and sympathy in regard to this sort of experience; I have always been prevented by fatigue. We work at piece rates, the rates are very tough, as is normal in a period of economic crisis; nothing in my past life has prepared me for this sort of effort, and shearing is, I think, one of the hardest jobs that the women do. I am still far from reaching the fixed rates, which, besides, are very often almost impossible to attain, even for the good workers, since the timing is not based on common sense, yet there is an average that I should reach and haven't as yet; I have even greater difficulty because since I am here first of all to observe and understand,

I cannot produce this mental void inside me, this absence of thought indispensable to the slaves of modern machinery.

"Before I went into this factory, I had finished a long essay that *Critique* will soon publish (and it will probably be its last issue). . . .

"I attended a discussion of the *R.P.* [*La Révolution prolétarienne*] on the C.G.T.'s project and was shocked to see that nobody even questioned the very principle behind the project, that is, of an economy directed by a central power that manipulates the working masses as it wishes.

"I forgot to tell you, in connection with my factory, that since I have been here not *one single time* have I heard anyone talk about social problems, neither about the trade unions nor the parties. In the canteen, where I eat sometimes, I have seen only a few newspapers, all bourgeois. And yet it seems to me the management is very liberal. Only once was there a small incident: someone at the factory door had handed out some leaflets about the Citroën affair signed 'The trade union section of the factory.' All of the women and most of the men workers took these leaflets with visible satisfaction, the satisfaction that slaves always get from a piece of bravado without any risks. But there was nothing else. . . . I asked a worker if there really was a trade union section in the factory; all I got in reply was a shrug of his shoulders and a knowing smile. They complain about the fixed rates, the lack of work, and many other things; but these are complaints, and that is all. As for the idea of resistance, no matter how faint, that never occurs to anyone. Yet, as regards the fixed rates, there should be some way of defending oneself to some small degree, even without the trade union, just with a little cunning and above all solidarity; but solidarity is largely lacking. . . ."

It was perhaps also during this week of rest that she wrote to one of her former students at Le Puy, a girl to whom she had already written several times the year before.* Simone was amazed that this student knew she was working in a factory—she had only told a few people—and asked her not to say anything about it. She warned her against the possible temptation of imitating her, describing the brutalizing fatigue and telling her that in the factory one lives "in perpetual humiliating subordination, forever at the orders of foremen." "Nevertheless, and although I suffer from it all, I am more glad than I can say to be where I am. I have wanted it for I don't know how many years. . . . Above all, I feel I have escaped from a world of abstractions to find myself among real men—some good and some bad, but with real goodness or badness. Goodness especially, when it exists in a factory, is something real; because the least act of kindness . . . calls for a victory over fatigue and the

*See pp. 200–202, 211–213, 217.

obsession with pay. . . . And thought, too, calls for an almost miraculous effort of rising above the conditions of one's life. . . . Apart from all that, I find the machines themselves highly attractive and interesting. I should add that I am in the factory chiefly to inform myself on a certain number of very definite points with which I am concerned . . ."

The greater part of the letter is devoted to affectionate and reasonable advice. Simone was worried about her young friend's inclinations. "Your letter dismayed me. If the knowledge of as many sensations as possible continues to be your main objective—as a passing phase it is normal at your age—you won't get far. . . . There are people who have lived by and for sensations; André Gide is an example. They really are the dupes of life. . . . For the reality of life is not sensation but activity —I mean activity both in thought and in action. People who live by sensations are parasites, both materially and morally, in relation to those who work and create. . . . I must add that the latter, who don't seek sensations, experience in fact much livelier, profounder, less artificial and truer ones than those who seek them. Finally, as far as I am concerned, the cultivation of sensations implies an egoism that revolts me. . . .

"As regards love, I have no advice to give you but at least I have some warnings. Love is a serious thing, and it often means pledging one's own life and also that of another human being, forever. Indeed, it always means that, unless one of the two treats the other as a plaything; and in that case, which is a very common one, love is something odious. . . . I can tell you that when, at your age, and later on too, I was tempted to try to get to know love, I decided not to—telling myself that it was better not to commit my life in a direction impossible to foresee until I was sufficiently mature to know what, in a general way, I wished from life and what I expect from it. . . . I will add that love seems to me to involve an even more terrifying risk than that of blindly pledging one's own existence; I mean the risk, if one is the object of a profound love, of becoming the arbiter of another human existence. My conclusion (which I offer you solely for information), is not that one should avoid love, but that one should not seek it, and above all when one is very young. At that age it is much better not to meet it, I believe. . . . What matters is not to bungle one's life. . . ."[31]

On Monday, March 18, Simone went back to work. Léon, the foreman, whom Jacquot had replaced had returned. Yet in her "Journal" it is not said that he became angry and shouted at her as he did in January. But Simone is still afraid of the mistakes she might make. Still tired, she is constantly surprised at her recourse to daydreaming, which slows up her work. On Wednesday, forbidding herself to think, she finally manages to work a little faster but with "bitterness in her heart."[32] For a few days she attains, it seems to her, quite a fast tempo ("uninterrupted tempo"). But on March 27 she has so violent a headache that every movement hurts her. On the twenty-ninth she writes:[33] "They have left me complete freedom—they treat me like someone condemned to death," and one of her fellow workers says to her, "Maybe you'll have to look for work? Poor Simone!" So it seems that her being laid off has been decided on.

Who had decided it? Was it Simone herself? It is quite possible. She could have wanted to leave Alsthom for at least two reasons: first of all, to extend the scope of her experience by working elsewhere, and, secondly, to put herself even more authentically in the position of a worker by getting hired through her own efforts in a factory where no one would protect her and nobody would really know her. On the other hand, it is also possible that since she generally worked too slowly, since she "muffed the goodies,"* the foreman of her workshop or the other foremen thought they could no longer keep her without amazing the other workers. Each worker can see quite well and minutely how the other worker performs.

An accident on the job was perhaps the occasion for her quitting the factory. On Wednesday, April 2, the last day on which her "Journal" speaks of her work at Alsthom, she notes: "I scraped my hands (a bad cut)."[34] A certificate issued by an insurance company on April 5 affirms that she was injured on the job and that the doctor of the Alsthom Company treated her.

After April 5, she no longer returned to work at Alsthom. The certificate of service she received states that she had worked at Alsthom from December 4, 1934, to April 5, 1935.

Having become an unemployed worker or regarding herself as such, Simone began looking for work. She went first of all to Issy and Malakoff; then she looked for work in Saint-Cloud. In the course of her peregrinations she met two workers (metal fitters who were also looking for work), with whom she had a conversation—"extraordinarily free, easygoing, at some level above the miseries of existence which are the predominant preoccupation of the slaves, above all the women."[35] She notes: "Total feeling of comradeship. For the first time in my life, in short. No barrier, either in the class difference (since it is suppressed), or sexual difference. Miraculous."[36] No doubt this was one of the rare moments of happiness that her condition as a worker procured for her.

On another day, standing in the rain, she spoke to a woman worker who told her that she had let her thirteen-year-old son remain in school. "If he doesn't go to school, what will he become? A martyr like us."[37]

She landed a job quite soon. Someone, perhaps Souvarine, told her about the J. J. Carnaud et Forges de Basse-Indre factory at Boulogne-

---

*It was said that "the goodies were muffed" when one's salary, calculated on the basis of the number of pieces finished, was lower than the minimum salary.

Billancourt, describing it as a "nice little shop." She applied for a job there and went to work on Tuesday, April 11.

From the very first day, she realized that the nice little shop was actually a very large shop, and she considered it "a filthy, a very filthy workshop."[38] When she got to the personnel office, although she was happy despite her fears and "grateful to the shop as an unemployed worker who has finally found a berth," she saw five or six workers whose dejected aspect struck her. Most of them had already worked in this factory and had come back, apparently because they couldn't find work elsewhere. Simone questioned them; they did not tell her very much. She finally realized that this factory "is a jail (frantic speedup, a profusion of cut fingers, layoffs without the slightest twinge of conscience)."[39] They put her in a workshop where for the first time she saw a conveyor belt, which upset her very much. She was not assigned to the belt but to a stamping press. Working much harder than at Alsthom, she managed to turn out four hundred pieces an hour. But at four o'clock in the afternoon, the foreman—"a handsome fellow with an affable manner and voice"—came to tell her politely, "If you don't make eight hundred, I can't keep you on the job. If you make eight hundred in the two hours that are left, I would *agree perhaps* to keep you on the job. Some of these workers do twelve hundred pieces." Absolutely enraged, Simone worked as hard as she could and managed to do about six hundred pieces an hour. At five-thirty the foreman said to her, "That is not enough." He then told her to set out the pieces for another worker, who "did not say a word or give her a smile of greeting." At six o'clock, "gripped by a concentrated, cold fury," she sought out the factory manager and asked him whether she should return the next day. He replied, "Come back anyway, we'll see. But you have to work faster." In the dressing room Simone was amazed at seeing the other women workers gossiping and chattering, not seeming to be as angry as she. She walked on foot all the way to the Seine and sat down on a stone wall, gloomy, dejected, exhausted. She wondered whether, if she were condemned to such a life, she would be able to cross the Seine every day without throwing herself into it.[40]

The next morning they put her to work on the same machine. Desperately summoning up all her strength, she managed to make about six hundred and fifty pieces an hour. No doubt they still thought that too little because they put her on another machine where one had only to pass through thin metal bands "at top speed," being careful not to put in two at a time. Yet soon after she did put in two, since the bands were stuck together, and that stopped the machine, which had to be set again. The second time she did this they put her back on the first machine. Then, a moment later, they sent her to another workshop, the paint shop, a "small, quiet corner," where the workers didn't seem so harassed or concerned (whereas in the first workshop the workers did not dare raise their eyes from their work or speak to each other, which might mean the waste of a second). "I never would have thought that from one corner to another in the same shop there could be such a great difference."[41]

That evening she went home on a streetcar with a woman who worked at the conveyor belt. She told Simone that after some time, even just a year, a person no longer suffers from it. Simone thought that this "was the lowest stage of degradation." The woman explained how she and her fellow workers had let themselves be reduced to this slavery: "Five or six years ago," she said, "we could get seventy francs a day, and for seventy francs we'd have put up with anything, we would have croaked."[42]

It was in a letter to Souvarine, written the same night, that Simone tells this story. Since the story might trouble Souvarine, in order to reassure him, she told him that she hoped to remain all next week in the "quiet little corner."

As to the upshot of her experiences in this factory we have not much information, since the "Journal" is silent about it after the second day. Perhaps she was too tired all the time she spent there to be able to write in her journal. We only know that she stayed less than a month. She was fired on May 7.

When she was told that she was fired, she was not given any explanation. She returned at quitting time and asked the foreman of the shop why she had been fired. He answered, "I don't have to account to you for anything." On the work certificate they gave her they had written that she had been employed as a "packer."

After a few days spent in "the sinister prostration produced by my headaches," she again went looking for work. This time, it was harder and took much longer to find a job. Since she was not earning anything, still lived on her last pay, and didn't want to ask her parents for anything, the problem of eating soon arose.

She went the rounds of the factories—Renault at Boulogne-Billancourt, Luchaire at Saint-Ouen, Langlois at Ménilmontant, Salmson, Caudron, and Gévelot. Everywhere there were no jobs, or, rather, some of the workers who were waiting at the gate like her were hired but not she. She also went to Issy and Saint-Denis. The second time she traveled to Saint-Denis, she noted: "Painful to walk so much when one hasn't eaten. . . ."[43] During the third week of her search for a job she decided to spend only three francs and fifty centimes a day, transportation included. "Hunger becomes a permanent feeling. Is it more or less painful than working and eating? Unresolved problem. . . . Yes, all in all, more painful."[44]

She spoke with the unemployed workers who like her waited in front of the factories. Sometimes she would travel for some distance with one of them. Mme. Weil remembers that she had taken an imprudent walk on the deserted quays (the quays lower down along the river), with a worker who soon made certain proposals to her. He saw that he had made a mistake and did not insist. But she had given him her address. Two days later, very early in the morning, someone knocked at her door. She thought that perhaps it was he but this time she was afraid and did not open the door.[45]

I think that it was during this period of hunger but also relative leisure that she wrote her "Reply to Alain's Letter," part of which was published in *Sur la science.*[46]

In this letter she looked forward to "a thorough study of the instruments of labor, no longer from the technical point of view . . . but from the point of view of their relation to man and to human thought." She thought in fact that the liberation of the worker must be accomplished in the work itself, and that the work, in order to become that of a free man, must be pervaded by thought, invention, and judgment. One must therefore find machines of a different kind from those that now exist, or in any case make a new study and appraisal of those that exist, considering them not only in terms of their efficiency but also in terms of how much thought they permit or demand of the worker.

I had returned from Leysin in May. Simone asked me, since I lived near Saint-Denis, to go and see whether I could find some work there for her. I went but could not find anything.

I visited her parents one day—it was June 5, according to the "Factory Journal." I don't recollect if I knew I would meet her there or if I met her by chance. She had the intention of going again to apply for a job at Renault's and borrowed some makeup from me. In the waiting lines at the Renault gate she had heard it said that the man doing the hiring was swayed by the appearance of the women workers and preferably took on those who were pretty. For once, she wanted to be pretty. I put some rouge on her lips and rose-colored makeup on her cheeks; she was transformed. One saw how she could have looked if she had taken the slightest trouble to fix herself up. She asked me to accompany her to the Renault plant. This time, the clerk hired her without any difficulty.

The next morning, Simone left at an early hour for the factory, even though her work would not begin until two-thirty in the afternoon. (At Renault's, she was on the shift that worked from two-thirty in the afternoon to ten at night.) She wanted to look around before going to work. In the early-morning subway she was pale with apprehension. "If I have ever been frightened, it was on that day. I was thinking all the time of the shop filled with machine presses, the ten hours a day, and a rough foreman, and cut fingers, and the heat and my headaches. . . ." When she got to workshop 21, she felt that her determination was shaken. "But at least there are no presses—what luck!"[47]

In fact she worked on a milling machine. "When, three months earlier, I had heard someone tell a story about a milling cutter which had crossed a worker's hand, I had said to myself that with such a picture in my memory it would never be easy for me to work on a milling cutter: Yet, in this respect, I never had to overcome any fear at any moment."[48]

It seems that she did much better on the new machine than she had done on the presses. If at the end of the first two days she was exhausted, later on, for about twelve days, she observed that she was not tired, or not too much. Only on June 19[49] she was again very tired, and on the twentieth she notes: "I go to the shop with an excessively painful feeling; each step costs me (morally, on my way home it is physically). I am in that state of semibewilderment in which I am the designated victim for any sort of hard blow. . . ."[50] Actually, after only a moment, she has a bad accident; she cuts the end of her thumb. She is cared for in the infirmary and then goes back to work. The next morning she is in pain when she goes to the factory, but this time it is a pain that is more physical than moral. "Once again this feeling of 'sticking it out again today . . .' as at Alsthom. Today it comes to fifteen days that I am working here; and I tell myself that no doubt I cannot take it more than fifteen days. . . ."[51]

Her contract of employment has a clause that states that the trial period lasts one month. So she could think that at the end of a month she would be discharged for being too slow. Yet she would be kept on, which perhaps proves that she had made progress or that her new work suited her better. Leclerc, the foreman on the job, seems all in all to have been quite understanding and human.

On June 21 and the days after that, she encountered some difficulties due to the lack of boxes. There were not enough boxes in which to put the finished pieces; the workers would sometimes steal them from each other. Simone would often roam about in search of a box, which made her waste time. Wasting time meant both diminished output and wages.

She passed alternately from utter exhaustion to gaiety. On the twenty-first, returning from work, she fell asleep on the subway and found it painful to walk. "A distinct act of will for each step."[52] But after she got home (that evening, as an exception, she went to rue Auguste-Comte), she felt very gay and read until two in the morning. The next day, having come back from work without falling asleep in the subway and having felt that she still had some strength for walking, she notes: "Tired, though. But all in all happy. . . ."[53]

On the twenty-fifth and twenty-sixth she had to return to the infirmary. She had driven a metal shaving into her hand and the hand had become swollen. Was it then that she refused to follow the treatment ordered by the factory's doctor? Mme. Weil remembered this refusal and said that the doctor had been astonished that a worker dared to oppose him.

It was probably on the twenty-seventh that she had a strange emotion when getting on the bus.

"How is this that I, a slave, can get on this bus, use it by paying my twelve sous in the same way as anyone? What an extraordinary favor! If they had brutally forced me to get off . . . I think that it would have seemed completely natural to me. Slavery has made me completely lose the feeling of having rights. It seems to me a favor to have moments when I have nothing to bear in terms of human brutality. These moments are like the smiles of heaven, a chance gift. Let us hope that I keep this state of mind, which is so reasonable."[54]

One does not find anything about her work between June 27 and July 4. Perhaps the abscess on her hand gave her a few days of rest. She is back at work again on Thursday, July 4. "Did not return to my milling machine, thank heavens!" She is put to work on a small machine "that trims the grooves cut in screws."[55]

The next morning she is given a leave ("what happiness!"). In the morning, before going to work, she had felt utterly exhausted. "A headache, exhaustion (also anxiety, which does not help matters . . .). No more than three weeks! Yes, but three weeks means countless times a day! And I no longer have courage except for one day, one single day. And again, gritting one's teeth with the courage of despair."[56] Had she decided to stop working at the end of July? In any event she would hold on longer and would work again in August.

On the following week, from July 7 to 12, it is clear that she is again at work on the milling machine. She manages on Wednesday to achieve an "uninterrupted rhythm." But on Thursday "shattered, crushed by the effort of the day before," she goes very slowly.[57]

On Saturday, July 13, a day of rest, she attends a meeting of the militants associated with *La Révolution prolétarienne*. "Louzon did not recognize me. He says that my face looks different. 'You look tougher.' "[58]

On Wednesday, July 17, she notes: "Returned. Weather cold. Less suffering (moral) than I had feared. I find it easy to put on the yoke . . ."[59] But at the end of the week, on Saturday, she writes: "Violent headaches—state of distress. In the afternoon, better (but cried at B.'s house . . .)."[60] So she had gone to see Boris Souvarine and had not been able to conceal her distress.

The next week her milling machine broke down more than once and earned her some tongue-lashings from the machine-setters. After a reprimand from one of them on Wednesday morning, she writes: "This episode froze my heart for some time, because all I asked was to think of him as a comrade . . ."[61]

The same day, a moment later, she learned that she would be paid that day and not the next one, as she had thought. This makes her very happy. "I won't have to go without eating . . . Also, at noon, I won't have to draw back from anything (pack of cigaretes, pudding)."[62]

On Thursday, "Painful morning. My legs were hurting. I'm fed up, fed up . . ." However, about noon, not wanting "to end up with a bad conscience," she takes "herself in hand."[63]

But the next day she notes: "dizziness, fits of vertigo—work without thinking."[64] She really feels for about two or two and a half hours that she is about to faint. In the end, she decides to go slower and feels better.

On the next Monday (July 29) an order given by the "machine-setter with glasses" in a tone of unquestioned authority, and which she obeys without saying a word, gives rise in her, when she leaves work, "to a tide of anger and bitterness that in the course of such an existence is always there at the bottom of one's feelings."[65]

On the same day she writes: "It is this evening or tomorrow that I must escape."[66] So it really appears that she had thought of quitting work on July 29 or 30. Yet she was still working on Wednesday and again on Monday, August 5, and the following days.

On Monday, August 5: "Return infinitely more painful than I could have believed. The days seem an eternity to me. Heat . . . Headache . . . This is the 'cushy job'; one must work fast, and I can't manage it. . . . The feeling of being crushed, bitterness of degrading work, disgust. Also the fear, always, of jamming the milling machine."[67] However, it is on the occasion of the feared accident, the jamming of the milling machine, that she gains a precious victory. "I managed for the first time to change the cutter myself, without any help, and Philippe said that it was right in the center. A victory, even better than working fast. I also learned, after another bad experience, to adjust the screw of the vise and the handle myself."[68]

The next day, Tuesday, she thought she was going to faint again—the shop was so hot and the air so stifling.[69]

The "Factory Journal" also mentions work on Wednesday and Thursday. After this, there is no more mention of work at Renault's. If the work certificate which was given her on August 23 states that she worked at the Renault plant from June 6 to August 22, 1935, a letter she wrote to me in the month of August would seem to indicate that she stopped working before the National Conference of the Alliance against War, which was held at Saint-Denis on August 10 and 11, 1935.

Immediately after being freed from work, she drew up a balance sheet of her experience.

"What did I gain from this experience? The feeling that I do not possess any right, whatever it might be, to anything whatever. . . . The ability to be morally self-sufficient, to live, without feeling inwardly humiliated in my own eyes, in a state of latent and perpetual humiliation; to taste each moment of freedom or comradeship to the full. . . .

"I could have been shattered. I nearly was. . . . I arose each morning with anguish, I went to the factory with dread; I worked like a slave; the noonday interruption was like a laceration; then went home at quarter to six, worried about getting enough sleep (which I never did), and getting up early enough. Time was an intolerable burden. The fear—the dread—of what was to come never ceased oppressing me until Saturday afternoon and Sunday morning. And the object of this fear was the *orders.*"[70]

In a letter to Albertine Thévenon, she would say that there are two factors in industrial slavery: the speedup and the orders.[71] The orders can humiliate you, when they are given in a certain way. But above all they are feared because at each instant they can impose something new and difficult; and the difficult thing that they impose is generally the obligation to attain a certain speed in a new job of work. So one ceaselessly expects and ceaselessly fears a job that can prove difficult or impossible; and the fact that one can always be ordered about, while always living in fear, is a humiliation.

Just as Alain in the war had found that the worst of it was not the danger or physical discomforts but the slavery, so Simone, in the factory, above all suffered from the humiliation. "The capital fact is not the suffering but the humiliation."[72] "The feeling of personal dignity as it has been formed by society is *shattered.* One must forge another kind . . ."[73]

The factory is an army barracks. Simone was not incapable of being amenable in certain circumstances. She had contempt for anyone who could not obey.[74] But she was essentially proud and wanted to know why things were done in a certain way. She suffered from contempt; and her awkwardness exposed her to reprimands and to not being given due consideration in a place where one is chiefly respected for one's skill or physical strength. Besides, she had always had the desire to understand, to decide, to invent, and, finally, to think; and now she had to accept at each instant not thinking and being manipulated by someone else's thought like an object.

It is certain that she suffered more than others would have suffered. This year of factory work was for her a martyrdom. Which does not mean that the observations she made in the course of this experience are not appropriate and correct. Monatte said that he had at first considered her experience with astonishment; he said to himself, "Her judgment cannot be correct, since she suffers much more than the ordinary worker." Yet he ended up thinking that she had seen, in spite of this, more profoundly than one usually sees.

One encounters in the "Journal" some moments of raw anger—("my machine-setter, this young bastard";[75] "I have five thousand of these filthy pieces to make."[76]) And certainly she did not lack the courage to resist, even at the price of going hungry. But she did not want to be discharged. She wanted to put herself in the situation of the worker, who, for example, because she has children, does not dare run the risk of being fired. Furthermore, it was not for herself that she was there but in order to solve problems that were significant for the fate of all of the oppressed. What she would never have tolerated for herself, she was obliged to bear because, for the good of others, she had to know and understand. Moreover, her reaction—and this was a great surprise to her—was not, in general, revolt and anger but submission and docility.

In a letter written to Albertine Thévenon after the end of the year of factory work, she would say: "What working in a factory meant for me personally was as follows. It meant that all the external reasons (which I had previously thought internal), upon which were based my sense of personal dignity, my self-respect, were radically destroyed within two or three weeks by the daily experience of brutal constraint. And don't imagine that this provoked in me any rebellious action. No, on the contrary; it produced the last thing I expected from me—docility. The resigned docility of a beast of burden. It seemed to me that I was born to wait for, and receive, and carry out orders—that I had never done and never would do anything else. I am not proud of this confession. . . . When I was kept away from work by illness, I became fully aware of the degradation into which I was falling, and I swore to myself that I would go on enduring the life until the day when I was able to pull myself together in spite of it. And I kept my word. Slowly and painfully, in and through slavery, I reconquered the sense of my human dignity—a sense that this time relied upon nothing outside myself . . ."[77]

Did she find in this experience what she had sought? Did she learn how the worker can become free in his or her very work? It does not seem so. She certainly concluded—she had already guessed it—that a certain slavery, at present, is tied to the material conditions and the very instruments of work: the machines. "In all the other forms of slavery, the slavery is in the circumstances. Only here it is carried into the work itself."[78] No doubt she had hoped that one might find ways of changing this state of affairs, that one might invent new machines, of a different kind, and a new technique. But she could not clearly see what one ought to do; she saw only the necessity to study certain problems, and the solution was still far away. She wrote, on the subject of the workers: "The class of those who *do not count*—in any situation—in anyone's eyes . . . and who will never count, whatever happens to it (despite the last verse of the first stanza of the "Internationale")."[79] She wrote this as the summation of what she had learned from her experience as a worker.

Her political pessimism was reinforced even more. She no longer believed in either revolution or reform. A little later she would write that reform and revolution are words bereft of any meaning.[80] The same day that she received her work certificate, on August 23, she wrote to Claude Jamet, her old classmate at the Ecole Normale: "The revolution is not possible, because the revolutionary leaders are ineffective dolts. And it is not desirable because they are traitors. Too stupid to win a victory; and if they did win, they would oppress again, as in Russia . . ."

Jamet, on receiving this letter, wrote this comment for himself: "This is what S. Weil thinks. It is sad. Why not hateful? Because it is Simone and she has the right. She, a saint, who gives everything. The heroine of tomorrow, or whenever you wish. A mind that really wants to do everything good for the workers, except to lie . . ."[81]

She had discovered, from her own example, that "an obviously inexorable and invincible oppression does not engender rebellion as an immediate reaction but rather submission."[82] This discovery was to help to reinforce her doubts about the future of liberty. So long as one thinks that oppression automatically engenders rebellion, one is sure that oppression can never last for long. But when one sees that this is not so, one realizes that for liberty there are dark nights that can last very long.

So she had not found, so it seems, what she was looking for: the means for a real liberation of the workers. But she learned certain things about herself and about the human condition in general. She realized that social prestige (the external reasons for which one is esteemed), had more importance, even for herself, than she had thought; that this prestige is of fundamental importance for all human beings; and that when it no longer exists, it is terribly hard not to lose one's sense of dignity. "One always needs, for oneself, some *external* signs of one's own value."[83] She had sworn to reconquer the sense of her dignity as a human being, and she achieved this. But, as she would write later in a letter to the manager of a factory, this feeling had always to be reconquered when she was a worker because time after time the very conditions of a worker's existence destroyed it.[84]

She had learned certain things about herself and human nature. What's more, she had changed. She realized this. If already in January she had written that from now on a certain lightness of heart would no longer be possible for her and her feeling about life was no longer the same,[85] she thought this even more in the following months. "I have lost my gaiety, in this [factory] existence." She adds: "And, nevertheless, I am glad to have lived through it."[86]

This year of sufferings was not without its joys. Simone at times had pleasant moments on the job. She notes them down as objectively as she notes down the painful ones. (If she mentions a painful experience, it is not to complain or to be moved to self-pity; she wants her "Journal" to exist for her as a testimony of what the worker's condition actually is. For the same reason, she did not want to neglect whatever was joyful in it.) Moreover, she would sometimes visit her friends. More than once she went to see Boris Souvarine and Suzanne Aron and also visited Martinet. Souvarine would sometimes come to see her, when she had written him that he could come. She even went to dinner with Detœuf (though only after having left his factory). She visited book shops, bought books (on her meager salary), and read. She went to the exhibition of Italian art. On Easter Sunday (April 21) she went to a church in the hope (which will be disappointed) of hearing the Gregorian chants. During her stay at Montana, a letter tells us that she did some skiing.

The Saint-Denis conference on August 10 and 11 did give her some of the joys of friendship. This conference, which had as its goal the struggle against war, brought together sections of the Socialist party, the "Communist radical section" of Saint-Denis (led by Doriot, an organization of Communist party dissidents), various trade union (among them the United Federation of Teachers) and pacifist organizations, and anarchists. Many of Simone's friends were there; among others, Urbain Thévenon, Pierre Arnaud, Serret, Patri, Collinet, and most of the militants associated with *La Révolution prolétarienne:* Louzon, Chambelland, Yvon, Charbit, Lazarévitch, etc. Simone could not talk with all of them. On the first day she saw Thévenon but could not talk to him because she didn't want to leave Lazarévitch, whom she had not seen for three years; and the next day she could not find him in the large hall where the meeting was being held. It was during the course of this conference that she met Carpentier, whom she was to meet again on the Aragon front one year later during the war in Spain.

Reading her journal, one realizes the interest she has in all human beings. She notes down everything she could learn about the life of her fellow workers, both men and women, and describes their behavior for herself. It is true that this was part of the inquiry that she was making into the workers' condition, yet one can see that she looks around her with a clearsighted sympathy not devoid of humor. One also sees what she usually is so good at concealing: her extreme sensitivity, her need for a benevolent, friendly, and fraternal environment. A simple smile did her inexpressible good. A foreman looks at her as he passes by, no doubt with pity, as she is miserably putting some big bolts in an empty crate and she writes: "Never will I forget this man."[87]

One of the reasons she had wanted to be a worker was certainly that she had thought she would find real human fraternity in the factory. And one of the things that certainly disappointed her was not finding as much fraternity as she had imagined. She will say, when speaking of the factory: "There only one knows what human fraternity is. But there is little, very little. Most often, even the relations between comrades reflects the harshness that dominates everything there."[88]

9

Bourges. The Beginning of the Popular Front (1935-1936)

Some days after having left the factory, Simone wrote to Albertine Thévenon.

"Dear Albertine,

"I hope you're not angry with me. I wanted to write you a long letter.... But I just had been taken on in an industrial jail, and the weight of this existence once again struck down on me. I have been free of it for some days now, but I still feel tired of it. I am going to take a freighter for a trip along the coasts of Spain, for only the sea can wash away all this accumulated fatigue. I will try to write you a longer letter soon."

So she had decided to take a freighter for a trip along the coasts of Spain. She left with her parents; they reached Spain on August 25. They went together to San Sebastián and Santander. She left her parents to take a boat at Pasajes, a small port not far from San Sebastián. They had agreed to meet again at Vigo, where the ship would put into port and to which her parents would travel by train.

The boat was very small and very uncomfortable and the sea was rough. Simone suffered from headaches. On the boat there were a certain number of French students whom she found unbearable and with whom she argued constantly. On the other hand, she enjoyed talking with one of the crew, the fireman. When she reached Vigo, her physical state was so poor that her parents advised her to stay with them, and she consented. She regretted it at times during the following weeks: "When I think I could be sailing!"

Her parents took her with them to Portugal, to Viana do Castelo. They had gone there in 1934 and just above Viana had discovered an admirably situated hotel from which one had a view of the sea, the mouth of a river, and the mountains. Simone found that the hotel was much too good for her and moved into a small pension in a nearby village. Her parents got off at Viana to join her again and took walks with her. According to what Mme. Weil has said, Viana is a charming little village that is completely white. One day, while on the square, they saw a group of musicians arrive who began to play and sing, and they saw men behind some barred windows listening. It was the local jail. These musicians often came to give concerts for the prisoners. Simone asked someone, "Can you give them cigarettes?" And the man replied, "Of course." They then went and bought many cigarettes and gave them to the prisoners.

According to Mme. Weil the place where Simone saw a procession around the fishermen's boats must have been located between Viana do Castelo and Porto. It was there that, as her autobiographical letter to Father Perrin says, she made the first of "three contacts with Christianity that have really counted."

The story she told him is well known. "I had been taken by my parents to Portugal, and while there I left them to go alone to a little village. . . . Being . . . in a wretched state physically, I entered the little Portuguese village, which, alas, was very wretched too, on the very day of the festival of its patron saint. . . . The wives of the fishermen were, in procession, making a tour of all the ships, carrying candles and singing what must certainly be very ancient hymns of a heart-rending sadness. . . . There the conviction was suddenly borne in upon me that Christianity is pre-eminently the religion of slaves, that slaves cannot help belonging to it, and I among others."[1]

She left Portugal with her parents on September 22 and returned to Paris. A few days later she left for Bourges, where she had been appointed professor of philosophy at the girls' lycée. (She had requested the post from the Ministry of Education on May 31.)

Mme. Weil accompanied her to help her find a place to live, but stayed only a few days in Bourges. According to J. Cabaud,[2] Simone lived with Mlle. Alice Angrand, a teacher of English. She certainly had to do her own cooking, for as soon as she returned to Paris Mme. Weil sent her daughter a suitcase in which were packed not only books and linen but also kitchen utensils; and the first letters she wrote her were full of advice on how to prepare certain simple dishes quickly.

In a letter mailed on October 13, Simone tells her mother: "Everything is going well here. I feel more at ease in this town than I have been in the other provincial towns." Actually, her relations with Mlle. Angrand were excellent. And her relations with her colleagues and the administration of the lycée were also generally good during the year at Bourges.

She had about a dozen students in her philosophy class. She also gave a course in Greek to the students in the fifth form. According to statements gathered by Cabaud, it seems that among the students at Bourges there was a little less enthusiasm and veneration for her than among those at Le Puy, Roanne, and even Auxerre. They would sometimes express their disagreement with her ideas; and sometimes they slipped into her desk drawer documents the reading of which, they thought, would not be very pleasant for her—for example, certain conservative or reactionary magazines. In general, however, they liked "little Weil" quite well and took a lively interest in her courses.

In the outlines of the courses that have been found, those that can be dated for the year at Bourges with certainty or great likelihood show that more than ever she offered her students the concrete, living examples to be found in literary works, novels, or poetry. She restricted herself less and less to philosophical abstractions. She referred not only to the great classic writers—Homer, Corneille, Racine, Rousseau, Goethe, and Balzac (*A Village Priest, Beatrice,* and, above all, *Colonel Chabert*), Stendhal, Hugo (*Les Misérables*), Tolstoy (*Resurrection*)—but also to contemporary authors: Valéry, Claudel, Saint-Exupéry (*Night Flight*), Pierre Hamp (*Glück auf!*), Johan Bojer (*The Last Viking*), and Emile Guillaumin (*La Vie d'un simple*).

Her memories of her year of factory work were now mixed up with her philosophical analyses. The name of Mouquet appears in her lecture notes, as well as certain words that she had heard the workers utter. The problem of affliction and humiliation often arises. She writes, for example: "Only the unfortunate have the happiness of knowing the price of human fraternity." (She does not say that only they know human fraternity, but that only they know its price.)

"What makes one experience human value: humiliation, degradation, slavery, sin, and error. Great idea that is at the foundation of the Catholic religion (Pascal)."

She wanted to get her students to understand that a man's misfortune can also come from something he has done that is good and that behaving properly can lead to degradation, at least externally.

"Is it dangerous to do evil but not to do good? Naive."

"Colonel Chabert ... Humility attracts insolence. ... Some fine deeds can plunge one into a situation that is degrading. ..."

In her teaching that year one can hear the sound of a restrained sob. Before this, when she spoke of social problems, the dominant emotion was more one of indignation.

Outside of her classes Simone spent most of her time, as was her habit, in helping those who needed help and searching for everything that could instruct her on the condition of the underprivileged classes.

The purpose of the first letter she wrote from Bourges to her mother (on October 10) was to obtain help for a certain young German refugee whom other refugees from the S.A.P. had tried to persuade to return to Germany. Fortunately for him, he remained in France. Simone had learned that Germany was demanding his extradition.

"My dear Mime,

"Sensational turn of events in the Emil business. The League for the

Rights of Man has informed J. that the German government has asked the French government for his extradition (Emil's). Reason unknown. Besides what he has actually done in Sarre, he says that comrades who have been caught have naturally accused the émigrés of all sorts of crimes. General panic, of course; it is thought that, if he's not handed over, he will be expelled in any case.

"Aside from this, of course, he would be in no danger in Germany!

"The party [obviously, the S.A.P.] continues to ignore him, or at least not to lavish anything but advice on him. They advise him to go to Norway. And it is up to me to supply the money for the journey, that goes without saying. After all, it would have cost as much if he had to be kept here for several months. . . . I beg you to give him 900 francs when he comes (the money for the journey and a small supplement . . .). It's possible that he might think it dangerous to come to the house (I don't know whether he is in hiding). In that case he will telephone to tell where you can meet him. . . ."

In November she wrote again about this refugee:

"Let J. tell you quite calmly everything he has to say about E. [Emil], so that it is all very clear. Then, when you leave him, I authorize you to tell him that in my eyes the party [S.A.P.], which is incarnated in his person, has *no* excuse in this affair. Unless, of course, his revelations change the aspect of the question. But that is hardly possible. Watch out for his sex-appeal* . . . and his blarney. . . ."

Shortly after, Trotsky's son, Léon Sédov, appealed for help for another refugee. Mme. Weil forwarded a letter from the "Crown Prince" to her daughter. "What do you say about this letter from the Crown Prince?" she wrote. "What do you want to do?"

Simone answered: "We cannot let a fellow croak who has had the superhuman physical and moral strength to stand firm for seven years and then escape after that. I've written to him to go and see you. Try to find out exactly to what degree the necessity is urgent and give him between 200 and 500 francs for me (I will return them on my coming trip through Paris). As for you, do what you wish. As for putting the touch on other people, I don't see anyone who is touchable. Let him know that this is a loan. Don't hesitate to go as high as 500 francs for me, if it is absolutely necessary. (Either one belongs to the Salvation Army or one doesn't.)

". . . By the way, any news of 'Papa'?"

Almost at the same time (in the second half of November, it would seem), two young German refugees, Emil's friends, had turned to Simone for help. Simone wrote a short note to her parents:

"Received a letter from two of Emil's pals. An appeal for help. If they come to rue Auguste-Comte, they should be given *good words*, advice

---

*English in the original.

and *sous* (taken from my funds, of course). They say that they wrote to me because they have no other *Ausweg.* That above all the problem of a place to sleep is terribly crucial . . ."

A little later she would ask for news about the "two young fellows." A letter from Mme. Weil written on January 5, 1936, would inform her that they had finally found a place to live, had also gotten work as servants, and were "quite happy."

These examples of Simone's generosity are known to us since she had to write to her parents on these occasions. But there must have been many others of which we have no information. Cabaud points out that at Bourges she was sometimes seen pushing a baby carriage to help certain working-class families and that she lavished care on a disabled beggar whose presence in the local hospital had been mentioned by a colleague.[3]

But during the year at Bourges she also devoted a great deal of her time to trying to increase her knowledge on the conditions of work among the oppressed classes. She was still obsessed by her experience of the previous year. All through the year she would describe it in long letters: a letter to Albertine Thévenon, the draft of a letter to Jules Romains, and a number of letters to an engineer who was the manager of a factory. She still felt a profound bitterness about it, but at the same time was more attracted than ever to factories, as if fascinated and unable to stop thinking about them. She did not give up the dream of a factory that would be the place where one could make contact with real life. Albertine Thévenon had told her in a letter that once, when seeing a factory, she had experienced a feeling of joy—arriving at Saint-Chamond as night was falling, she had suddenly seen a factory lit up inside, in which the machines, with their driving belts and pulleys, cast their shadow through the glass panes; she had the feeling of being at home, for she was the daughter of workers. Simone answered her letter, saying: "What you wrote about the factory went straight to my heart. I felt the same as you, ever since I was a child. That is why I had to go there in the end, and it grieved me, before I went to the factory, that you did not understand my wish. But once you get there, how different it is! As a result, I now see the social problem in this way: what a factory ought to be is something akin to what you felt that day at Saint-Chamond, and what I have so often felt—a place in which one makes a hard, painful, but nevertheless joyful contact with real life. Not the gloomy place it is, where people only obey orders and have all their humanity crushed and are degraded to something lower than the machines."[4]

Thus she wanted to find out how a factory could become this place where one collides joyously, though harshly, with real life. For this reason she wanted to study further the factory's modern techniques and organization.

A cousin of Mlle. Angrand's was the owner and manager of a factory at Vierzon. Simone, Cabaud says,[5] asked Mlle. Angrand to obtain permission for her to visit this factory. The permission was granted; she visited the factory and was guided through it by one of the employees, staying there all afternoon on November 28. She wrote to her mother on the thirtieth: "Thursday, visit to a factory in Vierzon (*very* interesting)."

One of her students was the daughter of M. Magdélénat, the owner and administrator of the Rosières Foundries. In her letter of November 30 Simone informs her mother that on the following Thursday they would come for her in a car to take her to Rosières Foundries. "It is quite different from standing for an hour in the rain in front of the personnel office, and then they deign to tell you, 'Come back tomorrow.' " The fact that they were now so considerate was a bitter reminder of how she had been treated some months earlier.

The headmistress of the lycée, Mme. Laignel, had most likely been instrumental in obtaining the authorization to visit this factory, since she went along with Simone. M. Magdélénat's wife and older son and the wife of a magistrate of Bourges were also with them. Simone wanted to see everything; she questioned everyone with tireless zeal. After the visit, the group went to the office of M. Bernard, an engineer and technical manager of the factory. "Simone Weil immediately began to argue. She simply could not agree that wages should not be the same for everybody. 'If you were allowed to decide the matter,' Bernard asked her, 'what would you do?' 'The first thing I'd do if I had a free hand? I would post the directors' salaries in the factory.' "[6]

She undoubtedly returned to the Rosières Foundries the following week, though this time alone, for in a letter she mailed on December 16 to her mother she says that she has once again seen the technical manager of the foundry.[7] "We talked for two and a half hours. He told me a lot of very interesting things. On my side, I think I opened his eyes to some small matters. But he most likely closed them very tight an hour after I left. . . ."

M. Bernard had started a small magazine for the workers in the plant which was called *Entre nous.* Simone asked him if she could write an article for it. He must have told her that she could send him an article and that he would decide whether it was appropriate and could be published.

She also asked him if he would possibly agree to hire her as a worker in his factory. He must have told her that he did not in principle exclude the possibility of hiring her. As a result, she thought that it would be best not to go back to Rosières, for fear, if one day she should enter the factory as a worker, of being recognized by the workers as someone who knew their boss.

It was no doubt about this time (perhaps on December 8) that Simone moved into a new house. Until then she had lived at 8 avenue d'Orléans; she moved into 7 place Gordaine, in a room that she rented from a milliner. It was a sparsely furnished attic room—an iron bed and a deal table—that looked out over roofs and chimneys. It was heated by a wood-burning stove. The stairway up to it must have been rather steep and in need of repair because Mme. Weil wrote to her daughter: "I want you to pay attention to the stove and try not to stumble on that stairway." And in another letter: "Pay attention to the stove and the stairway! I will put this in every letter." Mme. Weil had gone to Bourges to help her daughter move into the new room.

Cabaud says[8] that the milliner had a brother who would sometimes take books from Simone's room to read. One day he carried off Kierkegaard's *Diary of a Seducer.* The title had probably led him to expect a racy novel. He must have been very disappointed and brought the book back without having read very much of it.

Simone's room was of course in great disorder. She could not get herself to devote to housecleaning the time she could employ at what she regarded as more important work. As usual she left her money lying around on the table and bed. One day her money disappeared. She told a colleague about it and remarked, quite simply, "Whoever took it undoubtedly needed it."[9]

Before the Christmas vacations she sent the engineer at the Rosières plant the article she wanted to publish in *Entre nous.* It was called "An Appeal to the Workers at Rosières."[10] She invited the workers to write to her and to tell her what they experienced in the factory: whether they suffered from the monotony of the work, the necessity to work fast, the necessity of obeying their foremen's orders; whether or not they were interested in their jobs; whether or not they felt surrounded by a fraternal atmosphere; and when they left the factory, whether they felt gay or exhausted, etc. The letters she asked them to write to her were not to be signed, and she even promised them that in using the information she found in these letters she would arrange it so that it would be impossible to guess who the writers were.

Her health was a source of worry to her parents and certainly to her, too. During her first days at Bourges she had a cough. The cough soon disappeared, but her headaches persisted. While making an effort to reassure her parents ("Everything goes well, even very well, extraordinarily well, I must tell you, so that you will consent to believe that things are going pretty well"), she thought of going for a rest during the Christmas holidays either in Montana with Mme. de Jager or "in Catalonia" (that is, the Catalonian part of the Pyrenees).

At the end of November she received a letter from Madeleine Fouilloux, her best student at Auxerre, with whom she had remained in touch. It was perhaps from this letter that she learned that it would be possible for her and Madeleine Fouilloux to be engaged as *au pair* teachers in a children's boarding school at Font-Romeu during the end of the year holidays. She decided to spend her leave at Font-Romeu under these conditions with Madeleine Fouilloux. (Her generosity forced her to be economical, and she felt that the climate of Font-Romeu, at 5,400 feet in the mountains, would be good for her.)

Mme. Weil sent her a suitcase containing ski clothes, linen, warm slippers, and above all a great many sweaters. She also sent a medical certificate issued by Louis Ramond, a doctor at the Laënnec Hospital, a fine doctor whom Simone had had to consult and whom she again consulted afterward. This certificate permitted Simone to extend her holiday a little. (It would have even permitted her to take three weeks, but she was satisfied with about two.)

It was most likely during this Christmas holiday that she wrote the long letter to Albertine Thévenon from which we have quoted some passages. It was also perhaps at this time that she wrote the draft of a letter to Jules Romains, the novelist, in which she describes both the beauty and inhumanity of factory work. She used this description, reworking it somewhat, in an article entitled "An Experience of Factory Life," which she wrote in Marseilles in 1941.[11]

On January 8 she left Font-Romeu, stopped over for the night at Toulouse, and returned to Bourges. On her return, the reply of the Rosières' engineer was waiting for her. He refused to publish her "Appeal to the Workers at Rosières," since in his opinion this open letter was of such a nature as to excite class feelings. It is true that Simone had spoken at length to the workers of their sufferings, quite remorselessly, giving them to understand that their condition was a misfortune, on the presumption that they would not dare to complain and were constrained to hide their real feelings.

She then felt that there was not much chance of her being hired at this factory. So she felt freer about returning to Rosières to question M. Bernard again, for she no longer feared being recognized by the workers.

She wrote in reply to the engineer on January 13,[12] defending to some extent what she had written. She said, among other things, that the spirit that animated this piece of writing was "purely and simply the Christian spirit." She also said that to give expression from time to time to class feeling would not excite it but instead would modify and soften the bitterness.

She had hoped with all her heart, by collaborating with *Entre nous*, to be able to provide moral support for the workers at the Rosières Foundries, helping them to preserve or rediscover their sense of dignity. She thought that her experience during the last year would give her the ability to write "in such a way as to alleviate a little the weight of humiliations that life inflicts every day upon the workers. . . ." (Yet one might wonder whether the workers would have felt their humiliation alleviated at seeing themselves regarded as so completely wretched and unfortunate. This is a difficult problem. One runs the risk of wounding people by ignoring their misery, and one also runs the risk of wounding them even more by speaking of it with too much pity.) She ended her letters with these words: "If you are no longer disposed to hire me, if M. Magdélénat is against it, I will certainly come to Rosières. . . ."

On January 31, having received a reply from M. Bernard that led her to believe she would certainly not be hired, she wrote and told him that she would come to see him on Friday, February 14. In the meantime she spoke to him again of her experience in the factory, saying: "It is very difficult to judge from above, and it is very difficult to act from below. That, I believe, is in general one of the essential causes of human misery. And that is why I myself wanted to go right to the bottom and will perhaps return there. And that is why I so much want to be able to collaborate with some company, from below, with the man who directs it. . . . It is encouraging for me, who have chosen, deliberately and almost without hope, to adopt the point of view of those at the bottom, to be able to talk frankly with a man like you."[13] As one can see, she felt neither hostility (on a personal level), nor disdain, but rather esteem and sympathy for M. Bernard; and she hoped to collaborate "from below" with the manager of a factory.

So she went on February 14 to see M. Bernard, though afterward she had the impression that she had not been able to make herself understood. She wrote to him again on March 3.[14] In this letter, she continues to tell him about her experiences and the lessons that could be drawn from them. She suggests that there be started in the factory an exchange of views between the workers and their bosses, the workers proposing improvements and the bosses and managers possibly explaining why these ameliorations were difficult or even impossible to put into effect. (This is what would now be called arbitration or workers' participation.)

She wrote again on March 16.[15] She again explained her position to M. Bernard, so that everything might be clear between them and he make no mistake as to her feelings and stand in social and political matters. "I long with all my heart for the most radical possible transformation of the present regime in the direction of a greater equality. . . . I do not at all believe that what is nowadays called revolution can bring this about. After a so-called working-class revolution, just as much as before it, the workers at R. will go on obeying passively—so long as the system of production is based on passive obedience. Whether the manager at R. takes orders from a managing director who represents a few capitalists or from a so-called Socialist 'State Trust' makes no difference, except that in the first case the factory is not in the same hands as the police, the army, the prisons, etc., and in the second case it is. The inequality . . . is therefore not lessened but accentuated.

". . . The problem as I see it, quite independently of the political regime, is to progress from total subordination to a certain mixture of subordination and cooperation, with complete cooperation as the ideal . . ."

After this she said something that should have shown M. Bernard what her attitude toward the sit-in strikes of June 1936 would be:

"When the victims of social oppression do in fact revolt, they have my sympathy, though unmixed with any hope. . . . Nevertheless, I have absolutely no desire to stir up a spirit of revolt—not so much in the interests of social order but because I am concerned for the moral interests of the oppressed. . . . If they rebel at one moment, they will fall on their knees the moment after. . . . The spirit I want to encourage is precisely that spirit of collaboration for which you argue in the criticism of my article."

She was not without pity for the person to whom she was trying to communicate her experience and who she felt was at times shaken by her observations. "I feel a certain guilt about you, because in the event, which is after all a likely one, of our discussions coming to nothing, all I shall have done will be to pass on to you some painful preoccupations. This thought distresses me. You are a relatively happy man, and happiness in my eyes is precious and worthy of respect. I do not want to spread around me to no purpose the indelible bitterness with which my experience has left me."

M. Bernard once again asked Simone to come and see him at the Rosières plant. But the Easter holidays were fast approaching. So she put off her visit until her return from the holidays. Speaking of Easter, she said to him: "Don't imagine that my social preoccupations destroy all my joy in life. At this time of the year, above all, I never forget that 'Christ is risen.' (Metaphorically speaking, of course.)"[16]

Simone also wanted to become more deeply conversant with the life of the farmers. She had become friendly with one of her colleagues, Mme. Coulomb, and also her husband. She often took long walks with them. "One day she begged a peasant to let her drive his plow, which she immediately overturned. The peasant was furious. Simone Weil offered him a cigarette, which he refused; she and the Coulombs left, and she didn't recover her usual cheery mood for some time."[17]

Mme. Coulomb had a pupil whose parents, M. and Mme. Belleville, were farmers. They had a small farm at Carron de Gron near Baugy in the Cher region where they did everything themselves: planting, haymaking, harvesting, and raising livestock. Simone asked them if she could come to visit them and work with them. They told her she could come whenever she wished.

She arrived one morning in March. (It was perhaps March 6 because Mme. Weil, in a letter of March 5, mentions that Simone will spend the next day working in the fields.) It was still quite cold. She had not told them she was coming, for she was afraid that they might change the house's routine on her account. After drinking a cup of coffee without sugar, she asked them to put her to work. They assigned her to digging up the beet roots and then cutting them off the stalks, which was very hard work for a woman. After that she prepared the fodder for the cows, piled up the manure, drew water for the trough. She also tried to milk the cows, but admitted that this was too hard for her. Of course she wanted to be allowed to try to plow; she was determined to learn how to do it. The Bellevilles found that she was not clumsy and quickly adapted herself to everything, but of course she lacked practice.[18]

She helped Mme. Belleville prepare the noonday meal, insisting on this so that she could watch her and prevent her from adding anything to their everyday fare. "She ate very little," the family said. "But what a lot of questions! How do you manage? How much do you make? Do you think you are happy?" She asked them to sum up "their desires," a question that embarrassed them.[19]

She returned more than once to Carron de Gron during the month of March. She asked the family if she could live with them, if necessary even paying for her meals and lodgings. "But she had one condition: that she would be free at any hour of the day or night to go out and mingle with the lowest classes. They refused. 'Anyone who knew the country would know that that was impossible,' they said. 'After she left, life would have been impossible for us.' "[20]

The Bellevilles, who were certainly very fine people, nevertheless found Simone hard to take, and at the end of about a month Mme. Belleville went to see M. Coulomb at Bourges. "She found it very hard to come to the point: she was very sorry, but she did not want to have Mlle. Weil any longer. She never washed her hands before milking the cows; she never changed her clothes; and, worst of all, in the fields she never stopped talking about the future martyrdom of the Jews, poverty, deportations, and about the terrible war she foresaw in the near future. When they offered her a fine cream cheese, she pushed it away, saying that the little Indochinese were hungry." It is difficult to know whether these explanations are actually those Mme. Belleville gave at that time to M. Coulomb, or whether later on she believed she recalled all this, unconsciously mixing together in her memories what she had learned about Simone and the actual fate of the Jews during the war. It is quite amazing that Simone spoke so much about the Jews' coming martyrdom; at this time she never mentioned it. And one wonders whether she also said at this time: "The important thing is to be nothing. Those who do not believe are closer to the truth than those who believe. Everything is a lie."[21] As for not washing her hands before milking the cows, it is quite likely that, if she did it this way, it was because she thought that

that was how peasants behaved and was afraid to humiliate them by asking to wash her hands.

Mme. Belleville has written (again to Cabaud): "My husband and I used to say: the poor young girl, so much study has driven her out of her wits; and we were sorry for her; while really it was we who were out of our depth. But what could we do? All the intellectuals we knew put barriers between themselves and the peasants. Simone Weil threw down these barriers and put herself on our level."[22] It seems apparent that this excellent woman, in her humility, felt a sense of shame when she found out who Simone Weil was. But her sentiments and those of her husband are quite understandable. It seemed to them that Simone lacked common sense. And Simone herself, when she spoke later about the madness of love, would have readily agreed that the search for justice can drag one beyond what is reasonable. Yet, just as she did when she addressed the workers of the Rosières factory in her "appeal," there could have been some ineptness in the way she spoke to those she wanted to help. No doubt she let the Bellevilles see that she considered them poor and wretched. ("What I want is to live the life of the poor," she had said to them, "to share their work, live with their troubles, eat at their table."[23]) And certainly this way of looking at them did not please them. As Cabaud says: "They were small peasants who worked hard all day long and who were happy in their way. On the other hand, they did not believe they could do anything about the troubles of the world, and Simone Weil's lectures made them feel 'neurasthenic.' "[24]

So Simone did not return to Carron de Gron at the end of March or the beginning of April. But, according to Mlle. Ouvrard, one of her colleagues, she "worked as a servant girl at Levet—a small town about twenty kilometers south of Bourges—on a farm whose owners had connections with the Young Social Groups."

André Weil, who was then a professor at the University of Strasbourg, told his sister in February, so it seems, that she could apply for a grant from the Rockefeller Foundation for the school year 1936–1937. Simone was tempted by this suggestion. She was very tired; she admitted this to her parents in February and March, and at the end of March she wrote to M. Bernard that she barely had the strength to teach her class.[25] A letter—or rather the draft of a letter that she wrote during the year at Bourges, exactly when I don't know—shows us that she felt her capacity for work had been diminishing progressively for several years, and this greatly troubled her. She put no value on living for its own sake but in order to do certain things, and she felt haunted and dogged by time. Here is what she says in this draft of a letter:

"For some years now I have seen my capacity for work diminish progressively due to a bad physical condition. Today it is as it were nil, to the point that I have resolved to take a year's rest at the end of the school year. If I manage to build up the physical resources that would permit me to work and live with the intensity I require, I hope that I will regain a little of all the time I have so deplorably lost."

So it is understandable that she had accepted the idea of applying for a Rockefeller Foundation grant or some other type of grant. Her mother, who had looked into the matter, had learned that there were other grants Simone could obtain. Simone wrote to her on March 1:

"I would like you to get more information about the Rockefeller grant. Then I may decide to go and see Fauconnet [professor of sociology at the Sorbonne]. After all, I am working on technical and economic problems, isn't that true? They could perhaps send me to the Tennessee Valley. . . . If I went to America with André, that could be interesting. Only, what about you. . . .

"This week my headaches weren't so bad, not as bad as at other times. Now things are better for me. . . .

"Could you ask the Alexandres under what conditions one requests a year's leave for reasons of health? Perhaps it can be done at the end of October?

"Thanks infinitely for the provisions and many, many sweet kisses to both of you."

(Simone had most likely written these last, especially tender words because her mother's last letters had filled her with pity for her. At times Mme. Weil was almost desperate when she had no news from her. Simone had some difficulty in writing letters, even to her family, and furthermore, during this second trimester of the school year, as we have seen, she was overwhelmed with fatigue. Her letters had also been infrequent in January and February. It is true that she sometimes went to Paris on Thursday and Friday, which to some extent explains the infrequency of her letters.)

Going off and on to Paris, she must have told one of her friends the projects she had mapped out for herself for the school year 1936–1937. This friend must have expressed dismay at the "schemes" she thought she could resort to. I imagine that it was in these circumstances that she wrote him this poignant letter:

"The other day I considerably shocked and no doubt surprised you even more by my uncertainties concerning the program for the coming year—and you were quite right, of course. After hesitating, I have decided to mention this again so that you may understand everything.

"My situation is the following. I am not up to doing anything, whatever it might be, and this goes for all kinds of work. I cannot do any work without a great effort, without the anguish of the swimmer who wonders whether he will have the strength to reach the shore. And besides, even when I expend all my energy, I cannot do anything as it should be done. All this to a degree that grows and grows, all in all, as time goes by; at least that's my feeling about it. Besides, since nonetheless I live, reflect, go forward, I become more and more aware of what I carry in my belly;

and if I must speak to you with complete sincerity, I have the conviction that it contains the germs of great things. This contradiction involves a despair that has brought me to the point of letting my thought dwell with some complaisance on the schemes that have shocked you.

"You may wonder why I have not instead turned to the solution you suggested—that of falling back on my parents. To tell the truth, it has not even crossed my mind. During my last years in school (before entering the Ecole Normale), I suffered keenly from my material dependence on my parents, and since I have seen that I can earn some money, I resolved never again to depend on them; and once I make up my mind about something, I stop thinking about it entirely. Since you mentioned it to me, I have examined the problem. There are some considerations that I can and must leave to one side; but what is decisive here is that in this way I shall not find real rest. One's family is a precious thing, provided it is kept at a little distance; if not, it can stifle you. Above all when I am in bad health, the presence of my parents is for me a very painful burden, since in their presence I cannot let myself go, etc., etc. All this would not be an obstacle if my parents could understand it, but they can't. And I cannot on one hand ask for their help, and on the other reject their attendance.

"So then, as you say, there is no way out. Or rather this is the way out: keep on pushing myself as long as it will be possible for me—and when the disproportion between the tasks that have to be accomplished and my ability to work will have become too great, then die. And take away with me what I bear inside me, as undoubtedly has happened to many people over the centuries who were worth a good deal more than I.

"Every time that I go through a period of headaches, I ask myself whether the moment to die has not come. More than once, I found myself about to decide to die, for fear of a decay worse than death; to the point that, to avoid the risk of succumbing under the blows of an irrational depression, I decided never to carry through such a resolution (save under exceptional circumstances) until after the lapse of six months or a year. Add to all this the fact that since the headaches lessened enough to give me a feeling of freedom of mind, I threw myself into life with so much ardor and passion that a new aggravation of my state of mind is at each turn something analogous, with all due allowances, to what a death sentence would mean for a person overflowing with youth and vitality. Keep in mind also the terrible temptation I feel when my courage gives out, to use my headaches as an alibi, an excuse for my idleness and all my failings; and the remorse I feel over the emotion or fear of having succumbed to this temptation. And that's how it is. These lines may give you an insight into my particular misfortune —since each human being has a misfortune.

"But above all don't let all this worry you. Try to understand, and then don't think about it anymore. For me life is still beautiful, nonetheless. Or rather life is still supremely beautiful in my eyes—but for me less and less accessible.

"One more thing, since I am on this subject. I don't like to mention my headaches to you or to let you see them. If you don't want to risk often being unjust to me, don't forget that many things such as an ineptness in speaking or acting, a lack of presence of mind, thoughtlessness, inertia, etc., can simply be the effect upon me of physical sufferings that I manage to overcome enough so that they are not outwardly perceptible. Of course that does not mean that one should excuse everything I do, far from it. I would prefer you to be too severe rather than too indulgent in my regard."

On March 20 Alain published in *Vigilance* (the bulletin of the Committee of Vigilance of Anti-Fascist Intellectuals) a "Questionnaire Concerning Recent International Events." (Hitler had just remilitarized the Rhineland.) He posed ten questions, the last one being: "The men who speak of honor and dignity as being more precious than life—are they disposed to be the first to risk their lives? And what should one think of them if they are not?"

Simone felt that she had to answer this last question. She regarded it as very important, because the words honor and dignity are the sort that move men deeply and so are perhaps "the most deadly in the vocabulary." In a reply that she most likely sent to *Vigilance* and that was later published in her book, *Écrits historiques et politiques* ("Reply to a Question of Alain," pp. 244–46; variants on pp. 394–97), she maintained that it is never through war that individuals can defend their dignity, at least when dignity means self-esteem. "War is never a way to avoid having contempt for oneself. It cannot be such a resource for noncombatants, since they do not share in the danger. . . . Nor can it be such a resource for combatants, since they have been compelled to fight. . . ." And if one intends by dignity being respected by others and not being humiliated, Simone observes indignantly that in society the people in the lower classes are humiliated every day. "The principle according to which one must reject humiliation at the price of life . . . would be subversive of all social order. . . ."

During the Easter holidays, which began on April 5, she took a trip with her mother. Mme. Weil remembers having gone with her to Bordeaux and staying in the Landes during this holiday. They visited a small factory in the Landes.

On her return to Bourges, Simone wrote to M. Bernard. She could not yet name a date for her proposed visit to the Rosières plant. Moreover, she again hesitated to go there, having some hope of being accepted one day as a worker there.

In the meantime, she spoke to him of the problem that is posed when workers must be laid off. At all events, she hoped that such layoffs would never be arbitrary and that they would be guided by certain rules. The arbitrary usually is done out of an obligation to please the boss, and such an obligation is intolerable. "You see, it is not subordination in itself that shocks me, but certain forms of subordination that entail intolerable moral consequences." She also said that she cannot accept the idea that "the subordinate plays almost the part of an inert thing manipulated by someone else's intelligence."[26]

M. Bernard proposed that she spend a whole day at the Rosières plant so that she could see everything firsthand. Nothing could have given her greater pleasure. No longer hesitating, she told him that she would come on Thursday, April 30, or the day after.

Touched after this visit by M. Bernard's generosity, she decided to write some articles for his little magazine. Not articles like the "Appeal to the Workers at Rosières," but articles written in "my best-behaved prose, as far as I am able." She remembered an old project: making the masterpieces of Greek poetry accessible to the widest possible audience. She had felt, when she worked in the factory, that this poetry "would be a hundred times closer to the people, if they could know it, than both classical and modern French literature." To begin the project, she chose to recount the story of Sophocles's *Antigone.* "If I have done what I intended to do," she wrote to him, "it should be able to interest and move everyone—from the manager to the last of the workers."[27]

M. Bernard accepted the article and asked her what name he should put on it. Simone would have signed her own name, were it not for the possibility of eventually being hired as a worker in the factory. Still having some small hopes of being hired, she decided to sign it Cleanthes, in memory of the Stoic philosopher who had also worked with his hands as a water-carrier.[28]

The article, "Antigone," appeared in *Entre nous* on May 16. It was reprinted later in *La Source grecque.*[29]

From then on, Simone continued to write more articles of the same kind. She wrote one on *Electra,* which was published in the new edition of *La Source grecque* in 1963 and began another on *Philoctetes.* She also planned to write a series of articles about the creation of Greek science which would be "comprehensible and interesting to any unskilled worker."

She had declared that she would return to the Rosières plant on June 12. She was to bring her article on *Electra* with her. But news of the sit-in strikes made the desire to go to Paris irresistible. She wrote to M. Bernard on June 10 that she was forced to leave for Paris; she added that in any case it was better so, "because if I found myself among your workers at this moment, I could not resist offering them warm congratulations."

She could not and did not want to hide her joy: "You will realize, I think, what feelings of unspeakable joy and relief this splendid strike movement has given me. The consequences will be what they will be. But they cannot destroy the value of these lovely days of joy and fraternity, nor the relief the workers have felt at being for once given way to by those who dominate them."[30]

M. Bernard's reaction to this took the form of a brief, dignified, and very severe letter despite its outward politeness and moderate tone:[31]

"Mademoiselle,

"If the events you rejoice over had developed in the opposite sense I believe, since my reactions are not one way only, that I should not have experienced 'feelings of unspeakable joy and relief' at seeing the workers give way to the employers.

"At any rate, I am quite certain it would have been impossible for me to express those feelings to you.

"I must ask you, Mademoiselle, to accept my regret at being unable without falsehood to close with any expressions beyond those of courtesy."

In her reply, Simone defended herself against the charge of moral indelicacy. She had not trampled on wretched victims. The owners were neither in prison nor in exile. She even believed that the movement in progress could be good for them, for their souls, just as it was for the souls of the workers. "What ought I to have done? Not feel that gladness? But I think it legitimate. I never at any time had any illusion about the possible results of the strikes; I did nothing to promote or prolong them; but at least I could share the pure and profound joy that inspired my comrades in slavery."

She asked him, as a last request, to send back her letters. "I shall probably decide in the end to write something about industrial labor. Would you be so kind as to return to me all the letters in which I spoke about the condition of the workers? They include a number of facts and impressions and ideas, some of which I might not be able to recall. Thanks in advance." M. Bernard returned the letters; and that is how their relationship came to an end.

The strikes that followed the victory of the Popular Front in the elections of April 26 and May 3, 1936, had begun in May. Starting in certain factories in the provinces, they had quickly spread to Paris, and at the beginning of June all the large metallurgical factories in the Paris region were on strike. A new form of strike had been discovered: the sit-in strike, the takeover of the factory. The workers camped at their places of work. Food was brought to them; in some factories, hammocks were stretched between the machines. They spent their time as best they could, talking, arguing, playing cards, and singing; they often brought in their families to visit the factory. There was a joyous, enthusiastic, fraternal atmosphere. Simone visited several factories; she was transfigured. Among others she visited the Sautter-Harlé factory; she made a tour of the workshops on the arm of a worker who was famous as a woman chaser. The other workers whispered to him, "She looks pretty good, this last one," which made him fly into a rage.

She also visited the Renault plant, where she had worked. In an article published a few days later in *La Révolution prolétarienne* and entitled "The Life and Strike of the Metal Workers," she says: "I have been to see pals in a factory I once worked in for several months. I spent some hours with them. What joy to go into a factory with the smiling authorization of the worker who guards the door. What a joy to see there so many smiles and to hear so many words of fraternal welcome. How much one feels among comrades in these workshops where, when I worked there, each person felt so alone at his machine! What a joy to walk freely through the workshops . . . to talk, to eat a snack. What a joy to hear, instead of the merciless racket of the machines, music, songs, and laughter."

She adds: "Of course, this life that is so hard will start all over again in a few days. But nobody thinks about it, everyone behaves like soldiers on leave during the war. And besides, whatever may happen later on, one will still have had this experience."

The article was printed in the June 10 issue of *La Révolution prolétarienne* (but this issue probably appeared a bit late). It was later reprinted in pamphlet form by Prudhommeaux in *Les Cahiers de "Terre libre"* (No. 7, July 15, 1936) with the title "On the Job, Memoirs of an Exploited Worker." It was also reproduced later in *La Condition ouvrière.*

Since she had to write very quickly, she used certain passages from her "Factory Journal." Perhaps she had even written the section dealing with her memories as a worker beforehand. The part she wrote right then is the one that deals with the strike under way and the strikers' demands. She felt that they should voluntarily limit these demands but seize this opportunity to institute "workers' control" in the factories. "The bosses cannot grant unlimited satisfaction, that is clear; so at least they should not be the sole judges of what they can do or say they can do. The workers should set up everywhere control commissions that can check the account books."

During these days she went to see Auguste Detœuf. She had a very lively discussion with him. Detœuf felt that the strike movement was rife with all sorts of dangers. After this meeting she felt that she had not been able to state her views clearly and so wrote to him.[32] She felt strongly about being understood by him, not only because she felt friendly toward him but also because, knowing she would not be hired by Rosières, she had formed the project of again becoming a worker at Detœuf's plant and so collaborating with him in certain attempts at factory reform.

In her letter, she admits that the situation provoked by the strikes is dangerous. "The present wave of strikes is based on despair. That is why it cannot be reasonable." But she adds: "And yet I think that if things go well, that is to say, if the workers return to work fairly soon and with the feeling of having won a victory, the situation will be favorable in a little time for attempting some reforms in the factories."

She advises Detœuf to institute some sort of workers' control as being advantageous to the bosses themselves, since only this sort of satisfaction can make tolerable for the workers a resumption of work under conditions that at bottom would not be very much different from the previous ones.

She realizes that Detœuf doubts the value of her experience because he attributed to her a repugnance for manual labor and discipline. She assures him that she had no repugnance for manual work in itself, nor for obedience and discipline in themselves. "On the contrary, I have always been strongly attracted to manual work (though it is true I am not gifted for it), and especially to the most laborious jobs." She recalls that, long before working in a factory, she had made an effort to become familiar with work in the fields—haymaking, harvesting, threshing, digging up potatoes—and that, despite crushing fatigue, she had experienced profound joy in doing them. She also says that she is capable of submitting gladly to any discipline, so long as it is humane. "I entered the factory with a ridiculous amount of good will and discovered soon enough that nothing could be more out of place."

She wants to help him to understand his own workers—"which evidently presupposes first of all that I am not mistaken in thinking I understand them myself." She is not absolutely certain that she did indeed understand the workers.

She had to return to Bourges that Friday evening, but she returned to Paris on Wednesday or Thursday of the following week, and on Friday, June 19, she returned to the Renault plant. The evening of the same day she again wrote to Detœuf.

"Dear Sir,

"This morning I managed to get into the Renault works clandestinely, in spite of the strict control. I thought it might be useful to you to let you know my impressions."

She tells him that the workers know nothing about the negotiations under way and think that Renault is refusing to accept a collective agreement. "There reigns," she says, "an extraordinary atmosphere of distrust and suspicion." She returns to her idea that the only way out is the establishment of some form of workers' control. "It is inadmissible and in the last resort impossible that one irresponsible social category should impose its wishes by force and that the employers, who bear the whole responsibility, should be obliged to yield. There must be either a certain joint responsibility or else a ruthless re-establishment of hierarchy, which would no doubt involve bloodshed no matter how it was effected."

She ends by saying: "I shall no doubt come back to Paris tomorrow for twenty-four hours. It is extremely trying and nerve-wracking to be kept in the provinces at a time like this."

So she returned more than once to Paris during the month of June. On one of these visits she must have met Victor Serge, who, thanks to the campaigns organized for him outside of Russia, had at last been allowed to leave Russia and was now in France.

Simone stayed in Paris as long as possible. She had no desire at all to return to Bourges for the distribution of prizes. The headmistress of the lycée had to force her to return, saying that otherwise she could not pay her her salary. Simone gave in reluctantly, but warned the headmistress that she didn't have any suitable clothes to wear for such a formal ceremony. On the day of the distribution of prizes, after everyone was already seated in the hall, they saw a door open and Simone appeared in her old raincoat and worn, misshapen shoes. Her students immediately clustered around her, trying to hide her as much as possible. The headmistress, Mme. Laignel, had been well disposed toward Simone throughout the school year. In the report sent to the Ministry of Education on December 3, 1935, she said that Simone appeared "to give her lessons with great sureness of method." The reports of the other educational officials and inspectors expressed more mixed feelings. The academic inspector recognized that this young teacher fulfilled her obligations satisfactorily (although in his opinion the students did not participate enough in the class work and Simone spoke in too monotonous a voice). He also said that "Mlle. Weil's general appearance is certainly not very elegant" and that in the town "Mlle. Weil's attitude has provoked astonishment." He obviously wanted her to be sent somewhere else. "Mlle. Weil has asked for a post in the north of France; she would like to live in a working-class and industrial environment." The rector spoke of her more indulgently, but he expressed the same desire. He said that Simone seemed to him a trifle out of her element at Bourges and that it would be a good idea "to send her to an industrial area, as she herself wishes."[33]

Nine of Simone's students presented themselves for the *bachot*. According to Cabaud, there were only three failures. In short, it was a success for her. After the oral exams, which took place in Paris, Simone took one of her students to see Chaplin's *Modern Times,* which she admired very much. She claimed that only Chaplin understood the workers' condition in our epoch. She would also say—no doubt, jokingly—that to her knowledge he was the only great Jew, along with Spinoza.

10

The Spanish Civil War, the Popular Front, and the First Trip to Italy (1936-1937)

Both in Spain and France Popular Front governments were in power. The Spanish Popular Front, created after the French Popular Front, had been victorious before it in the elections held in February 1936. The revolt of the Spanish generals against their government erupted on July 17 and 18. Even before the end of July, the certainty had spread that Italian planes were being sent to the rebels. On its side, the Spanish government asked the French government for help. This put Léon Blum in a cruelly embarrassing situation. Certain parties or organizations that supported his government, above all the Communists, forcefully demanded that arms and military equipment be sent to the legal government of Spain. But other groups, such as the Radical party, were hostile to any form of intervention. Intervention could lead to war with the Axis powers; it could also lead to a civil war in France. Furthermore, the English government, which Léon Blum had consulted, made it quite clear that it would not stand by France if it granted military assistance to republican Spain.

One can imagine the interest and attention with which Simone followed these events. For her, war was the worst of all evils and from the start she approved of Léon Blum's efforts to avoid a war between the nations. But if she did not want to do anything to expose others to the dangers of war, she felt that she was free to expose herself. There was nothing more to be thought about the Spanish Civil War; it had begun and was a fact. Like Alain in 1914, Simone believed that when one could no longer prevent war, one must take one's share of the misfortune along with the group to which one belonged. She was to write to Bernanos in 1938: "In July, 1936, I was in Paris. I don't love war; but what has always seemed to me most horrible in war is the position of those in the rear. When I realized that, try as I would, I could not prevent myself from participating morally in that war—in other words, from hoping all day and every day for the victory of one side and the defeat of the other—I decided that, for me, Paris was the rear. . . ."[1]

Returning one evening from a meeting, she said to her parents, "I'm leaving for Spain." Seeing their despair, she added, "You needn't worry; I'm going as a journalist." She had in fact obtained journalist's credentials. But she was determined to do something more than just report the war.

Her parents decided that they would also leave and would go first to Perpignan, where they hoped to find some way of getting across the frontier. They took her to the railroad station and then went to the headquarters of the railroad workers' union. There they found unionists who knew Simone. They told them, "Simone has left for Spain, and we want to follow her." The trade unionists approved of their idea: "She will do something silly; you should follow her." They gave them introductions to railroad workers they knew in Perpignan. The next morning Dr. and Mme. Weil took the train to Perpignan, where they were warmly welcomed by the railroad workers.

Simone passed over the frontier at Port-Bou on the eighth of August. From Port-Bou she sent her parents a postcard, addressed to them *poste restante* at Perpignan: "All goes well, except that there was no train connection for Barcelona. I had to wait for two and three-quarter hours. Marvelous weather. Everything is calm. *Salud!*"

The next day she sent them a telegram from Barcelona to Perpignan: "Perfect. Complete calm."

On August 10 she sent a letter-card:

"Dear parents,

"I beg you to be completely reassured. This is the same Barcelona we are familiar with. People are infinitely less upset here (me too) than I was in Paris. This sojourn has already done me good. Apart from that, getting across the frontier is becoming more difficult. There is a need for doctors, it seems. But I want you to rest on the French side and think of me as being in the process of peacefully getting fit again in a lovely climate. This is always a stirring country. But I'll leave the details for my return. If there are any sensational stories in the French press, don't believe them. Things are going forward little by little, that is the simple fact. The international problem is the dominant one, but as always people think of it much less than in Paris.

"Write me for the time being in care of J. . . .

"Kisses."

On August 11:

"Dear family,

"All's well. Everything is calm, as usual. Nobody is being killed. I still don't have a stable address. I feel fine. No headaches. I have spent a few days studying socialized production.

"*Salud!*"

She also sent several undated postcards or notes to Perpignan which do not seem to have gotten through the mails.

A letter-card:

"Dear parents,

"I'm still writing to you at Perpignan because I have not received any letters from you. I've changed my address twice. In care of Señor X. is stable, but this afternoon I'm going with two French pals I met here who know Spanish to take a look at the small farms around Sitgès and Villanova, where the peasants have pooled their cultivations. That will make communication difficult. It will also prolong my stay for a few days. But it's interesting, and there is no danger at all. They say that even at the front everything is calm. (But they won't let you go there.) Write me still in care of Señor X. . . . Kisses."

Then two notes. The first: "Dear parents— Everything still fine. No time to write. I'm in Barcelona again. No news from you. Undoubtedly letters don't get over from your side. I remind you of my address: care of Sr. X. . . . You could perhaps send a telegram. Everything is calm and I am feeling fine."

The second: "Dear family,

"I take advantage of this opportunity to send you a direct message. Things are going very well. I'm knocking about the small farms. I expect to come back in a week. Don't worry, do you hear me!

"Still no word from you.

"Kisses."

Finally a postcard whose date is illegible and that was sent to Perpignan *poste restante,* then on to Barcelona, and finally forwarded to Sitgès:

"Everything is still going very well. The front is quiet. They don't allow journalists to go there or, generally speaking, foreigners, because they are an encumbrance. I haven't yet found a way to see what I want in Barcelona (all such negotiations are terribly complicated), but I shall do so directly. The city is peaceful. I shall no longer write to you so often, for it is really useless under these circumstances. Write in care of Sr. X. . . .

"Kisses."

One should not take everything that one reads in these letters at face value. Simone obviously intends to reassure her parents and to prepare them for a lack of news from her, so they would have no reason to become upset. While she was sending them these letters she was trying to put into execution some projects that were much less reassuring.

One of the first steps she took was to try to find Julián Gorkin. Gorkin, who had played a role in the insurrection of October 1934, had after it been forced to flee from Spain and take refuge in France. In Paris he had heard talk about Simone Weil (from Boris Souvarine, Michel Collinet, and Colette Audry, among others), but never met her. He had returned to Spain in October 1935. He was one of the leaders of the P.O.U.M. (Partido obrero de unificación marxista, or the Party of Marxist Unity), chiefly composed of dissidents from the Communist party.

The founder of the P.O.U.M. was Joaquín Maurin, Souvarine's brother-in-law. Maurin had mysteriously disappeared around the first days of the civil war. He had left to give a series of lectures in Galicia and was there when the generals' insurrection broke out; since then, nothing more was heard of him. Since the insurrection had been almost immediately victorious in Galicia, his friends believed that either he had gone into hiding or he had been arrested and perhaps shot. Gorkin had been chosen to replace him in the international secretariat of the party and also as the editor of their newspaper *Batalla* and member of the Central Committee of the Militia, which conducted the war.

Gorkin was in his office when Simone Weil walked in. She introduced herself and said to him, "I have a proposal to make to you; I hope that you won't reject it. I offer to go into Franco's territory to find out whether Maurin is dead or alive and, if he is alive, whether there is a way of saving him." Gorkin said to her, "Simone, you don't know what you are asking of me. Your devotion is extraordinary, but you don't speak Spanish and your physical type is not that of the women of this country. You would be discovered immediately. You are offering yourself as a sacrifice, and not only will you be lost but you may compromise Maurin. I would never take the responsibility of giving you this mission. You would have a ninety percent chance of sacrificing yourself for nothing." Simone became angry, protesting that she had every right to sacrifice herself if she wished and arguing that Maurin was Souvarine's brother-in-law and Gorkin's own best friend. The argument lasted for more than an hour and was quite painful. Seeing at last that she could gain nothing by it, she left.

Not having succeeded in getting her project accepted, she then tried to join the militia of the C.N.T. (la Confederación nacional del Trabajo, or the National Confederation of Workers, the central anarchist trade union movement). She left with some journalists but afterward separated from them. She went down through Lérida and reached Pina in the Aragon, on the banks of the Ebro River. It was in this region that the Durruti column was based. It is quite possible that Simone was already there when she wrote to her parents some of the notes I have already quoted from, because she was there on August 14 and on the fifteenth participated in a conversation between the peasants of Pina and the militiamen. (See Simone's "Spanish Journal," published in *Ecrits historiques et politiques,* pp. 209–16.)

Later on, she told of having asked one of the leaders (Durruti, perhaps), "When are you taking Saragossa?" He replied, "Tomorrow." She said, "I would like to see that." (She was listed officially as a journalist.) Most likely that is how she managed to get to the front.

Buenaventura Durruti, the chief leader of the Catalan anarchist unions, was in charge of the most important C.N.T. militia formation stationed on the left bank of the Ebro River. His general headquarters were in the rear at Bujaraloz, but he was undoubtedly often seen at Pina. Simone heard him give a speech to the peasants of Pina on Sunday, August 16.

Alongside the Catalan and Aragonese battalions a small international group had been formed, "a kind of commando group entrusted with dangerous missions and composed of French, Italians, Bulgarians, and Frenchified Spaniards."[2] (According to Simone's "Spanish Journal," there were also some Germans.) This group did not then contain more than twenty-five men; later, it grew much larger. Among these who belonged to it were two Frenchmen whom Simone knew (or, more exactly, I believe, a Belgian and a Frenchman: Ridel and Carpentier). She asked if she could stay with this international group and was immediately accepted.

Carpentier, a former corporal in the colonial army, taught her how to handle her rifle. At night when she slept with the group, Ridel and Carpentier would take turns staying up to protect her, if necessary. But they never told her about this, for she would have been very annoyed at the idea.

On August 16, after Durruti's speech, it seems, she joined those who were accompanying him. First she went to Osera, where Durruti issued some orders, and then to his general headquarters at Bujaraloz. She returned to Pina in a car the next morning.[3]

On that same day, Monday, August 17, she was writing to Souvarine: "Haven't heard a rifle shot yet." At that very moment she heard a dreadful roar! A plane was bombing them. She grabbed her rifle and ran out with the others. They were ordered to lie down in the cornfield. She stretched out in the deep mud to shoot up in the sky. After a few minutes they were ordered back in; the planes were too high, and it was useless to shoot at them. They all went to look at the aerial bomb: it was very small and had made a hole only about a half yard in circumference. Simone wrote: "I wasn't at all upset by all this excitement."

On the same day, this group, or part of it, decided to cross the Ebro in a boat so as to burn three enemy corpses that were lying on the right bank. On this bank, a Franco column was in the vicinity. The leaders who commanded the group at first did not want to take Simone with them. They had noticed her clumsiness (during target practice, her comrades had avoided walking anywhere near her rifle's line of fire). In the opinion of these leaders, her shortsightedness was a defect that automatically eliminated her. But she protested, got angry, insisting so much that they ended by taking her along. (One of her comrades, when he saw her obstinacy, said, "Oh Lord, deliver us from mousy women!") Just as they were about to cross the Ebro, she asked Carpentier if he would put a bullet in the chamber of her rifle.

After having looked for the corpses, the patrol divided up. Some of them went back across the river; the others, including Simone, stayed on the right bank, arguing about a surprise attack they were planning to pull off. Finally they decided to defer this action till the next day. They also started to go back across the river. Just then they noticed a house. One of the chiefs, Pascual, said, very seriously, "We're going to look for melons." Simone then described what happened: "We walked through the brush. Heat, a little anxiety. I think it's idiotic. Suddenly I realize that we are on a mission (against the house). Then I'm *very* excited (I don't know how useful all this is, and I know that if you are captured, you're shot). We divide into two groups. The chief, Ridel, and three Germans crawl on their bellies all the way to the house. We, behind in the ditches (afterward the chief bawls us out: we should have gone all the way to the house). We wait. We hear someone talking. . . . Exhausting tension. Then we see some of our buddies coming back without hiding; we join them and go quietly back across the river. This mistaken maneuver could have cost them their lives." Simone would later write: "This expedition is the first and *only* time that I was frightened during my stay at Pina."

On Wednesday they decided to go across the river the following day. This time it was to blow up the railroad line by which the enemy received its supplies—perhaps also to try to hold the area until the arrival of another republican column that was based on the right bank of the Ebro, farther south. That evening, the military adviser who was the main leader of the group, Louis Berthomieu (a French captain), gathered the group together and asked the members if they were agreed about this mission. At first, they kept silent. He insisted that they tell them him what they thought. Ridel said, "Well then, we're all agreed."

This time, too, according to Mercier, who was there, "Simone stormed and demanded of the leaders and the whole group that she be included in the expedition. She declared that she had come to Spain not as a tourist or an observer but to fight, and assured them that she would hold her own with the rest of the group."

They left before dawn on August 19, at two-thirty in the morning. There were twenty in the group. They crossed the Ebro twice—the boat not being large enough to carry them all at once—then they took up positions under trees and bushes so as not to be seen by the planes. Berthomieu sent some patrols out to reconnoiter. He put Simone in a hut he had found. Simone stayed there a while, then came out to go and eat with her comrades the "java" that had been prepared by a German who'd been appointed the cook. Some of the scouts, who had gone to a peasant's house (no doubt the same one they had gone to before), returned to report that the Phalangists had seen them on their previous reconnaissance. Berthomieu decided that they had to return to this house and take the peasant family back with them. He assembled the militiamen who were there and said to Simone, "You, stay with the cook." She said that she did not dare to protest. But Mercier claims that she did protest, wanting to face whatever dangers the others did. (It was no doubt to try to protect her that Berthomieu assigned her to help with the cooking.) Whatever may have been the case, she resigned herself to it. "Besides, this expedition only half-pleased me." The others left, and she watched them depart with anguish in her heart. The German cook proposed to her that they go to a small entrenchment beneath a tree that had been Ridel and Carpentier's command post. They waited. "From time to time, the German let out a sigh. He was frightened, visibly. Not me. But how everything around me seemed to have an intense existence! A war without prisoners. If you are captured, you are shot." Their comrades returned, bringing with them a peasant, his son, and a six-teen-year-old boy. An Italian anarchist raised his clenched fist while staring significantly at the boys. The son made the gesture demanded of him but "visibly against his will." The peasant turned back to look for his family. "We all returned to our respective places. An aerial reconnaissance. We took cover, hugged the ground. Louis started cursing about the lack of caution. I stretched out on my back, looked up at the leaves, the blue sky. A very beautiful day. If they capture me, they will kill me. . . . But it is what we deserve. Our troops have shed a lot of blood. I am morally an accomplice."

It was no doubt this moment of waiting and meditation she alluded to after her return from Spain, when she told me that at one time, just when she thought that perhaps their retreat would be cut off and they would be killed, the world had looked extraordinarily beautiful to her.

After some instants of calm, the planes returned and began to bomb. Simone first took shelter in the hut, then she came out to go toward the automatic rifle. Berthomieu sent her back again to the mess hut (it was most likely then that she protested). "Finally the peasant's family arrived (three daughters, an eight-year-old boy), all of them terrified (they were bombing pretty accurately). They thawed a bit. Very fearful. Concerned about the livestock they had left behind at the farm (they ended by taking them to Pina). Obviously not sympathizers of the Popular Front."

The next morning Simone's nearsightedness played a cruel trick on her. They were still bivouacked in the bushes, on the right bank of the Ebro. They had started a fire in order to cook their meal in a hole dug in the ground, so as to screen any flames that might give their position away. A huge pot or frying pan had been placed at ground level over this fire of covered coals. Simone did not see it and put her foot right into the boiling oil. Her foot was protected by her boot but the lower part of her left leg and the instep were seriously burned. When Carpentier removed her stocking, the skin remained stuck to the wool. They had to help her walk to the boat, which then took her to Pina.

But that very evening, "all bandaged but suffering like a martyr (the burn was quite deep), she returned with the men who brought the rations."[4] It took all her friends' diplomacy to persuade her to get back in the boat. They could see that her teeth were chattering. Carpentier, who thought her condition was serious, took her back to Pina.

So she was in the hospital, or rather what the militiamen called a hospital. It was installed in a school. They had put a bandage on Simone that did not even cover the entire burnt area, and they told her that she must keep it on for three days. The next morning the male nurse gave her a treatment. "Drink this and walk up and down for about twenty minutes." It was a purge. Simone told him, "I can't walk." He said, "This order comes from the head doctor." The head doctor was a barber. Simone realized that it would be better for her to be treated somewhere else. She took her knapsack and dragged herself down the road. She met a colonel; he took her in his car in the direction of Barcelona, giving her a lift for some distance. After that she was taken in charge by another man in a car, a Swiss trade unionist, Pierre Robert. Before reaching Barcelona, they had to stop and spend the night at a hotel. The owner of the hotel, perhaps as a crude joke, gave them only one room, and they had to make do. (Simone must have been less upset by this than she had been at Barcelona, where, as we shall see, she had to spend a night under similar circumstances. She no doubt had met Pierre Robert before and knew that he was not the sort of person to abuse such a situation.) The next day they reached Barcelona.

(Later Simone met Pierre Robert in Paris, at the Capoulade Café on boulevard Saint-Michel. She had just come from a play at the Odéon and was with some friends. Pierre Robert saw her and said, "Ah, Simone, how are you?" Afterward, she said in an offhand way to the others, "Oh, that's a fellow I spent a night with in Spain.")

Thanks to the railroad workers at Perpignan, Dr. and Mme. Weil had been able to slip across the border on August 14. Two workers had escorted them to the frontier and had handed them over to Spanish railroad men. They reached Barcelona. All or nearly all the hotels had been requisitioned and were occupied by organizations. Someone accosted them on the street and said, "Are you French? You are making a mistake to come here. You can't possibly imagine what is going on here." They wandered about, carrying their knapsacks, searching for a hotel. Finally, someone pointed out a mysterious pension. All the curtains were drawn and the whole place was dark. A lady came to open the door, asked them who they were, and gave them a room. The windows in this room were repaired with wads of newspaper, and the walls were riddled with bullet holes. They came down to eat; there was very little light, they could barely see shadows sitting at the tables, and nobody said a word. Finally they went to bed. The next morning they found out that this pension was a refuge where people in danger were hiding out.

They did not want to stay there, so they left again with their knapsacks on their backs. They went to one of the addresses Simone had given them. They found a woman boarder who seemed very annoyed when they mentioned Simone. She went to find a small redheaded young man, who told them, "Your daughter is not here; she left with some journalists. But I'll show you the room where she slept." He showed them a room that in fact was not the one she had slept in. Simone told them later that the only available bed was in this young man's room and that she had had to spend the night there. She had hardly slept at all, not being calm enough. Yet she knew that among the anarchists, they respected the woman's wishes. (This rooming house was certainly occupied by anarchists.)

The Weils finally found a hotel. They continued to search for Simone. They went to the P.O.U.M.'s headquarters. Gorkin remembers that one day he saw an old couple sitting modestly in the antichamber to his office. When he passed by, they followed him with their eyes but did not dare speak to him. He asked a militiaman who they were. The man said, "They've asked for you, but they see that you are so busy that they don't want to bother you." Gorkin went over to them; they told him they were Simone's parents and were looking for her. Gorkin welcomed this "really sweet" couple as best he could, but he could not tell them anything precise about where Simone might be. According to Mme. Weil, he told them, in substance: "She left with some journalists, but she parted from them en route and we don't know where she ended up." He also gave them the addresses of organizations that might possibly give them information as to her whereabouts.

They wandered from one organization to another. They went to the offices of the *Solidaridad obrera*. Everywhere they left their address. A journalist said to them, "Are you Simone Weil's parents? You will never see her again." They had heard people say that the Moroccan soldiers with Franco's army raped women and tortured their prisoners. At the end of five or six days they received a postcard signed "Aunt Louise," which said: "I have seen Simone, I've tweaked her ears, because she has done some foolish things; she is wounded, but you will see her soon." "Aunt Louise" was an old anarchist woman who had gotten their address from *Solidaridad obrera*. They spent half of their nights on the ramblas in front of the P.O.U.M.'s headquarters, since the convoys coming from the front arrived at night. Simone arrived during the day. They were seated at a table, having lunch when Simone arrived, smiling, radiant: "Here I am." She told them what had happened to her. The doctor said, "Let's see your leg." They went up to her parents' room, and the doctor was appalled when he saw so large a wound that the bandage only partly covered and that could easily become infected.

They then went to see Miravitlès, who felt that she should be gotten into a hospital. He drove them in a car to Sitgès. The military hospital was set up in the Hotel Terramar, one of the best hotels in Sitgès. At the very start, the doctor in charge was hostile. He gave Simone a small room in the back, even though the rooms looking out on the sea were empty. And he hurt her a lot when he changed her bandages. Dr. Weil did not dare intervene, for the hospital was directed by this Spanish doctor. But a few days later, Simone's teeth were chattering and her wound was suppurating. Dr. Weil took her temperature, saw that she had a fever, went to see his Spanish colleague, and demanded that he come immediately to see what was under the bandage. Then he waited; nobody came. The Weils realized that this could not go on and that they had to take Simone out of the hospital.

Michel Collinet was then in Sitgès with his wife. They came to visit Simone every day. They had a car. The Weils asked them to come and get Simone and take her in their car to their pension, where they, Dr. and Mme. Weil, were also staying. Collinet came; Dr. Weil and Collinet carried Simone to the car. The doctor in charge of the hospital was furious and pursued them with a thermometer in his hand, wanting, a trifle late, to take Simone's temperature. She was laughing. Collinet told the doctor, "I don't like Fascists very much, so you'd do best to keep quiet."

(Collinet believes that the patients who were thought to be anarchists were regarded with hostility in this hospital. The people in charge were probably reactionaries. It was also possible that the hospital was under the control of the U.G.T. [*Unión general de trabajadores*], the rival of the C.N.T. and at that time dominated by the Communists.)

They took Simone to the pension where the Weils were staying, and there her father could at last take care of her. If she had stayed in this hospital, the aggravation of her condition could have resulted in the amputation of her leg.

While at the pension, about September 5, Simone heard of the republicans' defeat in their raid on Majorca and what had followed it in Sitgès: the execution of nine presumed Fascists to avenge the nine boys from Sitgès who had been killed in the raid. She was very angry about this. Later, in her letter to Bernanos she was to say: "I was at Sitgès when the militiamen returned, defeated, from the raid on Majorca. They had been decimated. Out of forty young boys from Sitgès nine were dead, as was learnt when the remaining thirty-one came back. The very next night there were nine revenge operations. In that little town, in which nothing at all had happened in July, they killed nine so-called Fascists. Among the nine was a baker, aged about thirty, whose crime, so I was told, was that he had not joined the 'Somaten' militia [the meaning of this slogan is obscure. Possibly "We are ready" (*Somos atentos*)]. His old father, whose only child and only support he was, went mad."[5]

At Sitgès, Simone received a visit from Ridel and Carpentier. They told her about certain events that had taken place at the front after she had left. They were the ones who told her the story of the young fifteen-year-old Phalangist of whom she speaks in her letter to Bernanos. The militiamen had found him on the battlefield after the engagement, pretending to be dead. They had taken him with them, but in the rear he was executed. On him they had found a Phalange membership card, scapularies, and a letter from his mother, who scolded him. Durruti lectured him, it seems, for an hour, telling him of the beauties of the anarchist ideal and offering to spare his life if he agreed to join the militia. "Durruti gave this child twenty-four hours to think it over, and when the time was up, he said no and was shot." Simone added: "Yet Durruti was in some ways an admirable man. Although I only heard of it afterward, the death of this little hero never ceased to weigh on my conscience."

When she began to get better and could walk a bit, Collinet put his car at her disposal. He drove her to Barcelona several times. That is how she was able to visit certain factories, which she discusses at the end of her "Spanish Journal."

According to Collinet, she was very pessimistic about the future of the Spanish revolution. She thought, as she had when she wrote her article on war, that when a spontaneous uprising turns into an organized war, Caesarism supplants the revolution—and that if Franco was not victorious, Spain would probably become another Russia. Yet she had every intention of returning to combat as soon as possible.

But these somber forecasts were told to only a few people. For example, when Carpentier saw her at Sitgès, he was not struck by any great pessimism on her part.

Her father and mother tried to persuade her to return to France. They told her that she would receive much better medical treatment there, her leg would be cured more quickly, and then if she wished, she could come back to Spain. They begged everyone who came to see her to advise her to do this. Ridel and Carpentier, among others, joined their efforts to those of her parents. At last she let herself be convinced.

Dr. and Mme. Weil no doubt saw Gorkin again, for he recalls having facilitated their departure from Sitgès and Spain. In the name of the Central Committee of the Anti-Fascist Militia he provided them with the safe conduct that was necessary to cross the border. This was on September 22. He also got them a car with which to fetch Simone from Sitgès and bring her back to Barcelona. They crossed the border with their daughter at Port-Bou on September 25 and returned to Paris.

Painful as it was, Simone's accident saved her life. Soon after, the international group, which had grown much larger, was cut to pieces at Perdiguera. Few managed to escape. Several women had joined the group after the period when Simone was there, and they were all killed at Perdiguera.

During the days she had spent at the front, there had not been any real fighting there. When she met her parents again at Barcelona and

Mme. Weil was perturbed at seeing the rifle she was carrying, she said to her, "Don't get upset, I never used it." She had in fact not used it, but she did not get a chance. Had she resolved not to fire it? Why, then, had she asked Carpentier to load it for her? Certainly she would have fired it with regret. When I saw her again after her return and she told me about her adventure as a soldier, I remember saying to her (with the idea of dissuading her from going to Spain again, and also because of the idea I had of her), that her real concern was certainly not to kill people. She did not deny it; but neither did she say that she was determined not to use her weapon. She said, "Fortunately, I am so near-sighted that I don't run the risk of killing anyone, even when I shoot at them." This proves, it seems to me, that she would have shot her rifle if she had received the order, but she would have done it with the uncertainty of hitting the target and hoping, in her heart of hearts, that she wouldn't hit it.

For once in her life she was happy about being clumsy. In participating in this war, what she wanted above all was to confront danger. She certainly also wanted the republicans to win and thought that she could help her comrades in some way. But she had a deep repugnance to killing, even in the normal conditions of a war. Or rather these very conditions must have seemed dreadful to her, since they force you to kill unknown, perhaps innocent people. She would have fired her rifle more readily at someone whom she knew to be an oppressor of the people. She was torn between the desire to be a good soldier and the thought that her bullet could kill some "poor boy" whom chance had put in the enemy camp. She had an even greater horror of all the blood shed uselessly, outside all law or justice, in this atrocious civil war. The republicans had shed a great deal of blood, as had their adversaries. When, at the front, she wrote: "Our side has shed a lot of blood, morally I am an accomplice," it is clear that she already thought that certain republicans had committed crimes.

If she had been confronted by atrocities or unjustified executions, she would have been ready to pass over into the camp of the victims. When she had to be present at the execution of a priest (it is not certain when this took place, most likely before her arrival at Pina), she wondered whether she wouldn't have intervened to prevent the execution even at the risk of being shot herself. But she did not have to run this risk, for by a lucky chance the execution did not take place.[6]

(She was later to tell Gilbert Kahn, apropos of the resolutions one makes in advance which tend to weaken one's determination at the moment of action, that when she was in the car with those who were going to execute the priest, instead of making a resolution, she had concentrated her attention on what her existence would be like if she watched this execution without saying anything.)[7]

Yet she still remained a strong supporter of the side she had chosen.

On her return to Paris she participated in meetings organized by the S.I.A. (le Secours international antifasciste, or the International Anti-Fascist Rescue Committee). For example, they held a meeting in support of republican Spain in a movie house on avenue Emile Zola; Mme. Weil, Maurice Schumann, and Collinet attended. Simone spoke at this meeting; she wore the red and black scarf of the C.N.T.-F.A.I. (Federación anarquista ibérica, the political organization that included the most active anarchist militants and whose aim was to maintain the integrity of anarchist ideas in the C.N.T.). According to Collinet, she attacked the Stalinists, both Spanish and French, and energetically defended the Spanish anarchists and the social advances they had made in Catalonia. Moreover, Cabaud claims,[8] she came to Bourges still wearing her militiaman's cap and scarf and asked some former colleagues or former students if it would not be possible to steal some cannons from the arsenal at Bourges and send them to Spain. (It is true that Cabaud tells this story, but he does so with many reservations.) Mme. Weil recalls a meeting at the Winter Vélodrome at which Jouhaux spoke and Simone had the job of seating people in the stadium. She was wearing the mechanic's dungarees that were the militiamen's uniform, with the C.N.T. inscription. However, during the course of this meeting, at the moment when they stood up to sing the "Internationale," Simone put a newspaper on the floor and sat down on it, and Mme. Weil followed her example. She was opposed to these rituals insisted upon at meetings by certain political parties and unions. At the congress of the C.G.T.U. in September 1933, she and Charbit had been physically threatened, Mme. Weil said, because they would not stand up for each rendition of the "Internationale."

Besides, it is probable that at this meeting she heard some speeches of which she did not approve. Jouhaux was then in agreement with the Communists on the war in Spain; he criticized nonintervention. On the other hand, Simone supported nonintervention and the policy of Léon Blum. She had approved of this policy from the beginning. She will later say: "Even when I was in Aragon, in Catalonia, in the midst of the atmosphere of combat, among militants who had no words severe enough to describe Blum's politics, I approved of this policy."[9] She thought that a war between nations was the greatest evil. She was ready to sacrifice herself personally to help the Spanish people but not to sacrifice peace.

Almost immediately after her return from Spain, she wrote a resolutely pacifist article that was published in *Vigilance* on October 27, 1936.[10] In this article, entitled "Do We Have to Grease Our Combat Boots?" she struck hard at those who accepted the risk of transforming the Spanish Civil War into an international war. Her participation in the war in Spain had given her the right to support pacifism without being criticized for cowardice, and to scorn those who, on the contrary, accepted the risk of war while not fighting in the war themselves. "Since the war in Spain, one hears on all sides the sort of thing that unfortunately takes us back twenty-two years. It would appear that this time we will shoulder our packs for law, liberty, and civilization, not to mention the fact that it will, of course, be the last of all wars. . . . What is at stake here? Are you trying to prove to yourselves that you are not cowards? Comrades, you can go to Spain and fight. . . . You can find plenty of rifles there. . . . Or are you defending an ideal? Well, comrades, ask yourselves this question: can any war bring to the world more justice, more liberty, more well-being?"

Blum's opponents maintained that it would suffice to speak out firmly and the Fascist powers would retreat. "A singular lack of logic! Fascism, they say, is war. What does this mean but that the Fascist states will not retreat. . . .? Unless we retreat. Yes, we must retreat and we shall retreat when confronted by war. Not because we are cowards. Once again, let us say that all those who are afraid to look like cowards in their own eyes are free to get themselves killed in Spain. . . ."

Far from considering Léon Blum too pacifist, she felt that he was not pacifist enough and that the logic of his political position should have taken him much further. Since he had had to decide—and after so much heartache!—not to give military support to republican Spain, he should be even more determined not to start a war to defend the Versailles Treaty or to honor the clauses in the pacts of alliance. Simone wrote two more articles, which nonetheless she did not publish, though they were published later in *Ecrits historiques et politiques:* "The Politics of Neutrality and Mutual Assistance" and "Nonintervention Generalized." (They are perhaps two different drafts for a single projected article.) In the first article she said: "We have let our dear comrades endanger their lives for a cause that is ours as well as theirs. . . . All this in order to avoid a European war. . . . What we have not done for our dear comrades in Spain, we should not do for Czechoslovakia, Russia, or any other state. In the presence of a conflict that is quite poignant for us, we have allowed the government to proclaim its neutrality. So it should not then believe it can speak to us about mutual assistance. . . ." In the second article: "My intention is not to join in the violent attacks that have crashed down on our comrade Léon Blum. I recognize the necessities that have determined his actions. As hard and bitter as they were, I admire the moral courage that permitted him to submit to them despite all the declamations. . . . But in nearly all the speeches Léon Blum has delivered since the beginning of the Spanish War, side by side with profoundly moving statements about war and peace I find other statements that have a disquieting sound. . . . I defy anyone, no matter who, including Léon Blum himself, to explain why the reasons which dissuade us from intervening in Spain would have less force if it were a question of Czechoslovakia being invaded by the Germans." It is possible that these two articles were written a little later, during the first months of 1937.

For a long time Simone had the intention of returning to Spain. Her parents asked all those who had some influence over her to dissuade her. Carpentier, who went to see them when he returned from Spain, remembers that they begged him to do so. They also went to visit Detœuf, among others. Detœuf told them, "Unfortunately I have no influence over her."

They took her to Cadenat, a surgeon, who for medical reasons advised her not to go back to Spain. He then said something to her in a whisper—no doubt that she did not have the right to do this to her parents. She burst into sobs; later, she reproached herself for having let herself go like this. But it is quite likely that it wasn't Cadenat's arguments, even the last one, that made her change her mind.

She explains what changed her mind in her letter to Bernanos; it was the fact that the Spanish Civil War had become a war between states, a war between Russia on one side and Germany and Italy on the other.[11] Furthermore, what she had learned since her return confirmed her in the idea that the necessities of war quickly destroy the initial goal and force the combatants to neglect the concern for justice, liberty, and humanity that made them undertake the war. "The necessities, the atmosphere of civil war prevail over the aspirations which one tries to defend by means of civil war."[12] It was not more than a month after she had left Spain, toward the end of October or the beginning of November, when she began an article that she never finished, "Displeasing Reflections."[13] In it she demonstrates that everything that the Spanish republicans and their friends detested—military constraint, police constraint, constraint on the job, the lies spread by the press—that all this they had been forced to re-establish because of the necessities of war.

Undoubtedly she had some scruples about publishing such an article. Perhaps that is why she never finished it. But civil war seemed to her by now almost as unacceptable as a war between nations. In the article "Do We Have to Grease Our Combat Boots?" she wrote: "If the misfortune of our times demands that civil war today becomes a war like any other, and almost inevitably tied to an international war, one can only come to one conclusion: one must also avoid civil war."

She advised supporting all efforts to re-establish peace in Spain. When there were some attempts at mediation or negotiation in 1937 or 1938, she was in favor of negotiation and for stopping the war at any price.

In any event, during the third trimester of 1936, she could not return to Spain, for her leg was not completely healed. She had to request a leave of three months from the Ministry of Education (in September, from Spain she had sent the ministry a Spanish doctor's certificate attesting to the fact that she was incapacitated by second- and third-degree burns). At the end of each trimester during the school year of 1936–1937, she had to renew this request for leave because almost all year she had suffered from her wound and her headaches had been more violent than ever. On December 15, Dr. Weil wrote on the certificate that accompanied her request: "She is not yet cured of her anemia and still suffers from violent headaches and excessive general fatigue. Besides this, her left leg, which had a very extended burn . . . still pains her a great deal." On March 26, Dr. Ducrey of Montana will attest that she still suffered from the result of her burn.[14]

Thus freed of all professional duties and not being able to return immediately to Spain, she resumed her efforts for amelioration of the workers' condition. On October 23, 1936, she published in *Le Libertaire*, the weekly of the Anarchist Union, an article entitled "The Declaration of the C.G.T."

The C.G.T. had promulgated an appeal for calm, proposing to replace strikes by the procedures of conciliation and arbitration. Simone believed that one should not abuse the strike, but she maintained that one must not completely abandon the strike weapon. On the one hand, the continual agitation in the factories seemed to her dangerous; it favored interests that either were not those of the workers or were directly opposed to their interests. "The Communist party is interested in maintaining a permanent effervescence in the factories, so as to have a means of blackmailing the government on the question of foreign policy. On the other hand, the most aggressive employers have an interest in the fact that permanent disorders will dismay the population and drive all those who are not consciously revolutionary toward Fascism." Yet there is the further fact that as a group the workers "would again count for nothing if they handed over all the rights to the 'procedures of conciliation and arbitration.' "

She thought that one could not take away certain rights from the employers; however, the workers must defend their rights. There was only one solution to these problems—it was "an energetic, prudent, methodical, coordinated trade union action, with a well-defined objective: workers' control."

On November 25, 26, and 27, she attended the congress of unification of the Federation of Metal Workers. She wrote an article about it —"The Congress of the Metal Workers"—which appeared in *Le Libertaire* on December 4. The congress disappointed her. "As usual, the congress slid over the poignant, urgent problems that are imposed on the workers every day. . . . When one knows what a factory is . . . one is stupefied at the scant amount of connection there is between the daily life of the workers and the discussions of their own organization.

". . . One would have to seriously discuss obligatory arbitration. . . . One would have to speak about the work tempos, attempt to establish a trade union control that would prevent the workers from being degraded . . . while still keeping production at a reasonable level. One would have to examine the problem of discipline, and the ways of safeguarding the dignity of the workers . . . without compromising the orderly system necessary for production. . . . Above all one would have to talk about a slogan that was being imposed by the facts: workers' control. . . ."

She advised them to organize small study groups inside the workshops that would examine all concrete problems, and she concluded: "The working class must give proof of its capacity. Without this the conquests of June will vanish like a dream. . . ."

I believe it was at this time that she wrote the "Open Letter to a Trade Unionist," which was published in *La Condition ouvrière*. [15] In it she expresses the same preoccupation that she did at the end of the article on the congress of metal workers. She addresses herself to one of the four million workers who, after June 1936, had joined the C.G.T. (which had grown, in the space of a year, from about a million to five million members). Simone reminds this newcomer what his situation had been before June, when he was alone and incapable of struggling against oppression. She tells him that he is no longer alone, that he has become strong, thanks to the unions, but that as a result of this he has certain duties. "If you have begun to be treated like a man, you owe it to the trade unions. In the future, you will not deserve to be treated like a man unless you are a good unionist. . . . You have acquired certain responsibilities. . . . You must now work to make yourself capable of assuming them; without this, the newly acquired advantages will vanish one fine day like a dream. One does not preserve one's rights except if one is capable of exercising them as one should."

No doubt it was in this period that one must also place a piece of writing addressed to teachers, "Brutal Reflections." It shows her absolutely hostile to the influence of the university graduates, the intellectuals, in the workers' trade union organizations. "The question has been asked whether the university graduates do not run the risk of being drowned in the C.G.T. But I hope that they always will be drowned. The day on which their presence will become felt in the orientation of our General Labor Confederation I will be tempted to tear up my membership card. . . . Or do you want them to put their intelligence at the disposal of the working class? Very well. Without having any illusions, however, as to the value of the gift. . . . But as for playing a role, even a modest one, in the life of the workers' organizations, that must not be and will not be possible except for those who have assimilated their spirit. . . . If they bring with them the university spirit, they must be drowned and they will be. . . ."

Finally, it was no doubt also at this time that she wrote the "Letter to the Indochinese," in which she describes for the first time, I believe, what she felt on reading Louis Roubaud's inquiry in *Le Petit Parisien:* "I shall never forget it. It was at the time of the Colonial Exposition. The bloody incident at Yen-Bay, followed by a bloody repression, had reminded France that there was an Indochina. *Le Petit Parisien* published a courageous and documented inquiry written by Louis Roubaud on its first page. I bought it every morning; while I ate breakfast, I would hastily devour Louis Roubaud's article. I saw how the coolies were recruited, how they were beaten, how the white overseers would maim or kill Annamite workers by kicking them, right in front of their comrades, who were too terrorized to intervene. Tears of shame stifled me, I could no longer eat. . . . Since then I have never been able to think of Indochina without having a feeling of shame for my country."

She says that the coming to power of the Popular Front and "the so evidently generous and humane spirit of the head of the government" permits people for the first time to hope that Indochina will cease to be a source of shame to informed Frenchmen. But the work of the Socialists in this regard must be supported, because this work will encounter great obstacles. Simone hopes that the Indochinese will make use of the very paper in which her letter appeared, in order to let the French know what their complaints are. I don't know in what newspaper this letter was to appear, and whether it actually did get published.

The C.G.T., having become the sole nationwide trade union movement, had as its leaders Jouhaux and Belin, the former being the secretary general and the latter assistant secretary general. Their offices stood opposite each other. Simone got into contact with Belin, for whom she had a great deal of sympathy. He had founded a weekly newspaper, *Syndicats,* of which she said in some drafts for letters: "At present, in the C.G.T., it is only around *Syndicats* that one finds serious men." "It is around *Syndicats* that one finds the only comrades whom I consider among the responsible militants of our trade union organizations—which are, when it comes to organizations, the only ones that interest me."

She went more than once to see Belin at the C.G.T. headquarters. He recalls that she would sit in a corner, modestly, wearing her small beret, and that she spoke in a fragile, delicate voice and seemed very retiring and weak . . . (She had changed a lot since the days when Cancouët had called her the "Terror." It is true that she had perhaps always been humble with workers, and perhaps even with the representatives of workers' organizations.)

She asked to be entrusted by the C.G.T. with an inquiry into the factories in the North and was given the assignment. This inquiry was supposed to take place toward the end of December and the beginning of January. In any event, on December 27, 1936, she was in Lille. On that day she wrote to her parents that she did not yet know when she would be back. She had encountered certain difficulties. "Among several difficulties, the people of Lille (who would think it?) are nearly as precise as Spaniards."

She later wrote a report based on this inquiry: "Observations on the Lessons To Be Drawn from Conflicts in the North."[16] This report is remarkable for its impartiality, good sense, and the courage it displays in resisting demagogic statements. After a series of strikes, some of which had been without any precise objectives, the employers in the North had fought for the right to impose sanctions. "It would be absurd," Simone says, "to consider, as has been done until now in official statements, the complaints of the employers to be entirely false; for they are not. They are certainly exaggerated, but they contain an element of incontestable truth." She points out certain abuses committed by the workers' delegates. "Elected to supervise the application of the social laws, they soon became a power in the factories and strayed very far from their presumed mission." One of the results of these abuses was that the majority of the technicians and clerks have gone over to the antiworking-class camp. The employers were no longer afraid that they might have to run the factories without them. She concludes that any strike is dangerous in the present period and that the normal subordination of the union delegates to the union must be re-established, and, finally, that it is necessary for the C.G.T. to study seriously the problem of discipline and output in the factories. "Slavery has to a large extent disappeared; the system bound up with the slavery has disappeared at the same time. We can only congratulate ourselves. But industry cannot live without order and system. Thus the question that is posed is of a new order, compatible with the newly acquired liberties.... For the rest, the absence of sanctions cannot be perpetuated without a serious and real danger to production; nor is it in the workers' moral interest that they should not feel responsible for the accomplishment of their work. So one must obtain discipline, order, and sanctions that do not re-establish the arbitrary rule of the employers that existed before June."

After her inquiry, she had to see Jouhaux. When she returned from this meeting, she told her parents, "Now I am definitely lost in Jouhaux's eyes. He asked me for an account of my expenses. I told him that I had refused to accept anything. It seems to me that that made a very bad impression on him."

As we have seen, one of her report's conclusions was that one must begin to study the question of a new order and a new discipline in industrial enterprises. She herself wanted to contribute to this study and so wrote an article entitled "Principles for a Project for a New Inner Regime in Industrial Enterprises." She probably showed this text to Belin; a draft or copy of it has been found and was published in *La Condition ouvrière* (pp. 207–13). She claimed that whatever the social setup might be, there will always be the question of compromising between two opposed needs. "The working out of a new inner regime for industrial enterprises poses a problem whose chief elements are determined in part by the actual social setup but which, in its essence, is bound up with the existence of large industry, independent of the social setup. It consists in establishing a new equilibrium, within the framework of each enterprise, between the rights that the workers can legitimately demand insofar as they are human beings and the material interests of production." Whatever the social structure might be, the discipline of an enterprise must rest on the coexistence of *two well-defined powers:* the management, which has the responsibility of procuring materials and overseeing production, and the trade union section, which must enforce a respect for the workers' lives, health, and dignity.

On January 8, 1937, the rumor started that German troops had landed in Spanish Morocco, and it was believed that French Morocco was being threatened. The French press became very excited and envisaged the serious consequences that the necessity of defending Morocco might entail. Simone, nervous about anything that could lead to a war, wrote two articles with the intention of proving that France had no right to Morocco and, consequently, did not have to go to war to defend nonexistent rights. The first of these articles, which was published in *Syndicats* on February 4, was simply a brief history of the events that had permitted France to establish its protectorate in Morocco. Of course, Simone emphasizes everything that is least edifying in this history (the secret agreement with England, and the violations of the Algésiras Pact). The second article, which was published in February in *Vigilance,* "Morocco, or Prescription in the Matter of Theft,"[17] is more violent and bristles with bitterly ironic observations. The theft at issue is the one France committed by making Morocco a French protectorate. Simone piles up the sarcasms. She calls Morocco "this so essentially French province" and pretends to become indignant that Germany seems to want to tear the Moroccan population away "from the traditions inherited from its Gaulish ancestors." The Algésiras Pact, she says, "had not a trace of justification, since it did not grant Morocco to France; this point should be obvious to any average intelligence," etc.

The same day on which the second of these articles appeared in *Vigilance,* Simone published in *La Révolution prolétarienne* a report on the congress she had attended on February 5, 6, and 7, the congress of the trade union organizations in the Paris region. Since the massive increase in its members that had taken place after June 1936, this central organization's membership had grown to a million. These million members had sent about eight hundred delegates to attend the sessions held in Huyghens Stadium.

She was at first tempted, she says, to sum up the impression that this congress left her with by saying: "It was a congress of the C.G.T.U. . . . Not so much because of the debates but because at certain times one rediscovered an atmosphere, so familiar to some of us, that smacks both of a political rally and a religious ceremony. The comrades who have never left the 'old house' (that is, the C.G.T. before 1936), were completely disoriented. They saw with astonishment these movements of mass ritual, the standing up, the lifting of fists, the singing of the "Internationale," the sitting down again. . . . Those who had passed through the C.G.T.U. found all this familiar, only too familiar. They also recognized the organized claques or cheering sections, the prearranged murmur of excitement before certain speeches, the whole art of stage-managing imported from Moscow."

However, she realized that it was not purely and simply a congress of the C.G.T.U. "People could speak, be heard, and make statements —not without some uproar, not without interruptions, of course— which in the C.G.T.U. would have almost surely led to the massacre of their enunciator. . . . One can even—some people did—abstain from participating in the ritual manifestations and not be threatened with getting your face bashed in. . . . In this same hall about three years ago a militant from the building trades had kindly promised to put a bullet through the skin of a member of a minority who committed the crime of not lifting his fist while singing the 'Internationale.' " (The minority member must have been Charbit.)

She observes that nobody reproached the Union's leaders for not having made the revolution in June. "It would appear that all the militants are agreed about simply wanting the consolidation and extension of the reforms that have been won. Should one conclude that they have lost contact with the rank and file? On the contrary, I believe that as a whole the working masses simply want reforms." She was sorry that they had not discussed certain problems, particularly workers' control; but an important discussion had taken place on the question of the U.S.S.R.

The Union's leadership had inserted in the "report on tasks" a sentence which pointed out that the "vanguard of Fascism" had been "liquidated" in the U.S.S.R., and another sentence which affirmed that the new Soviet constitution was "the most democratic in the world." "One can manage to tolerate a great deal of ignominy," Simone says, "but the first of these statements, coming on top of the bloody playacting in Moscow, somewhat overflows the measure. . . ." "The bloody playacting in Moscow" refers to the second of the big show trials in Moscow, which took place January 3, 1937. (The first trial had taken place in August 1936.)

The attack against these statements had been launched by those whom Simone called "our side," that is to say, by the militants of *La Révolution prolétarienne:* Hagnauer, Fronty, Delsol, Charbit, and Guigui. "Charbit, armed with quotations from *l'Humanité,* presented the following dilemma: either the accusations of the last trial are correct, and in that case one is in the presence of a regime in which all the founders —save for one—have betrayed, and also of a series of scandals indicating a corruption to which nothing in the capitalist states can be compared; or they are false, and this trial is proof of an oppression unequaled in history or present-day events. . . ." (Charbit had prepared his speech with Simone.)

The elimination from the report of these statements was finally obtained. But Hénaff, the person who reported on coming tasks, had let slip some statements that Simone emphasized. "He said that we must let the Russians take care of their traitors and be chiefly concerned about those here who want to carry out that same necessary task. In the light of what traitor means in today's special vocabulary, all this promises some fine days ahead. I believe that we would do well to abstain, just as a precaution, from taking a stroll in the Bois de Boulogne." (A crime had been committed in the Bois de Boulogne. The victim was undoubtedly an anarchist or syndicalist.)

The victory that was won in the argument over the U.S.S.R. by the militants of the *R.P.* was somewhat annulled on the next day. First of all, by the complacence or passivity with which the majority of the membership listened to the speech of the Soviet delegate. "Impossible to describe the brutality, the baseness with which the Russian delegate expressed himself, for many long minutes, concerning the last batch of Russian leaders who have been shot. The claque worked efficiently. Our people kept silent. . . . They were dispersed throughout the hall; they had not established contact; they were paralyzed by rage or disgust. This apology for the death sentences was saluted by the 'Internationale' sung standing up. . . . Some people remained seated. . . . Nevertheless, one is not proud about singing the 'Internationale' to applaud death sentences. . . ."

Afterward the elections put the finishing touches to the Communist party's annexation of the Union. The list presented by the executive committee and elected contained twenty-two former C.G.T.U. members as against thirteen former C.G.T. members. "The typographers' union, basing its argument on a circular sent out by the C.G.T. executive, demanded parity; this demand clashed with the sincere feeling for unity that reigned in the hall; somebody replied, 'There are no more former C.G.T.U. members or former C.G.T. members.' In short, it is quite obvious that since there are no longer any different factions, there is no longer any reason for preventing one faction from destroying the other."

After this bitter reflection and a few more observations, Simone concludes that the C.G.T. is in danger. "There is no doubt that a C.G.T. subjected to the Communist party would be a mere appendage of the Russian state, an instrument of blackmail vis-à-vis the government . . . that the C.G.T. would then become in our country the principal factor for 'sacred union,' chauvinism, and war. From now on, all this begins to be true."

While being anxious over the future of the C.G.T., or rather, more accurately, precisely because of these anxieties, she wanted to see the Christian workers of the C.F.T.C. (la Confédération française des travailleurs chrétiens, or the French Confederation of Christian Workers) join the main trade union movement. She thought that they would provide a counterweight to the growing influence of the Communists. During the first two weeks of March she probably wrote a long letter to Emmanuel Mounier, who was the chief editor of *Esprit,* a Catholic magazine. She discussed these two questions: "Is a plurality of trade union organizations indispensable for liberty?" and "Is the spirit of the C.G.T. incompatible with Christian morality?"

On the first point, she said that not only the plurality of trade union organizations does not help liberty but on the contrary "the necessities of propaganda, under the conditions imposed by competition, stifles freedom." But she mostly discussed the second point. She admitted that the C.G.T., though not being a party or really having a doctrine, had a spirit, an ideal, and traditions. This spirit, ideal, and traditions—were they incompatible with the morality taught by the Catholic Church or, more generally, with Christian morality? She did not think so.

"For my part, I am personally not a Catholic; but I consider the Christian idea, which has its roots in Greek thought and in the course of the centuries has nourished all of our European civilization, as something that one cannot renounce without becoming degraded: this does not prevent me from feeling at home in the C.G.T. Our trade unionism does not preach hate; it was not hatred that inspired its precursors, its founders, and its pioneers. . . .

"I will permit myself, however, to say to the Catholics in the C.F.T.C. . . . that they are less scrupulous in other areas than in that of trade union action. Is there a nation that is founded on love? I mean on the love of foreigners? . . . In fact, Christians are not separated from the nation even in periods when the nation's entire activity is determined by hatred—I mean in time of war. In my opinion, one does not have the right to plead the purity of principles when one defends this right more jealously in the areas where it agrees with a certain conformism than in those where it scandalizes and shocks.

". . . The most urgent matter, in the majority of cases, even from the Christian standpoint, is not that the workers rise to a greatness of soul that permits them to love even their persecutors, but rather that they throw off the deadly passivity, the pitiable resignation due to which they are reduced to an inhuman misery. Because, according to Aristotle's formula, echoed again by Saint Thomas Aquinas, and which became a doctrine of the Church, virtue presupposes a certain comfortable standard of physical well-being. . . .

"Should the classes 'struggle' or 'collaborate'? There is much that is artificial in this opposition of the two terms. Who can deny that there is this collaboration between the classes? When a worker works, he collaborates with his boss; in order not to collaborate, he would have to stay out on strike all the time. . . . Who can also deny that there is a war between the classes? . . . The ideal of the manager of a factory, from the point of view of profit and loss, would be that of workers who supply very intensive work and do not consume. The ideal of a worker, as a man, is to furnish an effort that does not exhaust him and, in the long run, his vital resources, and to live reasonably well. There is an opposition. . . .

"So there is both collaboration and struggle. It is a fact, a fact that cannot be contested unless one wishes to lie.

"Who more than the militants of the C.G.T. desire a full and complete collaboration among the various elements of an industrial enterprise? This is even, quite precisely, their ideal. . . . What they criticize in those who recommend collaboration is not the desire for collaboration, but rather for having found a fine term to disguise trickery and slavery. For them, full and real collaboration . . . is an objective whose conditions can only be achieved by struggle.

"At bottom I believe that the only thing that can shock a Christian about the C.G.T.'s spirit is its tendency to a certain demagogy, to shift all faults onto the adversary, in all circumstances and on all points. But this is not the sole property of the C.G.T. The same thing occurs in all human groups that struggle against others, not only trade unions but also parties, nations, and churches . . . and the duty to react against this sort of demagogy is not specifically Christian; it is the duty of all men who think. . . ."

During this same period—the first months of 1937—Simone continued her efforts with a view to setting up a study of the inner regime in factories, a regime that, while being compatible with order and discipline, would conserve and consolidate the conquests of June. On February 11, she published in *Syndicats* the article "A Crisis of Authority?" which is a kind of addendum to her report on the factories of the North and her "Principles for a Project for a New Inner Regime in Industrial Enterprises." She made an effort to be just at one and the same time to the workers' aspirations and the employers' needs insofar as they were legitimate.

But it was not enough to affirm the legitimacy of these two opposed exigencies; one had to find out how to reconcile them in practice in the concrete details of work in the factory. It was as a preparation for deeper study of this subject that Simone studied the Taylor system. On February 23, she gave a lecture on industrial rationalization to a working-class audience. (The text has been published in *La Condition ouvrière*, pp. 215 –32.) This system, invented by Taylor, she claims, is the one that is still employed in the factories. That is why it must be studied, because "one must start from the present-day regime in order to conceive of a better one." What one must look for is a regime and system of work that would be acceptable at the same time to production and to the worker. "A factory must be organized in such a way that the raw materials that it utilizes result in products that are neither too rare, nor too costly and defective, and at the same time that the men who enter it in the morning do not come out diminished either physically or morally in the evening, nor at the end of a day, a year, or twenty years." Now "nobody has even begun to solve [this problem], since nobody has even posed it." "If we took over the factories tomorrow, we would not know what to do with them and we would be forced to organize them just as they are organized at present."

She put the workers on guard against the mistake of confusing this problem with that of property and profit. "The workers can force the management of a factory to recognize their rights without depriving the owners of the factory either of their title to the property or their profits; and, reciprocally, the workers could be deprived of their rights in a factory that would be collectively owned."

This problem of the internal organization of the factory is the one whose solution she had sought for some years now. She declares here that she does not know the solution and that it will only be found through gradual, piecemeal experience in the factories themselves. "I myself have no solution to present to you. This is not something that can be improvised wholesale on paper. It is only in the factories that little by little one can succeed in conceiving a system of this kind. ... precisely as the bosses, managers, and technicians in the enterprise have succeeded little by little in conceiving and perfecting the present system." The study and critique of the Taylor system will only show how to pose the problem.

She then presented the history of Taylor's studies, whose characteristics and intentions she described without indulgence. She demonstrated, with a feeling of indignation, what the effects of this system are. "Starting from a certain limit, it is much more serious for the human organism to increase the speed of work, as Taylor does, than to increase the work's duration."

As for the so-called scientific character of Taylorism, she also put the workers on guard against the experts. "Nothing is easier for an industrialist than to buy an expert, and when the employer is the state, nothing is easier for it than imposing this or that scientific rule. ... So the workers must not have any confidence in the experts, the intellectuals, or technicians when it comes to regulating what for them has such vital importance."

Finally, Simone wrote, no doubt in the first two weeks of March, another article for *Syndicats,* entitled "The Strike of the Roman Plebs." This article, which appeared on March 18, was intended to prove that peaceful resistance to oppression can be effective. What Simone calls the strike of the Roman plebs is their refusal to continue to enlist in the army, and the preparations they made to leave Rome in the fifth century before Christ. It is known that the patricians, to make them change their minds, were forced to accept the institution of tribunes. Thus the plebs had compelled their oppressors to grant their demands without shedding a drop of blood.

During this period she wrote more than once to Belin. Drafts and copies of letters that certainly were addressed to him have been found. She speaks of several different subjects. For example, she is indignant about certain sanctions, inflicted on the workers by trade union delegates. "As for that which concerns the quarantines inflicted on the workers by the delegates, I can assure you that at Renault's the quarantine was a normal part of the arsenal of sanctions of the regime of control. As for myself, whatever might be the cause of the sanction and whoever might be the victim (even if he is not a union member, even if he is a member of the *Croix-de-feu*), I consider it a scandalous abuse of power. I don't know whether you realize the moral sufferings that a day's work done under these conditions means. . . ."

She was upset about the rumors concerning a "political unification," which would no doubt be the unification of the Socialist and Communist parties. She thought, it seems, that in this case the Socialist party would be taken over by the Communist party, as she saw the C.G.T. already had been (trade union unity, which she had longed for so much, had had this result). "The rumor of which I spoke to you (political unity) has been confirmed. If you have any influence in the party [the Socialist party, apparently], this would be the time to exert it, in the name of the bitter experience that we have had in the C.G.T."

Speaking of the nationalizations, she says: "As for that, I have my own personal view: it is that even capitalism is better than a totalitarian state of the U.S.S.R. type, toward which certain socialists would like to lead us straightaway."

By far the longest of these letters, and the one she wanted to write most carefully (there are at least five drafts) is devoted chiefly to an argument against Belin's opinions on French foreign policy and national defense. Although he was, among the leaders of the C.G.T., one of the most resolutely pacifist, Belin felt that it was impossible not to defend Czechoslovakia if it were to be attacked by Hitler.

"It is with pained surprise," Simone wrote, "that I have learned the other day that in your opinion too, it is impossible to permit Czechoslovakia to be crushed; or, put in another way, it is legitimate to eventually start a war for Czechoslovakia. You too, then—like Blum, like Bergery, like the Communists and Jouhaux, like the right, like everyone. I defy you to give me one single reason that proves that it is not absurd that a single young boy from our country should die at twenty for Czechoslovakia. . . ."

She was not afraid to express all her ideas on the subject of war: "I think—and don't you think so, too?—that defeat is not a worse catastrophe than a victorious war; they are two quite similar catastrophes. . . . Lacking a general limitation of armaments . . . a limitation or progressive decrease in French armaments would not increase the risks of war; it would only increase the risk of defeat in case of war, and I refuse to attach any importance to that.

"I also affirm that a defeat without a war is preferable to a victorious war. What will prevent us, every time that an actual or latent diplomatic conflict threatens to become a war, from granting the adversary the avowed or secret, symbolic, or real objectives that he proposes to attain by a military victory?

"Such a diplomacy would fail in a situation where the adversary wants war for war's sake. But nothing allows us to affirm that Hitler wants war for war's sake. . . ."

So Simone, in her hopeless defense of peace, proposes an "experiment" that she herself says has never yet been tried: give the enemy, without war, all the advantages that he asks for. She questions herself in one of the drafts for the letter: "Can one avoid war in this way? This is not proven. But it has never been done, and one can try it. . . ." In the last draft she thinks of an objection that one is often tempted to advance: "You will tell me that in this way one is in danger of gradually encouraging the enemy so that one leads him to make demands even more serious than a war? At first it will be difficult; the concessions must really go very far to cost us as much as a war. But let us admit this risk. The risk of leading the adversary . . . to unacceptable demands is not greater than the risk of exasperating him by resistance. We must try to maneuver between the two alternatives. . . ."

One may judge that the experiment proposed by Simone would have been imprudent. But there is at least one point on which she is realistic and clear: she affirms that there is a contradiction between the social policy that the Popular Front is trying to put into practice and the necessities of national defense faced by the Nazi threat. If one is resolved to resist Germany and not to yield anything to it, the armaments race cannot help but destroy the results of the workers' victory in June. "You are not right, I am convinced, if you think that even a moderate social policy can be prolonged in the present international situation. . . . In the years that are coming, it will be a question of keeping up with Germany, and that can only be done by undergoing privations and constraints almost equal to those imposed by Hitler."

Broadening the scope of the problem, she shows Belin that one cannot really transform the proletarian condition except by acting on the fundamental elements that determine it. These givens are: "the necessities that are implied by the equipping of a country with a view to war, necessities whose effective weight surpasses by far the burden of the manufacture of war materials in themselves; the organization of industrial work, which reduces the social function of a large mass of workers to something equivalent to slavery; the general structure of the economy, which entails privations and overwork much beyond the real necessities, due to the role given those branches of the economy which do not contribute anything to the development of bodies and minds; the structure, function, and power of the state." These are the chief factors of misery and oppression. Neither "reforms" nor "revolution" touch them. Above all the first factor is important. "I believe that the military question is the determining one, above all others."

Both revolutionaries and reformists think that one can change the workers' condition without changing the fundamental elements in it. "I think that this method is illusory. The principal elements being what they are . . . it is impossible to find solutions palpably closer to popular aspirations than those of the right.

"For years now this is how I have thought, and that is why I have always kept more or less at a distance even from those political groups or others that are most sympathetic to me as regards their aspirations. Since the beginning of the Popular Front, I have regarded its propaganda and that of the organizations that belong to it as almost entirely demagogic, and I have abstained from taking even a small part in the propaganda effort that led to the electoral victory in May. The June movement, because of the miraculous change that it wrought in the general atmosphere, made me believe in completely new possibilities; but I realize with growing distress that this fine enthusiasm will never succeed in crystallizing itself into anything concrete.

"I don't consider a concrete thing the fact that they have loosened the vise of social constraint, that they have gained a little well-being, free time, and liberty. Certainly this is very fine, and I rejoice every day in the thought that they no longer suffer in the factories as they suffered the year when I lived this existence. But nothing has been changed in the structure of the social machinery, and when the enthusiasm of June will have died away, the vise will no doubt be tightened at least as harshly as before. . . ."

She predicts the financial difficulties to which the Popular Front government would succumb. "*It is not true* that they are delivered from the obsession with bookkeeping that dominates the politics of the right. Quite the contrary, the drama of the government is that it must return right now to this obsession that it had mistakenly thought it had gotten rid of. They have not carried through a methodical inflation, the only way to subordinate bookkeeping to the economy. They will return to the worries about balancing the budget, loans, 'confidence,' the preoccupation with preserving the stimulant of capitalistic profit, the specter of a commercial balance. . . ."

The last of these drafted letters ends with these somber predictions: "I predict—and we can both take note of this—that we shall enter a period in which one will see throughout the country the most incredible absurdities—and they will appear natural. There will be less and less civilian life. Military preoccupations will more and more dominate all the everyday aspects of existence. . . .

"Capitalism will be destroyed, but not by the working class. It will be destroyed by the development of national defense in each country, and replaced by the totalitarian state. That is the revolution we shall have. Someday, fortunately, iron, copper, and manganese will become very scarce in our world.

"There is, moreover, a rather curious passage in a recent book by Jouhaux and company.[18] It explains that the idea of a 'planned economy' was born among the trade union leaders because of the difficulties encountered by industrial mobilization. So this is indeed a war economy. The 'plan' [published by the C.G.T.] had always given me this impression, and here is a naive confirmation of it. . . ."

It is likely that none of these five drafts ever resulted in a letter that was actually sent, save perhaps the last, for one sees that Simone takes from one or the other letter the same arguments and often almost in the same terms. They must have been written from the end of February to about the middle of March. In the next-to-the-last draft Simone told Belin that she was leaving Paris for some time. So the last letter was probably written at Montana.

Her headaches had in fact become so bad that she had decided to try a treatment advised by her father and which was given at a hospital at Montana. Moreover, Montana was on the road to Italy, and before the grave events she foresaw, she wanted to see Italy.

She probably left on March 11. The hospital in which she was treated was the Moubra, run by Dr. Ducrey. The day Simone left, Dr. Weil wrote to Dr. Ducrey to offer him some advice about the treatment. But in her first letter to her parents, Simone wrote: "I really would have liked Biri to be here to take over the treatment. . . . Of course there is no 'Bofarul' here, yet nonetheless I would have much preferred Biri." (Bofarul is the name that Simone bestowed on the Spanish doctor in the Terramar Hospital, either because that was his real name or because she had nicknamed him that.) Her parents immediately decided to join her. They left for Montana on March 20 and stayed there for about two weeks.

During the time they spent with her, Simone took a trip with her father to consult a famous opthalmologist in Zurich. She took advantage of their stay there to stop at the Einsiedeln Abbey, where she could hear Gregorian chants. Easter fell on March 28; so she probably heard the Easter services at Einsiedeln. To hear Gregorian chants was a joy for her, but not to the same extent for Dr. Weil. He found the chants monotonous and confessed that he could not, like her, sit for hours on end listening to them.

In the first letter she wrote them from Montana, Simone had asked her parents to bring her some books. So she had the intention of working during her treatment. It was no doubt at Montana that certain articles were written or completed.

The first article she could have written (unless she had written it just before her departure) was one that was published in the *Feuilles libres de la quinzaine* on March 25 and entitled "Blood Flows in Tunisia" (reprinted in *Ecrits historiques et politiques*, pp. 336–38). Some Tunisian miners had gone on strike at Metlaoui and on March 4 had occupied the grounds of the mining establishment. The gendarmes had ordered them to leave, and when they did not obey, had fired at them. There had been between fifteen to twenty deaths. Simone's article was aflame with indignation. She pointed out the indifference of the French, even the French of "the left," to the misery of the colonial people. She spoke with bitter irony: oh, of course, the colonials are too far away! Their misery, as great as it might be, moves us less than the fate of a Parisian metal worker who does not get his 15 percent increase in pay. Besides, they are used to suffering; that is well known. Furthermore, there is nothing spectacular, generally, about their sufferings. The government of the Popular Front has until now limited its colonial policy to the dissolution of the "Etoile nord-africaine," a nationalist organization—that is, to a repressive measure—and the fault can be laid less to the government than to all Frenchmen. If Léon Blum "had the impression that we are more concerned about colonial slavery than the pay for government functionaries, he surely would have devoted to the colonies the time he has spent preparing a fine speech to the functionaries."

The article's conclusion is both harsh and prophetic: "When I think of a possible war, I must admit that the dismay and horror such a prospect evokes in me is mingled with a rather comforting thought. It is that a European war can serve as the signal for the great revenge of the colonial peoples, which will punish our unconcern, our indifference, and our cruelty."

She may also have written or finished at Montana the long and remarkable article "Let Us Not Start Another Trojan War," which was published in two parts on April 1 and 15 in the *Nouveaux Cahiers* (a bimonthly magazine, founded by Detœuf, whose first issue had appeared on March 15). In this article she demonstrated the absurdity of wars, since the fiercest conflicts are usually those that don't have a definable objective. It is precisely because they don't have a definable objective that one cannot put clearly in the balance the goal of the war as against what it will cost. Hence, struggles without any measure and without any possible compromise, wars in which quite soon the chief motivation is simply the war itself and what it already has cost.

In Troy, according to a certain Greek poet, there had been only the phantom of Helen, and they fought for ten years over this phantom. In our epoch, capitalized words such as Nation and State and often words ending in *ism,* such as capitalism, socialism, and fascism, have played Helen's role. Simone presents as examples of "lethal absurdities" the use of the word "nation" and the opposition set up between "fascism" and "communism." As examples of real opposition, which one must however define and so limit, since these are not oppositions between absolutes, she cites the opposition between order and liberty, between dictatorship and democracy, and the opposition between social classes. The class struggle certainly has meaning, but it is a struggle and not a war, and it is not effective except to the extent to which it is precisely not a war. When, submitting to the mirage of meaningless entities, one believes that it is necessary to transform it into a war, when one aims at the annihilation of the adversary regarded as an absolute evil, the class struggle leads, after bloody upheavals, to illusory results. It is only effective if it is seen as a permanent but limited struggle with the aim of re-establishing an equilibrium that is constantly being disrupted.

In this article Simone came upon an idea that she had perhaps just discovered or that at least appeared to her more clearly than before: it is that in one sense prestige is not an empty matter. It is tied to the nature of power, and power is tied, to a certain degree, to order. "The necessity for a power is tangible, palpable, because life cannot be lived without order; but the allocation of power is arbitrary because all men are alike, or very nearly. Yet power must not seem to be arbitrarily allocated, for if it appeared to be arbitrary there would be no power. Therefore prestige, which is basically illusion, is of the very essence of power. . . . Power, in order to be stable, must appear as something absolute, intangible. . . . If Priam and Hector had delivered Helen to the Greeks, this might merely have increased the Greeks' desire to sack a town that seemed so ill prepared to defend itself; they would also have risked a general uprising in Troy—not because the Trojans would have been upset by the surrender of Helen, but because it would have suggested to them that their chiefs could not be so very powerful. . . ."

This idea seems to entail the blackest pessimism. If order presupposes prestige, and if the search for prestige produces merciless wars, what hope do we have? But Simone thought that life is made up of miracles and that one must ceaselessly hunt down those empty words and things that are the causes of war. Moreover, to choose peace does not mean that one has given up all forms of struggle. "The relations between social forces are essentially variable, and the underprivileged will always seek to alter them; it is wrong to enforce an artificial stabilization. What is required is discrimination between the imaginary and the real, so as to diminish the risks of war, without giving up the struggle that, according to Heraclitus, is the condition of life itself."

This excellent article, the expression of a mind that was becoming more and more rich, nuanced, and complex, is dominated by the idea of equilibrium. What must be sought, according to Simone, are not the illusory paradises that would be established once and for all by the victory of an absolute good over an absolute evil; there are always precarious equilibriums between forces that are necessary to both sides, forces constantly being reborn and that can be just *within certain limits.* One must always keep an eye on both scales and work to add weight to the scale that has become too light.

At the same time Simone continued to defend the policy of peace inside the C.G.T. She wrote two articles for *Syndicats,* one appearing on April 8, "National Prestige and Working-class Honor"; the other, "The Dangers of War and the Workers' Conquests," appearing on April 22. In the first, she expressed an idea that one can already find in her "Reply to a Question of Alain's": those who speak of national honor and the impossibility of bearing certain humiliations are the same people who find it natural that people in the lower classes should have to bear so many humiliations. The honor that the workers must defend is "the honor of those who are at the bottom of the social scale," and not national honor. In the second, she developed the idea that she had maintained in her letter to Belin: it will be impossible to keep the social conquests of June if a foreign policy of force and prestige is pursued.

She then began an article which she did not finish and which seems to have also been intended for *Syndicats,* "French and German Relations." "It is only with dismay and fear in one's heart," she says, "that one can bring up the problem of French and German relations. One's heart is gripped by anxiety but also by regret, I would even say remorse. Did not the advent of the Popular Front arouse immense hopes, not only in social matters but also in terms of international policy?" She wants the C.G.T. to make an effort to supervise and orient foreign policy. "The C.G.T. must contribute, in a very large measure, . . . toward orienting the foreign policy of our country. There is no question as to the direction in which it should exert its influence. 'Peace,' Jouhaux has said, 'cannot be defended by a preventive war. It can be defended only by the means of peace.' We must simply put this formula of the secretary of C.G.T. into practice."

Among the patients at the hospital there was a medical student, Jean Posternak, whose room was, according to Simone, "the center of social life at Moubra." He had a phonograph and records. Simone experienced divine pleasure listening to Bach's *Brandenburg Concerti* conducted by Busch, especially the Andante of the fourth concerto. Posternak knew Italy very well; he gave her some useful information for the trip she planned to take and in particular gave her the address of a young Italian in Rome, the son of an important Fascist functionary. Simone wanted very much to get to know and understand the state of mind of a young Fascist.

The headmistress of the Bourges lycée informed her that she could profit from certain advantages offered by a certain governmental decree; she could resume work in July, which would have permitted her, for almost no work at all, to be paid during her leave. Simone refused to accept this advantage. Just as she had in March, again in June she requested a prolongation of her leave until the end of the school year.

Since her medical treatment had ended—it did not have any great effect on her, it seems—she left for Italy.

This journey through Italy was to be one of the happiest chapters in her life. She left on April 23. She first stopped at Pallanza. She walked for several hours along the banks of the lake in the direction of Switzerland and then, since she had gone too far to return on foot, she got a lift from a cart that was transporting bags of flour. Not speaking very much Italian, she could barely talk to the driver, "a young lad who looked very pleasant," but she could understand that he was not a Fascist. It was her first friendly contact with the Italian people.

She took the boat to go from Pallanza to Stresa. When she reached Stresa late in the evening, she was invited by an Italian teacher, whom she had met on the boat, to spend the night at her house. This teacher lived in a small village on the mountain, an hour from Stresa. Simone found herself staying with a passionately Fascist family, who subjected her to some ardent Fascist propaganda. But she was able to see "how people live, are housed, eat, and think in a village that is poor, though a trifle above the peasant level." This second contact with the Italian people was less pleasing than the first.

On the twenty-sixth she left Stresa for Milan. Since she arrived at the same time as the *Re Imperatore* [the King Emperor, as the Fascists called the king of Italy], who had come to close the exposition-fair, all the hotels were booked and full and she thought at first that she would not find a room. However, she ended up finding "a charming room for eight lire, between the delicious Piazza Beccaria and the no less delicious Piazza Fontana." After a short time she felt that she had been born in Milan, she was so much at home there. She wrote to her parents: "I know everything that one must know: where one can buy the best *Café expresso con panna* [Italian coffee with cream] for 80 centesimi, where it is good to get a *capuccino* on the terrace (this word made me dream for a long time, until I boldly ordered one and saw arrive a *café-crème* in the style of the Maison du Café), where for a lira one can buy first-rate ices, and where the *brodo* and macaroni are delectable. I have the profoundest pity for the unfortunates sitting in the restaurant of the Gallery Victor-Emmanuel, eating a meal for twenty lire and unfamiliar with the taste of *pasta al sugo* for one lira a portion."

To Posternak she wrote: "Milan is the kind of populous city I really like. . . . The people here are very nice. I am writing this at a delightful little café in Piazza Beccaria; just now the waiter was looking over my shoulder at what I was writing and when I looked up, his smile was charming: . . ."[19]

The day after her arrival in Milan she went to hear Verdi's *Aida* at La Scala. She had to stand in line for a ticket and then discovered there was only standing room. "That reminded me," she says, "of the heroic times of the Colonne concerts." As for Verdi's music, she wrote to her parents: "Very pleasant music, but properly speaking I don't really admire it. Always a trifle ridiculous."

She returned to La Scala soon after to hear Donizetti's *L'Elisir d'A- more.* "It is completely delightful. A very spiritual libretto, music of perfect grace. Very moving also to think that Stendhal must have heard, with delight, this same music in this same hall. (And La Scala is truly beautiful.)" This time she was seated.

She also spent a delicious evening at the "charming little marionette theater" in Piazza Beccaria. "I would give fifty *Aidas* for a show like this."

She prolonged her stay in Milan. First of all because it was raining, which made it pleasanter to stay in a large town than to travel through the country. And then she really did not want to leave Milan."I like it too much, too much. Not counting the fact that I do not see, when all is said and done, any valid reason for not spending my whole life in the church of Santa Maria delle Grazie, looking at Leonardo's *Last Supper.* . . ."

She would write to Posternak that she thinks she has found the secret of the composition of the *Last Supper,* after having looked at it for a long time. "There is a point on the hair on the right side of Christ's head toward which all the perspective lines of the roof converge and also, approximately, the lines formed by the apostles' hands on each side of him. But this convergence (which is discreetly emphasized by the arc above the window, of whose circle the same point is the center) exists only in the two-dimensional space which it evokes. Thus there is a double composition . . . ; and the eye is led back from everywhere toward the face of Christ, by a secret, unperceived influence that helps to make his serenity appear supernatural. . . ." She thought that Leonardo had a secret and that the secret was a Pythagorean conception of life.

She was happy to discover that there is a painting of him (the *Portrait of a Musician*) at the Ambrosiana, and she admired the "extraordinary ceiling with foliage" that he had painted in the Castello. At the Brera she was struck by the Christ in foreshortened perspective painted by Mantegna.

She wandered about the working-class districts. "Milan," she wrote to Posternak, "has some industrial suburban landscapes which are very moving; at least, they are to me. I spent hours among them. I possess the gift (which I purchased dearly) of reading the eyes of a shift of workers beginning or ending their day's work. And I had the opportunity to make use of this gift. It was the day after the official announcement of an all-around wage increase from 10 to 12 percent. (The day's papers were full of grateful acknowledgments.) Alas! What I read in their eyes was what I used to read in my fellow workers' eyes, and what was visible in my own, at the most painful moments. . . . Whatever gain may have been realized this time, the sense of servitude in labor has not been dispelled, but only muffled. . . ."

Finally she left Milan for Bologna. She visited Bologna in the company of a friend of her brother's. From Bologna she could not resist the temptation of taking the trains that offered trips to Ferrara and Ravenna. "Two really beautiful towns," she wrote to Posternak. "Do you remember the Diamanti palace? At Ravenna— it was market day— humanity was beautiful too, especially the young peasants. When Providence places beautiful people among beautiful things, it is a superabundance of grace. Every day, in this country, one notes in certain men of the people a nobility and a simplicity of manner and attitude that compel admiration."

Having returned to Bologna, she left there for Florence. She had already been in Florence for some days and was just about to leave when she wrote to her parents:

"Dear family,

"I believe that this time I'm a bit late. It's because I changed lodgings three times and wasn't able to buy ink until yesterday. On my arrival, Florence was packed. A horrible room for twelve lire, with meals twenty-five lire; I took the meals for two days and it was pretty awful. After that, a room for eight lire, but without light or air; finally a new room for eight lire, quite nice and very near the Duomo. I eat in a *fiaschetteria:* what a name and what charming things! . . ."

She did not like the Duomo, at least from the outside. "At first, I must confess the covering of white marble and green marble had the effect of fine crockery. Then I became used to it, but I still don't like it. I love the baptistery and the bell tower, and San Lorenzo (chiefly the old sacristy), Santa Maria Novella, and many other things (chiefly the bridges over the Arno). Until now I've spent most of my time in the Medici Chapel. I did not expect the effect that it had on me. It is too moving an art, like Beethoven. I did not think that *Dawn* and *Night* were so painful, the awakening and sleep of a slave for whom life is too bitter. *Dawn* has vividly evoked my own awakenings, when I was a worker and lived on rue Lacourbe.

"I didn't feel, when I was there, the need to go elsewhere and see something else. Nonetheless, I have been faithful to the appointment I had made with Giorgione's *Concert* at the Pitti Palace gallery. (I don't know what idiots have labeled it Titian; where does one find in Titian a hermaphroditic adolescent like the one who is listening, and such faraway looks like that of the man at the clavichord?)"

Although she had a horror of museums, she could not resist the Uffizi. "I've rediscovered the *Knight of Malta,* which I had promised myself to see for a long time (it wasn't in Paris), and Vinci's *Annunciation* (which was). There are a lot of Titians that are very beautiful. The Botticelli room is overwhelming, above all the *Primavera.* But nothing of all this equals the *Concert,* even distantly."

She was enchanted by Benvenuto Cellini's *Perseus* and above all by the figures sculpted around its base ("The naked virgin who says: *Ut vincas clypeum do tibi casta soror;* the miraculous genie who flies without wings. . . .")

She went to see San Miniato, of which her mother had spoken. "It is really delightful. There are on the right side some marvelous frescoes (a young saint on her knees, wrapped in her blond hair). They sang (not very well) Gregorian chants. Oh, but Florence is beautiful from high up there, with the sun setting! . . . The Viale dei Colli is full of aromatic odors that go to your head, above all with the view of all those slopes covered with olive trees. . . ."

She also went to hear Rossini's *Signor Bruschino.* "A happy surprise: there were tickets for seats at fifteen and ten lire. It is a kind of vaudeville to music. Very, very pretty." She also heard by chance some very beautiful organ music at Santa Croce.

She had to leave soon because she wanted to be in Rome in time for Pentecost and the religious music she hoped to hear there. "Perhaps I will spend a few days at Gubbio, where there is a festival. (That is where St. Francis converted the wolf)." But she expected to stay in Florence again on her return trip, after having seen Rome and Umbria. "Certainly," she says, "I must have lived in Florence in some previous existence."

From Rome she again writes to her parents:

". . . I've been in Rome for three and a half days and it seems like a whole epoch. I felt at home here more quickly than in the other towns I've been to and I had expected the contrary. Perhaps it is because the first thing I did here was to listen to some good music. I arrived about noon on Saturday and congratulated myself on having the rest of the day to look for a hotel. But after I'd gotten my breath, bought and studied a town-plan, and had lunch, it was already two-thirty. In the train from Milan to Bologna I had met a priest (that very type of shrewd, subtle Italian priest; he told me some interesting things about the present 'Stimmung,' and he spoke freely after I told him, as I do actually believe, that in the end the right will probably win in France), and this priest also told me that one can hear Gregorian plainsong at Sant' Anselmo. Finding on the map that the way to Sant' Anselmo (the Aventine) was by the Forum, the Colosseum, and the Palatine, I decided to take my chances going there and to walk. On the way I saw advertise- ments for the Adriano (which has replaced the Augusteo as a concert hall) announcing religious music on the same evening, sung by the choir of the Greek Catholic Church of Zagreb. (Not to be missed if it comes to Paris!) The Palatine, with its new excavations, being on my way, I went there and walked among the ancient stones all the way to the far end. (Impression of overwhelming grandeur.) At the end, no way out —so I had to go all the way back to the Viale Imperiale and then retrace my steps all along the street outside the enclosure. All this under a blazing sun and cursing the vaunted Fascist organization. Reached S. Anselmo at six o'clock, just in time for a very impressive liturgical ceremony that lasted an hour. On the way I had inquired at several hotels, which were all full. On leaving S. Anselmo (which is a pure jewel of a Benedictine monastery looking down on the Tiber), I went to the Adriano (part of the way by streetcar). There was just time to dine and go to the concert (seat 3 lire). Marvelous choral singing, rather of the Ukrainian type. Music by modern composers but, as was plain to hear, entirely based upon old liturgical themes. Coming out at midnight I still had to find somewhere to sleep. . . . I crossed the Tiber again and in the end luckily found a hotel, where I still am. I had left my rucksack at a restaurant near the station, which complicated things. . . ."

One sees how Simone could fill her days. The next days will be just as full. In her eagerness not to miss anything that was beautiful or interesting she seems indefatigable.

The day after her arrival, on May 16, she hears the Pentecostal Mass at St. Peter's, with the choir of young boys from the Sistine. "I don't know whose music it was, but doubtless Palestrina's. The music, the voices, the words of the liturgy, the architecture, the crowd, some kneel- ing, which included many men and women of the people, the latter with kerchiefs on their heads—there you have the comprehensive art that Wagner was seeking." She speaks of this ceremony to Posternak with the same enthusiasm, adding that "there is nothing more beautiful than the texts of the Catholic liturgy. . . ."

She says to her mother: "I seem to remember you don't like St. Peter's. Certainly it was considerably spoiled by the idiot pope who altered the original plan of Bramante and Michelangelo (a cross with four equal limbs); but even as it is I love it immeasurably, as well as the piazza in front of it. It really deserves to be the universal church of Christianity. I have seen nothing else in Italian architecture to approach Michelangelo's divine cupola. Brunelleschi's cupolas in Florence (the Duomo and even San Lorenzo, which is much better) are not nearly so good. The pope kneeling in prayer before the dome and just over the ashes of St. Peter is very beautiful. (Who the deuce did him?)"

After the Mass, she went to an exhibition of the Catholic Press, where she had her ticket stamped[20] and which in any case was interesting. In the afternoon she again went to Sant' Anselmo for Vespers. And then to St. Peters, still for Vespers. Not far from St. Peter's, she found "a very sympathetic trattoria, with delicious wines." She went to get her rucksack near the station and brought it back to her hotel. "At the end of a day like this, spent entirely listening to religious music, one has a very good feeling. If Paradise is like St. Peter's with the Sistine choir, it's worth going there."

On the Monday of Pentecost she again went to hear Mass at St. Peter's. When she came out, she wandered about for a long time in the streets around the Vatican looking for a missal, but she could not find one. "There was nothing anywhere except horrible little books with the most insipid Italian texts. This is something I would never have imagined in advance." She went again to Sant' Anselmo, where she was disappointed to discover there was no ceremony for Vespers. Then she walked, by way of the Capitol, the Forum, and the 'Forum of Imperial Italy,' to the house of the young man who had been told about her by Posternak. He was a student and a very ardent Fascist, but "otherwise pleasant, cordial, and very naive."

Then she returned to her hotel, which was near Ponte Umberto. But she went out again to finish off the evening in a movie. The film was over, but after it they put on a little comedy. "I didn't understand anything, but it was quite pleasant."

"After all that," she wrote her parents on Wednesday, "this morning my foot hurt and I was limping . . . (That burn doesn't seem to want to heal. . . .)" Despite the pain in her foot, she spent three hours in the Vatican Museum. In the Pinacoteca she saw "a St. Jerome by Vinci, painted on wood—extraordinary," and for this one painting she would give all the rest of the Pinacoteca twenty times over. "This *St. Jerome* and Giorgione's *Concert* at the Pitti and the foreshortened Christ at the Brera will be the three really intense memories I shall keep from the museums of Italian paintings."

She looked at Raphael's frescoes and admired them, but she felt no need to contemplate them for hours on end. At last she had the joy of seeing the Sistine Chapel. But, unfortunately, more than a third of the frescoes were hidden by scaffolding. In order to see more clearly what was left to see, she half-lay on her back on the benches, following advice her brother had given her. "But in my case it ended in a sharp altercation with the guard!"

That night she went to the theater. "A well-acted play, quite good (and interesting from the standpoint of the attitude of the regime). I was only able to follow it dimly." After the theater, she went to look at the Colosseum again. "There was a half moon and a clear sky. Unfortunately, also a good many electric lights. All the same, the Colosseum at night is impressive. I stayed there for about three quarters of an hour and when I remembered that it would be a good idea to go back, I was just able to catch the streetcar, which must have been the last one."

On the following days she returned to the Vatican Museum several times to see the Greek statues. She also went several times to other museums with Greek sculpture: the Barraco, the Capitoline, and the National Museum at the Baths of Diocletian. "I got dead drunk on Greek statues," she writes to her parents. And to Posternak: "They are the only things more beautiful than Michelangelo, at least those of the purest style." The memory of these Greek statues, along with the Pentecostal Mass at St. Peter's, (would) form an essential part of her enduring memory of Rome.

She again met the Fascist student. "The poor fellow," she tells her parents, "I must have left him, I think, gasping." She goes into greater detail about this meeting in a letter to Posternak: "I would be very interested to know what he said about it, if he has written to you since. . . . I think that if you could have been there behind a screen, you'd have had a good laugh. For my part, I have very much wanted for a long time to have a frank conversation with exactly the sort of young man he is —that is to say, holding the opinions you know and at the same time possessing intelligence and personality, so that he is not a mere echo. He seemed to me to be like that; with one of those characters that always interest me, full of repressed ardor and unavowed ambitions. So I'm grateful to you for the introduction; but I doubt if he has any such feeling.

"He thinks that my legitimate and normal place in society is in the depths of a salt mine. (He would send me there, I think, if he is consistent, as soon as his people govern France.) And I quite agree with him. If I had any choice in the matter, I would prefer hardship and starvation in a salt mine to living with the narrow and limited horizon of these young people. I should feel the mine less suffocating than that atmosphere—the nationalistic obsession, the adoration of power in its most brutal form, namely the collectivity . . . the camouflaged deification of death."

After having gone once more to the theater ("splendid audience," "an infinitely sympathetic people"), she left Rome for Umbria.

In the train from Rome to Terontola (the junction point for Assisi), she spoke to and fraternized with "some splendid types of young working men, back from Abyssinia." "One of them, who spoke French, told me that he would soon be going to Paris. I gave him my address. The result: an hour later he proposed that we get married when he comes to France. I told him that I had not known him long enough."

What she sees in Umbria overshadows everything she has already seen in Italy, which, however, had been so beautiful. She writes to her parents: "When I saw Perugia and Assisi, all the rest of Italy was wiped out for me. Never would I have dreamed of such a countryside, so splendid a race of men, and such moving chapels. You might indeed have lost me forever, because, about an hour and a quarter above Assisi, there is a chapel on the mountain, an old hermitage of St. Francis, which was shown me by a young Franciscan glowing with faith; when he saw the impression this place made on me, he told me the story of a woman in the fifteenth century who had gone up there dressed as a man, had been admitted as a Franciscan, and had lived there for twenty years. They discovered her real sex only after her death, and the Church then beatified her. If I had known this story before going up, who knows whether I might not have provided a new version of it? St. Francis knew how to choose the places he lived in. Nothing in the world so sweet, so serene, so happy as the Umbrian countryside when seen from on high."

She would say the same thing to Posternak: "At Assisi I forgot all about Milan, Florence, Rome, and the rest; I was so overcome by such graceful landscapes, so miraculously evangelical and Franciscan, . . . and those noble examples of the human race, the Umbrian peasants—so well favored, so healthy, so vigorous and happy and gentle. . . . A conundrum: everything in and around Assisi is Franciscan—everything, except what has been put up in honor of St. Francis (apart from the lovely Giotto frescoes); so that one might believe Providence had created those smiling fields and those humble and touching little chapels in preparation for his appearance. Did you notice that the chapel where he prayed, in Santa Maria degli Angeli (the abominable great church built around it), is a little marvel of architecture? As superior to the works of the majority of famous architects as a popular song is to those of the majority of famous musicians."

It was in this small chapel that Simone had the second of three contacts with Catholicism that she later remembered as having truly meant something to her. She does not mention what happened there either in her letters to her parents or the letters to Posternak, but she was to speak of it in 1942 to Father Perrin: "In 1937 I had two marvelous days at Assisi. There, alone in the little twelfth-century Romanesque chapel of Santa Maria degli Angeli, an incomparable marvel of purity where Saint Francis often used to pray, something stronger than I compelled me for the first time to go down on my knees."[21]

She returned after this to Florence to attend the Maggio Musicale. Whatever had been her pain at leaving Umbria, this return to Florence was a delight. "I had the feeling of coming back to my native town after a short journey. Nowhere do I feel so much at home as here." She went at least twice to see San Miniato—"in my opinion, the most beautiful of Florence's churches"; she revisited "the old sacristy of San Lorenzo, the Donatellos, the bas-reliefs of the Campanile, the Giotto frescoes at Santa Croce, Giorgione's *Concert,* the *David,* the *Dawn* and *Night*"; she again saw the church of Carmine. ("Oh, how beautiful Masaccio's frescoes are!") She went up to Fiesole. In between her walks, she read the poetry of Dante, Petrarch, Michelangelo, and Lorenzo the Magnificent. She also read Galileo and Machiavelli. She bought Galileo's complete works and said: "I spent some luminous hours one afternoon perusing his extraordinary original insights about uniformly accelerated motion. That is as esthetically pleasing as anything, especially when one reads it here."

She went to the Casa del Fascio [local Fascist headquarters], having been taken there "by one of the founders of the Florence Fascio—a railroad man by profession and a former trade unionist," with whom she had struck up a chance conversation on the terrace of a café. She made an effort to know and judge Fascism impartially. She told Posternak: "In the Casa del Fascio there is an information bureau for foreigners, run by a young intellectual—sincere, intelligent, and, of course, attractive (they are chosen for that). In his office I met a marquis of one of the oldest Florentine families—very rich, very Fascist, very interesting. Among the things he told me (I did not hide my opinions), some were sympathetic, others less so." And further on: "In other ways, apart from this exaltation of war, there are many things in the system that would appeal to me. But—as I think I have explained to you—I believe the system has an essential need for this exaltation; which shocks me not so much for humanitarian reasons as because it rings false. The seduction of war is only too real, but it has nothing to do with all these hollow words; which, moreover, seem even more hollow in this country and among this people."

She tells Posternak how on the day she went to Fiesole a worker there started talking to her as she was waiting for the return bus. "Seeing the books in my hand, he said he would have liked to study but he had a very humble job, he was a mason; and further, that Fiesole certainly had a lovely situation and life would be fine, only he earned really too little and his life was too hard—all this in the most unaffected way and with a gay smile. I asked him if he had a family and he replied that he was too fond of liberty to want to marry and that, since he was mad about music, he went for walks every Sunday with some companions and his guitar (so there's a man who cannot often be thinking about the things that preoccupy your friend). How can one help loving such a people?"

It was on the evening of the day when she went up to Fiesole that she heard *The Marriage of Figaro* conducted by Bruno Walter. It was the penultimate opera of the Maggio Musicale, which continued into June. She wrote to her parents: "*The Marriage of Figaro*, with Bruno Walter conducting, was beyond all possible adjectives, and so appropriate to Florence! . . . I had a great wish to burst out laughing when Cherubino angrily flings his military equipment on the floor; how can they let that be played here?"

But the impression left by Mozart faded when she heard the last opera of the festival, Monteverdi's *L'Incoronazione di Poppea*, "played in the Boboli garden amphitheater under the stars with the Pitti Palace for background." This was "one of those marvels whose memory will persist for a lifetime." "The audience was cool (a pack of brutes). Luckily, however, my enjoyment was enough to fill a whole amphitheater. Music of such simplicity, serenity, and sweetness, of such dancing movement. . . . You remember my reaction when you put anything at all on the phonograph after Bach?" she says to Posternak. "Well, there are melodies of Monteverdi that I would admire even after the famous andante."

She probably heard *L'Incoronazione di Poppea* on June 3. On June 11 she was still in Florence. Her ticket could be used until the sixteenth. She planned on stopping in Lucca and Leghorn, perhaps also in Pisa, Genoa, and Milan, but I don't know whether she was able to realize this program. On the sixteenth she left Italy and returned to France via Switzerland.

Throughout her journey in Italy she used the same passport that she had used the previous year and that bore the stamps of the Central Committee of the Anti-Fascist Militia of Catalonia. If someone had inspected it, this proof of her connection with an organization that was waging war against Fascism could perhaps have caused her some trouble. But apparently nobody ever noticed it.

I believe that it was during this journey—though it could possibly have happened on her return to Italy the following year—that something happened about which she later told me. While she was in some Italian town that I cannot identify she spoke one day with a poor fellow who seemed very hungry and completely demoralized; the difficulties of life had made him very cynical. Doubtless because he had understood that she was an enemy of Fascism he warned her that the Fascists paid a lot of money to anyone who denounced an anti-Fascist. Far from being startled into caution, she told him that she had fought in Spain in the ranks of the anti-Fascists. When I asked her why she had done that, this is what she said, approximately: "I thought that a show of confidence in him could reawaken in him the emotions of honor, pride, dignity." Something of that sort must have taken place or perhaps he was not so lacking in principles as he appeared, for he did not denounce her.

I also recall that after her first journey to Italy she said to me, with a smile, "I went there to see if I could meet Tommaso Cavalieri but I never did meet him." (Tommaso Cavalieri was the young man to whom some of Michelangelo's poems are addressed.) To Posternak she had written: "Ever since I've been in Florence, I've been looking around to see if I can recognize Tommaso Cavalieri, but I haven't seen him yet. Perhaps it's just as well, because if I did meet him, I should have to be dragged away from Florence by main force." Of course she was joking.

But I doubt that it was completely a joke. She most likely wished to express the admiration she felt for such beautiful and good human beings. Such a relationship seemed to her the very essence of an inspiring friendship. Indeed, the spectacle of human beauty has been a source of inspiration for more than one saintly or wise soul.

11

Saint-Quentin, Solesmes, and the Second Trip to Italy (1937-1938)

Scarcely had she returned from Italy than Simone was chagrined to learn of the taking of Bilbao by Franco's army on June 19. A few days later, on June 22, another very sad event for her took place in France: the resignation of Léon Blum's government. He was succeeded by a Chautemps ministry, in which he figured as vice president of the Council. In some people's eyes the Popular Front continued, but for others it was dead. Simone held the latter opinion; at least she felt that the enthusiasm of June 1936 was gone and that the government that would go down in history under the name of the Popular Front government was a thing of the past. On this occasion she wrote "Meditations on a Corpse."[1]

In this article, which she did not publish at the time, she drew lessons from the experience that France had lived through from June 1936 to June 1937, "this brief history that was a happy dream for many and a nightmare for some." In her view, this history demonstrates the capital importance of imagination in social life; for "everything rests on the imagination." What had changed between June 1936 and the period that preceded it? Almost nothing in the situations of real life but rather in the emotions and state of mind. "Imagination is always the fabric of social life and the dynamic of history. The influence of real needs and compulsions, of real interests and materials, is indirect because the crowd is never conscious of it. . . . Human crowds do not pay attention. . . . Anyone who invented a method of assembly that could avoid the extinction of thought in each of the participants would make a revolution in human history comparable to the discovery of fire, or of the wheel. . . . In the meantime, imagination remains and will remain a factor in human affairs whose real importance it is impossible to exaggerate. But its effects are very different according to how it is manipulated, or not manipulated. . . ."

She thought that Léon Blum's fault was not having known how to utilize the enthusiasm of June and the state of the country's imagination at this period in order to take the measures that this enthusiasm rendered possible and that were necessary to make it yield results—for example, certain financial measures. The crowd could not see the necessity for these measures, but he should have seen it and taken them precisely at the moment when the people were in motion. This shortcoming was not the result of a lack of intelligence. "To say nothing of Léon Blum's sincerity and sympathy and morality, which rightly endear him to all who are not blinded by prejudice, where shall we find, in French politics, his intellectual equal?" But, she believes, a properly political intelligence was lacking in this remarkable man. He is one of those who have not studied deeply enough the material inherent to his art. "The material of political art is the double perspective, ever shifting between the real conditions of social equilibrium and the movements of collective imagination." In order to act upon the real conditions of social equilibrium, the politician must make use of the collective imagination as a kind of motor force, though without sharing its illusions. "He may feel legitimate scruples against working opinion up artificially and by the use of lies, as is done in totalitarian states, and indeed in the others, too, but he need not scruple to make use of the existing currents of opinion that he is impotent to change. He can use them only by transposing them. . . . It can happen that, for lack of some reform that seems quite minute, a great current of opinion breaks and passes away like a dream."

She ended by meditating on Social Democracy, which everywhere has shown itself to have "the same identical virtues and to be undermined by the same weaknesses." "But it is always dangerous to have a doctrine behind you, and especially one that includes the dogma of progress and an unshakable confidence in history and in the masses. Marx is not a good author for forming the capacity of judgment; Machiavelli is better."

It was the financial situation that had brought about Léon Blum's downfall. Consequently it was doubtless at the same time and on this occasion that Simone wrote "Some Meditations about Economy: Sketch for an Apology on Bankruptcy."[2] This article also was not published at the time.

In her opinion, financial and economic difficulties cannot cause a government's collapse. A great many facts lead one to believe that "economic collapses do not occur, but that in certain cases a political crisis is brought on or aggravated by an unsound economic condition, which is quite a different thing." The difference lies in the fact that the economic crisis produces the political crisis not directly or necessarily but through the intermediary of the imagination. One must comprehend the apparent effect of economic crises by analogy with the effect of military defeats. They often result in the fall of the government in the country that has suffered them, and yet usually they do not make it materially impossible for the government to continue. If they bring about its fall, it is because they undermine or destroy "the prestige of power, which is far more important than force in the strict sense of the word in securing popular obedience." In a government that knows how to maintain its prestige and preserve the appearance of force, an economic or financial crisis cannot bring about a collapse.

It is not less true, however, that the economic situation plays a considerable role. But in order to act effectively on the economy one must have some conception of the equilibrium inherent in economy. Now although there was formed, thanks to the Greeks and the Renaissance Florentines, the idea of equilibrium in certain arts, the idea of the equilibrium proper to economy has not yet been found. We have only a cheap equivalent: the idea of financial equilibrium. It is thought that a great deal can be done for economic equilibrium by making an effort to preserve the financial equilibrium, which involves the payment of debts. But in fact rightly considered, so soon as capital, whether in land or any other form, is remunerated, the endeavor to achieve financial equilibrium becomes a permanent factor of disequilibrium. "Capital invested at 4 percent is quintupled in a hundred years; but if the income is reinvested, there is a geometrical progression so rapid that an interest of 3 percent will multiply capital a hundredfold in two centuries." It is therefore "mathematically impossible for a society based upon money and loans at interest to maintain financial probity for two centuries" because that would put all its resources into the hands of a few people. ... "The payment of debts is necessary for social order. The nonpayment of debts is quite equally necessary for social order." In the history of all societies, it is necessary at certain moments to cancel debts.

I believe that it was also in this same period that she wrote "Meditation on Obedience and Liberty."[3] In it can be found memories of Florence and the reading she had done there, and this article can be seen as the result of her reflections on the nature of power, on the underlying causes that make it possible or bring about its collapse and on the role that the imagination plays in these causes.

She maintained that if Florence, through Galileo, was able to give mankind the idea of force, there has not yet been developed a clear idea of "social force." Social organization presents the paradoxical spectacle of a great number of men obeying a few men or even one alone, as though, in this domain, the ounce is heavier than the pound. Marxists believe that they have found the key to this enigma in economy; but obedience and command are phenomena for which the conditions of production do not provide a sufficient explanation. The obedience of the larger to the smaller number will always appear an inexplicable fact so long as one does not understand that numbers, in the social world, do not comprise a force, at least in ordinary circumstances. "Numbers, whatever our imagination may lead us to believe, make for weakness.

. . . No doubt, on all occasions, those who give orders are fewer than those who take them. But precisely because they are few, they form a whole. . . . It is only possible to establish cohesion among a limited number of men. Beyond that, there is no longer anything but a juxtaposition of individuals—that is to say, weakness."

There are, however, moments when this is not so: "At certain moments in history, a great gust of wind sweeps over the masses; their breath, their words, their movements are fused together to form a whole. Then nothing can resist them. . . . We all witnessed a miracle of this kind in June 1936." But these moments do not last. "The mass dissolves once more into individuals; the memory of its victory fades." Crowds are once again kept in a condition of obedience by "the feeling of irremediable impotence."

This feeling of impotence is natural to the person accustomed to obey. "It is impossible for the most heroically staunch mind to preserve the consciousness of inward value when there is no external fact on which this consciousness can be based. Christ himself, when he found himself abandoned by everybody, mocked, despised, his life counting for nothing, lost for a moment the feeling of his mission. . . . It seems to those who obey that some mysterious inferiority has predestined them to obey for all eternity. . . ."

These reflections are already quite close to those that she will have some years later on affliction, and at the same time they remind us of those evoked during the year of factory work. A profound pessimism in regard to the social order appears in the ending of this essay. "Social force cannot be exerted without lies. That is why all that is highest in human life, every effort of thought, every effort of love, has a corrosive action on the established order." "Social order, though necessary, is essentially bad, whatever kind it may be. You cannot reproach those whom it crushes for undermining it as much as they can. . . . Neither can you reproach those who organize in order to defend it. . . . The struggles between fellow citizens do not spring from a lack of understanding or good will . . . ; they are in the nature of things. . . . For anyone who loves liberty, it is not desirable that they should disappear, but only that they should stay on this side of a certain limit of violence."

This justification of limited struggles, which can already be found in "Let Us Not Start Another Trojan War," generally agrees with Alain's idea that there is no social state that can render the citizen's vigilance and resistance definitively useless. Order is necessary without being good; one must neither destroy it nor stop struggling to alleviate its effects as much as possible.

Simone also did not publish this third article. She seemed at this time to be uninterested in exerting an influence. She thought that France was tired of politics; she wrote to Posternak during this summer: "Contrary to what you supposed, France has never been so calm. Everyone has lost interest in politics, from sheer fatigue; for the past year the interest has been too intense. I see no harm in this lull, but I pray that the gods won't break it by raising the curtain on the great international drama."

She herself seemed a little less absorbed than before by politics and the social struggle. Ever since her journey to Italy, she felt a nostalgia for the country she had seen and began to think about the arts, the beauty of works of art, poetry, and the theater. "My feeling," she wrote to Posternak, "when I think of Italy can only be described by the word '*Heimweh.*' I cannot read the name of Giotto, for instance, or think of the name of a street in Florence without being stirred. And the impression of the *Incoronazione* is still with me so that I feel that even in my dying moment I shall give thought to the scene of the death of Seneca."

(She told me with great emotion about this scene of Seneca's death, reciting for me the words of Seneca's friends: "*Non morir, non morir Seneca, no. Io per me morir non vò. Questa vita è dolce troppo* . . . ["Don't die, don't die, Seneca. For my part, I do not want to die. This life is too sweet . . ."], and she described Seneca's unshakable determination in the face of the supplications of his friends.)

Since her return she had gone to see Giraudoux's play *Electra.* (She saw the play with Marcel Moré and Jean Wahl, the philosopher. It was on this occasion that she made Wahl's acquaintance. He had heard people talking about her and asked Moré to introduce him to her. Moré, who knew her through the group of the *Nouveaux Cahiers,* had taken both of them to this performance of *Electra.*)

Yet this play, which she had liked very much, had not completely satisfied her. She dreamed of another possible *Electra,* an *Electra* which she perhaps could write. She also had an idea for a statue. She said to Posternak in her letter: "As you observe, Giraudoux's *Electra* is not mine. (Who will bring mine to light?) . . . Why have I not the infinite number of existences I need, in order to devote one of them to the theater! I am also haunted by the idea for a statue. . . . A statue of Justice: a naked woman, standing, her knees a little bent from fatigue (sometimes I see her kneeling, with chained feet, but that would not be so sculptural), her hands chained behind her back, leaning—with a serene face in spite of all—toward scales (sculpted in high relief in front of her) with unequal arms, which hold two equal weights at unequal levels."

It seems that she may have actually tried to do some pieces of sculpture. Pierre Dantu, who saw her quite frequently in 1937 and 1938, recalls that one day when he had gone to see her at Chevreuse, she showed him some very simple sculptures she had made in small sandstones she had collected.

Yet her concern about social matters appeared even in her dreams of the arts. If she thought of a statue, it was a statue of Justice. If she thought of a play about Electra, it was an *Electra* in which, even more than in Giraudoux's, it would have been shown that virtue, conscience, and love can have a destructive effect in society by opposing the lie on which society lives.

In fact she sketched an outline of this Electra in a draft of a letter to Giraudoux which she wrote at this time. She told Giraudoux that although she did not know him, she could not help but tell him the thoughts his play had inspired in her. She did not hide from him the fact that in her opinion this play was less perfect than *La Guerre de Troie n'aura pas lieu* [in English, *Tiger at the Gates*], even though it "scintillated with beauties." And precisely because it was not perfect, it made her dream of other possible Electras. To cite only one feature in this sketch of a play, it ends in a scene where the little Eumenides sing in praise of virtue —"without which they would have so few dreadful catastrophes to savor on this earth."

In the end she decided not to send this letter to Giraudoux. As for the possible *Electra,* she did not write it. But soon after her return from Italy, she wrote a poem, "Prométhée."[4] Later she (would) say that Italy aroused again in her "the vocation for poetry, which was suppressed since my adolescence."[5] She sent "Prométhée" to Posternak in the letter she wrote him during the course of the summer. She also sent it to Paul Valéry, whom she did not know but had always admired and whose judgment meant a great deal to her. Valéry thanked her in September with a letter that contained some criticisms but also great praise. "I have only compliments for you on the firmness of the ensemble, its plenitude and its strength of movement. Many of your lines are quite felicitous. And finally, what is essential, there is in this 'Prométhée' a will of composition to which I attach the greatest importance, in view of the rarity of this concern in poetry. . . . By composition I mean something else than the logical or chronological sequence that flows from a subject. I am thinking of a much subtler quality, the rarest there is, and that even the greatest poets have in general ignored. . . ."[6]

Simone showed me this letter and asked me whether I did not find it astonishing that someone who wrote such a letter did not have any desire to meet the person to whom it was sent. She surely would have been happy to meet Valéry.

In the following year she was to send him another poem, "A un jour," which was longer and which she thought was better. But this time he did not reply.

The congress of the National Teachers' Union took place in Paris, from August 2 to 5. Urbain Thévenon attended it. It was most likely on this occasion that Simone saw him for the last time. Thevénon hesitated to phone her; but then he made up his mind and went to see her at rue Auguste-Comte. They went to see the movie *Potemkin* together. They were, he says, completely separate persons; they no longer understood each other immediately and effortlessly as they had in the past. They no longer felt any desire to ask each other where they stood and what they felt about things. They spent that afternoon simply enjoying each other's presence, feeling that they should not spoil the small amount of time that they had to be together. They seemed to know tacitly that they would understand each other if they spoke. Perhaps just a spark would have sufficed to set off a lively flow of ideas. But they spoke very little and did not discuss anything. Thévenon thought that they would have the chance to do this later on, that the moment was not opportune or ripe. He did not know that this was the last time that he would see her.

Simone had made a request to be reinstated as a teacher for the school year of 1937–1938. She was appointed to Saint-Quentin, a post she had wanted and requested for some time (both because Saint-Quentin is a working-class town and because it is very near Paris). Before leaving to start her work, she, undoubtedly at Detœuf's request, wrote an article entitled "The Worker's Condition."[7] Detœuf's magazine, the *Nouveaux Cahiers,* had published a series of articles on the condition of workers in various countries; a synthesis of these inquiries had to be made and the conclusions drawn. This is what Simone did in this article, which is dated September 1937. It was not published as such in the *Nouveaux Cahiers,* but it inspired an article the magazine published on November 15, 1937, without the author's name and entitled "Conclusions."

Simone summed up what the inquiries had shown: that there were great differences and great inequalities in the fate of workers depending on the countries involved. The result of these inequalities was that the countries where the worker's condition has been improved are at a disadvantage in international competition. This demonstrates how necessary it is that the social progress achieved in one country should be followed by similar advances in the other countries, and how urgent it is to obtain international agreements and rules on this point; without this, the advances can be endangered in the very country where they have been achieved. (She saw that the workers' conquests in June 1936 could not be maintained very long if they placed France in too marked a state of inferiority on the plane of international competition.)

At the girls' lycée at Saint-Quentin, where she taught from October, she gave courses in philosophy and Greek. She had nine students in her philosophy class and two or three in Greek. As regards philosophy, if one can judge from the extracts Cabaud presents from one of the students' notebooks[8] (the notebook is Mme. Brion-Delaporte's), she continued to follow the method she had used at Bourges: she made them read literary rather than purely philosophical works, with the aim of teaching them to think about concrete circumstances and cases.

Guillaumin's *La Vie d'un simple* inspired her to say this: "For joy to reign on earth without changing the laws of necessity, it is not the big things that must be changed but the little things, which for the soul are precisely the big things."

She took advantage of the brief leave on All Saints' Day to go to Amsterdam, where she spent a long time in the museum. (Rembrandt was one of the painters who spoke to her soul, as she was to write a little later to Posternak.[9]

Since she came to Paris almost every week she was able quite regularly to attend the meetings of "the *Nouveaux Cahiers* group." She had belonged to this group since it was formed around Detœuf in the spring of 1936. It was not a group defined by a doctrine. It had come into existence due to meetings between some industrialists, who, starting in 1934 (after February 6), had tried to pool their ideas on the necessary social reforms. In the spring of 1936, just before the elections, this small group of industrialists, brought into existence by Detœuf, had contacted men of different professions, some of whom belonged to parties and organizations (for example, to the Socialist party, the Committee of Vigilance of Anti-Fascist Intellectuals, the Christian trade unions, and the C.G.T.), while others belonged to no party or group but had knowledge of the fundamentals of certain problems. They had gotten into the habit of meeting every Monday night, at first in the Café de Flore (which before this had been a meeting place for the members of Action Française, and a little later became a place where the existentialists would get together), and then in a café near Saint-Sulpice. Each of the regulars could bring to the meetings a friend who he felt would be interested in that night's discussion and would have something to contribute to it. All that was asked of the participants was that they approach the problems without any a priori prejudices or distrust. Finally the magazine the *Nouveaux Cahiers* was founded in March 1937. The group had hopes of reaching a wider public.

Simone was already going to these meetings during the final months of her year at Bourges, and she attended them again during the winter of 1936–1937. (In any event, she also attended some meetings of the Polytechnical Center of Economic Studies, also called X-Crise, where the participants were in part the same persons who went to the meetings of the *Nouveaux Cahiers*.) Starting in October 1937, the meetings of the *Nouveaux Cahiers* group, which had been interrupted during the summer, were resumed and she went to them fairly regularly. Leafing through the magazine one can see that she was there on Monday, October 25; Monday, November 8; Monday, December 6; and Monday, December 20. But she must have attended them more often because the *Nouveaux Cahiers* only occasionally printed news about the group's sessions.

At the October 25 session the subject under discussion was "The Effect of Foreigners and Foreign Powers in France." Professor Vermeil spoke on German racism. Simone observed that in the professor's talk the racist idea appeared in two greatly different aspects. At one point it was "the idea that all groups of the German race or language belong at bottom to Germany," and at another "the idea, *quite different,* that the

German race is superior to any other race and that, as such, must dominate all of them." The first idea, Simone said, can be unreasonable in certain instances, but it is not objectionable in itself. As for the second, it is perhaps only a propaganda theme for internal use, destined to "keep the German people in breathless suspense with the mirage of a great future," for it is contradicted by the peaceful speeches directed specifically at foreign opinion. When does Hitler's government lie? Is it when it speaks to the people outside or when it speaks to the Germans? It can be in its interest to conceal its plan for aggression as long as possible, outside the country; but it can also be interested in keeping the Germans in a state of mind that is useful to him, while avoiding the risks of war. In short, "if the real aims of Hitler's government are perhaps less reasonable than he says in his speeches aimed at the outside world, why . . . would they not be even much more reasonable than his speeches for internal use lead one to believe?" These remarks show what her attitude toward Nazism was at that time. She made an effort to be just and to think objectively about this subject, as about all others. Many will say that she was deluding herself and that subsequent events have proven this quite clearly. She thought so herself later on. But it was precisely these subsequent events that had not yet taken place, and one must wonder, taking into account the facts we then had at our disposal, whether Simone's moderation was not reasonable. When war or peace is at stake, one cannot take into account too many possibilities nor reason too rigorously.

About the end of 1937, or perhaps the beginning of 1938, Simone wrote "Who Is Responsible for the Anti-French Maneuvers?"[10] She wanted to defend Messali Hadj, who had been arrested and sentenced to two years in jail. She had already been indignant when the first government of the Popular Front had dissolved the *Etoile nord-africaine,* an organization founded by Messali Hadj that brought together many Algerian workers living in France. It was because he had been accused of having reconstituted this organization under the name "Party of the Algerian People" that Messali had been sentenced. The court had not prosecuted him on the charge of "anti-French maneuvers." Simone declared that it was actually the French state itself and not Messali that was guilty of anti-French maneuvers in Algeria, because its policy made France hateful. Once again she violently attacked the French in general and the anti-Fascists in particular for their indifference to the colonial problem.

I think that it was also toward the end of 1937 or the beginning of 1938 that she wrote two important fragments that were published later in *Oppression and Liberty:* the fragment that has been entitled "On the Contradictions of Marxism," and another that she herself entitled "Critical Examination of the Ideas of Revolution and Progress."

The first of these fragments begins like this: "To my mind, it is not events that make a revision of Marxism a necessity; it is Marx's doctrine, which, because of the gaps and inconsistencies it contains, is and has always been far inferior to the role people wanted to make it play. Which does not mean that either then or since has anything better been thought of." Now the magazine *Essais et combats* in its November 1937 issue had published an inquiry: "Does Marxism Have To Be Revised?" "The profound and unexpected upheavals that the world has undergone since the beginning of the century and above all since 1914, incite us to pose the following questions: 1. Do you think that the experience of these upheavals and overturns has brought to light in the Marxist doctrine points that are false or have become decrepit, or even inadequacies? 2. What are your opinions on this? . . . 3. Would you set forth briefly the elements of a revolutionary revision of Marxism or a new Socialist theory?" After these questions the magazine published a list of prominent figures to whom this questionnaire had been sent and announced that the replies it received would be published in full. Simone Weil and many of her friends were on this list.

I therefore believe that the text "On the Contradictions of Marxism" is a draft answer to this questionnaire. It could have been written during the last two months of 1937 or the first months of 1938.

Simone Weil maintained that it was not as measured against events but in itself that Marxist doctrine was defective; or rather she thought that "the body of writings by Marx, Engels, and those who have taken them as guides does not constitute a doctrine."

Certainly events have confronted Marxism with a "flagrant refutation." But this refutation was hardly useful; "in Marx's doctrine itself the chief contradiction was so glaring that it is surprising that neither he, nor his friends, nor his followers became aware of it." There is in fact a manifest contradiction between the Marxist theory of revolution (a theory based on historical analyses that Simone considered well founded) and Marx's belief in the imminence of a liberating revolution.

The Marxist conception of revolution can be expressed in this way: "A revolution takes place at the moment when it is already nearly achieved; it is when the structure of a society has ceased to correspond to its institutions that the institutions change. . . . Notably, the section of society that the revolution places in power is the same as that which already, before the revolution, although victimized by the prevailing institutions, actually played the most active role. Broadly speaking, 'historical materialism'. . . means that institutions are determined by the actual mechanism of the relations between men, which in turn depends on the form taken at each moment by the relations between man and nature, that is to say, on the way in which production is accomplished. . . ."

Now what is shown by Marx's analysis of the regime he had before his eyes (and which has developed even more since then)? It proves that if there is oppression, it is because the role of the workers in production is most often that of mere cogs; that they are reduced to this role due to the fact that "the development of technology has taken away the privilege of skill from man and transferred it to inert matter"; that if the workers are not paid according to the value of their labor, this is simply the result of the "reversal of the relationship between subject and object," a reversal that subordinates man to the machine. And as far as the state is concerned, Marx's analysis shows that if the state is oppressive, this comes from its very nature, from the fact that it is composed of three permanent bodies that recruit themselves by co-option: namely, the army, the police, and the bureaucracy. "The interests of these three bodies are different from those of the population and consequently opposed to them." What should we conclude from all this? "The conclusion forces itself on the mind: nothing of all this can be abolished by means of a revolution; on the contrary, all this must disappear before a revolution can take place; or if it does take place beforehand, it will only be an apparent revolution that will leave oppression intact or even aggravate it. . . . How, given big industry, machinery, and the degradation of manual work, could the workers be anything but mere cogs in the factories? How, if they continued to be mere cogs, could they at the same time become the 'ruling class'? How, given the techniques of war, policing, and administration, could the military, police, and administrative functions cease to be specialized callings, professions, and consequently the prerogative of 'permanent bodies, distinct from the population'? . . . Or else must we posit a transformation of industry, of machinery, of the technique of manual labor, of administration and war? But such transformations are slow, gradual; they are not the result of a revolution."

So should there be a revision of Marxism? "One cannot revise something that does not exist, and there has never been such a thing as Marxism, but only a series of incompatible assertions, some of them well founded, others not; unfortunately, the best founded are the least agreeable. . . ."

In its questionnaire *Essais et combats* emphasized that the revisions with which the inquiry was concerned were *revolutionary* revisions of Marxism. ("We employ the term *revolutionary* revisions to make it clear that in our sense attempts like those of Bernstein or De Man have presented their evidence in the opposite direction. . . .") Simone replied: "But what do we understand by the word 'revolutionary'? . . . Does being a revolutionary mean expecting in the near future some blessed catastrophe, some upheaval that realizes on this earth a part of the promises contained in the Gospels, and gives us finally a society wherein the last shall be the first? If that is what it means, then I am not a revolutionary, for such a future—which incidentally would overwhelm me with joy—is to my mind, if not impossible, at any rate altogether improbable." If being a revolutionary means "calling forth by one's wishes and helping by one's acts everything that can alleviate or lift the weight that presses upon the mass of men," then in that event it is a matter of "an ideal, a value judgment, something willed, and not an interpretation of human history and the social mechanism." What has this revolutionary will taken from Marx? It has taken that which precisely has almost been forgotten by the Marxists: "The glorification of productive labor, conceived as man's highest activity; the affirmation that only a society in which the act of work brought all of man's faculties into play, in which the man who works was considered of prime importance, would realize human greatness to the full."

The text entitled "Critical Examination of the Ideas of Revolution and Progress" has quite close connections with "On the Contradictions of Marxism," particularly for what it contains about revolutions; it could therefore have been written in the same period or a period just a little later than this one.

Headaches were torturing her more and more. About the middle of January she had to ask for a sick leave. This leave was granted to her for two months, but she was to ask for its renewal for the rest of the school year, and then for the following year, 1938–1939, and again for 1939–1940. In fact, she never again would go back to teaching.

Having returned to Paris, she continued, despite the state of her health, to be active in the *Nouveaux Cahiers* group. Since the group was not very well organized, the need was felt to entrust the study of certain problems to specialized commissions. Simone was part of a commission charged with studying educational reform. The first project that this commission presented dealt with educational scholarships. The majority of the commission's members had approved of this project, but Simone had disagreed. It was discussed at a general session of the *Nouveaux Cahiers* group on Monday, January 31. The project rested on the principle that it was necessary to establish a selection of students that would assure "the access to leading executive careers of all those who were worthy of them"; or, differently put, that one must permit poor children, thanks to an increase in scholarships, to get a higher education and so attain executive positions. Now Simone, like Alain, thought that the problem is not one of giving the possibility of rising higher only to those who appear gifted but that of giving everyone a suitable level of education. She advocated a prolongation of the required education to eighteen years of age. To elevate only a few would have as its result skimming the cream in some way from the working and peasant classes, depriving them of their best persons and making them pass continually to the other side of the class barrier. It was in fact a strange conception of equality that consists in regarding as the most democratic a society where the mass is ignorant, oppressed, and wretched, but in which a chosen few from the mass of people could become masters of the others, rather than a society in which the main endeavor is to raise the general level. The equality of *possibilities* is not a *real* equality, above all when such possibilities are only present at the beginning of one's life. Alain contended that a good education must be provided for as long a time as possible and for all children; that one must endeavor to raise the level even of those who do not seem especially gifted; that education is made for man and not simply to ensure the recruitment of the society's ruling classes.

On January 17, 1938, Detœuf had given a public lecture in the hall of the Society of Geography on the subject, "The Construction of Trade Unionism." The text of this lecture was published in part in the *Nouveaux Cahiers* of February 15, and a discussion of it took place in the group on February 28. One can find a full account of this discussion, written by Marcel Moré, in the *Nouveaux Cahiers* of May 1.

According to Moré, this session was "one of the liveliest and most moving" that had been held since the foundation of the *Nouveaux Cahiers*. "The question being debated was one that was a great source of contention, and one felt that the debaters facing each other were involved in the debate in a profoundly human way." Simone spoke at the very start of the discussion and criticized Detœuf's views. He had advocated the establishment for the workers of a single obligatory and apolitical trade union and another obligatory, apolitical union, also the only one, for the employers. Simone explained why this kind of syndicalism seemed to her undesirable. "Detœuf's system would . . . apparently be the most complete democracy, but in reality it would be the most complete bureaucracy." It could only make the mass of workers more passive and dependent. Whatever there is in working-class trade unionism of liberty, will, energy, attachment to an ideal, attachment to dignity —all this would disappear in a large organization imposed from on high and about which the workers would no longer have the feeling that it belonged to them. Besides, it is not enough to declare that the union will be apolitical for it to be so in reality. "Even if it did not play an obvious political role, any trade union will be subjected indirectly to the pressure of the state and sometimes even that of a foreign state."

Moreover, she pointed out that Detœuf's idea was unfortunately in the process of being realized. By describing what was happening in the C.G.T., she made it clear that French trade unionism was evolving toward the establishment of a single, obligatory union. But, according to her, this meant that trade unionism was on its way to destruction. No doubt such an evolution could avoid conflicts and serve social peace. But social peace is not an absolute good or the only good; under certain circumstances struggle can be legitimate. If the causes for revolt persist —and they would no doubt persist, since what is painful in the workers' condition cannot be simply summed up by questions of material interest —if therefore feelings of inner revolt continue to exist, the day will come when "savage, anarchic, illegal" strikes and demonstrations will take place in spite of the trade unions. (Today this view can appear prophetic.)

One of the arguments she had used to demonstrate the decadence of the C.G.T. was that it seemed willing to accept the "Modern Work Statute," a collection of laws proposed by the government. An unpublished text that Simone was to write in February 1938 proves that she regarded this statute as marking the end of the period that had started in June 1936.

"June 1936 marked a date in the history of the French working class and the C.G.T. February 1938, I believe, will also mark a date, because of the discussion on a Work Statute." The victory of June 1936 seemed like a fairy tale. "And today—what has happened? When did things change? Nobody could tell you exactly but the fairy tale is far away. No law has yet been abrogated since the summer of 1936. But power has very quietly, without the slightest noise, changed sides, and one of these days we shall only have to open our eyes to see before us the fact that is the hardest to admit: the weakness of the working class. Victorious without having fought, or almost, we are on the point, it seems, of seeing ourselves defeated without a struggle. That will happen if the Work Statute is adopted as a whole, or even close in form to what the government proposes, and is effectively applied."

This statute included the regulation of the right to strike. A strike could not be decided upon except inside the enterprise and after a vote taken by the entire body of workers. They could be forced to vote by fines. A new vote could be taken every eight days to decide whether the strike should continue.

As she had already decided in 1934, it was now the struggle for the colonial peoples and the struggle for the preservation of peace to which she would devote almost all of her efforts. Trade union problems, about which she had again become excited after the events of 1936, had once more lost much of their interest for her, since it seemed to her that the trade union movement was slowly dying. In particular, the Communist party's persistent influence on and control of the workers had profoundly disappointed her and dashed her hopes. In a letter to Posternak, which she doubtless wrote toward the end of March 1938, she said: "The spirit of June 1936 is dead, or rather putrefying. The persistent hold of the Communist party over the workers is what is most distressing for anyone who has dedicated some of his love and hope to the working class. This hold was scarcely less strong when I was at Montana; but what is disheartening is that it has persisted. The strikes in the industries working for national defense are a scandal. If their motive was pacifist, they would have the beauty that goes with any vigorous assertion of faith; but most of these metal workers are very far from being pacifists. Almost all of them are in favor of armaments, and especially the Communists; and yet they hold up production in order to increase wages which are already abnormally high in the working class; this is probably a complicated maneuver of the Communist party, which wants to join the government and push it into a war."

At least, she thought, one should try to defend the colonial peoples and also try to save the peace. In the article "These Palpitating Limbs of the Country," which she published in *Vigilance* on March 10, she once again defended Messali Hadj and the *Etoile nord-Africaine.*[11] "The majority of Frenchmen do not know under what conditions the Algerian workers who work in our country live and have lived, above all before June 1936. . . . The *Etoile nord-Africaine* has been able to give these men a feeling of dignity, a goal, an organization, and an ideal. . . . The *Etoile nord-africaine* marched in serried ranks in the procession of July 14, 1936, providing perhaps the most poignant spectacle on a day rich with emotion." Simone had participated in this procession. She concludes with the observation that there is a connection between the problem of the colonies and the preservation of peace in Europe. The punishment of the French for their indifference to the colonial peoples will perhaps be that they will have to go to war in Europe because of these very people.

She seems to have thought that Hitler might go to war for the colonies. But Hitler had undoubtedly understood that the future lies with the massive powers, with those who have their colonies all around them or even within their borders. What he wanted first of all, it seems, was not the distant colonies; it was to aggrandize Germany in Europe.

In fact a few days after the publication of this article, an event occurred that considerably extended German living space and was a great blow to peace: the Anschluss. On March 12 German troops entered Vienna, and on the thirteenth Austria was annexed by Germany. With other anti-Fascist intellectuals, Simone immediately signed a declaration that was an appeal for negotiation, an appeal that was designed, if possible, to stop the race to war. This declaration was published by *Feuilles libres de la quinzaine* in its March 25 issue. It is quite possible that Simone may have drafted it, since she usually refused to sign a petition or declaration that she had not written herself. Moreover, the style seems indeed to be hers. It reads in part: ". . . Everyone's safety . . . demands that a decisive effort for peace interrupt the senseless race to war.

"We, anti-Fascists of all political shadings and opinions, deeply regret that the Popular Front governments have had little desire to perform the task of negotiating with the Fascist adversary when that should have been their foremost activity. We profoundly regret that they have left the real initiative, for something on which perhaps the entire future of humanity depends, to a conservative government such as the present British government—and we do not overlook any of the suspicions that can be held against it. Nevertheless, since we are convinced that the moment has come to choose between peace and war, we salute with sympathy Neville Chamberlain's efforts. . . .

"One must say, however distasteful it may seem, that Chamberlain's policy—inasmuch as it endeavors to put a stop to the deadly armaments race—is actually the *only* one that by means of effective negotiation makes an attempt to bring about the pacification of Europe.

"We call upon the French government to join resolutely in this action, and after having by this means realized an initial international détente, it should orient the negotiations, in conformity with the popular will, toward a just settlement of the majority of European and colonial conflicts, the precondition and point of departure for progressive and controlled disarmament."

Anschluss had rendered Czechoslovakia's situation even more shaky and dangerous. As we have seen, Simone had for a long time envisaged the possibility of an attack by Hitler on this country. But she hoped above all that the war could be avoided. In a letter she wrote to Posternak about the end of March, she said: "At the moment, there are two possibilities. One is war with Germany for the sake of Czechoslovakia. Public opinion is scarcely interested in that remote country, but the Quai d'Orsay resolutely prefers war to German hegemony in central Europe; and as for the Communist party, any Franco-German war suits its book. . . . What may prevent violent measures is the generally recognized weakness of the French army. The other possibility is an antidemocratic *coup d'état* supported by Daladier and the army and accompanied by a very violent outbreak of anti-Semitism (of which there are signs everywhere), and by brutal measures against the parties and organizations of the left. Of the two possibilities I prefer the latter, since it would be less murderous of French youth as a whole."

She continued to think that nothing could be worse than a war. Moreover, her disinterestedness made her prefer, of the two evils, the one of which she personally would be the victim.

She knew Bergery, who was the chief editor of the weekly *La Flèche.* She had already spoken to him about the problem of Czechoslovakia. After reading an article by him in *La Flèche* on this question—probably the article published in its April 1, 1938, issue—she set about writing him a letter to prove to him that his position, though extremely pacifist, was not pacifist enough.[12] Bergery connected the problem of Czechoslovakia to that of Germany's dominance in central Europe and its hegemony in Europe. He thought that such hegemony would tempt Germany to attack France and that this was a sufficient reason to oppose it, even if, in other respects, the reasons for refusing Germany the annexation of the Germans in the Sudetenland might seem questionable. So Simone posed this problem: Is it true that German hegemony in Europe would tempt Germany to attack France? "Nobody can really set aside this fear; nobody can take it lightly. Yet a firm attitude on France's part, however adeptly handled, can also lead to war, and the war to defeat, invasion, and their extreme consequences. One can therefore consider that both positions, in the worst of eventualities, can lead to the same final result (but, it seems to me, with much less of a train of slaughters and disasters in Europe and the world in the first instance). It is a matter of knowing whether the worst consequences would be more probable with the first position rather than the second. ...."

She examined the probability of the worst outcome in both cases. In the second case, she thought that Hitler would not retreat when faced by a war. In the first, it was possible that despite everything Germany would not attack France. "Such a possibility surely cannot be excluded. It is also possible that in such a case France would carry through within its own borders, provided that it goes to the trouble, an effort of culture, civilization, and social renewal, without Germany obstructing it. No doubt the superiority of German armed forces would lead France to adopt certain laws of exclusion, chiefly against Communists and Jews— which is, in my eyes and probably in the eyes of the majority of Frenchmen, nearly an indifferent matter in itself. One can quite well conceive that nothing essential would be affected."

She wrote at the end: "Can I tell you my whole idea? A war in Europe would be a certain misfortune, in all cases, for everyone and from all points of view. The hegemony of Germany in Europe, bitter as such a prospect may be, could in the long run not be a misfortune for Europe. If one takes into account that National Socialism, in its present, extremely tense form, cannot endure, one can conceive that such a hegemony, in the coming course of history, will have several possible consequences, not all of which are disastrous."

Before finishing this long letter she again mentions the colonial problem, which she never forgets. "The greatest obstacle to this policy of retreat is that France is an empire. But this is a dishonorable impediment because it is not a question for France of preserving its independence but rather the dependency in which it keeps millions of men. If France wishes to adopt this policy without seeing itself purely and simply robbed of its colonial empire, this policy must be accompanied by a rapid evolution of its colonies to a much broader autonomy and a different system of rule. As for myself, that would be a sufficient reason, if I had no other, to want such a change in orientation; for, I must confess, to my way of feeling, there would be less shame for France even to lose part of its independence than to continue trampling the Arabs, Indochinese, and others underfoot. ...."

Yet she thought about the problem of national defense. Henri Bouché, one of Alain's former students and a member of the *Nouveaux Cahiers* group, had given a lecture on March 28 in the hall of the Geographical Society on the "French Problem of National Defense." Simone was present and wrote on the subject, either for herself or because she wanted to write an article, "Reflections on Bouché's Lecture," which was published later.[13] The problem that has to be solved, she felt, is "how to render a possible invasion so difficult that the idea of such an invasion does not constitute a temptation in the neighboring states." (This question shows that she took Bergery's argument into account.) Now Bouché had advocated decentralization as a method of passive defense against airplanes. Simone felt that one could enlarge this idea and extend it to the whole conception of the defense of a territory. She thought that the most effective means of defense would be not only the decentralization of economic, political, and social life in France but the decentralization of an eventual armed resistance, "a certain form of resistance that would tend more to guerrilla warfare than to regular warfare." "Do not form fronts, do not lay siege to cities; harass the enemy, break up his communications, attack him always where he least expects it, demoralize him, and stimulate the resistance by a series of small but victorious actions." (These opinions, which were relatively new at that time, have since met with striking confirmation. The guerrilla method has in our century permitted several peoples to reconquer their independence or defend it.)

But such a method of waging war presupposes "real civic spirit, a vivid awareness, among all Frenchmen, of the benefits of liberty." Simone observes that unfortunately we have not yet reached that point and that the dictatorships "have great prestige among a far from negligible part of the population, starting with the workers and intellectuals."

One must also, she says, consider the colonies, which Bouché hardly mentioned. Because it is the existence of a French Empire that compels France to preserve and develop offensive armament. It is obvious to Simone that if the present form of the French Empire is maintained, France is sure to lose its colonies, with or without a world war. "It would be infinitely preferable that this took place without a war; but even without a war such a possibility is not desirable from any point of view." (It appears here that she did not look forward to complete separation of the colonies from the metropolitan center.) So that the envisaged method of defense could be applied both in the colonies and the metropolitan center, it was indispensable that the French Empire should evolve quickly in the direction taken by the British Empire.

Ever since her leave, Simone had been doing a lot of reading. From time to time she also went to see exhibitions of paintings. In her letter to Posternak, that is, toward the end of March or the beginning of April, she says that she has recently developed two new passions: for Lawrence of Arabia and Goya. Of Lawrence she says: "If you want to learn how to recognize that prodigious composite that produces an authentic hero —a perfectly lucid thinker, an artist, a scholar, and with all this a kind of saint as well—read his *Seven Pillars of Wisdom.* . . . Never since the *Iliad,* so far as I know, has a war been described with such sincerity and such complete absence of rhetoric, either of the heroic or hair-raising variety. In short, I don't know any historical figure in any age who expresses so fully what I admire. Military heroism is sufficiently rare, lucidity of mind is rarer still; the combination of the two is almost unprecedented."

She had seen some of Goya's paintings at an exhibition. He immediately joined that special group of painters who speak to the soul— Leonardo, Giotto, Masaccio, Georgione, and Rembrandt. "The works of the other painters evoke a higher or lower degree of pleasure and admiration, but until now it is only with these few that I have the feeling of a sort of immediate spiritual contact, the same feeling that I have with Bach, Monteverdi, Sophocles, Homer, etc."

Easter fell on the seventeenth of April. Simone wanted to hear the Gregorian chants. She had heard that at Solesmes the execution of these chants was very beautiful. It was not easy to attend the Easter services in the abbey's church because many pious people and music lovers reserved their seats in advance. Dr. Weil had to turn to someone he knew in the region; in this way he obtained two seats for his wife and daughter.

They spent ten days at Solesmes, from Palm Sunday to the Tuesday of Easter week. Mme. Weil did not attend all the services, but Simone did. Some people were amazed; they said to Mme. Weil, "She is not a Catholic and yet she goes to all the services more faithfully than anyone else."

Her headaches, which since January had never ceased making her suffer cruelly, did not prevent her from experiencing a profound joy at the beauty of the chants. Later, she wrote to Father Perrin: "I was suffering from splitting headaches; each sound hurt me like a blow; by an extreme effort of concentration I was able to rise above this wretched flesh, to leave it to suffer by itself, heaped up in a corner, and to find a pure and perfect joy in the unimaginable beauty of the chanting and the words. This experience enabled me by analogy to get a better understanding of the possibility of divine love in the midst of affliction. It goes without saying that in the course of these services the thought of the Passion of Christ entered into my being once and for all."[14]

So it was during these days that the concept of Christ's Passion profoundly affected her. Certainly she had often thought of it, though not with such intensity. It was also then that for the first time she got some notion of the supernatural power of the sacraments. This was inspired in her by the sight of a young Englishman who seemed surrounded by a truly angelic radiance after receiving communion. She called him "angel boy." He was indeed an angel for her, that is to say a messenger, because he told her about the seventeenth century English metaphysical poets, whose works would play an important part in her life. His name was John Vernon.

She also met another young Englishman at Solesmes, Charles B., whom she jokingly called "devil boy." He had dreams of becoming a writer. She talked with him about literature, especially *King Lear*. He was at Solesmes with his godmother, who soon after that came to visit the Weils in Paris.

Having returned to Paris on April 19, she undoubtedly immediately tried to procure the works of the metaphysical poets. But it was only gradually that these poems had an effect on her thought.

I remember that she spoke to me about "angel boy" and the radiance that beamed from his face. She also told me about George Herbert's poem "Love," so simple and expressive of such tender goodness, which soon caught her attention among all the other works of the metaphysical poets. She told me that it was "the most beautiful poem in the world." She recited it and also copied it out for me; but she didn't tell me that once when she had recited it she seemed to feel Christ's presence. In any event, this must have taken place only at the end of 1938,[15] but whenever it did happen, she never talked to me about it.

She reread *King Lear* and wrote to "devil boy" that the reasons she had for loving this play were not the same as his. A draft of this letter, written in English, has been found. In it she says that *King Lear* is more like the plays of Sophocles than any other work she knows, and that this should be the model for the work of our epoch, because ours is an epoch of real, not simply metaphysical affliction. No doubt affliction is always metaphysical; but it can be merely so, or indeed it can penetrate the soul through physical sufferings and humiliation. Christ's affliction, for example, was a real affliction: it was not until he had known the physical agony of the crucifixion, the shame of blows and mockery, that he uttered his immortal cry, a question that will always remain unanswered: "My God, why hast thou forsaken me?" The poetry expressing affliction is great only when that cry sounds through every word. So it does in the *Iliad;* and so it does at times in Aeschylus, nearly always in Sophocles, and in Shakespeare's *King Lear*. Lear is broken by the external world, and his suffering has something great in it inasmuch as he is broken but not crushed. And Sophocles's heroes are of the same breed.

"Devil boy" had sent her some of his literary work. She told him that he certainly had talent and that his talent could become genius, but only on certain conditions. The soul of genius is *caritas* in the Christian sense of that word, that is to say, the feeling that every human being is "all-important."* And she adds: "That, at least, is my creed."

*In English in original.

While the thoughts that Solesmes had inspired in her were working within her, she turned again to action. She was trying to find out what one could do when confronted by the threat of war; she wanted to associate herself with the resistance of those who had remained determined pacifists. In the *Feuilles libres de la quinzaine* of April 25 she is listed with others as one of the participants in an international pacifist meeting to be held in the Montcel Castle at Jouy-en-Josas from August 16 to 29. (I don't know whether she actually participated in this meeting.) On the same day, April 25, she took part in a discussion on national defense in the *Nouveaux Cahiers* group. She no doubt advocated the mode of defense which seemed to her most effective in making sure that the adversary would not be tempted to attack, that is, guerrilla warfare. Finally, about the same time she wrote "Europe at War for Czechoslovakia," which *Feuilles libres de la quinzaine* would publish on May 25.[16]

In this article she examines the Czechoslovakian problem from four standpoints: rights, the balance of power, French foreign commitments, and the dangers of war or the chances of peace. She tries to prove that from none of these standpoints does "the maintenance of the Czechoslovakian state as it presently exists seem to have the importance which has been attributed to it."

From the standpoint of rights she admits that if Germany annexed the Czech territories inhabited by Germans, Czechoslovakia would then be at its mercy and would become a satellite state. That would be an injustice. But on the other hand the status quo is an injustice inflicted on the Germans of the Sudetenland. Czechoslovakia could become a satellite without sacrificing its culture, its language, and its national characteristics. "The National-Socialist ideology is purely racist; its only universal content is its anti-Communism and anti-Semitism. The Czechs could outlaw the Communist party and exclude the Jews from the more important posts without losing anything essential to their national life. In short, injustice for injustice, since one must have one form of it in any case, we would choose the injustice that has less chance of leading to a war."

From the standpoint of the balance of power, the satisfaction of German demands would result, starting with Czechoslovakia, in all of central Europe falling under German influence, which would in turn have as its consequence German hegemony in Europe. But "if there has to be hegemony in central Europe, it is in the nature of things that this will be a German hegemony." Germany is the strongest power. "In 1918 she was just barely beaten, and by a formidable coalition. In any event, why should German hegemony be a worse prospect than French hegemony? It is true that Germany is totalitarian. But political regimes are unstable. . . ."

From the standpoint of diplomatic agreements—"Can one accept the fact that an entire generation of young Frenchmen should die for a pact that hasn't even been ratified?" "The pact of the S.D.N. constitutes a formal commitment; it has never determined, so to speak, any action, and it has tacitly been recognized as null and void at all the times that special clauses have been added to it. It is not more than a quarter of a century ago that France violated its signature when it took over Morocco, risking by this act a European war; it could very well do the same today to avoid a war. ...."

The most important question was in fact the last: Would the chances for peace be increased if France and England should solemnly guarantee the integrity of Czechoslovakia once again? But nothing is less certain and moreover it is a terrible risk to take. It would be infinitely preferable to accept the transformation of the Czechoslovakian state in order to satisfy the chief German objectives.

A new book by Bernanos, *Les Grands Cimetières sous la lune,* had just been published. It dealt with the Spanish Civil War, which was still going on. Bernanos, who had lived in Majorca, had seen what had happened on the Franco side of the war. A Catholic writer, a royalist, an admirer of the reactionary Drumont, he should have been sympathetic to the revolt of the Spanish generals against a republican government. But he had been appalled by the regime of terror that the Fascists had established in Majorca, and the great number of senseless executions that had taken place on that island, where nothing could justify such severe measures. In his book he denounced this mad intoxication with death. Simone felt impelled to write to him about the analogous experience she had had on the opposite side. In this letter [17] she describes some of the events she had seen or heard of when she was in Spain. These events, though they never reached the utter ignominy described by Bernanos, suffice to show, she says, that a certain atmosphere reigned equally in the two camps. Bernanos thought that fear had caused all these useless cruelties. Simone says: "Yes, it is true that fear played some part in all this butchery; but where I was, it did not appear to play the large part you assign to it. Men who seemed to be brave—there was one at least whose courage I personally witnessed—would retail with cheery fraternal chuckles at convivial mealtimes how many priests they had murdered, or how many 'fascists,' the latter being a very elastic term. My own feeling was that when once a certain class of people has been placed by the temporal and spiritual authorities outside the ranks of those whose life has value, then nothing comes more naturally to men than to kill. As soon as men know that they can kill without fear of punishment or blame, they kill; or at least they encourage the killer with approving smiles. ... The very purpose of the whole struggle is soon lost in an atmosphere of this sort. For the purpose can only be defined in terms of the public good, of the welfare of men—and men have become valueless. ...."

To her knowledge, Bernanos was the only person who "was exposed to the atmosphere of the civil war in Spain and resisted it." "What do I care that you are a royalist, a disciple of Drumont? You are incomparably nearer to me than my comrades of the Aragon militias—and yet I loved them."

She tells him about the disappointment she suffered because of her political and trade union activity. "From my childhood onward I sympathized with those organizations which claimed to be representative of the lowest and least regarded social strata, until the time when I realized that such organizations are of a kind to discourage all sympathy. . . ."

She also says that she is not a Catholic, though nothing Catholic or Christian has ever seemed alien to her. "I have sometimes told myself that if only there were a notice on church doors forbidding entry to anyone with an income above a certain figure, and that a low one, I would be converted at once. . . ."

When she had gone to Italy she had not seen Venice, both because of the lack of time and because Florence occupied too great a place in her thoughts. ("I have no heart left for loving Venice," she had written to Posternak, "because Florence has taken it.") Yet she wanted to see Venice. Her parents decided that they would go there for a while and that she would join them. But first she wanted to see her beloved Florence again.

She left with her parents on May 22, then separated from them and traveled to Florence as they went on to Venice.

Devil boy's godmother, whom she had seen again in Paris, had recommended a small pension that was mainly patronized by English widows and bachelors. Simone spent the first week of her stay in Florence at this pension, but it was a very bad week for her, for these charming ladies were forever on her neck and wanted to protect her, which annoyed her enormously. ("Miss P. has been very kind, full of all sorts of attentions," she wrote her parents. "You know how much I like that!") She finally discovered a small room in Fiesole, rented it, and felt more at ease.

On May 29 she wrote to her parents: "Tuesday evening, arrived at the pension (on foot) at 10:15. They didn't expect me; no room. They had me sleep (for the night) in the bathroom. Wednesday morning, excursion to the Pitti Palace and the Carmine. In the afternoon, Miss P. proposed that we have tea somewhere and I did not have the presence of mind to refuse. Went by streetcar to Piazza Michelangelo, which did not do me any good. On our return, to avoid going through that again and to make up for the offer of a snack, I brought Miss P. back in a cab. Coffee and aspirin. Theater Pergola (where my clothes were hardly suitable!). Haydn, a mediocre Haydn, in my opinion. Liturgical drama of the twelfth century, which would have been all beauty, splendid, if the idiot of an adapter had not thought it right to insert the orchestra everywhere, so that it almost drowned out the voices. He must think that they were Wagnerians in the twelfth century. It was the same good taste one encounters in the restoration of Greek statues at Rome. Just the same . . . So I was half enraptured, half furious. A sixteenth-century opera, not at all what I had thought but very funny, *opera buffa* in polyphony, with the characters of the *commedia dell'arte*. You see the characters make gestures, while a polyphonic chorus (of the madrigal type) sings each part; the voices of the men and women mingling at each moment. As *buffa* polyphony, it is unexpected. The next day Miss P. took me in the morning to the Cascine gardens, where there was a festival. In the afternoon, went out at six, made a tour of Piazza de la Signoria and ate spaghetti in a *fiaschetteria*. Friday morning, made a tour of San Lorenzo (the Medici Chapel) and Santa Maria Novella (Uccello). In the evening, Viale dei Colli on foot and returned by way of Piazza de la Signoria, with a stopover in the *fiaschetteria*. Saturday, didn't budge from my room, except to go get lire at the C.I.T. Fortunately I found *Pride and Prejudice* at the pension. Sunday morning (that is, this morning), the Bargello, a few minutes at Teatro Verdi (a meeting in honor of Spain), and a few more at Santa Croce. This afternoon Miss P. took me by car to Fiesole (she always takes a trip in a car on Sunday), where she treated me to tea with two of her friends." She concludes: "As you can see, I have not used my time very well. I hope to do better starting right now."

It is clear therefore that Simone attended another Maggio Musicale in Florence. She wrote again: "By the way, no *Euryanthe*. Replaced by a D'Annunzio play, since they suddenly remembered that he died this year. I have no desire for *Messe en ré* or Brahms."

On Friday of the following week she wrote that she had spent five beautiful and restful days in Feisole—without any books, save for her pocket edition of Dante.

She stayed four more days in Florence, so as to cancel the impression of her first week there, and then left for Padua. As soon as she arrived, she went to see Giotto's frescoes. That same evening she wrote to her parents: "I am already soused, completely soused, from drinking in Giotto." She intended to go to Castelfranco on the following day. But the next day she proposed that they meet in Padua, though teasing them a bit: "I want to see you, but I'm not sure this feeling will last. If you feel the same way, perhaps we can take advantage of it immediately. . . . If you don't come, that won't have the slightest importance; *above all* don't think that you are obliged to come if that doesn't suit you, or if it might tire you. . . ."

I don't know whether they came to Padua or simply met again in Venice. In any event, she joined them a few days later and moved into the Venetian pension, the Bucintoro, on the banks of the lagoon, where they were staying. The proprietress of the pension was a remarkable woman who was not overawed by Fascism and who would say things in a loud voice that were certainly not in keeping with the spirit of the regime. Painters stayed at this pension; before Simone's arrival, Zuloaga and Dufy had been there, but I don't know whether they were still there when she arrived, or whether she met them. Dr. Weil could not be away from Paris for too long, so he left for France on June 13. Simone stayed on with her mother, taking tours through Venice and the surrounding region.

They stayed for a while at Asolo, the "town with a hundred horizons," and while there went to a movie. A huge Fascist wearing a black shirt was selling tickets. Simone asked for the popular-priced seats, which cost a lira. He explained that there were only four rows of popular-priced seats and that in any case you could barely see anything from them. So Simone bought seats for two or three lire. After they entered the theater, she saw that there were many more rows of popular-priced seats than he had said. At the intermission, she went out to see him and said, "*Ha mentito Lei*" ["You lied"], fixing him with her piercing eyes. Furious, the Fascist stood up and made the gesture of crossing his wrists, which meant she would be thrown into jail. Simone said to him in Italian, "If you think I am afraid of you, you are fooling yourself." Then she left with her mother because the newsreel was just ending and they only wanted to see the audience's reaction to it. Simone told her mother, "Let's separate, for if they arrest me, it's better that you aren't with me." Her mother refused, and they returned to the hotel together; but nothing happened. The next day they were in a café when they saw the big Fascist walk in, but when he saw Simone, he made himself scarce.

It was at Asolo, in the small church of Sant'Angelo located a little outside the town, that Simone noticed an old fresco of which one could catch a glimpse here and there through the decay of a more recent fresco. What she saw of this old fresco seemed very beautiful. She spoke about it to several of the town's officials, the mayor among others, and she realized that nobody knew about it and that perhaps she was the first person to have seen it. In fact, people did not often go to this church, and photographs that had been taken the year before showed that the more recent fresco was then much less decayed and so one could see almost nothing of the older one. She visited the town's archives and looked through them, and since the faces in the older fresco appeared to her to be of an Asian type, she supposed that this painting could date from the tenth century, the epoch in which the Magyar invaders had occupied Asolo. This supposition appeared to her confirmed when subsequently in Verona she saw tenth-century frescoes in which the technique seemed to bear a similarity to that in the Asolo fresco.

She was to write a short article on this, in order if possible to attract attention to this fresco and make sure that steps would be taken to insure its preservation. But other events soon occupied her thoughts, and this article was published much later, in 1951.[18] At this time Cesare Fasola made a study of the Sant'Angelo frescoes.[19] He discovered that there were three layers of paintings (not two) in this church, and that the oldest fresco went back to the thirteenth century, which, moreover, was the time when the church was built. It would seem therefore that Simone's hypothesis was not confirmed. Yet she had been the first to draw attention to this work.

After Asolo she visited Verona with Mme. Weil. In the admirable amphitheater they went to a performance of Verdi's *Nabucco*. When some official personage arrived, the orchestra began to play "Giovinezza" and everyone in the theater stood up. Simone said to her mother, "Let's remain seated." The people hooted at them, shouting at them to stand up and finally forcing them to do so. Somebody said, "*Forestieri!*" ["Foreigners!"]

Then they traveled through the Tyrol, where Dr. Weil rejoined them on July 7. They stopped at several places, among others Madonna di Campiglio and Brunico. From the Tyrol they crossed the border into Switzerland on July 31. They lived for a few days in a small chalet in the mountains that they had rented. Simone did not like it up there and went down again to Montreux. There she met Posternak, who by this time was cured. She took an excursion in a car with him. She must have spoken to him about the Sant'Angelo fresco, and he must have asked her to send him a complete account of it, for it is no doubt to him that an unpublished letter is addressed in which, as in the article, she describes the fresco and presents the reasons for her hypothesis. She wrote this letter on the same day that she left Montreux with her parents. She most likely reached Paris on August 14.

12

The Inner Experience and the Renunciation of Pacifism (1938-1939)

In September she took part, with her brother, in a meeting of mathematicians of the Bourbaki group, which was held at Dieulefit in Drôme, near Valentia. After the meeting, she spent a few days with her parents in Switzerland, most likely in Geneva. If, as is probable, they stayed in Geneva, it was no doubt this year that they met Nguyên Van Danh, an Annamite whom they were to see quite often in Paris, Vichy, and Marseilles. This was the period of diplomatic negotiations that finally led to the meeting at Munich. Simone anxiously followed these negotiations. On September 15 her *Nouveaux Cahiers* friends published a special issue of their magazine, in which on one hand they advised the avoidance of measures of intimidation such as general mobilization, and, on the other, the enlarging of the objective of the negotiations, not confining it to the Czech problem, and trying to obtain a settlement of the international situation as a whole. Simone wrote to tell them that she approved of this advice.[1]

She returned to Paris just when the Munich agreement was signed, on September 30. She felt relieved. Nonetheless, her view of the future was dark. When I saw her, soon after news of the accord, she said to me, "Everything indicates that the war has not been averted, but merely postponed." She thought that the French and British governments by now considered war inevitable and were preparing for it, that they had put it off only because they did not feel they were ready for it.

The essays and articles that she wrote at this time reflect her sadness. The fragment entitled "The Disorder of Our Times," published in *Ecrits historiques et politiques,* was probably written after Munich. It expresses the anxiety of waiting, the uncertainty, and the painful loss of so many hopes. "The great expectations inherited from the three preceding centuries and above all from the last century, the hope of a progressive spread of knowledge, the hope of general well-being, the hope of democracy, the hope of peace, are all in the process of disintegrating rapidly." "The sense of security has been profoundly undermined.

However, this is not absolutely bad in itself; there can be no security for man on this earth, and beyond a certain measure the feeling of security is a dangerous illusion. ... But the total absence of security, above all when the calamities one fears are so out of proportion to the resources that can be furnished by intelligence, activity, and courage, is surely harmful to the health of the soul. ..."

(She had written to Posternak in the spring, speaking of the far from joyous circumstances that already existed: "For some years I have held the theory that joy is an indispensable ingredient in human life, for the health of the mind; so that a complete absence of joy would be equivalent to madness. ...")

After Munich, she thought that the French government had "thousands of reasons" for yielding.[2] But she also thought that "it is frightful for those Sudeten Germans who are not bedazzled by Hitler's regime; it is extremely painful for Czechoslovakia, which has no more than a shadow of national independence; and it is bitter for the democratic states, whose prestige and, consequently, security seem to have been diminished."[3] These reflections can be found in the article, "New Aspects of the Colonial Problem in the French Empire," which was written after Munich and published in *Essais et combats* in December 1938, and also in some fragments that can be regarded as variants of this article.[4]

If she wrote and published an article on the colonies at this time, it was because the colonial problem seemed to her to be almost the only subject where the situation still offered some hope. She hoped that Europe's parlous circumstances would at least favor a change in the destinies of the colonial peoples. It was now to France's interest that these peoples participate actively in political life and in the economic organization of their respective countries. They would therefore have something for themselves—something that another form of domination might jeopardize. Perhaps they could contribute wholeheartedly to the defense of their territories. "From the French point of view, such a policy is necessary; from the human point of view—which, be it said in passing, is naturally mine—whatever might be the consequences for France, it would have a good effect."

For the colonies, autonomy granted by France would be preferable, she thought, to the emancipation that would result from a victorious uprising. Autonomy "would permit the populations subjected today to so many intolerable constraints to achieve at least a partial liberty without being forced to descend to a frantic nationalism—in its turn imperialistic and blustering—an all-out industrialization based on the indefinitely prolonged misery of the masses of people, an exacerbated militarism, and the state's invasion of all social life." Simone in fact feared the development of nationalism among the colonial peoples after their eventual liberation. She particularly feared Arab nationalism.

It was somewhat at the same time, that is, before the end of 1938, that she wrote the fragment published in *Ecrits historiques et politiques,* after "The Disorder of Our Times." She was still a pacifist; but she thought that those who approve of the Munich policy are wrong to resort to mockery when their adversaries speak of humiliation. "In September a feeling of general humiliation swept France; what can be a better proof of this than that species of lethargic sleep into which all of us were subsequently plunged, the usual result of a recent humiliation? . . . We have been humiliated even more profoundly than in our concern with national prestige; every one of us has been subjected in the very center of our beings to that which is, in truth, the essence of any sort of humiliation—the abasement of thought before the power of factual reality. We search for ourselves as we still were yesterday and cannot find ourselves, not because we have been renewed by some effort of thought or action, but because between yesterday and today there occurred, outside of us and against our will, an event—this is what it means to be humiliated. . . . We have experienced the fact that men have the power, if they wish, to tear away our thoughts from the objects to which we applied them, and to force upon us an obsession that we have not chosen. . . ."

Never had her headaches been so violent as in the year 1938. They became especially bad toward the end of the year.[5] It was perhaps then that, fearing she had a brain tumor, she went to Clovis Vincent, a surgeon who operated on this kind of tumor. While sitting in his waiting room she said to her parents, "If he advises an operation, I want it done as quickly as possible." Her mother made some objection. Simone stared at her and said, "So you want me to go from breakdown to breakdown?" She dreaded madness more than anything else.

Her anguish at the thought of the breakdown by which she felt she was threatened was so great that at a certain point she was delivered from it only by resolving upon suicide under certain conditions and after a given trial period. She was to write to Joë Bousquet: "A time came when I thought my soul menaced, through exhaustion and an aggravation of the pain, by such a hideous and total breakdown that I spent several weeks of anguished uncertainty as to whether death was not my imperative duty—although it seemed to me appalling that my life should end in horror. As I told you, I was only able to calm myself by deciding to live conditionally, for a trial period."[6]

It was probably during the year at Bourges that she had made this resolution; but she suffered even more in 1938. The consultation did not help at all; he did not find the cause of the illness nor consequently, the remedy for it.

What is certain is that she suffered greatly during the last months of this year. At the most painful moments she would often recite the poem

"Love," fixing all her attention on this poem, and clinging with all her soul to the tenderness it contains. "I used to think I was merely reciting a beautiful poem," she would later say, "but without my knowing it the recitation had the virtue of a prayer."[7] At one time, about the middle of November,[8] when she recited it she had the feeling that Christ was present. "A presence more personal, more certain, and more real than that of a human being," she will write to Joë Bousquet.[9] It was not an apparition. She will say to Father Perrin: "Moreover, in this sudden possession of me by Christ, neither my senses nor my imagination had any part; I only felt in the midst of my suffering the presence of love, like that which one can read in the smile on a beloved face."[10]

How much this event astonished her and how little she was prepared for it, she was to tell both Father Perrin and Joë Bousquet. "In my arguments about the insolubility of the problem of God, I had never foreseen the possibility of that, of a real contact, person to person, here below, between a human being and God. I had vaguely heard tell of things of this kind, but I had never believed in them. In the *Fioretti* the accounts of apparitions rather put me off if anything, like the miracles in the Gospel. . . . I had never read the mystics. . . . God in his mercy had prevented me from reading the mystics, so that it should be evident to me that I had not invented this absolutely unexpected contact."[11]

Here we are astonished ourselves and are brought, as it were, to a standstill by the account of an event that remains impenetrable to us. It surprises us as much as the event surprised her. It is hard to understand why, given her ideas until that moment, she did not regard this feeling of Christ's presence as a purely subjective impression; why she thought that Christ had really been present. It does not suffice to remember that for some time now she had loved certain aspects of Christianity. One can love Christ without considering him a divine, transcendent being who can appear personally in our existence. One can admire Christian morality and Catholic liturgy without seeing in them anything more than the creations of human genius.

It is not enough to point to her physical suffering or certain disappointments in the sphere of morality. She may have had the impression of having failed in her attempts at political and social action, or at least of having been deluded in her hopes; but that had been true for a long time. Moreover, the person involved was Simone Weil, not some weakling. It is hard to believe that she would give way and look for consolation in the other world. She was much too much on guard against this kind of temptation, and had too much strength of soul to take refuge in a consoling illusion.

If she had already been a believer, one would have less difficulty in understanding her faith in this event, though some of that difficulty would persist. For even a believer, if he has had the feeling of Christ's presence, can doubt whether Christ has actually appeared before him. And this is true even more for a nonbeliever.

That is what makes this an astonishing event. I don't mean Christ's manifestation, which would obviously be an event of a supernatural order; I speak of the fact that she believed in the reality of this manifestation. In truth, this mystery is one that surrounds mystical experience in general. It is usually accompanied by a feeling of certainty: the certainty of having touched something real that lies beyond subjectivity. One has touched something that lies beyond oneself; beyond, though not as one touches palpable objects—beyond but within oneself. *Interior intimo meo.* One has been in contact with a reality that can only be attained through the inner life, which, however, goes far beyond what one is in oneself. One has touched in one's self something much greater and more ancient than the self.

But what is mystical experience and how much credit can be accorded it? Are there not people who are called mystics, yet whose thoughts seem to be simply unreasonable, irrational, and disorderly? Isn't it true that one can procure by means of drugs experiences that are called mystical? In fact it would appear that this word has been greatly abused; its meaning must undoubtedly be restricted and narrowed. I believe that what permits us to distinguish the true mystic from those who often resemble him is the quality of saintliness. A pure love, a love that does not seek egotistical satisfactions, that seeks the good of others, that does not confuse what is truly other with what one desires for oneself, such a love can be believed when it declares that it has encountered a reality that goes beyond itself and is not a thing of this world. In all true mystics the detachment from the self accompanies the experience of the absolute. Among the mystics of India, too, I believe that this is the case, for the "self" they speak of is not the empirical self.

So if some ordinary person tells me that he has encountered God, I don't believe it. But when a saint tells me, I must pay great attention to what he or she says. Because a saint is someone who knows how to resist the assaults of the ego and the imagination. The saintliness of the life is therefore the criterion; because if there is saintliness it is manifested in the life. The reason for believing in Simone Weil's mystical experience is embodied in her life.

She was not yet a believer but perhaps there had already occurred a certain change in her philosophical ideas. Alain's philosophy was voluntarist in nature. The philosophy of mysticism is the exact opposite of voluntarism. ("The mystical," Father de Guibert says very accurately, "describes the aspect of passivity that is found in all inner life.") And it is striking to see how often philosophies of a mystical nature have immediately followed philosophies of a voluntarist nature. For example, Descartes was followed by Pascal, Spinoza, and Malebranche. As though, in digging out a philosophy of the will, one reaches a point where it is completely reversed. Perhaps philosophical reflection based on Alain's doctrine but reaching a point where this doctrine seemed to be reversed played a role not in the feeling of a presence that Simone had at a certain moment, but in the fact that she subsequently regarded this feeling as not being something purely subjective.

It is possible, however, in view of what she says of the surprise she felt at this event, that she had not been at all prepared for it. But from that moment on her meditation would turn toward the study of everything that could explain and legitimatize such an experience. She would try to discover the reasons for believing that there is an absolute source of goodness and truth beyond the human mind. She could have discovered, in this way, only artificial and forced reasons. But, on the contrary, she discovered a philosophy so harmoniously beautiful and so full of manifest truths that it can be considered a second proof of the authenticity of her experience, the first proof being her life and character.

She would show that in our life and our thought there are certain inspirations which we cannot draw from ourselves and which do not come from the external world, so that we must indeed believe that we sometimes have had contact with something higher. "The experience of the transcendent; this seems contradictory, and yet the transcendent cannot be known except by contact, since our faculties cannot manufacture it."[12]

She continued to attend the meetings of the *Nouveaux Cahiers* group. She had been there on October 10 when there was a discussion of France's foreign policy after Munich.[13] On November 21 she participated in a debate about Jewish immigration to Palestine and the terrorism with which the Arabs fought against this immigration. Simone feared Arab nationalism, as I have said, but she also feared Jewish nationalism. Her contribution to the debate is summarized as follows by Tarde: "S. Weil sees another danger in the Jewish move to Palestine: why create a new nationality? We already suffer from the existence of young nations, which were born in the nineteenth century and are animated by an exasperated nationalism. (One recalls Lamartine's observation on Italian unification: let us not create another Prussia to the southeast of France.) So one should not give birth today to a nation that, fifty years from now, could become a menace to the Near East and the world. The existence of an ancient Jewish tradition in Palestine is precisely a reason for creating a Jewish homeland somewhere else than in Jerusalem."[14]

She also participated in the activities of other groups. On November 17 she spoke to the Parisian group from *Essais et combats* on "War, the Grave of the Revolution."[15]

Before leaving the year 1938, I want to mention again several events that took place or could have taken place in the course of this year, but that I am unable to place with greater precision. According to Mme. Weil, in 1938 Simone had the intention of going to Indochina, in order to find out for herself about the people's living conditions. She knew several Indochinese. Her parents went to see one of them, a prince, to ask him to dissuade her from doing this. He agreed with them that it would be foolhardy. Nguyên Van Danh, after he met her, also advised her against it. Finally she gave up the idea.

Speaking to some young Annamites, she was astonished to learn that these young people knew nothing about the 1930 revolt or the repression that had followed this revolt.[16]

She sometimes went with Nguyên Van Danh to attend lectures on the colonies. Often what the speaker said filled her with indignation and she wanted to take the floor. Danh would keep her from speaking to avoid stirring up trouble.

It was most likely in 1938 that she told me about her meeting with André Malraux. She had talked with him and had not been able to get him to agree that Stalin's regime was as oppressive as the Fascist regimes. Malraux seemed to treat Russia as a thing apart. The same things that he condemned in other countries he would not consent to condemn, or not to the same extent, when it was a question of the Communist regime. (Perhaps he condemned these things privately, but he did not want to say them openly.)

It was also perhaps in 1938 that Simone took me one day to the Ecole Normale, on rue d'Ulm, to meet the German instructor, a young German who, I believe, was named Fuchs. She had told me that he was being persecuted by students at the Ecole because he came from the country where Hitler ruled. Certainly Simone had as little sympathy as anyone else for Hitler, but she thought it rather cowardly to satisfy one's anger against him by persecuting a German who was alone in France and without any power. She pitied any individual victim of collective passion. She told me that in the school's annual review, Hitler had been the chief target for attacks and mockery. "Now," she said, "the review is traditionally devoted to mocking the director and the administration. So far as I know, Hitler is not the director of the Ecole normale supérieure." She wanted to alleviate the German assistant's distress over these insults by giving him some possibility of normal relations with the French. The conversation with him was cordial. We did not mention politics. We spoke about contemporary German philosophy (phenomenology, the philosophy of existence, etc.), and he gave us a lot of interesting information.

The year 1938, so painful from so many points of view, nevertheless brought Simone some joy, besides the joys she had had hearing the Gregorian chants at Solesmes and on her journey in Italy. Mme. Weil recalls that in 1938, for a concert conducted by Toscanini at which all the seats had been sold and which she and Simone thought that they would not be able to attend, they had finally gotten two excellent seats that had been returned at the last moment. "There are some joys," Simone said, "that come unexpectedly and for which one cannot be prepared."

In 1938 David Garnett published the letters of Colonel T. E. Lawrence. Simone, who loved Lawrence so much, certainly purchased this book as soon as she heard of its publication. After having read it, she felt impelled to write to David Garnett, although she did not know him and only knew that he had edited these letters and had been a friend of T. E. Lawrence's. Some drafts of a letter written in English and addressed to him have been found.

She told him that after reading *The Seven Pillars of Wisdom* she had immediately recognized that Lawrence is the only famous man, not only of our times but, so far as she knew, of all times, whom she could wholeheartedly love and admire. In fact, the majority of historical figures are disappointing for her in one way or another, because she longed to find in them a coming together of virtues that seem to be incompatible. On the one hand, the virtues she recognizes (what she would call her standards) are all opposed to the rules for effective action among men; and, on the other, not to act seems to her a proof of weakness. Thus she is always torn between admiration and horror when she considers the glorious exploits described by history; cruelty, or the fact of using human beings like raw material, is just as horrible to her as weakness. But Lawrence had as his standards the same values in which she believed, and he nevertheless acted in a great, heroic and glorious fashion. Of course, he could not act in perfect conformity with his standards; yet almost always he tried not to betray them any more than was necessary. And when he did betray them, he was fully aware of it, recognizing it with an intellectual clarity even more heroic than his most heroic deeds.

She compared him to Tolstoy and St. Francis of Assisi, who had also been soldiers. But they had renounced the deeds of warfare since they had turned toward another ideal. Yet Lawrence had continued to be a soldier, while upholding an ideal that was not the soldier's ideal. Like the author of the *Iliad,* he was able to describe war as it is seen by a man whose real values are those of peace. She told Garnett that she wanted to write an article on Lawrence for the *Nouveaux Cahiers* and with this in mind asked him for certain information. I don't know whether the letter was sent and, if it was, whether Garnett replied.

I remember that she spoke to me about Lawrence and that, showing me a charming sketch of his profile in her copy of *Seven Pillars,* she remarked that he looked like an angel. She could not bear the idea that he was dead. She told me that she could not stop hoping that he wasn't really dead and that she might meet him some day. Given his character and the sort of life he had led, she thought that the story of his death might even be another false story, a rumor that he himself had started so as to be able to disappear, escape his fame, become even more anonymous than when he had hidden under the name of Ross, and so, alone and free, become even more completely lost in the crowd.

Since she had been on leave, that is, since January 1938, her greater free time had permitted her more than ever before to satisfy her hunger for reading and study. She profited from it to enlarge, diversify, and fortify her culture, seeking in past centuries for a perspective, a firm and correct standard by which to judge present-day events. During the years that preceded the war she read an enormous quantity of works, above all in history. She read or reread a great number of ancient historians (Herodotus, Thucydides, Polybius, Diodorus of Sicily, Plutarch, Appian, and the Latins—Caesar, Titus Livy, Tacitus, etc.). She read many accounts, chronicles, memoirs, and documents that dealt with the Middle Ages or modern times—for example, the *Chanson de la Croisade,* the *Chronicles of Charles VI* by Juvénal des Ursins, the *Story of Charles VI* by the anonymous monk of Saint-Denis, Richelieu's *Memoirs,* Saint-Réal's *Conspiracy of the Spaniards against the Republic of Venice,* Liselotte's (the Palatine) letters, Pepys's *Diary,* etc. She also read or reread certain poets—for example, Ovid and Juvenal, Plautus and Terence, Maurice Scève, Agrippa d'Aubigné, and Théophile. She reread the *Iliad,* Aeschylus, and Sophocles.

A good part of her reading was devoted to the history of religions. I remember that she came to the National Library to consult the Egyptian *Book of the Dead* and other Egyptian religious texts. It was also at that time, I believe, that she read the entire *Old Testament* and was more than once indignant over what she found in it.

I remember in fact that before the war (I cannot say whether it was in 1938 or 1939), she pointed out to me what was shocking in certain Biblical accounts. I recall in particular two subjects that aroused her anger and indignation: the reason for which God withdrew his favor from Saul, and a story concerning the prophet Elisha.

According to the Bible, the reason God rejected Saul was that he had not fully obeyed the order God had given him to exterminate the Amalekites down to the last man. God had said: "You shall put to death men and women, children and nurslings, cows, sheep, camels and donkeys" (I Samuel 15:3). Saul having spared the king of the Amalekites and part of the livestock, God had turned away from him (I Samuel 15:7–33).

Simone was not surprised to find accounts of massacres in the Bible. She knew that there does not exist a people that at some point cannot be heard boasting about having exterminated its adversaries. She also knew that the massacres of which a people may boast did not necessarily take place, that the stories could be exaggerated. What filled her with indignation was the fact that the order for the extermination is presented in the Bible as God's order and that neither the person who wrote this story nor the majority of those who read it, including Christians, had found it repugnant to admit that God could give such an order.

As for Elisha, the Bible recounts that, some children having mocked him by calling him "Baldhead," he cursed them and after this curse two bears came out of a wood and dismembered forty-two of these children (II Kings 2:23–24). Simone had a great love for children. Here again it was not for her a matter of knowing whether the story was true or false. What shocked her was that one could accept and admire it. She thought that such a story put in question not only Elisha but the idea one had of God, since God, through this dreadful miracle, shows that he approves of his prophet's curse.

It was she who made me notice these things. I had read and reread the New Testament but I knew very little about the Old Testament; in particular, I had never read all of the historical books. And perhaps, if I had read them, I would have been blind to what is cruel in these stories, because having learned the "sacred story" very young, I was accustomed like many others to regard the enemies of Israel and of the prophets as bad. My sympathy for the Gnostics did not at first come from the fact that they criticized the Old Testament but from the fact that their doctrines are not without some relation to Plato's ideas, and above all that they had inspired the theology of St. Paul and the fourth book of the Gospel. On the other hand, Simone, if she had some sympathy for Marcion and the Cathars, this was first of all and perhaps above all because of their criticism of the Old Testament.

Nonetheless she admired some parts of the Bible—for example, certain psalms, the Song of Songs, Isaiah, Daniel, and above all Job. When reading the Book of Job, she noticed the lack of consistency that is apparent in the present text of the book owing to the intervention of Elihu. She said to me, "I can't understand it; God condemns Job's friends, and he says nothing against Elihu, who said the same things as they did." Thus she had an inkling of the hypothesis that the majority of interpreters have now accepted: that the character of Elihu and his speeches have been added to the original text.

It was to discover the possible sources of the Book of Job that she asked me, a little later, to bring her the *Choix de textes religieux assyrobabyloniens* published by Dhorme.[17] She wanted to read one of the poems contained in this book, "The Suffering Just Man." But this, I believe, was at the beginning of the war. But let us return to the first months of 1939.

It was probably at the beginning of 1939 that I brought her the collection of *Manichean Homilies,* found in Fayum. When she returned the *Homilies,* she said to me roughly as follows, "It's remarkable that the religious teachers have never, in the presence of death, an attitude of defiance, of contempt for death; that, although being firm toward men, they complain to God in their prayers and manifest their sadness." She had been struck by the fact that Mani complained to God while in prison. This seemed to her the sign of real courage, because real courage does not keep one from loving life and does not demand that one blind oneself.

It took only six months for Hitler to violate the commitment he had made at Munich. He had guaranteed the independence of Czechoslovakia; on March 15 German troops entered Prague. From then on things became clear to those who had believed in the possibility of peace. Some of those who changed their opinion did it radically and without the slightest nuance. They thought: it is now proven that agreements with Hitler are useless; the only relation that can exist between Germany and the other states is one of force.

For Simone it was also a great turning point; but she did not draw such radical conclusions from the event, or at least not immediately, because she was more cautious and more truly human. She was not one of those who clung to pacifism, desperately shutting her eyes to the reality, but she did not think that negotiations were now useless. She felt that one had to halt Hitler's progress, but without neglecting to try to do it through negotiations. This can be seen in her "Reflections with a View to an Estimate," which she wrote after England had adopted conscription, that is, after April 27, 1939.[18]

In "Reflections" she recognized that if war breaks out, it will most likely be a war among nations for their very existence and not for some limited goal. It is true that for many centuries now we have become accustomed to see the failure of attempts at universal conquest. But the history of a more distant past shows that at least one of these attempts succeeded: Rome's attempt in ancient times. That is enough to give us the right to ask whether the disappearance of the free nations is a fictive danger, as the optimists believe.

However, it should be clear that when a nation fights for its very existence, it can have only the guarantee of its security as its aim. This "sounds innocent, but what in reality it means is the elimination of the danger that caused the war; and that danger is another nation or other nations." Thus the democratic powers would necessarily have as their objective the annihilation of Germany as a nation, and the annihilation of such a country implies either that some other country will acquire universal domination, which would be no less of an evil in its hands or, more probably, since there seems to be no country of sufficient caliber for the role, that would mean "the total ruin of Europe, which will thereafter no doubt become, in its turn, a colonial territory."

Thus war would be a catastrophe, not only in itself but because of the sort of peace that would follow it. Unfortunately the existence of such a situation renders negotiations very difficult, for the slightest concession "leads to loss of prestige, which diminishes, for the nation

consenting to it, its chances of defending its independence." Prestige
is truly a power, perhaps indeed in the last analysis it is the essence of
power; and a great nation that would have made every possible concession until it had nothing to defend except its own existence, would
probably by that very fact have become incapable of defending it."

We are already no longer truly in a state of peace since the change
in British policy, of which the institution of conscription is the proof.
Are we already in "the state of war danger," as the Germans put it? We
can hope that we are still in an intermediate state between peace and
the danger of war and that there still remain some possibilities of avoiding the conflict. Certainly Hitler will go as far as he can in the direction
of universal domination. Already, by the ties that he has established with
Italy and Spain, he has nearly reconstituted the empire of Charles V.
Besides, he possesses something that neither Charles V, Louis XIV, or
Napoleon possessed, and that is the essential instrument of a vast domination: the state in its most perfected form. He has also rediscovered
the methods by which Rome had extended its power in the past: "In fact,
between the manner of development of Roman domination, especially
during the second century B.C., and the rise of Hitlerian domination
there are some astonishing analogies."

Yet there remains a reason for hope. "For the resemblance of the
Third Reich to republican Rome of the second century does not extend
to their inner regimes. In internal affairs it is imperial Rome that resembles Germany." But if the Empire preserved the conquests of republican
Rome, it did not conquer much itself. Rome's power of expansion no
longer existed when it was under imperial rule. One can also find a great
analogy between the inner regime of Germany and that of Soviet Russia.
Now the flaws of the Soviet regime have made Russia less and less
redoubtable to its neighbors than in the past. So one can hope that the
same progressive weakening of Germany will occur due to the work of
its own regime. If Europe can hold out for ten or fifteen years without
a war, the danger will probably have passed at the end of this time.

"It is absolutely necessary, therefore, to hold out for as long as the
German system is still in its phase of expansion. . . . But to hold out does
not mean to refuse ever to retreat; a rigid determination never to give
way at all during the next ten years would probably mean war. To hold
out means sometimes to stand firm, sometimes to give way, sometimes
even to advance a little, so as not to offer one's opponent an obstacle
that he feels can only be overcome by desperate violence, nor yet one
that seems so weak that he can do what he likes. Until recently we were,
or seemed to be, in danger of provoking desperate violence, but now the
second risk is greater. There is a danger that our opponent will go so
far that we may be reduced to the choice between enslavement and war."

She therefore advises being rather firm in negotiations, while still
hoping that skillful negotiations will perhaps permit the avoidance of

war. She does not regret her past pacifism, but she thinks that this pacifism, which had its legitimate reasons, no longer has any meaning, since France has missed the opportunity to be generous when she could be so without any danger. "Only ten years ago she had the power to behave with generosity in Europe; even three years ago she could still at least have behaved with moderation; today she is able to do neither because she is not strong enough. . . ."

Thus "our aims in every sphere, whether political or social, national or international, must at present, if they are reasonable, be limited by the maneuvers to which, as a result of our faults in the past, we are condemned to resort in our foreign policy." But it does not at all follow that this policy will be sufficient. "It is a defensive tactic and, as we know, to remain long on the defensive is bad tactics and bad for morale. . . . Some kind of offensive is indispensable. We, too, must have a positive force—but not in the field of violence and the appetite for power. . . . It is right to demand from France a policy of generosity, but she no longer has it in her power to be generous to Germany and its clients. One is not generous to those who are stronger than oneself; one is generous, if at all, to those who are at one's mercy."

Those whom France has at its mercy are the colonial peoples. So once again Simone's conclusion is that it is necessary to change the regime imposed on these peoples. Since one cannot defend oneself against the threat of subjugation except by making an appeal to the love of liberty, France must "be seen by her own citizens and by all men as an ever-flowing source of liberty." "There must not be a single genuine lover of freedom in the whole world who can have a valid reason for hating France; all serious men who love liberty must be able to be glad that France exists. We think this is now the case, but we are mistaken; it is our responsibility that this should begin to be so."

She did not publish this article, perhaps because the situation evolved so quickly that she soon considered her advice useless.

Parallel with these reflections and most likely written at about the same time are the drafts for a long letter that Simone addressed, or had the intention of addressing, to an Italian friend.[19] Probably commenting on Hitler's violation of the Munich agreement, this friend had written to her that there are different ways of not keeping faith with a treaty and that if Caesar, Augustus, and Richelieu built something solid, it was because they had not committed vulgar breaches of faith. However, Simone's estimate of these three historical figures was quite different from her friend's. She was especially concerned to prove to him that he was mistaken as regards Caesar and Augustus in particular and the policy of ancient Rome in general. Her reading or rereading of so many ancient historians had not been in vain. She had drawn from this a vision of ancient history as personal—and as shocking to many people—as her vision of the Bible. She had perceived that Roman policy, usually so highly thought of, was in many instances perfidious and merciless. In particular she had studied very carefully the history of Caesar's victory over Ariovistus, perhaps because her friend Guillaume de Tarde, in the *Nouveaux Cahiers* of April 1, had compared Ariovistus's methods to Hitler's. For her, it was Caesar whose methods should be compared to Hitler's, at least as regards bad faith.

She therefore tells her friend the story of Caesar's victory over Ariovistus, in her view a victory gained by betrayal. She tries to prove to him that starting with the Second Punic War, Rome's history is full of acts of brigandage. As an example of Roman perfidy, she recounts the history of the destruction of Carthage. She recalls that Augustus, when he was still called Octavius, had been guilty of deceit; and later on when he was Augustus, "the unbelievably base adulation that was the rule under his regime made it quite difficult to estimate his policy and give an account of it." And finally she sums up her attitude toward the Roman Empire as a whole, saying: "The Roman Empire is in my view the most dreadful phenomenon for the development of humanity that can be found in history, since it practically killed, by suppressing their traces, a number of civilizations and the entire prodigious exchange of ideas in the Mediterranean basin that had gone to making the greatness of what is called antiquity; but it is also the vastest phenomenon we have known and one of the most lasting. Hence I conclude that it is not accurate to say, despite all that you bring forward, that brigandage is powerless to establish solid systems."

(In her "Reflections with a View to an Estimate," she also says something akin to this: "I believe the Roman conquests, with their atrocious material or spiritual annihilation of entire peoples, to have been history's great disaster. . . .")

For the breaking of a promise to become a means of establishing a solid conquest in her opinion it must fulfill one of these three conditions: either be so exceptional and surrounded by such shadowy circumstances as not to be noticed by people who do not look at things closely; or have as its result the almost total massacre of those who could object to it; or be the act of someone so powerful that nobody would dare to criticize him or even notice it. The failure to keep one's word that her correspondent mentioned (probably Hitler's act as regards Czechoslovakia) does not fall, she says, in any of these categories. So she believes that it is "a misstep and even a serious mistake." "Unless, however," she adds, "the third condition might be close to being realized, which is possible."

In these drafts, as in "Reflections with a View to an Estimate," she cites as an example of cynicism but also frankness and lucidity the words the Athenians addressed to the inhabitants of the island of Melos, words she would often quote after this, and which she says she had found recently in Thucydides. As in the "Reflections," she also says that it is not true that force is powerless to annihilate spiritual values. "It annihilates them very quickly and very easily. People always point to the nationalities that have survived centuries of oppression; but there are many, many more that have not survived. . . . How many religions have also been annihilated by force. . . .! There is nothing in the world so precious but nothing more fragile, which perishes so easily, or which is so difficult or even impossible to revive, as the vital warmth of a human environment, this atmosphere that bathes and nourishes thoughts and virtues." One thinks of what she will write a little later on the subject of the city. Also when she says: "It is by a kind of miracle that there arises on a given land, at certain moments, forms of social life where constraint does not destroy this delicate and fragile thing that is an environment favorable to the development of the soul. There has to be a social life that is not overly centralized, laws that limit injustice, and, to the extent that authority is exercised arbitrarily, a desire for obedience that permits one to submit without abasing oneself."

She believes that excessive centralization would some day be supplanted by decentralization, but that this change was not near at hand. "I don't think that this will happen very soon, nor perhaps even in a future that is on the scale of a human life; and above all I am completely convinced that centralization, once it is established anywhere, will not disappear before having killed—not paralyzed momentarily but killed—all sorts of precious things. . . . "The material conditions of a dispersed life will not come into existence before a long time has elapsed, nor will the destroyed spiritual values be easily revived. Undoubtedly other spiritual values will spring up, but not before a long time has gone by. . . ."

About violence, she says; "Violence is often necessary but in my view there is greatness only in gentle behavior."

Speaking of affliction (this in connection with the afflictions that had struck certain Italian Jews, since in Italy Jews were also beginning to be persecuted): "It must be said that unless one is sustained by some form of fanaticism, which makes everything easy and without value (notably this singular fanaticism about History that today is the sole living faith), to bear decently any change of fortune, either good or bad, is a masterpiece of the highest virtue. And, in a general way, it is not easy to bear up under affliction; for an attitude of defiance does not suit man's condition, which forces him to bow to necessity, and this submission must never penetrate to the soul without incurring the penalty of destroying all that which is human."

Toward the end of this spring, Simone fell ill with pleurisy. Dr. Louis Ramond treated her and would come and sit for long spells at her bedside, talking to her.

When she was cured, Ramond insisted that she take a vacation in the mountains. She agreed to follow his orders on the condition that she could stop over in Geneva to see the exhibition of the Prado's master-pieces, which had been sent to Geneva in February 1939. The war in Spain having ended at the beginning of April, the paintings were now on exhibition before being returned to Spain.

She left with her parents at the end of July and spent about fifteen days in Geneva. Every day she would go to look at the Velásquezes and contemplate them for hours on end. After this, she went with her parents to Peïra-Cava, a town in the mountains above Nice. They had the intention of staying there through the winter. But war was declared during the first days of September. The Weils returned to Paris.

13

The First Year of the War
(1939-1940)

When I saw Simone again in September, she spoke to me about the part played by England in the declaration of war. She thought that England had been the principal factor and that now it was the British government that was inciting the French government to resistance and standing firm, after having for a long time held it in check. She was not angry about this; quite the contrary, she thought that the English were right and that we must follow them loyally and back them up at every step.

But she still believed that in order to resist Hitler, we must be bolstered by the feeling that our cause was absolutely pure and just. She was still tormented by the problem of the colonies. The fragment published in *Ecrits historiques et politiques* after "Reflections With a View to an Estimate" is a good expression of her thoughts at this time.[1] Moreover, it seems to me that it must have been written in this period, soon after the declaration of war.

"In order to carry through the struggle that pits the only two large European countries that have remained democratic against a regime of total domination . . . before all else we must have a good conscience. We should not think that because we are less brutal, less violent, less inhuman than those we are confronting, that we will prevail. Brutality, violence, and inhumanity have immense prestige. . . . The contrary virtues, so as to have an equivalent prestige, must be exercised in a constant and effective manner. Whoever is only incapable of being as brutal, violent, and inhuman as the adversary, yet without exercising the opposite virtues, is inferior to this adversary in both inner strength and prestige; and he will not hold his own against him."

She concludes that, to fight effectively, it is not sufficient to defend a less stifling regime than the totalitarian regimes one opposes. "We must take our stand from an environment in which all activity is actually and effectively channeled in a direction that is the very opposite of tyranny. Our propaganda cannot be made up of words; to be effective, it must be based on dazzlingly self-evident realities." This conclusion recalls that of "Reflections With a View to an Estimate." It is clear that in her mind the dazzlingly self-evident realities on which our propaganda must be based were measures favorable to the colonies.

When mentioning propaganda, she was thinking perhaps of what Jean Giraudoux, who had just been appointed Commissioner General of Information, was then doing to support the French cause. Most likely Giraudoux's speeches—charming, sensitive but not very effective— were in her view a form of propaganda composed of not much more than words.

She always managed to hear or read Giraudoux's speeches. Following a speech on "The Duties of the Women of France," which he delivered on November 26, 1939, over the radio and of which *Le Temps* published extracts the next day, she felt impelled to write to him about it. Among other things Giraudoux had said: "France has an empire of one hundred and ten million men and a colonial domain attached to its metropolitan center by ties that are not those of subordination and exploitation. . . ." It was this judgment that, in Simone's eyes, was untrue, and such a lie seemed to her to weaken France's cause. She wrote to Giraudoux: "I did not hear your speech; I read it in *Le Temps.* There is a passage in it that caused me acute pain. I have always been proud of you as one of those whose names can be mentioned when one is looking for reasons why present-day France can be loved; and that is why I would wish you always to speak the truth, even on the radio. No doubt you believe what you say is the truth; but I wish with all my heart that I could persuade you to ask yourself if it is so when you assert that France's colonial dominions are not bound to her by ties of subordination and exploitation.

"I would give my life and more if it was possible to believe that this is true; for it is dreadful to feel guilty through involuntary complicity. But it is not true. To any informed person who has studied the question it is as clear as day that things are not as you describe them."

She then cites some examples of the oppression to which the natives are subjected in certain French colonies and concludes by saying: "I realize that this letter exposes me, under the decree of May 24, 1938, to from one to five years in prison. I don't feel in danger; but suppose I were, what do I care? Perpetual prison could not hurt me more than the fact of being unable, owing to the colonies, to think that France's cause is just."

So she still had divided feelings. If she no longer had any hesitation about deciding that it was necessary to fight Hitler, she nonetheless felt, sadly, that France's cause was not entirely just. On the other hand, she could not bear, once again, to be in the rear, a mere civilian. She forged plans for undertakings that, while serving both France's cause and that of other peoples, would have permitted her to be in the front lines. (It was then forbidden for civilians to go to the front.)

She had been shocked to learn that a revolt of students in Prague had been brutally repressed by the Germans. She worked out a project for parachuting troops and arms into Czechoslovakia. She thought that they could get the people to rise up against the Germans and help those in prison. She presented her plan to a number of important political figures, always adding that, if it were adopted, she absolutely insisted on participating in the action. She swore that if it were performed without her, she would throw herself under a bus. Every day, for many weeks, she bought the newspapers and anxiously looked through the stories to see whether her plan had been put into execution, and she thought that her last day had perhaps come. She confessed all this to her mother soon after, when she realized that her plan had obviously been rejected.

One of those she had approached with her plan was Henri Bouché. Actively engaged in work in the aviation field, he could give her technical advice and put her in contact with some of the people who had the power to get her plan adopted. (He mentioned it later, with a smile, as a plan that was utterly impossible. He has said to Simone, "But this plan will kill the very people you wish to help." And Simone had replied, "So be it, they will die, but they will die with dignity.") She also spoke of it several times to Noble Hall, an Englishman and perhaps a diplomat assigned to Paris whom she was to meet some years later in New York.

It is probable that, in her efforts to get her plan adopted in official circles, she was often hampered by her long-standing reputation of being a Communist. They had no confidence in her. It was also on this occasion that she wrote a declaration that we have quoted earlier, in which she says that she has never been a member of the Communist party. It was then too that she asked me to look through the copies of *L'Humanité* for August and September 1933 for a paragraph that demanded the expulsion from France "of Trotsky, the White Guards, Prader, and Simone Weil." She wanted to have the exact reference. These lines could serve as proof that for a long time the Communists had considered her one of their enemies.

I could not find this paragraph; but I did find another passage, where, with regard to the congress at Rheims, she was attacked in *L'Humanité* in August 1933. She told me that this passage was just as suitable as the other and fitted her purpose.

André Weil had been sent on a scientific mission to the Scandinavian countries in April 1939 by the Caisse des Recherches. When France entered the war, he was in Finland with his wife Eveline, whom he had married in 1937. He had decided a long time ago not to participate in the war that he, like everyone else, had foreseen. He believed—thinking he was in accord with the teachings of the *Gita*—that duty is an individual matter and that his duty to himself was to be a mathematician and not to fight in a war. He sent Eveline back to France, while he stayed on in Helsinki.

When Simone heard that her brother intended to stay in Finland, she was more inclined to blame herself than him. She felt responsible for his decision, believing that he had been inspired by the extreme pacifist position she had long held. She was full of remorse.

As she waited for the putting into effect of the "parachute plan," she worked on two long essays, one on the Roman Empire and the other on the *Iliad.* The first, called "Some Reflections on the Origins of Hitlerism,"[2] had a direct connection with the war that had just begun. It was intended to demonstrate the objectives that the French and English should pursue in this war.

A clear awareness of the goal to be pursued obviously depended on the idea one had as to the deep-going causes for the conflict. Now one might regard this war as having been provoked by an eternally aggressive power, a power that was dangerous by nature—Germany. (Which is what Pierre de Lanux had argued in the pages of *Nouveaux Cahiers.*) In that case, the war's objective could only be the destruction of Germany as a nation. Or it may have been provoked by a plan for universal conquest, a plan favored by certain aspects of contemporary civilization and certain characteristics of the modern state much more than by a particular nation's characteristics. In this latter case, the war's objective must be the establishment of an international system that would make such a plan impossible not only for Germany but for any other country.

It can be said that, in line with her habit of going quickly to the core of a problem, Simone already saw the questions that would arise after the war. She realized that what threatened the world was not just Hitlerian Germany—it was the state of civilization that had rendered the Hitlerian enterprise possible; and that, consequently, this threat would not be abolished by an eventual victory of the democratic countries, unless there was a clear awareness of what was at stake and ways to ward it off were found.

The question posed by this long and remarkable essay is basically this: Should humanity desire universal domination? We have been raised to admire Rome, its conquests and empire; but we do not fully realize what the Roman Empire actually was. When the methods with which Rome conquered the world are reproduced before our eyes, we do not recognize them and they fill us with horror. We must distrust more than ever the prospects for the unification of the world and try to form some idea of what the method and consequences of such a unification would be. And we cannot form this idea unless we examine attentively and without prejudice the only universal domination that the world has known, the only one that succeeded in establishing itself and in lasting—Roman dominion.

That is why this essay is much more about ancient Rome than about

Hitler. Most of it is devoted to describing the methods that Rome employed to extend and maintain its conquests. As for the part that concerns the permanence and changes in national characteristics (that is, the refutation of the then current statements about "eternal France" and "eternal Germany"), this is only an introduction that, besides, must have been written after the rest of the essay and is solely intended to link it more closely to the political situation at that moment.

The part of the essay that was written first, and indeed was the only part published at that time, is the one that follows the introduction and became the second part in the definitive version—"Hitler and Roman Foreign Policy." Here the problem is essentially that of Rome. Hitler is only evoked when the perfidy and callousness of Roman policy calls his methods to mind.

We already know Simone's opinion on certain events in Roman history; she had already spoken of the sacking of the towns of Epirius, the destruction of Carthage, the way in which Caesar's victory over Ariovistus was won. She again discusses Epirius and Carthage (she had also explained how Caesar's victory over Ariovistus took place, but in the introduction); and she adds to this some other facts of the same kind, that is, more examples of bad faith and cruelty: the taking of Cartagena, the siege of Numantia, Rome's policy toward Greece.

Besides, she again emphasizes the Romans' great concern for Rome's prestige. "The first principle of Roman policy . . . was to maintain the maximum degree of prestige in all circumstances and at any cost. There is indeed no other way by which a limited power can proceed to universal domination; for no single people can possess in reality sufficient forces to dominate many other peoples. . . . That is why the Romans exhausted themselves in an interminable war against a little town whose existence was no threat. . . . That is also why they never agreed to discuss peace except after a crushing victory."

The power of opinion is immense in both politics and war. Rome not only has always been anxious to preserve the prestige of its power, it also was always able to invest this power with an appearance of legality. Pretexts are not useless, even when they are transparent and cannot fool anyone, provided they are put forward by those who are stronger. "Might is nearly always in the wrong if it is silent when the victim invokes his rights. . . . On the other hand, even if the pretexts are grossly contradictory and hypocritical, they are plausible enough when used by the stronger."

Finally, the Romans possessed "a skill at which neither Richelieu nor Louis XIV nor Napoleon were completely adept." "It was the skill of maintaining in their behavior toward other nations a rhythm that at one moment lulls them into apparent tranquillity and at the next moment paralyzes them with anxiety and confusion, without ever allowing them to rest in any intermediary state. . . . Above all, they concentrated on the essential point: a lightning rapidity of attack. . . . On each occasion the victims of this treatment . . . were stricken with dismay and confusion that prevented them from putting up any effective defense. But everything was done to encourage the witnesses of these executions to feel easy about their own immediate prospects."

This part of the essay was published by *Nouveaux Cahiers* in its January 1, 1940, issue.

The next part, "Hitler and the Internal Regime of the Roman Empire," was already in galleys when the censorship forbade its publication. It is perhaps even more convincing than the first part, for it sets out to demonstrate the misdeeds of universal conquest. The long and profound decadence that was caused for the subjugated peoples in the Roman Empire by a single, centralized domination cannot be denied. "Finally, if we consider the long centuries and the vast area of the Roman Empire and compare these centuries with the ones that preceded it and the ones that followed the barbarian invasions, we perceive to what extent the Mediterranean basin was reduced to spiritual sterility by the totalitarian State." The Roman peace was soon the peace of the desert, of a world from which had vanished, together with political liberty and diversity, the creative inspiration that produces great art, great literary works, science, and philosophy. Many centuries had to pass before the superior forms of human life were reborn.

It should be observed that when it was a question of the internal regime, it was to the Roman Empire that Simone compared Hitler's government, whereas when it came to foreign policy, she compared Hitler's methods to those of the Roman republic. In fact she felt, and had already said this in her "Reflections With a View to an Estimate," that the resemblance between Hitler's policy and that of the Romans was not total. "The principal difference is that he has established a totalitarian dictatorship before becoming master of the world, and this will probably prevent him from conquering the world; for it seems that a totalitarian dictatorship is better at oppressing its own subjects than at conquering many new ones." So she was not without hope as regards the final outcome of the war. Hitler had stifled liberty too early in his own country. It was the Roman republic that had conquered the world, not the Rome that itself had lost its liberty.

In her conclusion she denies that one must excuse the Romans on the pretext that morality changes and that certain acts that have become inadmissible were forgivable in the past. "There is no ground for believing that morality has ever changed." Indeed this is what Alain thought. She quotes from three ancient Egyptian texts and also from the Greeks to show that the purest forms of morality have always been known. And even if morality has changed, this would not justify speaking of Rome with admiration in our epoch. "If I admire, or even excuse, a brutal act committed two thousand years ago, it means that my thought, today, is lacking in the virtue of humanity. Man is not divided into compartments, and it is impossible to admire certain methods employed in the past without awakening in oneself a disposition to copy them. . . ."

The traditional admiration for Rome is usually explained by the fact that Rome, having abolished the different cultures in the Mediterranean basin, save for Greek culture that it had not abolished but that it relegated to second place, had inevitably imposed and transmitted its own culture. Roman culture was almost the only culture known during the Middle Ages in the West. "The influence of Christianity might have been a sufficient counterweight, if the one influence could have been separated from the other; but unfortunately Rome had adopted Christianity after a few centuries and established it officially in the subject nations, and in this way she contracted an alliance with it by which it was contaminated. It was a second misfortune that Christianity's place of origin bequeathed to it a heritage of texts that often express a cruelty, a will to domination, an inhuman contempt for conquered or potentially conquered enemies, and a respect for force, which are extraordinarily congenial with the Roman spirit. . . . The twofold Hebraic and Roman tradition has in great measure negated, for two thousand years, the divine inspiration of Christianity. . . ."

French culture itself has been to a great degree pervaded by the Roman ideal. Certainly France "has had many minds of the first order that have been neither servants nor worshippers of force." From the fifteenth to the seventeenth centuries, one can name Villon, Rabelais, Là Boétie, Montaigne, Maurice Scève, Agrippa d'Aubigné, Théophile, Cardinal de Retz, Descartes, and Pascal. But the heroes of Corneille and Racine ordinarily see greatness in terms of the Roman model: the glory of triumphing, conquering, dominating instead of serving justice and the public welfare. And the statesmen and leaders who have governed France and are still held up for our admiration, especially Louis XIV and Napoleon, have often copied Rome's methods.

Probably it was these pages, in which certain aspects of French thought and political policy were criticized, that motivated the censor's interdiction. Simone begins here to refute the current affirmations about "eternal France" and "eternal Germany," as she would do in the introduction finally added to the essay. She shows that it is France that, in great measure, is at the source of the development of nationalism since the beginning of the nineteenth century. "Every people that turns itself into a nation by submitting to a centralized, bureaucratic, military State becomes immediately and long remains a scourge to its neighbors and the world. This phenomenon is not connected with Germanic blood but with the structure of the modern State. . . . But a phenomenon that has long been familiar must now begin to cause anxiety to all thoughtful minds. . . . Every new development of the last three centuries has brought men closer to a state of affairs in which absolutely nothing would be recognized in the whole world as possessing a claim to obedience except the authority of the State."

The only way to limit the power and ambition of the state would be to institute a supranational authority that could, if the situation arose, exempt the citizens and subjects of a state from the duty of obedience toward this state. "International order presupposes some kind of federalism among nations, and also inside each great nation. A fortiori, the link between colonies and their metropolis should be made a federal one, instead of a relationship of simple subordination."

If Germany were to be conquered without such an order being established, the respite enjoyed by the European peoples would most likely not last very long. Europe "might collapse from exhaustion into a state of general disorder and bloodshed, from which Russia perhaps would profit. . . ." On the other hand, to impose a system of order that Germany would not accept presupposes a constraint maintained over a long period of time. "A long and continuous effort is impossible for a coalition; so it would have to be the task of a single nation. . . ."

If this nation were to be France, "she would be punished for her presumption by another war, which would perhaps annihilate her. But let us assume it to be within her power. Then would she not lose all her wisdom, her freedom, and her humanity in straining her national resources to the limit in the effort to fulfill such an enormous task? . . . In other words, Hitler's system would not disappear; it would simply migrate, with all its characteristic aims and methods, to France. . . .

"The victory of those who are armed to defend a just cause is not necessarily a just victory; it is not the cause for which men took up arms that makes a victory more just or less, it is the order that is established when arms are laid down." It is desirable that the German nation be broken up, but with the proviso that this is not maintained by force. "The only condition which can make this possible is that the victors, if that is what we are destined to be, should accept for themselves the same transformation that they impose upon the vanquished.

"It is inevitable, anyway, that a day will come when the tendency to centralization that humanity has followed for several centuries will change into the opposite tendency; for everything in nature has its limit beyond which it cannot go. There are two types of decentralized organization about which history gives us fairly full information: the small city and the feudal society. Neither of them offers a guarantee against tyranny or war, but each of them does more than the centralization of Roman and modern times to stimulate and favor the better forms of human life."

Thus, for her, the conditions for a just peace after the war were decentralization—or, as we would say now, regionalization—and federalism between the nations and within one's own government.

In the same spirit as "Reflections on the Origins of Hitlerism,"

Simone wrote some fragments of an article that she never finished, "Reflections on Barbarism."[3] Did she write it before the article on Hitler and the Romans, at the same time, or a little later? I don't know. This article was also intended for *Nouveaux Cahiers.*

On the one hand, she wanted to demonstrate that if one calls barbarians the peoples who remained outside of civilization or, if one wishes, the peoples of primitive civilizations, Hitler was not properly speaking a barbarian. "It requires an extremely civilized State, but a basely civilized State so to speak, such as Rome, to bring forth in those it threatens and in those it conquers this moral breakdown, which not only destroys in advance all hope of effective resistance but also disrupts brutally and finally, the continuity of spiritual life. . . . Our situation in Europe is not that of civilized men fighting a barbarian but the much more difficult and dangerous one of independent countries threatened with colonization. . . ." On the other hand, she wanted to show that what is called barbarism, in the moral sense, is not typical of certain epochs or certain peoples. "I would suggest that barbarism be considered as a permanent and universal human characteristic that becomes more or less pronounced according to the play of circumstances. . . . I would be prepared to present this postulate: that we are always barbarous toward the weak. Or at least, in order not to deny all efficacy to virtue, one might put it that we are always barbarous toward the weak unless we make an effort of generosity that is as rare as genius."

No particular people is essentially barbarous, in the moral sense. Nor is any "particular social class predestined as the one and only bearer of civilization." The key to history is not the idea of class, as Marx believed, but the idea of force. "I believe that the concept of force must be made central in any attempt to think clearly about human relations, just as the concept of relation is central to mathematics."

It was this concept of force that would give Simone the means to construct a powerful and original psychology. It would permit her to cast a new light on a universally admired poem that had been the subject of innumerable commentaries, a poem about which one would have thought there was nothing further to be said: *The Iliad.*

"The Iliad, or the Poem of Force,"[4] is one of Simone's very rare articles, among those that she published herself, in which the subject is not directly political or social and does not have a close connection with the actual situation in which she wrote it. There is the problem of war, but not of the war against Hitler. There is the problem of misery and affliction, but it is the misery and affliction of the Trojans and Greeks, or affliction in general. Certainly circumstances contributed to the fact that Simone had focused her attention on affliction, and even more intensely than was usual for her. But, apparently, her main concern was to understand the *Iliad.*

The passages from the *Iliad* quoted in this article were translated by

Simone herself. Since she translated line by line, never inserting into a line of the French translation a word that was part of the following line in the Greek (she observed one day that it is often by the line arrangement that a poet succeeds in expressing a given emotion), and since she also wanted to preserve the original word order as much as possible, she often spent a half-hour translating a single line. The final result shows that this effort at precision was worth all the trouble. I believe that never before has a translation so completely captured the human tenderness and pity that pervades the *Iliad*. All that one saw in this poem up until now was the depiction of heroic deeds. It never has been observed that much more often than what we call heroism, the poem depicts human beings who either let themselves be carried away by the intoxication of their own power and force or are cruelly overpowered by affliction and the force of others. That accent of "incurable bitterness" which one hears so often in her translation had never been heard before. "It is in this," she says, "that the *Iliad* is absolutely unique, in this bitterness that proceeds from tenderness and that spreads over the whole human race, as evenly as the sun's clarity. Never does the tone lose its coloring of bitterness; yet never does the bitterness fall to the level of mere complaint. Justice and love, which have hardly any place in this study of extremes and unjust acts of violence, nevertheless bathe the work in their light without ever becoming noticeable themselves, except as a kind of accent."

For this reason the *Iliad* is not simply a beautiful poem. Or rather, it is a beautiful poem because it is first of all a poem based on lucid thought and humanity, justice and charity.

What the poet shows us and what struck Simone is essentially the weakness of the human soul, of any human soul in the face of force and violence. Whether he employs force or undergoes it, man is transformed by it. Sometimes, by a miracle of courage or love, he escapes the basest transformations produced by the contact with force and violence, yet he cannot avoid being harmed by it. Simone says of the *Iliad:* "Its bitterness is the only justifiable bitterness, for it springs from the subjections of the human spirit to force, that is, in the last analysis, to matter. This subjection is the common lot, although each spirit will bear it differently, in proportion to its own virtue. No one in the *Iliad* is spared by it, as no one on earth is. No one who succumbs to it is by virtue of this fact regarded with contempt. Whoever, within his own soul and in human relations, escapes the domination of force is loved but loved sorrowfully because of the threat of destruction that constantly hangs over him."

It is the same in Greek tragedy: "Here the shame of the coerced spirit is neither disguised, nor enveloped in facile pity, nor held up to scorn; here more than one spirit bruised and degraded by misfortune is offered for our admiration."

The same is true of the Gospels: "The Gospels are the last marvelous expression of the Greek genius. . . . The accounts of the Passion show that a divine spirit, incarnate, is changed by misfortune, trembles before suffering and death, feels itself, in the depths of its agony, to be cut off from man and God. The sense of human misery gives the Gospels that accent of simplicity that is the mark of Greek genius. . . . This accent cannot be separated from the idea that inspired the Gospels, for the sense of human misery is a precondition of justice and love. . . . Only he who has measured the dominion of force, and knows how not to respect it, is capable of love and justice."

Simone briefly contrasts this attitude to that of the Romans and Hebrews. "Strangers, enemies, conquered peoples, subjects, slaves, were objects of contempt to the Romans. . . . With the Hebrews, misfortune was a sure indication of sin and hence a legitimate object of contempt; to them a vanquished enemy was abhorrent to God himself . . . a view that made cruelty permissible and indeed indispensable. . . . Throughout twenty centuries of Christianity, the Romans and Hebrews have been admired, read, imitated . . . their works have yielded an appropriate quotation every time anybody had a crime he wanted to justify."

Furthermore, she thinks that the spirit of the Gospels has not been transmitted in its pure state to the Christians. "To undergo suffering and death joyfully was from the very beginning considered a sign of grace in the Christian martyrs—as though grace could do more for a human being than it could for Christ. . . . The only people who can give the impression of having risen to a higher plane, who seem superior to ordinary human misery, are the people who resort to the aids of illusion, exaltation, fanaticism, to conceal the harshness of destiny from their own eyes. The man who does not wear the armor of the lie cannot experience force without being touched by it to the very soul. Grace can prevent this touch from corrupting him, but it cannot spare him the wound." In this essay Simone found the accent of all the writing she did in her last years.

She continued her studies in the history of religions. It was certainly around the beginning of the war when I brought her, on her request, a volume of the *Choix de textes religieux assyro-babyloniens* translated by Dhorme. She wanted to read the "The Suffering Just Man." Not being able to go to her house on the same day that I had borrowed the book from the library but only two or three days later, I took advantage of this to peruse some of the texts it contained. I was above all interested in *The Epic of Gilgamesh* and found that certain parts of this poem were very beautiful. When I gave Simone the book, I said to her, as a joke, "I'm giving you the 'The Suffering Just Man,' but don't take *Gilgamesh*—that's mine." We used to find it amusing to contend for the possession of great men and beautiful works; we would say, "I leave that one to you, but this one is mine."

Some days later, in the letter in which she asked me to look for the paragraph in *L'Humanité,* she told me that thanks to Dhorme's anthology (where the texts are not only translated but also transcribed), she was in the process of learning Babylonian without a grammar or dictionary and that *Gilgamesh* had now become her personal property.

"I have been studying Babylonian for two afternoons, boning up on *Gilgamesh,* and I've transformed Dhorme's translation (the most beautiful passages) into a juxtalinear translation (word for word). Of course, without a grammar or dictionary. You see what a ridiculously easy language it is! I imagine that you will know it perfectly well within a month. (But it isn't as beautiful as Greek!) In the meantime, I hope you won't tell me that *Gilgamesh* is yours.

"See you soon, *ib-ri.*" (*Ib-ri,* I should imagine, means friend in Babylonian.)

She was particularly delighted by the naive way in which Gilgamesh, when he sees his friend dead, suddenly has the revelation that he himself will die and runs away in order to search for the secret of immortality. (He will not find this secret, or having found it he will lose it; the poem ends with a bitter description of the miserable condition of the dead.)

Some time later she read the *Bhagavad-Gita.* According to her autobiographical letter to Father Perrin, she read it in the spring of 1940. It is astonishing that she had never read it earlier, for she had often seen it in her brother's hands. Her brother, when a student at the Ecole Normale, had studied Sanskrit and, on the recommendation of Sylvain Lévi, had read the entire *Gita* in the original and had greatly admired it.

(It is also astonishing that, curious as she was, she had never read the Spanish mystics. Her brother had brought back the works of St. Teresa after a journey to Spain in 1934, and he was also interested in St. John of the Cross. But Simone always had too little time for all the things she would have liked to do.)

Still, she managed to read the *Bhagavad-Gita* just at the moment when this poem answered precisely all the questions that she was thinking about. When she spoke to me about it, it was perhaps at the beginning of the German offensive. She told me that this poem had a burning pertinence to what was just happening because it dealt with the question of knowing whether a man who has pity for others and whom war fills with horror, Arjuna, must nonetheless go fight in the war. She herself had already answered this question in the affirmative, but this did not stop her from being tormented by pity. Arjuna's problem was hers. It is clear that she had read with extreme attention Krishna's words that prove to Arjuna that he must fight and that if he does so in a certain way, a man can still remain pure.

During the following years she must have never stopped meditating upon Krishna's teachings. She was struck by the resemblance between the spirit of the *Gita* and the Christian spirit, and instead of her admiration for this poem turning her away from Christianity, it brought her even closer.

From this time on, when we spoke about religion, she would often use Krishna's name instead of God or Christ. It seemed to me that this was due to a certain feeling of shyness.

She also continued to read historical books and documents. She rejoiced when she encountered in history an important figure who had the rare strength of soul not to exercise all the power at his disposal. I believe that it was around the end of 1939 that she told me about Theodoric, king of the Goths, and Gaston Phœbus, the Count of Foix. She admired both of them, the former because he had ruled without ever committing any acts of injustice, as even his enemies had testified, and the latter because, after having conquered his enemy the Duke de Berry, he had nonetheless ceded to him the government of Languedoc out of a love of peace and the public good. Gaston Phœbus was for her one of those rare examples of men who had freely consented not to rule in every place where they held the power.

Finally the account of the conspiracy of the Spaniards against Venice, which she had found in Saint-Réal, occupied more and more of her thought. She said that Otway and others had not understood the nobility of the motive that, according to Saint-Réal, led Jaffier to denounce the plot: it was pity for the city of Venice. An emotion so rare must have seemed impossible to them, so in fact they had invented other motives. But it was precisely this motive that formed the beauty of this story, and it seemed to her that she was the first person to have perceived it. I believe that she began to write her play *Venise sauvée* even before her departure from Paris. It is true that Mme. Weil said that she had started it during their flight; but I tend to believe that, since she had left all her papers in Paris and was not sure that she would ever retrieve them, during their flight she wanted to write again the already written parts of her play and continue it.

No doubt it was just before the war or at the start of the war that Dr. Weil read an article on larval sinusitis in a medical journal and showed it to Simone. The symptoms of this illness, as they were described, seemed to the doctor to be the same as the illness from which she suffered. After she read the article, she said to her father, "It seems that that might in fact be it." They contacted the author of the article (Mme. Weil could not tell me the doctor's name, but, according to Cabaud,[5] his name was Vernet), and Simone began to follow the treatment that he advised (doses of cocaine administered to the sinuses). This treatment seemed to do her some good. But it was soon interrupted, since the doctor was called up for military service. It was perhaps due to this treatment, even though it was interrupted, that she was to suffer a little less during the last years of her life. Yet it appears that her headaches had already been a little less violent after the end of 1938, even before the treatment.

On November 30 Finland was attacked by Russia. André Weil had gone for a walk around a building that housed an anti-aircraft battery and the Finns suspected he was a spy and arrested him. In his rooms they found some correspondence with colleagues in Moscow, and this confirmed the police in the belief that he was a spy in the pay of the Russians. They also found in his quarters texts written in mysterious signs, which only reinforced their suspicions. These were texts that had been stenotyped by Eveline; she had learned the Grandjean stenotype system, and her husband, to give her practice, had dictated one of Balzac's novels, *Cousin Bette,* to her. He was in great danger of being shot as a spy. But since they could not prove that he was a spy, they at last decided to expel him. He was taken to the Swedish border and handed over to the Swedish border police. In Sweden, he was detained for some time at the border, at Haparanda. His guards loaned him a sweater and a small woolen cap, for it was extremely cold.

One of Simone's friends was in Sweden. He wrote to Simone telling her that he was sorry that he had not been told about this mishap sooner. If he had been, he might have been able to do something, but the way things looked now André was, in his opinion, in danger of being shot by a firing squad. When she got this letter, Simone burst into tears. With her mother, she went to see a Swedish professor who was in Paris and was just about to return to Stockholm; they asked him to take them along as his secretaries (this was the only way they could possibly leave immediately for Sweden). He did not say one word in reply and did nothing during the entire meeting but shake his head negatively from side to side with an imperturbable smile on his face. Only when they got up to leave did he open his mouth and say, *"Au revoir, Madame."*

So they had to stay in Paris and wait for news; and much more reassuring news soon arrived. The friend who had written had been mistaken: André ran no risk of being shot in Sweden; he had been in danger in Finland. He was no longer regarded as a spy. But since he had sent a letter to the French legation there asking to be repatriated and sent to the front, the Swedes decided to return him to France.

About the end of January he was put on a boat that was going to England. When he got off the boat, an agent of the English Intelligence Service was waiting for him and stayed with him until he embarked again for France. Having met a Frenchman who was boarding the same ship and was a functionary of the French Secret Service, the Englishman said to him, "Since you are returning to France, would you please accompany M. Weil. That will save us the trouble of sending someone along with him."

On the ship the Secret Service agent told André that he was sorry but he had to keep him locked up in his cabin all night. Before disembarking at Le Havre, he said to him, "If you want to write to your parents, give me the letter, for I'll be obliged to hand you over to the police." André wrote to his parents: "Get me a lawyer, any lawyer, provided he is not named Cohen or Levy." His parents chose a lawyer named Bloch! He was a veteran of the First World War; perhaps this is why they considered it right to overlook their son's advice.

This lawyer's parlor was crammed with furniture covered with red plush. According to Mme. Weil, this was the parlor Simone was thinking of when she spoke, in the "Prologue," of these "bourgeois parlors full of trinkets and red plush." She spent many hours there with her parents when they went to see the lawyer. They often had to wait a long time before being able to speak to him.

Charged with failure to report for military duty, André was first sent to the civilian prison at Le Havre. He remained there for about three weeks. At the start they did not permit him to receive any books or to get paper on which to do his mathematical problems. He wrote to his parents that if he were deprived of the means to read and write, he did not know what he might do. His parents, his wife, and Simone, terribly frightened and alarmed, all rushed to Le Havre. A letter from Dr. Bercher, who was in Le Havre and had been able to see André, had led them to believe they could visit him. But when they got to Le Havre, they were told, "Our orders are very strict: nobody can see him." But André found a way of informing them that the desperate tone of his letter was purely intended for the prison officials. He hoped by this ruse to obtain the materials with which he could work. This attempt to startle the prison officials had a different result; fearing that he might commit suicide, they put two companions in his cell, whom he found quite amusing. One of them was a poacher.

Simone made an appeal to de Tarde. She had already told him of the situation her brother was in; she wrote to him:

"You know what effect solitude, silence, and a lack of work can have on any human being; but my brother, especially, has never, I think, remained idle for an hour in his whole life, and he is accustomed to uninterrupted intellectual activity.

"Perhaps you know someone who by a telephone call, either to the prefect or the civil prison at Le Havre, could settle the whole thing. . . . Getting a little paper would seem a very small thing to ask for; to grant it should not cause them great trouble; the deprivation of this little thing can have destructive and lasting effects; yet it is often precisely things of this kind that are impossible to obtain, and without one ever finding out why. . . ."

I don't know whether de Tarde succeeded in getting André the materials he needed to work with, or whether this request simply became pointless when the justice department of the military took over the affair and André was transferred to the military prison at Rouen. There he could work. Simone went to see him with her parents or her sister-in-law as often as this was permissible. They could visit him twice a week, but each time only two visitors were admitted, so that the Weils did not all go at the same time. So they soon got to know the waiting room in the railroad station at Rouen very well. Mme. Weil said that when Simone spoke of the railroad station waiting room in the "Prologue," it was probably this waiting room she was thinking of.

(So, in the "Prologue," when she lists the places where she feels she is condemned to live and that visibly fill her with horror—a prison cell, a station waiting room, a parlor crammed with trinkets and red plush —two of these places are those in which she spent a good deal of time during this period. They remained in her memory as horrible places because of the anxiety she had felt over her brother.)

When she did see him, it was through two iron grilles separated by a space in which a prison guard walked up and down. They had to shout to make themselves heard. One day she said something to him in Greek, and the guard rushed over: "It is forbidden to speak in a foreign language here."

Between these visits she wrote to him, most often about mathematics or subjects far from his present troubles. It was not only to distract him; she wanted to share his ideas and knowledge, to renew the intellectual understanding that had united them when they were children. Perhaps for a long time neither of them had had enough free time in which to exchange ideas. She also hoped that by telling him her ideas about mathematics, it might perhaps induce him to do the sort of research she wanted to see undertaken, or to provoke replies from him that would be extremely interesting in themselves. This is how she came to write the letters or drafts for letters, some of which have been published in *Sur la science.*[6]

She believed that there was a connection between social oppression and the fact that the higher mathematics are inaccessible to laymen. She also thought that this inaccessible, impenetrable nature of higher mathematics was due in part to their being too abstract, too often reduced to algebra, and too separated from intuition. To bring them closer, if possible, to concrete perception was a task to which she would have devoted her entire life, if she had several lives to live.

"Present-day mathematics, considered either as a science or as an art, seems to me to be singularly far from the world. Could not an effort of reflection and criticism bring it closer? ... It is one of the goals to which I would have loved to devote my entire life; but, alas, I have several goals. And not only do I have but one life but, as you well know, I don't even have a life to devote to anything whatever; nothing but discontinuous moments, short and far apart. The only remedy for this is metempsychosis. Let us hope that my future reincarnations will suffice to satisfy my many different longings."[7]

Owing to its concreteness, Greek mathematics seemed to her the ideal mathematics. She thought that the Greeks had rejected algebra and that they had consciously preferred geometry. She too preferred geometry. She thought that "God, according to the statements of the Pythagorians, is a perpetual geometer, but not an algebraist."[8]

If the Greeks attached great value to mathematical reasoning, it was insofar as it allowed them to make an effective study of concrete problems. "Not that they were avid for technical applications, but because their sole objective was to obtain a clearer conception of the identity of structure between the human mind and the universe. Purity of soul was the sole concern; 'to imitate God' was the way to it; the study of mathematics helped to imitate God insofar as it looked at the universe as subjected to mathematical laws, which made the geometer into an imitator of the supreme legislator."[9]

Their mathematics was truly an art. "It truly was based on hard material, a material that existed, like those of all the arts without exception . . . ; this material was space really given, imposed as a factual condition on all the actions of men. Their geometry was a science of nature."[10] (She had said the same thing about Descartes' geometry in her doctoral thesis.)

Simone did not believe that the discovery of incommensurables had been a great shock to the Pythagorians, as certain historians imagine. She suggests that the number they spoke of, when they said that everything is number, was a relationship. The fact that certain spatial relationships could not be expressed in rational numbers was therefore not considered a failure of their theories.

Her brother having spoken to her about Neitzsche, whom he admired for his genius as a writer, she told him (in a draft of a letter that was never sent): "We are quite far apart on the subject of Nietzsche. He inspires in me no inclination to treat him lightly; only an invincible, almost physical revulsion. Even when he expresses things that I believe, he is literally intolerable to me."[11] She thought that he did not understand Greece. "He is utterly wrong about Dionysus—not to speak of the opposition to Apollo, which is pure fantasy, since the Greeks mixed them together in their myths and appeared sometimes to consider them identical. Has he taken into account what Herodotus says . . . that Dionysus is Osiris? Hence it is God whom man must imitate to save his soul, who has joined man in suffering and death, and whom man can and must join in perfection and felicity. Exactly like Christ."[12]

Certainly the Greeks had a grim and painful conception of human existence—"like all those who keep their eyes open." "But their sadness had an object; it had a meaning *in relation to* the felicity that is the natural allotment of the soul and of which it is deprived by the harsh constraints of this world. Pain and sorrow never appear among them except as the defeat of an aspiration to felicity. It is in this sense only that (as Nietzsche says) there was among them a mixture of sorrow and joy; because the feeling of being born for felicity is still a happy feeling, even if it remains miserably impotent, and it appears more purely in misfortune. On the contrary, for so many modern men . . . there is a sadness in itself, a sadness linked to the absence of this very sense of happiness. . . . To my way of looking at it, madness is essentially the total privation of joy and the very idea of joy."[13]

In her view, anguish did not exist among the Greeks. They "were on another plane; they had grace." "What they had intensely was the feeling of exile, the feeling that the soul is exiled in the world. It is this part of them that passed over into Christianity. But such a feeling does not produce anguish—only bitterness. They have also had, more than any other people, the sense of necessity and its dominion that is impossible to combat. But this feeling, bitterer than all else, excludes anguish."[14] Besides, the soul must learn "to recognize its country in the very place of its exile," as the Stoics had understood.[15]

Since her brother had asked whether there was mysticism in Plato and in general among the Greeks, she replied (also in a draft of a letter which she did not send); "As for the problem of mysticism in Greece, there are things that must be clearly understood. There are people who simply were seized by states of ecstasy; there are those who, moreover, study these states almost exclusively, describe them minutely, classify them, even to a certain extent provoke them. The latter are generally called mystics. . . . In this sense there is no trace of mysticism before the neo-Platonists and the Gnostics. . . . But if one calls mysticism the fact of having these states of ecstasy, of attaching a high value to them, and if not provoking them, at least attempting to put oneself, whenever possible, in that state of mind, then Plato, first of all, is a mystic. . . . Moreover, when he says, praising the μανία inspired by the gods, that Dionysus inspired these mysteries, he testifies to the existence of a mystical tradition. For this μανία can only consist in ecstatic states. . . ."[16]

Speaking of Greece, she asked her brother in one of her letters whether he knew Autran's thesis, according to which the Phoenicians were Dravidians. "His arguments, which are philological, don't seem beneath contempt, insofar as one can judge without knowing the Dravidian language. . . . But the thesis is very seductive—even too seductive in the sense that it gives an extremely simple explanation for the analogies between Greek thought and Indian thought. . . . Whatever the case might be, how can one avoid being nostalgic for an epoch in which the same ideas existed everywhere . . . in which ideas circulated over a prodigiously large area, and in which there was all the richness that diversity produces? Today, as under the Roman Empire, uniformity has had its leveling effect everywhere . . . and at the same time ideas have almost stopped circulating. Enough! Perhaps a thousand years from now this will be a trifle improved."[17]

Decidedly she had turned toward the past, not the future. "I thank you for telling me that the future needs me; but, as I see it, it has no more need of me than I have of it. If only I had a machine to travel through time, I would turn not toward the future but toward the past. And I would not even stop among the Greeks; I would at least go all the way to the epoch of the Aegean-Cretans. But this very thought has the effect on me that a mirage has upon a man lost in a desert. It makes me thirsty. It is best not to think of it, since one is caught on this minuscule planet that will become great, fertile, and varied as it was in the past only a long time after us—if it ever will."[18]

She also wrote to her brother about Cardinal de Retz and Théophile. Of Retz she said that his great concern for fidelity and honor, as well as his concern for the public welfare, had dominated all of his intrigues. "The direction of all his activity was a desperate attempt to destroy Richelieu's work. . . . In France, Spain, and England, this beginning of the seventeenth century was something of extraordinary luminosity; an indefinable inspiration attained its culminating point and suddenly perished, never to reappear again. For my part, except for Racine, I don't value anything that came after 1660 (right down to our day) as much as that which dates from before it. I don't count Corneille, whom in any case I value very little. . . ."[19]

She quoted some of Théophile's verses and said that for her, along with Villon, Maurice Scève, and Racine, he ranks high above all other French poets.

The warden of the prison enjoyed talking to Simone, whose intelligence he admired. While talking about one thing or another, she would slip in the fact that her brother was a genius and that it was necessary that he be able to work. As a result, they encountered no difficulties in sending him books crammed with mathematical signs, which usually would have aroused fears during wartime. He worked so well that later on, according to his wife Eveline, he used to look back regretfully to his days in the prison at Rouen.

Simone would have ardently loved to take her brother's place in jail. In a sense, she envied him because he was there. Laughing, she told him that she would never forgive him for having known the inside of a prison cell before she did. She promised that if the sentence he was given meant he would have to stay in prison, she would slap one of the judges or the prosecutor so that she would be thrown in prison, too.

Among the texts she sent to him while he was in prison there was also George Herbert's poem "Love." Yet he did not realize the change that had been taking place in her philosophical and religious ideas. It was not until he saw her again two years later in America that he became aware of it.

When he was just about to go to trial, she wrote a draft of a letter to give him some wise advice. (André Weil thinks that this letter was not sent.) "It is obvious," she said, "from the way you write (legal recourse —solemn protest!!! etc.) that you still believe you are in the most beautiful days of the Popular Front. You should convince yourself that that time is past, dead, as distant as the Egyptian revolution of 2000 B.C. . . . A heavy, opaque, stifling atmosphere has settled over the country, so that people are now bored stiff and dissatisfied with everything, but on the other hand are disposed to swallow *no matter what* without protest and even without surprise." She recalls that the recent decree-laws permit the government to inflict very severe punishments for acts and statements that previously would have seemed tame. She gives some examples of the courts' severity. "The conclusion is that it would be idiotic on your part to sound off before the Council of War or anywhere else. In such a situation, there are only two positions to take: to slip through the holes in the net, or to be convicted as the result of deliberate statements, after having chosen the occasion, the moment, and the way of doing so. For you, it is obviously not the moment to get convicted, since you have chosen to return and to conform to the law. . . ."

She added: "Although I feel enormous regret about this transformation of the country, I don't dislike all its aspects; for principles are not made to be invoked publicly but within oneself, in order to decide one's proper line of conduct; and, just between us, the 'Popular Front' style was very bad French. The Louis XIII style is much more beautiful."[20]

André went to trial on May 3. His lawyer did not defend him well at all, in his opinion and his family's. Simone had given him advice that he unfortunately did not follow. But even if he had been well represented in court, the sentence would most likely have been the same. The period and the instructions of the government weighed in the direction of severity. André was sentenced to five years in prison. He did not want to appeal the sentence; he asked to be sent to a combat unit, which would involve a suspension of the punishment until the end of hostilities. As a result, he was freed and sent to an infantry regiment at Cherbourg. Before joining his regiment, he was able to spend a weekend with his family in Rouen.

In the drafts of one of the letters that Simone intended to send her brother, as we have seen, she mentioned the Gnostics. What did she know about them at this time? What had she read of their works or about them? I don't know. I believe that we never talked about them. The first person to talk to me about them was my boss at the National Library, Amand Rastoul. He was a convinced Catholic and I often argued with

him. I asked him one day why the Church, instead of basing itself on
Plato, who is so close to Christianity, had chosen to base itself on
Aristotle, who is so far from it. "I believe that the Church," he answered,
"distrusted Plato because he had been used by the Gnostics."

Learning in this way that the Gnostics were Platonists, I felt sympathy for them and looked for whatever texts they might have handed
down. One of the first I read was the *Odes of Solomon,* those Christian
poems that of course are not by Solomon but doubtless by a follower
of Valentinian (and so I believe it is possible that they are by Valentinian
himself). I thought very highly of this poetry that celebrated grace and
that seemed to me to be pervaded by the spirit of St. Paul and St. John
the Evangelist.

This took place about the beginning of the war, for Rastoul retired
as head of the General Catalogue in 1939, if I am not mistaken. (He was
still in charge of the Catalogue when he spoke to me about the Gnostics.) Yet I don't recollect having spoken to Simone either about the *Odes
of Solomon* or about the Gnostics in general. Perhaps, during our meetings, our talk was too taken up with the war. But perhaps it may also be
because I didn't know that she was particularly interested in the idea of
grace. I knew that she didn't like Luther; she had spoken once with
distrust about St. Paul; I believe that her philosophy was still that of
Alain's, a philosophy that was completely founded on the will. I certainly
knew that she was becoming more and more interested in religions and
also that she profoundly loved Christ. But one can profoundly love
Christ without believing in God, or at least without believing in the God
of grace. There are in Simone's *Notebooks* (those she wrote in Marseilles
and after that) many ideas that I did not at all know she had—but did
she already have them then? I was quite surprised when I read, after the
war, the volume entitled *Gravity and Grace.*

I was not the only one who had not perceived the extent to which
her ideas had changed, the ideas that formed the groundwork of her
philosophy. I am not aware whether anyone had become aware of this,
though I do know that many of those who knew her well and had seen
her in Paris during the years 1938, 1939, and 1940—for example, her
parents, her brother, Mme. de Jager's daughters, Dr. Bercher, and René
Château—did not notice then the essential place that religion had taken
in her thought. Her parents did not see this until they reached Marseilles and her brother only in America.

People were misled by the fact that Alain's former students would
frequently use certain religious expressions and also by the fact that
Simone had always spoken about God, meaning by this the God of the
philosophers, he whom one seeks but who does not seek you. Furthermore, her love for religious art and her sympathy for Christianity was
an old story. All this prevented people from seeing the change.

Jean Wahl, the philosopher, went to see her during the first months of the war and had quite a long conversation with her, the only long conversation that they ever had. She spoke to him about the *Iliad,* force, and Christianity. When he left, he asked himself whether she was a Christian. It was not clear that she was. She was evidently interested in Christianity, but it did not appear certain that she believed in it.

During the period her brother was in prison Simone often went, with her mother, to listen to the trials at the Palace of Justice. She wanted to learn something about the procedures so as to be more effective in helping her brother or other people in legal trouble. She also studied the penal code, and I believe that it was during this period that she drafted the unpublished essay entitled "Some Remarks on the Subject of the Penal Code." This essay deals with two punishments that particularly filled her with indignation: solitary confinement and confinement in a penal colony. Of solitary confinement, she said: "Cultivated men, who have at their disposal a language that they know to the bottom and a well-stocked memory, can, with great strength of character, stand up to some extent under the assaults of this punishment; but the intelligence of men without culture inevitably perishes in solitude and complete silence. . . ." The greater part of this essay deals with the penal colony, which consists in enforced residence for life in a desolate region, almost without resources, in French Guiana. This could be applied to those sentenced for minor but repeated crimes. For example, since the decree of November 12, 1938, any foreigner who was arrested and given an expulsion order and did not obey this order could be transported to a penal colony if over a period of ten years he had already been sentenced three times, one of the sentences being for at least a year in prison, for disobeying the police measures concerning him. "Transportation to a penal colony," Simone says, "is a barbarous measure that France should regard as unworthy of preservation. One cannot conceive of it being justifiable except for those who trade in and exploit prostitutes. . . . For ordinary crimes, it is absurd and cruel to want to punish repeaters as severely and even more severely than the most hateful crimes are punished."

I believe that it was also during this period that, having lost all hope of seeing her parachute project accepted, she worked out another project, the "Project for a Formation of Front-Line Nurses." The presentation of this project, as it has been published in her book *Ecrits de Londres* (pp. 187–95), was written or rewritten in America. But she had written a first version of it before the German offensive in May 1940.

She suffered when she thought of all those who were wounded on the battlefields and for whom it was of capital importance to receive speedy assistance. Many of those who died might have survived if they could have been treated immediately, even if the treatment was only rudimentary. As for those among the wounded who were too seriously hurt to be saved, the idea of their solitary, forsaken agony was unbearable to her. So she suggested the organization of a small group of nurses who, having decided to sacrifice their lives, would devote themselves to treating and helping the wounded and dying in the midst of combat. Of course, she would insist on being allowed to join this group; and of course she also realized that most of these women would be killed.

This project would be judged impossible to put into practice by most of those to whom she presented it over the course of the next few years, and some of these declared that it was insane. One is tempted to see it as a result of her will to immolate herself, carried to an almost abnormal point, which Rees believes he sees in her from 1940 on.[21] Yet it was not merely a mad transport of love and pity that inspired her scheme but also a realistic reflection on the conditions necessary to a military victory. She asked herself what the democratic countries could oppose to all that which in the totalitarian countries was the sort of thing that excited the imagination. "It is necessary to remember to what an extent moral factors are essential in the present war. . . . Hitler has never lost sight of the essential necessity of impressing and exciting the imagination. . . . One of his best instruments in this regard are such special formations as the S.S. and the parachute groups. . . . These formations are composed of picked men selected for special tasks, ready not only to risk their lives but also to die. . . . We cannot copy Hitler's methods. . . . But . . . we must find equivalents. It is perhaps almost a vital necessity."[22]

"Our enemies are driven," she says, "by idolatry, an ersatz form of religious faith. Our victory perhaps has as its condition the presence among us of a similar inspiration, but authentic and pure. . . . A courage that is not kindled by the desire to kill, which at the point of the greatest peril can bear the prolonged sight of wounded and dying men, is certainly of a rarer quality than that typical of the young, fanaticized S.S."[23]

So one must give the example of pure courage, courage not excited by the desire to kill. But where can one find nurses with such rare courage who at the same time would possess the necessary tenderness to perform their tasks properly? "Women always run the risk of becoming a hindrance unless they possess a great amount of cold and virile determination that would prevent them from being concerned about themselves in whatever situation arose. This cold determination is rarely found in the same human being together with the tenderness required to comfort suffering and the agony of death. But no matter how rare it is, it still can be found."[24]

In fact she felt that she herself was such a woman. (And not without reason. She had the most tender of souls combined with the staunchest, most courageous qualities.) She knew that persons of this kind could give such an undertaking a lopsided quality, and she seemed to anticipate the accusation of insanity. "A woman cannot conceive the determination to propose herself for the task outlined here unless she possesses

375

both tenderness and this cold determination, or, indeed, unless she is unbalanced." But "those who are in the last category could easily be weeded out before they reached the front lines and were under fire."[25]

A senator whom her parents knew was a member of the Senatorial Army Commission. Dr. and Mme. Weil asked him to receive Simone and, in order to calm her anxiety, her great need to participate in the war, to tell her that he would present her project to this commission. So he received Simone in a very friendly way and soon after told her, or so it seemed, that her project had been given a favorable report by the commission. Mme. Weil doubted that the project had really received a favorable report. But, rightly or wrongly, Simone was convinced that it had. That is why she was to write later on to Maurice Schumann, when sending him the project, and say that just at the moment of the invasion of France the project had come close to being used, but that things had gone too fast.[26]

The German offensive in the West was unleashed on May 10. As is known, it took only a few days for the Germans to overcome the resistance of the Dutch and Belgians and to penetrate into France. I saw Simone during this period. She passionately wished that the government would be able to "galvanize" the population and thought that everyone should help it. She insisted on the word "galvanize." "Do you understand what that means?" she kept saying.

She spoke of the importance of public opinion in the war, observing, for example, that when an army unit is encircled as the result of a flanking movement of the enemy, the enemy is also caught between two lines of fire, so that the encirclement is in some sense reciprocal. The important thing is to realize this and not to lose courage. (The danger of encirclement above all lies in the discouragement that might overtake one of the adversaries, who feels encircled when the other, who might also have this feeling, does not have it.) She also said that bombardments are much less dangerous than a man who runs after you with a knife in his hand.

She was thinking about strategic problems. When the Germans reached the English Channel, she admired the German general staff for having understood that the essential thing was to get to the sea as quickly as possible in order to divide and disrupt the enemy armies. She thought that in 1914 the German high command had made a mistake by attempting before all else to capture Paris. The capture of Paris was not so important. The French and Germans were exhausted, the French wanting to bar the road to Paris, the Germans wanting to reach it, matching mistakes as if they were playing a game in which he who loses wins.

When Weygand was made commander in chief of the army, she made this astonishing remark to me, "Do you know in whose place I would like to be? I would like to be in Weygand's shoes."

From their apartment on rue Auguste-Comte, the Weils could day and night hear and see the tide of pedestrians and cars that flowed down the boulevard Saint-Michel, headed for the south. These were Belgians and Frenchmen from the north who were crossing Paris to seek refuge in the south of France, or at least to the south of Paris.

I had tried to rent a room in the provinces for my mother and, finding nothing near Paris (I had looked at first in Etampes and Evreux, but all the rooms for rent in this region had already been taken), I had written to a hotel in Domme in the Dordogne region, whose address someone had given me. They had a room at this hotel. My mother moved into it, and I subsequently managed to arrange for my father to go and join her. When the Germans were approaching Paris, Simone, who knew that I was alone in my apartment, urgently advised me to leave Enghien and come stay in her apartment. I packed my suitcase and arrived at rue Auguste-Comte. I believe I slept there for two nights, in a maid's room on the seventh floor in which I had already slept once or twice when I was a student. During the day I went to my job at the National Library. I can no longer recall whether it was in the morning or the afternoon that a bombing took place. I think it was early in the morning. Simone took me out on the terrace and we saw the smoke rising to the west of Paris.

(In the course of the previous bombardment, she had taken Adèle out on the terrace.)

She was absolutely determined not to leave. She must have been tortured when she saw her parents' anxiety over this, especially her father's. But she was unshakable. "I don't want to run away," she would say. One afternoon, which must have been the tenth of June, she went to the place de L'Opéra to listen to the conversations among the people clustered on the square. Many people said, "We don't have to go. The Germans are not savages; it will not be impossible to come to some understanding with them." She returned, quite dismayed and astonished: "So it's just the good people who are leaving?" Yet she held to her resolve not to leave Paris. She hoped that the city would be defended.

If the remarks of those who were resigned in advance to German domination dismayed her, she had no hatred for the German people and above all pitied the young Germans who had been regimented and turned into fanatics. I recall that during one of the meals she wondered out loud what would happen if a young German parachutist landed on the terrace of their apartment and asked her parents what they would do about it. Calmly and practically, her father answered that, if possible, he would hand him over to the police. Simone declared that she could not go on eating with someone who had such intentions. I thought at first that she was joking, but she seemed to be speaking quite seriously and in fact stopped eating. To get her to continue eating her father finally promised that he would not hand over the young parachutist to the police if that eventuality should arise.

At the National Library all the personnel had received an order to prepare to leave. We understood that it was more in the form of a permission than an order and that one could remain in Paris. However, I was convinced that Paris would not be destroyed and that one was safer here than on the trains and highways. But it was still believed that the front would be stabilized either on the Loire or somewhere south of Paris, and I feared being separated for a long time, perhaps even years, from my family, and forced to live under the rule of the Germans, like people in the occupied regions during the First World War. Besides, I wanted to go and see what had happened to my sister, who was sick and being treated in the region of Orléans. Her husband, who had been called up, could not help her. I did everything possible to persuade Simone to leave, but nothing could convince her. Mme. Weil urgently advised me not to stay in Paris and to take care of my family. I finally decided to take the train that we had been told about. Simone gave me her poem "A un jour" and accompanied me to the subway.

I soon regretted this departure, which was useless in terms of what I had envisaged and which simply left me with a painful memory. Certainly, my sister had great need of help, as I discovered later on. But having been badly informed as to where I should be to catch the right train, I could not get into the Austerlitz station, which was surrounded by a huge crowd; I had to leave from the Lyons station and that forced me to make a detour to reach Orléans, and so the Germans were there before me.

On the thirteenth of June, having left their apartment to do some shopping, Simone and her parents saw official announcements posted in the streets that declared that Paris was an open city. Simone then at last yielded to her parents' wish and, without even returning home to pack a suitcase, they went to the Lyons station. A crowd surrounded it and the railroad guards would not let anyone in; one train was still there and it was full of passengers. Mme. Weil got the idea of telling the man guarding the gate that her husband was a doctor and that he could be useful in a convoy. (Or perhaps—this is what André Weil thinks—she persuaded the doctor to say he was the convoy's doctor.) The clerk agreed to let just the doctor in, but the doctor said, "Not without my wife and daughter." So he allowed all three of them to go through the gate. The train was packed, yet they still managed to squeeze in. The next day, the fourteenth of June, the Germans entered Paris.

As they were leaving Paris, Simone said to her parents, "I would prefer that you thought you will never come back here again." On the train she was sorry she had left. "If they don't defend Paris," she said, "maybe they will at least defend the outskirts." She already wanted to get off the train at Montereau. Mme. Weil pointed out to her that if a new line of defense was formed, it would undoubtedly be on the Loire. This argument convinced her and she agreed to go as far as Nevers.

There they met the Detœuf family and Boris Souvarine. It was thanks to Detœuf that they could sleep in a miller's house that had been abandoned by its owner. They also met Dieudonné, a friend of André's, who offered to loan them money if they needed any and warned them that the Germans would get there soon. Simone again said, "I'm not leaving." She hoped that Nevers would be defended.

The Germans arrived that night. They saw the panzer divisions go clanking by. Simone felt that it was quite frightful. When she met Germans, she would not lift her head or look at them. There were no newspapers, and people said that it was forbidden to listen to the radio. The rumor spread that all of France was occupied. One day the Weils read a leaflet that said that the people must return to their homes and that there were no trains, but if one got on the main highway one could find trucks and other vehicles. They decided to start walking along the highway to get back to Paris. But on the street they met a former pupil of Simone's, one of her students at Bourges. Simone said to her, "Do you have a radio?" She replied, "Yes, but I don't dare turn it on." Simone said to her, "I'll go to your house and I'll turn it on."

When she returned, she told them, "It's not true that all of France is occupied. My opinion is that we should leave on foot and try to reach the free zone." They bought some baskets to give them the look of peasants. In any event, nobody asked them anything when they left Nevers. They walked for several miles. Simone's skirt was scraping against her leg and finally opened up a wound. Someone passing on the highway shouted at them, "Where are you going?" They replied, "We would like to go to the unoccupied zone." The man was the owner of a garage. He offered to transport them, but only if they paid for the gas. The doctor had money with him; it was the only thing they had. The garage owner could not take them immediately, but he made an appointment to meet them the next morning in a café. They were then in a small village that was full of young Germans. They did not know where to sleep and spent the night in the café. The next morning they waited for a long time; at last the garage man came looking for them and drove them to Vichy.

Simone had gotten into the habit of sleeping on the floor in Nevers. She continued to do this until she was hospitalized in London. In order to justify it, she told her parents that one must adapt oneself immediately to a style of life that could become a necessity. She said, "From now on we probably won't get the chance to sleep in a bed." I wonder whether this was the real reason. I tend to believe that she was thinking of the life that the soldiers were leading and did not want to be more privileged than they were.

It was the beginning of July when they reached Vichy. This was the period when Marshal Pétain set up his government. Simone soon met people she knew. Among others, she met former comrades who, having always been pacifists, still followed these ideas; they approved of the armistice, though they still hoped that a republican government would be formed that would maintain liberty and achieve certain reforms. She violently objected to their ideas. One of them told me later that her mind seemed in disarray, that she seemed to be sickened by rage. In fact she was terribly angry about everything that had happened and everything she saw. She thought that Paul Reynaud should not have resigned, that parliament should not have given up its powers and should not have asked for an armistice, that France should have continued to fight.

The violence of her chagrin and revolt upset the people she met and spoke to. Some people avoided her. Other people who had admired her before this treated her with glacial coldness when she spoke to them. There were also misunderstandings; she had an appointment with the Alexandres, who as it turned out could not come; she perhaps thought that they didn't want to see her.

She had several meetings with her old comrade Guindey, who was a high official of the ministry of finances and whose duties permitted him to travel between Paris and Vichy. She spoke to him of her poem "A un jour," which she had left in Paris, and asked him if he could go to her house on the rue Auguste-Comte, get it, and bring it back to her. He promised to do this. It was perhaps through him that she sent her address to Adèle Dubreuil. She also met Henri Cartan, a friend of her brother's, who told her that her brother was in England. A boat had picked up the soldiers who were grouped on the shores of the English Channel; it was supposed to take them to Brest, but it had been forced to change its course and had sailed for a British port.

Simone wondered whether her brother could return to France without running the risk of being put in prison again. Since the armistice had interrupted hostilities, was the suspended sentence still in force? She consulted with two lawyers, including the man who had defended André; they both said that he could return without any fear. But she looked into the penal code on her own and found an article that seemed to indicate that he would indeed be in danger. She showed it to the lawyers, who admitted that she was right. She then sent her brother a telegram advising him to stay in England. According to Mme. Weil, this telegram was a masterpiece of camouflage. Simone carefully weighed each word she used so that it would be quite clear to André but could not be understood by anyone else.

She also met Nguyên Van Danh in Vichy. He had been summoned as a representative of the Red Cross to handle the cases of prisoners of war from the colonies. He was making efforts to get them freed and in the meanwhile was doing all he could to ameliorate their living conditions in the prison camps. Simone accompanied him to the Japanese embassy, to which he had gone, almost clandestinely, to ask the Japanese to intercede with the Germans for these prisoners. He also wrote an official memorandum about the situation of the colonial combatants in captivity and about those who had been demobilized without any resources; Simone helped him draft this memorandum.

A French general in the medical corps, to whom Danh had spoken about this problem, had said, "When there are one million eight hundred thousand French prisoners, you don't expect us to worry our heads over a few natives." Burning with anger and indignation, Danh wanted to hand in his resignation.

Simone told him that it was the only thing to do. So he wrote a letter of resignation, but Marshal Pétain's private secretary promised Danh that they would give instructions to do what he asked and convinced him to withdraw his resignation.

Simone sent me a postcard from Vichy to Domme on which the address was incomplete and so I never received it. From my end, I wrote to her from Domme, asking her to tell me what had happened and how she was. This letter, addressed to Paris, was forwarded to Vichy, undoubtedly by Adèle, who, with her husband, had moved into the Weils' apartment to make sure that it was not requisitioned. Simone answered my letter on August 6:

"Dear Simone,

"I sent you a postcard addressed to Domme, just like that. Get it at the post office if they haven't delivered it to you. I sent you all my latest news and I asked you to send me a copy of my verses if you took them with you, because, due to the circumstances that you will find described on the above-mentioned postcard, we left Paris with empty hands, having left our place not knowing that we would go to catch a train. I really love this sort of a departure, but it does have its drawbacks. I was very happy to hear from you. Write me again: 3 rue du Bourbonnais, Vichy. I shall write you a real letter one of these days. Tell me what you are doing now—if you are writing—if you are thinking of Krishna. The *Gita* is unfortunately one of the many things I did not bring along with me. And I have almost forgotten my Babylonian! Χαιρε . . ."

This postcard, addressed to Domme, was forwarded to me at Enghien, to which in the meantime I had returned. It reached me after a long delay (surely more than a month, perhaps even two months or more), and when I replied, Simone had left Vichy. She never got my reply. It was only toward the end of the year, when she was in Marseilles, that the correspondence between us, through the so-called "family" cards, could be resumed regularly.

Ever since the armistice had been signed, she had resolved to go to England to join those who were continuing the fight. But it was not possible to get to England directly; one had to go through some other country. To get out of France, she thought of being sent as a professor either abroad or to the colonies. In any event, as we have seen, she had long desired to visit the colonies. On the nineteenth of August she presented a request for a post to the Ministry of Education:

"Mlle. Simone Weil, former student of the Ecole Normale (rue d'Ulm), graduate in philosophy, and professor of philosophy at the girls' lycée of Saint-Quentin, on leave since January 1938, has the honor to solicit the Minister of Education for her reassignment in the educational system and her appointment to a post either abroad or in the colonies. Vichy, August 19, 1940. [Signed] Simone Weil."

While awaiting a reply—she doubted, however, that she would receive one and had only made this request in order to force the ministry to take a stand—she wanted to reach that part of the country from which one could leave France, having decided to leave it in any event. With her parents, she first went to Toulouse. Most likely they hoped to get out of France by way of Spain, or, already knowing perhaps that André had decided not to follow Simone's advice and was returning to France, they thought that he might come back by way of Spain. They stayed in Toulouse for about two weeks, from the latter part of August to the beginning of September.

Before leaving Toulouse, she wrote two letters to Guindey. In the first, she sent him her poem "A un jour," which she had reconstituted from memory and entrusted to him. She hoped that he could get it published in some magazine. She also spoke to him about her "Reflections on the Causes of Liberty and Social Oppression," which had been written in 1934 and which had been left behind in Paris.

"Dear friend,

"I got your note just in time because I was about to leave Toulouse. I'm going to Algiers, while waiting for something else.

"My memory has returned and I reconstituted the verses I left in Paris. I have even improved three or four lines by some retouchings, so the Paris text is no longer valid.

"But I would like to know the variants to assure myself that outside of those due to premeditated will, there are no others due to a fault in my memory. But I don't think so. Nevertheless I want to ask you, if it's not too much trouble, to get the text left in Paris and hold on to it.

"I am sending you the one I reconstructed here, which I consider the definitive version. Events have given this poem a great deal of pertinence. . . .

"I think that it is worth publishing, and I believe that those who will read it will think so, too. But I'm leaving, and I don't know whether I shall ever return to the European continent. My heart does little to urge me back.

"If either at Vichy or Paris you happen to meet people who are more or less literary, I would like you to give them this poem so that they could publish it. It doesn't matter where, provided that it be under such

conditions that whatever may be left in France of 'honest folk' can read
it. Magazines such as *Mercure de France, N.R.F.,* and the *Revue des Deux
Mondes* would be quite suitable. If my name is not advisable in the
present circumstances, just invent any sort of pseudonym, or you can
use three stars. I don't care a bit. I don't want any literary notoriety and
I no longer have the impression that this poem belongs to me in any way
whatsoever. I only want it to be read because in my opinion it would be
a pity that it should simply and purely disappear. It must be easy for you
in Vichy to get the present addresses of famous writers. You could send
it to them. What does it matter that you don't know them, nor I for that
matter? If it is worth anything, it will speak for itself.

"In 1938 I sent Valéry a very imperfect version of it. He did not
answer me. Before that, the same year, I had sent him another poem
entitled "Prometheus," quite inferior to it, and he wrote me a very
friendly and flattering letter.[27] I would send him this poem in its present
version if I had his address. . . .

"Moreover, there is in Paris in my briefcase a prose piece, very long,
typewritten, whose title I forget, but it has a quotation from Spinoza as
an epigraph. It is essentially an analysis of political and social oppression, its permanent causes, its mechanism, and its present forms. It
dates from 1934. It too is very pertinent today. It surely is good enough
not to be lost, I think. But I don't know whether it would be prudent
to take it home with you. Read it and evaluate it yourself. . . . I really
regret now that I didn't publish it. I wanted first of all to rewrite it
because of its imperfect form, and my physical state always prevented
me from doing so. It can't be published now. But the poem can be
published, I believe. I entrust it to you. Don't forget it. Because I will
not be concerned about it anymore, and although one cannot foresee
what the future will bring, I leave without any prospect of returning.
And it's not just because of the circumstances. I have always thought
that one day I would leave like this.

"You can write in care of *poste restante* in Casablanca. I will keep you
informed about my movements as much as possible.

"Your friend."

She wrote to Guindey again the very next day to indicate a mistake
in the text she had sent and also to give some pointers in regard to
possible differences between the text she had sent and the one left in
Paris.

Guindey certainly received these letters at Vichy. When he was back
in Paris, he went to the apartment on rue Auguste-Comte and Adèle
Dubreuil gave him the briefcase containing the writings in question. He
looked at them at home and when he himself left France in 1942, he put
them in trustworthy hands. After the war, he returned them to Dr. and
Mme. Weil.

These letters to Guindey show that Simone at that time was confident that she could quickly travel to North Africa. Besides the application she had presented to the ministry, she had also asked for a visa for Portugal and had written, either from Vichy or Toulouse, to one of her old Ecole Normale classmates, Hourcade, then stationed at Lisbon, asking him to make certain contacts to facilitate her request for a visa. She had only asked for a visa for a short stay; her plan was either to go to Morocco by way of Portugal or to go directly from Portugal to England.

14

Marseilles I
(1940-1941)

At that time Marseilles was the great escape gateway at which the majority of those who wanted to flee from France were gathered. Dr. and Mme. Weil and Simone had left Toulouse for Marseilles, where they arrived in September, just a bit before September 15. They stayed at first in a family pension, where they remained for about a month.

It was perhaps during the first days after her arrival that Simone decided to write to Emile Dermenghem, the author of some remarkable studies of the Muslim world. Actually, she still thought that her chances of leaving quickly for Morocco were quite good when she wrote the draft of her letter to Dermenghem, and, besides, since he wrote regularly for *Cahiers du Sud,* it is quite possible that in Marseilles she was able to obtain his address.

"Dear Sir:

"I hope you forgive me for writing to you without knowing you. After reading the remarkable article you wrote about Morocco for *Esprit,* various notes dealing with Muslim affairs in several magazines, the collection of fasi folklore that you edited with an Arab, I have a great deal of admiration and sympathy for you. . . .

"I permit myself to address you now because I expect to go to North Africa and, if possible, to Morocco. Besides, I have requested a position as a teacher; I don't count very much on getting it; but, in any case I shall try to go. For a long time now I have wanted to know something else besides Europe; and certainly the present events are not the sort to weaken this desire. For some time I have felt more and more attracted to what still remains of Oriental culture and particularly to Muslim culture. I would be enormously grateful to you if you could furnish me with some information as to things and people that it would be interesting to get to know in Morocco. As for the people, I am thinking of the French and Arabs, but of course, above all, the latter.

"I chiefly want to find out about two things: what is the real character of the regime imposed on the population, and what effects it has upon their minds and spirits; what remains alive, authentic, truly interesting, a vestige of a more glorious past and perhaps the presage of a better future, beneath the colonial oppression. . . ."

But Simone soon began to doubt that she could obtain a visa for Portugal. Hourcade had tried to do what he was asked to do, but nothing had come of it. He had also written to Simone. She wanted to thank him, tell him that her request had not yet had the success she had hoped, and explain to him that her plan was not to stay long in Portugal. For he had thought that she wanted to find refuge there. During the course of the first month of her stay in Marseilles she wrote this draft for a letter:

"My dear Hourcade,

"I thank you for your letter and for having gone to the bank. In fact I got the paper that I wanted; until now nothing seems to have come of it and I am starting to despair of putting it through.

"What I desire for myself is not exactly a chance to relax. If that were the case I certainly would not have bothered you; even less would I have thought of asking for your help with such insistence. What I wrote to you could, I know, have led to getting this wrong idea, but since you know me I thought that you would interpret my words differently. Of course it is quite a long time since we have seen each other. But neither the years nor illness have changed me so much that I would consider my well-being and my comfort as of even slightest importance in the midst of such a tremendous upheaval. What I am looking for is not precisely a refuge. Or if I do want a refuge, it is a refuge to protect me not from events but from my own imagination.

"My imagination is always working in a fashion quite painful for me. The thought of the hardships, misfortunes, and dangers in which I have no part fills me with a mixture of horror, pity, shame, and remorse that has deprived me of all freedom of mind; the perception of the reality would deliver me from all this. For example, the deaths caused by the bombing of Paris did not cause me any emotion, simply because I was there. However, the days during which the battle in Flanders took place were atrocious for me. You surely must have experienced similar emotions since you were in Morocco.

"These statements should suffice, I imagine, to help you understand my state of mind and the fact that, in Europe's present condition, I am not looking for a chance to relax but only for a different kind of tension.

"I fervently desire a change of atmosphere. A few weeks in Portugal would please me enormously. You know from my last letter that I ask for only a short-term visa and I do not have the intention, once I am there, of trying to prolong it, or only for very little. I really want to stay only a short time in this beautiful country, so worthy of being loved.

"I realize that you can't do very much. But if you ever see a chance of doing something for me, I ask you with extreme insistence to do it. You could without any hesitation intervene in my favor since I don't in any case have the intention, even if life here becomes extremely difficult, of increasing the number of unfortunates who take advantage of the admirable hospitality . . ."

The draft stops here. It shows that for Simone Portugal as well as North Africa would have been just places of passage. What she wanted was to be where one could share the dangers of war.

One of the refugees who were in the family pension told her that people were leaving with Siamese visas. You left, he claimed, as though you were going to Siam, but once you were out of Marseilles you could go where you wished. On September 17 Simone persuaded her parents to go with her to the Siamese legation. There they sold them very expensive visas, but subsequently they were told that these visas didn't permit them to leave, for they would have to leave on Siamese ships and none were available. Simone was ashamed to have dragged her parents into this absurd adventure.

The family pension was on the sea and not far from the camp of Mazargues, in which Indochinese workers were gathered. Simone soon got in touch with them. One morning Mme. Weil saw about thirty Annamites seated in a row along the sea wall. They had come to see Simone, since that was the day they could leave the camp; not wanting to disturb her, they were waiting until she awoke.

These Indochinese were the ones whom Minister Mandel had brought to France during the "phony war" to work in the factories, especially the gunpowder factories. After the armistice, they had trickled back to Marseilles. Their camp was the future prison of Baumettes, then under construction, and it had neither heat nor electricity. According to Dr. Bercher, one Indochinese told Simone that he had signed up to see France but had not seen anything. Since his arrival, he said, "I live in the dark and I am terribly bored." Simone "repeated these words in a voice that was also rendered dark by emotion."

In their camp, "one of the commonest punishments was not physically cruel, but, it appears, many of them were terribly hurt by it. It consisted in shaving their heads, but only half of their heads."[1]

In the course of the following winter these Annamites were employed one day to clear the snow off the streets. Dr. Bercher wrote: "One day when it snowed they scattered these men from the tropics all over the streets of Marseilles, with the task, so it seems, of clearing away the snow. This broke Simone's heart. 'There was nothing more lamentable,' she told me when we met in July, "than these poor people, standing there in the middle of the snow, in their torn, ragged clothes, with not the faintest idea what they were supposed to do!'[2] (It is quite possible that they hadn't even told them that they had to clear it away!) And what were they supposed to use to do this?"

Simone wrote several times to C., a friend of Belin's, who was in a ministry at Vichy, to try to get something done for them. In the draft for one of these letters she points out the painful conditions of their life and denounces the exploitation of their work by certain contractors in Marseilles.

"Dear comrade,

"I thank you very much for your letter. I know how you and Belin feel and I have complete confidence in you. Unfortunately, up until now there has been no amelioration in the condition of the Indochinese, either in regard to their physical sufferings or their lack of freedom. Perhaps you still do not have the time to deal with them. Or you have given orders that have not been carried out? Whatever may be the case, I am simply pointing out the facts to you.

"There is something concerning them that it might be useful to mention. At their camp they perform different jobs of work that are awarded after bidding to various contractors. These contractors do not hire workers but have the work done by the Annamites themselves, whom the commandants put at their disposal. For the Annamites this work is forced labor performed free of charge; no wages are paid.

"When I learned about this, I asked myself who profits from this economizing on wages. If it is the French State, the arrangement seems to me legitimate, provided it is humanely carried out; which, unfortunately, is not the case, for I have been told that sick Annamites, whom the doctor refuses to put on the sick list, are frequently compelled to do this work and when they do not work hard enough, are beaten by the French overseers. (And keep this well in mind—by the French overseers, not by the Annamite supervisors.) But I also wonder whether this economizing on wages is not profitable to the contractors. In Marseilles everything is possible. I mention this just to put you on the alert."

According to Bercher, she handled things so adeptly "that the insignificant, unofficial, and persecuted person she herself was managed to get the camp commandant (an old colonial administrator) transferred, and then after that, under a new commandant, things weren't so bad."[3]

At the beginning of October, André Weil informed his family that he would arrive at Marseilles by boat. The Weils learned that on the boat he was taking there were sick and wounded; they thought he was wounded. They went to the port to meet him. Mme. Weil told an ensign who was there that she had come to look for her son and was afraid that she wouldn't find him in the crowd. The ensign amiably offered to help her look for him. A moment later Simone heard a policeman say, "I am looking for two people: so-and-so and André Weil." She thought that they were going to arrest her brother. Before debarkation began the Weils saw André standing at the rail with some other passengers. They went to the edge of the pier and shouted to him, "Oscar is with us, he's waiting for you." Oscar was their private name for the police, which they used when they didn't want other people to understand them. André disappeared and returned a moment later. He had gone to his cabin and had thrown into the sea a tube of toothpaste containing a message entrusted to him by a friend in England. He got off the ship. Simone and her mother (they had sent the doctor away, since they felt he was not up to this sort of situation) had arranged to sneak him through, and the policeman looking for him didn't see a thing. They took him to the pension and managed to get him in without his having to sign the register. But two or three days later he said that he wanted to go and pick up his discharge pay and his "Pétain" (the name given to the civilian clothes issued to all demobilized soldiers).* His parents and Simone told him, "You're crazy, you're going to be arrested." He insisted and went to pick up his discharge pay and "Pétain," and nothing at all happened to him. The policeman who was looking for him when the ship arrived undoubtedly had been asked by the obliging ensign to find him and bring him to Mme. Weil.

André remained for only a short while in Marseilles. He left for Clermont-Ferrand, where the University of Strasbourg, on whose faculty he was, had been shifted. He found a great many friends there. They asked him, "Isn't it dangerous for you to show up here?" He replied, more or less, "My case is not very clear, but that is precisely why I want to show myself everywhere and appear as though I were perfectly at ease. They will think: He could not be so calm unless he has received some assurances." This method was a complete success. André got his wife, who was in the occupied zone, to join him; she crossed the demarcation line clandestinely. He then obtained passports for both of them. In January he returned to Marseilles with Eveline and embarked on the *Winnipeg,* a transatlantic merchant ship that carried passengers and took them to the Antilles. From there, they easily reached New York.

About the middle of October Simone and her parents moved in to an apartment that they had rented at 8 rue des Catalans. It had a beautiful view over the sea and the Catalans beach. Her parents did not tell Simone how much it had cost to rent it; if she had known, she would have refused to live there.

When they had moved in, they sent Adèle a list of everything they wanted from among the things left behind in their Paris apartment. Mme. Weil had discovered that through Cook's Agency one still could ship cases across the demarcation line. Adèle could send three shipments of cases containing their linen, clothes, silver, and, above all, manuscripts and books.

Of course the manuscripts and books were for Simone. She had sent Adèle a long list headed by the request: "All of my manuscripts." And then, if I remember correctly: "All of my Greek books, all of my Latin

*Doubtless because of a decision made by Marshal Pétain.

books, and all of my books in English and Italian." After this came a long list of French books.

Adèle and her husband had no trouble finding the manuscripts. They put in a packing case all the papers in Simone's handwriting that they found in the apartment. But they did have trouble finding the books. The titles Simone had given them were not always exactly the ones on the books; in certain cases Simone had put down equivalent titles but in a different form. Adèle or her husband wrote me a note, asking me to come and help them. So one day I went to the apartment. All the manuscripts were already in the packing case, and I helped them find the books.

The concierge for the building did not like the idea that they were shipping out these cases. She was afraid that she would be held responsible for the gradual emptying of the apartment. At the third shipment she went to get a policeman so that he would stop the truck on which the cases were loaded. It was a horse-drawn truck, since gasoline was scarce. The policeman came, but when he found out what was at stake he wanted nothing to do with it. He turned his back and gazed in the other direction. The driver of the truck said to Adèle, "So, what should I do?" She told him, "Go ahead, leave." He whipped up the horses and left. So the third shipment reached its destination like the other two, without mishap.

But after that Adèle no longer dared send off cases. Besides, this possibility was most likely done away with. But the essentials had been saved; the manuscripts and books had left, I believe, in the first shipment.

So the room that Simone occupied on the rue des Catalans was soon full of papers and books. On its walls she hung some photographs of statues and Giorgione's *Concert,* the painting she had seen at the Pitti Palace that she loved so much.[4]

She had not received a reply to her request for a post. However, according to her service record that was sent to me by the Ministry of National Education,[5] she had been appointed a professor at the girls' lycée in Constantine starting on October 1, 1940. But she never knew about this appointment; for some reason, the information never reached her. About the second week in October or November she wrote to the Minister of Public Education:

"Dear Sir:

"Having taken a leave of absence for reasons of health in January 1938, and having renewed it for a year in July 1938, and again for a year in July 1939—my leave therefore expired in July 1940—I requested a post last August, preferably in Algeria.

"I have conjectured that the text called 'the Statutory Regulation on

Jews,' which I read some time ago in the press,* perhaps has some bearing on the fact that I did not receive a reply. It is for this reason that I would like to understand this text, so that I can be clear about my own situation. I do not know the definition of the word Jew; this subject has never been part of my program of studies. True, the text says whoever has had three Jewish grandparents is to be considered a Jew; but this clarification only puts the difficulty back for two generations.

"Does this word designate a religion? I have never entered a synagogue and I have never witnessed a Jewish religious ceremony. As for my grandparents, I recall that my paternal grandmother went to synagogue; I believe I have heard it said that this was also true of my paternal grandfather; I know that my mother's parents were both freethinkers. If it is a question of the religion of my grandparents, I have thus had, so it seems, only two Jewish grandparents, which would place me beyond the reach of the statute.

"Does this word designate a race? I have no reason to suppose that I have any sort of tie, either through my father or my mother, with the people who lived in Palestine two thousand years ago. Besides, when one reads in Josephus how Titus exterminated this people, one finds it hard to believe that many of their descendants were left. The twelve hundred thousand human beings who were in Jerusalem at the time of the siege, and who came mostly from outside on the occasion of the feast of the Passover, were in fact almost the entire population of Palestine. The Romans took pains to massacre eleven hundred thousand Jews and transported the rest as slaves, and, subsequently, the majority of these slaves perished in the circuses. So the Jews who at this moment lived outside Palestine are the only Jews who could have had descendants.

"As far back as memory can go my father's family has lived in Alsace; no family tradition, to my knowledge, tells us whether they arrived in distant times from some other country. My mother's family lived before this in a country with a Slavic population, and nothing leads me to suppose that it was composed of any group but Slavs.

"Perhaps one must apply the definition of the statute to my grandparents themselves and find out whether each of them has had at least three grandparents of the Jewish religion? It would seem to me to be quite difficult to obtain unequivocal information on this particular point.

"For the rest, one can conceive of the inheritance of a race, but it is difficult to conceive of the inheritance of a religion. As for myself, who do not practice any religion and never have done so, I have not inherited anything of the Jewish religion. Having pretty much learned to read by reading French writers of the seventeenth century, such as Racine and

---

*The statute concerning the Jews was issued on October 3, 1940.

Pascal, and having had my mind impregnated at an age when I never heard talk of the Jews, if there is a religious tradition that I regard as my patrimony, it is the Catholic tradition.

"The Christian, French, Hellenic tradition is mine; the Hebrew tradition is foreign to me; no text of a law can change that for me. If nonetheless the law demands that I regard the term 'Jew,' whose meaning I do not know, as an epithet applicable to my person, I am disposed to submit to it as to any other law. But then I want to be officially informed, since I do not possess any criterion susceptible of resolving this point.

"If it is otherwise, I want to benefit from the rights that are granted me by the contract implied by my title as a graduate of the Ecole Normale."

Obviously this letter did not mean that Simone was not in solidarity with other Jews. The arguments she raises in regard to race were valuable for all Jews. On the contrary, she was mocking the "Statutory Regulations on Jews" and the confused ideas on which all anti-Semitic racism rests.

It is true that she declares that she has nothing to do with the Jewish *religion*. But many of those whom one calls Jews are in the same situation. She was really foreign to this religion and knew it very imperfectly.[6] But if she says this in her letter, it was not in order to confide in the minister in regard to her position on the subject of religion and even less in order to avoid persecution (because she knew very well that it was not a religion that was being persecuted); it was only to demonstrate the difficulty of defining the word "Jew."

This letter never received a reply.

On December 5 she sent me one of those postcards that were then used as the only form of correspondence between the free and occupied zones, and on which it was permitted to complete only certain printed formulas in one's own hand. Only two lines were left for messages that did not fit the formulas. Simone informed me that her parents, her brother, and she were in good health. In the two lines reserved for free correspondence she wrote: "What have you done with my poem and the other literature? Perhaps you can tell me what you have of mine, and if there is some way of getting it back? Tell us the news and tell me if you are working."

(She had not received my reply to her postcard from Vichy.)

What I had of hers was her poem "A un jour" and also the typewritten copy her mother had given me in 1934 of "Reflections on the Causes of Freedom and Social Oppression." I no longer remember how I managed to send them to her; no doubt I gave them to Adèle so that she could put them in one of the packing cases. What I do recall is that, fearing that the copy of the "Reflections" might be lost and thinking that it was perhaps the only copy of this essay left, I took the precaution of copying the entire essay before sending it off. I still have this copy. When I saw Simone the next year I told her that I had copied her study on oppression before sending it; she told me that I shouldn't have bothered and that it would have been better if I had used the time for my own work.

The *Cahiers du Sud,* published at Marseilles, was certainly the most important literary magazine in the free zone. Ballard, its editor in chief, was not afraid to publish Jewish writers and others who were known for their hostility to the Vichy government. Simone at first thought of publishing one of her poems, perhaps "A un jour," in this magazine. (She had most likely not yet received the package I sent her, but, as we have seen, she had recomposed the poem from memory.) She brought it to Ballard, who told her that it resembled Le Franc de Pompignan's work. He had the impression that he had vexed her (but Mme. Weil said that she had laughed over it). He said to her, "If you prefer, it smacks a bit of Cocteau, but for my part I prefer Le Franc de Pompignan. Right now, in the *Cahiers* we want poetry with a newer form." He thought that a magazine should have a certain tendency and that poetry written in classical form was not in line with his magazine's tendency.

She submitted no other poems; but she gave Ballard her article on the *Iliad,* since it was impossible to publish it in Paris owing to the German invasion. Ballard accepted it with joy. From the start, he was more drawn to her prose than to her poetry.

So "The Iliad, or the Poem of Force" appeared in *Cahiers du Sud* in December 1940 and January 1941.[7] Simone signed it with the pseudonym Emile Novis, which is a rough anagram of her name. From this time on she often visited the *Cahiers'* office and so met the other people who wrote for the magazine. This is how she made the acquaintance of the poet Jean Tortel and soon became close friends with him and his family.

It was perhaps also at *Cahiers du Sud* that she got to know Jean Lambert, André Gide's son-in-law. As he tells the story,[8] he would often go up to her room in the morning, after he had had a swim at the Catalans beach. They had long conversations about the Greeks and about beauty. She claimed, he says, "to perceive the presence of God in everything on earth that is beautiful," and he completely agreed with this theology. Sometimes she would recite her own verses for him, while the many-voiced sounds from the beach washed into her room, forming a kind of chorus that accompanied her monotone voice. He learned about her plans for the future; while waiting to find a way to get to England, she again wanted to work at some sort of manual labor so as to share men's common fate. As he listened to her, he felt that he lived a selfish life and for the first time was ashamed of himself. (Who would not be ashamed of himself in Simone's presence, after seeing the sort of life she led?)

Jean Lambert met Gilbert Kahn, whom he had known as a student at Henri IV. He told him that Simone Weil was in Marseilles. Kahn then lived at Montpellier, but he sometimes came to Marseilles. He went to see Simone around Christmas in 1940. He would see her again from time to time and then very often when he began living at Aix, that is, during the 1941–1942 winter. In the spring of 1941 he took the three photographs of Simone that we have of her at Marseilles. (In one photograph we see her standing up, wearing her beret and a large cape. In the other two she is seated at a table in a café; in one photograph Jean Lambert is next to her and in the other Lanza del Vasto.)

It was also about Christmas 1940 that she began seeing the Honnorats. Pierre Honnorat, a mathematician and a fellow student of André's at the Ecole Normale, had known her for a long time. His sister, Hélène Honnorat, a teacher at the girls' lycée in Marseilles, had been a student at the Duruy lycée at the same time as Simone, but, since she was four years younger, in a lower class. Having learned that she was at Marseilles, they went to visit her. Hélène Honnorat was a fervent Catholic; she discussed religion with Simone. Simone told her, "I am as close to Catholicism as it is possible to be without however being a Catholic." She was to tell her just before her departure from Marseilles, "I never thought that I could draw closer to Catholicism, and yet I have drawn much, much closer."

Hélène Honnorat offered to introduce her into Catholic circles in Marseilles. Simone gladly accepted. It was through Hélène that a little later she met Father Perrin and, through Father Perrin, Gustave Thibon.

By chance, while walking on the Canebière, she met Camille Marcoux, her comrade at the Ecole Normale. Marcoux visited her home. It seemed to him that she was mainly occupied with mathematics. Not even for an instant did he get the slightest sense of her religious preoccupations. When she went to the Dominican convent, he did not hear about it. He was very surprised later, when he read *Gravity and Grace.*

(Mme. Weil said about all this that Simone never talked about religion even with her parents. Yet she did not hide her ideas, since before leaving Marseilles she asked her mother to copy part of her *Notebooks.* But she did not talk about religion, or only talked about it to certain people.)

I imagine that it was also at the beginning of 1941 that she met René Daumal, whom she had known in *cagne.* He had been studying Sanskrit for quite a long time. He loaned her some notes on Sanskrit grammar and the *Gita,* which he had copied out by hand. She then began to study Sanskrit. He worked with Mme. de Salzmann and it was through him that Simone met Lanza del Vasto.

Shortly after having met Simone, Ballard spoke to her about a special issue that he was preparing on the "genius of Occitan." He says that this project "set her afire." He loaned her a booklet on Catharism by Déodat Roché;[9] she soon felt impelled to write to Roché. On January 23, 1941, she sent him the letter that the *Cahiers d'études cathares* published twice and that was also published in *Pensées sans ordre concernant l'amour de Dieu.*[10]

She told him that for a long time she had been attracted to the Cathars and that one of the chief reasons for this was their judgment of the Old Testament. She believed with Roché that the worship of power had caused the Hebrews to lose the idea of good and evil. "I have always been kept away from Christianity because it ranked these stories, so full of pitiless cruelty, as sacred texts. . . . I have never been able to understand how it is possible for a reasonable mind to look upon the Jehovah of the Bible and the Father invoked in the Gospel as one and the same being. The influence of the Old Testament and of the Roman Empire, whose tradition was continued by the Papacy, are to my mind the two essential sources of the corruption of Christianity."

She thought that Catharism has been "the last living expression in Europe of pre-Roman antiquity." Before the Roman conquest, there existed one and the same thought, expressed in different forms "in the mysteries and initiatory sects of Egypt, Thrace, Greece, and Persia"; a thought of which Plato has left us the most perfect written expression. "It is from this thought that Christianity issued; but only the Gnostics, Manicheans, and Cathars seem to have really kept faith with it."

She observes, however, that "there is something more in the Manicheans than in antiquity, or at least than in the antiquity known to us; there are some magnificent conceptions, such as the descent of divinity among men and the rending of the spirit and its dispersal throughout matter." Thus the Manichean-Cathar current adds something to ancient thought. "But what above all makes the fact of Catharism a sort of miracle is that it was a religion and not simply a philosophy. I mean to say that around Toulouse in the twelfth century the highest thought dwelt within a whole human environment and not only in the minds of a certain number of individuals."

In Roché's booklet she had read with joy that Catharism could be regarded as a Christian Pythagoreanism or Platonism. "In my eyes, there is nothing that surpasses Plato. Simple intellectual curiosity cannot give one contact with the thought of Pythagoras and Plato, because in regard to thought of that kind knowledge and adhesion are one single act of the mind. I believe it is the same as regards Catharism."

Did she mean to say by this that she is a follower of Catharism? One must be clear about this. As a religion, Catharism is dead and cannot be revived. She would say so in her *Notebooks:* "One cannot, in fact, be a supporter of that which doesn't exist. For example, one cannot be in favor of the re-establishment of the Carolingian dynasty on the throne of France, or a follower of the Catharist religion, or of the Order of the Templars."[11] What she agreed with, in a sense, and what she wanted to see revived, was "this form of thought," and what she meant by this form of thought was evidently a Christianity in which the Greek, Platonic element would be accentuated and the heritage of the Old Testament would be lessened. Such in her eyes was Cathar Christianity. It is not certain that she was mistaken to see it in this way.

I myself have studied this subject for about thirty years—not, properly speaking, Catharism but rather Gnosticism, with which Catharism is connected. (It probably has connections owing to historical descent and certainly because of a similarity in ideas.) Now, after having granted some particle of truth to the fashionable theories—for one cannot avoid, when one begins a study, at first following the current ideas on the subject—I have come to the conclusion that Gnosticism issued out of Christianity and was an attempt to develop its Hellenic element by diminishing the element of Judaism that it conserved.

During the first days of March the Weils received a telegram from André announcing that he and his wife Eveline had reached America. They had impatiently awaited this news. Simone wrote to her brother: "We were all very happy to receive your telegram, because for the past two weeks we have been thinking too much about you, and that was not pleasant. Right now we can at least forget your existence most of the time, as is normal. A brother is like a tooth; it is a good thing, provided one is not forced to become aware too often that it exists. We even go so far as to ask ourselves whether Oscar, by chance, is in Martinique these days. . . ." (As I have said, Oscar was their code name for the police.)

She told her brother that for her part she had no desire to go to America, except if she were certain to be able to return to Europe with the necessary means to realize her project. This was her project for the organization of a group of front-line nurses.

"Your parents would like to request information from you about the voyage to America. As for me, my attitude has not changed. I don't wish to stay in America for a whole pile of reasons, all of which I can't go into but all of which are excellent. As for you, your case is special; to begin with, you had special reasons for leaving France; and then, as I said the other day to a young friend from Cavaillès, a philosopher who knew you at Strasbourg—and this point of view seemed to surprise him—a mathematician is so rare an animal that he deserves to be preserved be it only on the score of curiosity. . . . Therefore, with all the exceptions granted in your case, I think that since the hospitality of the Americans is in the nature of things limited, the French, who have until now lived quite peacefully, should not be the ones to take advantage of it. Their hospitality is a purely philanthropic matter, and it is repugnant to me to be the object of philanthropy. . . . It is more flattering, taking it all in all, to be the object of persecution. Moreover, I know myself, and unless I could sink, for example, into the heart of Turkestan (which seems to me at the moment quite difficult), the fact of being far from Europe would make me suffer to the point of losing all moral equilibrium. Being in France, the stories for instance about famine in France don't upset me; even if a real famine occurred, I would undergo it like the others and my imagination would not be unduly affected by it; but in America, even though theoretically I know very well the exaggerations that newspapers are capable of, reading articles on this subject would upset me enormously. Whether it be simply from an instinct of self-preservation or not, I must above all avoid going over there to live.

"I make an exception for only one circumstance: the circumstance in which the voyage would permit me to realize my project. But as to this I want *certainty* (setting aside obviously unforeseeable changes that might take place while I am en route, at sea). There are three problems: the money, the official authorizations, and the material means. Your parents say they are ready to provide the solution for the first, that is, the money. You can, where you are, obtain 1. the assurance that the material means exist (at least at the time when you send me the information); 2. the *formal promise* that official authorizations will be granted. . . . I would leave only on these two conditions. Without them, I would prefer staying in France. I count on you for a precise reply—and above all an exact one, you understand? I count on you not to fill me with false hopes, with the idea that it is in my interest to make the journey. It would be a very bad calculation, and it would certainly not be the right thing to do."

She made all sorts of efforts to help not only the Annamites in the Mazargues camp but also people who were in the camps in which, at the beginning of the war, all foreigners living in France had been gathered. These were in large part anti-Fascists, who had been driven from their own countries by the victory of Fascism. Simone had written about them to Belin and Belin's comrade, a functionary in a ministry at Vichy, to whom she had sent her complaints about the treatment of the Indochinese. In the same letter from which I have quoted a passage about the Indochinese, she said to him:

"I must now speak to you of a problem that is no longer within your jurisdiction; I have already written to Belin about this: these are the camps for foreigners. I have before my eyes at this moment confidential documents from the Center of American Relief for Intellectuals. . . . They are filled with horrors. Just think of the effect that these documents must have upon the Americans, upon a nation from which France, in its misfortune, is forced at the moment to expect assistance and pity.

"I am sending you extracts copied *word for word* from these documents that I have before my eyes. I don't dare send you the documents themselves. Until now my letters to you have all arrived; I don't know whether it would be the same for a letter containing typewritten documents. ...."

Since there had been no amelioration in the condition of the poor unfortunates imprisoned in the camps, on March 10 she wrote a letter in English to Admiral Leahy, United States ambassador to Vichy.

"Excellency:

"I am emboldened to write to you by the thought that I am going to speak for many Frenchmen and Frenchwomen who, in all parts of the country, in all classes of the population, are thinking many things which they cannot say. They feel deeply grateful for America's generosity, but think that such generosity, to be wise, should be subject to some conditions. ...

"In the first place, of course, no help given to France should be in the least harmful or dangerous to the cause of England. Many men and women in France would gladly starve if they felt that through starvation they could be useful to England. ...

"We have not yet felt hunger. It may come, of course, even tomorrow; but many people have complained before they were hungry. I am sure of that; for I am living with my father and mother in Marseilles, which has been for some time, I believe, the town in the whole non-occupied zone where food is most scarce; my father and I have both lost our situation, so we take care to spend very little money; we had absolutely no food in store; we have never, up till now—and I mean literally never—stood in a 'queue'; yet till now we have eaten, not well, of course, but enough. So I think I can say that there is as yet no hunger in France. ...

"The second condition, I think, to which American generosity should be subject is a better treatment of aliens in this country. You know, of course, all the facts about the bad treatment of aliens in France, the concentration camps, etc.—facts which I, as a Frenchwoman, can scarcely bear to think upon for very shame. In spite of all official promises, these shameful things are still going on. I even happen to know that in the *'camp du Vernet'* there has been lately an aggravation.

"For the sake of these unhappy people, for the sake, also, of the French men and women to whom honor is dearer than food, I think America should refuse to give any help till these cruel treatments have really ceased. ...."

As can be seen from this letter—and this is confirmed by various witnesses—she never stood on the "queues" to obtain food. Not only did she forbid herself this but she had persuaded her parents never to do it, declaring that she would never eat food obtained in this way. She also scorned the black market—one day she asked, "What would Socrates have thought of the black market?"—and forced herself scrupulously to obey the laws in this domain, living on the few ration coupons she kept for herself after giving away most of them to other people.

The second secretary of the American embassy at Vichy wrote to her on April 10 and said that when the ambassador, who was for the moment absent, would return, her letter would be brought to his attention.

In her letter to Admiral Leahy Simone mentions the camp at Vernet. Some foreigners she knew had given her information about this camp, among others a certain Nicolas who had been imprisoned there in July 1940 and later had been freed. (This was most likely Nicolas Lazaré-vitch. Since he was a Belgian, at a certain point he had been sent to the camp. Simone must have seen him at Toulouse at the beginning of September 1940, and then saw him again perhaps at Marseilles.) This Nicolas had told her, both in person and in letters, about a Spaniard named Antonio who was in this camp. He praised him highly and also said that he didn't have any acquaintances outside the camp and so never received either letters or packages. Simone decided to send him a package and to write to him. So the same day that she wrote to Admiral Leahy she also wrote to Antonio:

"Dear Sir:

"You will doubtless be surprised to receive a letter from someone you don't know; but your former companion at the camp, Nicolas, spoke to me about you in such a way that I felt I knew you. . . .

"I have been in your beautiful country for a short time in the past. . . . I think that it was in your region. I have never forgotten the peasants whom I saw in that countryside. . . . That is why, when Nicolas spoke to me about you, it seemed to me that I had known you for a long time.

"He told me that you had no one and that you don't receive any help. That is why I would like to do something for you; unfortunately I cannot do very much. I am sending you a package. I hope that I have chosen things that you will like; it is quite difficult these days to find things to send.

"I am sorry that I can't write to you in Spanish. If you don't know enough French to read this letter, I hope that you will find someone who can translate it for you. You can answer me in Spanish.

"With my best wishes and cordial salutations,
        "Simone Weil."

Antonio must have thanked her and told her that he feared she had deprived herself for him. She wrote to him again on March 17:

"Dear Sir:

"Your letter gave me great pleasure, because reading it I felt trans-ported again to Spain; and I have already told you how much I love Spain, the Spanish language, their way of thinking and expressing themselves that exists there and in no other part of Europe.

"A friend has loaned me for a few months a collection of Spanish folk songs. I have copied some of them out, so beautiful do I think them. There is no other country where there exists such poetry among the people. You certainly know much more about this than I; but would it perhaps please you if from time to time, I copy out one or two of them for you? . . . In return, you could write me some of them from memory, each time that you write to me.

"I would like to be able to send you books; but one cannot find Spanish books in Marseilles. I know this because I have looked for them for myself. If by chance, however, I manage to find some, would you like them?

"I have sent you a small package. I hope that it will reach you soon in good condition and that what I have chosen will please you.

"Don't be afraid that I am depriving myself for you. It gives me such pleasure to send you something from time to time, and what gives one pleasure is not a deprivation.

"The little that I can do does not deserve any thanks. If I were in a camp and you were free, you would behave in the same way toward me. . . .

"One day we shall perhaps be able to meet and get to know each other in some other way than through letters. It would be a great joy for me.

"Very cordially,
    "Simone Weil."

Deeply moved by this very warm and friendly letter, Antonio must have expressed his gratitude and friendship so fervently that Simone was perhaps a trifle embarrassed by it. I imagine that it was he who asked if he could address her informally with the "tu," because in the very next letter, written on April 22, Simone uses the informal form of address. (This was the custom, as we have seen, among Spanish anarchists, and Antonio most likely was an anarchist or had been one.) She accepts this, yet one feels a slight uneasiness in the first lines of her letter. She would like to say something that she doesn't say because "it is not the moment." No doubt she didn't want to show him any coldness, since he was in a miserable situation, but she was already afraid that the young Spaniard had become too attached to her.

"Dear friend:

"Forgive me if I have not written sooner. I have been very busy. You have understood my thought in my last two letters very well, at least the essential of my thought. There would be a great many things to be said about this, but this is not the moment.

"The weather here is marvelous; there are floods of light over the sea and the trees are covered with leaves. I am glad to know you get joy out of looking at the mountains. So long as there are such things as the sea, the mountains, the wind, sun, stars, moon, and sky one cannot be completely wretched. And if one were deprived of all that and put in a dungeon, knowing that such things exist, that they are beautiful and that others enjoy them freely must always be a consolation.

"The fact that you are capable, in the place where you are, of feeling such joy shows that you have been able to preserve what is best in you. They can make you suffer, but they cannot do you any real harm. It is a great joy for me and I am happy to have gotten into contact with you.

" . . . Forgive me for not having had the time as yet to send you some books. I have sent you a package; perhaps you have already received it. I shall send you another quite soon.

"I am copying out some folk songs for you. With friendly greetings."

So she thought that what is best in man is revealed by his ability to experience joy despite a miserable fate. She placed a character like Antonio's very high in her esteem; he never complained in his letters; he spoke a great deal about nature, and in a charming fashion. He was the Spanish peasant of whom, in a letter to Father Perrin, she will say that she regards him as not being very far from saintliness.[12]

Simone also exchanged letters with an Austrian, Frantzl K., a peasant from the Tyrol, who had also been in the camp at Vernet but had been able to get out thanks to the efforts of some monks at Annecy who had hired him as a gardener. He had been friends at the Vernet camp with an Austrian lawyer, Richard R., who had been freed before him and whom Simone had become acquainted with in Marseilles. (She made more than one effort to help R. with the American consulate. Sometimes she would return from the consulate in tears because she had to wait so long and the discussions were so nerve-wracking.) R. had finally obtained his visa; he had left Marseilles and, by way of Casablanca and Martinique, had traveled to New York, when Simone wrote this draft of a letter originally in German, to Frantzl:

"Dear Herr K.,

"I am sending you a raincoat; I hope that it fits you. If you need anything else, write to me and tell me. I have also sent you some money; don't be offended, I beg you. You should at least have a little money, for unfortunately in this world one cannot live without money. Do not thank me for it, I beg you. What I can do for you is so little and, as I have already told you, it is a debt. Your thanks would make me feel ashamed.

"Instead, I have a reason to thank you. Your letter moved me a great deal.

"I have received a letter from Richard R., sent from Casablanca. Things are going well for him. Your liberation made him very happy. I have written to him what you told me to tell him and have given him your address. . . .

"Although Annecy is beautiful, you are surely feeling homesick. Unfortunately I don't know your beautiful country. I would love to go there some day. In other times, how beautiful life must be in your mountain villages! I hope that you will again taste that happiness. ...

"With cordial greetings ..."

Another draft of a letter to Frantzl comes after April 6. K. was a poet; he had sent some of his verses to Simone.

"Dear Herr K.:

"Pardon me, I beg you, for answering so late. I received your letters of March 11 and 18 and April 6, but I wanted to wait until I had news of Herr R. Now I have received a postcard from Martinique; he is fine. He was at Martinique on March 18. I hope that we will soon receive letters from New York. He will certainly write to you; he will not forget you, because he has a real feeling of friendship for you. ...

"Every time that I look at your postcard from Annecy, it gives me a feeling of joy to know that there are in the world such marvelously beautiful things and that you live among them. As for myself, I can never think of my country without chagrin, because my country is Paris. But a large city like Paris, although it is so beautiful, has surely deserved much more misfortune than the mountain villages in the Tyrol or in Styria. ...

"Believe me, if our correspondence is a joy and a consolation for you, it is so for me, too. All human beings who love real peace are strangers now in a strange world and must find consolation from each other.

"With cordial greetings.

"If you need some money or anything else, tell me, I beg you, without hesitating (and naturally without thanking me)."

It was perhaps around the month of March that Simone wrote a "Note on the Penal Colony Punishment Inflicted on Foreigners," which she had meant to send to Monsignor Delay, the bishop of Marseilles, and which was perhaps sent to him. She described everything that was cruel in this punishment of banishment to a penal colony. We have seen that she already demanded its abolition in a declaration entitled "Some Remarks on the Subject of the French Penal Code." She observes that this punishment was applied to foreigners in September 1939 in Marseilles and also in February 1941. She concludes that Marshal Pétain should be asked to do the following things: 1. abolish banishment as a punishment for repeated criminal offenders who are living in France as foreigners; 2. pardon all foreigners already sentenced to banishment for such criminal conduct.

It seems that it was at the beginning of April that Simone wrote this undated letter to her brother:

"My dear brother,

"Just to let you know that we are still alive. ... If you read in the papers that we are all dead of hunger, don't believe a word of it. We like to imagine you dipping huge, heavily buttered tarts in cups of chocolate and at the same time shedding huge tears while thinking of us. You would never admit the huge tears, but we are convinced that you shed them, and this idea makes us laugh a lot."

She told him that she had discovered a different method from that of Archimedes for the quadrature of the parabola. She asked him whether Neugebauer had published any new works on ancient mathematics or astronomy; and if he had published them and would send them to the Philosophical Society at Marseilles, she would gladly report on them.

She advised her brother that one of their cousins, who had also passed through Marseilles and was about to take a ship for America, would bring him an issue of *Cahiers du Sud* (no doubt the issue that contained the second part of her essay on the *Iliad*). She had also entrusted to this cousin her plan for the group of front-line nurses, so that he could give it to André. But since he was afraid that this document might be compromising, he had gotten rid of it en route.

At the Society of Philosophical Studies in Marseilles, two lectures (the last of the 1940–1941 series) particularly interested Simone: a lecture by Marcel Brion on painting and philosophy in China; and another lecture by the dean of the faculty of medicine, Lucien Cornil, on Hippocrates. Moreover, the president of this society, Gaston Berger, defended his doctoral thesis at Aix, and Simone attended this discussion. She wrote an article on these three subjects, which under the title "Philosophy" was published in the *Cahiers du Sud* of May 1941 (No. 235, pp. 288–94).

As to Brion's lecture, it appeared to her that the author, who repeatedly contrasted the East with the West and wanted to show Oriental philosophy as foreign to Europeans, instead had shown how close this philosophy was to ours. "Each Taoist formula awakens in us a resonance, and these texts evoke in turn Heraclitus, Protagoras, Plato, the Cynics, the Stoics, Christianity, and Jean-Jacques Rousseau. Not that Taoist thought isn't original, profound, and new for a European; but, like everything that is truly great, it is at once new and familiar; as Plato said, we remember having known it on the other side of the sky."

Also, Oriental art, in its relation to philosophy, is not so different from ours. If it is tied to a philosophy, our art is also, among the great creators. "Could real art be anything else but a method for establishing a certain relationship between the world and itself, between itself and itself, that is to say, the equivalent of a philosophy? Certainly many Western artists have conceived of art in another manner, but they are no doubt not the greatest." It is true that the Chinese painters have so great a need for the infinite that this need drove them to dissolve forms, whereas the Greeks search everywhere for the definite and limited. "However, it is still the same human need. Man cannot console himself that the infinite is not given to him, and he has more than one way of fabricating, through the finite, an equivalent of the infinite; a fabrication that is perhaps the definition of art." She adds: "But if M. Brion, in presenting Chinese art to us as foreign, makes it appear so close to us, this is the best praise of his description."

M. Cornil did not present Hippocrates as distant but rather as very close to us. "What is closer to us than Greece? It is closer to us than ourselves. It is doubtful that we have a single important idea that was not clearly conceived of by the Greeks."

Hippocrates had gotten the idea for the experimental method. But his greatness lies, as Cornil shows, "not in the fondness for experiments, because there were in his time a number of excellent empirics, not in the attachment to philosophy, because a number of philosophers spoke about medicine, but in the methodical use of philosophical and particularly Pythagorean thought for a perpetual investigation of experience.

"In a sense, Greek science is much closer to ours than we think, and it is anything but a rough sketch. . . . But in another sense Greek science is far from us, far above us. . . . Among the Greeks, the epic, drama, architecture, sculpture, the conception of the universe and natural laws, astronomy, mechanics, physics, politics, medicine, and the idea of virtue —each of these things bore at its center the idea of the equilibrium that accompanies proportion. . . . In Greece, the idea of equilibrium oriented all scientific research toward the good, and of course, medicine, more than any other. M. Cornil has shown by his numerous quotations that in Hippocrates's view virtue and even saintliness form a part of the definition of true medicine."

The defense of M. Berger's thesis also transported his auditors to Greece. But it had not been a question of Greece particularly. "Yet in following the discussion . . . one necessarily thought of Plato. M. Berger's method, which consists, when he encounters an idea, an affirmation in his mind, not in asking himself whether it is true or false but what it means, is the very method used by Socrates. . . . There can only be two kinds of philosophers—those who employ this method and those who construct at their pleasure a representation of the universe; only these last have what is properly called a system, whose value can only consist in a certain poetic beauty, above all in the marvelously incisive formulas with which the exposition of some of these philosophers is strewn, as is the case with Aristotle and Hegel. But the former are the true masters of thought. . . . And a singular fact—the philosophers who follow this method are all oriented toward salvation."

Here Simone expresses briefly her conception of philosophy and of the history of philosophy. This conception can already be discerned in her courses, especially in the lessons in philosophy published by Mme. Reynaud,[13] and it derives from even further off yet, from Alain. But she now expresses it a little differently and with even greater conviction.

There can only be two kinds of philosophy: the philosophers with systems on one side, and, on the other, those who are attached to the Platonic tradition and whose whole study is oriented toward salvation. These are the true masters of thought. They are even, in Simone's eyes, the only ones who really deserve the name of philosophers. It is in an unpublished text, probably written in Marseilles[14] and entitled "Some Reflections on the Idea of Value," that she developed this conception of philosophy.

"The idea of value," she says, "is at the center of philosophy. All reflection that deals with the idea of value, or the hierarchy of values, is philosophic; every effort of thought that deals with another object than value is, when examined closely, alien to philosophy."

One cannot renounce the posing and questioning of values. "For the mind is essentially and forever, in whatever way it is disposed, a tension toward value; it cannot regard the idea itself of value as uncertain without regarding its own existence as uncertain, which is impossible for it." One cannot renounce reflecting on values, comparing them, and trying to establish an order among them, a hierarchy. But this reflection is extremely difficult. "For since the mind is a tension toward some value, how can it detach itself from the value toward which it is straining in order to consider it, judge it, and put it at its proper level in regard to other values? This detachment demands an effort, and every effort of the mind is a striving toward a value. Thus in order to achieve this detachment, the mind must regard this detachment itself as the supreme value. But in order to see in detachment a value superior to all others, one must already be detached from all the other values. This is a vicious circle that makes the task of reflection seem to be a miracle; the word grace expresses this miraculous nature."

It can be seen from this that philosophy does not consist in the acquisition of various forms of knowledge but in a change of one's entire soul. "Reflection presupposes a transformation in the orientation of the soul, which we call detachment. . . . Detachment is a renouncement of all possible goals without exception, a renouncement that sets a void in place of the future, as would the imminent approach of death; that is why in the ancient mysteries, in Platonic philosophy, in the Sanskrit texts, in the Christian religion, and quite probably always and everywhere, detachment has always been compared to death and the initiation into wisdom has been regarded as a kind of passage through death. . . . But the detachment that is in question here does not lack an object; detached thought has as its object the establishment of a true hierarchy among values . . .; it has as its object a way of living, a better life, not elsewhere but in this world and immediately. . . . In this sense, philosophy is oriented toward life by passing through death. . . ."

Therefore philosophical reflection is very different from science, but it is no less certain; indeed it is just the opposite of vagueness and uncertainty. "The rigor and certitude of philosophical investigation are as great as they can be; the sciences are far from coming close to them. Should one conclude from this that philosophical reflection is infallible? Yes, it is infallible to the degree that it is actually carried out." This certainly is a way of viewing the matter that is absolutely contrary to common opinion. "One generally sees only conjectures in philosophy. What produces this opinion are the contradictions between the systems and within each system. It is generally believed that each philosophy has a system that contradicts all the others. Now, quite far from this being the case, there exists a philosophical tradition that is probably as ancient as humanity and that, one must hope, will last as long as humanity will; from this tradition, as from a common source, are inspired, it is true, not all those who call themselves philosophers but several among them, so that their thought is nearly the same. Plato is no doubt the most perfect representative of this tradition; the *Bhagavad-Gita* is inspired by the same tradition, and one can easily find Egyptian and Chinese texts that can be named alongside these. In Europe in modern times one must cite Descartes and Kant; among the most recent thinkers, Lagneau and Alain in France and Husserl in Germany. This philosophic tradition is what we call philosophy. Far from being able to reproach it for its differences, it is one, eternal, and not susceptible to progress. The sole renewal of which it is capable is that of expression, when a man expresses himself to himself and expresses himself to those around him in terms that are related to the conditions of the epoch, the civilization, and the environment in which he lives. It is desirable that such a transformation take place from age to age, and this is the only reason that makes it worth the trouble to write on this subject after Plato wrote. . . ."

As for the contradictions within the doctrines, this is inherent in all philosophical thought. "Far from being an imperfection of philosophical thought, it is an essential characteristic without which there is only a false appearance of philosophy. For true philosophy does not build anything; its object is given to it—it is our thoughts; it only makes, as Plato says, an inventory of them; if in the course of the inventory it encounters certain contradictions, it is not its task to suppress them, unless it intends to lie. Philosophers who try to construct systems in order to eliminate contradictions are those who in appearance justify the opinion that philosophy is something conjectural; because such systems can be varied to infinity, and there is no reason to choose one rather than another. But from the point of view of knowledge, these systems are even lower than conjectures, since conjectures are inferior thoughts, and these systems are not thoughts. One cannot even think them. One cannot do this, since if one could, be it for an instant, one would during this instant eliminate the contradictions that the system seems to resolve, and one cannot eliminate them. The contradictions that reflection finds in thought when it makes an inventory of it are essential to thought, including the thought of the fabricators of systems; these contradictions are present in their thought even at the time they elaborate or describe their systems, but they employ words in a way that is not in conformity with their thought, and do this out of an excess of ambition. Thus those who deny the reality of the external world, at the very moment that they say that they deny it, have toward the reality of their table and chair the same feeling as any peasant whatsoever; they establish the same difference between their perceptions and their dreams as any peasant whatsoever.... Decisive progress will be achieved when one decides to present honestly the contradictions essential to thought instead of vainly trying to set them aside."

One can set these reflections on the idea of value side by side with the "Letter to the *Cahiers du Sud* on the Responsibilities of Literature," which was probably written about the same time, that is, about April or May 1941, and also dealt with the problem of value.

Léon-Gabriel Gros had published two articles in *Cahiers du Sud,* in October 1940 and March 1941, in which he argued against the thesis, almost official at that time, of a responsibility of the writers in the national disaster of 1940. Simone felt it necessary to inform the magazine that she didn't have the same opinion as Gros, even though she had no sympathy for those who supported the opposite thesis. "I am impelled," she said, "to return to the subject, in defense of a point of view opposed to that of the review, and of almost everyone I sympathize with, and seeming, unfortunately, to resemble the one held by people for whom I feel no sympathy at all."

She believed that the writers did have a responsibility in the misfortunes of our century. "The essential characteristic of the first half of the twentieth century is the growing weakness, and almost the disappearance, of the idea of value.... Dadaism and surrealism are extreme cases; they represented the intoxication of total license.... The surrealists have set up non-oriented thought as a model; they have chosen the total absence of value as their supreme value.... The other writers of the same and the preceding period have gone less far, but almost all of them ... have been more or less affected by the same disease, the enfeeblement of the sense of value. Such words as spontaneity, sincerity, gratuitousness, richness, enrichment—words that imply an almost total indifference to contrasts of value—have come more often from their pens than words that contain a reference to good and evil.... Words like virtue, nobility, honor, honesty, and generosity have become almost impossible to use or else have acquired bastard meanings.... In a general way, the literature of the twentieth century is essentially psychological and psychology consists in describing states of the soul by displaying them all on the same plane without any discrimination of value, as though good and evil were external to them, as though the effort toward the good could be absent at any moment from the thought of men."

Simone recognizes that writers don't have to teach morality. "But they do have to express the human condition. And nothing concerns human life so essentially, for every man at every moment, as good and evil." It is true that a certain morality is even more foreign to good than amorality. "Those who are now blaming the eminent writers are worth infinitely less than they. ... If our present suffering ever leads to a revival, this will not be brought about through slogans but in silence and moral loneliness, through pain, misery, and terror in the profoundest depths of each man's spirit." This letter was published in *Cahiers du Sud* much later, in 1951.[15]

Jean Tortel put Simone in touch with a Resistance network. I don't know exactly what network this was. Tortel himself knew it only from the outside and was not able to give me much information about it. However, it is clear that the network was quickly tracked down and Simone was questioned a number of times by the police. These interrogations must have taken place in 1941, in April or the beginning of May.

It was due to the fact that she had been told that this organization could get her to England that Simone had wanted to join it. She had to fill out an application with information about herself. Simone filled it out, writing down her entire *curriculum vitae,* with a brief description of her ideas and plans. She attended one or even several clandestine meetings. But there was a traitor in the organization and the police were tipped off. Early one morning the bell rang at the door of their apartment and Mme. Weil found herself in the presence of four policemen. They asked to see Simone; Mme. Weil went to wake her. She told her with a smile and without apparent emotion—Simone congratulated her afterward on her steady nerves—that some policemen were there and wanted to see her. They showed Simone the application she had filled out and questioned her. They showed her some photographs: did she know any of these people? She recognized one of the faces, but told the policemen that she didn't know a single one. They asked her who had put her in touch with this organization; she said that it was someone with whom she had struck up a conversation while waiting for a bus and that she didn't know him in any other way. They asked her for a description of this unknown person; she gave them a made-up, very vague description. With a touch of humor, one of the policemen summed it up: "In short, no particular distinguishing marks." They then wanted to search her room, which was full of manuscripts. (Mme. Weil felt inwardly sorry for them, having to sift through this great mass of papers.) They stayed there all morning examining the manuscripts and then left. One of the policemen, after the search, said to Mme. Weil, "Tell your husband not to be upset so much; it's not worth it."

Simone had made some extracts from "Reflections on the Causes of

Freedom and Social Oppression" under the title "Critique of Marxism," and Mme. Weil had typed them up. Before leaving, one of the policemen asked Simone to give him a copy of this with a dedication, which she willingly did. Afterward, she said to her mother, "Don't you think he asked for a dedication in order to get a sample of my handwriting?" Her mother pointed out that if all he had wanted were samples of her handwriting, her room was full of them. The policemen were also interested in a draft of the letter to Admiral Leahy. They asked Simone to translate it for them, and she did.

Soon after, she was summoned to the police station. Since she thought that they might have decided to arrest her, she packed a small suitcase with some clothes and a copy of the *Iliad.* Her parents went with her, waiting for her on the terrace of a café just across from the police station.

A military examining magistrate questioned her. He asked her abruptly, without beating around the bush, "What are your feelings in regard to England?" Simone burst into laughter and declared, "My feelings in regard to England are feelings of the greatest sympathy." A trifle disconcerted by the fact that she didn't hide these feelings and that he could not surprise her, he said to her, "I can understand that before you may have had sympathy for England, but after Mers el-Kébir. . . ."* She replied that she had not changed and tried to show him that England should be supported. They discussed this for some time. He then said, "You are carrying on pro-English propaganda." She denied this. "You see," he said, "though knowing what a risk you are taking, you still tell me your pro-English feelings, so wouldn't you try to get other people to share these feelings in a more ordinary situation?" "If someone asks me what my feelings are," she replied, "I don't hide them; but I don't tell them to someone who doesn't expressly question me about them."

He asked her about the application, in which she had spoken of her plan for a group of front-line nurses. He said of this plan: "That's a very good tactical idea. Did you attend the Staff College?" "No more," she said, "than a lot of people who are concerned about the war."

To Simone's great astonishment, he decided not to arrest her. Her parents saw her come out accompanied by a policeman and then enter another building. Finally they let her go.

She was summoned by the police two more times. Each time she packed her suitcase, telling herself, "This time they'll put me in," and her parents again went to mount guard at the small café. The policemen tried to conquer her by wearing her out. They let her sit for a very long time in a corner, and now and then they would say to her, "If you tell

---

*A reference to the time the British navy attacked and sank the French warships that were in this port in Algeria.

us what you know, we won't do anything to you, but if you continue to keep silent, that can be very serious for you." They gave her some examples: "So-and-so told us everything he knew; so we didn't bother him." She repeated, "I have nothing to add to my declarations." They confronted her with someone whom she knew very well; both Simone and this man behaved as if they had never seen each other before. She was very careful not to say anything that was true, instead saying anything that popped into her head, since she knew that with a single particle of truth they could uncover a great deal of the truth. (Alain had once told us how in a certain colony, most likely Indochina, the native servants always lied as a precaution, knowing that one could always return to a lie and prove that it was false, whereas once the truth was said, one could not go back and prove it to be false. On the contrary, it is easy to confirm the truth and to proceed from there to other truths.) At last an irritated policeman said to her, "You are a little bitch. You know that I could have you thrown into jail together with a bunch of whores." She replied, "I have always wanted to know that environment and I can't see any better way than going to prison to find out about it." Another policeman said to the first, "I told you that we can't get anything out of her." They tried to play on her emotions by showing her her parents, who were waiting for her across the street: "Doesn't that mean anything to you, seeing your poor parents waiting for you?" In the end they let her go.

In a letter to her brother written on May 21, Simone alludes to these interrogations that she calls, in their code, "conversations with Oscar." She describes them with amusement, indulgence, and serenity, not accusing Oscar, that is, the police, of having been harsh with her. Instead, she seemed to think of him as rather bizarre, lazy, and insufficiently conscientious in his work:

"Your mother has told you of my conversations with Oscar. One of them occurred at our place; he was interested in my books and manuscripts. Then three times at his place. He was bizarre. Now he was polite, now agreeable, and now angry in quick succession, but above all terribly lazy and not very conscientious. He spoke of inviting me to his house for a rather prolonged stay, but after that it never came up again and I really believe that he forgot all about it. But one can never be sure with him because you know how crazy he is, but the probability is so faint that I don't even take account of it in my plans. Somebody showed him my letter in which I spoke of my plan for common work with Doris, which you know about; that shocked him a bit, but he didn't bear a grudge. What also contributed to making our relations a bit tempestuous is that I thought he was much too inquisitive and indiscreet. But in the end, that is up until now, we seem to understand each other not too badly."

The "plan of common work with Doris" was the plan to get to

England. In the code arranged beforehand between Simone and André, "Doris" stood for England.

Simone was not pretending when she accepted with calm, almost with pleasure, the possibility of being arrested; she had no fear at all of prison. But her parents had lived in anguish and always feared the dangers into which her heroism and her mad devotion could sweep her. At the time of these interrogations, Mme. Weil sighed and said to Tortel in a moment of particular anxiety, "Monsieur, if you ever have a daughter, pray to God that she isn't a saint."

Simone, when someone expressed sympathy for her parents, would at times flippantly say, "Another one who belongs to my parents' protective association!" Yet she had a profound feeling of pity for them. But she could not renounce the road she felt she had to follow.

Every time that someone among Simone's friends or acquaintances shipped out to America, she asked them again to take to her brother the "Project for the Organization of Front-Line Nurses," which she was afraid had not yet reached him, or to convey to him certain information about what she wanted to do and what she was sure she could accomplish if she got to America. In her letter of May 21 she tells him that Mme. Rapkine (the wife of a scholar who was André Weil's friend), who was about to leave for America, would provide him with details on her projects.

"My frame of mind is still the same; I want to go to America only if I can realize my project; otherwise, I am infinitely better off here. If I were over there and trapped in the impossibility of doing what I want to, I would be crushed by despair. . . ."

For a long time now she had wanted to know at first hand how the agricultural laborer lived by submitting herself to this life, just as she had experienced the life of the factory worker. She had told me about it once, in 1937, but then she had to wait until she was in better physical condition, for she thought that the work of the agricultural laborer was even more demanding than the work she had done in the factories. About the spring of 1941 she thought perhaps that she was in danger of not having much more time in which to realize her plan. She spoke about it to Hélène Honnorat. Hélène knew Father Perrin, a Domenican who gave devoted assistance to many of the people who had found refuge in Marseilles; she felt that he could help Simone find a job as an agricultural laborer in the region.

Father Perrin, who had been traveling for some time, returned to Marseilles at the beginning of June. On his return he may have found a letter from Hélène Honnorat, or perhaps she had gone to see him. Or perhaps Simone had written to him, mentioning her friendship with Hélène and her recommendation. At any rate, there is a short letter of his to Simone on June 3, in which he explains his tardiness by the fact that he had just returned the day before and tells her that he will be very happy to help her carry out her plan. "Your friend has perhaps told you of my love for Israel, and its present misfortunes can only increase this desire to serve it." He proposes that she come to see him on the following Saturday. So there is no doubt that on June 7 Simone met him for the first time.

He has spoken of this first meeting in the introduction to *Waiting for God.* [16] "Right at the start Simone Weil spoke to me of her love for the 'unfortunate' and her desire to share their fate, to live as they did, this time not in a factory but as a part of the agricultural proletariat. . . . This is what brought me, somewhat later, to put her into contact with G. Thibon."

Simone was deeply impressed by this meeting with the almost blind priest, who was then ascetically thin and spoke in a very gentle, sweet voice. He immediately inspired her with both trust and friendship. She got into the habit of visiting him regularly, not only to find out what had happened to his efforts to get her a job but also to tell him of the religious problems that preoccupied her.

As to these visits, Father Perrin wrote: "She used to come to see me as often as it was possible for both of us to fit it in. . . . With her extreme consideration for others, she used to wait quietly in the passage, letting two or perhaps three people pass before her. After they had gone we talked for whatever moments remained. On a few rare occasions she asked me to see her at a friend's house in order to have more time and freedom of spirit."[17]

At the start she did not seem to consider the problem of baptism and the formal joining of the Church. "Her love of Christ seemed to be enough for her, and the extremely superficial idea she had of the Church and Catholics was not of a nature to suggest the slightest question in her mind."[18] However, "the question of baptism came up very soon,"[19] and from then on it returned as the central subject of their conversations.[20] One may suppose that it was Father Perrin who first oriented their conversations in this direction. Besides, Simone wrote to him a little later: "If I had not met you, I should never have considered the problem of baptism as a practical problem."[21]

From their very first meetings she told him about the difficulties she had in attaching herself exclusively to Christianity and the great admiration she had for other religious traditions. She says this in a fragment of a letter published by Father Perrin: "From the time of our first interviews I explained to you my difficulties concerning the other religions. You told me that no doubt with time these difficulties would lose their importance in my eyes."[22] Contrary to Father Perrin's expectation, these difficulties did not lessen with the passage of time. She would also very early in their relationship express her judgment on the Old Testament. "At the center of all her oppositions was her attitude to Israel, it was the key to all of her resistance."[23]

Antonio had been transferred from the camp at Vernet to another camp at Djelfa in Algeria. He wrote to Simone, who answered him on June 5:

"Dear friend,

"No doubt you have received the letter I wrote to you to the camp at Vernet; I imagine that they forwarded it to you. Forgive me for having gone so long without writing to you; I have been very busy; I have written a great deal (on philosophical subjects; I am also writing a play); I have also had some troubles, but now that is over. I often thought of you, but I did not have a free mind to be able to write. I hope you didn't think that I had forgotten you. . . ."

(The troubles she mentions are certainly her interrogations at police headquarters.)

"I am very unhappy that they have sent you off to where you are now, if the climate is bad for you. . . . Do you need any warm clothes for the night, if the nights are cold? . . . Have you enough blankets? Is the nourishment sufficient? Can one send you packages from France?

"I am afraid that the nature surrounding you there may not be as beautiful as in the Pyrenees. As I am writing to you, the sun is setting in the Mediterranean. I hope that you see each day things as beautiful, you and all those who are capable of enjoying what is beautiful. Fortunately, the sky is beautiful everywhere. . . .

". . . Where you are located, do you have any contacts with the Arabs? I believe that the Spaniards and the Arabs have much in common; and that certainly those things that make me love Spain so much can also be found among the Arabs, at least among the best of them. I would really love to see Algeria; I have requested a safe-conduct but they didn't grant it to me. . . ."

She ends the letter, saying: "Would it be useful to you if I sent you a bit of money from time to time? We know each other well enough now, I hope, so that I can ask you this without offending you. I wouldn't want to offend you for anything in the world. But between people who think as we do this would be an absolutely natural thing to do."

A letter written by Simone to Gilbert Kahn on June 30 informs us that she had had the intention of going to Carcassone to hear the Gregorian chants, but could not do so because she was forced to use the money set aside for that for some other purpose. It is easy to guess what the money was used for. If it was not for money orders sent to Frantzl, it was certainly for something of that kind.

(The chants she longed to hear were those of the monks in the Abbey d'En-Calcat at Dourgne in the Tarn region. She had the joy of hearing them the very next year, and when going to the Dourgne in the spring of 1942 she stopped over at Carcassone.)

She returned to Kahn a copy of Alain's book *Entretiens au bord de la mer,* which he had loaned her, and told him that it had been very useful to her. He had also loaned her Alain's book *Les Dieux,* or loaned it to her a little later. She does not mention it in this letter, but Kahn recalled that she liked *Les Dieux* less than the *Entretiens.* She felt that in *Les Dieux* Alain was Hegelian and found it hard to forgive him for being inspired in this book more by Hegel than by Plato. One day she told Kahn that there was in Alain's thought a part that seemed integral to her beliefs and another part that she no longer accepted.

She already had the hope of being taken on during the summer at Gustave Thibon's farm. Father Perrin had made an effort to find her a job as an agricultural laborer; but since he felt that an experience of this kind should be undertaken with some sort of supervision, he had turned to one of his friends, Gustave Thibon, a Catholic writer who had a farm in the Ardèche. He had written to tell him that a young Jewish woman, a philosophy graduate and a left-wing militant, excluded from the university by the laws of Vichy, wanted to work for a while in the country as a farmhand and that he hoped that she could work on his farm under his supervision. Thibon's reply had perhaps not yet arrived. Simone wrote to Kahn: "I think that I am going to obtain—through the intervention of a Domenican who has understood my desire very well, and for whom I have written, for eventual publication in a Catholic magazine, some reflections on factory work—a job as a servant on a farm. This will be a very sudden change in my way of life, but Krishna will not be farther from me, since he was the beloved of the milkmaids. . . . This job will be in the Ardèche region. That will not bring us closer together. I don't know when it will begin. I imagine that you too will work in agriculture during your vacation. But, I hope, in a less lowly position. Lowly conditions suit me, but this is due to a special vocation."

The "reflections on factory work," which she says here she had written for Father Perrin and which were destined for a Catholic magazine, form the article in *La Condition ouvrière* entitled "Experience of Factory Life."[24] This article was in fact published in Marseilles after Simone's departure, in the Catholic magazine *Economie et humanisme* and under the title "Reflections on Factory Life."[25]

As Simone had feared, the spectacle of nature at Djelfa did not give Antonio the same joys as had nature in the Pyrenees. Simone wrote to him in June or the beginning of July: "I am very sorry that the spectacle of nature around you does not give you the same joy as it did at Vernet. But perhaps, with time, you will learn to see as much beauty in it, because beauty takes many different forms. In any case, you always have the sky and the light in which you can find joy, since you are one of those rare beings who know how to find joy in the beautiful things that surround you."

She asked him again to tell her if he needed anything and also to describe his life and how he spent his time. Having received his reply, she wrote to him on July 21:

"I want to thank you for having told me about your daily life. Do you still miss the birds of the Pyrenees? I don't know whether silence is not more beautiful than all the songs. When the sun sets or rises in a vast landscape, there is no more complete harmony than silence. Even if men talk and make noise around them, one can hear the silence that glides above and that extends as far as the sky. I am happy that you have pure water; pure water is a beautiful thing. The nights must be very clear and full of stars in Africa. Do you look at the stars a lot? Do you know them? Plato said that sight is not truly precious unless it helps us to know the stars, the planets, the moon, and the sun. For my part, I am ashamed to say that I don't know all the constellations and their names. Some months ago I got a map of the sky in order to put an end to my ignorance. But I have not studied it; because I then thought that I had no need of books to look at the sky and that I can, by looking at it often and for a long time, manage without help to recognize the groups of stars and the movement of the sky, like the shepherds who invented astronomy some thousands of years ago. There is no greater joy for me than looking at the sky on a clear night with an attention so concentrated that all my other thoughts disappear; then one can think that the stars enter into one's soul."

It seems that Simone loved above all in nature the purity of mineral things, or the void of silence, of immense and luminous space, or the strange, distant splendor of the stars. She says of them: "The stars, those marvelous, brilliant, inaccessible objects, at least as remote as the horizon . . . which we can neither change nor touch, and which, in turn, touch only our eyes, are what is furthest away from us and closest to us."[26] In her letter of June 30 to Gilbert Kahn she also told him that she had bought an atlas for the stars, but that soon after she had resolved not to learn their forms and names in this way and wanted, when looking at the sky, to learn by herself to recognize the forms, as had been done by the Babylonian shepherds. She told me somewhat the same thing a few months later at Poët, when, before a beautiful starry sky, I wanted to teach her the names of the constellations and stars of the first magnitude.

Since she had sent some money to Antonio, she went to great lengths to overcome Antonio's scruples about accepting it:

"I have sent you a money order; I will send you money orders from time to time according to your needs and my possibilities. I don't think you should have any scruples or hesitations on this matter. When I have a little money in my hands, I never have the impression that this money belongs to me. It just happens to be there. And if I send it to you, I don't get the feeling that I have given it away. It simply passes from my hands to those of someone else who needs it, and I have the feeling that I am not at all involved. I would really prefer that money was like water and that it flowed off by itself whenever there was a little too much of it.

"In fact, when you get this money order, don't think that you have gotten something from me but simply that a little money has fallen into your hands. That has nothing to do with me. You and me, what we give to each other and receive from each other are thoughts and emotions in the form of letters. This exchange takes place between us because we feel and think in the same way about many things. As for the rest, always tell me what you need and I will do what it is possible for me to do; because this does not at all involve our personal relations with each other. I think that you understand me and that you feel as I do about this subject."

Antonio was, like Frantzl, a poet. He had sent Simone a poem. (She told him she had liked the poem and the emotion it expressed very much.)

Since about the month of May, Nguyên Van Danh had been in Marseilles. He had been sent there to organize the embarkation of a certain number of Indochinese soldiers who were to be repatriated. He was also dealing with the camps in which these soldiers and the Indochinese civilian laborers were gathered. He had written a number of official memoranda about the camps, asking that all Indochinese be repatriated or, if not, that they be sent to Algeria, or at least that they be employed in factories or on farms and be hired by individuals—they would then receive better food and would learn a trade. Simone tried to help him, as she had helped him at Vichy. They went to see the Japanese consul together and asked him to write to the Japanese ambassador at Vichy. They also continued to hope to persuade the Japanese ambassador to intervene with the Germans to free the Indochinese prisoners, or at least to improve their living conditions. They went to the prefecture together. Simone took Danh to see Father Perrin, who advised them to write to the papal nuncio at Vichy.

Danh saw that Simone would bring to the camp at Mazargues everything she could scrape up in terms of food, clothing, ration coupons, stripping both herself and her parents (with their consent). He tried to convince her to moderate her generosity, telling her that what she could give was only a drop in the ocean and might lead to jealousies since they could not help everyone; that the most effective action was to keep after the authorities so as to obtain some general measures for the prisoners.

It was not easy to get ships for repatriating the soldiers, since there was a dearth of ships. But finally, at the beginning of August, Danh could embark for Saigon with 2,500 Indochinese workers. An hour before the ship sailed, he went to see the Weils. He brought them a chicken; Simone refused to eat it, saying that she had promised herself not to eat expensive things. Her parents also refused, saying that they had already dined. He had to eat it by himself. Then he left to go to the boat and Simone walked part of the way with him.

Perhaps she had dreamed of leaving with him in order to reach England by this roundabout route. She had told him, as she had in 1938, that she wanted to go to Indochina. But Mme. Weil had asked Danh to dissuade her. As a result, he had said to her, "Perhaps it will be possible for all of you to come together, you and your parents; but first I must get there and see what the situation is. When I get there, I shall write to you and tell you whether you can come." The first available ships were reserved for the soldiers and functionaries; they took almost no ordinary passengers.

When Danh reached Indochina, he did not forget his promise to write to the Weils. But his ship had taken almost three months to reach Saigon, for it had been forced to go all the way around Africa. The moment he arrived was almost the same moment that Japan entered the war. From then on communications were cut off and the letter sent to the Weils never got to them. Even during his voyage, Danh had written more than once to Simone at the various ports of call, but none of these letters ever reached her.

Simone had given him, both at Vichy and Marseilles, some of her writings: some poems, a few essays on social problems, and some others on religious problems. He took them with him to Indochina. But these manuscripts were to disappear when his house was looted by soldiers in 1945.

Dr. Bercher, who was working as ship's doctor on transatlantic vessels, often came to Marseilles. He was there in July 1941. He took long walks with Simone between Goudes, Cassis and Baumettes, "in the delicious massif of Marseilles-Veyre, which somehow manages to unite the rocks of Greece with the fiords of Norway."[27]

They often talked about religion. The question that most concerned Simone was to know whether, according to Catholic dogma, one could be saved outside the Church.

"This preoccupation had assumed maximum intensity, without really being new. Since 1938, or perhaps even before, I had already told her of an opinion that had been expressed before me, quite a long time ago, by a Benedictine nun (my sister). According to this opinion, not only those just ones who belong in the Church are saved but also those who, outside the Church, both in space and time, have known how to be just.

"I had insisted, quite happy about it: 'But that is a very liberal opinion!' And my sister had reiterated it, firmly.

"My sister, whom I had seen again a few years later, in another convent (near Rome), had again expressed the same opinion. The chaplain father attached to the convent had also confirmed it.

"When she learned of this in 1938, Simone had not only been very interested but had also insisted: 'Could you ask her again?'

"This seemed completely useless to me. And soon after it became very difficult to travel to Italy just to ask some idle questions."

In 1938 Simone had no doubt appeared to be interested only incidentally in this question and out of simple curiosity, since Bercher—he told me this several times—had not realized, before their conversations at Marseilles, the intensity of her religious preoccupations. But in Marseilles the question of knowing whether the Church admitted salvation outside the Church was for Simone manifestly a question of prime importance. Apparently during her conversations with Father Perrin she had not received an unequivocal answer to this question.

"In short, Simone was haunted by the idea of finding a liberal theologian. About 1938 or 1939 she had asked me:

" 'Do you know any theologians?'

"My goodness, I don't! I gave you the opinion of my Benedictines. But I don't know whether they are theologians." (In fact we had become cautious about the use of the word 'theologian,' since the time a priest, questioned by Simone on the massacres committed by the Chosen People, had prudently advised Simone to address herself to . . . a theologian.)

"However, it is evident that for a priest of the visible Church the difficulty that Simone posed was an extreme one. It is one thing to recognize, theoretically, the probable reality of a latent Christianity, and it is quite another to allow a specific person not to enter the official Church!"

And Dr. Bercher continues, speaking to Father Perrin, to whom these notes were first addressed: "In short, Simone reproached you . . . no, one cannot call it a reproach, she suffered because you could not, on occasion, step outside the visible Church and become a minister of the complete Church. She confided this to me at least twice, with visible suffering (her voice became hoarser), and of course, without naming you.

" 'Yet they still have got something!' she said. 'To convince someone of their conception, they imagine that the other person has already acquired precisely this conception.'

"If it were not a trifle irreverent, one could schematize the situation as follows:

"The priestly argument: The greatest good on this earth is baptism; and you do not want to accept baptism; hence you have deprived yourself of the greatest good.

"Simone's reply: Impeccable logic. I would be convinced of the conclusion but for the fact that I do not believe in the premise.

"I would not permit myself to say this if, on this matter of formal entry into the Church, Simone had not confided in me at this time: 'I don't think that this would bring me anything.' "

Along with these reflections on the Church and baptism, Simone often talked with Bercher about more specific religious questions. For example, she spoke to him about the translation of the Our Father prayer; she defended her translation of the word *epiousios*[28] with the word "supernatural."

"She told me that she had submitted this point to a priest (who could only be you), and that he had said that there is in fact in the Church an opinion in favor of 'supernatural bread.'

" '—So, you are sure of this opinion?'

" '—But don't you see! It is the bread of the spirit. Otherwise one cannot understand such a break in the order of concerns. . . .'

"Then, after a few minutes of silence, as if her mind had played over the meaning of the word 'bread': 'Don't you feel,' Simone said, 'how noble the expression 'to earn his bread' is and how base the expression 'to earn his beefsteak.'?"

She was amazed that nuns were permitted in imagination to talk with Christ. Bercher had told her that, according to his sister (the Benedictine), cloistered nuns spoke with Christ at certain moments as they would have spoken to a friend. "She began to protest—with words that I won't repeat, but that I understood to say that in such a thing there could only be error and imagination. . . . She concluded, 'What astonishes me is that they permit them to do this.' "

Bercher often told her that she was a heretic. He says to Father Perrin in his notes:

"You tell me, Monsieur, that a priest flabbergasted Simone by telling her that she was a heretic.

"When I read this, I thanked heaven for having been only what I am —which excluded all priestliness—for I told her this at least ten times.

"The basic thing here seemed to me to be the desire for purity. It is the source of all heresies, I told her. Remember the Cathars! Man is not pure but a 'sinner.' And the sinner must stink a bit, at the least.

"Simone didn't deny this, but she didn't give in to my point either."

One day she told Bercher in confidence how she had wanted to take communion.

"One day in 1940 Simone told me that at some time and in some church, neither of which I can now recall, she was suddenly seized by a great desire to take communion too.

"For my part, extremely convinced of what I had just said about the human condition, I could only protest.

" 'But . . . but one can't do it like that! One must be in a "state of grace"!'

"At this there came a reply whose words I can't precisely reproduce, since they were mumbled, but that sounded like 'I was' or 'I am.' I had understood 'I am'—and in the sense of not being in such a state just at this moment when the others were taking communion or at the present time, but at all times.

" '—Are you sure of this?'

" 'Yes.'

"And soon after this, she wrote to you that 'for me all sin must be a mortal sin.' "

Among Simone's preoccupations there was one that Bercher, both as a doctor and a friend, did not at all like; he had the feeling that she was obsessed by the desire not to eat.

"To Simone, eating seemed a base and disgusting function. . . . I had told Simone that during its sleep of hibernation the marmot, which does not eat anything, grows heavier—of course if one takes into account the weight of its excrement. (Medical students learn this in physiology; the explanation is in the lungs' fixation of part of the oxygen inhaled.) Well, this marmot seemed to Simone a very fine thing to take as a model!

"I also told Simone a story that I had heard from my sister, the story of a nun who had gone for a very long time without eating. 'She nourished herself on the holy eucharist,' my sister had said. Simone found this story quite reasonable.

"When I told these stories to Simone, I wasn't very happy with myself. I had the sensation that I was both giving her pleasure and doing her *harm.* That was how it was with this creature who was at war with her own life. If you did one side of her good, you wounded the other side.

" . . . This was a year of 'alimentary restrictions,' to employ the euphemism. . . . The result was that people thought more than ever about food. Simone found this extremely disgusting. She detested the subject of 'rations,' on which, she said, whenever people met, the conversation 'fell as if propelled by the law of gravity.' "

Bercher recalls that she felt it beneath one's dignity to "queue up" to obtain food. He also says that she was the only person he knew who took the official ration allotments seriously; she considered culpable any attempt to increase her ration, saying that this would diminish other people's ration. "And, of course, her own ration was greatly diminished by the gifts she gave, notably the packages to the camps in which Vichy had gathered Hitler's enemies."

He wondered, at least for a time, whether she was not suffering from some illness, either of the body or the psyche. ("Doctors are quite familiar with the symptom called 'refusal of nourishment.' ") Yet it seems to me that the reason Simone gave for refusing to increase her ration was the real one. Certainly she had never eaten very much, but no doubt never until the war (except when she had been a worker and unemployed) had she carried her privations as far as she did now. So I believe that the cause was above all in the circumstances produced by the times, circumstances with which her extreme sense of charity, combined with her inflexible logic, was confronted. For it is indeed true that when there is too little food for a determined number of people, whoever eats more than his share reduces other people's share. Moreover, there was perhaps in her, as Bercher thinks, a desire for mortification, not just to mortify herself but in order to share in the misfortune in which she knew so many people were engulfed.

In July or the first days of August she also met Jean Rabaut, who was now in Marseilles. She told him of her visits to the Dominicans and let him know (with some reticence, it seemed to him) that she frequented or had frequented certain Gaullist circles. She judged severely those Jews who had accepted segregation. "I would much more prefer to go to jail than to a ghetto," she said.[29] She had not registered as a Jew despite the decree of June 2 ordering the registration of all Jews in the free zone.

During the same period she exchanged some letters with Gustave Thibon, whom she had not met as yet. He had at first tried to refuse what Father Perrin had asked of him; then he had agreed to employ Simone on his farm; or rather he had proposed that she spend a few weeks at his house "in order to get some idea of the different kinds of agricultural work while she was waiting to become a real farmhand for a large landowner in the vicinity."[30] Simone wanted him to know that she was ready to do all kinds of work, even the most demanding and painful, and hoped that she would not be coddled. "I ardently wish to be able to do all that may be asked of me, without benefitting by any consideration. . . . I am not worrying as to the consequences of such work, but as to whether I shall be able to carry it out. . . . In any case I hope not to fail in that resolution that enables one to go to the very limits of one's strength. . . ." "I want my time and the current of my thoughts, insofar as they depend on my body, to be subjected to the same necessities as those that weigh upon no matter what farmhand. . . ."

So as to explain this wish to him, she told him that in her view "intellectual culture, far from giving a right to privileges, constitutes in itself a privilege that is almost frightening and that in turn involves terrible responsibilities." She wanted to prove to herself that she really thought like this by shouldering, at least for a time, "a burden such as those who have no part in this privilege have to bear all their lives."[31]

René Daumal and his wife Véra were to leave for Poët, a small village in the Hautes-Alpes situated at about 3,600 feet, and spend the summer there. Simone, to whom they had told of this plan, wanted to see this region and stay there for a while too, in the event her own plans had not been realized. But when she saw that Thibon had agreed to take her, she wrote to tell them that she probably would not accompany them. "It seems that he is going to offer me, as I wish, a job as a servant on the farm. . . . The word 'wish' is completely inappropriate, because I don't wish at all to do this; it will certainly be hard morally and physically, and a part of myself is frightened by it. But since I can't realize my other project, I feel that I must do this. And not having Krishna at my beck and call to tell me whether this is truly my *dharma,* I am compelled to go along with my feelings. Besides, my feeling is in accord with the social order at the present moment. If it seems good to the French people at this moment that I should be among the *Sudras,* * it is perhaps good that I conform to this."[32]

She had to meet Thibon in Avignon on August 7. On the third she again wrote to René and Véra Daumal to tell them that she had left the *Gita* and other "treasures" that they had loaned her at the office of the *Cahiers du Sud.* "Treasures of inestimable price, of which I have absorbed very little. Let us hope that Krishna will one day give me another chance."

She did not know whether she would ever see them again, if one of her two projects (work as a farm laborer or getting out of France) actually came to fruition. And she thanked them for having been "the source of a precious stimulant for several things—Sanskrit being one of them."

"We met just when I began to thirst for this language and this thought and now, when we may never see each other again, the memory of both of you and that of the months of mingled happiness and sorrow which have composed this year are for me no longer separable from the form of these Sanskrit characters. I hope never to stop loving these characters, which are sacred and which perhaps have never served as the vehicle of anything base.

"Say goodbye for me, when you leave them, to those plains and hills around Allauch—I believe I shall never forget how they received the clear light of the dawn."

She also asked them to bid goodbye for her to Lanza del Vasto, if she should never see him again.[33]

On the sixth of August she was just on the point of leaving for Avignon and Saint-Marcel. Before her departure, she wrote to Antonio and Gilbert Kahn. To Antonio she wrote:

"Dear friend,

"I hope that you received the money order, the books, and the letter I sent you.

"I write you a few words in haste to tell you that I am about to change my address. My new address will be: Mlle. Simone Weil, in care of M. Thibon, Saint-Marcel d'Ardèche. . . .

"This is a village where I am going to work in the fields. I hope that I can stand up under this work better than your friend Nicolas; I think that he is physically exhausted and very miserable. But some friends are taking care of him and I believe that his condition is improving.

---

*Hindu word for lowest caste, that of servants.

"I am quite afraid that physical fatigue may often prevent me from writing letters. If this is so, don't become concerned; I will be thinking of you in any case. . . ."

To Gilbert Kahn:

"Dear friend,

"I am still in Marseilles, but I leave tomorrow for Saint-Marcel in the Ardèche. . . . Are you going to the Ardèche, or have you already gone there? It would give me great pleasure to see you, provided that you don't forget that I am now more or less a farm girl; we must behave in conformity with our respective social ranks. . . . If all goes well, I should be a complete farm girl in October, but it will be at Maillane (Mistral's native town) and will last, I believe, for a year."

She then made this painful confession: "Your remarks about the effects of physical fatigue on the intelligence interested me. I can say that I have felt this in the most literal sense, as someone who has suffered and is about to suffer the same thing. . . .

"I also expect to witness the extinction of my intelligence owing to fatigue. Nonetheless, I regard physical work as a purification—but a purification in the order of suffering and humiliation. One can also find in it, in its very depths, instants of profound, nourishing joy that cannot be equaled elsewhere.

"Why should I attach so much value to this part of my intelligence that almost anyone, using whips and chains, or walls and bars, or a bit of paper covered with certain characters, could deprive me of? If this part is everything, then I am completely a thing of almost no value and so why should I spare myself? If there is something irreducible, it is that which has an infinite value. I am going to see whether this is so."

15

Marseilles II
(1941-1942)

The next day, on August 7, Simone left Marseilles to go to meet Thibon. She took advantage of her stop at Avignon to see the frescoes in the Palace of the Popes.

She was to meet Thibon at Avignon, as had been agreed, and to travel with him to Saint-Marcel. He has described his impressions of this first meeting. "I don't want to talk," he says, "about her physical appearance—she was not ugly, as has been said, but prematurely bent and old looking due to asceticism and illness, and her magnificent eyes alone triumphed in this shipwreck of beauty. Nor will I dwell on the way she was outfitted and her incredible baggage—she had a superb ignorance not only as to the canons of elegance but extending to the most elementary practices that enable a person to pass unnoticed. I will merely say that this first contact aroused feelings in me which, though certainly quite different from antipathy, were nonetheless painful. I had the impression of being face to face with an individual who was radically foreign to all my ways of feeling and thinking and to all that, for me, represents the meaning and savor of life. . . ."[1]

The first conversation he had with her did not seem to promise easy relations. "At first," he says, "our relationship was friendly but uncomfortable. On the concrete plane we disagreed on practically everything. She went on arguing ad infinitum in an inexorably monotonous voice, and I emerged from these endless discussions literally worn out."[2]

However, even from the first meeting, he felt "an unconditional respect" for someone whose unique stature he dimly discerned despite all their emotional and intellectual divergences. "This feeling of veneration increased still more when, after having left her for a few moments to receive a visitor, I returned to find her sitting on a tree trunk in front of the house, lost in contemplation of the valley of the Rhone. Then I saw her gaze gradually emerge from the vision in order to come back to ordinary sight; the intensity and purity of that gaze were such that one felt that she was contemplating interior depths at the same time as the magnificent perspective that opened at her feet, and that the beauty of her soul corresponded with the tender majesty of the landscape."[3]

When he had to proceed to the question of her new quarters, it was not easy to come to an agreement. "Finding our modest house too comfortable, she refused the room I was offering her and wanted at all costs to sleep out of doors. Then it was I who became vexed, and after long discussions she ended by giving way. The next day a compromise was reached. At that time my wife's parents had a little half-ruined house on the banks of the Rhone and we settled her in there, not without a few complications for everyone. It would all have been so much simpler otherwise!"[4]

In this connection, Thibon remarks that Simone was detached, but that she was not detached from her own detachment. "She, who when her pleasure or her needs were involved would not have allowed anyone to make the slightest sacrifice on her behalf, did not seem to realize the complications and even sufferings she caused in the lives of others as soon as it was a matter of realizing her vocation for self-effacement."[5] "She wanted to forget herself and would come upon herself in this very forgetfulness; she loved her neighbor with all her being, and in her devotion she often overlooked the real desires and needs of others."[6] "This soul, who wanted to be flexible to every movement of the divine will, could not bear the course of events or the kindness of her friends changing by one inch the position of the stakes with which her own will had marked her path of immolation. . . . And the way she mounted guard around her void still paid witness to a terrible preoccupation with herself . . . her *ego,* as it were, was like a word that she may perhaps have succeeded in *obliterating,* but that was still *underlined.* "[7]

It is true that she had a great concern for the higher part of herself. If she tried to annihilate her natural ego, there was another ego that she respected, the hidden transcendental "I," the part of the soul that is "on the other side of the curtain," the side of the supernatural. It is also true that she sometimes was guilty of what Thibon calls "the failure to open to external reality";[8] she did not always understand others, despite her extreme desire to understand them. Yet I have never seen her sacrifice others to her own search for discomfort and misfortune, except perhaps in small things (she could cause, as Thibon says, complications for them). Did she sometimes cause sufferings because of her will for immolation? Only to the degree that people loved her and suffered at seeing her suffer or expose herself to dangers. It was this kind of suffering that she could not prevent causing her family, especially her parents. It is only too true, as Thibon says, that her heroic follies and extravagances tortured them and kept them in constant anxiety.[9] But it would not be just to say that she did not take this into account. She was deeply troubled by it and tried to soften their trials as much as possible.

So she lived in a small, isolated, half-ruined house, which she called "my fairy tale house." She would remember it later with poignant regret, for she was very happy there. In a letter of August 10, she described it to her parents:

"Dear family,

"I write to you under the most colorful circumstances, the sort of color that I look for; in a large, low-ceiling room, with a floor of beaten earth mixed with pebbles, at the edge of a wood, with a large chimney and fireplace and a small window, sitting beside a fire that I am feeding after having sawed off a piece of firewood, and on which I try, quite ineffectively, to boil water for my tea. The water comes from a spring about a hundred and fifty yards from the house. It is truly an abandoned house, where I am alone and nobody has entered for many years. They had told me that it was swarming with rats, but although they certainly swarmed at some time, for they have left traces everywhere, fortunately they are not doing so now. I spent the better part of the day yesterday eliminating these traces, the spiders' webs, and most of the dust in the two rooms, the one I am in right now and the one where I sleep. I sleep in my sleeping bag, but on a bed made of boards with a mattress stuffed with pine needles. . . .

"You can see from here the Rhone valley from one end of the horizon to the other (not from my house, but a little higher up), and there is a marvelous Romanesque church nearby. . . ."

She again expresses her enthusiasm and happiness in a letter of August 15:

"The beaten earth is perhaps not exactly beaten earth but pebbles that have been mixed together and packed down. I've gotten rid of all traces of the rats. . . . Here I eat potatoes boiled in water on the wood fire (indescribably delicious, and I managed to do it very well), onions, beets, tomatoes, fruits, and sometimes eggs, all this given to me by the Thibons, who have a tendency to load me down with food to the extent of their available means and even beyond that (since even here one doesn't swim in abundance). I also often eat with them, where one eats very well. Tomorrow I'm going to eat mayonnaise made with pounded garlic! . . .

"Admirable landscape, delicious air, rest, leisure, solitude, fresh fruits and vegetables, spring water, wood fires—nothing but sensual pleasures. And nothing to produce nightmares, far from it. The only danger I run is losing myself among these sensual pleasures. . . ."

(The fear that there might still be rats in the house had perhaps given Simone's parents nightmares, or indeed they feared that she herself had had some.)

She realized quite soon that she was being treated as a friend, not as a worker or apprentice. On the tenth of August she told her parents: "Here, from the point of view of work, it is even less serious than I had supposed. Since my arrival, I have only worked two hours. In short, this is a vacation." On the fifteenth of August: "I have been doing some Greek with Thibon. I'm still not working. . . ."

However, she managed to persuade them to let her work on certain days. Thibon says that she worked the earth "with an inflexible energy."[10] He initiated her into work in the fields, "where her clumsiness was only equaled by her good will—the latter ending by triumphing over the former."[11] She also helped a bit in the housework, not without clumsiness there, too. "The way she held the plates when washing up," says Thibon, "which was as careful as it was unnatural, was enough to set me off in fits of irresistible laughter."[12] Each morning she would come up from her small house to Thibon's and try to make herself useful. She often shared their meals. "But she usually refused those things that town-dwellers could not have."[13] "Some days she did not appear at table and fed on the wild fruit she found in the countryside."[14] Of course she kept strictly to the ration regulations; she was indignant because a baker, thinking to please her, had offered her a little bread without asking for the ration coupons.

In the evening, she would sit with Thibon on a stone bench near the fountain and read with him some pages of Plato in the Greek text, helping Thibon, who, having educated himself, didn't know Greek as well as she did. He speaks, quite rightly, of her tremendous gifts as a teacher.

"She knew how to place herself on the level of no matter what pupil in order to teach no matter what subject. I can imagine her carrying out the duties of an elementary schoolteacher just as well as those of a university professor! Whether she was teaching the rule of three to a backward village urchin or initiating me into the more arcane aspects of Platonic philosophy, she brought to the task and tried to obtain from her pupil that quality of extreme attention that, in her doctrine, is closely associated with prayer."[15]

A warm friendship soon sprang up between Simone and Thibon. He realized that if she had at first shown the "uncomfortable side of her nature,"[16] she gained infinitely when one got to know her. What he has written about her is full of admiration and profound friendship. "I have witnessed too much of the daily unfolding of her existence to be left with the slightest doubt as to the authenticity of her spiritual vocation; her faith and detachment were expressed in her actions, sometimes with a disconcerting disregard for the practical, but always with absolute generosity. . . . Her asceticism might seem exaggerated in our day of half-measures; nevertheless, it was free from any emotional excess.[17] Never did the word "supernatural" seem to Thibon more swollen with reality than in contact with her. They did not always agree, especially on political questions or on the subject of certain writers and philosophers (for example, he admired Nietzsche); but the disagreements did not get in the way of their friendship, even when their arguments grew quite heated. She was not offended by a refusal to accept or agree with her ideas. "The most blunt contradictions or the refusal no less blunt to continue a discussion—two things of which I made a habit with her —didn't meet with those expressions of wounded self-love that in the intellectual world are still more frequent than expressions of intelligence itself. I always found her unshakable (she was, as it were, barred and bolted in her opinions), I never found her touchy. . . ."[18]

If there had been disagreements between them, if the way she had of "refusing to make any concession whatever to the requirements and conventions of social life"[19]—for example, she always used to say everything she thought to everybody and in all circumstances—could be wounding, if her company was not exactly restful, Simone also had "some delightful moments when she let herself go and relaxed."[20] "In intimacy she was a charming and lively companion; she knew how to joke without bad taste and could be ironical without unkindness. Her extraordinary learning, so deeply assimilated that it can hardly be distinguished from the expression of her inner life, gave her conversation an unforgettable charm."[21] "She knew how to share in a family festivity, would joke with her friends and even occasionally allow herself some slight sensual treat. The Achilles' heel of her asceticism was smoking. Of all the things belonging to material life, tobacco was the only one that one was almost certain she would accept."[22]

She had a feeling of friendship not only for Thibon but also for his wife and his father. She spoke of his wife's kindness in her letters to her parents. She described his father as "an admirable man, a peasant since his infancy and who has never ceased being one, who passionately loves nature and his work and has read and reflected all of his life."[23] The only thing for which she could criticize this family (if this could be considered a criticism) was that the Thibons had a tendency to protect her as though she were their daughter. She wrote to her parents: "All three of them are a little too inclined for my taste (but not for yours) to behave toward me in *loco parentis.*"[24]

Thibon gave Simone the works of St. John of the Cross in Spanish and she began to read them.

On August 23 she wrote to Antonio. To him, too, she spoke enthusiastically about the life she led in the small house. "I go to fetch the water from the spring, the firewood in the pine woods, I eat vegetables just taken from the earth and cooked on a wood fire; and I continually see the light of the sun shine in a different way on the valley and the hills; and then, at night, immense stretches of starry sky. One cannot be closer to nature and, as you say, it envelops one with beauty, light, and joy."

In one of his letters Antonio had advised her not to deprive herself for him, telling her that the life of one healthy being was worth more than that of two anemics. This phrase pained Simone. "Are you sick, then? As for me, though I'm not sick, I haven't much strength and vitality; I hope that you have much more than I.

"However," she adds, "don't worry; I never deprive myself of necessities. I've sent you another money order, because I have a bit of money at the moment. . . .

"As for everything you say about the attitude that a man must have when facing happiness and misfortune, I think just as you do. But I think that you put it into practice better than I do. I admire you a great deal because of this."

A few days after Simone's departure for Saint-Marcel, her parents had left Marseilles in turn to go to Poët, perhaps with the Daumals, or in any event to join them there. Simone, after having thought that she had to give up the idea of making this journey, had decided to spend at least a few days at Poët so as to enjoy the sight of the mountains. She had written to her parents in the letter of August 10: "Absolutely forbidden for you to look at the mountains before I get there." (She pretended, as a joke, to be jealous of any beautiful sight that she could not see.)

Her parents having intended to go and see her but then temporarily having given up this plan, Simone had written to them about August 24:

"I'm glad that you didn't come here because that would have been quite tiring for you; from all other points of view, I greatly regret it. Above all, for two reasons. First of all, Thibon's father (a completely astonishing man, as I've told you) . . . is very tired, somewhat ill, and refuses to let us call a doctor; Biri could induce him by way of a friendly conversation to let himself be examined and put his gift for diagnosis to good use. . . . Second, if the project of a journey does not come off, it doesn't seem to me a bad idea to settle down here. After I will have spent six months or a year at Maillane (if I can stand up to it) and will have learned how to work, you could very easily settle here and live very well, almost without any expenses. Biri would very often have a chance to give his advice, it seems, and no doubt gifts in kind would flow in. You could perhaps move in here even as early as this winter, though I must stay in Maillane, and I could rejoin you in the spring or summer.

"When we're together, we could cultivate some vegetables on a piece of land, with Thibon's help and advice (one can find uncultivated land for nothing), I could work now and then for the neighbors, and perhaps I could also sometimes use my pedagogic abilities in exchange for gifts in kind.

"This seems to me to be a healthy, prudent, and sensible life. But in order to consider it seriously, you must see the country hereabouts."

(When she spoke of their plans for a journey that might not come off, this was evidently their departure for America.)

She hesitated once again about going to Poët, for she thought she might be working at Maillane about September 10.

"As for me at Poët, I am quite uncertain about it. I would love to see the place. However, I'm also frightened by the fatigue of the journey and above all the change of altitude on my return, when I will begin doing the hardest sort of work.

"I have to begin the grape harvest at Maillane about September 10. I could go to Poët in a few days (the time to receive your reply), work in the harvest, return here about September 5 or 6 (perhaps with you?), spend two or three days here to make the transition, and then go to Maillane. That would be worth it, or would it be too tiring for me? Think it over and advise me."

She envisaged spending a few days at Poët, provided she could participate in the work of the harvest and so pay for her own food.

"Of course, if I do come to Poët, I want your *word of honor* that I'll be really fed by my own work and that you don't and won't give me more money for my food. No sort of arrangement like the one at Auxerre; you remember, don't you?"

She asked them to convey her friendly greetings to the Daumals. She was sorry that they couldn't meet Thibon's father. "They [the Daumals] would above all be extremely interested in the things he told me concerning certain moments of more heightened consciousness than those of ordinary life, which sometimes seize him."

In a postscript, she adds: "I believe in short that it wouldn't be very sensible for me to come. . . . I have ended by getting a little work here (not every day!). I stand up better than I had thought I would. I believe that I would do very well in the harvest at Poët. It is the journey and change of altitude that trouble me. But if it is very beautiful, I would love to come. . . ."

Mme. Weil answered her immediately, on August 26. She advised Simone not to come to Poët; the journey and the change of altitude could tire her out at a time when she should husband her strength. Mme. Weil proposed that she herself would come to Saint-Marcel with the doctor.

So Simone's parents arrived at Saint-Marcel most likely on September 2 and stayed there until the tenth or eleventh of the month. Simone had written to them that there was a small hotel in the village and they no doubt stayed there.

When they saw the house she lived in, they were upset at the thought that she lived alone in an isolated house, near woods where one sometimes saw vagabonds. But Simone would not hear of changing houses. The doctor treated some people in the village. One old woman, who didn't know that the Weils were friends of Thibon, spoke about him to Mme. Weil. She said, "He has his mistress living next to him! She is a crazy woman who lives in a hut!"

Simone talked to Thibon about Antonio and asked him to approach the authorities at Vichy and try to do something for him. On this occasion, she wanted him to swear that he would never try to do anything for her if she were imprisoned. But only the evening before he had promised her parents the exact opposite. He said to her, "Would you be happy if I were in prison while you were free?" "She raised her head a little and replied with a restrained gleam in her eyes, 'I couldn't bear it.' I think these were the most affectionate words she ever said to me."[25]

It was decided that Simone would begin working in the grape harvest not on September 10, as she had thought, but a little later and at Saint-Julien-de-Peyrolas, a village in the Gard near Saint-Marcel. It was also decided that before her departure for Saint-Julien she would accompany her parents on their return to Poët and spend a few days with them.

She had written to me at the beginning of June asking me to tell her what was happening to me. "What are you doing? Are you working? You must develop the work that you began for a thesis. It is worth it, you know. You must finish it and publish it. There is somebody quite good here named G. Berger; a philosophy thesis of his has just been published in Paris. Could we see you this summer, if you can take a trip to the mountains? Everything's going well for us here. Write me. Tell me what you're doing, what you're reading, what you're thinking."

She wrote to me again on August 7, giving me her address at Saint-Marcel and telling me that her parents were leaving for Poët. She added: "It's very likely, though not certain, that I will leave Ardèche and spend some days with them. This autumn I transform myself—if Krishna looks kindly on me—into an agricultural worker or farm servant. During August I am preparing for this transformation."

Since I had been ill, I spent a month each summer in the mountains. This year once again the doctor who was treating me felt that a sojourn at a high altitude would do me good and gave me a certificate that allowed me to go to the Alps, in the free zone. So I obtained an authorization to travel to the free zone, though not without having to be examined by a German doctor, which I had not expected. I went to Huez in the Isère region. From there, I wrote to Simone. I made some jokes about her new transformation into a farmhand and compared her to Vishnu, the god of multiple avatars. I told her that I doubted the job of farmhand or farm servant really was what suited her and asked her if she really needed to do this. I told her about the things she could do and for which she was certainly more necessary than for agriculture. And, finally, I regretted that she didn't have the sort of egotism with which I was even too richly endowed and remarked that, without a little egotism, one could not live amid the horrors of our epoch. She answered me from Saint-Marcel on September 7 with a long letter, the only long letter I ever received from her—and unfortunately, I have not preserved it in its entirety!

A probably unnecessary fear made me tear up one sheet of it when I came back by train from Huez to Paris. As we approached the line of demarcation between the two zones, I saw the people on the train begin tearing up papers and letters and throwing the pieces out the windows. They were telling each other that the Germans, when one passed across the line, searched in the suitcases and packs and examined the papers they found, either to be sure that one was not carrying any correspondence across or for some other reason. I remembered then that in Simone's letter there was a page with the names and addresses of two people for whom she had asked me to perform certain errands. These errands were not at all compromising, yet one of them at least could appear quite astonishing and be regarded as a camouflaged message; what's more, Simone could easily be suspected of Resistance activity. I thought, wrongly perhaps, but had no time to think it over, that it was better to tear up the page after having memorized the addresses of these people. I felt very sorry I had done this when, once we passed the line of demarcation, I saw that the Germans on guard there didn't ask anyone to open their mountain packs.

Furthermore, Simone had filled the second of the two double sheets of this letter in an order that was not the normal order for pages—that is why she numbered them*—and it seems that there are two breaks in continuity, although, according to my memory of it, I had only torn up a single sheet.

Here is what she said to me in the parts of this letter that remained:
"Dear Simone,

"Your comparison with Vishnu is completely to the point since, being incarnated in Krishna, he was a herdsman; and there is a verse about Krishna in a Sanskrit text that I reproduce forthwith: 'Well beloved, the girls who guard the cows call him; child, the old women call him; sovereign master, the gods call him.' So, as a farm girl, I would have the right to call him well beloved; it's pleasant to think that I can. I have been doing some work on Sanskrit these last months and have read some verses of the *Gita* in the original text, which makes him even dearer to me. I have also learned to love the *Upanishads*.

"My place—how can it be defined? If it is from the outside, you know very well that the government of my country judges that in teaching and intellectual activity I exert a noxious influence and that I must go back to productive work. Is it not in a general way—and at least if some other duty does not come before it—a good thing to submit? It seems to me that it is. If one looks at things from the inside—yes, I have a *need* to do

*Or rather she had wanted to number them; but she must have mixed them up, so that she tried to erase the numbers she had originally put on the last pages.

this. Else where would I find the strength to decide to do something in which I foresee, perhaps mistakenly, difficulties, hardship, fatigue, and suffering? I haven't in me the energy to undergo pain and to suffer except when an inner necessity drives me that I feel I cannot avoid without betraying myself. When to this inner necessity an outer necessity is added, what power does it not acquire? Don't you feel how much this resolution helps me bear the misfortunes of the moment? The fatigues of my body and my soul are transformed into nourishment for a people who are hungry.

"As for myself, you know that I never regretted going into the factory; since that time I have congratulated myself every day for having had the strength; this time I feel myself pushed just as imperiously.

"There is something else I would prefer to do—but until now that has been materially impossible for me. I will tell you about it if we can meet.

"It is true, I feel that there are things that I can do, but I don't yet see clearly enough which ones (although I see several, indeed too many); but I feel that this must come first. I also felt this way about the factory, and I was right. If I were so weak as to retreat before the harshness of the life that awaits me, I know that I could then never do anything else.

"In any case, it's possible that they will fire me after a short while because of my inadequacy at the work. That will be for me, morally, a very hard blow; I can't tell you how strongly I feel about this. (I'm not yet a farm worker; I will begin, I think, in a week. . . .)

"I can't tell you how much I hope that you continue to work in philosophy. You should get a leave of absence and a scholarship for the doctorate. . . . What you call egotism is only the inner solitude indispensable to all creation and shows that you are ready for work. You aren't egotistic, since the horror of the epoch penetrates into you. But you shouldn't be overcome by it. Horror is an infernal emotion, I mean to say that it proceeds from the inferno. If one passes through it, then one day one must come out of it. But the more the mass of destructions is horrible, the more doing one's work is essential, the more the thought of a task to be done awakens love. What a reward to do something (or prepare to do it) at a time when each instant is crowded with deaths! There is only that, or to die oneself; but to die cannot be voluntary.

"Try to love this beautiful country in which you live; it is innocent of the horrors that are taking place in it. For my part, I try to love the sky. . . ."

When Simone spoke in this letter of the other things that she would prefer to do, they were her plans to take part in the war, and particularly her plan for the organization of a group of front-line nurses.

As regards her immediate plans it seems that between the start and the end of this letter there had been a slight change as to the date she foresaw for the beginning of her work in the grape harvest. In fact at the end she told me that she would be in Poët the following Tuesday, that is to say, on September 11. So she left with her parents for Poët, no doubt on September 10 or 11, and stayed there for about twelve days.

On the eleventh she wrote to de Tarde. On leaving Marseilles for Saint-Marcel she had sent him a "family" postcard on which she told him that she was going to be metamorphosed into a farm worker. When she reached Poët, she wrote him a long letter:

"Dear friend,

"I haven't yet been transformed into a farm worker. That will happen only toward the end of October, at a truck gardener's about three kilometers from Saint-Rémy-de-Provence. My address will then be, if everything goes well and I manage to bear up (*inch' Allah!*): in care of M.R. . . . I won't learn how to work at this place, as I would have passionately hoped. At least I believe that I can manage it, since this type of work, however painful, demands more, I imagine, the capacity to suffer and endure than physical strength. If they don't lay me off—and except for events that would put other ideas in my head—I count on staying a year. After—always with the same reservation—perhaps I shall find something more interesting; or perhaps I shall settle with my parents in a village provided with houses and abandoned fields and I could grow some vegetables for myself, with a little help and advice.

"Don't you own some land? Couldn't you hire me, if the occasion should arise, if I had spent the year before working for a landowner who doesn't know me and will only be concerned that I do a satisfactory job?

"Before going to work for this truck gardener, I intend to work for a month in the grape harvest in a village of the Gard region called Saint-Julien. . . ."

She then told him about Thibon and the delightful month she had spent alone in an abandoned house. "I thought I was in a Grimm's fairy tale. But above all I rested, though I also managed, from time to time, to heft a spade and a hoe (to clear away the weeds around the vines) for an hour and even several, and I did better than I had expected."

She tells him of her cordial feelings for the peasant environment. "In the course of my life, I've already been in contact several times with peasant life, always with a strong feeling of sympathy. But now I hope to have a serious contact with this world."

She hopes de Tarde will inform her if he hears of "things to do that are preferable to cultivating potatoes and beans. By preferable, you know very well I don't mean less demanding and difficult."

"I wonder," she says, "what Bouché could have found as work that excites him. I must say that for me the thought of transforming the efforts of my body and soul into potatoes and things of that kind among

Men and women workers at the Alsthom plant where Simone Weil worked for several months in 1934–1935. This photo was taken during the famous sit-in strikes in 1936.

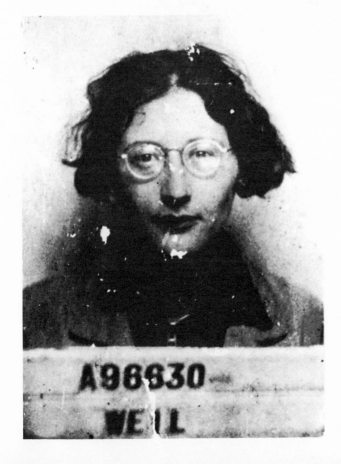

Simone Weil, photograph for identity card at the Renault plant, 1935.

Simone skiing, most likely at Montana, 1935.

Two photos of Simone
Weil in Spain after
her return from the
front, 1936.

Simone and her mother at Sitges, 1936.

The Terramar Palace, which was turned into a hospital during
the Spanish Civil War and where Simone Weil was treated at
Sitges. *(Photo L. Roison.)*

Crucifix in the Basilica of Santa Chiara at Assisi. This is the image of Christ which, it is said, spoke to St. Francis. Simone Weil visited Assisi in 1937.

The Abbey of Saint-Pierre at Solesmes. Simone attended all the holy services there during the Easter week of 1938.

Venice, Riva degli Schiavoni, on the Grand Canal. To the right the
Pensione Bucintoro, where Simone Weil stayed in June 1938.

Love.

Love bade me welcome; yet my soul drew back,
    Guiltie of dust and sin.
But quick-ey'd Love, observing me grow slack
    From my first entrance in,
Drew nearer to me, sweetly questioning
    If I lack'd anything.

A guest, I answer'd, worthy to be here.
    Love said, You shall be he.
I, the unkinde, ungrateful? Ah, my deare,
    I cannot look on thee.
Love took my hand and smiling did reply:
    Who made the eyes but I?

Truth, Lord; but I have marr'd them; let my shame
    Go where it doth deserve.
And know you not, says Love, who bore the blame?
    My deare, then I will serve.
You must sit down, says Love, and taste my meat.
    So I did sit and eat.

george Herbert.
1593. 1634.

"Love" by George Herbert, copied by Simone Weil. It was while reciting this poem that she experienced, no doubt in November 1938, the feeling of Christ's presence.

Simone Weil in Marseilles,
spring, 1941.

Simone in Marseilles, spring, 1941, sitting in a café with Jean Lambert.

Simone in Marseilles, spring, 1941, with Lanza del Vasto.

Saint-Julien–de–Peyrolas, in the Gard area, where
Simone Weil worked as a grape harvester in 1941.

Simone Weil, date unknown.

Hélène Honnorat (1913–1967).

Ruins of Montségur, last bastion of Occitan and Cathar resistance.

Simone Weil in New York, 1942.

Simone Weil's pass in London.
(*Snark International.*)

FRANCE COMBATTANTE

LAISSEZ-PASSER

No. *1663*   Nom *lle Weil*

Prenoms *Simone*

Grade ou Profession *Redactrice*

Bureau ou Service *C. N. I*

Londres le *30 Mars 1943*

Le Chef du Service de Sécurité

a people who may go hungry is the only thing that can excite me at this moment—save for one other. . . ."

(This other thing is obviously to work as a front-line nurse.)

"Without the horror of affliction that at this time submerges so many parts of the earthly globe, the present situation, as far as it concerns me personally, would suit me completely. The government of my country could not do me a greater good than forbidding me from being active in the intellectual professions and so making thought for me a gratuitous affair, as it should be. Since my adolescence I dreamed of the marriage of St. Francis with poverty, but I felt that I must not go to the trouble of marrying it, since one day it would come to take me by force and it would be better so. . . ."

About the middle of September I went to spend two or three days with her at Poët. (In fact, two days, I believe: I arrived in the afternoon, spent the whole next day at Poët, and probably the next morning.)

These two days, the last days I saw her, have remained in my memory like a bright flash of felicity in the midst of a very somber period. They were spent in gaiety, the camaraderie of shared work, and in conversations in which what was said was said in a hurry since we had too little time for everything we wanted to say. Simone would write to me afterward: "I will always remember those few days at Poët; it is marvelous and astonishing that one still could have that sort of thing."

Although she looked rather tired, she had lost none of her humor and we really had some good laughs together. Yet I felt that I could discern once or twice something sad beneath her gaiety, for instance when she joked about her fatigue. What struck me most of all at this meeting was a gentleness and serenity that I had never known in her to this extent. She could still become indignant, but so much less than before. With a more tender, wiser goodness, she had become a person whose company was, more than ever, extremely charming. Even more than before one felt good and at ease with her. Perhaps the atmosphere of the mountains, so pure during those beautiful autumn days and according so well with Simone's purity, also contributed to the sweetness of these last days together.

As usual, she knew a lot about the events of the war and about everything that was going on. She also talked to me about her life at Marseilles, her troubles with the police, and her plans. I was astonished when she explained her project for the organization of front-line nurses, which she had not mentioned to me in Paris. I would have been terribly frightened if I had not thought that this madly generous plan was no doubt unrealizable. With the idea that it was impossible, I admit I had not given it too great an importance. I did not realize the enormous significance it had for her.

She was very pessimistic about the future of civilization. She foresaw a long period of decadence. She said to me, "There will be no hope for men until they return to the caves."

She told me that she still was trying to understand the science of our times. She was not sure that science had overcome the crisis into which it had entered when Michelson's and Morley's experiments on the speed of light had introduced a contradiction in it. She wondered whether Einstein had really done away with the contradiction or had only "covered it up." She tended toward the second hypothesis.

We talked about philosophy. Speaking about Hegel, I said to her that Hegel's dialectic was far from inspiring me with confidence but that nevertheless one is tempted to establish a dialectic since on certain questions, for example, on human liberty, two contradictory affirmations can both be true and should be simultaneously maintained. One is then tempted to try to find out whether each is true or false according to where one places it. She wholeheartedly approved of this and told me that that was exactly what she thought.

We talked about Alain. She was still profoundly attached to him, but felt that there was something lacking in his doctrine. "Alain's shortcoming," she told me, "is to have rejected pain."

When anyone spoke to her about her health, she would pass it off with some joking remark. But, as I have said, sometimes it seemed to me that her light tone gave off a sad note, as if something in her had moaned in spite of herself. Yet, if she could not completely suppress the moans of nature, she did not take them into account in her behavior. Simply from this point of view, she was hard on herself; she treated herself cruelly. I was surprised to learn that she slept on the floor. Her mother told me this, and she herself confirmed it, advising me, as a joke, to greet her as Plato, it is said, greeted Diogenes: "If you get up early and go into the kitchen, you will see a dog lying on the floor in the corner and you will say to him, 'Good day, dog.' " I asked her why she inflicted such an absurd hardship on herself, and she could not give me any reason for it.

We worked together to help the people in the town dig up the potatoes. Among those who were working with us there was a young shepherd who went out of his way to be sweet and kind to me. Simone pretended to be jealous and said gaily, "It's always like that!" Which was not at all true. (Actually, she had been more than once very deeply loved, and much more than I could ever have been loved. Love is less blind than it is said to be. If she once wrote, speaking to herself: "It is not by chance that you have never been loved,"[26] that was when she was about twenty-five years old. And even then, I believe, she was mistaken. It was due to an excess of humility that she thought she was not loved. She would have been even more mistaken if she had said this later on, for she was loved very much during these last years.)

Dr. and Mme. Weil seemed to be very popular among the people in the village. I recall that on the evening of my arrival a woman there had promised to make them a present of a large tart. The tart was finished rather late in the evening. I had already gone to sleep because, having walked up the hill that runs from Briançon to Embrun, I was rather tired. Simone came to wake me, but I didn't want to get up; half asleep, I protested. "Some job waking you," Simone said. She finally succeeded, and I went down to eat the tart. She herself hardly ate any of it.

When we parted, she gave me the manuscript of her play, *Venise sauvée,* telling me to take it to Huez, read it, and send it back to her before returning to Paris. She wanted to know what I thought of it. I don't remember what I wrote to her about it; no doubt that I found it quite beautiful and that she must absolutely finish it. Actually, I did think it was beautiful, but I must confess that I was not as impressed by it as I was later when I read *Gravity and Grace, Waiting for God,* or the *Notebooks*; nor as I was when I read "Reflections on the Causes of Liberty and Social Oppression." Yet its subject is sublime. But this fine play was unfinished then, and she left it that way.

Simone wrote her brother from Poët. He had made some contacts in America to arrange matters so that his parents and sister could go there. Simone still hesitated about leaving Europe. André had not been able to give her the assurance that she could return to Europe and to a place where it would be possible for her to participate in the war. Consequently her letter deals in large part with reminding her brother of what she hoped for and why she was still hesitant.

Using masked, circuitous language, she mentioned her "request for a post," that is, her desire to go to England; and she also spoke about the ideas that had come to her "concerning certain passages in Tacitus," that is, her project for the group of front-line nurses. (She had in fact discovered in Tacitus that the ancient Germans had the custom of placing a young girl surrounded by an elite of young warriors in the front lines during a battle.)[27] She told him that Mme. Rapkine would have explained all this to him.

"As for our plans for the journey, I am beginning to be a bit undecided. It is indeed quite irksome that you have had no reply on my request for a post. Mme. Rapkine will have explained to you in detail, I think, the sort of work I'm thinking of, and particularly the ideas that have occurred to me concerning certain passages in Tacitus on the methods of combat of the barbarian and semi-nomadic tribes in the first century. In my opinion, this is a problem to be solved that should be very interesting to scholars and specialists. But it may well be that such work is not very pressing and up-to-minute. In that case, it would be useless for me to insist on wanting to obtain a post. After all, cultivating vegetables and potatoes here is perhaps more useful under present-day circumstances. For some time now, and above all during these last weeks, I think of this more and more. Give me your opinion about all this.

"As for our parents, it seems to me that if they would settle down in a village where your father could become popular because of his medical ability, they would have the opportunity to live well and quietly without being uprooted. I've gotten the idea, in case we stay in France, that they settle down in the autumn either here in the mountains or in a village of the Ardèche where I have friends. . . . I would spend the autumn, winter, and perhaps spring with the truck gardener I told you about, then I would rejoin them and we would grow vegetables with the help and advice of friends and neighbors, combining this occupation with some part-time medicine and teaching. As for the particular research about which Mme. Rapkine has spoken to you, I surely am not giving it up; I think about it more and more; but I begin to wonder whether I wouldn't have a better chance to pursue it by staying here instead of leaving."

In conclusion, she tells her brother to continue his efforts to obtain the visas but not to try too hard to get them quickly. But she adds a postscript: "P.S. Very important: when reading this letter, keep in mind the date. During the three weeks that will pass before it reaches you, my impressions may change. As regards myself, I desire *ardently* to go where I would be better placed for the studies about which Mme. Rapkine has told you. Do you think that it is better for this purpose to stay or to leave? At this moment I'm uncertain; but you can make a better judgment on the basis of the objective data at the moment you receive this letter than in terms of what I say in it."

While she was at Poët she memorized the Greek text of the Our Father. She had read it to Thibon during the month of August and they had promised each other to learn it by heart. Yet she had not done it immediately. "Some weeks later," she writes in her autobiographical letter, "as I was turning over the pages of the Gospel, I said to myself that since I had promised to do this thing and it was good, I ought to do it. I did it. The infinite sweetness of the Greek text so took hold of me that for several days I could not stop myself from saying it over and over all the time."[28]

This happened a week before she began working in the grape harvest, so it must have been about September 15. This was the first time in her life that she had prayed.

"Since that time," she wrote in the same letter, "I have made a practice of saying it once each morning with absolute attention. If during the recitation my attention wanders or goes to sleep in the minutest degree, I begin again until I have succeeded in going through it once with absolutely pure attention. Sometimes it comes about that I say it again out of sheer pleasure, but I only do it if I really feel the impulse."[29]

As to the virtue of this practice, which surprised her every time, she has left a testimony that describes certain profoundly mystical impressions:

"At times the very first words tear my thoughts from my body and transport them to a place outside space where there is neither perspective nor point of view. Space opens up. The infinity of the ordinary expanses of perception is replaced by an infinity to the second or sometimes the third degree. At the same time, filling every part of this infinity, there is silence, a silence that is not an absence of sound but that is the object of a positive sensation, more positive than that of sound. Noises, if there are any, only reach me after crossing this silence.[30]

"Sometimes, also, during this recitation or at other moments, Christ is present with me in person, but his presence is infinitely more real, more poignant, and clearer than on that first occasion when he took possession of me."[31]

Before leaving for Poët she had asked Thibon to give her his unpublished writings so that she could read them calmly in the mountains. Just before coming back down to the plain she wrote him a long letter, from which he quoted some passages.[32] After having thanked him for everything he had done for her ("I cannot find adequate words to thank you for your kindness to me—with just this one reservation, that it far exceeds all reasonable measure"), she spoke to him about his writings. "They contain, to my mind, things of the highest order (which for me means a great deal); but not very many; not nearly as many as the praise of your friends would lead one to think. You fully realize, for you know me well enough for that, that in such judgments no consideration can prevent me from being as honest as it is in my power to be. . . . Friendship, gratitude, and other such sentiments cannot serve to diminish but only to augment my scrupulous care and attention in trying to make a right evaluation. . . . You have already experienced the dark night, but it is my belief that a great deal of it still remains for you to pass through before you give your true measure; for you are far from having attained in expression, and hence in thought, to the degree of utter stripping, nakedness, and piercing force that is indispensable to the kind of works that you intend to write. . . ."[33]

She knew that she was taking a risk in writing this way, for Thibon's friendship was precious to her. She admitted to him later that she had thought that his friendship for her would not survive the reading of this letter. But this was not so. Thibon was grateful for her frankness. Simone admired him for this and cherished him even more.

She left Poët on September 19 or 20 and went to Saint-Marcel to stay with the Thibons. That night she slept in their house and the next morning they accompanied her to Saint-Julien.

It was on Thibon's recommendation that she had been taken on as one of the crew of grape harvesters of a grape-grower in this area. "She was not treated," Thibon says, "as an anonymous laborer; her employers put her up in their house and she had her meals with them. . . . But at work she was not given any special consideration and shared the lot of the laborers in everything."[34] And from the day of her arrival, in the afternoon, she worked. And on each of the following days she did her eight hours. During the second week of the grape harvest, the work was interrupted by three days of rain. She took advantage of this to write to Antonio on October 2:

"I am at this moment a grape harvester working for a farmer who has only grape vines on his land. . . . The work seems to me very hard, but the people I am with are very good. The nature around me is very beautiful, with a horizon lined with hills and mountains. And the tiredness is a tiredness that is healthy for the soul, which puts me into more complete contact with nature, and in the depths of which one finds profound joys. I love this life. . . ."

Still thinking of the month she had spent at Saint-Marcel alone in her little house, she writes to Antonio:

"I really love to live alone: I was very happy for a month to be completely alone in a small house all to myself, and I would gladly stay there like that for a long time. I would also be very happy to live in that way for some time with a man or woman friend; but I have never had the opportunity to do so. Perhaps some day I will have the chance to do this with you? One can always dream; it doesn't harm any one. But what I want for you is that you should be free and happy, in some place where that might be possible. . . ."

One would have to have Simone's purity not to have thought that in writing this she ran the danger of arousing in poor Antonio an unrealizable dream.

She also says that certain steps had been taken in official quarters so that Antonio could be sent back to France. (This was no doubt the effort made through Thibon's intervention.) "This effort could easily fail; one can't put too much hope in it. I didn't want to mention it at all; but I think it's better that you know about it, because of what you have written me about the departure of three hundred Spaniards for Spain. If by chance it is successful . . . it would be best that you don't make some other decision. . . ."

On October 3 she wrote to Pierre Honnorat. "I am here, transformed into a worker in a grape harvest—hard work, but I love it. . . . I feel more and more that this is really what I ought to do. The reason would be impossible to explain; and why should I try to explain it? That which one feels one must do, a poem or a grape harvest, one must do, and that's that. . . ."

A little later, to Hélène Honnorat who had asked her, "But after all,

Simone, why do you do this, with what you bear within you and what you have to say?" she would say in reply, "There are things that I would not be able to say if I had not done these things."[35]

During the time when the rain had stopped work, Simone also wrote to her parents:

"They say here that I am doing my job as a grape harvester in the normal fashion. Last Wednesday, which was the last day of work (since it's been raining, on Monday, too, we didn't do anything), I did my eight hours without great fatigue; I don't know whether it will continue like this. We are still eating a lot and extremely well. Thanks for the chocolates, which gave the children much pleasure. . . .

"Of course I'll write and tell you if there is any change in my health."

Dr. and Mme. Weil had thought of renting a house at Saint-Julien. "I know nothing more," Simone wrote, "about a house to rent, except that going on the basis of what I am told here this idea becomes more and more alluring (save for better possibilities). . . ."

One or two days later, on Sunday, October 5, she wrote to them again to send them the names and addresses of two refugees to whom she wanted them to send a package of rye bread. One was interned in a camp in Vernet, the other was in Marseilles.

She adds: "We only worked three days this week because of the rain. My employers, always very nice to me, say that I am working as well as the others, but that isn't my impression. I feel fine.

"Don't stop telling me everything that's happening at Poët, where I would really like to be if I could at the same time be here, since I often get great joy from the work of grape harvesting. . . .

"Stay in that blessed corner where you are as long as you can. . . .

"I just bought a pair of magnificent sandals for fifty francs. . . . No point in sending stockings. . . ."

She soon noticed that these magnificent sandals were cutting into her feet. According to Thibon, the straps made her ankles bleed and left two deep marks.[36] Yet she wore them to the end of the grape harvest.

On that same Sunday, October 5, she wrote to Gilbert Kahn. To him she admitted a great tiredness that she had not mentioned to her parents.

"I work eight hours a day, except for the days when it rains, which have been frequent enough to permit me a certain amount of intellectual activity. My employer and his family, with whom I live and eat, are excellent people and very considerate. They tell me that 'I am keeping my end up' in the work, which gives me great pleasure but unfortunately doesn't at all tally with my personal impression. In any case, if I am not too inferior to the others, it is only at the price of a great effort. Sometimes I am crushed by fatigue, but I find in it a kind of purification. Right at the very bottom of my exhaustion I encounter joys that nothing else could give me and that prevent me from regretting the inevitable dwindling of my intellectual acuity. . . ."

A little later she would confess to Thibon: "One day I asked myself whether I wasn't dead and fallen into hell without noticing it, and whether hell did not consist in picking grapes eternally. . . ."[37]

Each morning, before work, she recited the Our Father. She often recited it while she was working in the vineyard.[38]

M. A. Rieu, her employer, expressing his admiration for her energy, said simply, "She has a lot of self-respect."[39] He testified later to her determination and courage in an interesting letter to Eugène Fleuré.[40]

"Our first impression on seeing her had not been a very happy one. When we saw how downcast she was, we did not think she would be able to stand up under the hard work. Her will and her courage have given us the lie, for she stood up to it and did work equal to that of the other vine cutters. And she did it under painful moral and physical conditions."

She refused to have a room to herself. "We put her in the dining room; after many arguments, we were able to slide a small mattress under her sleeping bag that must not have been occupied too often, since she would spend quite a long time writing owing to her large correspondence." Her room had become "a regular flea market."

M. Rieu recalls the trouble they had in getting her to eat. "As for food, we always had to watch her like a hawk, for otherwise she would have only eaten not very nourishing food (onions, raw tomatoes). Her health seemed quite impaired, and she often had very bad headaches.

". . . Despite so much deprivation and distress, she managed to do as much work as the other workers. We understood that sometimes she was utterly exhausted, but she always kept going. We have seen her lying under the vine-trunk as she kept on cutting off the grapes."

Her parents came to see her at Saint-Julien. "But she did not want to miss an hour of the harvest to stay with them."

"After work, her charity make her radiant; she would take two or three of the young grape pickers and teach them, or gave advice to the older workers in accordance with their different occupations.

"She was interested in everything that happened on the farm. Her incredible will drove her to want to do everything: in the morning she wanted to milk the cow and in the evening she would wash the dishes and clean the vegetables. She even tried to enter a grape vat (which is not easy). When a horse was being shod, she carefully watched the whole procedure. In the evenings or on days of rain, she took an interest in the children's homework, helped them with their penmanship, and watched over their games."

They had noticed her interest in religious matters. "She wanted a prayer book for the Mass, asked us if our children said their prayers every morning and every night; and on the first Sunday she wanted to go to Mass.

"But on the other Sundays she spent her time walking in the more deserted part of the countryside. In the evening, after dinner, when night had fallen, she would put on her cape and go to sit on the bench in the garden and stayed there for a long time looking at the stars (or so we thought) and smoking a cigarette."

They felt that she was mysterious. "For us, not knowing her, we thought her mysterious (we thought she was a scholar, but not so learned a scholar as she was). . . . For us Simone Weil was at that time an enigma, we did not understand her. But we admired her iron determination and her boundless charity. . . ."

From Saint-Julien, before mid-October, Simone wrote to Father Perrin and thanked him for having "opened the earth" for her. Father Perrin replied and asked her: "When shall I have the joy of 'opening the heavens' for you?" However, he added that in this matter (that is, the question of baptism), one must neither see nor desire anything but the will of God.

On October 18, the grape harvest was about to end. Simone wrote Xavier Vallat, Commissioner of Jewish Affairs, a letter of thanks at once ironic and sincere:

"Dear Sir:

"I should consider you, I imagine, as being in some way my leader; because, although I have not yet understood very well what one means today in legal terms by a Jew, in view of the fact that the Ministry of Public Education has not replied, although I am a graduate of the Ecole Normale in philosophy, to the request for a post that I made in July 1940 at the expiration of sick leave, I am forced to suppose, as the reason for this silence, the presumption of Jewish origin that attaches to my name. It is true that they have also abstained from paying me the indemnity provided for in such cases by the statute concerning Jews; which gives me a lively feeling of satisfaction at having no part in the country's financial difficulties. Whatever the case may be, I believe that I must render an account to you as to what I am presently doing.

"The government has proclaimed its desire that Jews should go into production, and preferably go to work on the land. Even though I do not consider myself a Jew, since I have never set foot in a synagogue, have been raised by my free-thinking parents with no religious observances of any kind, have no feeling of attraction for the Jewish religion and no attachment to Jewish tradition, and have been nourished since my early childhood only on the Hellenic, Christian, and French tradition, nevertheless I have obeyed.

"I am at this moment working in a grape harvest; I have cut grapes eight hours a day every day for four weeks, in the employ of a grape-grower in the Gard region. My employer has honored me by saying that

I hold up my end of the work. He has even given me the highest praise that a farmer can give a young woman who comes from the city, telling me that I could marry a farmer. He does not know, it is true, that simply because of my name I have an original defect that it would be inhuman for me to transmit to children.

"I still have a week of grape harvesting to do. After this I expect to go and work as a farm laborer for a truck gardener. . . . One cannot, I believe, obey more completely.

"I consider the statute concerning the Jews in a general way as being unjust and absurd, for how can one believe that a university graduate in mathematics could harm children who study geometry by the mere fact that three of his grandparents attended a synagogue?

"But, in my particular case, I would like to express the sincere gratitude I feel toward the government for having removed me from the social category of intellectuals and given me the land and, with it, all of nature. For only those possess nature and the land who have been penetrated by it through the daily suffering of their limbs broken by fatigue. The days, months, seasons, the celestial vault . . . belong to those who must cross the space of time that each day separates the rising from the setting of the sun by going painfully from fatigue to fatigue. These people . . . live through each day, they do not dream it.

"The government, which in my eyes you represent, has given me all this. You and the other rulers . . . have given me what you do not possess. You have given me the infinitely precious gift of poverty, which you do not possess either.

". . . You must certainly not receive many letters of thanks from those who find themselves in my situation. That perhaps makes the few minutes that you have lost reading my letter worthwhile."

(If in this letter Simone boldly affirms that she doesn't consider herself a Jew, it is not in order to disassociate herself in practice from the Jews—she would not disassociate herself from anyone, above all not from people being persecuted, and in Marseilles she did much to help Jews—nor in any way to deny her origins; nor is it to affirm a religious conviction that would have no interest for the Commissioner of Jewish Affairs. Instead, she did this in order to emphasize again the difficulty of defining the word "Jew," and to show quite clearly that she does not understand its significance and considers the statute concerning the Jews absurd and incomprehensible.)

The grape harvest ended on October 23. The next day Simone's employer gave her a certificate stating that he had employed her from September 22 to October 23 and was satisfied with her work.

After this, she spent a few days at Saint-Marcel with the Thibons. Before Thibon she counted out the money she had earned picking grapes. He told her that he knew very well where that money was going to be spent—meaning on people she wished to help. She replied gaily, hinting at her weaknesses, "But I shall certainly *also* buy a few books!"[41]

It was through Thibon that she learned that her truck gardener, whose farm was between Maillane and Saint-Rémy-de-Provence and who had in principle agreed to hire her for the following months, had changed his mind. He had decided to employ only people from his town, since he did not want to feed his workers. So Simone had to give up her plan of working as a farmhand during the winter of 1941–1942.

Her parents had returned to Marseilles. She rejoined them. She lived there again for six months that, even in a life as full as hers always was, were among the most fertile. It was during this period that she wrote the major part of the *Notebooks* of Marseilles. In fact it becomes quite clear that the period of the grape harvest corresponds to *Notebook* IV and the beginning of *Notebook* V. Thus the notebooks from V to XI— that is to say, Volumes II and III in the French edition—were written during the winter of 1941–1942 and the beginning of the spring of 1942.

In the course of this period she also wrote numerous essays and articles: three articles for *Cahiers du Sud*; two for *Le Génie d'Oc* (the special issue of *Cahiers du Sud*); five essays that appear in *Waiting for God*; the majority of the essays that go to form *Intimations of Christianity* and some of those that have appeared in *La Source grecque* (in particular "God in Plato"); four of the essays published in *Pensées sans ordre concernant l'amour de Dieu*; and, finally, "Condition première d'un travail non servile," published in *La Condition ouvrière.*

Besides this, she gave lectures or rather oral expositions followed by discussions. During this winter Father Perrin organized some meetings where she "read and commented upon some texts that seemed to her the most beautiful and revelatory in Greek thought."[42] These meetings were held in the crypt of a convent of Dominicans. It was undoubtedly for these expositions that Simone wrote "God in Plato"[43] and most of the essays that were published later in the collections *Intuitions préchrétiennes*[44] and *La Source grecque.* It is true that in writing them, she also had a further plan: that of collecting in a book the most beautiful non-Christian writings on the love of God.[45]

She went to Mass regularly on Sunday. She would usually meet friends there, especially Hélène Honnorat. But sometimes she went to an early-morning Mass rather than High Mass, so as to be there alone.

She asked Hélène to introduce her to some priests. Hélène put her in touch with all those she knew. "I arranged," she says, "as many meetings as possible. She had made a tour of all the canons and all the reverend fathers whom I happened to know at the time in Marseilles, and I also gave her for Catholic circles (since she had a kind of shyness about this) a series of set replies, somewhat like the modest confidants in classical tragedy.''[46] Simone never tired of putting questions to these men of the Church. She wanted to know exactly what the dogmas of the Catholic faith were. She discovered that it was very difficult to know them with exactitude; a certain dogma may be a matter of strict faith for one priest, the same dogma may not be so at all for another priest.

She would dine now and then with the Honnorats. To put her at her ease, Mme. Honnorat said to her, "Simone, just drop by, it's no big affair, just soup and another dish." Simone replied, "Either soup or the dish," and she didn't eat any more than she said she would. When she ate dinner with them, she would also sleep over because of the curfew. They would prepare a bed for her but she would sleep on the rug next to the bed. Mme. Honnorat would lay out on the floor, so that it would be less hard for her, all the thickest blankets she could gather together.[47]

I am not sure whether it was during this winter that she was put into contact (I don't know by whom) with the Resistance network called Christian Witness. She participated in the circulation of clandestine literature. One day when she was carrying a suitcase full of pamphlets, just as she was getting off the streetcar the badly locked suitcase opened and the pamphlets scattered all over the street, with all the passers-by looking on. Simone did not get upset; she quietly picked up all the pamphlets.

On November 15 she wrote to Antonio. She had waited before writing to him so as to have some news about the efforts she had urged Thibon to make on his behalf. "Finally I've received a letter; but I have simply been told that there are no results as yet, that one must wait, that things there are very difficult at present, but everything possible will be done."

He had once mentioned Plato in a letter. "Do you know enough French to read Plato translated into French? . . . Nothing is more beautiful than Plato; such reading, for those who are able to understand him, can give one happiness even in the most miserable circumstances."

She spoke to him about St. John of the Cross. "It is a blend of poetry and prose, both extremely beautiful. The thought, expressed in different words, is often very close to Plato's."

She copied out a beautiful *copla* for him and told him that she had sent him a little money. "If you need anything else, write to me, I beg you, don't have any hesitation."

In November or December she wrote to Thibon. He had come to Marseilles and she had met him with Father Perrin, who had undoubtedly talked to her about baptism. "You must have guessed that Father Perrin's words yesterday evening greatly troubled me. They almost gave me the impression that I had not been quite straightforward with him, though I have always tried to tell him the truth. The thought that I might disappoint him and thus cause him any pain is extremely distressing to me because of my affection for him, and because I am grateful for the charity that leads him to desire my good. Yet I cannot enter the Church just to avoid causing him pain. . . ."[48]

When Father Perrin spoke "of communicating to me the fullness of the Lord," Simone says that she doesn't understand exactly what he is talking about. Did he mean to speak of that which only saints can possess? Nobody has ever said that the sacraments in themselves have the power to bestow sanctity. "But if Father Perrin was speaking of such communication of God as any convinced Catholic has received, I do not think that in my case this still has to come. . . ."

She also said: "At this moment, I should be more ready to die for the Church, if one day before long it should need anyone to die for it, than I should be to enter it. To die does not commit one to anything, if one can say such a thing; it does not contain anything in the nature of a lie."[49]

On October 19 she had written to me on an interzone postcard during her month of work at the grape harvest: "I am now, if one believes my employer, a fully accomplished grape harvester. . . . I shall remember those few days at Poët. . . ." She wrote to me again on December 1 to tell me that her plan to work at growing vegetables had not gone through. "I have simply set about again to read and write; but although I have plenty of leisure, my old enemy laziness (which my tendency to lie sometimes makes me call fatigue) seriously hampers me. . . ."

Whatever she might think of her "laziness," she worked very hard. It is difficult to know at exactly what time the various essays and articles she wrote that winter were composed; but the comparison of these texts with the *Notebooks* permits us certain conjectures. It seems, for example, that the two articles about science written for *Cahiers du Sud* were written before the end of 1941. They correspond to some research that can be found in *Notebook* V. (*Notebook* VII is the first that is dated 1942. The end of *Notebook* VI already seems to be in January 1942, but all of *Notebook* V is in 1941).[50]

The first of these articles[51] is a review of *L'Avenir de la science* [The Future of Science], a collection in which are included essays by Louis de Broglie, André Thérive, Raymond Charmet, Pierre Devaux, Daniel-Rops, and Father Sertillanges (Paris: Plon, 1941). Simone was chiefly concerned with criticizing the picture Daniel-Rops had drawn of a future in which men would have almost no work to do, and the conception Louis de Broglie had of the contributions of science to philosophy.

While praising Daniel-Rops for his clarity and talent, she thinks that his forecasts, analogous to those that had been spread by the "New Order" group,[52] and also to those of the Marxists, are most uncertain. "A people subjected to a short period of compulsory unpaid labor," she says, "will not really work except under pressure from a despotic central power and under the threat of severe punishments, unless other truly

effective stimulants can be discovered. . . . And as for the long years of
leisure, one must be naive, especially today, not to reflect that some
people would devote them to the one sport that really inflames men, the
sport whose objective is domination over other men; . . . since this sport
calls for unlimited resources, in armaments and other things, the period
of compulsory labor would soon be prolonged to a whole lifetime. . . ."

As for Louis de Broglie, his conception of the relation between
philosophy and science is unworthy of such a mind as his. As he represents them, the contributions of science to philosophy are misleading.
Contemporary science does not need to teach philosophers that determinism is simply a postulate, since it never was anything else for them.
In the same way, philosophers have always known that the procedures
of observation have a disturbing effect on the phenomenon observed
and that, in consequence, knowledge of the phenomenon can only be
imperfect. The principal reason that science cannot make a new contribution to philosophy is that novelties are, properly speaking, impossible
in philosophy. "When a man introduces a new thought into philosophy,
it can hardly be anything except a new accent upon some thought that
is not only eternal by right but ancient in fact. . . ."

The other article, "Reflections on the Quantum Theory,"[53] deals
with a book by Max Planck, *Initiations à la physique* (Paris: Flammarion,
1941). It contains, it is said, an error with regard to the basis for the
quantum theory. Simone believes that it is because Planck only employs
numerical, discontinuous probability, that he had to introduce the idea
of the quantum of energy; he did not entertain the idea of a continuous
probability. Now continuous probability was known to scientists, and
Planck knew it. However, Simone had posed a question on this subject
to her brother in her letter of May 21, 1941,[54] and since André Weil had
no doubt answered that she was mistaken and the basis of the quantum
theory was not what she thought, she had made some objections to this
reply in her letter from Poët: "Your reply concerning Planck has not
satisfied me. . . . I've read a collection of Planck's lectures, one of which
is entitled 'The Genesis of the Quantum Theory'; I've also read the part
dealing with quanta in his physics textbook in four volumes; in both he
says explicitly that it is probability that demands the discontinuous; he
does not make any allusion to the least attempt to employ probability
to preserve continuity. . . ." It is therefore possible that Planck himself
gave rise to a false interpretation by the way in which he presents his
theory in his popular books on the subject.

Whatever the case may be, and setting this point aside, it is well to
consider what Simone Weil says about contemporary science in this
article. For example, she shows that ever-increasing specialization
makes the necessary control over and verification of scientific theories
more and more difficult. The scientist has for a judge no more than what

amounts to a small "village," in which he finds himself shut up with other scientists of his specialty. In this village everybody knows everybody else; and although these specialists are dispersed throughout the world, it is in fact a small circle in which gossip circulates and friendships and enmities play their part. In so small a circle, general opinion does not offer the guarantees that general opinion might offer in a larger environment; it has less chance of controlling certain extravagances by reason. This holds a danger for the future; for one must not forget that once before a brilliant science, the science of the Greeks, perished for long centuries. The need for specialization, in proportion to the growth of science, perhaps signifies that there is a limit to the development of science.

It is more difficult to decide when the short article, "Morality and Literature," which was not published by *Cahiers du Sud* until 1944, was actually written.[55] Though it is close in its subject matter to the "Letter to *Cahiers du Sud* on the Responsibilities of Literature," it does not seem to be of the same period. It no longer deals with a question of *value*. The idea on which Simone now insists is that nothing is as beautiful and marvelous as the good, nothing more dreary and boring than evil; but that this must be understood as *real* good and evil. In fiction this relationship is reversed. In fiction, it is good that appears boring and evil that appears interesting and attractive. Now literature only presents us with fictions; because of this, immorality seems to be an inseparable part of literature. One must be at least a genius to present in the form of fiction "something equivalent to the actual density of reality."

So it is useless to seek for a remedy for the immorality of literature. "The only remedy is genius, and the source of this is not within the reach of our efforts." But what can and ought to be corrected is "the usurpation by writers of the function of spiritual guidance, for which they are totally unsuited." "For centuries the function of director of conscience had been exclusively in the hands of the priests. They often performed it atrociously badly, as the fires of the Inquisition testify, but at least they had some title to it. In reality, it is only the greatest saints who can perform it, as it is only the greatest geniuses among writers. But all priests, by virtue of their profession, speak in the name of the saints, and look to them for inspiration, and try to imitate and follow them. . . . When, as a result of what was called the Enlightenment in the eighteenth century, the priests had in fact almost entirely lost this function of guidance, their place was taken by writers and scientists. In both cases, it is equally absurd. . . ."

The idea for this article could have come to Simone during the period of the grape harvest work. Indeed, one finds toward the end of *Notebook* IV: "Literature and morality. Imaginary evil is romantic, fanciful, varied; real evil dreary, monotonous, barren, and boring. Imaginary good is boring; real good is always new, fresh, marvelous intoxicating. . . . Thus 'imaginative literature' is either boring or immoral (or a mixture of both). It manages to escape this alternative only by passing in some way, by the force of art, to the side of reality—which genius alone can do. . . ."[56]

This article is also mentioned in *Notebook* VII, written in January or February 1942. So it appears that she wrote it between October 1941 and February 1942.

At Christmas Simone sent the children of her "boss" at Saint-Julien a letter and some small figures for their holy crib. She also wrote a letter and sent some books to the Lorrainaise peasant girl who had sought refuge at Saint-Julien, whom Simone had undertaken to teach during the grape harvest, and of whom Thibon had already said that while Simone was presenting some marvelous commentaries on the *Upanishads,* she was bored to death but concealed it out of politeness and shyness.[57] This young girl thanked Simone in a charming letter in which she recalled their conversations at the end of the work days. "I don't think I am flattering you when I tell you that you are a good teacher. My confidence in you was so great that I was not afraid to ask you any sort of questions, sometimes naive, and let you see how little education I had. . . ." She says that since then someone else has loaned her books and that she was grateful to him, "but he does not have the simplicity of Simone." It is clear that Simone, by her simplicity and kindness, had been able to put this shy, modest soul at her ease.

The poem "Nécessité" was written by Simone about the month of July 1941; "La Porte" probably at the time of the grape harvest; "La Mer" would seem to have been written in November or December 1941; and, finally, Simone probably composed the short poem "Les Astres" in December, a little after "La Mer."[58]

At the beginning of January 1942, she sent me "Les Astres" on an interzone postcard; the poem just fit on the postcard. She also sent it to Antonio, with a letter in which she spoke to him about the Stoics:

"The Greek philosophers whom one calls Stoics say that one must love fate; that one must love everything that fate brings, even when it brings misfortune. Since my childhood, it has always seemed to me that this is truly the most beautiful virtue. . . .

"You possess it to a very high degree, and I cannot tell you how much I admire you for this. But I would like to see you finally stop suffering. I would like to be in your place, and that you might be in mine. . . . Certainly I would not bear the suffering as well as you, because I have less firmness of soul; but I think that more than me you deserve the spectacle of the sea, freedom, and everything that fate does not grant you at this moment. I'm sorry that it is not really in my power to change places with you. . . ."

It was on January 9 that she wrote Father Perrin the first of the letters

that have been published in *Waiting for God.*[59] This letter concerns
baptism, or rather Simone's personal position in regard to baptism. She
knew that Father Perrin wanted to baptize her. No doubt she had already
explained to him why she didn't think she could give him this joy. If she
had decided to write to him, when she often had the chance to see him,
it was certainly because she wanted to clarify her position definitively,
not only for Father Perrin but also for herself.

She says that she has recently questioned herself on the will of God
and on the way in which one could manage to conform to it. She
distinguishes three manifestations of this will. The first is external necessity, that of events that do not depend on us. The second is duty,
which concerns personal things and which ordinarily is clear and manifest. The third are the inspirations that God sends us. "God rewards the
soul that thinks of him with attention and love, and he rewards it by
exercising a compulsion upon it. . . . We have to abandon ourselves to
the pressure, to run to the exact spot whither it impels us and not go
one step further, even in the direction of what is good. . . ."

She believes that "only those who are above a certain level of spirituality can participate in the sacraments as such." But she thinks that she
is below this level. And besides it seems to her that the will of God is
that she should not enter the Church "at present." Certainly, she experienced a great joy at hearing Father Perrin say to her that her thoughts
were not incompatible with belonging to the Church. But she cannot
help wondering whether, in a period of materialism, God does not wish
"there to be some men and women who have given themselves to him
and to Christ and who yet remain outside the Church."

"In any case, when I think of the act by which I should enter the
Church as something concrete, which might happen quite soon, nothing
gives me more pain than the idea of separating myself from the immense
and unfortunate multitude of unbelievers. . . . I don't think in any case
that I would ever enter a religious order, because that would separate
me from ordinary people by a habit."

She feels that this last sentence could wound Father Perrin. So she
adds: "There are some human beings for whom such a separation has
no serious disadvantages, because they are already separated from ordinary folk by their natural purity of soul. As for me, on the contrary, as
I think I told you, I bear within me the germ of all possible crimes, or
nearly all. . . ."

She concludes: "One thing is absolutely certain. It is that if one day
it comes about that I love God enough to deserve the grace of baptism,
I shall receive this grace on that very day, infallibly, in the form God
wills, either by means of baptism in the strict sense of the word or in
some other manner. . . ."

This letter would seem to bring to an end the exchanges of views on
baptism. However, Simone judged it necessary to return to this ques-

tion. A few days later she sent Father Perrin another letter,[60] which she calls a postscript.

She tells him that the obstacles of an intellectual order that stop her at the Church's threshold have not been completely eliminated. Some of them are still there. These obstacles could be reduced to the following: "What frightens me is the Church as a social structure. . . . I am afraid of the Church patriotism that exists in Catholic circles. . . . There are some saints who approved of the Crusades or the Inquisition. I cannot help thinking that they were in the wrong. I cannot go against the light of conscience. If I think that on this point I see more clearly than they did, I who am so beneath them, then I must admit that in this matter they were blinded by something powerful. This something was the Church seen as a social structure. . . ."

Simone knows very well that it is inevitable that the Church should be a social structure; but "insofar as it is a social structure, it belongs to the Prince of this world." The social is irreducibly the domain of the devil.

"There is a Catholic circle ready to give an eager welcome to whoever enters it. Well, I don't want to be adopted into a circle. . . . In saying I don't want this, I am expressing myself badly, for I should like it very much; I should find it all delightful. But I feel that it is not permissible for me. I feel that it is necessary and ordained that I should be alone, a stranger and an exile in relation to every human circle without exception. . . ."

Her ability to merge with almost any milieu, in order to know the people in it and love them for what they are, implies that she doesn't belong to any group.

One feels that she regrets not being able to participate in the sacraments. (She had an ardent desire to take communion.) But it is perhaps not inconceivable, she says, that for certain persons "the desire for and deprivation of the sacraments might constitute a contact more pure than actual participation."

She sometimes is tempted to put herself entirely in Father Perrin's hands. But when all is said and done, she cannot do this; she does not have the right.

"If I had my eternal salvation placed in front of me on this table, and if I only had to stretch out my hand to take it, I would not put out my hand so long as I had not thought I had received the order to do so. . . ."

At the beginning of February she wrote to Antonio. She was just about to make a new attempt to procure him a job that would permit him to be freed. A certain organization would eventually propose to offer him a work contract, but first he must send Simone certain information.

She wrote to him again a little later to tell him that she had once again made a request and to prepare him for the proposal that would be offered him if this request were successful.

"I am acquainted here with a Dominican monk who is an admirable man, a Christian in the true sense of the word. That is to say, his way of understanding life does not differ much from yours and mine. He is very tied to a religious community that is in Algeria . . . and, it seems, has influence with the government of Algeria. I have written about your case to the superior of this community, through this Dominican.

"I told them that to my knowledge you don't have any religious faith but that in my opinion there is a great similarity between your Stoicism and their faith, and that they should do something for you.

"For your part, I think, I am even certain that you can accept their help, because what they will do for you will be done in a spirit of pure fraternity. . . ."

About the middle of February, she wrote to me: "Forgive me for not having acknowledged sooner receiving the books, for which I must thank you enormously. I have gone through a period in which I lost the sense of time. . . . Not, unfortunately, that I've done very much during this period. . . . I've done nothing new in verse. Would you replace *tirez* with *levez* in the last verse? I had written to Dieudonné that he should find out about the Research Fund; since I had expressed myself very warmly about you, he thought that I wanted some sort of intervention and not just information, and he has alerted C., whom you, it seems, sent packing. You were wrong: we had already talked about that at Poët, and you should have guessed that I am the only person to blame in this affair. Blame me to your heart's content, insofar as one can do this on a postcard, and try to make C. understand, if you can, that your bad humor was mistaken in its direction."

On this postcard she adds: "I recommend to you the works of the philosopher Teitaro Suzuki on Zen Buddhism, in English; it is extremely curious. The *Gita* in the text (I can now read it a little) is of an incomparable splendor. I am just rediscovering Heraclitus. The world is full of beautiful things. Fortunately . . . Think well of Krishna."

She had discovered Suzuki thanks to Daumal, who was then translating the second series of the *Essays in Zen Buddhism* (London: Luzac, 1933).

She wrote to Thibon very often. One of these letters, of which he quotes a sentence in *Simone Weil As We Knew Her*, seems to be from this period when she reproached herself for having lost the idea of time. For she begs his pardon at the start for not having written for "an infinite stretch of time" ("I have fallen into a kind of abyss in which I've lost the idea of time. Being forgetful of time is my great temptation. . . .") It is in this letter that she says to him: "Our differences must not lessen our friendship, and our friendship should not attenuate our differences."[61]

A little later, that is, toward the end of February or the beginning of March, she asked him to look for work for her in case she did not leave France. "The spring is coming. If I don't go, I want to work. May I ask you to start now to find me something? Don't pay any attention to the injunctions Father Perrin gave you last summer to find me something where the conditions of life are not too hard. He didn't know me at that time. . . . If I hit upon a place where life is intolerable, there is nothing to prove that that will be bad for me. . . ."[62]

I imagine that it was roughly around this time, in February or March, that she wrote the two articles destined for the special issue that Ballard had been preparing for a year: *Le Génie d'Oc et l'homme méditerranéen.* In fact, in the last part of *Notebook* VIII,[63] soon after the first passages dealing with Suzuki,[64] one finds in the margin of certain thoughts the word "Oc,"[65] and one can see that these thoughts are taken up again, in a sometimes only slightly different form, in the articles in the *Génie d'Oc.* Also in *Notebook* IX, at the beginning, one can read thoughts analogous to those in these articles.[66]

The first article is entitled *L'Agonie d'une civilization vue à travers un poème épique.*[67] This epic poem is the *Song of the Crusade against the Albigensians.* Simone shows that in this poem there are all sorts of signs which attest to the value of the civilization that was destroyed by this Crusade. "Nothing is more cruel to the past than the commonplace which asserts that spiritual values cannot be destroyed by force; on the strength of this belief, civilizations that have been destroyed by force of arms are denied the name of civilizations; and there is no risk of our being refuted by the dead. In this way we kill once again something that has perished. . . ."

The second article, entitled "What Makes Up the Occitan Inspiration?"[68] begins by a critique of the idea of progress, a critique analogous to observations found in *Notebook* VIII.[69] The idea of progress orients us toward the future; but it is not in the future that we can find that which is better than ourselves. "The future is empty and is filled by our imagination. Our imagination can only picture a perfection on our scale. It is just as imperfect as we are ourselves. . . ." What presents us with something really better and what can lift us up is the past. The eternal alone being invulnerable to time, what survives of the past contains a part of the eternal relatively greater than the present and above all than the future. It is toward ancient Greece that we Europeans ought to turn to look for the source of spirituality that is really ours.

To return to Greece is what was done by Romanesque civilization. The Renaissance of the eleventh and twelfth centuries was the true Renaissance. "The Greek spirit was reborn in the Christian form that is its truth." The other, false Renaissance soon produced Humanism; people thought "that they could turn away from Christianity toward the Greek spirit, although the two are in one and the same place." Between the true and false Renaissance, what had happened? "Many crimes and errors. Perhaps the decisive crime was the murder of this country of the *langue d'oc* on whose soil we are now living."

"The essence of the Languedocian inspiration is identical with that of Greek inspiration. It consists in the understanding of force. This understanding goes only with supernatural courage. . . . To understand force is to recognize that it is almost absolutely supreme in this world, and yet to reject it with loathing and contempt. This contempt is the other face of the compassion that goes out to everything that is exposed to the ravages of force."

The Cathars "carried the horror of force to the point of practicing nonviolence and to the doctrine that sees everything associated with the domain of force as originating in evil: namely, everything carnal and everything social. That was going far, but no further than the Gospel. . . ."

At the end of the winter and the beginning of the spring, Simone wrote two more letters to Antonio. It was still quite cold when she wrote the first, but in the second she says: "Spring is coming now."

She feels very sorry for him: "From what you tell me about the sources of consolation that you possess, I can see very well that you have the joy won from suffering. This is the most beautiful. In finding this joy, you come together in the same place with the true sages who existed before the Christian era, and the true saints who came after it. They were able to lift their souls to the place, unknown to most men, where pain is joy and joy is pain. It is from this place too that the true poets have risen. True poetry comes from there. You are the brother of all those people. But I would also like you to know a little pure joy—joy that is only joy. For that I think that it would suffice that you be free in the midst of a beautiful countryside. It is a small thing; why should it be so hard to obtain?"

Before the end of March she was almost sure that she would soon be leaving. Indeed, before her trip to Dourgne she wrote me: "Don't send me anything more until I write to you." She had copied out for me on her letter the end of *Venise sauvée*, which she told me she had corrected and, she hoped, had improved.

Easter fell on April 5. She had decided to do what she had not been able to do the year before, that is, go to Dourgne in the Tarn to hear the Gregorian chants at the Benedictine Abbey of En-Calcat.

She wanted to stop off first at Carcassonne. This is where the writer Joë Bousquet lived. He had worked with Ballard to prepare the publication of the *Génie d'Oc* issue. He had been badly wounded in the First World War; he had been struck by a bullet in the spinal column and since 1918 had been completely paralyzed, nailed to his bed and tormented by physical suffering. Simone wanted to meet him. Moreover, still concerned with finding out whether her ideas were or were not compatible with belonging to the Church, she wanted to question the monk F. Vidal, who was then, or became, Superior of the Great Seminary of Carcassonne and whom Hélène Honnorat knew. She also wanted to see again her old comrades from the Ecole Normale, Lucien and Suzette Roubaud.

She left with Ballard on one of the last evenings of March. As they traveled on the train, she spoke to him about the mythology of the moon, explaining its intricacies. They reached Bousquet's house quite late, most likely at eleven or twelve o'clock at night.[70] They spoke to him for about two hours; then Ballard left. Simone remained with Joë Bousquet and went on talking until three or four in the morning. He then offered Simone a bed on which to rest; as usual, she refused all comfort and slept for a few hours on a mat in a small room next to Bousquet's bedroom.

Although, according to the monk Vidal, she stayed for several days in Carcassonne, I do not think that she saw Joë Bousquet again. This single conversation she had with Bousquet was enough to create a deep friendship. Each had recognized in the other a courage that was like his own. Simone had spoken to Bousquet, among other things, of her "plan for a formation of front-line nurses" and had asked him to write her a letter about it. She thought that his experience and testimony as a former officer could help to get her project considered seriously.

For three mornings in a row she went to see the monk Vidal. Giving Hélène Honnorat as a reference, she told him that she wanted to know whether he considered her ready to be baptized. She asked him to explain the main outlines of Catholic dogma to her.

"I gave her," the monk Vidal says, "a rapid description of the mysteries to which our minds must adhere, mysteries whose content we could never exhaust but which we must gain a deeper knowledge of by study and prayer. . . .

"She listened to me, quiet, attentive, interrupting me rarely just to have me explain one point or another in detail. I pointed out to her that these dogmas did not present any difficulty for my thought; she agreed with this and seemed happy about it, perhaps a bit surprised.

"I invited her to return on the following morning. She was very punctual. She told me about some of her difficulties. She was very hard on the Hebrews of the Old Testament. Among other things she said, 'You quote Job to me; but Job was not a Jew.' And again: "If Christ had been incarnated in India, they would have worshipped him."

"She was also very harsh toward Yahweh, the 'God of the armies,' a cruel God who gave the order to exterminate the people of the land of Canaan, etc. And she would not admit that one could explain these things, which revolted her, by the harshness of customs in that period, or by the necessity to preserve the Jews from any contact that could have altered the purity of their monotheistic faith.

"I found in her, not in her heart which I found very open to charity (in the evangelical sense of love) but in her spirit, something crude, rigid, and intransigent for which she reproached the Jewish people.

"She returned once again, always very punctual, the next day, no doubt interested by the exchange of views we had had.

"I don't know how I came to speak of natural and Christian 'virtues.' She asked me to list them. I cited for her as natural virtues—the integrity of the conscience, goodness of heart, the force of will, delicacy of feelings and manners, good manners as being the flower of charity (love). For the Christian virtues I named humility and purity. After a moment of silence, she said to me very simply, 'I practice all that. And what you call grace (the supernatural help of God and a life of intimacy with him), I have this, too; I have experienced this benefit, by whatever name you wish to call it.'

"She then told me, without insisting but quite definitely, that Christ had possessed her one day and had revealed himself in her, so fully did she believe in his divinity. On this point her faith and certainty were absolute. I forbade myself from questioning her, out of respect for the secret of her soul. Now I know to what she alluded.

"She presented me with a series of problems, some of which are described in *Her Letter to a Priest.*

"Obviously we needed more time than we had at our disposal to examine all these problems, to try to settle them with even some measure of approximation. . . . The very richness of her discourse paid witness to the vigor of her thought, the probity of her study, the rather dismaying extent of her scholarship . . . and the progress she would have to make before being able to adhere to the Catholic faith.

"Finally she forcefully declared that she would continue to teach and write, even after her baptism, what she believed to be incarnations of the Word before Jesus; she cited Melchisedech, Osiris, and Krishna. . . .

"It was very clear that she was not ready for baptism. I told her this and urged her to reflect, become more informed, and pray.

"It has been written that if she had been humble, she would have embraced the Catholic faith. I am not of this opinion. Simone Weil was not kept back by the pride of the intellectual. She submitted herself docilely to the truth she had discovered. But it was necessary for her to have discovered it and for her to have good reasons to admit its being well founded. Yet she had come alone and by her own efforts, thanks to her illuminations, to the possession of certain truths of the Catholic faith. A vigorous, exigent, personal mind, which was rather thwarted and troubled by her very great learning, it would have taken time for her to simplify her thought and assimilate aspects of the truth unfamiliar to her mind. She was not accustomed to our categories.

"When I told her that in order to be baptized she had to wait some more, she was no doubt disappointed, but did not let any of this show. On her return to Marseilles she confided her astonishment to Hélène Honnorat: 'As our conversations proceeded, I saw myself getting further and further away from baptism.' "[71]

The monk Vidal thought that at the time he had seen Simone she certainly wanted baptism and that it was not right to say that she had always refused it. It is true that she wanted it, for she wanted to participate in the sacraments. But she was afraid that among the necessary conditions there would be those to which she could not subscribe. Hélène and Pierre Honnorat told me that Father Perrin was ready to baptize her but that she had not accepted it.

During these days at Carcassonne Simone also went one evening to see the Roubauds, her old classmates. Cabaud has told the story of this encounter: "She wore rough homespun; her bare feet were in sandals. Remote, far from all fleshly concerns, she seemed to her hosts like a saint of the Middle Ages. They spent the evening together. Jean Paulhan [the French writer and one of the editors of the famous literary magazine *Nouvelle Revue Française*] was there, too. Looking much older, she had come with a school exercise book under her arm. She first expressed certain political opinions. She had never declared herself a Jew, she said, because she thought she ought not to. She also spoke, with a kind of childish pride, about her experience as a grape picker. . . . Her preoccupation with mysticism was apparent to each of us."

She spoke a bit about her projects. According to Cabaud, she appears to have said: "I want to be truly useful. I want to go wherever there is the greatest possible danger . . . where my life will be least protected." When she had left, those who were there, he says, had a feeling of uneasiness. "Her lack of interest in earthly and secular affairs, the new light in which she presented herself, aroused a curious emotion."[72]

She arrived at Dourgne on Maundy Thursday. She took part in the service. In the afternoon she went to consult with the Benedictine Dom Clément Jacob on the religious problems that preoccupied her. On the following days she divided her time between attendance at the religious ceremonies and her conversations with Father Clément.

These conversations seem to have been quite painful for both of them. Father Clément did not conceal the fact that in his opinion she was a heretic.[73] According to Hélène and Pierre Honnorat, this was a turning point for her; until then, despite all her objections, she had thought she was going toward the Church.

She had given Father Clément a series of questions.[74] While affirming her faith in the mysteries of the Trinity, the Incarnation and the Eucharist, in this questionnaire she said that she didn't see *any* possibility of ever adhering to the Christian conception of history. She asked what exactly are those opinions of Marcion to which one cannot agree without being anathema; whether one is anathema when one thinks that there could be incarnations of the Word before Christ; whether one is anathema when one thinks that the source from which has issued the commandment for Israel to destroy the towns, massacre the people, and exterminate the prisoners and children was not God; whether one is anathema when one considers as at least doubtful the opinion that the true knowledge of God is more widespread in Christianity than it was in antiquity and is at present in non-Christian countries such as India.

Father Clément, in a letter to Mme. Denise Azam,[75] said that he replied to these questions in conformity with the thought of the Church; that he felt he discerned in Simone "much more respect, confidence, a certain feeling—unconscious—of superiority (the certainty of being right), of fastidiousness and disappointment"; that on his part he had been surprised by her physical appearance (her dress, her voluntary lack of femininity); that he had had an awkward desire to convince, the annoyance of feeling himself overborne, and a touch of irritation. He tells how in the course of the discussion Simone had quoted, translating it freely, a verse from the Gospel: "You have taken away the key of knowledge" (Luke 11:52). She translated it as "You have lost the keys of knowledge"; he had claimed that this was not in the Gospel, but she had given him the chapter and verse.

He was to write to someone: "There was in her moral and intellectual exigencies a rigor that left her no escape route. . . . Now that I better understand who she was, I think that she nevertheless has found what she was searching for." And in another letter: "Much has been said about her eminent intellectual gifts, but I believe the most striking thing about her was the nobility, integrity, and purity of her soul."

Hélène Honnorat took Simone to the Abbey Sainte-Scholastique to meet Sister Colombe, a nun who had studied medicine before becoming a Benedictine. According to Hélène, Simone was very moved by this nun's personality and observations; she felt great admiration and sympathy for her.

Some fifteen years ago, in a letter dated January 15, 1956, Sister Colombe was kind enough, on the request of Hélène Honnorat, to write and tell me what she recalled of this meeting. To her great regret she could not remember what she and Simone had said to each other, but she did recall her attitude very well. "She came into this small parlor, enveloped in a large, sailor-blue cape, a Basque beret plopped untidily over her hair, which was a bit wild, standing in a very self-effacing manner behind Hélène. . . . Yet her silence, the quality of her attention—this is what I have not forgotten. This emanated from her at first sight, along with her seriousness, and her authenticity. Afterward, much later, when reading her books, I remembered this: she had the poverty of those who are searching. . . ."

Simone attended all the services, from Maundy Thursday to Sunday.

On Good Friday she was astonished to learn that at the convent's hostelry the people had eaten codfish and vegetables. "On Good Friday! A bit of dry bread, if that. . . ." She judged that a good many of the faithful didn't take their religion very seriously. For example, she was very indignant at hearing them talk about their trifling affairs on coming out of the services. On Easter Sunday she went to Matins with Hélène and heard the *Salve festa dies*. She asked for the words and music of this chant.

She returned to Marseilles after Easter. The abundance of what she wrote during the last months she spent in Marseilles has no equal except for the huge amount of writing she did in London. She seemed to be in a hurry, like someone who is about to leave with the presentiment of a probable death and wants to say everything beforehand. She had acquired such mastery of her thought and her style that the words, continually beautiful and pure and with profound human resonances, flowed naturally from her pen. Speaking of the last conversation he had with her, Thibon says, "Her mouth uttered thoughts as a tree gives its fruit."[76] In the same way, what she wrote at this time seems to have come to her quite naturally and without any effort. (Yet how much effort and discipline lay behind this well-earned facility!)

According to Father Perrin,[77] it was without a doubt during this month of April that she wrote "Reflections on the Right Use of School Studies with a View to the Love of God,"[78] and "Forms of the Implicit Love of God.[79] As for the essay "The Three Sons of Noah and the History of Mediterranean Civilization,"[80] Father Perrin says: "This idea had come to her, it seems, toward the end of her stay in Marseilles."[81] (And actually, the idea does not appear in the *Notebooks*, if I am not mistaken, before page 233 of Volume III.) As for the "Love of God and Affliction,"[82] Father Perrin believes that this beautiful text was written in the spring of 1942,[83] that is, in March, April, or the beginning of May. (I believe that it was in April or the first days of May, because of the analogies with certain passages in the *Notebooks*,[84] and with letters that Simone wrote to Father Perrin and Thibon just at the time of her departure.)[85]

Moreover, Simone must have written at this time, or at least put together, part of the texts that form *Intuitions préchrétiennes* (she would complete this collection of essays in Casablanca), and part of the notes on folklore that Father Perrin has given to the National Library. It seems quite possible that also written at this time, or not much later, were the first four essays published in *Pensées sans ordre*: "Thoughts without Order on the Love of God," "Christianity and the Life of the Fields," "Reflections without Order on the Love of God," and "Israel and the Gentiles."[86] And finally I believe that the article "A Prime Condition for Non-Servile Work,"[87] must also be placed in this period.

There can be no question of analyzing here such a great number of writings. Besides, they are too well known and too beautiful to be summarized. I will speak only of the last texts I have cited, in order to justify the dates at which I propose placing them.

The three essays, "Reflections without Order on the Love of God," "Thoughts without Order Concerning the Love of God," and "Christianity and the Life of the Fields" form a group. "Thoughts without Order" could, from the standpoint of the sequence of ideas, be put at the end of the "Reflections without Order." (It takes up again, in order to develop it, the idea that evil in us can only be diminished by the attention brought to bear on a perfectly pure thing.) In turn, "Christianity and the Life of the Fields" is connected to the end of "Thoughts without Order." This sequence of texts leads to a reflection on the condition of the workers and to a search for motivations that could render bearable their necessarily monotonous activity, an activity without joy because it has as its goal only the simple preservation of existence. Simone thought that the only motivations that could sustain the workers and would not be lies are those one can find in contemplation, in intuitive attention brought to bear on sensible things insofar as they reflect truths concerning God. "That is not possible except by a symbolism that would permit one to read divine truths in the circumstances of daily life and work."[88]

It is also in terms of this search and with suggestions of this kind that the article "A Prime Condition for Non-Servile Work," deals (this article was meant for the magazine *Economie et humanisme*). Here, too, Simone maintains that "only one thing makes monotony bearable; it is the light of eternity and beauty."[89] "The people have as much need of poetry as of bread. . . . They have a need that the daily substance of their lives might itself be poetry. . . . And this poetry can only be religion. . . ."[90] Of course, she did not think that it was enough to teach the workers a symbolism that permitted them to see God through the palpable images that their work offered them. She thought that one should provide them with their material necessities and job security, protect them from injustice and arbitrary actions, and, finally, outlaw "rationalized" or Taylorized work. "The base kind of attention demanded by Taylorized work is incompatible with any other form of attention, because it empties the soul of everything but the concern for speed. This kind of work cannot be transformed—it must be abolished."[91] But in her opinion one must reject all illusions about the future, every idea that, like the idea of revolution, makes life bearable at the price of a lie. Much more than religion, the revolution is the opium of the people.

The point of departure for this research and theory could well be something that Simone heard some farm workers say during her month of grape harvesting. "At the end of a year's work you haven't done anything. But you've survived."—"As for me, if it were a matter of working simply in order to survive, I just couldn't do it. . . ."[92] These words, combined with her experience of the monotony of work as a grape-picker, no doubt incited her to try to discover a way that makes work of this kind more bearable.

One would therefore be tempted to place the writing of these essays a little after the period of the grape harvest. But on reading the *Notebooks* one notices that it is somewhat toward the end of Volume III (in the French edition) that one finds passages analogous to certain passages in the essays, and so these must have been written toward the end of her stay in Marseilles.[93] In particular, on page 279 of volume III one finds some words that could be the first title Simone had thought of for "Prime Condition": "An Essential Condition for Non-Servile Work."

As for the essay "Israel and the Gentiles," it seems also to be of this period in that it takes its commentary from Greek texts and from her notes on folklore so as to prove that true religion had been known even outside of Christianity and had even been better known among the Gentiles than among the Jews. It is linked with the same order of ideas as in *Intuitions préchrétiennes*. It is also clear from the *Notebooks* that she had reread or at least had again gone through the Old Testament just before the end of her stay in Marseilles.[94]

On the thirteenth of April she wrote to Joë Bousquet.[95] She now thought that she would most likely be leaving about the end of April and was somewhat concerned not to have received the letter he had promised her for the front-line nurses project. She also sent him the finished part of *Venise sauvée* and some poems, not only so that he could give her his opinion on them but so that he could preserve these writings if she were to leave and, more particularly, if she should die.

"I was very moved," she says, "to see that you had paid real attention to some pages I had shown you. . . . Attention is the rarest and purest form of generosity. It is given to very few minds to notice that things and beings exist. Since my childhood I have not wanted anything else but to receive the complete revelation of this before dying."

She ends her letter by offering her services to get him a drug he might need. This offer would not deserve mention if Bousquet's reply ("It heartens me to think that you proposed to do for me what most men have not dared to offer me"[96]) didn't allow us to suppose that it was perhaps a drug meant to put an end to his sufferings when and if they became unendurable. Not that Simone approved of suicide; on the contrary, in many passages in the *Notebooks* she condemns it.[97] But perhaps she felt that to kill oneself to escape intense and irremediable physical pain is not a real suicide and that one is not forbidden to do it.[98]

Father Perrin had left Marseilles, having been given a mission at Montpellier. (It was because this put him into contact with students that Simone composed for him her "Reflections on the Right Use of School

Studies.") She wrote to him on April 16.[99] She still thought that she would leave France at the end of April.

This letter confirms what Simone's parents and her brother believed to be the reasons that made her decide to leave France. She assuredly wanted to get her parents to a safe place, and she knew that they would not leave without her. This was one of the reasons for her departure, but it was not the principal one. (In the situation that then existed she could still think that if her parents settled in a village, they would not be in any grave danger.) The principal reason, as can be seen from this letter, and as will also be seen from a postcard she sent from Casablanca to de Tarde and from the letters she wrote in New York, and, finally, from the memories of her family, was the desire to be employed in actions useful in the war and, particularly, the hope of realizing her project for a formation of front-line nurses.

She says to Father Perrin: "I do not in the least wish to leave. I shall leave with anguish. The calculations as to the probabilities that are making me decide are so uncertain that they scarcely give me support. The thought guiding me, and that has been in my mind for years, so that I dare not dismiss it although there is little chance of carrying it out, is fairly close to the project with which you had the great generosity to help me a few months ago, and which did not succeed."

The project with which Father Perrin had helped her was certainly that of becoming a farmhand. The project that has been on her mind for years is that of being part of a corps of nurses with the task of caring for the wounded and helping the dying on the battlefield.

But, in any case, she had not completely made up her mind to leave. What made her hesitate was the fear that the conditions of life and the dangers would become worse in Marseilles after her departure and that she would find herself in the position of someone who had run away from danger and misfortune.

"Although the time is near, I have not yet made my decision quite irrevocably. . . .

"You know that for me there is no question in this departure of an escape from suffering and danger. My anguish comes precisely from the fear that, in spite of myself and unwittingly, by going I shall be doing what I want above everything else not to do—that is to say, run away. Up till now we have lived here peacefully. If this peace is destroyed just after I have gone away, it will be frightful for me. . . . If you know anything that might throw any light on what is going to happen, I count on you to tell me."

She must have seen Thibon for the last time before the end of April, in Marseilles.[100] They talked together almost all night. "I had the impression," he says, "of being in the presence of an absolutely transparent soul that was ready to be reabsorbed into original light. I can still hear Simone Weil's voice in the deserted streets of Marseilles as she took me back to my hotel in the early hours of the morning; she was speaking of the Gospel; her mouth uttered thoughts as a tree gives its fruit."[101] She also went to say goodbye to him at the railroad station and rather carelessly handed him a package or a folder containing the *Notebooks*; she wanted him to keep them in his house.

Thibon, greatly saddened by the prospect of not seeing her again, at least for a long time, wrote her a letter on April 27 in which he told her of his sorrow, his friendship for her, and in which he mentioned the *Notebooks* that he had just started to read.

Her departure was not as near as she had thought. During the last days of April or perhaps on the first of May, she wrote to Joë Bousquet: "My departure has been deferred from day to day, so that I am still here. But this time I think it will really be this Wednesday or Thursday. . . ."[102]

So she thought at the beginning of May that she would leave on the sixth or seventh. But a few days later she wrote to Thibon:

"Our departure has been delayed until about the fifteenth of May. Until then many things can happen. Our farewells were premature. Let us not do it again before I am in Casablanca. There, things will be rather clear."

Concerning the sorrow that separation causes she says to him: "All sorrow, especially if it concerns me personally, is, as it were, enveloped on all sides with a layer of indifference. Unfortunately this is not detachment. It is an exhaustion of sensibility due to an accumulation of sufferings, no doubt not great in themselves but disproportionate to the vital energy. This indifference is an imitation of detachment and results from a biological process . . . and it has no value."

And concerning the very friendly letter he had written to her: "The first impression I had from your letter was that there must be some mistake or misunderstanding, otherwise such words could not be addressed to me. My second thought was that I must lie a great deal without knowing it for such a mistake to be possible. My third thought was one of very real and deep gratitude because, in spite of everything, such words seem to infuse additional life. But who knows whether that really does good or harm? . . . In any case, there is in me something stronger than the illusions of pride, something which prevents me from believing words of this kind or even remembering them. . . ."[103]

Among other documents needed to obtain the visas it was necessary to present the police records. Long before this, Simone had asked that hers be sent to her; then she had forgotten about this request. One day she was summoned by the police commissioner. She thought that it was perhaps about the old affair of the Resistance network. But she also had another, even more serious reason for anxiety. To get a German refugee a ration card, she had induced her father to sign a medical certificate in which everything was false. She feared that this was why she was summoned, and, going to the police station with Mme. Weil, she was disconsolate at the thought that she might have compromised her father. But when she walked into the commissioner's office, the commissioner, very amiable, handed her the police records, which had just arrived. Leaving his office, Simone was seized by a fit of uncontrollable laughter.

Finally the departure could be foreseen for May 14. On the twelfth, Simone wrote her remarkable farewell letter to Joë Bousquet.[104] On May 2 he had sent her the letter about the project of front-line nurses,[105] which he had promised. In it he had said that he thought that this project was realizable provided that some of its points were made clearer and more detailed. Simone thanked him for the help that this letter might give her. "If your letter is effective, as I hope, you will have done it not for me but for others through me, for your younger brothers who should be infinitely dear to you since the same fate has struck them. Perhaps some of them will owe you, just before the moment of death, the solace of an exchange of sympathy."

Bousquet had written her in April: "I would like to read some of your mystical impressions. . . . I don't fear in you that sort of feminine lenience that all your aspirations deny. It is because you would not be weak without doing violence to yourself that I expect much from any mystical abandon that you would have grudgingly yielded to."[106] It is because of this request that for the first time she breaks the silence she had maintained on her mystical experience. In this first spiritual autobiography (preceding by two days the long autobiographical letter to Father Perrin), she tells Joë Bousquet what, it seems, she had never told anyone else, and what, after this, she tells in confidence only to Father Perrin: how, and under what circumstances, Christ was revealed to her.

She also speaks of Joë Bousquet's destiny and his ideas, with which she was not fully in accord. "When you say that you don't feel the difference between good and evil, your words are not serious if taken literally because you are speaking of another man in you, who is clearly the evil in you. . . . What you mean is that you have not yet consented to recognize this difference as the distinction between good and evil." She predicts that a moment will come, perhaps quite soon, when he will have to be possessed by good, and if not, he will fall into evil. This moment comes for each of us. As for evil, she says: "The root of evil . . . is daydreaming."

With her letter she sent him George Herbert's poem "Love." Before leaving she also sent him books by Swinburne and T. E. Lawrence, as well as the New Testament in Greek and the poem of the Holy Grail.

Two days later she writes to Father Perrin the other remarkable letter and spiritual autobiography that he published in *Waiting for God.* This letter is so well known that I shall not spend too much time on it. It not only contains the story of Simone's journey as regards Christianity, an account that we have used and quoted more than once, but also a summation of the reasons that force her to remain outside the Church save perhaps at the moment of death.

She had never had, even once or for an instant, the feeling that God wanted her in the Church. She believes that Christianity is Catholic by right but not in fact.

"So many things exist outside it, so many things that I love and do not want to give up, so many things that God loves, otherwise they would not be in existence. . . . I should like to draw your attention to one point. It is that there is an absolutely insurmountable obstacle to the incarnation of Christianity. It is the use of the two little words *"anathema sit."* . . . I remain with all those things that cannot enter the Church, the universal repository, on account of those two little words. I remain with them all the more because my own intelligence is numbered with them. . . . The proper function of the intelligence demands total freedom. . . . In order that the present attitude of the Church might be effective and that she might really penetrate like a wedge into social existence, she would have to say openly that she had changed or wished to change. . . . After the fall of the Roman Empire, which had been totalitarian, it was the Church that was the first to establish a rough sort of totalitarianism in Europe in the thirteenth century, after the war with the Albigenses. . . . And the motive power of this totalitarianism was the use of those two little words: *'anathema sit.'*

She wishes him all possible good things except the cross. For she does not love her neighbor as herself, since she can never succeed in wishing affliction on someone else. "One cannot fail more seriously in the second of the two essential commandments. And as to the first, I fail to observe it in a still more horrible manner, for every time I think of the crucifixion of Christ I commit the sin of envy."

She closes with: "Believe me more than ever and forever in my filial and tenderly grateful friendship."

She had sent him a few days before her departure "The Love of God and Affliction."[107] She had sent to Solange B., who was working as his secretary because his sight was so poor, part of *Intuitions préchrétiennes.*[108] Just at the moment of departure, she asked someone, no doubt Hélène Honnorat, to give him "Forms of the Implicit Love of God."[109]

On May 14 the Weils sailed on the steamship *Maréchal-Lyautey.* Simone spent her last night in Marseilles at the house of the Honnorats. She left Hélène some packages to send for her: for Joë Bousquet, Thibon, and René Nelli, who had loaned her a collection of the works of the troubadours. The Honnorats accompanied her to the boat. They said to her, "We'll be seeing you, Simone, in this world or the next." She said, "No, in the other, one doesn't see anyone."[110] Pointing to the sea, she smiled and said to Hélène, who doubtless regretted the fact that she had not been baptized, "If we are torpedoed, what a beautiful baptismal fount!"

16

New York
(1942)

Not having slept very much during the last nights she spent in Marseilles, Simone rested on the boat. She also wrote some letters. In sight of Oran she finished a letter to Thibon that she had undoubtedly started before sailing. "It seems quite definite that I shall leave. Soon there will be distance between us. Let us love this distance that is wholly woven of friendship, for those who don't love each other cannot be separated.

"You have been, you are, and you always will be a great deal to me.

"There is nothing I admire so much in you as your friendship for me. These words may look like excessive pride, but you know me well enough to see in them an exactly opposite meaning. . . .

"Our departure is becoming more and more definite. The extraordinary beauty of an ocean voyage still prevents me from feeling the laceration. . . ."[1]

To Antonio she wrote:

"Today I am forced to write you something that, I fear, will give you great sorrow. It rends my heart to think of it. In my last letter I mentioned the efforts made by my parents to go to America, and I told you that I could not refuse to accompany them. But I didn't think that these efforts would succeed. They did, and we have very quickly found, by chance, places on a boat.

"I am making this journey across the sea that you found to be so beautiful. As the marvelous presence of the sea all around me fills my entire soul, I think of you.

"What dismays me is that letters take much more time to come from America than from Marseilles. . . . But we shall nonetheless continue writing to each other. Above all, we shall remain united by our thoughts. I shall think of you every day.

"Have you written to the Mexican counsul? If not, do it soon. I have gotten word about you to someone who has an important position in the consulate.

"If that succeeds, perhaps we can meet again on the American continent.

"I bid the stars, the moon, the sun, the blue of the sky, the wind, the birds, the light, and the immensity of space, I bid all this, which always remains with one, I bid all this transmit to you my thoughts about you and give you each day the joy that I wish for you and that you so fully merit.

"Forgive me for not having been able to do anything for you and now for going so far away. . . .

"Believe in my deep friendship.

"P.S. I left Mme. Bercher some money for you, and I hope to be able to send her some again in the future. . . ."

The postscript was surely written in Casablanca, but at the beginning the letter is dated from Oran.

Finally, she wrote to me on an interzone postcard.

"I hope that you've received my last card, on which I sent you some verses. You will see by the postmark on this one that our plan has succeeded. I'm not sorry about it, since this is what I wanted, but I have an immense sorrow in me. You will easily understand this. You no doubt have some of this, too.

"I fervently hope that all will go well for you and that you can bring out of yourself, for everyone's benefit, what you bear within you.

"Perhaps I've never said this to you but in the past the reading of your outline for a thesis had a profound effect on me.

"I also fervently hope that you are happy to the extent that your destiny and your vocation allow.

"You know that I will always think of you."

At Oran the passengers were not permitted to go ashore. They could only send letters. (The postcard I received postmarked Oran was sent on May 18.) The boat then sailed directly to Casablanca. The passports of Simone and the doctor show that they arrived at Casablanca on May 20.

The passengers who, according to Cabaud, numbered nine hundred,[2] were then quartered for the most part in a camp at Aïn-Seba, on the outskirts of Casablanca. They were there for seventeen days. In two large halls they slept on the cement floor, wrapped in their blankets. They had a garden where the rabbis, who were mostly Polish, would gather each morning to say their prayers. Simone observed with astonishment their unfamiliar ritual movements and gestures. The passengers were very badly fed, and many of them became a bit sick because of the food, Dr. Weil among others.

Simone does not seem to have been very sympathetic to her companions in the exodus. Writing to Hélène Honnorat, she said that Father Perrin, if he could have seen them, would have been pained by the spectacle they presented.

"Only the thought of having left France continues to lacerate me."

They could leave the camp but had to ask for official permission, and Simone rarely did this. She went out only once to see Dr. Bercher's wife. (The doctor, who worked as a ship's doctor, was at sea; his wife lived in Casablanca.) While she was out of the camp this one time, perhaps she tried to see the inside of a mosque but failed, for in her letter to Hélène Honnorat she says: "It will reassure you no doubt to know that Europeans here don't have the right to enter the mosques. So I have not prayed to Allah."

She wrote from morning to night, monopolizing one of the camp's few chairs in order to do this. When she had to leave her chair, her mother or father sat down on it to hold it for her. In the morning they would rise before everyone else and at night they would go to bed last —all because of the chair. People were amazed and asked her parents, "What does your daughter do? Is she a journalist?" She was in fact writing commentaries on the Pythagorean texts that form the last part of *Intuitions préchrétiennes*[3] and that she wanted to send to Father Perrin.

On May 26 she wrote to him for the last time.[4] Just before she left Marseilles he had written her a short letter in which, after having quoted St. Paul on divine mercy (*"Deus qui dives est in misericordia propter nimiam charitatem suam . . ."* [Ephesians 2:4], he had said that she was better suited than another to taste the immense joy of Redemption and added: "Although I don't doubt your spiritual incorporation in Christ the Lord, the day of your baptism will be for me a great joy." Simone replied that she hoped she had not given him the impression that she misunderstood God's mercy. She knows this mercy with the certainty of experience— she has touched it. She believes that it is manifest in affliction as well as in joy. "If, by an absurd hypothesis, I were to die without ever having committed any serious faults and yet were to fall to the bottom of hell, I should nevertheless owe God an infinite debt of gratitude for his infinite mercy, on account of my earthly life, and that notwithstanding the fact that I am such a poor unsatisfactory creature. . . . For already here below we receive the capacity for loving God and for representing him to ourselves with complete certainty as having the substance of real, eternal, perfect, and infinite joy. . . . What more can we ask or desire?" Although her imagination, mutilated by long suffering, cannot accept the idea of salvation as something possible for her, there is nothing she lacks. She has a certitude that is always perfectly secure.

"There is only one time," she says, "when I really no longer know anything of this certitude. It is when I am in contact with the affliction of other people, those who are indifferent or unknown to me as much as the others, perhaps even more, including those from the most remote ages of antiquity. This contact causes me such atrocious pain . . . that as a result the love of God becomes almost impossible for me for a while. It would take very little more to make me say impossible. . . . I reassure myself a little by remembering that Christ wept on foreseeing the horrors of the destruction of Jerusalem. I hope he will forgive me my compassion."

As regards baptism, she says: "You have hurt me by writing that the day of my baptism would be a great joy for you. After having received so much from you, it is in my power to give you joy; and yet it doesn't enter my head for a second to do so. I can do nothing about this. I really believe that only God has the power to prevent me from giving you joy."

She tells him again of her infinite gratitude. "I think that, except for you, all those human beings for whom I have made it easy to hurt me through my friendship have amused themselves by doing so, frequently or occasionally, consciously or unconsciously, but all of them at some time or another. When I recognized it to be conscious, I took a knife and cut out the friendship, without however warning the person involved. They didn't behave like this out of malice, but as a result of the well-known phenomenon that makes hens rush upon one of their number if it is wounded, attacking and pecking at it. . . . My situation with regard to you is like that of a beggar . . . who for the space of a year had been going at intervals to a prosperous house where he was given bread, and who for the first time in his life had not suffered humiliation. . . ."

Yet she is not going to give him any signs of her gratitude except to say things about him that might give him every reason to be irritated with her, things that she had no right to say and about which, however, she didn't dare keep silent since she had thought them. Rightly or wrongly, she thinks she can detect a bias in some of his attitudes, above all a certain unwillingness to admit the possibility of implicit faith in special cases. When she told him of unbelievers who are able to accept misfortune as part of the order of the world, this does not have the same effect upon him as when it is a question of Christians who accept misfortune as being the will of God. "Yet it is the same thing." Simone was upset one day when he used the word "false" when he meant to say "nonorthodox." She thinks that she can discern in him a "serious imperfection"; but imperfection does not in the least suit Father Perrin— it is like a "wrong note in a beautiful song."

She believes that this imperfection is his attachment to the Church as to an earthly country. "The children of God should not have any other country here below but the universe itself, with the totality of all the reasoning creatures it ever has contained, contains, or ever will contain. . . . Our love should stretch as widely across all space. . . ." Our epoch demands that universality, which in the past could be implicit, must now be fully explicit. It demands a new kind of saintliness. God's friends have the obligation to produce the genius to invent this new saintliness. "The world needs saints who have genius, just as a plague-stricken town needs doctors. Where there is a need, there is also an obligation."

As for herself, she is only a rotten instrument. "I am too worn out. And even if I believed in the possibility of God's consenting to repair the mutilations of my nature, I could not bring myself to ask it of him. . . . Such a request would seem to me an offense against the infinitely tender Love that has made me the gift of affliction."

But the thoughts she bears within her are perhaps worth much more than she herself. "If no one consents to take any notice of the thoughts that, though I cannot explain why, have been placed in so inadequate a being as myself, they will be buried with me. . . . The fact that they happen to be in me prevents people from paying any attention to them. I see no one but you whom I can implore to give them attention. I should like you to transfer the charity you have so generously bestowed on me to that which I bear within me. . . . It is a great sorrow for me to fear that the thoughts that have descended into me should be condemned to death through the contagion of my inadequacy and my wretchedness."

Having entrusted him with the care of her thought, she again affirms her filial gratitude and boundless friendship.

She addressed this letter to Mlle. Solange B., asking her to give it to Father Perrin. And with the same letter she sent him the commentaries on the Pythagorean texts written at Casablanca; the "Reflections on the Right Use of School Studies," which she had forgotten to give him before her departure; a translation of the dialogue between Electra and Orestes rediscovered among her papers and more complete than the one she had already given him; and no doubt also the notes on folklore, the extracts from Egyptian and Chinese religious texts, and the "Note on the Primitive Relations of Christianity and non-Hebraic Religions," that is, the texts which Father Perrin later donated to the National Library. In her letter to Mlle. B.,[5] she asks her to read Father Perrin these words, which she hopes will not grieve him too much.

"In finishing the work on the Pythagoreans, I felt definitively and certainly, as far as a human being has the right to use these two words, that my vocation imposes upon me the necessity of remaining outside the Church, without so much as committing myself in any way, even implicitly, to her or to the dogmas of Christianity, in any case for as long as I am not quite incapable of intellectual work. And that is in order that I may serve God and the Christian faith in the realm of the intelligence. The degree of intellectual honesty that is obligatory for me, by reason of my particular vocation, demands that my thought should be indifferent to all ideas without exception . . .; it must be equally welcoming and equally reserved with regard to all of them."

She said again near the end of the letter: "It is for the service of Christ as the Truth that I deprive myself of sharing in his flesh in the way he has instituted. He deprives me of it, to be more exact, for never up till now have I had even for a second the impression of there being any choice. I am as certain as a human being has the right to be that I am deprived in this way for my whole life; except perhaps—only perhaps —if circumstances make intellectual work definitively and totally impossible for me."

She also wrote to Thibon: "It indeed seems now that the moment has come to say farewell. It won't be easy for me to often get news from you. I hope that fate will spare the house at Saint-Marcel in which live three beings I love. This is something enormously precious to me. Human existence is so fragile and so vulnerable a thing that I cannot love without trembling. ...."[6]

In his letter of April 27, Thibon had written to her that he had found in her notebooks things that he had already thought and others that were new to him but at the same time familiar, because without possessing them, he had anticipated them. She replied that since that's the way it was, these things belonged to him. "I hope that after undergoing a transmutation in you they will appear one day in one of your books. Because it is certainly much more preferable for an idea to join its fortune to yours than to mine. I have the feeling that my fortune here below will never be good. (Not that I count on it being better elsewhere; I don't think that.) I am not someone with whom it is good to cast one's lot. Human beings have always more or less sensed this; yet, I don't know by what mystery, ideas seem to have less discernment." If her ideas found "a good residence" in Thibon, this would decrease her feeling of responsibility and the crushing weight of the thought that she is incapable of serving the truth to the extent that it appears in her. About her notebooks, she also says: "If during three or four years you don't hear any further talk about me, consider that you own them as your complete property. ...."

She only regrets not being able to entrust him with everything she has within her that has not yet been elaborated. "But fortunately what is in me either is without value or else resides outside of me in a perfect form, in a pure place where it cannot be harmed and from which it can always descend again. ...."

She does not forget that he has said and written to her some comforting words, even when one cannot believe them, which is her case. "They are nonetheless a support. Too much perhaps. ...."

She sent him the end of *Venise sauvée* and informed him that she had asked someone to send him her poems and the "Reflections on the Causes of Liberty and Social Oppression." If this last work interested him, he could do with it what he wished. "For example, if you find it in accord with the taste of our friends on rue Marengo, you could have them cut out a few slices." (The friends on rue Marengo were the people who ran the magazine *Economie et humanisme.*)

She wrote a few more farewell letters and postcards. To Gilbert Kahn: "I have in fact really left, as you can see. I hope that this won't prevent you from getting ideas about Lagneau, Alain, and perception. I don't remember any more whether in this connection I thought of telling you that when Alain read Maine de Biran, he recognized his own thought; although he said (which is a very profound insight), that instead of effort Maine de Biran should have used the word labor."

She preferred that he not read the notebooks she had left with Thibon. "The connection between their contents and the subjects you are concerned with is not distant, yet very hidden, and one does not find it at all clearly indicated. You will not see much more in them than some risky speculations on theological themes. . . ."

To de Tarde she wrote: "I am accompanying my parents, who are going to rejoin my brother. I have gone with them because I have some plans for work that I hope to carry out. . . ."

Just on the eve of her departure from Casablanca, she wrote to me:

"I have left Marseilles, not without a real wrench and sense of laceration. The thought of going away from you was not unconnected with this feeling. May you be good, not unhappy, and use your time well. I commend you with fervor to the diverse divinities of every origin we hold in common. . . . I fear that they don't heed me, but I am sure that they love you. . . . Study them thoroughly. As for myself, I don't count very much on having the time to study them in the present circumstances. At least I do hope that I will have some work to do.

"I am thinking of you as I look at Orion, which you once pointed out to me and which immediately became my personal property.

"Farewell.

"To be surrounded on all sides by the Mediterranean is a marvelous experience. One wouldn't mind, I think, spending one's entire life in this way (at least so it seems). . . ."

She sailed for America with her parents on June 7 on a Portuguese ship, the *S.S. Serpa Pinto*.[7] The crossing lasted almost a month. They stopped at Bermuda, and while they were there a ball was given on the boat.

Simone did not talk very much with the other passengers. Having escaped after a long period of anxiety and privation, they gave themselves up without restraint to the pleasures of eating and whatever other pleasures they could find on board. Simone called the boat the "floating brothel." She had chosen to travel fourth class and suffered a great deal, particularly at night. In the end, not being able to stand it anymore, she began to sleep on the deck.

One of the few passengers she had anything to do with was Professor Léon Herrmann, a Latinist, with whom she had already talked in Casablanca. This professor thought that Christianity had been known in ancient Rome and had already had followers there very soon after the crucifixion of Christ. In the notes she had sent from Casablanca to Father Perrin, she mentioned his ideas.

She also talked with a young student, Jacques Kaplan, a recent baccalaureate graduate who, since he was a scout, took care of the poorest refugee children. He told Jacques Cabaud: "She was very pleasant, very protective, very sarcastic. What especially struck me was the astonishing contrast between her and normal people—or, rather, ordinary people. She couldn't stand the cabin-class passengers because they openly enjoyed the comforts that those in steerage were deprived of. She took an interest in me because, being a 'scout,' I volunteered to take charge of the refugee children in the hold."[8]

She kept in touch with him. It was in New York no doubt that she wrote him a short note in which she scolded him in a gently teasing tone for not doing something he had promised to do for her.[9]

She also became fond of a young mental deficient whom she continued to see while she lived in New York.

The *S.S. Serpa Pinto* disembarked its passengers in New York on July 6. The Weil family lived at first in a hotel; then they moved into an apartment at 549 Riverside Drive. This apartment had a fine view of the Hudson River, but it did not have many doors. The Weils gave their daughter the only room that was closed by a door so that she could work in peace.

Soon after their arrival, André Weil, who knew what the possibilities for such a voyage were, and who moreover wanted to protect his sister from herself, had told her that her plan to leave again for England would be very difficult, if not impossible, to realize. For her, this was a very hard blow. Other people during her first days in America also told her that she was under an illusion; entry into England was strictly controlled and limited. Terribly disappointed, she nevertheless began taking steps to try to obtain what she wanted.

It was undoubtedly very soon after her arrival that she wrote to Jacques Maritain. She wrote to him twice during the month of July. She forwarded to him some letters from Father Perrin and Dom Jacob, explained her plans to him, and sent her project for the group of front-line nurses, along with a copy of Joë Bousquet's letter about this. (She hoped that Maritain could put her into contact with some authorities who might become interested in this plan; that perhaps he would talk to President Roosevelt about it, and even arrange an interview with Roosevelt for her.) Maritain was then traveling; the letters took some time to reach him, so he replied on August 4. His reply was very friendly. He told Simone that her project was inspired by a lofty and noble concept—that he could not judge whether it was practicable but that he hoped with all his heart that he could help her meet with the appropriate authorities. He advised her to go and see Alexandre Koyré, the philosopher, who was about to leave for London and could take her project with him and show it to the leaders of the Free French movement.

Since Simone had also spoken to him of her "spiritual position," he advised her to get in touch with Father Couturier, a Dominican, who at that moment was not in New York but would return soon.

While awaiting Maritain's reply, Simone had also taken other steps. On July 29 she had sent her plan to Admiral Leahy. He had left France in May 1942 and now was the head of President Roosevelt's special staff. She soon received a reply, dated August 3, which came from the Combined Chiefs of Staff, Washington, and was signed by a commander in the U.S. Navy, or his assistant. This informed Simone that Admiral Leahy had indeed received her letter, that he also thanked her for the documents it contained, and that her plan had been sent on to the services that dealt with such matters.

On July 29 she wrote to an English captain who on July 14 had spoken about France with great warmth on American radio. The draft of this letter, written in English, has been found. After having thanked the captain for what he had said, she told him that in view of the sympathy he had shown for the French people, she was taking the liberty of asking a favor of him:

"It is a very hard thing to leave one's country in distress. Although my parents, who wanted to escape anti-Semitism, put great pressure upon me to make me go with them, I would never have left France without the hope that through coming here I could take a greater part in the struggle, the danger, and the suffering of this war.

"I was taking some part over there. I lived in Marseille [sic] since the defeat, and had some important responsibility in the diffusion of what the *New York Times* called the most important underground publication in France: *Les Cahiers du Témoignage chrétien.*

"Yet it did not seem enough. I wanted more. I hoped to get it by coming here. Now I find myself among comfort and security, far from the danger and the hunger, and I feel a deserter. I cannot bear that. If it was to last a long time, it seems to me that it would break my heart. . . .

"I came here with a plan, which I am including in this letter. I beg you to read it attentively. I think it must please you.

"I would wish to put it in practice in a group of French, or English, or American women. . . .

"If that is not practicable, I wish to be sent again to France with precise instructions and a mission—dangerous by choice—in the underground work. . . .

"I think I could even go back legally—with a secret mission.

"I would welcome *any* degree of danger if only I could do something really useful. My life is of no value to me so long as Paris, my native city, is subject to German domination. Nor do I wish my town to be freed only with the blood of others. . . ."

The captain invited Simone to dine with him at his hotel. His letter did not indicate clearly whether this was an invitation to lunch or dinner. To be sure not to miss the appointment, Simone was at the hotel at lunch-time, but it was for dinner, and the captain, who had gone out, only returned at seven o'clock. I don't know what he said to Simone about what she hoped to do, but he probably could not do very much for her.

She also wrote to old classmates who were in London in the Free French organization. On July 28 she wrote to Jacques Soustelle, whom she had known slightly at the Ecole Normale. On July 30 she sent two letters to Maurice Schumann, her old *cagne* classmate at Henri IV. One of these letters must have been sent by regular mail; she entrusted the other to Captain Mendès-France.

In the first letter she tells Maurice Schumann, as she had told the English captain, the plan she had had when she left France. "Although urged by my parents, who wanted to escape anti-Semitism without being separated from me, I would never have left if I had known how difficult it is to get from New York to London. . . ."

She tells him that, when leaving, she had obeyed two ideas, one or the other of which she would like to be able to put into practice. One of them is set forth in the paper that she sent him (the plan for the organization of a group of front-line nurses). The other is based on the idea that she could act more effectively in underground work by leaving France and returning with precise instructions and a precise mission— preferably a dangerous one. The first condition for being able to carry out either of these ideas would be that she be permitted to go to London. She appeals to him as an old comrade and classmate to get her out of the painful moral situation in which she finds herself.[10]

In the other letter she mainly elaborates her second proposal, that of carrying out a mission in France. "I would willingly undertake a mission of sabotage. And as for the transmission of general instructions, I would be all the more suitable for that because I only left France on May 14 of this year and was in contact with the underground movements. In particular I know well, since I have worked with him, the organizer of the paper *Les Cahiers du Témoignage chrétien.* . . . I beg you get me over to London. Don't leave me to die of grief here."

She asked the same thing of Soustelle. She also wrote to Mme. Rosin, with whom the Weils had had very friendly relations in Paris and Montana and who now lived in London. She hoped that Mme. Rosin would perhaps find some way of getting her the authorization she wanted.

When she had received Maritain's letter, she went to see Koyré. He knew people who were working with de Gaulle in London; he wrote to them, asking them to send for her and get her over to England.

While she waited, she champed at the bit. She had read in the papers that in Marseilles on July 14 a patriotic demonstration had been broken up by the police and that there were not only arrests but two persons had been killed and a number wounded. She had been so deeply moved by this that she went two days without eating. What she had feared appeared to have taken place: the situation in Marseilles seemed to have gotten much worse after her departure. The people she met would say to her, "How lucky you are to be here!" She was furious with them and could not bear them.

She told her mother, "I can't go on living like this. If this must go on, I'll go to work in the south with the blacks, and there I am sure I will die because I can't stand this life."

She was absolutely set on leaving. "If I could do it through the Nazis," she told Souvarine, "I would do it!" She harassed all those who she thought had some power to get her to England. She often went to the offices of the Free French movement and the French consulate. It was doubtless at the office of the Free French Delegation that she met Lieutenant Roussy de Sales, who directed propaganda for France in the War Department. She saw him several times. She showed him her plan for the formation of a group of front-line nurses; it seems that he approved of this plan, at least to a certain degree, because she made a point of his approval in her English presentation of the project. But apparently this approval did not suffice to procure the necessary authorization.

In the waiting room at the French consulate, she met a Frenchwoman whom she had known in Marseilles and who also wanted to leave for England. Brought together by their common aim, from then on they met quite often. They both decided to take a course in First Aid. A diploma from this course could further the success of their efforts to get to England. (In Paris, before the defeat, Simone had already taken a course that gave some notion of the nursing profession—perhaps a Red Cross course.) They enrolled in a course in Harlem; except for them, all the other students were black.

Besides this, she went to the public libraries, studying folklore, making an effort also to "dig into the hidden recesses of theology," as she said in a letter to Bercher.

She wrote a few articles in English. An article has been found on the problems in the French colonies ("Concerning Problems in the French Empire"); another about the bad treatment to which black prisoners of war were subjected in Germany ("Treatment of Negro War-Prisoners from the French Army"); and reflections on the state of mind in France and on Gaullism as a political movement.

In New York she again met Noble Hall, the Englishman she had known in Paris and to whom she had spoken of her plan for parachuting into Czechoslovakia. Noble Hall and his wife happened by chance to be in America when the law was passed forbidding persons past a certain age from sailing for England. Being older than the prescribed age, they could not return home. Simone gave Noble Hall one of her articles in English so that he could correct the English, and he did so gladly.

She happened to meet a man named Reeves, who could recommend articles to various magazines. She brought him one of her articles, no doubt the one that dealt with the state of mind in France. A little later, when she was leaving New York, she asked her parents to give him after her departure "Concerning Problems in the French Empire" and "Treatment of Negro War-Prisoners from the French Army." If these articles were accepted, she wanted the first one to be signed with her own name and the second with a pseudonym—Francis Brown. She also asked that very little about her be put in the biographical notes and that nothing should indicate that the two articles were by the same author.

Her parents took the articles to Reeves after her departure. But he finally returned them, along with the article that Simone had given him. None of the magazines he was in contact with had accepted them.

She often visited the churches, above all a Catholic church near her house (Corpus Christi) and a Baptist church in Harlem. She regularly attended Mass on Sunday and often during the week. One Sunday she went to the Catholic Mass first, then to the Baptist ceremony, and in the afternoon she wanted to go to a black synagogue. (There was a small congregation of Ethiopian Jews who had a synagogue she wanted to see. This was the only time she ever went into a synagogue.)

The first time that she went to a Catholic church in America she returned and told her mother, "Have you ever seen anything like it! You pay to get in!"

In a letter to Bercher, no doubt sent in September, she spoke about her visits to the Baptist church: "Every Sunday I go to a Baptist church in Harlem. I am the only white person in the church. After a service of one or two hours, when the atmosphere is established, the religious fervor of the minister and the congregation explodes into dances much like the Charleston, exclamations, cries and the singing of spirituals. That's really worth seeing. A true and moving expression of faith, it seems to me."

Bercher claims that if she had stayed in America she would surely have become a black. Indeed, sympathizing as always with the people at the bottom, she would have willingly shared the life of the black population. Now it is easy, when one lives in this way, soon to be considered by the whites as also being partially of black origin.

She still was trying to find out whether or not her ideas were compatible with belonging to the Church. With this in mind, she had a number of meetings with theologians. Among others she saw several times Dietrich von Hildebrand, a professor of philosophy at Fordham University, to whom Father Perrin had directed her. Since she declared that the spirit of Christianity was closer in spirit to the mind of Greece than that of the Old Testament, he thought at first that she had been tainted by the malady of anti-Semitism propagated by the Nazis. He later realized that this was not so and that her opposition to the Old Testament rested on arguments akin to those of the Gnostics. He did not consider this opinion any more acceptable.[11] She also met Father Oesterreicher. With him, the discussion seems to have become particularly heated and vehement. He had the impression that she thought that the mysteries of Christianity had been better expressed by the Greek philosophers and poets than in the New Testament. This impression does not seem correct, unless Simone had on that day put forward ideas that are different from those in her writings.[12]

Her parents had gone to visit her brother, who was teaching in a college in Pennsylvania, and she wrote to them:

"I have seen the Jesuit to whom the nun from the convent in Brooklyn sent me. After an hour of theological discussion, he explained to me that to his great regret he traveled too often to be able to have repeated meetings with me, and that another Jesuit there, whom he named, would deal with me. That reminded me of 'It's noon, time to go to lunch.' I wonder whether this other fellow will pass me on to a third, and so on, until none of them is left. I feel sorry for them.

"He told me that after I had expended sufficient effort in understanding them, I could certainly read the stories of the massacres in the Old Testament in the proper spirit, given the fact that he doesn't encounter any difficulty."

Soon after she wrote to her brother:

"I have become aware that even in the minds of priests, Catholicism doesn't have fixed frontiers. It is at once rigid and imprecise. There are things of 'strict faith,' but it is impossible to know which they are. If one questions several priests educated in theology as to whether such and such a proposition is 'of strict faith,' some say yes, others 'I think so,' and still others 'I'd say no.' . . .

"Personally, I haven't yet been able to discover whether a priest who baptized me would or would not be committing sacrilege."

Eveline, her sister-in-law, was pregnant and expected to give birth soon. Simone named this future infant "Patapon." She wrote to her parents that she intended to advise her brother to have the infant baptized.

"If Eveline wished it, I would write to André on the matter of baptism. I don't see what objections he could have. He is not one of those people who makes atheism into a religion. . . . I don't see in the name of what he could have even the slightest reason to refuse. I can't imagine the possibility that Patapon, having reached the age of manhood (or womanhood), whatever his state of mind might be, could regret that we have done this for him. There is some point in saying that this can do him good (above all socially), and in any event it cannot do him any harm.

"Not that I am sorry that I wasn't baptized. For otherwise I would not be able to fulfill what seems to be one of my missions on earth, namely, to decrease the time in purgatory for several Jesuits and others by forcing them through the torture of reflection. But there is little probability that Patapon is destined to follow me in this task. At least I hope this for him and his immediate relations. . . ."

She adds: "Since the letters arrive at Haverford and are then forwarded, I suppose that Father Perrin, after having gotten to know the prose sent from Casablanca, has arrived at Father O.'s conclusion as to my spiritual affiliation (the devil via Marcion), and that the absence of letters is explained in this way. . . ." She ends by saying: "Don't forget Krishna."

She had less and less hope of being able to leave for England. On September 10 she wrote to Thibon, from whom she had received a letter (it was the first she had received from France): "Your letter has awakened a very painful echo in me. I have far more considerable reasons for heartbreak, since for me the separation is from an entire country and a country that contains almost everything I love. And above all, I myself am the cause of this separation. I had resolved to leave partly because of my parents but most of all because of a project that had been in my thoughts for years and that I had hoped to realize here. . . . I knew that the probability was remote, but I didn't dare take the responsibility of giving up even the slightest opportunity, because this idea seems to me to have been sent me by God. For this reason, I decided, not without pain and anguish, to leave. But up until now all my efforts have been fruitless. That forcibly impresses upon me the feeling that I have made a mistake about the will of God, or lack the faith to accomplish it. In both cases, there is a defect in obedience. So the pain of separation is made intolerably sharp and bitter by the added sense of my shortcomings. . . .

"If you happen to pray for me, ask that I get the chance to accomplish either the thought for which I have come here, or something similar; and if I am not worthy, that it might be granted me to become worthy. . . .

"At this moment the mere recollection of the streets of Marseilles or of my little house by the Rhone pierces my heart. . . ."[13]

She had perhaps written to President Roosevelt when she had sent him the plan for her formation of a front-line nurses' group. The White House replied that a recent discovery concerning the use of blood plasma had already improved the treatment given the wounded at the front.[14]

The birth of Patapon, who turned out to be a girl (Sylvie), took place on September 12. It appears that immediately after having heard the news, Simone wrote her brother a letter in which she advised him to have Sylvie baptized.

"I would not hesitate for a second," she says, "if I had a child to have it baptized by a priest. There would be only one reason to hesitate: if the child might regret it later on. Sylvie would not have the shadow of a reason to regret having been baptized by a priest unless she later turned toward a fanatical Judaism, which isn't very probable. If she turns to atheism, Buddhism, Catharism, Hinduism, or Taoism, what would it matter to her that she had been baptized? If she turns to Christianity, Catholic or Protestant, which is indeed her right, she will be very happy about it. If her fiancé is a Jew, an atheist, Buddhist, etc., her baptism will not be an inconvenience; she will not be responsible for it. If a more or less anti-Semitic piece of legislation grants advantages to baptized half-Jews, it will be agreeable for her, probably, to enjoy these advantages without having done anything cowardly. In summation, I believe that if she is not baptized, in twenty years she may be discontented with you."

In the same letter she says that she has gotten to know a broad-minded and very intelligent French Dominican, Father Couturier. (Maritain, as we recall, had told her to go and see this priest, whenever he might be in New York.) She advises André to entrust the religious instruction of Alain, Eveline's son, to this priest and offers to write to him about it.

Her brother no doubt having answered her immediately, since she had asked him to do so, she then wrote the draft of a letter to Father Couturier on September 15. This draft is the first outline for the *Letter to a Priest.*[15] To begin with, she asks Father Couturier whether he could give her advice about Alain, or even take over his religious education. Then, taking advantage of the opportunity, she tells him that she would like to talk to him when he is free about her own affairs, and in the meanwhile she tells him in detail what she would like to ask him.

"I would like," she says, "for you to tell me, after study and reflection and in a precise and completely certain manner, if a priest legitimately can or cannot grant baptism to a person who has the following opinions and could not be persuaded to abandon them. . . . I don't ask for a discussion of these opinions in terms of their fundamental merits. I would like first of all a precise and certain answer as to the compatibility or incompatibility of each of these opinions with membership in the Catholic Church. All these opinions, in my mind, are accompanied by a question mark. . . . But those of my thoughts that accord with the teachings of the Church are also accompanied in me by a question mark, and to the same degree."

She then makes a list of her "supposed heresies." This list is not as long as the one that is found in *Letter to a Priest;* it has only fifteen points instead of thirty-five. These fifteen points are all found in *Letter to a Priest*, where they are often more fully developed and placed in a different order. She ends by saying: "All this is far from being a game for me. I have been drawn since childhood to the Catholic faith. I have thought about these things for years, with all the intensity of love and attention at my disposal—a lamentably feeble intensity, unfortunately for me, owing to my imperfection, but that always continues to grow, it seems to me. Now to the extent that it grows, the thoughts that keep me apart from the Church assume in me ever greater force. (The thoughts that drew me to it follow the same progression, of course.) Hence I have, it seems to me, but a very weak hope or none at all of ever receiving the sacraments, unless the Church modifies the conditions under which it grants them. I hope that one day it will do so, because I believe that for it it is a matter of life or death; but I don't expect that this can happen in my lifetime. . . ."

It was about this time, that is, in mid-September, that Simone seems to have regained some hope of sailing for London. Her parents having written her that they would open a bottle of burgundy when she comes to see her niece, she replied, most likely on September 17: "The hope of departure has bucked up my morale, but not to that point, especially since I dare not believe it until I am actually on the boat." Also a letter she wrote to the Honnorats on September 23 shows that just a few days before she had again felt it possible to enjoy things. Speaking of what is beautiful, good, and interesting in New York, she says: "For almost three months now my state of mind has made me absolutely incapable of enjoying all this or almost anything whatever. Only in the last few days did I feel capable of this, since I believe I see a chance of working."

It was certainly a letter from Maurice Schumann that had given her some hope. He had spoken about her to André Philip, Commissioner of the Interior and Labor in the National Committee of the Free French movement. Philip had judged the plan for a corps of front-line nurses impractical, but he seemed disposed to bring Simone to London and to entrust her with some kind of work. It was then that she wrote to Maurice Schumann the undated letter sent from New York:

"Your letter brought me great encouragement at a time when the distress of being so far away from the scene of struggle and suffering . . . was becoming very hard to bear. . . .

"A thousand thanks for having spoken to André Philip about me. I am glad he is well disposed toward me. I very much hope I shall see him if he comes here. . . .

"The suffering all over the world obsesses me and overwhelms me to the point of annihilating my faculties, and the only way I can revive them and release myself from the obsession is by getting for myself a large share of danger and hardship. . . . I beseech you to get for me, if you can, the amount of hardship and danger that can save me from being wasted by sterile grief. That is a necessary condition before I can exert my capacity for work.

"I would accept any provisional work anywhere—propaganda or press, for example, or anything else. But if it was a job not involving a high degree of hardship and danger, I could only accept it provisionally; otherwise I should be consumed by the same grief in London as in New York. . . . It is not, I am certain, a question of character only, but of vocation. . . ."

She tells Schumann that she has had an evolution that runs parallel to his. True enough, she has not been baptized, but she feels that she is not lying when she says that she is Catholic in the etymological sense of the word. "I adhere totally to the mysteries of the Christian faith, with the only kind of adherence that seems to me appropriate for mysteries. This adherence is love, not affirmation. Certainly I belong to Christ— or so I hope and believe. But I am kept outside the Church by philosophical difficulties that I fear are irreducible. They do not concern the mysteries themselves but the accretions of definitions with which the Church has seen fit to clothe them in the course of centuries, and above all the use in this connection of the words *'anathema sit.'* . . ."

A few days later she received a letter from André Philip and also a letter from Jacques Soustelle, both of which confirmed Schumann's.

I imagine that it was also around mid-September or in the second half of the month that she wrote to Dr. Bercher. He was then on the *S.S. Oregon,* a ship immobilized in port by the American blockade of Guadeloupe in the West Indies, as were all Vichy ships that were found in the Western hemisphere at the moment of Laval's declaration: "I am for a German victory." This letter is not dated, but Simone indicates in it that she already had hopes of seeing her plans succeed.

"I am quite happy," she says, "to have gotten word from you, although your situation seems quite wretched. You must be really fed up, knowing that your son is growing and his character forming far from you. . . . I am fed up too, seriously. . . . I was much happier when we took walks together. . . . I'm trying to put through my little plans, which you know about, and so I haven't looked for work here, since I expected to leave New York, barring unforeseen obstacles, not too long from now. . . ." It was in this letter that she described the church in Harlem.

In her letter of September 23 to the Honnorats, she says: "I was very glad to receive your letter. It did me good at a moment when I was crushed by the pain of being so far away from France and so uncertain about the fate of those I love, by the obsession with the misfortunes that I no longer have the comfort of sharing, by the remorse of having deprived myself of this consolation, and by the grief of failing in my plans for work.

"At present I have some hopes of obtaining, if not the kind of work for which I had hoped—no influential person here wants to accept my arguments on this point—at least something else that can perhaps somewhat satisfy me. . . . I hope to leave New York in about a month to reach my place of work. . . . My parents will send you the news about me. . . . As usual, they dream of going with me, but, practically, that can't be arranged."

She also wrote about New York: "If France's situation didn't make its memory obsessive, my stay in New York could be very pleasant and very interesting. I always feel at home in a big city. Seen from above, the skyscrapers are marvelous, with a chaotic beauty that resembles that of rock cliffs or crags. From street level most of them are ugly, except for the Rockefeller buildings, which have come off perfectly. But beautiful or ugly, the streets are always extremely attractive. And Harlem is a very interesting place. . . ."

Finally she asked them if the letters she sent from Casablanca to Father Perrin had been lost, or "if their envelopes had given off too sharp a smell of sulfur," or if something had happened to him. She hoped that anything but this last possibility was the case.

On September 23 and the subsequent days she took the examination for which she had prepared by following the course in First Aid. After this, she spent the last days of the month at her brother's house.

When they showed her Sylvie, she exclaimed to the infant, "How beautiful you are in your angel's robe!" She asked permission to give her her bottle and did it very well.

When she spoke to André about Christianity and told him that if certain problems hadn't kept her outside the Church, she would have been baptized, he said to her, "I can only see one problem: it is that you would have exactly the same reasons for adhering to Hinduism, Buddhism, or Taoism, etc." She seemed to approve of this objection. I say "seemed" because I wonder what the meaning of this apparent approval was. In some of her writings,[16] she says that the tradition to which it is good for Europeans to adhere is the Christian tradition rediscovered in its purity, that is, united with the Greek tradition. If, in the absolute, she placed other traditions at the same level, if she says that non-European peoples must preserve their own religions and find in them what we find in Christianity, she does not, however, seem to have thought that for herself and for Europeans in general the choice was free and a matter of indifference. Certainly she loved Krishna, but Krishna's story certainly moved her much less than Christ's,[17] and if she often uses his name when she speaks or writes to others, in her *Notebooks* she mentions him much less often than Christ. (He is scarcely mentioned at all in the American *Notebooks*.) And it is in the *Notebooks* that she speaks for herself without any concern about making herself understood by someone else or of modestly veiling what she really believes.

The significance of this approval was perhaps that she fully recognized the value of certain non-Christian religions and that in her view the Church did not recognize this, or not sufficiently. Indeed, this was one of the reasons that made it difficult for her to enter the Church. But this did not exactly mean that she personally had just as many reasons to embrace all these different religions.

After three or four days she left. When Eveline said to her, "Well, we'll be seeing you, Simone," she puckered her lips and smiled, as she often did, and, looking straight at Eveline, said, "No, goodbye." She was sure of not returning.

Back in New York on September 30, the day after that she wrote to her parents, who had stayed with their son, telling them to say hello to Sylvie for her and joking about the demons that since her visit she claimed must now inhabit her niece: "Greetings to Sylvie and to the seven demons who must be living in her since my visit."

Mme. Souvarine, who saw her often when Dr. and Mme. Weil were staying with André, says that she talked a great deal about Sylvie, with the idea that this child would be a consolation to her parents when she herself had left.

She had not forgotten the problem of Alain's religious education. She studied a religious manual to assure herself that the teaching of Christian doctrine, if performed intelligently, would not be harmful to a child. She wrote to her brother, probably during the month of October:

"I studied hard the *Manual of Piety* that cast its shadow over Pierre Honnorat's childhood, and I've concluded that the two troublesome things for children are the confession and the daily prayer.

"As for the confession, you must really convince Alain once and for all . . . that he need not worry about it. That he should not torture himself for fear of forgetting something, or go into great detail, or force himself to say things which are annoying to say, when they can be dealt with in general terms.

"As for prayers, I believe that the Our Father said once a day but said with the greatest possible attention is the most that can be expected of a child, and perhaps even of an adult. The 'acts of faith,' etc., in these books of piety are really frightful. . . ."

She had written a letter to Father Couturier in the second half of September that, unlike the draft prepared on September 15, dealt almost solely with Alain. For she had devoted another letter, the long *Letter to a Priest,* to finding out whether her opinions were or were not compatible with belonging to the Church, and this was sent to Father Couturier just when she was leaving. So she wrote to the father about Alain and the reply she must have received in the course of the month of October, either in writing or in direct conversation, was a favorable one. He agreed to do something about Alain. After Simone's departure and during the Christmas holidays, he gave André and Eveline advice about Alain's religious education and he himself prepared him for his first communion the following spring. Sylvie was baptized in New York a little later.

With the hope of leaving for England, Simone seems to have been visited by inspiration and began writing in her notebooks again. In fact the major part of the American notebooks seem to have been written in October 1942 or the period around this month. True enough, it is difficult to establish with certainty the chronology of the texts published in *La Connaissance surnaturelle* (Paris: Gallimard, 1950). This would require a minute study that cannot be done at this point. But it seems to me, provisionally, that of the seven notebooks regarded as having been written in America,[18] at least four, *Notebooks* IV to VII, were written in the month of October 1942.[19] However, *Notebook* III was terminated in October, as is shown by Simone's note at the end of the manuscript.[20] It can therefore be supposed that this notebook, which was ended in October, had been started in September. For the previous period there only remain *Notebooks* I and II. Now *Notebook* I[21] seems to have been begun at Marseilles and continued at Casablanca; and *Notebook* II,[22] outside of certain passages that were written before her arrival in New York,[23] is in great measure composed of notes taken in the libraries. It is therefore true that her great sadness and grief had made Simone almost incapable of working for about two and a half months.

It is in *Notebook* V that one finds the terrible prayer:

"Father, in the name of Christ grant me this.

"That I may be unable to will any bodily movement, or even any attempt at movement, like a total paralytic. That I may be incapable of receiving any sensation. . . . That I may be unable to make the slightest connection between two thoughts. . . .

"Father, in the name of Christ grant me all this in reality. . . ."

She asks God to strip away her will, her sensibility, her intelligence, even love itself insofar as her love is something in her. "May all this be stripped away from me, devoured by God, transformed into Christ's substance, and given for food to afflicted men whose body and soul lack every kind of nourishment. And let me be a paralytic—blind, deaf, witless, and utterly decrepit.

"Father, effect this transformation now, in the name of Christ; and although I ask it with imperfect faith, grant this request as if it were made with perfect faith.

"Father, since thou art the Good and I am mediocrity, rend this body and soul away from me to make them into things for your use, and let nothing remain of me, forever, except this rending itself, or else nothingness."

She realizes that one does not voluntarily ask for such things. "One comes to it in spite of oneself. In spite of oneself, but one consents." Such a prayer only has value if the Spirit compels one to utter it. Then, speaking of consent, of the union of the soul with God, she offers this sad thought:

"But all these spiritual phenomena are absolutely beyond my competence. . . . They are reserved for those who possess, to begin with, the elementary moral virtues. I can only speak of them at random. And I cannot even sincerely tell myself that I am speaking at random."[24]

André Philip landed in America in October. Simone had an interview with him. As a result, it was understood that she would join his staff, on which there was also Louis Closon, a friend of André's. Simone's conversation with Philip filled her with admiration for him and gratitude, since he was making it possible for her to get to England.

Departure was near. Knowing that her parents would be deeply troubled and upset, she was particularly loving toward them. She would often hug them. They in fact began to make plans to try to follow her to England. But she was afraid that if they took any official steps now her own departure might be compromised and asked them not to do anything until she had left.

On November 4 she wrote to her brother, mainly about their parents. "The fact that they look quite young does not prevent them from being elderly and tired and needing a good deal of coddling. Young people can fall and get up again but with them, if they ever crack, that may be the end. . . . My departure will unfortunately be a great sorrow for them. . . ."

She wrote her great letter to Father Couturier (*Letter to a Priest*). She also wrote to Jean Wahl. He had escaped from the occupied zone and arrived in Marseilles just after Simone's departure, and later on they missed each other again in New York. He had sent her a letter in which he seemed to say that certain Frenchmen, who had gotten to America, thought Simone was in sympathy with Vichy.

"You speak mysteriously," she wrote, "in a way that seems to imply that certain people are spreading strange rumors about me. Is it being said, by any chance, that I am sympathetic to Vichy? If so, you can deny it. In June 1940 I fervently hoped that Paris would be defended, and I only left after I had seen with consternation the placards declaring it an open city. I stopped at Nevers in the hope that there would be a front on the Loire. I was dismayed again by the news of the armistice, after which I immediately resolved to try to get to England. I tried every possibility that offered itself, including dangerous ones. When I left France, it was solely with the idea of getting to England. Meanwhile, before leaving France, I took part in the distribution of illegal literature. As soon as I arrived here I wore everybody out with supplications to be sent to England, and at last I am going there, thanks to André Philip, who has found a job for me with him (incidentally, he is a very, very fine person, completely first-rate). Ever since the day when I decided, after a very painful inner struggle, that in spite of my pacifist inclinations it had become an overriding obligation in my eyes to work for Hitler's destruction, with or without any chance of success, ever since that day I have never swerved from my resolve; and that day was the one on which Hitler entered Prague. . . . My decision was tardy, perhaps. Indeed, I think so, and I bitterly reproach myself for it. But anyhow, since I adopted this position, I haven't budged. . . .

"What may have given rise to such rumors is the fact that I don't much like to hear perfectly comfortable people using words like coward and traitor about people in France getting by as best they can in a terrible situation. There is only a small number of Frenchmen who almost certainly deserve such epithets. . . . There was a collective act of cowardice and betrayal, namely the armistice; the whole nation bears the responsibility, including Paul Reynaud, who ought never to have resigned. I myself was immediately appalled by the armistice, but in spite of that, I think that all the French, including myself, are as much to blame for it as Pétain. From what I saw at the time, the nation as a whole welcomed the armistice with relief. . . . On the other hand, I think that since then, Pétain has done just about as much as the general situation and his own physical and mental state allowed to limit the damage. The word traitor should only be used about those of whom one feels certain that they desire Germany's victory and are doing what they can to that end. As for the others, some of those who are prepared to work with Vichy or even with the Germans may have honorable motives that are justified by particular situations. And others may be constrained by pressures that they could only resist if they were heroes. Most of the people here, however, who set themselves up as judges have never had an opportunity to find out if they themselves are heroes. . . ."

She would have liked very much to discuss philosophical problems with Wahl. She gave him a kind of summary of her thoughts on the history of philosophy and religion:

"I believe that one identical thought is to be found—expressed very precisely and with only slight differences of modality—in the ancient mythologies; in the philosophies of Pherecydes, Thales, Anaximander, Heraclitus, Pythagoras, Plato, and the Greek Stoics; in the Greek poetry of the great age; in universal folklore; in the *Upanishads* and the *Bhaga-vad-Gita;* in the Chinese Taoist writings and in certain currents of Buddhism; in what remains of the sacred writings of Egypt; in the dogmas of the Christian faith and in the writings of the greatest Christian mystics, especially St. John of the Cross; and in certain heresies, especially the Cathar and Manichean tradition. I believe that this thought is the truth, and that it today requires a modern and Western form of expression. That is to say, it should be expressed through the only approximately good thing we can call our own, namely science. This is all the less difficult because it is itself the origin of science. . . .

"As regards the Jews, I think that Moses knew this wisdom and refused it, because, like Maurras, he conceived of religion as a simple instrument of national greatness; but when the Jewish nation had been destroyed by Nebuchadnezzar, the Jews, completely disoriented and scattered among many nations, received this wisdom in the form of foreign influences and introduced it, so far as was possible, into their religion. . . .

"I think that the first eleven chapters of Genesis (up to Abraham) can only be a translation, mutilated and recast, of an Egyptian sacred book; that Abel, Enoch, and Noah are gods, and that Noah is identical with Osiris, Dionysus, and Prometheus. I think that Shem, Ham, and Japheth correspond, if not to three races, at least to three human families, three forms of civilization; and that Ham alone witnessed the nakedness and intoxication of Noah, that is to say, received the revelation of mystical thought. . . .

"The 'Hamitic' stream of thought is traceable everywhere as a thread of light all through prehistory and history. . . . But it is everywhere threatened with destruction by pride and the will to domination, the spirit of Japheth and Shem. It had been almost destroyed throughout the whole of the Roman Empire at the time of the birth of Christ, who was a perfect and consequently a divine expression of it, to judge by the writings that he inspired. Today, Hitler and many others are trying to abolish it throughout the world.

"I will not hide from you that the 'existentialist' line of thought appears to me, so far as I know it, to be on the wrong side; on the side that is alien in thought to the revelation received and transmitted by Noah—on the side of force. . . ."[25]

She asked her parents to say goodbye for her to several people she had not been able to see and to write to Antonio for her.

She sailed on November 10 on a Swedish freighter. Her parents were not allowed to go aboard the ship; they had to say goodbye in a kind of long open shed that ran along the dock. As they parted, Simone said, "If I had several lives, I would have devoted one of them to you, but I have only one life."

17

London
(1942-1943)

The crossing from New York to Liverpool took about fifteen days. Soon after her arrival Simone wrote to her parents: "The voyage was pleasant. A lot of rolling, but nobody on board was seasick. A few extremely cold days, but the ship was heated. No incidents. Morale good."[1]

May Mesnet was able to question one of her travel companions, E. A. Kirby, an Englishman and district officer in the fire brigade. What he told her adds a few strokes to the brief picture given us by Simone. The sea was not too rough considering the time of the year. There were ten passengers aboard. In this small group, brought closer together by the common danger and the unusual nature of a crossing in wartime, Simone as a rule became a kind of leader and would think of what to do. In the evenings she would gather the group together and tell folk tales. She encouraged the others to tell the same sort of stories, if they happened to know any. She longed for a moonlit night so that they could have their meetings on the deck; but usually the sky was overcast. But one night her wish was granted—though some of the passengers were much less delighted than she, since clear weather was favorable to torpedo boat attacks. She dragged her companions out on the deck, near the prow, and told them folk tales.

E. A. Kirby remembers having discussed God and human misfortune with Simone. Once, when he pointed out to her that she didn't eat enough, she said that she didn't have the right to eat more than her compatriots back in France. She seemed obsessed with the idea of getting to France, as if she had a special mission to help the French people.

The Allied landing in North Africa took place on November 8. Some of the passengers expressed the hope that the war would end soon. Simone reminded them that even when the war was over, there would still be many problems and indeed a great deal of suffering.

Having reached Liverpool around the twenty-fifth of November, she was immediately sent with her companions to a clearing center popularly known as the "patriotic school," which was situated on the outskirts of London. All those who landed in England were kept there by the security services for a few days so they could be questioned and to identify possible spies or persons whose presence was undesirable in wartime. Generally one stayed there from six to ten days, but Simone was kept for eighteen and a half days. Was this because her old activity as a determined pacifist was known to the English police? Or was it because they remembered her brother's decision at the start of the war? Simone appears to say that it was chiefly due to the latter, for in recounting her misadventure to her parents, she adds: "Antigone as usual!"[2]

But living conditions at the center were not too bad. "At any rate, we were very well treated," Simone says, "and it was quite comfortable."[3] She learned how to play volley ball; and she amused herself or rather tried to amuse the others by playing pranks. One night, when they had all gone to bed, Simone dressed up as a ghost to entertain them. Yet time seemed to pass very slowly; it was absolutely forbidden to write, telephone, or telegraph. Finally Maurice Schumann was informed that her detention was being prolonged; he intervened and got her released.

So on December 14 Simone was free in London. She stayed temporarily in the barracks that housed the Free French women volunteers. She went to see Schumann and Closon; she knew Schumann but had not seen him for some time, while this was her first meeting with Closon. On the sixteenth she visited her friends the Rosins. It was from their place that she wrote her first letter to her parents. As can be seen from this letter, she was well received by Schumann and Closon ("Schumann was very sweet, and Closon welcomed me as if we had been pals for ten years"), but she already realized that it would be difficult to put her plans into effect. "My own little plans don't seem to be very popular. This will undoubtedly please you. I still don't know at all what my job will be, or whether I'll be in civvies or in uniform. . . . But I am infinitely and totally happy to have crossed the ocean again. Only, so far, I still continue to regret, for myself (for you it's an entirely different matter), the decision I made last May. . . ." She regretted all the more having left Marseilles, since the former free zone in France was now occupied by the Germans; and so now more than ever she had the unendurable impression that she had run away.

She gives her parents to understand that it won't be easy for them to get authorizations to come to England. They themselves were becoming aware of this. Immediately after her departure, they presented applications both to the Free French Delegation and the British consulate, and in both cases were turned down. Later on André Philip did everything in his power to help them get the authorization to leave, but he never succeeded.

Philip decided that Simone should work in the civilian department as an editor and gave Closon, who directed his cabinet and handled all activities concerning France, the job of finding work for her. At the start Closon was somewhat uncertain and embarrassed, but he soon realized that what she should do was write. She was boiling with ideas. So she was given a small office in which she was alone and could write in peace. This particular department had been installed in a private house at 19 Hill Street.

In France, the Resistance committees were developing projects for the reorganization of the country after the war, and these projects were being sent on to London. Philip told Simone to examine some of them.

Although terribly disappointed at being employed in this way, and not in the least intending to give up her plans for dangerous missions, which in fact she continued to request, nevertheless, with her boundless good will, Simone immediately set to work. She examined the documents that had been given to her and so was led to express her own ideas on the problems they dealt with. The sheer amount of what she wrote in London in a few months is almost beyond belief. She must have written day and night, scarcely taking the time to sleep. More than once she spent the entire night in her office, where she voluntarily locked herself in. Not only did she write the "papers" published in *Ecrits de Londres*—"Human Personality" [originally published in French as '*La personne et le sacré*'], "Are We Fighting for Justice?" "The Legitimacy of the Provisional Government," "Draft for a Statement of Human Obligations," "Remarks on the New Constitutional Project," "Essential Ideas for a New Constitution," "A War of Religions," "Reflections on Revolt," "Note on the General Suppression of Political Parties"—but she also wrote the book entitled *The Need for Roots*,[4] "Is There a Marxist Doctrine?" and the fragments connected with it;[5] "Concerning the Colonial Problem in Its Relation to the Destiny of the French People";[6] "Notes on Cleanthes, Pherecydes, Anaximander, and Philolaus";[7] a translation of extracts from the *Upanishads;*[8] the "Theory of the Sacraments" and the profession of faith that was published under the title "Last Text,"[9] the London notebook;[10] certain unpublished reports; and finally some "observations" that are also unpublished and deal with an essay on Hitler.

It is difficult to establish whether some of these writings were not done, at least in part, after she entered the hospital. The doctor who treated her in the hospital had given strict orders that she was not to do anything at all; and he had agreed to relax this order only for the letters she wrote to her family. But it is quite likely that she didn't always obey this prescription. In any event, except for the end of the London notebook, we don't see any clear signs (especially in the handwriting) that would allow us to affirm that certain works were composed in the hospital. Until a minute study of these manuscripts can be carried out, all that one can say is that it is possible that all these works were written between the middle of December and the middle of April, that is to say, over a period of four months.

She wrote almost without any changes or erasures, as if swept along by a firm and continuous inspiration. Her handwriting is always slowly formed, regular, and pure. She expressed her ideas, which were often daring and paradoxical, with an ever-increasing tranquil assurance.

It is out of the question to try to analyze here and in detail all the various writings of this period. Besides, one can find in them many ideas that she already had expressed before. Yet in these last writings she has become fully conscious of her philosophical and religious thought and expresses its essentials. There is no doubt at all that she wanted to sketch the broad outlines of a doctrine. "A doctrine does not suffice," she says, "but it is indispensable to have one, if only to avoid being misled by false doctrines."[11] This sentence is the beginning of an unfinished, scarcely begun draft that bears the title "Sketch for the Foundation of a Doctrine (Chiefly for the Use of Study Groups in France)."

She does lay the foundations of a doctrine in the text entitled "Profession of Faith,"[12] which is the prologue to the "Draft for a Statement of Human Obligations" and which seems to have been written expressly as a proposed examination for Resistance groups. This profession of faith begins with the words: "There is a reality located outside the world, that is to say, outside space and time, outside man's mental universe, outside the entire domain that human faculties can reach. Corresponding to this reality, at the center of the human heart, is a longing for an absolute good, a longing that is always there and is never satisfied by any object in this world."

By "a reality located outside this world," she obviously means God. However, in this profession of faith, she never names God; she always refers to him, as in the beginning, by such expressions as "a reality other than that of this world," "the other reality," "the reality located beyond all human faculties," and "the reality alien to this world." The reason that she avoids naming God can be found in a note written in London: "To gather people behind Christian aspirations. . . . It is necessary to try to define them in terms that an atheist might adhere to completely, and do this without depriving these aspirations of what is specific to them. . . . One would have to propose something precise, specific, and acceptable to Catholics, Protestants, and atheists—not as a compromise . . . and from then on demand that the Resistance organizations . . . declare whether this is their orientation. . . . Even a professed Christian needs this sort of translation. . . ."[13]

The "Profession of Faith" was by its spirit intended to inspire the activity of all the men to whom some power in society would be entrusted. Evidently, it had to be acceptable to all men of good will, including those who are or think they are atheists. Yet Simone makes it clear that this is not a question of compromise; that this interpretation must not strip Christian aspirations of what is peculiar to them; that in fact this interpretation is needed by Christians themselves. So she does not intend to deviate from Christianity but rather to express its very depths. She does not in any way wish to obliterate God, but on the contrary wants to define him by a description that, in her view, is essential to the idea of the true God. For her, two things are essential to this idea: one is that God is the Good, and the other is that he is outside the world, at least in a sense.

Does his existence outside of the world, that is to say, his transcendence, simply mean that he is a personal God? It does not seem so. Besides, in more than one of her writings she affirms that there are in God at one and the same time personal and impersonal aspects.[14] In "Human Personality" she speaks of a "higher good" that is impersonal.[15] In "Is There a Marxist Doctrine?" she says that certain Buddhists who exclude the notion of a personal God have nevertheless elevated themselves to the mystical life.[16] Now the faith whose essentials she wishes to define here is assuredly, in her eyes, the faith common to all mystics.

So the affirmation that absolute good is located outside the world does not at all mean that God is a personal God. Instead it means—and this can be seen in the *Notebooks*—that the entire world is a domain that stands outside the Good, at least in one sense. The world (if one leaves aside thinking beings) does not contain any specific cause that tends toward the good. It is governed by another principle—necessity—and there is not the slightest rent or loophole in the fabric of necessity. In this world God is silent, God does not intervene, God is absent from the world, except for those human beings who turn their attention and their love toward him.

Thus the "Profession of Faith" seems to present this concept as the first proposition, the basis of the doctrine that Simone Weil wanted to develop and elaborate. Besides, it is certain that a clear separation between good and necessity, God and the world, is a characteristic trait of her religious thought. Yet this separation is not absolute, as we shall see; in her view, necessity's indifference to the good is willed by good itself. But the separation must first be posited. There are two domains, and in the one where necessity reigns good is, as it were, prevented from reigning directly. In Simone's thought, this profound division is bound up with more than one preoccupation. In the first place, it is evident that Simone wants to preserve the scientific vision of the world. She is anxious to leave intact the pure determinism that is the postulate of science and of all objective knowledge. What's more, she admires and loves pure necessity. This necessity without regard for the good or for us, harsh as it may be, she considers beautiful and believes that one must love it, accept it in everything that does not depend on us. This separation of the two domains is also in keeping with her rigorous conception of the Good. With Kant, she believes that good must never be conceived on the basis of what is shown us by fact; good is as irreducible to fact as the latter is to good. And with Plato, she criticizes those who don't know "how great is the real difference between the necessary and the good. . . ."[17] What especially moves her is the idea that to put good in the world—"in front of the curtain," as she expresses it—would mean to fail in the respect and compassion that one owes the unfortunate; for it would mean that one believed that misfortune is always a just punishment. Finally, she wants to safeguard the purity of the love directed to God. This God exiled from the world is the only God for whom love can be really pure.[18] A God who was powerful in the world could not be loved with a love that didn't have some admixture of base feelings. To set God beyond the world is the same as only wanting to love him through Christ. Thus science by presenting its conception of the world as pure necessity not only is not contrary to Christianity but actually is indispensable to it; it is part of true religion.

Alain regretted the fact that Christians included power among the list of divine attributes; it seemed to him that love for God was spoiled by this. Simone preserves the idea of divine omnipotence, but she believes that the God who possesses this omnipotence does not exercise it. In the world, he has abdicated from it in favor of necessity. Even in men's souls the presence of God is but an infinitesimal speck, for the soul as well as the body is subjected to necessity, even though it be a necessity that is different from that which governs the body. The soul escapes necessity only to the extent that a ray of light coming from another world falls upon it, and on the condition that this light is desired or that one consents to receiving it.

God, even in the soul, is but a beggar. He calls to men in secret, but if they don't answer his call, he will not allow himself to compel their souls. This God, foreign to the world, who can deposit in the soul only an infinitesimal germ of pure good, this God who is present only in the most secret recesses of the heart and like a beggar, this God whose reality seems so weak and so close to unreality, is the God whom Simone Weil loves with a love that consumes her. No doubt precisely because he seems so weak. Sometimes she says that even if he did not exist at all, it would be necessary to love and serve him more than any existing thing because he is the good.

If one says that the good exists outside the world is that the same as saying that the world is bad? Certainly not. Necessity is simply indifferent to good. And far from being bad, necessity is for us the tool of the good because by accepting it we submit our person to an impersonal order. Necessity allows us to overcome our imagination, which makes the self or person the center of the world. Of the two limitations that God has imposed on himself, the world's necessity and the autonomy of thinking beings, the former seems to have been given us in order to free us from the latter. The real enemy of salvation is the latter. Sin resides in the self, in that which says "I" in ourselves. It is this particular being that does not know how to bow to necessity or to the good because of its need to preserve and aggrandize itself. It is this kind of inner necessity that has the appearance of freedom.

What is sacred in man, and quite far from anything connected with the self, is the faculty of going beyond the self in order to consent to impersonal truth, impersonal good, and justice. It is because of this faculty that one must not destroy, unjustly wound, or despise a human being. By killing a man one often prevents him from becoming perfect enough to consent to the annihilation of his self.

The self is not annihilated by committing suicide but by accepting the good in everything that depends on us and by accepting necessity in everything that does not. By submitting to good and necessity, we gradually succeed in breaking up our personal autonomy, that is to say, our apparent freedom, in order to gain true freedom, which is linked to good and truth.

One must therefore reinterpret divine *power*. This power is compounded of mystery and paradox, and it is not power as we conceive of it. Moreover, this reinterpretation will lead to other reinterpretations. And it especially leads to a new image of God's creation of the world.

The problem of knowing how to view God's creation of the world was confronted by the first Christians, or at least many of them; and by all those who, attentive to the many passages in the Gospels and St. Paul where God and the world are set in opposition, asked themselves how to reconcile this opposition with the idea that the world came from God. The Gnostics tried to answer this question, or at least to underline it, by many myths; they have many accounts of the Creation, inspired by the account of Genesis but profoundly modifying it. It is not surprising that Simone in turn should have confronted this problem. She solved (or underlined it) by means of an original idea or, rather, by an admirable myth that had rarely been thought of before her. She says that for God creation did not consist in extending but rather in withdrawing himself. He did not create outside himself beings who did not exist before, thus extending the domain in which to exercise his power. On the contrary, he left outside himself a domain that before was within him and was himself, and in which he no longer intervenes or does so only under certain conditions. One domain, or rather two domains: the one in which he does not intervene, namely, the world that he has entrusted to necessity, and the one in which he intervenes only under certain conditions, namely, the souls of thinking beings. In both domains, he has limited himself. Thus already in the creation, as in the Incarnation and Redemption, God has "emptied himself of his divinity." He has humbled himself, obliterated himself for the sake of love, so as to make free and generous love possible in other beings, too.

(Perhaps a rare example of an analogous theory can be found in Isaac Luria, the sixteenth-century Cabalist, and, above all, in his disciple Hayim Vital.[19] The Cabala is in certain respects a Jewish Gnosticism; the fact that this Gnosticism does not appear with any certainty until well after Christian Gnosticism seems to suggest that it was influenced by the latter. Perhaps one can also find traces of this theory in the *Chaldaean Oracles*,[20] texts from the second century that probably come from a so-called pagan Gnosticism. This so-called pagan Gnosticism also appears only after Christian Gnosticism and may have been influenced by it. Miklos Vetö has pointed out that analogous thoughts can also be found in the writings of Hamann and Schelling.[21])

God has withdrawn from thinking beings so that they may love him freely. But thinking beings who are separated from him and cast into space and time cannot love him without a terrible wrench. Separated from the unity, the universality that is the condition of true thought, they have become subject to error and injustice because they see things in a false perspective, starting from a center that is not the true center. Original sin is not something apart from the Creation and which came afterward; it is inseparable from it. It is the very existence of the distinct, thinking human being that is guilty. That is why, in speaking of the self's need to renounce itself, Simone Weil refers to this by the forceful term of "decreation." By withdrawing, God has allowed us to exist; he has done so for the sake of love and so that we ourselves, for the sake of love, can renounce the being he has given us.

But what is this being he has given us? Is it veritable being? More than once Simone says that the ego is in reality nothing, that man's being is non-being. And indeed, what is left that could properly be considered man? From the start the personality seems dissolved, split on one hand between the power to reject good, a power that is the self itself but is only a false power—because in one way or another we do in the end obey God, if not for the love of good, then by being subjugated by necessity—and, on the other, the power to accept good that, basically, is identical with good itself, identical with God. For only God can love God. The love of God within us is not ourselves, it is the son of God, reincarnated once again. That which within us can accept good is not less distinct from the self than God. In the end, the self exists in neither instance. In the first, the self is only a deceptive appearance, and, in the second, it is not the self that exists but God. In the same way, man's freedom is not in the least his freedom, but God's. And again, in the same way, true immortality is not in the least the immortality of the individual soul but the eternity of God. The eternal part of the soul mingles with God at death and even before in life; the part of the soul that is not eternal falls into nothingness at death and was already nothingness in life.

For some people this conclusion makes Simone Weil's doctrine unacceptable. For example Miklos Vetö, whose book is certainly the most complete and thorough study of this doctrine, finally decides that it contains "a mortal threat" because in the last analysis it suppresses "any center of individual existence." "A basic continuity," Vetö states, "must remain in the decreated man and his previous non-decreated personality, since he owes his second birth exclusively to the efforts made during his non-decreated life and to the consent whose faculty was always within him."[22] At first sight this objection seems quite sensible. But one might ask oneself whether the identity and continuity of the self is included among those things that we can clearly define for ourselves. What kind of existence is the existence of the self? What kind of existence is the existence of the mind? "I am a thing that thinks," Descartes said. But is a thing that thinks still a thing or is it even a being? Are we not forced to dissolve the self when we want to describe the life of thought and its perpetual surmounting and renunciation of itself?

And, after all, the continuity of the self seems even less assured in certain parts of the New Testament than in Simone Weil. For she at least connects the new birth with certain conditions fulfilled in the person. Whereas in the Gospel of St. John and in St. Paul it often seems that the new birth derives solely from God's decision and predestination. Where then is the continuity between the new man and the old? The change seems even more complete and total. Where is the neutral center that could choose between good and evil and yet remain identical throughout all these changes?

The self is and is not; freedom is and is not; the spirit is and is not. Perhaps one ought to say of God that he is and is not. Because he is the Good and his mode of existence is that of the Good.

But we cannot undertake to debate this doctrine here. It is extremely difficult for us, and in any case such a discussion is not within the scope of this book. A doctrine of this sort certainly contains paradoxes and even contradictions. Yet we would have to examine it and decide whether these contradictions are not the sort that are inevitable for the human mind. Kant singled out some of these irreducible contradictions, but his list is far from complete. Simone, too, as we recall, maintained that on certain points contradiction cannot be avoided if one doesn't want to lie to oneself. For her, this fact represents one of the proofs of a transcendent reality. The irreconcilable contradiction between two equally and certainly true affirmations shows us that absolute truth dwells on a higher plane, beyond our reach. This no doubt is also Plato's thought, and that is why so many of Plato's dialogues don't end in any positive conclusions but only in contradictions.

Perhaps there exists a level of thoughts or, rather, a level of problems, where truth can be expressed only through myths and beauty. This is perhaps another thing that Plato intended to say. In any event, on the subject of Simone Weil's religious doctrine one might repeat what she herself thought teachers should tell children on the subject of the Christian religion: "It is so beautiful that it must surely contain much that is true."[23] It is impossible not to feel the beauty of these writings, and where there is so much beauty, there is also truth.

Perhaps Simone herself, at times, attenuates the rigor of her fundamental affirmation as to the relationship between good and the world. In those texts that seem to be among the last she wrote before entering the hospital we find expressions that seem to suggest that good can be present in the world not only through the actions of certain men or in the shape of a necessity indifferent to the good, but also in another way. In the London notebook she says: "Something mysterious in the universe is the accomplice of those who love only the good."[24] In *The Need for Roots* she says that one must believe that the universe is in conformity with the divine will, not only because everything that is real in the end conforms with it, but also in the sense that in the universe, considered in its totality, "good outweighs evil."[25] It is through this belief that faith in Providence is expressed. Of course, "this can only be the universe in its totality, for unfortunately we cannot deny that there is evil in its individual aspects."[26] She also says that the laws of nature "are providentially arranged in such a way that, in the case of human creatures, the determination to search first and foremost for the kingdom and justice of the heavenly Father does not automatically lead to death."[27]

In the essay "Is There a Marxist Doctrine?" and the fragments connected with it, she points out that in certain instances the work of something infinitely small can be decisive. "Through this paradox is accomplished the wise persuasion that Plato speaks of, that persuasion by means of which divine Providence induces necessity to direct most things toward the good."[28]

Does this mean that the infinitely small that serves as God's instrument is simply the action of certain men? But how could the deeds of the saints be sufficient to direct "most of the things that take place"? She also reminds us that there is a unity, in the last resort, between necessity and good.[29]

It is true that she still maintains that *for us* there exists a profound and irreducible distinction between the two orders. "Good and necessity, as Plato said, are separated by an infinite distance. They have nothing in common. They are totally opposed. In spite of our being forced to assign them a unity, this unity is a mystery; it remains a secret to us."[30]

Vetö recognizes that in common with Plato and Kant she had "a certain prudence that consists in not following through to the end a speculative perspective that offers a beautiful idea, and in being humbly satisfied with the unfinished and incomplete."[31] In fact, we have said that she wanted to trace the broad outlines of a doctrine, but not that she wanted to construct a system. Her contradictions, at least the apparent ones, come from the fact that at times she comes to a halt and doesn't follow the development of an idea through to the end, so as not to go beyond the certainties of her own experience. In her eyes, being faithful to her experience was more important than eliminating all contradictions or following a logical development to its end.

But let us return to the "Profession of Faith." Simone believes that justice in society depends on this faith. If one does not understand that the true good is a reality located outside the world which cannot be reached by human faculties but toward which all men possess the power to turn, one cannot, in her opinion, behave justly with human beings. All those who, by their behavior, show that they unconditionally respect all human beings consciously or unconsciously possess this faith. The politics of justice cannot be separated from religion or, rather, from mysticism.

She is aware of the immense difficulty one encounters in thinking justly in the domain of politics. "Human intelligence—even in the case of the most intelligent—falls miserably short of the great problems of public life."[32] At the same time, however, she believes that this difficulty does not abolish the duty to seek solutions to these problems. If one cannot formulate a detailed program (in any event, programs are useless), one can at least try to establish certain guiding ideas.

In a "Draft for a Statement of Human Obligations," she sets out to define the rules that should inspire political life. This aim corresponds to one of the tasks that the fighting Free French movement had set for itself. One of the commissions set up by General de Gaulle, called the State Reform Commission, was drafting a new Declaration of the Rights of Man and Citizen, and turning for inspiration to the Declarations of 1789 and 1793, but modifying them. Simone certainly knew about this work, and doubtless it was because she considered the changes they had made in these Declarations not radical enough that she wrote this draft for a Statement of Obligations. For her it is the very idea of rights that should be replaced by something else, since this idea is so weak and diffuse that it cannot possibly fulfill the function one wants to assign to it; it must be replaced by the concepts of justice and obligation.

(It should be noted that in the new Declaration that was published in the press of the Free French movement on August 4, 1943, there is not only a list of rights but also a list of duties.[33] Perhaps they had to some extent taken Simone's ideas into account.)

The obligation to human beings has as its basis the respect owed to that part of the soul that in every man can rise above the self and attain the impersonal. But this respect can be expressed only by trying to satisfy both the needs of the body and the needs of the "earthly part of the soul." In order to define these obligations, it is enough to list these needs.

The needs of the body are easy to enumerate. As for the needs of the soul, perhaps no one has ever tried to make such a list. This is the new enterprise Simone tackles, and to it she brings all of her original and profound psychological knowledge and insight. As needs of the soul, she sets down not only freedom but also obedience, not only equality but also hierarchy, not only security but also risk, not only honor but also punishment.[34] Just like that of the body, the health of the soul rests on a balance, and each need is accompanied by an antithetical need.

She particularly stresses the linked, antithetical pair: freedom of opinion and truth. If these needs are to be respected she considers it necessary to prohibit all party propaganda, and any pressure by a group on its members that has as its intention the imposition of certain opinions (that is to say, any pressure exerted as the result of a concept of orthodoxy). And she also urges the formation of a court before which any writer or journalist guilty of knowingly publishing lies or easily avoidable inaccuracies could be summoned.

But the need she insists on at the greatest length, and the only one for which apparently there is no corresponding opposite need, is the need for roots. The major part of the book that the French publisher entitled *L'Enracinement* [in English, *The Need for Roots*] is of course devoted to the new and difficult task of defining this need and searching for the means by which it could be satisfied.

I can only refer the reader to this book. But I might point out, in order to assess and measure the long road traveled by Simone since her first political activities, that she now recognized the value of patriotism, provided that one's attachment to the nation is subject to certain limitations. Before all else, this attachment must be limited by the respect one owes to other nations; and then by the knowledge that the nation is only one of the environments that are vital to man (which does not exclude the fact that under certain circumstances the nation can demand a total sacrifice from him). Simone Weil hoped that in France importance would again be given to what is smaller than France—the region—and that people would also become attached to what is larger—Europe. Above all, so that the attachment to one's nation does not turn into the dominion of the totalitarian "great beast" over the individual, it is necessary that patriotism be accompanied by an inspiration and a faith that root man in another world. Each people must discover this faith in its own traditions and its own past. The preservation of the treasures of the past must be one of the chief preoccupations of those who are truly concerned about the life of their people. In France not only memories of 1789 (those from the beginning of the Revolution), but also those memories that were left Frenchmen from before the absolute monarchy and were embodied in certain attempts at Christian civilization in the Middle Ages, and other memories that antedate the Roman Empire and link us to Greece and the Orient, can be pure sources of spirituality.

If she changed in regard to certain matters, her desire to see the workers' and peasants' condition profoundly transformed did not alter in the slightest. What we have of *The Need for Roots*—for the book is incomplete—concludes with the idea that one must build a civilization in which work forms the spiritual center.

In the fragment in which she says that it is necessary to have a doctrine, she also declares that before attempting to express the true doctrine—the doctrine that is the "sole guide for all human problems" —it would be useful to clear away the others, that is, show the inadequacy of the doctrines that for the last two or three centuries have vied for men's minds and spirits.[35] Thus the essay "Is There a Marxist Doctrine?" which intended to prove the inadequacy of one of these doctrines, can be considered a kind of preface to the "Profession of Faith" and *The Need for Roots*.

In this unfinished essay she wages her last battle with Marxism. In it one encounters again the objections that for some time now she had raised against Marx: that his theory of revolutions contradicted his hope for a liberating revolution in the near future; that among the conditions that determine the structure of societies he neglects to include war (he only recognizes it in the form of class struggle); that his picture of the class struggle is simplistic, because men can at one and the same time be oppressors and oppressed, and so on. But this time she mainly develops the general and philosophical objections. At the base of Marxism she perceives a confused mixture of idealism and materialism. Now idealism and materialism should be joined, but in such a way that they do not intermingle. Marx seems to think that there exists in matter a tendency to automatically produce good, a kind of principle of progress toward the good. This is neither science nor true religion; it is an inferior form of religion.

She recognizes that Marx had insights that could only have been inspired by genius. Marxism is precious both for science and true religion insofar as it extends materialism to a knowledge of human events. Indeed, materialism is legitimate in regard to all the facts and events of the world, including all of man's natural thoughts. Only the supernatural eludes materialistic explanation. Marx conceived the idea of nonphysical matter, and this is an extremely fecund idea. (The idea of nonphysical matter is in fact implied in Simone's own psychological doctrine.)

Thus one must search in Marx for fragments of the truth; but these fragments do not constitute a doctrine. He did not develop his inspired ideas, and he set them side by side with weak and false theories. Simone speaks of Marx's errors with tranquil audacity and even a kind of compassion. If he contradicts himself, it is because his love of justice could not bear to be deprived of hope. He could not live without believing that a fully liberating revolution was at hand. But when one must choose between truth and life, one is under the obligation to choose the truth. What is more, true religion is not a religion without hope. Supernatural Good, although outside the world, is not incapable of descending to it and changing something in it. True, it descends to only an infinitesimal degree, but an infinitesimal act can under certain conditions be decisive.

One can also connect to *The Need for Roots,* either as preparations for or as complements of certain parts of this work, several other essays that were written in London. In "This War Is a War of Religions," Simone shows how only inspiration steeped "in a past pervaded with the light of mysticism"[36] permitted England to resist a Germany animated by nationalist idolatry. She goes on to say that one of the most important and urgent problems is that of inspiring people in servitude with a faith and a religion. In "Concerning the Colonial Problem in Its Relation to the Destiny of the French People," she says that "the problem of finding a doctrine or faith to inspire the French people . . . cannot be separated from the colonial problem."[37] The evil that has been inflicted on the colonies is precisely the evil of uprootedness. "It is only the radiance from the spiritual treasures of the past that can induce in the soul that state which is the necessary condition for receiving grace. . . . The loss of the past is equivalent to the loss of the supernatural."[38] She does not look forward to the colonies becoming nations in the European manner ("there are all too many nations in the world already"), but hopes that an honest meaning for the word *protectorate* will be found.

The incredibly beautiful essay, "La Personne et le sacré" [published in English under the title "Human Personality"] begins with a refutation of "personalism" that could be regarded as a more elaborate preface to the "Draft Statement of Human Obligations" than the "Profession of Faith." In "Are We Fighting for Justice?" Simone states that "one must be blind to set justice against charity, to believe . . . that there exists a charity beyond justice or a justice this side of charity."[39] In fact the need for justice springs from "a mad love." Those who possess it "bear within themselves a need as destructive to the natural balance of the soul as is hunger to the functioning of the physical organs."[40] This mad love "plunges one into dangers that could not be faced if one gave one's heart to anything at all in the world, whether it be a great cause, a Church, or a nation."

Writings of this kind must have seemed to her superiors in the Free French organization far removed from practical problems. Philip said, "Why doesn't she concentrate on something concrete, for instance, trade union problems, instead of remaining in generalities." Among the "papers" she wrote for the Free French fighting services, only one, it is said, had any practical consequences; this is the essay entitled "Reflections on the Rebellion." This is the only one that Philip was able to convince de Gaulle to read from start to finish, and Simone's proposal for the creation of a Supreme Council of the Rebellion played a part, it is claimed, in the decision to create in France a National Council of the Resistance, whose first meeting was held on May 27, 1943.

To tell the truth, the Supreme Council of the Rebellion that she proposed would have been an international, European council, not simply a national council. Furthermore, the National Council of the Resistance was organized, at least in part, with a purpose that had nothing in common with the aims that animated Simone Weil. At that time the political parties were coming back to life in France. Up until the end of 1942 only the Communist party had maintained its coherence and organization; since June 1941 it alone had entered the Resistance *as a party,* and it exerted a growing influence. At the beginning of 1943 the Socialist party was officially reconstituted; in January it asked de Gaulle that "the representatives of the various political parties and trade union movements that had been in the Resistance since June 1940 be allowed to participate in clandestine political activities." "This meant posing the principle," Henri Michel says, "of the resurrection of the political parties within the Resistance and the question of their recognition by General de Gaulle. It also meant the launching of the first idea of the National Council of the Resistance."[41] This council was in fact created to assemble not only the Resistance groups and the trade unions but also the political parties. (It is true that at the first meeting of the council Jean Moulin made it clear "that the presence of the representatives of the old political parties in the council must not be regarded as officially sanctioning said parties as they operated before the armistice";[42] yet the existence of these parties was nonetheless in fact recognized to some degree.) Simone, however, in her "Note on the General Suppression of Political Parties," had recommended their complete abolition.

This "Note" was no doubt written precisely because the question of the recognition of the parties had at that point been raised for the fighting Free French movement. The essay is interesting because of the discussion it contains on the subject of the foundation of democracy. Simone reminds us that the value that we correctly attribute to democracy is wholly based on Rousseau's argument concerning the general will; it should rule, he said, and make the laws not because it is the will of the majority but because it has greater chances of being just than any individual will, given the fact that men's thoughts ordinarily come to an agreement as to what is just and reasonable, whereas individual passions oppose and annul each other. Rousseau has pointed out that certain conditions are required for the general will to be able to take shape and express itself. Above all, the general will must derive from a great number of truly *independent* wills. What is necessary is a great number

of individuals each judging according to his own lights and not according to orders, otherwise the mechanism whereby their very number
abolishes the effect of individual passions would not come into play. If
people are grouped into parties, for example two or three parties, the
general will no longer is produced by a great number of individual wills
but rather only two or three; and it is much easier for two or three
people to agree on an injustice than it is for thousands (when thinking
independently). Little does it matter that these two or three party leaders represent thousands; that does not prevent their opinion from being
an individual one, subject to error and injustice. It is certainly inconsis-
tent to choose democracy as an ideal on the basis of Rousseau's arguments and at the same time reject the conditions without which his
reasoning is no longer valid. (The inconsistency is carried to an extreme
when attempts are made to identify democracy with one-party regimes.
Rousseau had said that the least one could do, if one could not prevent
the existence of parties, would be to multiply their number; indeed,
their multiplicity, besides allowing individuals to choose their own
party, increases the number of opinions that then confront each other
and must be compared.) Just like Rousseau, the men of 1789 rejected
"sections of the people," that is to say political parties. Therefore Simone goes back to the doctrine that is the foundation of the democratic
ideal. Can this doctrine be applied nowadays in all of its purity? Perhaps
one would have to exert such forceful coercion to prevent the formation
of parties that a dictatorial power would be needed. Perhaps true
democracy can only be found, as Rousseau believed, in the past and in
primitive societies rather than in our societies or in the future. (It has
been thought possible to separate *The Social Contract* from Rousseau's
other writings; but can it really be separated?) In any event, Simone's
recommendation as regards political parties was not accepted, and the
National Council of the Resistance turned out to be quite different from
the Supreme Council of the Rebellion that she had imagined.

Another practical problem arose at this time. In the fighting Free
French Movement the question was being debated as to whether after
the victory, the Vichy government, which had certain elements of legality, should be supplanted in the normal manner or should be overthrown in order to re-establish true legality. This led to reflections on
legitimacy. In this connection, Simone wrote the essay "Legitimacy of
the Provisional Government." One might seriously wonder whether
Philip felt an overwhelming desire to show this essay to General de
Gaulle, if indeed he himself ever saw it (he did not see all of Simone's
"papers"). For in it she says that in order for General de Gaulle's
government to have the necessary degree of legitimacy after the victory,
if he must continue in power for a certain period while awaiting the
formation of a Constituent Assembly, it is desirable that: 1. the general,
as well as his chief collaborators, pledge to submit all of the actions of

their provisional authority to a tribunal nominated by the Constituent Assembly, empowered to pronounce any sentence whatsoever, including death; 2. that to this he joins the pledge of not allowing in the country the formation of anything that might resemble an organized group of his supporters. Simone adds: "It would seem that the exercise of provisional power, thus conceived, implies the renunciation of any further political career. Preoccupation with a further career could alter the total purity indispensable to the exercise of provisional power under such dreadful circumstances. Similarly, it is desirable for France that once her balance is re-established she should be led by a Frenchman who has lived during her misfortune on her soil.[43]

Simone admired de Gaulle ("To have saved the country's honor at the moment it was enslaved . . . is infinitely more beautiful than any political career"),[44] but she dreaded the formation of a Gaullist party. Not only did she condemn political parties, but a party formed around a leader seemed to her particularly dangerous; she was afraid that such a party might be inclined toward Fascism.

Of the reports she was asked to write, one has been published in *Ecrits de Londres;*[45] it is entitled "Remarks on the New Draft for a Constitution." This was the draft prepared by the Commission for State Reform, one of the commissions set up by de Gaulle.[46] Simone observes that this text contains some felicitous innovations, but that it does not go very far. Everything considered, the proposed constitution is not as good as the one in 1875—so "no need to say more."

Against this draft she sets her own ideas on the subject. In the sketch for a constitution that she outlined,[47] in which there is no dearth of new proposals, what is perhaps most original is the very important role she assigns to the power of the judiciary. To begin with, the judiciary must control the legislative power, namely, make sure that the laws voted for by the chamber are always in conformity with the spirit of the "Fundamental Declaration." Then it also has the task of "punishing all that is evil and, more specifically, all that inflicts evil on the country"—for example, a journalist who lies, an employer who exploits his workers, the head of the government if he has committed a serious error in the exercise of his power. In fact the head of the government must be accountable not only to the legislative power, but "in case of error, he must not be overthrown but judged."[48]

Magistrates must also pass judgment on all deputies whose mandate has not been renewed; they must pass judgment on the President of the republic if, a referendum having disavowed him, someone then brings charges against him in connection with his administration. "The judges can be appointed to a case by anyone or can even appoint themselves." The Prime Minister will have to undergo compulsory judgment after five years in office. If anyone brings charges against the President of the republic after he has been disavowed, he may be sentenced to death.

"Judges must have much more of a spiritual, intellectual, historical, and social education than a juridical one . . . ; they should be much, much more numerous; they must always judge with equity. For them the law should only serve as a guide. This should also apply to previous judgments. But there should be a special court to judge the judges, and it should dispense extremely severe punishments. The legislators should also be able to summon before a court chosen from among their fellow members any judge guilty, in their eyes, of having violated the spirit of the laws."

Thus the legislative power watches over and restrains the judiciary, just as the latter watches over and restrains the legislative power; and both together watch over and restrain the executive. Conflicts between two of these powers are judged by the third (if a conflict between the government and one of the other two powers is at issue) or by a referendum (if it is a conflict between the legislative power and the judicial power).

This brief sketch not only shows Simone's concern for subjecting all the powers to very serious and redoubtable controls, but also expresses her preoccupation with the stability of power as a whole. The President of the republic, chosen by the magistrates from among the high magistrates, is, in principle, appointed for life. The Prime Minister, appointed by the President, can be dismissed after three months due to inadequacy; but after this lapse of time he cannot be dismissed for a certain period (five years, for example). At the same time, the President or any member of the Chamber of Deputies can bring him before a High Court.

Simone concludes: "All this sounds pretty fanciful, but it is not."

Some other reports she wrote have been preserved but have not yet been published. They deal with texts of various kinds sent from France to London by Resistance groups. One of them, a very short one, refers to a text dated September 15, 1942, and entitled "Report on the Present Situation." Simone declares that this report is "of no interest at present." She adds only one comment: that it would be dangerous to hold a plebiscite concerning a constitution drafted by a national committee appointed by de Gaulle at a time when de Gaulle is in power. "If de Gaulle wishes to propose a constitution, it would be necessary for him to relinquish power at the same time. The governmental function and the constitutional function are incompatible."

Four other, longer reports concern projects all of which originate with the same Resistance group. One dealt with "responsibilities and sanctions"; another with the "bases for a statute regarding French non-Christian minorities of foreign origin"; another with the formation of a future party and the structure of the government; and a final one with "the basis for Constitutional Reform."

In the first report the responsibilities and sanctions for the mistakes committed by the French before the war, during the war, and under the

Occupation were discussed. Simone judges this text as follows: "That which concerns the prewar and war periods seems reasonable" (the report said that the responsibilities incurred before and during the war, with the exception of some cases, were diffused, collective, and shared by the whole country). "That which concerns the Occupation is more attractive than cries for revenge. Nevertheless, they do not dare to state the problem clearly." In her view, the problem is first of all that of the nature of punishment in general, then that of true responsibilities and, finally, that of the penalties to be taken into consideration and the ways of preventing revenge from being unleashed by these procedures.

As for punishment, she says that it has a double nature: 1. it is a measure for the protection of public order; 2. it is a measure intended to work for the good of the culprit, to bring about his return to the realm of the good. "The second aspect is essential while the first is secondary. This cannot be denied when one has adopted as a rule of life the respect owed to all human beings without exception. Any punishment that is not, in regard to the culprit, a proof of respect is a worse crime than that committed by the criminal. It clearly follows that the punishment must aim, sooner or later, at evoking in the guilty man a movement of the soul that will lead him to recognize that the punishment is just and to submit to it freely." She concludes that one should inflict the death sentence only on those whose souls are prepared to die.

As for responsibilities, she believes that "the initial crime, that of capitulation in June 1940, from which almost all of the others have flowed automatically, is the collective crime of the entire nation"; and furthermore, one must not punish mistakes that can be traced to a situation in which heroism was lacking. "Conscience is already shocked by the fact that men, mobilized without their consent, can be punished . . . for mistakes that are connected with their lack of heroism. At least they know that they are subject to an authority that demands heroism of them. But in the absence of all legitimate authority—with a caricature of authority that systematically encouraged cowardice—the absence of courage cannot be regarded as a failing."

There is, true enough, a strong popular feeling in favor of stern measures. But the mistake that must not be made is to think that it is proper for the government to spill a little blood so as to stop the people from spilling a lot of it. "A murder committed by the government . . . is a hundred times worse, indeed infinitely worse, than a hundred murders committed by irresponsible individuals. It is as if a priest at the head of a school, knowing that his boys go and hang about the brothels every day and not knowing how to prevent it, were to offer to accompany them there once a month, on the condition that they abstain the rest of the time. That would be much worse.

"The greatest evil is not evil, but the mixture of good and evil. Christ came not to wipe out evil, but to effect a distinction between good and evil. As a consequence, this, too, is the duty of those who follow him."

One should punish only those Frenchmen who were guilty of collusion with the enemy before the armistice and those who, not content to endure servitude, gratuitously added to it without being forced to do so. Simone suggests that the severest penalty should be prison. "The government will then be able to say that violent death, which for our martyrs was the supreme honor, must not be shared by them with this despicable gang."

The project for a "Basis for a Statute Regarding French Non-Christian Minorities of Foreign Origin" in fact chiefly concerned the Jews. The authors of this project, while refuting various accusations leveled against them, considered it an irrefutable fact that the Jews constituted a distinct minority and maintained that due to this the majority could legitimately take measures to avoid possible inconveniences, such, for example, as the presence of too many Jews in the administration, or their presence in certain high positions, etc. Simone's comments on this project are as follows:

"The central idea is correct: that it is a matter not of knowing whether the Jewish minority has this or that characteristic, but whether it exists. Correct also is the idea that this minority has as a common bond the absence of the Christian heritage.

"However, it is dangerous to consider these accepted premises as stable and to make them correspond to a stable *modus vivendi*. The existence of such a minority does not represent a good thing; thus the objective must be to bring about its disappearance, and any *modus vivendi* must be a transition toward this objective. In this regard, official recognition of this minority's existence would be very bad because that would crystallize it."

The measures she considered desirable to facilitate this minority's disappearance, that is, to make it gradually melt into the aggregate of the nation, are mainly: "the encouragement of mixed marriages and a Christian upbringing for future Jewish generations."

"If a genuinely Christian inspiration—without the encroachment of dogma on intelligence—really impregnated the training, education, and upbringing of the youth in France, and even more the entire life of the country, neither the so-called Jewish religion nor the atheism typical of Jews emancipated from their religion would be strong enough to prevent contagion. . . .

"It is only in relation to inspiration of an authentic spirituality, which had already begun to pervade the life of the country, that protective measures against those who are incapable of participating would be appropriate. . . ."

The next project concerned on one hand the structure of the government and on the other the creation of a party that would be called the "Revolutionary Group of French Republicans" and would have been composed solely of people from the Resistance. Simone considers that the chart for the government's structure is very good, but as for the rest, "these people are completely, exclusively, and consciously Fascists."

"When they say that according to their intention their party would not be the only party, it is obvious that they are lying. And this is the only point on which they go to the trouble of making an apparent distinction between themselves and the Fascists. All the rest is unadulterated Fascism—without extenuation, and avowed. The elected leader who will be the head of the party will hold absolute power over the economic and cultural life of the country. They admit that they want to seize power by violence. . . . The cynicism with which all this is presented is scarcely believable. . . ."

Finally, the text entitled "The Basis for Constitutional Reform" involved first of all a critique of France's political past since 1789 and, above all, since 1875; and after that the draft for a new Constitution. As to the first part, Simone said:

"The critical part is good. The points contained in this summary are absolutely correct (in particular: total confusion of the various powers from 1875 until 1940, absence of the judiciary function, total lack of protection accorded to men in relation to the state)."

But her judgment of the proposed constitution is quite different:

"In the constitution the Fascist intention does not leap to the eye as much as it does in the paper on the party. Yet if one looks closely, it is nevertheless manifest.

"In passing, it might be said that this permits us to understand these people's real thoughts about the Jews. Realizing that German-style anti-Semitism is not popular in France at the moment, they pretend to be making a serious and objective study of the problem. But their sole aim is to form a crystallized Jewish minority, as a readily available reserve with a view to future atrocities.

"The constitution does not contain anything related to those very correct observations in the critical section—whose use therefore is simply polemical. No new judiciary organization, no protection of the citizen from the arbitrary actions of the state, no separation of powers.

"The president has the power. He is surrounded only by fictitious restraints. Both chambers, being regional, have no moral authority over the country as a whole. . . . The Senate, elected at two stages by thirds and for nine years, has zero prestige. The President has the right to *unlimited* dissolution of the government. The High Court is convoked only by the Senate. Its president and its chief members have been appointed by the head of the state. . . ."

The "Observations Concerning the Essay on Hitler" is also an essay written in London that has not yet been published. It was not meant for the Free French service. Someone (I don't know who) had shown Simone an essay on Hitler, and these observations were meant for the author of this essay.

The author has presented Hitler as a mediocre man who didn't understand anything about economics, a primitive leader, at once king, warrior, and thaumaturge. For Simone, Hitler is a nightmarish figure but not a mediocrity and even less a primitive leader.

"If Hitler is an 'average' man—mediocre and without culture—how does one explain that before the age of twenty-five he had such a clear vision of German foreign policy, especially as regards the inopportuneness of a war fleet and as regards the danger of the Austrian alliance?

"If Hitler despises economy, it probably is not simply because he understands nothing about it. It is because he *knows* (it is one of the notions of simple common sense that he clearly possesses and that can be called inspired since such ideas are so little understood) that economy is not an independent reality and as a result does not really have laws, since in economy as in all other spheres human affairs are ruled by force. . . .

"It seems to me difficult to deny that Hitler conceives, and conceives clearly, the laws of a kind of physics of human matter, laws that he has not invented but that before him were presented so forcibly and distinctly only by men of genius. He possesses an exact notion of the range of the power of force, something that the average man *never* has. . . .

"Hitler a primitive leader, at once king, warrior, and thaumaturge? Oh, not at all! Nothing could be less primitive than Hitler, who would be inconceivable without modern technique and the existence of *millions of uprooted men.* Primitive leaders, generally speaking, were legitimate leaders and ruled legitimately, that is to say within the limits set by traditions. Hitler's power is unlimited; this is where he becomes part of a nightmare. He is totally artificial and can only stay in power by killing souls under the terror—something that is never the case with traditional powers established by clearly defined conventions, forms, and rituals. . . . Hitler, you say, goes back to Cro-Magnon man. And what the devil do you know about Cro-Magnon man? How do you know whether his morality was not even purer than Christian morality? . . ."

She had written her parents on December 16 that she had fallen in love with London. But she admits that she had been in love with it even before she got there. On the twenty-first she writes: "I love this city more and more, this country and the people who inhabit it. . . . In one way, both the people and things here seem to me to be exactly as I think I expected them to be, and in another way perhaps better. Lawrence somewhere describes England with the words 'humor and kindness,' and one meets these two traits everywhere in the small incidents of daily life. . . . Especially *kindness.* . . . People's nerves are tense, but they control them out of self-respect and a true generosity toward others. It is possible that the war may have a lot to do with this."[49] On January 8: "I tenderly love this city with its wounds. . . . What strikes me most about these people, in their present situation, is a good humor that is neither spontaneous nor artificial but that comes from a feeling of fraternal and tender comradeship in a common ordeal."[50]

By the eighth of January she had not yet found a room she could rent. She told her parents to write to her in care of Mme. Rosin. Simone visited her every Sunday, but she was still living at the French volunteers' barracks.

She at last found a room in a very poor section of town, on Notting Hill, at 31 Portland Road, Holland Park, in the house of Mrs. Francis, a schoolteacher's widow who had two children. On January 22 Simone writes that her landlady is charming;[51] and on February 1 that her room is very pretty, "at the top of a cottage, with branches full of birds, and stars at night, just outside the window."[52]

At first she had lived in a room on the ground floor; but Mrs. Francis, seeing her so badly dressed, so thin and so tired, had thought that she might have financial difficulties and had offered her the room upstairs, which was less expensive.

Simone's relations with Mrs. Francis soon became very affectionate. They were greatly concerned about each other, each trying to persuade the other to be careful and take good care of her health. Mrs. Francis could hear Simone tossing in bed at night and knew that she suffered from headaches. She also saw that she worked too much; Simone often came home very late (when she did come home, for sometimes she spent the entire night at her office), and then would go right on working at home for part of the night. Mrs. Francis herself had a very hard life. During the day she worked outside, and in the evening she still had the housework to do. Returning late from the office, Simone would sometimes find her at the ironing board or busy with some chore. She would say to her, "You are not being good," and Mrs. Francis would answer, "Neither are you. I will rest if you take a rest, too."

Mrs. Francis's older son, David, was then fourteen, and her younger son, John, was nine. Simone, who had so much work to do, nevertheless found the time to take an interest in the children and help them with their studies. She would give David mathematical problems to solve and spelling exercises to John. John had to copy words into his notebook and in the evening place the notebook in front of her door. Sometimes he slipped in a note asking her if she wanted to come downstairs for tea. Whenever she accepted the invitation, Mrs. Francis prepared coffee for her because Simone didn't like tea, and at times she even managed to get her to accept a small slice of buttered bread. Simone would yield only after a fuss, for she wanted only margarine. The children were fond of her, especially the younger boy. John was very proud when she was satisfied with him. Often he could be found curled up at her door, waiting for "Miss Simone."

She was also concerned about their health. Thinking that the younger boy was so tired due to some glandular malfunction, on her own initiative she made an appointment for him at the infirmary at the Free French headquarters and accompanied Mrs. Francis there with the child.

She prepared and ate her meals in her room, which was furnished with a small gas cooker. She had gone to buy some pots with Mme. Rosin. There also was a gas stove to heat the room, but she never wanted to use it; she didn't have any heat. Her papers were spread everywhere, and she forbade the Francises to touch them when they had to clean up her room.

We can see from her letters that she would at times go for walks in London. On Sundays she spent hours in Hyde Park, watching the people listening to the public speakers there. She suggests that this is the last remaining vestige of the discussions in the agora in Athens.[53] She takes great delight, so she says, in the "utterly special atmosphere of the pubs in the working-class districts."[54] During her first weeks in London, before becoming too absorbed in her work, she went twice to the noon concert at the National Gallery and visited an amusing exhibition organized by the Food Ministry to encourage people to eat potatoes instead of imported foods. Toward the end of January she went to the theater and saw Shakespeare's *Twelfth Night* and shortly after that *King Lear.*

She was taken to see "the smallest house in London," a one-story house that was only the width of a door. She told her friends the Rosins that it was the nearest thing she knew to Diogenes's tub and that she would have liked to live there. One weekend she went camping with a woman friend on the outskirts of London, in the park of a convent. Unfortunately this excursion was not blessed by good weather. It began to rain and water seeped into the tent. The nuns offered the two campers shelter for the night. Simone declined the invitation and remained shivering and with chattering teeth under the soaked tent for the whole night.[55]

Every Sunday she went to see the Rosins. They put the bathroom at her disposal, and this made it possible for her to take a bath. She gave mathematics lessons to their son. She lunched with them, but ate very little. When they were able to obtain something that could not be easily found in the markets, she didn't want to touch it. There were also certain foods she refused because they were too good and the French people were starving.

Professor Fehling, a friend of the Rosins', found her less trenchant and more open to discussion than when he had met her at Montana. He felt that her thought and her being were attaining an ever greater harmony and that some of her too extreme, forced attitudes had disappeared. In January Simone wrote: "Mme. Rosin couldn't be kinder to me. Fehling is more and more pleasant."[56]

She developed a friendship not only with Louis Closon but also with his wife. They sometimes would invite her to their house for dinner along with other friends, whom she was glad to get to know. She wrote in April: "My pals, especially Schumann and the Closons, are always kind, even to an absurd degree. Mme. Closon is a remarkable woman; and he too is a man of great value. And one couldn't dream of a better comrade than Schumann."[57]

Although she loved London, or rather could have loved it if her mind had been free, and although she had the best relations with her friends and companions, she was not happy—indeed she was very unhappy. For she had come to England only in order to carry out her plans; and the obstacles she had encountered from the beginning had in no way been surmounted or seemed about to be surmounted. It is said that the plan for the formation of front-line nurses had been shown to de Gaulle and that he was supposed to have exclaimed, "But she is mad!" Other people also considered this project insane. She clearly felt that it had no chance of being accepted. By now she devoted all of her energy to the fulfillment of her second request, that she be sent to France with a special mission. But in this, too, she ran into objections so strong that they left her with scarcely any hope.

She saw Philip very infrequently, and there is no doubt that she never spoke with de Gaulle. Those whom she could hope to convince were Closon and Schumann.

Since she worked in Closon's department, she often had the opportunity to talk with him. He fully understood her aims; he himself would not have been able to bear staying in London all the time, safe and out of danger; and in fact he had made more than one journey to occupied France. Yet he never accepted the idea of sending Simone to France. She would have gotten herself captured, he says, and would have caused the capture of others. Furthermore, this was the opinion of all those who were in any way responsibile for these missions. It was believed that Simone's physical type and relative notoriety would make it easy to apprehend her. She would be arrested almost immediately and would involuntarily endanger the people who had received her and the people who had had any contact with her.

Schumann did not work at the Hill Street offices; he belonged to the National Commissariat of Information and worked at Carlton Gardens, where de Gaulle worked. But Simone saw him quite often. Not only did he have a great feeling of friendship for her, but he also understood her singular greatness, admired her genius, and venerated her saintliness. He would have liked to satisfy her request. But he was not the boss and didn't have as much power as she thought, and when he tried to support Simone's request, everyone told him that he was crazy. Moreover, he supported her unwillingly and against his better judgment, since he himself understood all the risks involved for her and for the people associated with her.

The long letter that she wrote to him[58] shows that he had met her arguments with the same objections raised by everybody else. She tried to persuade him that even if she were captured she would know how to die without betraying any secrets. But what people were afraid of was not her weakness; it is possible to give away information without speaking and without any failure of will—simply because one was seen in this or that place, or was followed, or as a result of a moment's absent-mindedness or ineptness.

Cavaillès, whom she had known at the Ecole Normale, was in London for two months, from about the middle of February to the middle of April. Simone had a conversation with him in Schumann's presence. She told him what she wanted to do. He didn't want to dishearten her completely. But afterward, when he was alone with Schumann, he told him that what she had requested was absolutely impossible. As far as he was concerned, if he were asked to take her with him or use her, he would refuse. He was even slightly irritated by her insistence. For him, there could be no question of a special vocation; he thought that each person must serve where he is placed and that it is not up to him to make decisions. He had abolished the intellectual in himself and was no longer anything but a soldier. As for Simone, he said, "This is a particular case of exceptional nobility, but today there are no more particular cases."

To tell the truth, she was torn between the feeling of having a special vocation and the conviction that it is not permissible to seek out affliction. She believed that real affliction is not what one brings down on oneself but what one endures out of necessity. Since childhood she had always had a very clear idea of what she wanted to do with her life. In a letter to Albertine Thévenon she had said: "Perhaps you cannot imagine what it means to see your whole life ahead of you and to form a firm and constant resolution to make something of it, to steer it from beginning to end by your will and effort in a specific direction. . . . And that is the way I am. . . ."[59] But later, just as she had understood that will is of no use without grace, she had also understood that the very fact of wanting a certain kind of life and a certain death prevented her from attaining them. Because the life and death she desired were the kind that are imposed by coercion, not the kind one chooses voluntarily. In her letter to Schumann, she says: "If affliction were defined by pain and death, it would have been easy for me, while in France, to fall into the enemy's hands. But affliction is defined first of all by necessity. It is only suffered by accident or by obligation. And obligation is nothing without an opportunity for fulfilling it. It was to find such an opportunity that I came to London."[60]

So she desired affliction, but at the same time she wanted to be driven to it by necessity. Can one say that she did not desire affliction? It seems indisputable to me that she sought it. Not, of course, because of a taste for affliction. But first of all because of a desire for justice. Since affliction exists in the world, she found it difficult to go without her share of it; and above all she believed that one must share in it so as to understand how one can really remedy it. Furthermore, she thought later on that only through affliction can one come to know the truth of existence, the complete and absolute truth. And indeed she says in her letter to Schumann:

"Leaving aside anything I may be allowed to do for the good of other people, life for me means nothing, and never has meant anything, at bottom, except as an expectation of the revelation of the truth.

"I feel a laceration that grows without surcease, both in my intellect and in the center of my heart, due to my inability to think with truth at the same time about the affliction of men, the perfection of God, and the bond between the two.

"I have the inner certainty that this truth, if it is ever granted to me, will only be revealed when I myself am physically in affliction, and in one of the extreme forms of affliction that exist at present.

"I am afraid that this may not happen to me. Even when I was a child and thought I was an atheist and a materialist, I always had within me the fear of failing, not in my life, but in my death.

"I am outside the truth; nothing human can take me there; and I am inwardly certain that God will not take me there in any other way than this. . . ."[61]

This then was the twofold need that made her cruelly dependent on others. She was sure that affliction and a certain kind of death were her vocation; but the war machine had to push her in the direction of her vocation; she could not go to meet it herself. Now, despite her protests, the machine was choosing other people in terms of their usefulness in a group action.

She had obtained an aviation manual and studied it; she had also gotten a parachutist's helmet. She also tried to learn how to drive a car, doubtless because that would have been useful if she were given a mission. Moreover, on January 14, 1943, a service communication had been sent the chief doctor of the Free French forces in London, asking him to examine Simone at her house. This decision to have her examined was certainly connected with her request for a mission, since in January, according to what Maurice Schumann told me, she did not seem ill.[62]

It was not Simone but rather one of her companions at work who was chosen by the Central Bureau of Intelligence and Action to be parachuted into France. Simone was very hurt. She tried to convince this companion to let her take her place. In the end, the mission was canceled, and Simone rejoiced. She was jealous of a danger that she wanted to keep all for herself.

When people explained to her the danger she might be for others, involuntarily and in spite of her enormous strength of character, if she were sent to France, she seemed deeply hurt and all of her hope was crushed.

So the same distress that had worn her out in New York tormented her again in London. She could perhaps have endured any distress that was not also a feeling of remorse, but that's what it was: she reproached herself "more and more grievously" for having left France.[63] I remember her telling me once that what she feared most in the world was remorse.

Her headaches, which in January had almost left her in peace, had started again. In her melancholy state, she ate less and less. The truth is that if she ate little, if she refused certain foods, claiming that the children in France didn't have them, it seems that she did not painstakingly calculate the amounts in terms of the rations, which, moreover, she couldn't possibly have known at that time. What is certain is that for some time now, besides having a small appetite, she had deprived herself because she didn't want to be one of the privileged.

Perhaps she was already sick in America. It is true that she had been X-rayed before leaving New York (and in Marseilles too). But incipient tuberculosis does not always appear clearly on the plates, and in order to get the authorization to leave she may have concealed any signs of fatigue or weakness. In any event, once she was in London, insufficient nourishment and excessive work, added to her despair and grief, no doubt had, before the start of spring, caused an illness about which one can only wonder why it took so long to attack so debilitated an organism. She certainly did not know what kind of illness she had, but she felt terribly tired and foresaw that she didn't have much time left. In her long letter to Schumann, she says: "In a short time my work here will be arrested by a triple limit. First, a moral limit: because the ever-increasing pain of feeling that I am not in my right place will end in spite of myself, I fear, by crippling my thought. Second, an intellectual limit: it is obvious that at the moment it reaches down to grip something concrete, my thought will be arrested by the lack of an object. Third, a physical limit: because my fatigue is increasing."[64]

Pressed for time, she desired all the more strongly to use what little remaining strength she had in an action that would allow her to meet her death, the death that fitted her. ("Oh Lord, give each his proper death," Rilke prayed.) "If I am allowed to make the journey I wish," Simone said to Schumann, "it would be a sufficient stimulus, I think, to erase all fatigue—unless the delay were too long."[65]

Jacques Kaplan, who had come to London from America and saw her toward the end of February,[66] "found a different Simone Weil from the one he had known: she was worn out and tense, her nerves seemed stretched to the breaking point."[67] Moreover, she had been feeling exhausted for a long time, and in fact she spoke to him of her lack of vital energy. (It is true that this feeling was partly due to her excessive demands on herself; she was aggrieved at not being able to do and think as much as she would have liked.) More than ever, she had the feeling at this time of being without strength or ability. She told Schumann that the continuous effort she had to put forth to summon up the little energy she had and direct it to what she had to do was "killing." She compared her condition to the periods of drying up that mystics experience; but she said that in her case this was not only confined to certain periods but was a permanent character trait. In her London notebooks she compares herself to the sterile stones on which wheat cannot germinate. She tells herself that the only possible way to make the seed of the divine word grow out of stones is to gather so carefully all the water that falls and to concentrate it so completely in the crevice where the seed lies that not a single drop will be lost for some other use, not even to preserve life. "But where to find the courage to deprive one's flesh and blood of the last drop of water so as to give it to the divine sprout? It is only under coercion that one can do such a thing."[68]

She also wants God to plunge her into slavery. She wants this but still fears that this desire may not be sincere. "The difficulty is to make the desire real."[69] In the same way, in her letter to Schumann she tortures herself by thinking that if she has not found what she was looking for when she came to London, it may not be that she has miscalculated; on the contrary, it may perhaps be that the weakness in her has calculated too well, without her being conscious of it. "Could it be that the coward in me has calculated too well? For my nature is cowardly. All that is painful and dangerous frightens me.... How can I help despising myself?"[70]

She went to Mass every Sunday and often during the week. Maurice Schumann sometimes went with her, but she would leave him at the threshold of the church because she preferred to be alone during the service. The regret she felt at not being able to participate in the sacraments, the desire she had to receive communion, was more intense than ever. This desire often led her to think about the sacraments and ask herself how they act upon the soul. That is why she wrote "Theory of the Sacraments,"[71] which she sent to Schumann and which is certainly one of the last things she wrote before entering the hospital. This essay is also connected with the question she had asked herself: What must one do to make a desire real? How can one really desire and not just imagine one's desires? In her eyes, the sacrament is a means by which one's desire for the good is put in touch with reality and becomes reality itself. But to achieve this it is necessary to believe in the virtue of the sacrament.

Her preoccupation with the sacraments is also expressed in the text incorrectly called "Last Text," which was perhaps written at about the same time.[72] This "Last Text" is a profession of faith that ends with a question. She sent it to a friend for her to show to priests and other religious persons she knew. In it she defines her position vis-à-vis the Church very clearly and firmly.

"I believe in God, the Trinity, the Incarnation, the Redemption, and the teachings of the Gospel.

"I believe, that is to say, not that I make mine what the Church says on these points, affirming them as one affirms the experiential facts or geometric theorems; but I adhere by love to the perfect, ungraspable truth that is contained within these mysteries. . . .

"I do not recognize any right of the Church to limit the workings of the intelligence or the illuminations achieved by love in the domain of thought.

"I recognize that the Church, as repository of the sacraments and guardian of the sacred texts, has the mission to formulate decisions on certain essential points, but solely for the purpose of guiding the faithful.

"I do not recognize her right to impose the commentaries by which she surrounds the mysteries of faith. . . .; even less that of using threats and fear in exercising her power to deny the sacraments so as to impose these commentaries."

Further on she says:

"I am certain that this language does not contain any sin. It is in thinking differently that I would commit a crime against my vocation, which demands absolute intellectual integrity."

She confesses that she has an intense and perpetually growing desire for communion. But in view of the attitude in which she perseveres, if the Church were to grant her baptism, that would mean that she would be breaking with a practice at least seventeen centuries old. It would then be necessary for this break to be officially recognized.

"If this break is right and desirable . . . it would be necessary for the Church and the world that it take place in a striking manner and not through the isolated initiative of a priest performing an obscure, unnoticed baptism.

"For this reason and many others of a similar nature, I have never until now presented a priest with a formal request for baptism.

"Nor do I do so now.

"Nevertheless I feel not the abstract but the practical, real, urgent need to know whether, if I were to request it, it would be granted or refused me."

The limit of fatigue had been reached. On April 15 a friend, having gone to visit her at her office, did not find her and learned that she had not been there the day before. She went to her house and found her lying unconscious on the floor of her room. She brought her to and wanted to call a doctor. At first Simone protested and tried to make her swear that she wouldn't tell anyone about the condition in which she had found her. Then she understood that she had to give in and would definitely be taken to a hospital. She telephoned Schumann, crying as she talked to him; the need to undergo medical treatment made the realization of her plans even more impossible, at least for a long time. Schumann tried to comfort her; he told her that she had to take care of herself and would soon recover and promised to visit her. The doctor gave orders to take her to Middlesex Hospital.

At first she was put in the large common ward. Three days later she was given a room to herself. Although the noise in the common ward had tired her very much, she had to be told that she was contagious to convince her to accept the private room; as always, she refused to accept any privileges.

Dr. Izad Bennett diagnosed a granular form of tuberculosis that consists in a multitude of small lesions. Both lungs were affected, but one lung more than the other. The doctor felt, however, that she had a good chance to recover.

He ordered absolute rest. To Mme. Closon and Schumann, who had gone to see Simone the day after she entered Middlesex, the doctor said that her treatment had to start at the hospital because the sanitariums were overcrowded and understaffed. In any event, Simone could not receive so well in the sanitarium as in the hospital the care based on the absolute immobility she needed. At the end of two months, he said, her condition would certainly be much improved, and then they could move her to a sanitarium.

After a few days of rest her coloring improved and she looked much better. But soon enough all progress stopped. The reason was that she ate too little.

From the start in the hospital it had become the practice to help her eat, since they wanted to relieve her of all effort. Moreover she was extremely weak and could barely lift her spoon. But she did not like to be helped. It annoyed her. Besides, either she could not eat or would eat very little. She never finished her meals and refused to eat certain foods. She was given milk but perhaps it did not agree with her, and, in any case, she had scruples about drinking it since she believed that milk should be given only to the children. Maurice Schumann said to her, "Right now, at this time, we are living under a war economy. Food is portioned out; before it is given to you, milk is given to all the children. It is precisely now that you should not be afraid of taking their share." But she continued to eat very little.

Visitors were permitted every day but only for a short time (only one visit, for ten minutes in principle but a little longer in fact). She made all those who came to see her promise not to tell her parents about her illness. She knew that if they heard of it they would be in torment and would no longer be able to endure being far from her; they would suffer cruelly for a long time and still would not be able to join her. Mme. Rosin also had to promise, although she felt guilty toward her friends the Weils for not informing them.

In the letter Simone wrote to her parents on April 17 not only did she not tell them about her illness, but in order to hide from them the fact that she was in a hospital, she took care to write her Portland Road address on the envelope. She was to do the same thing every time she wrote right up until her death.

In this letter she tells them about the beauty of spring in London. Before going into the hospital she had the joy of seeing the blossoms on the trees. Yet she cannot avoid showing her regret—"every day more and more bitterly and excruciatingly"—for having left France.[73] On the same day she writes to her brother: "Every day, I am more and more cruelly torn by regret and remorse. . . ."[74]

It is not only by concealing her address that she avoids worrying her parents. The letters she now writes them are framed in such a way that they will neither suspect where she is nor realize that she has stopped going to her office. She continues to talk about her friends, her colleagues, her work, and what is going on in London. Her letters are one long lie full of tenderness. But even before going to the hospital, one can discern a number of fibs in the things she tells them. And they, too, tried out of a feeling of tenderness—and in vain—to deceive her, sending her cables saying that they were "very happy," "perfectly happy."[75]

Even when she was so weak that she could barely hold a book or lift a spoon, she somehow managed to write to her parents without anything in her handwriting betraying her weakness. The steadiness of her writing, even in her last letters, is astonishing and presupposes an extraordinary act of will. As we have seen, although she had not asked for baptism, she had an urgent need to know whether it could be granted to someone who perseveres in the attitude she had taken. Someone asked Abbé de Naurois, chaplain of the Free French forces, to visit her. He visited her three times. In 1955 he was kind enough to write and tell me everything he remembered of those conversations. They took place, he believes, in May (or perhaps even as early as the end of April) and in June. After informing me that he had found it very difficult to follow Simone's thought ("I certainly was not," he says, " 'up to' understanding her very well"), he summarized his memories as follows:

"1. When I saw her for the first time, Simone Weil was already *very* debilitated, dreadfully thin, feverish, and exhausted. I obtained permission to visit her in my capacity as chaplain and, in principle, for only ten minutes (in fact I must have spent twenty minutes or a half-hour at her bedside each time I went to see her). She spoke rapidly in a low voice, in sentences interspersed with silences, following the course of a thought all of whose stages were not expressed in words. She did not seem to listen much to my answers. Besides, since she was so terribly tired, she undoubtedly found it difficult to marshal her ideas and express them clearly.

"2. Apart from the admiration I felt for her life as a witness, her rectitude, and her spirit of sacrifice, the very method of her thinking threw me off and sometimes irritated me. What confusion, I thought, between the principal propositions and the subordinate or interpolated clauses, what continuous swerves and strayings . . . the acrobatics of a squirrel in a revolving cage! At such moments I thought: all this discussion is useless; it would be a hundred times better to be a peasant with no more culture than a good country priest but at least some saintliness in me! Then I would have come to listen to her, remain silent, and pray . . . and that would be all!

"In fact she *wanted* to argue. And yet the best moment, the moment for which she herself waited was when, before leaving, I would bless her. Then the argumentative flood was suddenly arrested; and I had the powerful sense of a wholly docile, wholly ready soul that only apparently escaped through the subtleties of thought and analysis. I think that I blessed her every time—and that she herself had requested it since at least the second visit . . . and with such great seriousness and faith!"

Further on in the same letter Abbé de Naurois partly returns to what he had said previously:

"I should like now partially to correct what I said under point 2 about her way of thinking. It always dealt with faith, the Church, Christ, and the salvation also offered to 'unbelievers' . . . (After so many years I cannot describe it more accurately than that.) Her method, if I can use this word after emphasizing the *disjointedness* of her discourse, exasperated me (but I am sure that I never let her see this). Nevertheless, she remained within a *climate of truth;* the motive for her thinking was a passionate love of the living Truth. So I now want to modify the criticism I made above. If the approach of our consciousness toward the living God of Faith were a demonstration analogous to the proofs of physical science, then it is true, she reasoned badly—incapable as she was at least apparently and in her impaired state of health to order her thoughts, to define clearly each step, and to embrace both the domain of mystery and the unknown and the domain of the known. But, quite rightly, faith depends on Christ rather than resting on man. . . . Though seeming to turn back incessantly, to question again and again, to 'leap' from one perspective to another, and finally to entangle all the threads of her discourse, she ended by rendering the most authentic and humble witness to the Truth—the Truth that is Grace and that mocks our reasons. I am not afraid of that last word because I felt her *so humble,* so far from what one might have taken for an intellectual's pride, and at the same time so absolutely loyal!"

And he concludes: "The essential thing in my memory of her is the feeling, so strong and free of any admixture, which I had in her presence: the feeling of an extraordinarily pure and generous soul, to whom precisely because of its strength and rectitude the Lord had seemingly refused the tokens of Joy and Peace, preferring that she verify this truth to the bitter end: if God is and if he is love, *it is necessary that he be hidden* and that we must seek him 'manfully' in the Night. . . ."

Abbé de Naurois formally denies having said to Simone that she was full of pride, as someone claimed Simone had told her.[76]

According to one witness, Simone was at that point speaking of a dogma, or rather of an opinion that has often been considered a dogma, and had said that she could not accept the opinion that unbaptized infants, if they die just after birth, cannot enter paradise and remain forever in limbo.[77] In fact, we can see in her *Letter to a Priest* that she resisted this idea: "It is *probable* that the eternal destiny of two children who died a few days after birth, one baptised and the other not, is identical."[78] Perhaps Sylvie's birth had made Simone particularly interested in this problem. At any rate, she felt strongly about everything that concerned children.

But this was probably only one obstacle among the many separating her from Catholicism, and even this was not really an obstacle because this problem, it is said, has never been specifically defined by the Church. As it would seem from the "Last Text" and also from some letters to Father Perrin, the chief obstacle was the fact that she believed she had to preserve her freedom of thought. "I do not recognize any right on the part of the Church to limit the workings of the intellect or the illuminations achieved by love in the domain of thought.[79]

She had not asked Abbé de Naurois to baptize her. However, in the "Last Text" she says that even if a priest consented to baptize her, it would still not be what she desired, since it would not involve the Church. She did not believe that it was permissible for her to enter the Church as long as that could mean a limitation on her freedom of thought and study.

In any case, when she had written to Father Perrin and his secretary that she could not enter the Church, she had added: "except perhaps at the moment of death."[80] Indeed, if the desire to protect the independence of her thought was, as it seems, what kept her outside the Church, she had no reason to be afraid of entering it at the moment when she would no longer be able to think.

Perhaps she still had this inner reservation when she was in London. For someone told Mme. Closon, while Simone was still alive, that she had supposedly said, "If one day I am completely deprived of my will, in a coma, then they ought to baptize me."[81] (Mme. Closon was not absolutely certain that Simone had made this statement, but she felt that it was possible.)

One of the persons who visited Simone at the Middlesex Hospital has said that one day—apparently about the time of Abbé de Naurois's visits—she took some tap water and poured it over Simone's head while pronouncing the baptismal formula. It is difficult to speak with complete clarity about this event since at present this person does not want to be named and become involved in a controversy. But it is also difficult not to mention it at all since in fact the controversy has already begun. W. Rabi has devoted a study to this question in an article entitled "Simone Weil ou l'itinéraire d'une âme, les derniers jours, le baptême *in extremis*" ["Simone Weil or the Itinerary of a Soul, the last days and baptism *in extremis*"].[82] What I can say—and no doubt must say—is that having compared the reports cited by Rabi with the account told me personally by the person who claims to have baptized Simone, I believe that if this was actually done, it was done without Simone's attaching any great importance to it. This seems to me to be proven by the details of the account I was given, details that I wrote down immediately,[83] and by Simone's subsequent behavior. Actually, according to the story I was told, this baptism did not take place at Ashford, as Rabi assumes, but in London, at the hospital. Moreover, still according to the same account, Simone did not after this ask to receive the sacraments. This proves, in my opinion, that she did not consider the baptism a valid one. For, in a sense, if she wanted to be baptized, it was above all so as to be able to receive the sacraments. What is more, when she entered the sanitarium at Ashford and was questioned so that they could fill out her form, she asked that nothing be written under the heading "religion" and later told one of the doctors there that she preferred Catholicism but that there was still something that prevented her from saying that she was a Catholic. It appears therefore that she did not think of herself as having been baptized. She continued to think of herself as outside the Church, though very close to it.

(She certainly must have known that for an adult such a baptism is not valid unless the person requesting it is in imminent danger of death and does not have the time to turn to a priest. And it certainly appears that she did not request it. Furthermore, as long as she was in the hospital in London, it seems she did not think that she was in any immediate danger. She could still have turned to a priest. It was not the lack of time that made a normal baptism impossible but difficulties of a different order.)

Toward the end of May or the beginning of June she went back to reading Sanskrit in the *Gita*.[84] Mrs. Braham, who visited her in the hospital before the middle of June, [85] found her studying Sanskrit. (The Brahams were her brother's friends; Simone had called on them once, shortly after arriving in London.[86]) But Mme. Closon, the Rosins, and a colleague were her most frequent visitors. Mme. Rosin asked her what she might like in the way of food, so she could bring it to her; Simone at times said that she would really like some cherries, but there was nothing else she wanted.

Mme. Rosin says that she was always content and cheerful when they came to see her, and that her mind was very clear and remained clear until the very end. She also says that she was very beautiful, ethereal, transparent; it seemed that everything material in her had been abolished.

Schumann and Closon also visited her when they were in London. But they weren't always there during the time she spent in the hospital. Closon was away from the middle of April until about May 20,[87] and again from the end of May until approximately June 20.[88] Schumann was away from the end of May until about the end of June.

Perhaps what Schumann told me about how she appeared when he saw her in London is particularly true of the way she was in the hospital. He told me that she already was "a spirit almost completely released from the flesh, a spirit who was the Word." She seemed to think of herself as inspired, and in his opinion she really was. She did not argue; she spoke like a prophet, she taught and seemed to emanate the very breath of the spirit. She offered her words as a kind of life buoy that one was free to take or reject. One day she took his hand with a grave look on her face, as though she wanted the inspiration in her to flow into him, and she simply said, "The Father who is in heaven. . . ."

Mrs. Francis went to see her several times and brought her a small book of consoling thoughts. She would often say, "Get well soon and come back to us." Simone once replied; "I won't be here for long." She also said; "I cannot be happy or eat to my satisfaction when I feel that my people are suffering."

She received a visit one day from one of her old trade union comrades, Giugui, one of her "good pals." Sometimes comrades she had known in the Free French fighting services came to see her.

Generally, her friends took turns in coming to see her so that she never lacked for visitors. Yet on some days she may not have seen anyone but the nurses and so felt lonely and isolated. (Life in London during the war was as difficult as everywhere else; people were tired and had very little free time.) Among Simone's notes written in London there is a passage from a Persian poem she copied out—"Why, when I am ill, does none of you come to visit me/ When if your slave is ill, I hurry to see him?/ Crueler for me than illness is your contempt"[89]— which perhaps echoed a lament in herself.

About the middle of June the doctor observed that her recovery was much slower than he had foretold or, rather, that there was no improvement. Her fever had not gone down, the X-rays showed that the condition of her lungs was stationary, and her appetite was still very weak. He asked for a consultation with Dr. Young, a famous specialist. The latter confirmed the diagnosis. All that he prescribed was the discontinuance of certain measures that, though meant to spare Simone all effort, had only annoyed her. She was at last allowed to eat without help.

Starting at the end of June she began to say that she would like to be transferred to a sanitarium. She had the impression that she was suffocating in her room. Her window looked out on a corner of the street and it saddened her to see only stones. To Mme. Closon she said something like this, "How could I get better with this London air? This hospital atmosphere is perhaps the worst thing for me." She asked her to find her a sanitarium. She also asked Mme. Rosin. She advised them to make their inquiries without Dr. Bennett's knowledge because she no longer got along with him.

A conflict with the doctor was in fact inevitable, for by eating too little she was making her recovery impossible. Dr. Bennett later told a friend of André Weil's that she was the most difficult patient he had ever seen. Having heard, either from Simone or her friends, that she ate too little even before entering the hospital, he remarked that she had "let herself starve in an attic."[90]

Did she want to die? It is hard to believe that she did not realize the danger to which she was exposing herself by eating so little. After all, could not she perhaps want to commit suicide so as not to be an accomplice of those who kept her in London in conditions of safety that she considered dishonorable? In more than one instance she had condemned suicide, yet in her eyes this would perhaps not have been a real suicide. Perhaps she felt that to kill oneself to avoid dishonor was only an apparent suicide.[91] Unable to obtain the danger she felt obliged to face, she may have wanted to prove to herself that she was not running away from it, and the only way to do that was perhaps to face another danger, to risk death by an even more hazardous act that made it almost inevitable.

And yet, none of those who were with her in London, with the exception of Mme. Rosin, had the feeling that she wanted to die. Mme. Rosin herself has told me that this was only a personal impression and that Simone had never said that she wanted to die, that she did not refuse to eat and ate only very little while saying that she had no appetite. For Mme. Rosin it is clear that she did this because she wanted to die. But neither Mme. Closon nor Schumann nor any of the others who saw her at this time had this feeling. Mme. Aron told me that the coroner's inquest and the conclusions he reached had seemed an absurdity to all those who knew Simone in London. Certainly she was desperate and angry at not having been able to obtain a mission in France. This deep feeling of grief undoubtedly made her indifferent to her chances for recovery. But that she had a deliberate will to die, that she herself wished to decide her fate on such a crucial matter does not seem to accord with her general frame of mind since her thoughts had turned to religious doctrines. It would seem that she only wished to obey and to accept; she wanted to have no will. I was told that at the hospital she had sleeping pills at her disposal and that it would have been easy for her to commit suicide if she had wanted to. This same person, who saw her often, told me that there were actually many foods that Simone's stomach did not tolerate (she could only digest certain kinds of porridge). She also said—and Mme. Closon, too, has confirmed this—that at the hospital she often talked of the future, of what she would do after France was liberated, when she would have returned to France. In fact the letter Simone wrote to Louis Closon on July 26, 1943, which I will quote further on, shows that on that date she thought she might have several more years to live.

If on one hand she did not have the intention of committing suicide —the letter to Closon seems to prove as much—and if, on the other, she understood that by eating too little she was making sure she would not recover, how can one explain the fact that she persisted in her refusal both of hypernutrition and even normal nutrition? It seems to me that this can be explained only in two ways. For one thing, it is actually possible that, by dint of depriving herself, she could now only take in very small amounts of food. This is almost certainly true for the last weeks she spent in London and the eight days she was at Ashford. She suffered then from a disorder of the digestive system, and the treatment for this must have been extremely painful and embarrassing for her. It was perhaps in order to avoid these painful treatments that from that time on she accepted food only after making great difficulties and in extremely small amounts.

Another possibility is this: she had no doubt decided once and for all to eat very little so long as most of the French people were being subjected to restrictions in this sphere (restrictions that she perhaps exaggerated). She seems to have made this resolution when she left France. (In fact, on arriving in New York she had said to her parents, "I will not eat more than in Marseilles.") Perhaps she felt obliged to keep faith with this resolution even after falling ill, no matter what the risk. The Church can relieve one of a vow, but Simone, if she had made a vow, had no one who could relieve her of it. Furthermore, she may have thought that complete surrender to what one judges to be good can have extraordinary, miraculous effects. One sees in *The Need for Roots* that she did not deny the possibility of a miracle, understood as a physical phenomenon "necessitating as one of its prerequisites a total abandonment of the soul to either good or evil."[92] She wrote that for saints truth can become a part of life. She did not presume to regard herself as a saint, but perhaps she thought that this was true not only for saints. When she was in Marseilles, she had asked herself if it might not be possible to live without eating. It is therefore possible that she may have said to herself something like this: I must keep faith with the duty I feel, the obligation not to eat more than if I had remained in France, the obligation to share the fate of my compatriots; after that, whether I live or die does not depend on me—it depends on Providence, which is to say, on the eternal laws of this world, laws that do not forbid one from hoping to live under what may seem utterly desperate conditions.

If there is an element of truth in the idea that she wanted to die, that element would perhaps consist in this: that her sorrow made her to a great extent indifferent to what might happen to her. In a letter to her parents written on July 18 and speaking about the work she is doing, she says: "Since the time they refused to give me the job I wanted, that or something else (it makes no difference) . . ."[93] Now she may also have had this attitude of indifference with regard to recovery, and without having decided to die, she may not have fought enough against it. Yet it seems to me that in this connection one ought, possibly, to speak of obedience and not indifference. Starting at the end of July she certainly no longer had a choice; she had, it would seem, actually become incapable of eating normally. All that she could do now was to fulfill "the supreme act of total obedience,"[94] that is to say, the consent to die. Until then she had perhaps done nothing but remain obstinately faithful to what she regarded as an obligation, an order. She accepted the risk that this fidelity entailed, but there is nothing to prove that she had anything in mind but the fidelity itself.

She certainly did not fear death, as she has often shown. Perhaps she looked forward with a kind of joy to being delivered from herself. She is supposed to have said to someone, either at the end of her stay in the hospital or at Ashford, "You are like me, a badly cut-off piece of God. But soon I will no longer be cut off; I will be united and reattached." But whether death meant joy or sorrow for her, there is no doubt that she would not have risked it if she had not received the order to do so.

General de Gaulle had left for Algiers at the end of May. Philip, Schumann, and Closon had left with him. Simone heard talk of what was happening in Algiers, the rivalry between de Gaulle and Giraud, and she didn't like what she heard. Certain aspects of the politics of the fighting Free French movement had already displeased her. As early as May 10 she had written to her parents: "I will tell you now, though, that I have no practical responsibilities. And I prefer it that way."[95] On June 15 we can feel her indignation, although she is putting it humorously: "My pals are a long way off. They don't know their luck in escaping the rough side of my tongue; without knowing anything, I still have little doubt that they richly deserve it (like all the others. . . .) If you see Boris, be sure to tell him that I didn't have, don't have, and, I hope, never will have (I'd rather sleep under the bridges) any responsibility for anything

—either for good or evil."[96] Some days later, speaking apparently of what was happening among the leading circles of the Free French movement, she says that she is fed up with "all this inextricable absurdity."[97]

About June 29, Closon, who was back in London, went to see her. She had feared this meeting precisely because Closon was "such a good comrade."[98] She believed that she was no longer in agreement with him. There was, however, less disagreement than she had feared. She says to her parents: "Saw Closon. Divergences less than I feared. But I can speak only of him, personally."[99]

Her indignation grew in July and became so great that she resigned from her post despite the fact that she had no other source of income. On July 26 she wrote Closon a letter in which she confirmed her resignation, explaining it first of all by the fact that she had not been sent to France but also saying that at the moment of the country's liberation she wanted to be free of any ties with both the fighting Free French movement and the governmental cadres. At the close of this letter she speaks of her physical condition in a poignant manner.

"Dear friend,

"I forgot to ask you during our last meeting if you had informed Philip of my present situation—resigned and kept on the Hill Street roster only due to illness and in the name of philanthropy.

"If not, I ask you to do so when you see him, here or in Algiers.

"Although I turned down your proposal for an exchange of letters as ill befitting our friendship, my decision was as definitive as if it had been expressed to him in writing and officially.

"There has been no change in this regard, and I don't foresee the possibility of a change in the future.

"If I could one day rejoin my parents in North Africa, and if they were to take me on as a dependent (which they would do, of course), I would demand to be stricken from the roster of the Ministry of the Interior. At the same time I could ask to be readmitted into the Department of Public Education (from which Vichy has stricken me) and to be given a leave without pay.

"The Commissariat of the Interior is in charge of the French Resistance. There is only one way for me to be active in the French Resistance and only on one portion of the terrestrial globe. You know what I am talking about.

"When for four months one's temperature runs between 38 and 38.5 degrees, one puts such thoughts aside for the time being. I hope with all my heart that France will rid itself of its bacilli (at least those in green uniforms), and so fast that I can't catch up with her.

"Besides, I have always been told again and again that even in perfect health there is no possibility for me.

"Since that can be regarded as out of the question, I do not have,

I cannot have, and I do not wish to have any direct or indirect, or even very indirect, connection with the French Resistance.

"Don't tell me that if everyone were to take this stand, nothing would be accomplished. In point of fact this is not the case, and there is no danger at all in this respect. People differ in temperament, character, abilities, life objective, and vocation. I speak only for myself. Let others settle their differences with themselves and the universe as best they can.

"As for the postwar period, at the moment of liberation of the French territory I absolutely wish to have no official tie, no matter how indirect and far removed, with either the "fighting French movement" or with the governmental cadres.

"If I ever regain some ability to work, and if at that moment Philip —supposing that at such a time he will still be 'in place'—should feel the need to use my scribbles, he'll only have to throw any sort of research grant my way from any sort of research fund. For a task similar to the one I am doing here that would be a much more appropriate remuneration than inclusion in a regular ministerial position.

"That would surprise me very much. His often repeated statement: 'Get it off your chest' (which seems to imply: after that, you'll be available for serious matters), and his question: 'Why doesn't she tackle something concrete, such as trade union problems, instead of wallowing in generalities?' don't seem to indicate very great interest.

"Apart from this, there is nothing, absolutely nothing that I can do for him.

"Of the three offers of work that he made me during the four months I spent at Hill Street, one was so vague as to give me not the slightest inkling of what he wanted ('brain trust,' 'clearing of the ground of doctrines'), and the two others were impossible for me (a detailed 'plan' for French trade unionism— a study of the English trade union and working-class situation).

"These two tasks would have perfectly suited people—and there are some very eminent ones in the field—who, whether they know whereof they speak or not—almost always not—have mastered the art of writing brilliantly on a subject about which they are ignorant.

"Philip has misjudged the person.

"One day he complained to Schumann that 'he could not utilize my intelligence.' Indeed, he cannot. But that is easily mended. Intellects that can be utilized abound on the market. Mine—I assure you that I am speaking in all sincerity and am well acquainted with what I am talking about—is not at all exceptional. It has always been average.

"All intellects wholly, exclusively surrendered and consecrated to the truth cannot be utilized by any human being, even by the person in which it resides. I myself cannot utilize my own intelligence; so how could I put it at Philip's disposal? It is my intelligence that utilizes me, and it obeys without reserve—at least I hope that it's so—what seems to be the light of truth. It obeys day by day, instant by instant, and my will never has any influence on it.

"Such people, I believe, don't really have anything in common with ministers, even ministers like Philip.

"Thus I can be of no service to the commissariat as such or to Philip personally.

"Finally, I am anxious to point out in passing that I disapprove of the continuation—confirmed by de Gaulle in an interview—of something called 'the movement of fighting France'; wherever I may be, whether here or in Africa, I don't consider myself a part of it.

"I formally request you to communicate to Philip the contents of this letter. Show it to him if you think it is a good idea. It would, I think, be best.

"You know my feelings for Philip. He too, I believe, knows them. I don't believe that this letter is likely to cause any misunderstandings in that connection. Although I know him so little, I completely understand your friendship for him; that is all that needs to be said.

"A letter like this, in my condition, is madness. But it had to be written. I hope it will not trouble your sleep.

"Affectionate and bacilli-free kisses to Zette and Daniel.

"Sincerely,
"Simone Weil.

"P.S. This is no great loss for you.

"What I am going to say now expresses an old (but increasingly strong, especially, of course, for several months now) thought and permanent conviction. It is not the result of physical or moral depression.

"I am finished, broken, beyond all possibility of mending, and that independent of Koch's bacilli. The latter have only taken advantage of my lack of resistance and, of course, are busy demolishing it a little further.

"According to the most favorable hypothesis (to speak like everyone else; to me everything is equally good), the object may perhaps not be repaired but only temporarily glued together in such a way as to be able to function for a few more years. A small number of years.

"That, really, in my opinion—as certain an opinion as any can be in this domain—is to stretch possibilities to their extreme limit. If I don't generally speak like this it is because it seems futile to me and not because I ever think otherwise.

"I believe, I am almost convinced that even a temporary gluing-together could only be accomplished by my parents, not by anyone else.

"If it ever should take place, I will dedicate what little energy and life thus granted to me either to thinking and writing down what I have in me (even if there will be no one to consume it) or to some activity in the cannon-fodder line. I hope that you understand what I mean.

"I will not fritter myself away in any activity that has in any degree to do with politics, knowing that the amount of energy corresponding to an effective minimum in politics is as far beyond my reach as that which the explorers of Mt. Everest need.

"So that's that.

"Keep this well in mind: if certain words in my letter seem to imply an indirect criticism of you, that would be an incorrect interpretation. Until further notice I don't disapprove of anything either in your position or your activity. You have managed your life in your way; I in mine.

"Again, regards.

"S.W.

"If the opportunity arises, show this letter to Schumann (also the P.S.). And keep it."

Mme. Closon and Mme. Rosin had tried to gather information that might help them in finding a sanitarium. Mme. Closon had written to several establishments. Among those that did not require too long a waiting period—some replied that it would be necessary to wait at least three or four months—the only one about which the Closons had sufficiently precise information was the Grosvenor Sanatorium at Ashford in Kent. Its director was a Dr. Roberts, whose mother-in-law, Mme. Jones, was French. Simone applied for admittance. She was waiting for everything to be settled before telling Dr. Bennett.

But she was forced to act in a different way because one morning the doctor came in and told her quite peremptorily that, after having consulted with another specialist, he had decided to give her a pneumothorax and that he would begin the new treatment immediately. She told the doctor that she was in touch with a sanitarium and that she would no longer submit to any treatment at the hospital.

This refusal of the pneumothorax could be the clearest sign yet that she wanted to die. It definitely convinced the doctor that she was not cooperating with the efforts to cure her. Yet Mme. Closon has stated that she explained her refusal not only by her desire to leave the hospital but also with arguments about the medical value of the treatment. She wondered whether it was a good idea to sacrifice one lung when the other, already stricken, could some day also end up in very bad condition.

From that moment on Dr. Bennett himself deemed it useless to keep her at Middlesex any longer and felt that her place was in a sanitarium. On July 30 he wrote to the director of the Grosvenor Sanatorium, asking him to accept her.

During the next days she anxiously waited for the necessary steps to be completed. It was at this point that she suffered several digestive attacks, after which she ate less and less and became even weaker than before.

It was no doubt during the very last days of July or the beginning of August that she again saw Maurice Schumann, who had returned from Algiers. She had foreseen, a few days earlier, that unfortunately, at one time or another, she would hurt him.[100] And in fact she had a few violent, painful arguments with him. De Gaulle had claimed that only his movement had the right to represent France. According to Schumann, this was necessary because in order for France to negotiate with the Allies it had to be represented by a single authority. But Simone saw personal rivalries in the dissensions between de Gaulle and Giraud. By now it seemed quite certain to her that Gaullism was a kind of political party and she was afraid that this party might become fascist. She spoke of the deterioration of the fighting Free French movement, the state of erosion that had overtaken it. She also criticized Schumann with regard to his radio broadcasts. She reproached him for a statement that might incite hostility toward the German people as a whole, without discrimination. (Schumann thanked her for this warning: "Only she," he said, "could say this to me.") He had also spoken about the Russians in a way she did not approve of. She thought that one must not hide the truth concerning an ally because of the excuse that he is an ally. Finally, she held it against him that he had not been able to get her parachuted into France. She was in a state of rebellion against him and against Gaullism because they had not granted her the means of fulfilling her vocation. She reproached Schumann for not having been a good enough friend to her: shouldn't he have, if he really had been her friend, done what she requested instead of letting her die of grief in England? Finally, she told him that she would not forbid him to visit her, but she would never talk to him again. In fact, their last meeting was silent. He had brought her Vercors's novel *The Silence of the Sea;* she handed back the book in silence, refusing even to glance at it.

She got along very well with the nurses and the other employees at the hospital. It was only with the doctor and the people who had political responsibilities that she was difficult. In her letters to her parents, still trying to conceal from them the fact that she was shut up in a room and saw very few people, she tells them that she has become acquainted with "some young English girls, very young and very kind."[101] She obviously is referring to the nurses and other workers in the hospital. In her letter of August 4 she devotes some time to describing for them, with a mischievousness filled with both indulgence and kindness, the young girl who does the cleaning.[102]

Several months before her parents had applied for authorization to leave for Algiers, if they could not go to England. She had tried to help their request as best she could,[103] and at times knowing whether these attempts were successful was the only thing that still preoccupied her. As long as she had any hope of being cured, she thought, as we have seen, that she would try to join them in Algeria.

They had gone to spend some time with their son and spoke a lot about Sylvie in their letters to Simone. These descriptions of her niece filled her with joy; she thought all the time about Sylvie and her "sunny laughter."[104] She never grew tired of receiving details about her. "You cannot imagine what it means to me."[105]

What preoccupied her during these days when she felt her chances for living rapidly waning was the thought of the truths she had spoken and which it seemed to her had not been heard, and perhaps never would be. She was very pessimisitic about this. In one of her July letters she implies that nobody pays enough attention to her ideas. She is certain that there is in her "a deposit of pure gold that must be handed on." "Only I become more and more convinced, from experience and observing my contemporaries, that there is no one to receive it. . . . As for posterity, before there is a generation with muscle and the power of thought, the books and manuscripts of our epoch will surely have disappeared."[106]

She is quite well aware of the fact that some people consider her slightly touched in the head. She certainly knew this when she wrote "Are We Struggling for Justice?" (the article that dealt with 'mad love'). In her letter of August 4 she brings up the madmen or fools in Shakespeare and Velásquez—so tragic because only they know the truth but are not listened to by anyone because they are fools.[107]

Does this pessimism make her suffer? She declares that it does not. She believes that the truth exists in itself, in a place from whence it can always descend again. In her letter of July 18, when she doubts that she can hand on the pure gold deposited in her, she adds: "This does not distress me at all. The mine of gold is inexhaustible."[108]

Yet she could not, so it seems, help but regret that people's attention was directed to her person rather than to her thoughts. Just as in leaving Marseilles she had advised Father Perrin to concern himself with her thoughts rather than worry about her, so in her letter of August 4, having the presentiment of another journey, she regrets that people praise her intelligence rather than take a real interest in what she is saying. The laudatory remarks about her intelligence, she says, are *purposely* made so as to evade the question: "Is what she says true?" This is the question that she wanted to see asked. This was her final testament.

Dr. Roberts, the director of the Grosvenor Sanatorium, had raised some objections to her admission because his establishment took in chiefly workers; he was afraid that a professor would feel out of place there. He did not know that this particular professor had spent her whole life trying to share the workers' way of life and condition. Mme. Jones, who had come to see Simone at Middlesex, argued in her favor and was able to get her application accepted.

Before leaving the hospital, Simone carefully watched over the packing of her books and papers; she was anxious that certain things would be within reach. She appears to have thought that she still could manage to work in the sanitarium.

Yet she certainly no longer had any hope of getting better, of returning to some kind of normal existence, even for a few years, when she wrote a short letter to her parents, her last one. This letter is evidently intended to prepare them at first for the absence of news, and then for the news of her death.

"Darlings,

"Very little time or inspiration for letters now. They will be short, erratic, and far between. But you have another source of consolation."

She hoped they would be allowed to leave for Algeria.

"By the time you get this (unless it arrives quickly) perhaps you will also have the long-awaited cable. . . ." She confirms the friendship shown her by the Closons and says: "Au revoir, darlings. Heaps and heaps of love."[109]

On August 17 she was transferred to Ashford by ambulance. The trip that Mme. Closon had feared went well; from time to time Simone smiled at her. On arriving she expressed her happiness at seeing the countryside again. The room in which she was put (a room with two beds, though she was alone) looked out over meadows and trees. When she entered this room, she is supposed to have said, "A beautiful room to die in."

She was terribly thin and utterly exhausted. She was also running a very high temperature, which was to go down during the next days. On her patient's sheet, the doctor wrote: "Too ill to be properly examined." It was not hidden from Mme. Closon that it would definitely be impossible to cure her.

She was given over to the care of Dr. Henrietta Broderick. This doctor, according to an Ashford newspaper,[110] is supposed to have said after Simone's death:

"When Professor Weil came down, she was fully convinced that we would cure her. We did not consider her in an advanced stage of tuberculosis, and that she had a chance if she took food. I had a letter from Dr. Roberts [sic] of the Middlesex Hospital, in which he said that Professor Weil was starving herself, and that she kept repeating that her food was to be sent to the French prisoners of war."

On certain points the newspaper undoubtedly distorted Dr. Broderick's statement. Not only is "Dr. Roberts" a mistake for the name of Dr. Bennett, but it is also likely that at that moment or even earlier Simone was not fully convinced that she would get better. Nor were the doctors. As I said, a doctor at Ashford (perhaps Dr. Roberts) admitted to Mme. Closon that from the start there was no hope whatsoever. Later on Dr. Broderick told Jacques Cabaud that she had not been as optimistic as the newspaper had claimed.[111]

The same newspaper article went on as follows: " 'When she arrived,' Dr. Broderick continued, 'she was tired and registered no emotions. Later I gave her an examination; a nurse had to turn her over because she was so weak. I did not consider that the signs of tuberculosis in the chest coincided with the condition of the patient. Her limbs were stiff, and she wouldn't use them. She was slightly mentally unbalanced. On the morning of the eighteenth of August, the day after she was admitted, I tried to get her to take some food. She said she would try. She didn't have any, however, except for some tea and water. The reason she gave for not eating was that she couldn't eat when she thought of the French people starving in France. I consider the death due to cardiac failure due to degeneration through starvation, and not through pulmonary tuberculosis.' "

Perhaps this part of Dr. Broderick's statement was also somewhat distorted. Later on Dr. Broderick told May Mesnet that at Ashford Simone had preserved "a total lucidity of mind." The doctor also said that she had not absolutely refused all food, and that she had perhaps accepted some fruit or a small piece of chocolate.[112] I assume that this means that she accepted these things from time to time and not just once in eight days. The head nurse, Mrs. Wilks, according to the same article in the *Tuesday Express,* stated that Simone took very little food, but not that she did not take any at all.

Yet it does seem true that from the time she arrived at Ashford and perhaps already during the last days she spent at Middlesex, she had almost stopped eating. She said that she could not tolerate any solid food. When Mme. Closon returned to the sanitarium on the following Saturday (August 21), Dr. Broderick and Mme. Jones told her that it was very hard to feed her. "The doctor as well as the director of the sanitarium," Mme. Closon wrote just a few days later, "have told me that they found it very difficult to feed her because she could not tolerate milk—and said that she could not take any solid food; that she would try as best she could to accept any liquid food (concentrated chicken broth, egg yolk whipped in sherry, a very ripe peach) that she could hold.[113] That same Saturday Simone told Mme. Closon that perhaps she would be able to eat some mashed potatoes if they were prepared in the French manner, a purée like her mother used to make. Mme. Closon promised to return eight days later and make it for her.

The next day, Sunday, August 22, Simone received a visit from a colleague. Monday was a relatively good day. Tuesday, a day at the beginning of which "she had a few conversations and seemed quite lively,"[114] she fell into a coma at about five o'clock in the afternoon and did not regain consciousness. At about ten-thirty that night she expired.

"Her death must have been calm," Dr. Broderick told May Mesnet. "At the moment of the doctor's visit on the evening of her death, around eight o'clock, she was sleeping. She undoubtedly suffered a cardiac arrest in her sleep and looked quite peaceful.[115]

Dr. Broderick also told May Mesnet that physically Simone did not suffer at Ashford but that she must have suffered morally, since she was unable to do anything for herself and found it disagreeable to be waited upon by the nurses. "She often talked to Dr. Broderick because she maintained complete mental lucidity; her eyes kept their brilliance, and she could read and write. She seemed to have achieved complete detachment, knowing that she was going to die. She told the doctor that she was a philosopher and interested in humanity."[116]

As for her religious ideas, two Maidstone newspapers that ran articles on her death (one on the third and the other on the twelfth of September, 1943) said that, according to Dr. Broderick, she "had a curious religious outlook, and would say that she had no religion at all."[117] Here, too, it seems that Dr. Broderick's remarks have been misinterpreted. She told May Mesnet in 1954 that Simone refused to reply to the nurses when, for her dossier, they asked her what her religion was, but that to the doctor (was it Dr. Broderick or Dr. Roberts?) she said that she was Jewish and wanted to be a Catholic, but that there was still a point that was undecided.

Although she did not absolutely refuse all kinds of food—and as for the food that she did refuse she explained that she could not tolerate it— and also said that she would try to eat more, it was thought at the sanitarium that she had voluntarily refused to eat, either because she had said that she could not eat when thinking of her compatriots or because Dr. Bennett's letter had suggested this idea. As always when there is a suspicion that a death is not completely natural, an inquest was held by the coroner on August 27, and Dr. Broderick and Nurse Wilks had to appear as witnesses. I have already quoted their statements, at least as the *Tuesday Express* in Ashford reported them. The coroner issued a verdict of suicide. The death certificate indicates that the cause of death was "cardial failure due to myocardial degeneration of the heart muscles due to starvation and pulmonary tuberculosis"; to which was added the following sentence: "The deceased did kill and slay herself by refusing to eat whilst the balance of her mind was disturbed." This is the formula ordinarily used in such cases, since suicide is prohibited by English law.

This "suicide" seemed strange enough to be mentioned in the local newspaper.[118] The *Tuesday Express* of Ashford carried the news on the first page, with the headline "French Professor Starves Herself to Death." The two Maidstone newspapers I have mentioned, the *Kent Messenger* of September 3 and the *South Eastern Gazette* of September 12, published their articles with the headline "Death from Starvation: French Professor's Curious Sacrifice."

And yet, on the same day on which Simone was to die, Mme. Jones had written to Mme. Closon:

"I would have liked to see Dr. Broderick before writing to you, but she was very busy with two doctors from the Ministry of Health.

"I am very much afraid that Simone is very low. She did not open her eyes nor did she make any movement when I went to see her just a short while ago; and so far today she has not eaten anything but an egg yolk whipped in sherry and diluted with a little milk. Sunday evening I brought her some bread and butter boiled to a pulp; she herself explained to her private nurse how to fix it with some bouillon because she does not want any milk, and she ate some twice. She also ate some peaches and drank some sherry; she spoke to me at length, asking me not to tell her any longer what she ought to eat, saying that she was intelligent enough (I never doubted it!) to do her best and try to absorb more and more, etc. She also asked me if I could find a French cook and, also, to let her have a little butter roll in the morning—both impossible things to procure! When I had spoken to her about the mashed potatoes, she had said: Yes, if they are done the French way by a Frenchwoman. . . . Unfortunately I cannot go and meddle with the cooking or intervene in the duty rooms where the nurses prepare the special dishes. Today her nurse is very discouraged after she had a little hope on Sunday and yesterday morning.

"Four-thirty. I have just seen Dr. Broderick. She says that unfortunately nothing can be done anymore. I am desolate; it seems that this is the end for Simone. . . . Her breath is really all that she has left. If there is an emergency, we will call you tomorrow morning at Hill Street. But alas, I don't see what you could do.

"Please believe in my warmest sympathy for you and for our patient. . . ."

This letter seems to indicate that Simone was trying to eat and refused most foods only because she thought she could not tolerate them. It is true that if she wanted to die, at least if she wanted to from a certain moment on—perhaps when she thought she would never recover and had become a useless burden—she would not have said this and could have been covering it up by making excuses. The question of what she wanted at the end remains obscure, and no doubt we shall never know.

She was buried on August 30 in Ashford's New Cemetery in the section reserved for Catholics. Seven people attended the funeral. They were, I believe, Mme. Aron (who had arrived in London shortly before), Mme. Closon, Professor Fehling, Mrs. Francis, Mme. Rosin, Maurice Schumann, and a Frenchwoman from the Free French movement. A priest had been asked to come; he took the wrong train or missed his train and never arrived. Schumann had a missal; he knelt and read the prayers; Mme. Closon made the responses. Mrs. Francis threw into the grave a bouquet tied with a tricolor ribbon of France's colors. Afterward, before leaving Ashford, these friends gathered at the house of Mme. Jones.

Mme. Closon had sent a cable to André Weil, then a letter to Eveline Weil. André Weil immediately went to New York. Before leaving he had telephoned Dr. Bercher, who at the time was in Philadelphia, and asked him to come and meet him in New York. He went to see his parents and asked them if they had received any news about Simone recently. He could see that they didn't know anything and he didn't have the courage to tell them. The next day he got Louis Rougier to call them—and Rougier asked them whether it was true that Simone was so very ill. They answered that everything was fine. Yet, disturbed by this telephone call, they decided to send a cable. As Dr. Weil came downstairs with the cable, just as he stepped out of the elevator, he met his son, accompanied this time by Dr. Bercher. They told him the terrible news and went back upstairs with him to tell Mme. Weil.

Notes

Chapter 1. *Family and Childhood (1909–1925)*

1. The beginning of this letter and therefore its date are missing.
2. *La Connaissance surnaturelle* (Paris: Gallimard, 1950), p. 178.
3. *Cahiers,* III (Paris: Plon, 1956), p. 160.
4. Letter to Georges Bernanos, in S. Weil, *Ecrits historiques et politiques* (Paris: Gallimard, 1960), pp. 220–24. See also p. 109 of the same volume: "While still a child, in everything that I read or heard described, [I] always put myself instinctively, due to indignation rather than pity, in the place of all those who suffered constraint."
5. Letter to Georges Bernanos, in *Seventy Letters,* edited and translated by Richard Rees (New York: Oxford University Press, 1965).
6. Published in S. Weil, *Poèmes, suivis de Venise sauvée* (Paris: Gallimard, 1968), pp. 37–38.
7. *Waiting for God* (New York: Capricorn Books, 1959), p. 64.
8. Ibid.
9. *Cahiers,* I, new edition (Paris: Plon, 1970), p. 20.
10. Ibid.
11. P. Claudel, *l'Otage,* act III, scene II.
12. *Waiting for God,* p. 73.

Chapter 2. *The Encounter with Alain*

1. Alain, *Journal* (unpublished).
2. Letter of June 21, 1914.
3. *Seventy Letters* (New York: Oxford University Press, 1965), pp. 12–13.
4. M.-M. Davy, *Simone Weil* (Paris: Editions Universitaires, 1956), p. 13.
5. I have heard it said that one fellow student, to play a joke on her, sent her a series of love letters during the first year she attended Henri IV. A story Mme. Weil told me may be connected with this. Mme. Weil said that for some time during this first year Simone seemed depressed; then one day she told her that she had made an appointment with one of her classmates on the place du Panthéon and asked her mother to accompany her. Mme. Weil did go with her, but while Simone was talking with her classmate, she

stood some distance away and did not hear what was said. When Simone left her classmate and rejoined her mother, she said, "I think that he understands and things will be different from now on." After this, she was no longer bothered.

6. *Cahiers,* I, new edition (Paris: Plon, 1970), p. 277.

7. Alain, *Souvenirs concernant Jules Lagneau* (Paris: Gallimard, 1925), p. 158; cf. p. 54.

8. A. Maurois, *Mémoires* (Paris: Flammarion, 1948), vol. 1, p. 53. See also S. Pétrement, "Sur la religion d'Alain, avec quelques remarques concernant celle de Simone Weil," *Revue de métaphysique et de morale,* 60 (1955), pp. 306–30.

9. I call it a *topo* because it doesn't have numbered notes. But Alain assigned us a dissertation on the same subject, "The Beautiful and the Good." Could it be Simone's dissertation, which she subsequently took up again and refashioned as a *topo*?

10. *Notebooks,* II, translated by Arthur Wills (New York: G. P. Putnam's, 1965), p. 446. She also said (*Notebooks,* II, p. 406): "To perceive *purely,* without any admixture of dream or reverie (my idea when I was seventeen)." Though here it was more a question of the will to perceive well, which Alain inculcated in us, without any necessary reference to Spinoza.

11. *Waiting for God* (New York: Capricorn Books, 1959), p. 61.

12. *First and Last Notebooks,* edited and translated by Richard Rees (New York: Oxford University Press, 1970), p. 137.

13. These evaluations are to be found in a register kept at the Lycée Henri IV. For the third trimester of 1927–28 a transcript of Alain's evaluation, which was sent to Simone, has a longer text: "Excellent student; unusual strength of mind, broad culture. She will succeed brilliantly if she does not go down obscure paths. In any event, she will certainly be noticed."

Chapter 3. *Preparing for the Examination for the Ecole Normale (1925–1928)*

1. To tell the truth, this account astonishes me. It has also astonished many others—for example, Albertine Thévenon and André Weil. It is possible that Simone Canguilhem did not really understand the significance of the discussion she remembers.

2. *Memoirs of a Dutiful Daughter* (New York: Harper & Row, 1974).

3. Ibid., p. 243.

Chapter 4. *The Ecole Normale (1928–1931)*

1. Examination in physics, chemistry, and the natural sciences that ends the first year of medical studies; it later became the P.C.B. (physics, chemistry, and biology). Students in philosophy must pass an examination in the sciences before presenting themselves for the *agrégation* examination, which is the exam for a license to teach in the lycées and universities, and they usually chose the physics in the P.C.N. because it was the easiest one.

2. According to a report on the Congress written by Michel Alexandre. See *Libres Propos*, New Series, 3rd year, No. 4 (April 20, 1929), p. 177.
3. V.-H. Debidour, *Simone Weil, ou la transparence* (Paris: Plon, 1963), p. 24.
4. J. Cabaud, op cit., p. 34.
5. *Libres Propos*, New Series, 3rd year (1929), No. 5, pp. 237–41; and No. 8, pp. 387–92.
6. Paris: Gallimard, 1966.
7. Ibid., p. 55.
8. Ibid., p. 60.
9. Ibid., p. 62.
10. Ibid., p. 66.
11. Ibid., p. 71.
12. Ibid., p. 83.
13. Ibid.
14. Ibid., p. 84.
15. This dossier, which was kept at the Ministry of National Education until June 15, 1970, is now at the National·Archives, where the regulations now in force do not permit its examination.
16. J. Cabaud, op. cit., p. 39.

Chapter 5. *Le Puy (1931–1932)*

1. "Après la mort du Comité des 22" ["After the Death of the Committee of Twenty-Two"], *L'Effort* (January 2, 1932).
2. C. Claveyrolas, S. Faure, Y. Argaud, M. Dérieu, "Simone Weil professeur" [Simone Weil As a Teacher], *Foi et éducation* (May 1951), pp. 170–73.
3. J. Duperray, "Quand Simone Weil passa chez nous" ["When Simone Weil Stayed with Us"], *Les Lettres Nouvelles*, I (April–May 1964), p. 92.
4. Quoted by Mme. Weil in a letter to André Weil dated November 5.
5. Josette and Jean Cornec, "La voix de l'Enseignement du Finistère: Pourquoi nous quittons la C.G.T.U." ["The Teachers of Finistère: Why We Left the C.G.T.U."], *La Révolution prolétarienne* (April 1932), pp. 13, 109–20, 116.
6. "La marche vers l'unité syndicale: une réunion intersyndicale au Puy" ["Progress toward Trade Union Unity: An Inter-Union Meeting at Le Puy"].
7. *Bulletin de la section de la Haute-Loire du Syndicat national*, etc., No. 68 (November 1931), pp. 69–72.
8. According to Mme. Weil's letter to André, dated December 16, 1931.
9. See Piquemal's letter in *La Révolution prolétarienne*, 8th year, No. 125 (March 1932), pp. 20–84.
10. See Monatte's article, "La vie et la mort du Comité des 22," *La Révolution prolétarienne*, 7th year, No. 122 (December 1931), pp. 4/292–14/302; Thévenon's article, "Après la dissolution du Comité des 22," *L'Effort* (December 19, 1931); and Simone's "Après la mort du Comité des 22," *L'Effort* (January 2, 1932).
11. Letter of December 13.
12. Letter of December 11.
13. Letter of December 15.

14. Ibid.
15. Letter of December 14.
16. Letter of December 13.
17. Letter of December 14.
18. Ibid.
19. Ibid.
20. Letter of December 16.
21. *Bulletin de la section de la Haute-Loire du Syndicat des institutrices et instituteurs publics de France et des colonies,* 13th year, No. 70 (January–February 1932).
22. See the newspaper *La Haute-Loire* (February 20, 1932).
23. In its December 20, 1931, issue.
24. Letter of December 21, 1931.
25. *Le Mémorial* (December 20, 1931).
26. Same issue as the one that ran Vidal's article; see note number 24.
27. See note number 24.
28. C. Claveyrolas, S. Faure, Y. Argaud, and M. Dérieu, op. cit.
29. These documents can be found collected in the *Bulletin de la section de la Haute-Loire* (January–February 1932).
30. André Weil had written to his sister on January 14, in the letter where he calls her "the mushroom on the humus," that the University of Aligarh was collapsing and that he was thinking of returning to France by way of China and Russia.
31. C. Claveyrolas et al., op. cit.
32. See *La Haute-Loire* (February 10 and 11, 1932).
33. According to *La Haute-Loire* of February 20, out of 170 unemployed only 22 asked to benefit from the soup kitchen.
34. Mme. Weil's letter to her husband on December 21, 1931.
35. Mme. Weil's letters to her husband dated February 29 and March 3, 1932.
36. Mme. Weil's letter to her husband on March 4, 1932.
37. This article, published in *L'Effort* and entitled "The Modes of Exploitation," had these words at the end: *To be continued.* No second section, however, was ever published under the same title. But it is probable that the continuation is "Capital and the Worker"; and it can also be connected with the article on the visit to the mine, which expresses the same preoccupations.
38. Mme. Weil told me of a young carpenter who came to see Simone and to whom she gave lessons in mathematics. He undoubtedly wrote this letter. He was later to die of tuberculosis. During his illness, Simone visited him at the hospital.
39. Pages 11/107.
40. The theory held by Louzon in "The Reason for Economic Crises," *La Révolution prolétarienne,* 7th year, No. 115 (March 1931), pp. 5/69–10/74.

Chapter 6. Trip to Germany. Auxerres (1932–1933)

1. It was reprinted in *Ecrits historiques et politiques* (Paris: Gallimard, 1960), pp. 117–23.
2. Busseuil, whose real name was Finidori, had tried to dissuade Simone from going to Germany. Also no doubt Cancouët, and several others.

3. This extract is reprinted in *Ecrits historiques et politiques*, pp. 124–25.
4. Some extracts from this and other letters written by Simone to the Thévenons have been published by U. Thévenon in "Une étape de la vie de Simone Weil" ["A Stage in Simone Weil's Life"], *La Révolution prolétarienne*, No. 362 (May 1952), pp. 13/157–18/162.
5. *Op. cit.*, p. 73.
6. Ibid., pp. 73–74.
7. See *Ecrits historiques et politiques*, p. 142. In this collection the word "movements" was printed by mistake instead of "uprisings."
8. Ibid., p. 144.
9. Text published in *Libres Propos*. The text found in *La Révolution prolétarienne* and reprinted in *Ecrits historiques et politiques*, p. 145, is slightly different.
10. These articles are reprinted in *Ecrits historiques et politiques*, pp. 146–94.
11. The council met on the thirtieth, according to *L'Emancipation*, monthly bulletin of the Federation of Union Members in Lay Education, 29th year, No. 339 (January 22, 1933). Supplement of *L'Ecole émancipée*, 23rd year, No. 17.
12. *Le Travailleur de l'Enseignement*, 5th year, No. 5 (February 1933), pp. 8–9.
13. A Relief Committee had been organized to help these people. It had its office in a corner of the Labor Exchange where the trade union for utility (gas) workers of the Paris suburbs was.
14. According to Mme. Weil, certain stories about escapes had led Simone to think that it was not impossible to free a prisoner by taking his place. Moreover, Jean Rabaut, speaking of Simone, has written: "In 1933—according at least to what people told me—she had a plan to go to Germany to carry on underground work. She declared that the thought of the tortures to which militants were being subjected haunted her so much that she wanted to replace the sensation by the reality." *L'Age nouveau*, No. 61 (May 1951), p. 20.
15. "Some Remarks on the Reply of the M.O.R.," *L'Ecole émancipée*, 23rd year, No. 31 (May 7, 1933). See also *Ecrits historiques et politiques*, pp. 197–202.
16. Ibid.
17. Reprinted in *Ecrits historiques et politiques*, pp. 195–96.
18. Reprinted ibid., pp. 197–202.
19. *Oppression and Liberty* (London: Routledge & Kegan Paul, 1958), p. 25.
20. Ibid., p. 25.
21. Ibid., p. 127.
22. Ibid., p. 43.
23. Also called the "Opposition of Radial XV."
24. J. Rabaut, "Simone Weil and the Fourth International." Unpublished article.
25. This statement, which is followed by fourteen signatures, one of them Simone's, is found at the beginning of a mimeographed pamphlet entitled *Where Are We?* edited by Albert Treint, one of the signatories. It is not certain that the text published by Treint reproduces fully what Simone had written; some amendments may have been added. But the passages that I have quoted seem to be from her pen. It was on the basis of information furnished me by Jean Rabaut that this text was rediscovered.
26. M. Ducret, "A New Party," *Le Travailleur*, Belfort (November 26, 1932).

27. *Oppression and Liberty,* p. 25.
28. *L'Effort* (July 22, 1933).
29. *L'Ecole émancipée,* 23rd year, No. 42 (July 23, 1933). Reprinted in *Ecrits historiques et politiques,* pp. 203–8. At the end of this article, one can read: "Received on June 24."
30. See J. Malaubre's article, "Promenade 'à travers' le Front unique" ["A Stroll 'Through' the United Front"], *Bulletin of the Majority United Federation of Education,* No. 6 (February 1934).
31. See Cabaud, op. cit., p. 80.
32. Cabaud, op. cit., pp. 75 and 82.
33. These reports are quoted on the basis of Cabaud's account, op. cit., pp. 79–81.

Chapter 7. Roanne (1933–1934)

1. See *L'Effort* (August 12, 1933).
2. *Le Communiste,* monthly bulletin of the left Communist group, New Series, No. 2 (September 1, 1933), p. 8.
3. Louis Renard in *Le Travailleur,* Belfort, 2nd year, No. 79 (November 18, 1933), reproduced in the *Bulletin of the Majority of United Federation of Education,* No. 6 (February 1934), p. 30.
4. See *L'Emancipation,* monthly bulletin of the Federation of Union Members in Lay Education, 30th year, No. 352 (October 1, 1933). Supplement of *L'Ecole émancipée,* 24th year, No. 1, p. 16.
5. Unpublished article: "Simone Weil and the Fourth International."
6. Ibid. In *L'Age nouveau,* No. 61 (May 1951), p. 19, Rabaut sums up the account like this: "After a night session, during a stroll through Rheims, she began very seriously to praise monks and nuns. The others made polite fun of her." When she said that certain nuns were the best people she had ever known, Simone was evidently thinking of Edi Copeau.
7. "Simone Weil and the Fourth International."
8. *L'Age nouveau,* No. 61 (May 1951), p. 19.
9. She would question people untiringly and would try to push her inquiry to the very bottom. As Bercher puts it, she "emptied people out." Her curiosity, whose motives people did not always understand, was more than once badly received. Cancouët said that she liked to visit workers unexpectedly to see how they lived, and of course this annoyed their wives, who did not like being surprised in this way. Thévenon says that when she heard something good of someone she wanted to meet that person immediately, and that she would endure almost anything to find out what she wanted to know. Bercher told me that one day Louzon, irritated by her incessant questions, began to bang on the table and yelled, "But what is this? Am I being grilled by an examining magistrate?"
10. *L'Age nouveau,* loc. cit.
11. Printed in the volume *Oppression and Liberty* (London: Routledge & Kegan Paul, 1958), pp. 9–38.
12. J. Rabaut, in *L'Age nouveau,* No. 61 (May 1951), p. 20.
13. Ibid.

14. "La personne et la pensée de Simone Weil" ["Simone Weil's personality and thought"] *La Table ronde* (February 1948), pp. 312–21.
15. They were at first six, but one or two of the students had taken the course for only a short time.
16. *Les Lettres nouvelles* (June–July–August 1964), p. 130.
17. *Les Lettres nouvelles* (April–May 1964), pp. 85–102; (June–July–August 1964), pp. 123–38.
18. *L'Effort,* 17th year, No. 402 (October 28, 1933).
19. According to a letter of Simone's written from Roanne, probably in November 1933.
20. Reprinted in *Ecrits historiques et politiques* (Paris: Gallimard, 1960), pp. 229–39. See also the fragment that follows this article, on pp. 240–41, which is a variation of it.
21. Ibid., p. 233.
22. Ibid., pp. 236–37.
23. This last review was reprinted in *Oppression and Liberty,* pp. 45–53.
24. *Oppression and Liberty,* pp. 4–5.
25. *Le Contrat social,* Vol. XI, No. 3 (May–June 1967), p. 144.
26. *Les Lettres nouvelles* (June–July–August 1964), pp. 125–28.
27. Ibid., p. 128.
28. Ibid., pp. 135–36.
29. Ibid., p. 136.
30. Ibid., p. 137.
31. See J. Brezolles, *Cet ardent sanglot . . . pages de mon journal* (Paris: Beauchesne, 1970), pp. 206–7.
32. Ibid., pp. 128–30.
33. Duperray writes in *La Révolution prolétarienne* of February 25: "The twenty-four-hour general strike has been a formidable success throughout the country, but at Saint-Etienne a triumph."
34. See *Selected Essays, 1934–1943,* chosen and translated by Richard Rees (New York: Oxford University Press, 1962), pp. 55–72.
35. See *L'Ecole émancipée* (February 18 and 25, 1934).
36. See J. Cabaud, *Simone Weil: A Fellowship in Love* (London: Harvill Press, 1964), p. 102, and the testimony of Mme. Reynaud on French television on April 18, 1968.
37. Cabaud, op. cit., p. 102.
38. See J. Cabaud, op. cit., p. 103.
39. See *La Révolution prolétarienne* (Feb. 25, 1934), pp. 1–61.
40. J. Cabaud, op. cit., p. 105; Cabaud also quotes (p. 94) from another passage of Duperray's memoir that is not found in *Les Lettres nouvelles;* it is the account of a difference of opinion that had momentarily brought Simone and Arnaud into conflict. "On one occasion, she gave Pierre Arnaud, leader of the miners' union, a document that condemned the attitude of the Communist party. Arnaud lost his temper; his eyes flashing angrily, he shouted, 'Simone, take your filth away! I'm not a counter-revolutionary yet!' Simone Weil calmly handed him another petition, to raise funds for the anti-Fascist German refugees. Arnaud took the paper, read it, and said, 'Yes, that's all right, I'll sign that!' His hands were trembling. Simone protested, 'But, Pierre, it means the same thing!' 'No,

Simone,' he replied, and both stood speechless. With tightened lips, Simone handed him a fountain pen, and he spread the paper out on the table and signed it."

41. *Seventy Letters*, edited and translated by Richard Rees (New York: Oxford University Press, 1965).

Chapter 8. The Year of Factory Work (1934–1935)

1. *Waiting for God* (New York: Capricorn Books, 1959), pp. 66–67.
2. Ibid., p. 66.
3. *Cahiers*, I, New Edition (Paris: Plon, 1970), pp. 9–90.
4. Ibid., p. 13.
5. *First and Last Notebooks*, edited and translated by Richard Rees (New York: Oxford University Press, 1970).
6. "La prospective chez August Detœuf" ["August Detœuf's View of Things"], *Le Figaro* (May 31, 1967).
7. *Leçons de philosophie de Simone Weil (Roanne, 1933–1934)*, presented by A. Reynaud (Paris: Plon, 1959), p. 151.
8. Simone realized that they would not have kept her on the job without some protection from on high. See S. Weil, *La Condition ouvrière* (Paris: Gallimard, 1951), p. 24.
9. However, he would sometimes give Simone a job that she considered dangerous. See *La Condition ouvrière*, p. 37.
10. Ibid., p. 75.
11. Ibid., p. 82.
12. Ibid., p. 24.
13. This was a notebook in which I put down my ideas. I had had the imprudence of mentioning it to her (or perhaps she had managed, by her questions, to get me to admit it), and she wanted to see it. I had already refused to bring it to her, saying that what I had done was idiotic. In the end, I didn't show it to her because I thought she would make fun of me.
14. *La Condition ouvrière*, p. 40.
15. Ibid.
16. It was perhaps on Tuesday, December 18, that she did this work. See *La Condition ouvrière*, p. 40.
17. This title was not given to the essay until much later by Simone. Whatever it might have been, we always referred to it by that name.
18. *La Condition ouvrière*, p. 41.
19. Ibid., pp. 19–20; see also pp. 42–44.
20. Ibid., p. 42.
21. Ibid., p. 46.
22. Ibid., p. 51.
23. See S. Weil, *Oppression et liberté* (Paris: Gallimard, 1955), p. 8.
24. See *La Condition ouvrière*, pp. 15–17.
25. Ibid., p. 107; see p. 148.
26. Ibid., p. 148.
27. Ibid., p. 53.
28. Ibid., p. 58.
29. Ibid., p. 61.

30. Ibid.
31. This letter is printed in full in *La Condition ouvrière,* pp. 23–27. The date 1934 in this collection is somewhat wrong, since Simone says at the end of the letter "Enjoy the spring ..." Also in *Seventy Letters,* edited and translated by Richard Rees (New York: Oxford University Press, 1965).
32. *La Condition ouvrière,* p. 66.
33. Ibid., p. 70.
34. Ibid., p. 72.
35. Ibid., p. 79.
36. Ibid., p. 80.
37. Ibid., p. 78.
38. Ibid., p. 29.
39. Ibid., p. 82.
40. Ibid., pp. 81–82 and 29–30.
41. Ibid., p. 30.
42. Ibid., p. 30.
43. Ibid., p. 86.
44. Ibid.
45. See also ibid., p. 85.
46. S. Weil, *Sur la science* (Paris: Gallimard, 1966), pp. 111–15.
47. *La Condition ouvrière,* p. 86.
48. Ibid.
49. In her "Factory Journal," the dates from June 11 to 26 are slightly inexact as regards the days of the month. Simone has written Tuesday the twelfth for Tuesday the eleventh, Wednesday the thirteenth for Wednesday the twelfth, etc. The day she designated as Wednesday the twentieth was Wednesday the nineteenth. She was again mistaken, starting from July 17. "Wednesday the eighteenth" [of July] is in fact the seventeenth; "Tuesday the nineteenth" the eighteenth; "Friday the twentieth" the nineteenth. These errors show how terribly tired she was.
50. *La Condition ouvrière,* p. 88.
51. Ibid., p. 89.
52. Ibid., p. 89.
53. Ibid., p. 90.
54. Ibid., p. 92.
55. Ibid., p. 92.
56. Ibid.
57. Ibid., p. 93.
58. Ibid.
59. Ibid., p. 94.
60. Ibid., p. 96.
61. Ibid., p. 98.
62. Ibid.
63. Ibid., p. 99.
64. Ibid., p. 101.
65. Ibid., p. 102.
66. Ibid., p. 101.
67. Ibid., pp. 104–5.
68. Ibid., p. 105.

69. Ibid.
70. Ibid., pp. 106–7.
71. Ibid., p. 21.
72. Ibid., p. 107.
73. Ibid.
74. Ibid., p. 152.
75. Ibid., p. 87.
76. Ibid., p. 99.
77. Ibid., pp. 20–21.
78. Ibid., p. 124.
79. Ibid., p. 107.
80. In a draft of a letter to Belin.
81. *Feuilles libres de la quinzaine,* 2nd year, Nos. 22–25 (September 1936), p. 244. Simone would protest against the publication of this commentary. She wrote to the editor of *Feuilles libres:* "[I regret] that you have let pass these inadmissible epithets, which would not be appropriate except in an obituary."
82. *La Condition ouvrière,* p. 107.
83. Ibid.
84. Ibid., p. 133.
85. Ibid., p. 15.
86. Ibid., p. 22.
87. Ibid., p. 87.
88. Ibid., p. 22.

Chapter 9. Bourges. The Beginning of the Popular Front (1935–1936)

1. *Waiting for God* (New York: Capricorn Books, 1951), pp. 66–67.
2. *Simone Weil: A Fellowship in Love* (New York: Channel Press, 1964), p. 116.
3. J. Cabaud, op. cit., pp. 121 and 126.
4. *La Condition ouvrière,* (Paris: Gallimard, 1951), p. 15.
5. J. Cabaud, op. cit., p. 119.
6. Ibid., p. 133.
7. She writes: "I have again seen the technical manager of the foundry, whose daughter is in my class." That might make one think that it is M. Magdélénat. But it is M. Bernard whom she calls the technical manager (see *La Condition ouvrière,* p. 117). What she meant to say was: the technical manager of the foundry whose owner's daughter is in my class.
8. Cabaud, op. cit., p. 120.
9. Ibid., pp. 116–17.
10. Published in *La Condition ouvrière,* pp. 128–32, and *Seventy Letters,* edited and translated by Richard Rees (New York: Oxford University Press, 1965).
11. Published in *La Condition ouvrière,* pp. 241–59.
12. Ibid., pp. 125–27.
13. Ibid., pp. 132–35, and in *Seventy Letters.*
14. Ibid., pp. 135–43, and in *Seventy Letters.*

15. Ibid., and in *Seventy Letters.*
16. Ibid., p. 148.
17. J. Cabaud, op. cit., p. 126.
18. Ibid., p. 130.
19. Ibid.
20. Ibid., p. 131.
21. Ibid.
22. Ibid.
23. Ibid.
24. Ibid., p. 131.
25. *La Condition ouvrière,* p. 147.
26. Ibid., pp. 149–52.
27. Ibid., p. 154, and in *Seventy Letters.*
28. *La Condition ouvrière,* p. 155.
29. (Paris: Gallimard, 1953), pp. 57–62.
30. *La Condition ouvrière,* p. 157, and *Seventy Letters.*
31. *Seventy Letters.*
32. Letter published in *La Condition ouvrière,* pp. 181–84, and *Seventy Letters.*
33. See Cabaud, op. cit., pp. 120 and 123.

Chapter 10. The Spanish Civil War, the Popular Front, and the First Trip to Italy (1936–1937)

1. *Ecrits historiques et politiques* (Paris: Gallimard, 1960), p. 221; and *Seventy Letters,* edited and translated by Richard Rees (New York: Oxford University Press, 1965).
2. Louis Mercier, *"Contribution à la connaisance de Simone Weil,"* ["Contribution to Understanding Simone Weil"] *Le Dauphiné libéré* (November 16, 1949).
3. See *Ecrits historiques et politiques,* pp. 211–12.
4. Mercier, op. cit.
5. *Ecrits historiques et politiques,* p. 222, and *Seventy Letters.*
6. Ibid., p. 221.
7. There is also a passage in the *Cahiers,* III (Paris: Plon, 1956), p. 51, that seems to look back at this terrible moment. Here she seems to say that she had made a resolution, but that it was an *unformulated* resolution, not even formed inwardly.
8. *Simone Weil: A Fellowship in Love* (New York: Channel Press, 1964), p. 158.
9. *Ecrits historiques et politiques,* p. 252.
10. Ibid., pp. 248–49.
11. Ibid., p. 221, and in *Seventy Letters.*
12. *Ecrits historiques et politiques,* p. 218.
13. Ibid., pp. 218–19; variant, pp. 392–93.
14. See Cabaud, *L'Expérience vécue de Simone Weil* (Paris: Plon, 1957), p. 149.
15. *La Condition ouvrière* (Paris: Gallimard, 1951), pp. 175–79.
16. Ibid., pp. 197–205.
17. *Ecrits historiques et politiques,* pp. 331–35.
18. This is no doubt *La C.G.T., ce qu'elle est, ce qu'elle veut* by L. Jouhaux, M. Harmet, J. Duret (Paris: 1937), pp. 83–84.

19. For the letters to Posternak, see "Cinque lettere a uno studente . . ." *Nuovi Argomenti,* Rome, No. 20 (1953); and *Seventy Letters.*
20. The Italian government granted railroad tickets at reduced price on the occasion of certain exhibits. Simone no doubt had a ticket of this kind for the Catholic Press exhibition. Your ticket had to be stamped to prove you had attended the exhibition.
21. *Waiting for God* (New York: Capricorn Books, 1951), pp. 67–68.

Chapter 11. *Saint-Quentin, Solesmes, and the Second Trip to Italy (1937–1938)*

1. Published in *Selected Essays, 1934–35* (New York: Oxford University Press, 1962) under the title "A Note on Social Democracy."
2. Ibid., pp. 319–23.
3. *Oppression et Liberté (Paris: Gallimard, 1955), pp. 186–93.*
4. S. Weil, *Poèmes, suivis de Venise sauvée* (Paris: Gallimard, 1968), pp. 22–24.
5. In her fifth letter to Posternak, written in the spring of 1938.
6. See *Poèmes,* p. 10.
7. Published in the volume to which the same title is given: *La Condition ouvrière* (Paris: Gallimard, 1951). pp. 233–39.
8. Cabaud, *L'Expérience vécue de Simone Weil* (Paris: Plon, 1957), pp. 170–72.
9. In her fifth letter to Posternak, she says about Goya: "He immediately joined the small group of painters who speak to my soul—Vinci, Giotto, Masaccio, Giorgione, and Rembrandt."
10. *Ecrits historiques et politiques* (Paris: Gallimard, 1960), pp. 339–43.
11. Ibid., pp. 344–50.
12. Letter or draft of a letter published in ibid., pp. 283–89.
13. Ibid., pp. 279–82.
14. *Waiting for God* (New York: Capricorn Books, 1951), p. 68.
15. About the month of November 1938, according to the letter to Joë Bousquet published in *Pensées sans ordre concernant l'amour de Dieu* (Paris: Gallimard, 1962), p. 81.
16. Reprinted in *Ecrits historiques et politiques,* pp. 273–78.
17. *Seventy Letters,* edited and translated by Richard Rees (New York: Oxford University Press, 1965).
18. S. Weil, "The Romanesque Fresco in the Church of Sant'Angelo at Asolo," *Il Ponte,* Florence, 7th year (June 1951), pp. 612–13.
19. Ibid., pp. 614–51.

Chapter 12. *The Inner Experience and the Renunciation of Pacifism (1938–1939)*

1. See *Nouveaux Cahiers,* No. 32 (October 1–15, 1938), p. 20.
2. *Ecrits historiques et politiques* (Paris: Gallimard, 1960), p. 357.
3. Ibid., p. 354.
4. Ibid., pp. 351–60.
5. See *Cahiers,* I, New Edition (Paris: Plon, 1970), p. 272.

6. *Seventy Letters,* edited and translated by Richard Rees (New York: Oxford University Press, 1965).
7. *Waiting for God* (New York: Capricorn Books, 1951) pp. 68–69.
8. S. Weil, *Pensées sans ordre concernant l'amour de Dieu* (Paris: Gallimard, 1962), p. 81.
9. Ibid.
10. *Waiting for God,* p. 76; see also *Pensées sans ordre,* p. 81.
11. *Waiting for God,* pp. 76–77; see also *Pensées sans ordre,* p. 81.
12. *Notebooks,* II (Paris: Plon, 1953), p. 156.
13. See *Nouveaux Cahiers,* No. 33 (November 1, 1938), p. 18.
14. *Nouveaux Cahiers,* No. 38 (February 1, 1938), p. 20.
15. *Essais et combats* (December 1938), p. 2.
16. According to Dr. Bercher's unpublished notes.
17. *Etudes bibliques. Choix de textes religieux assyro-babyloniens,* transcription, translation and commentary by Father Paul Dhorme (Paris: J. Gabalda, 1907).
18. See *Ecrits historiques et politiques,* pp. 296–312.
19. *Ecrits historiques et politiques,* pp. 102–13.

Chapter 13. The First Year of the War (1939–1940)

1. *Ecrits historiques et politiques* (Paris: Gallimard, 1960), pp. 313–14.
2. Ibid., pp. 11–60; also *Selected Essays,* under the English title: "The Great Beast: Some Reflections on the Origins of Hitlerism, 1939–1940," pp. 88–144.
3. *Ecrits historiques et politiques,* pp. 63–65.
4. S. Weil, *La Source grecque* (Paris: Gallimard, 1953), pp. 11–42. In English, *Intimations of Christianity among the Ancient Greeks* (Boston: Beacon, 1957) and "The Iliad, or the Poem of Force," translated by Mary McCarthy, Pendle Hill Pamphlet, Wellingford, Pa., 1956.
5. Cabaud, p. 194.
6. (Paris: Gallimard, 1966), pp. 211–52.
7. This passage is in a letter or a draft that has not been published.
8. *Sur la science,* p. 212.
9. Ibid., pp. 219–20.
10. Ibid., p. 220.
11. Ibid., p. 231.
12. Ibid., p. 232.
13. Ibid., p. 241.
14. Ibid.
15. Ibid., p. 242.
16. Ibid., pp. 242–43.
17. Ibid., p. 221.
18. This passage is not in *Sur la Science.*
19. This passage has also not been published.
20. This draft letter was not published.
21. Richard Rees, *Simone Weil, a sketch for a portrait* (Southern Illinois University Press, Carbondale, 1966), p. 56.
22. *Ecrits de Londres et dernières lettres* (Paris: Gallimard, 1957), pp. 190–91.
23. Ibid., pp. 192–93.

24. Ibid., pp. 195–96.
25. Ibid.
26. Ibid., p. 186.
27. It was in 1937, but no doubt less than a year before sending the poem *"A un jour."*

Chapter 14. Marseilles I (1940–1941)

1. Dr. Bercher's unpublished notes.
2. Ibid.
3. Ibid.
4. See J. Lambert, *Les Vacances du coeur* (Paris: Gallimard, 1951), pp. 233–34.
5. This service record was sent to me on August 31, 1971.
6. It is certain that she had never been attracted to the Jewish religion. Even when she read the Old Testament carefully, it was not in order to gain knowledge of the Jewish religion but because she was more and more attracted to Christianity, which also considers the Old Testament a holy book. About 1934, she said one day to Bercher, as a joke, "Personally, I am an anti-Semite." They had discussed it later and she agreed that she was not really an anti-Semite and that the Jews she disliked were those who regarded themselves as Jews before all else and so separated themselves from other men. In short, what she disapproved of in Judaism was what could possibly lead to sectarianism or fanaticism.
7. This essay was published again in English in *Intimations of Christianity among the Ancient Greeks* (Boston: Beacon Press, 1958) and as a separate publication entitled *The Iliad, or The Poem of Force,* translated by Mary McCarthy (Pendle Hill Pamphlet, Wellingford, Pa., 1956).
8. J. Lambert, op. cit., pp. 233–35.
9. This was a booklet entitled *Le Catharisme* (Carcassonne: printed at de Gabelle, 1937). Reprinted in a revised and augmented edition (Toulouse: Institute of Occitaine Studies, 1947).
10. See also *Seventy Letters,* edited and translated by Richard Rees (New York: Oxford University Press, 1965).
11. *Notebooks,* Vol. II (New York: G. P. Putnam's, 1956), p. 350.
12. *Waiting for God,* (New York: Capricorn Books, 1951), p. 95.
13. *Leçons de philosophie de Simone Weil (Roanne, 1933–1934),* presented by A. Reynaud (Paris: Plon, 1959). See, for example, p. 209.
14. The comparison of a passage of this text with a passage in "Science and Us"—published as "Classical Science and After" in the volume entitled *On Science, Necessity and the Love of God* by Simone Weil, translated and edited by Richard Rees (New York: Oxford University Press, 1968)—leads us to think that it was written at the same time, that is, in the spring of 1941.
15. See *Cahiers du Sud,* 38th year, No. 310, pp. 426–30.
16. P. 14 of first French edition, *L'Attente de Dieu* (Paris: La Colombe, 1950).
17. *Simone Weil As We Knew Her* by J. B. Perrin and G. Thibon (London: Routledge & Kegan Paul, 1953), p. 35.
18. Ibid., p. 36.
19. Ibid.

20. Ibid., pp. 36–37.
21. *Waiting for God,* English edition, p. 70.
22. J. B. Perrin and G. Thibon, op. cit., p. 66.
23. Ibid., p. 59.
24. *La Condition ouvrière* (Paris: Gallimard, 1951), pp. 241–59.
25. *Economie et humanisme,* No. 2 (June–July 1942), pp. 187–204.
26. *On Science, Necessity and the Love of God,* p. 40.
27. These words, and all the quotations that follow, are taken from Dr. Bercher's unpublished notes (1950).
28. The meaning of the word, which is found only in the Our Father, has been discussed and until now it has never been established with certainty. St. Jerome translates it with the word *supersubstantialis* in the Gospel of Matthew and with *quotidianus* in the Gospel of Luke. A certain number of Church Fathers have interpreted *ho artos ho espiouios* to mean immaterial, spiritual bread, bread from on high.
29. See *"Simone Weil anarchiste et chrétienne," L'Age nouveau,* No. 61 (May 1951), p. 20.
30. J. B. Perrin and G. Thibon, op. cit., p. 116.
31. Ibid., pp. 114–15.
32. M.-M. Davy, *Simone Weil* (Paris: Editions universitaires, 1956), p. 32.
33. Ibid., pp. 38–39.

Chapter 15. *Marseilles II (1941–1942)*

1. J. B. Perrin and G. Thibon, *Simone Weil As We Knew Her* (London: Routledge & Kegan Paul, 1953), p. 116.
2. *Gravity and Grace,* trans. Emma Cranford, (London: Routledge & Kegan Paul, 1952), p. 4.
3. *Simone Weil As We Knew Her,* p. 116.
4. Ibid.
5. Ibid.
6. Ibid., p. 118.
7. Ibid., p. 119.
8. Ibid.
9. *Gravity and Grace,* p. 14.
10. Ibid., p. iv.
11. *Simone Weil As We Knew Her,* p. 124.
12. Ibid., p. 127.
13. Ibid., p. 125.
14. Ibid., p. 125.
15. Ibid., pp. 124–25.
16. Ibid., p. 120.
17. *Gravity and Grace,* pp. 5–6.
18. *Simone Weil As We Knew Her,* pp. 119–20.
19. *Gravity and Grace,* p. 7.
20. *Simone Weil As We Knew Her,* p. 120.
21. *Gravity and Grace,* p. iv.
22. Ibid., p. 127.
23. Letter of August 10.

24. Ibid.
25. *Simone Weil As We Knew Her*, p. 117.
26. *Cahiers*, I, New Edition (Paris: Plon, 1970), p.70.
27. *Ecrits de Londres et dernières lettres* (Paris: Gallimard, 1957), p. 194.
28. *Waiting for God* (New York: Capricorn Books, 1951), p. 71.
29. Ibid., p. 71.
30. Ibid., p. 72.
31. Ibid., p. 72.
32. *Simone Weil As We Knew Her.*
33. Ibid., pp. 122–23.
34. Ibid., pp. 128–29.
35. These words were quoted in a lecture given by Hélène Honnorat: "La conversion d'après Simone Weil." This lecture, which Hélène Honnorat delivered several times, was published in a slightly different form in several Catholic magazines, among others in the *Feuillets des Avents,* Castres (January 1972).
36. *Simone Weil As We Knew Her*, p. 129.
37. *La Pesanteur et la grâce* (Paris: Plon, 1947), p. vi., French edition.
38. *Waiting for God.*
39. G. Thibon in *Simone Weil As We Knew Her.*
40. E. Fleuré, *Simone Weil ouvrière* (Paris: F. Lanore, 1955), pp. 93–96.
41. *Simone Weil As We Knew Her*, p. 127.
42. *Attente de Dieu* (Paris: La Colombe, 1950), p. 14.
43. *On Science, Necessity and the Love of God,* translated and edited by Richard Rees (New York: Oxford University Press, 1968).
44. S. Weil, *Intuitions préchrétiennes.*
45. Ibid., p. 7.
46. "La conversion d'après Simone Weil," a lecture by Hélène Honnorat.
47. Ibid.
48. *Simone Weil As We Knew Her*, pp. 45–46.
49. A long extract from this letter has been published by Father Perrin in *Simone Weil As We Knew Her*, pp. 46–47.
50. *Notebook* V is the beginning of Volume II. *Notebook* VI, in the 1953 edition, begins on page 87; *Notebook* VII, on page 234; *Notebook* VIII on page 339. [All references here are to the French editions.]
51. Published in *Cahiers du Sud*, 29th year, No. 245 (April 1942), pp. 393, 303–8. Republished again in *On Science, Necessity and the Love of God,* edited and translated by Richard Rees, Oxford University Press, 1968, with the title "On Scientism: A Review," pp. 65–70.
52. Simone had in an unpublished fragment criticized the theses presented by the "New Order" group.
53. Published in *Cahiers du Sud*, 29th year, No. 251 (December 1942), pp. 102–19. Reprinted in *On Science, Necessity and the Love of God.*
54. See *Sur la science* (Paris: Gallimard, 1966), p. 254; and *Notebooks* I, (Paris: Gallimard), p. 111.
55. *Cahiers du Sud*, 31st year, No. 263 (January 1944), pp. 40–45; reprinted in *On Science, Necessity and the Love of God.*
56. *Notebooks*, I, pp. 143–44.
57. *Gravity and Grace*, pp. 6–7.

58. All in *Poèmes, suivis de Venise sauvée* (Paris: Gallimard, 1968).
59. Pp. 43–51.
60. *Waiting for God,* pp. 52–57.
61. *Simone Weil telle que nous l'avons connue* (Paris: La Colombe, 1952), p. 124, French edition of *Simone Weil As We Knew Her.*
62. Ibid., p. 130.
63. A great part of *Notebook* VIII was published in Vol. II (1953) of the *Notebooks.* But the last part is in Vol. III (1956). In this volume, *Notebook* VIII ends on p. 73; *Notebook* IX ends on p. 191; *Notebook* X ends on p. 279.
64. The first passages on Suzuki's work can be found starting on p. 381 of Vol. II (1953).
65. These thoughts are found on pp. 49, 52, 54, and 70 of Vol. III (1953).
66. For example, on pp. 82–84 of Vol. III (1956).
67. Published at first in No. 249 of *Cahiers du Sud,* 29th year (August–September–October 1942), pp. 99–107. This special number (*Le Génie d'Oc*), of which a certain number of copies were sold with another cover, as a separate work, appeared in February 1943. The article was reprinted in *Selected Essays: 1934–43,* edited and translated by Richard Rees (New York: Oxford University Press, 1962), under the title "A Medieval Epic Poem."
68. Published in the same special issue of *Cahiers du Sud* as cited in note 63, pp. 150–58; reprinted in English in *Selected Essays,* trans. Richard Rees (London: Oxford University Press, 1962), under the title "The Romanesque Renaissance."
69. *Notebooks* III (Paris: Plon, 1956), pp. 49–50.
70. In the short introduction he has written for the correspondence between Simone Weil and Joë Bousquet (*Cahiers du Sud,* 37th year, No. 304, 2nd Semester [1950], p. 420), Ballard says: "It was certainly two o'clock in the morning." But when I talked with him some years later he told me, "About eleven or twelve o'clock."
71. This letter was written to me by the monk F. Vidal on November 22, 1955.
72. J. Cabaud, *Simone Weil: A Fellowship in Love* (New York: Channel Press, 1964), p. 250.
73. This is what Hélène and Pierre Honnorat have told me. They probably also told Father Perrin this, for I imagine that this is what he alludes to on p. 37 of the French edition of *Waiting for God.*
74. Published in *Pensées sans ordre concernant l'amour de Dieu* (Paris: Gallimard, 1962), pp. 69–72.
75. Letter of October 9, 1955.
76. *Simone Weil As We Knew Her,* pp. 131–32.
77. See *Waiting for God,* pp. 113, 143.
78. Ibid., pp. 114–23.
79. Ibid., pp. 143–211.
80. Ibid., pp. 223–36.
81. Ibid., pp. 223–36.
82. Ibid., pp. 124–41.
83. Ibid., p. 124.
84. See, for example, in Vol. II, pp. 313–14, the remark on the feeling of culpability that affliction provokes; and on p. 329 a thought on the growth of the divine germ in the soul; and on pp. 278, 281, 283, 285, thoughts

on matter as the model of pure obedience. And it should be noticed that Joë Bousquet appears for the first time, if I am not mistaken, on p. 261.

85. In the letter to Thibon one finds the idea that separation is one form of friendship; in the letter to Father Perrin the idea that it is the Love of God that sends the gift of affliction.

86. *Pensées sans ordre concernant l'amour de Dieu,* pp. 13–62.

87. *La condition ouvrière* (Paris: Gallimard, 1951), pp. 261–73.

88. *Pensées sans ordre,* p. 17.

89. *La Condition ouvrière,* p. 265.

90. Ibid.

91. Ibid., p. 272.

92. *Notebooks,* I, p. 147.

93. See in particular pp. 276–80 of Vol. III. See also on p. 302–3, the idea that our being has for its substance the love that God feels for us, and on pages 316–17, the idea that it is the fear of God, not of the flesh, that turns us away from God—two ideas that can be found in "Reflections without Order."

94. *Notebooks,* II, trans. Arthur Wills, (London: Routledge & Kegan Paul, 1956), pp. 564–74.

95. *Cahiers du Sud,* 37th year, No. 304, 2nd Semester (1950), pp. 421–23.

96. Ibid., p. 426.

97. *Notebooks,* I, pp. 171, 175, 202, 230; II (1953), pp. 116, 180, 187; III (1956), p. 130. (All references to the French edition.)

98. According to *Notebook,* II, p. 171, she seems to think that suicide is permitted under certain circumstances. In *La Connaissance surnaturelle,* published in English as *First and Last Notebooks,* edited and translated by Richard Rees (New York: Oxford University Press, 1970), she remarks that Eusebius, the bishop and contemporary of Constantine, had only praise for Christian women who killed themselves to escape rape.

99. Letter published in *Waiting for God,* pp. 58–60.

100. He has said in the preface to the French edition of *Gravity and Grace* that he saw her for the last time at the beginning of May 1942. But it is difficult to date these memories exactly, and if it is indeed at this last meeting that she gave him her *Notebooks,* one must think that this meeting took place a little sooner, in view of what he says about the *Notebooks* in a letter of April 27.

101. *Simone Weil As We Knew Her,* pp. 131–32.

102. *Cahiers du Sud,* 37th year, No. 304, 2nd Semester (1950), p. 427.

103. *Simone Weil As We Knew Her,* pp. 136–37.

104. *Seventy Letters,* edited and translated by Richard Rees (New York: Oxford University Press, 1965).

105. Letter published in *Cahiers du Sud,* 37th year, No. 304, 2nd Semester (1950), pp. 431–38. Reprinted in *Pensées sans ordre,* pp. 73–84.

106. Ibid., p. 426.

107. *Waiting for God.*

108. Ibid., p. 92.

109. Ibid., p. 143.

110. She had made the same reply to Thibon. See the preface to *Gravity and Grace,* French edition, p. vi.

Chapter 16. New York (1942)

1. J. B. Perrin and G. Thibon, *Simone Weil As We Knew Her* (London: Routledge & Kegan Paul, 1953), pp. 132–33.
2. J. Cabaud, *Simone Weil: A Fellowship in Love* (New York: Channel Press, 1964), p. 274.
3. Pp. 108–71.
4. *Waiting for God* (New York: Capricorn Books, 1951), pp. 88–101.
5. Ibid., pp. 84–87.
6. In the preface to the French edition of *Gravity and Grace* (*La Pesanteur et la grâce* [Paris: Plon, 1947]), where he quotes most of this letter (pp. vii–ix), Thibon says that it was sent from Oran. Yet a copy that was shown to me by Mme. Weil is dated from Casablanca, and it seems indeed that the letter was written there. Thibon must have confused it with the previous letter.
7. According to a stamp on Simone's and her father's passports: "General Harbor Commissioner. Passed, sailed on June 7, 1942. Casablanca."
8. J. Cabaud, op. cit., p. 275.
9. J. Cabaud, *Simone Weil à New York et à Londres* (Paris: Plon, 1967), p. 21.
10. *Seventy Letters,* edited and translated by Richard Rees (New York: Oxford University Press, 1965).
11. See D. von Hildebrand's preface to J. Cabaud, *Simone Weil, die Logik der Liebe* (Freiburg-München, Munich: K. Alber, 1968), pp. 5–6.
12. J. Cabaud, *Simone Weil: A Fellowship in Love,* pp. 290–91.
13. This letter is published in part in *Simone Weil As We Knew Her,* p. 133.
14. See J. Cabaud, *Simone Weil à New York et à Londres,* p. 34.
15. S. Weil, *Letter to a Priest,* translated by A. F. Wills (New York: G. P. Putnam's Sons, 1954).
16. For example, in "In What Does the Occitan Inspiration Consist?" *Ecrits historiques et politiques* (Paris: Gallimard, 1960), pp. 76–77. And see *Ecrits de Londres,* p. 156.
17. See *Notebooks,* I (London, Routledge & Kegan Paul, 1956), p. 286: "If Krishna himself were troubled in spirit, as Christ was in the Gospels, wouldn't it be far more beautiful?"
18. These notebooks are in fact six in number, but they are numbered I to VII because one of them has two numbers: II and III.
19. *Notebook* IV begins on p. 71 of *La Connaissance surnaturelle* (after the blank space) and ends at the first blank space on p. 126. *Notebook* V goes from the middle of p. 167 to the second paragraph of p. 229. *Notebook* VI begins on p. 229 and ends on p. 274. *Notebook* VII begins on p. 274 and ends on p. 302. In *Notebook* IV one must make an exception for the passage that runs from p. 111 (starting with the blank space) to the middle of p. 114. These pages, written in another direction from the rest of the notebook, were probably copied from the Marseilles notebooks. The notes that run from the middle of p. 114 to the first blank space on p. 126 probably also predate most of this notebook.

20. This note has not been reproduced in the published version. *Notebook* III runs from the second blank space on p. 38 to the blank space on p. 71.
21. From p. 13 to the second blank space on p. 38.
22. From the first blank space on p. 126 to the middle of p. 167.
23. For example, one reads on p. 137: "Written on boat, on the high seas ..." Part of p. 126, written on a separate sheet, seems to be from the Marseilles period.
24. *First and Last Notebooks,* translated and edited by Richard Rees (New York: Oxford University Press, 1970).
25. Published in *Seventy Letters.*

Chapter 17. London (1942–1943)

1. *Ecrits de Londres et dernières lettres* (Paris: Gallimard, 1957), p. 219, and *Seventy Letters,* edited and translated by Richard Rees (New York: Oxford University Press, 1965), p. 162.
2. Ibid., p. 218; and see p. 243 in *Seventy Letters:* "Antigone has gone through some awful moments, it's true. But it didn't last. And it's far away now."
3. Ibid., p. 218; and p. 161 in *Seventy Letters.*
4. *The Need for Roots,* translated by Arthur Wills, with a preface by T. S. Eliot (New York: G. P. Putnam's Sons, 1952).
5. *Oppression and Liberty,* translated by Arthur Wills and John Petrie (London: Routledge and Kegan Paul, 1958).
6. *Ecrits historiques et politiques* (Paris: Gallimard, 1960), pp. 364–78.
7. *On Science, Necessity and the Love of God,* translated and edited by Richard Rees (New York: Oxford University Press, 1968).
8. *Cahiers,* I, New Edition (Paris: Plon, 1970), pp. 281–91.
9. *Pensées sans ordre concernant l'amour de Dieu* (Paris: Gallimard, 1962), pp. 113–58.
10. *La Connaissance surnaturelle* (Paris: Gallimard, 1950), pp. 303–37.
11. *Ecrits de Londres,* p. 151.
12. Ibid., pp. 74–80.
13. Ibid., pp. 169–70.
14. *Letter to a Priest,* translated by A. F. Wills (New York: G. P. Putnam's Sons, 1954), pp. 35–38.
15. *Ecrits de Londres,* pp. 19 and 43. Also *Selected Essays: 1934–43,* edited and translated by Richard Rees (New York: Oxford University Press, 1962), pp. 15 and 34.
16. *Oppression and Liberty,* p. 177.
17. Plato, *The Republic,* VI, 493 c.
18. *Ecrits de Londres,* p. 180.
19. Gershom G. Scholem, *On the Kabbalah and Its Symbolism* (New York: Schocken Books, 1960).
20. See H. Lewy, *Chaldaean oracles und theurgy* (Le Claire, The French Institute of Oriental Archaeology, 1959), pp. 322–31.
21. M. Vetö, *La métaphysique religieuse de Simone Weil* (Paris: J. Vrin, 1971), p. 20, note 8.
22. M. Vetö, op. cit., p. 145. See p. 84.
23. *The Need for Roots,* p. 93.

24. *La Connaissance surnaturelle,* p. 328, and *First and Last Notebooks,* translated and edited by Richard Rees (New York: Oxford University Press, 1970), p. 355.
25. *The Need for Roots,* p. 271.
26. Ibid.
27. Ibid., p. 270.
28. *Oppression and Liberty,* p. 166.
29. Ibid.
30. Ibid., p. 229.
31. M. Vetö, op. cit., p. 143.
32. *Ecrits des Londres,* p. 90.
33. See H. Michel and B. Mirkine-Guetzévitch, *Les Idées politiques et sociales de la Résistance* (Paris: Presses universitaires de France, 1954), pp. 283–87.
34. See *Ecrits des Londres,* pp. 80–84, and *The Need for Roots,* pp. 3–40.
35. *Ecrits des Londres,* p. 152.
36. *Ecrits des Londres,* p. 106, and *Selected Essays,* under the title "A War of Religions."
37. *Ecrits historiques et politiques,* p. 364, and *Selected Essays,* under the English title "East and West: Thoughts on the Colonial Problem."
38. Ibid., p. 375.
39. *Ecrits de Londres,* p. 50.
40. Ibid., p. 57.
41. H. Michel and B. Mirkine-Guetzévitch, op. cit., p. 32.
42. Ibid., pp. 34–35.
43. *Ecrits de Londres,* pp. 70–71.
44. Ibid., p. 71.
45. Pp. 85–92.
46. It is published in H. Michel and B. Mirkine-Guetzévitch, op. cit., pp. 299–301.
47. Under the title "Essential Ideas for a New Constitution," *Ecrits de Londres,* pp. 93–97.
48. I assume Simone means that he must be judged by magistrates. However, she also perhaps means that he must be judged by a tribunal selected by the Chamber of Deputies from among its own members.
49. *Ecrits de Londres,* p. 221, and *Seventy Letters,* pp. 165–66.
50. Ibid., p. 226, and *Seventy Letters,* pp. 165–66.
51. Ibid., p. 226.
52. Ibid., p. 229, and *Seventy Letters,* p. 180.
53. Ibid., p. 231, and *Seventy Letters,* p. 181.
54. Ibid.
55. J. Cabaud, *Simone Weil à New York et à Londres* (Paris: Plon, 1967), pp. 58–59.
56. *Ecrits de Londres,* p. 222, and *Seventy Letters.*
57. Ibid., p. 234, and *Seventy Letters.*
58. Ibid., pp. 201–15.
59. *La Condition ouvrière* (Paris: Gallimard, 1951), p. 18, and *Seventy Letters,* p. 19.
60. *Ecrits de Londres,* p. 214, and *Seventy Letters,* p. 179.
61. Ibid., pp. 213–14, and *Seventy Letters,* pp. 178–79.

62. See W. Rabi, "Simone Weil, ou l'itinéraire d'une âme" *Les Nouveaux Cahiers,* No. 26 (Autumn 1971), p. 54, note 15. This physician, Dr. Kac, strongly suspected that she might be tubercular and advised much more thorough examinations. But Simone was reticent, and no thorough examinations were made. He did not get the chance to mention his suspicions to Closon or Philip. Besides, Simone must have insisted that he do nothing that might hinder her request for a mission.

63. *Ecrits de Londres,* p. 226.

64. Ibid., p. 212, and *Seventy Letters,* pp. 177–78.

65. Ibid., p. 212–13, and *Seventy Letters,* p. 178.

66. In a letter dated March 1 Simone says that she has seen him. (Ibid., p. 213).

67. J. Cabaud, op. cit., p. 61.

68. *La Connaissance surnaturelle,* p. 321, and *First and Last Notebooks,* pp. 348–49.

69. Ibid.

70. *Ecrits de Londres,* p. 212–14, and *Seventy Letters,* p. 179.

71. *Pensées sans ordre concernant l'amour de Dieu,* pp. 133–47.

72. Ibid., pp. 149–55. One can only attempt to date this text through the handwriting. See J. Cabaud, op. cit., p. 342.

73. *Ecrits de Londres,* p. 233, and *Seventy Letters,* p. 183.

74. Ibid., p. 217, and *Seventy Letters,* p. 184.

75. English in original.

76. J. Cabaud, op. cit., pp. 340–41.

77. Ibid., pp. 72–74, French edition.

78. *Letter to a Priest,* p. 67, French edition.

79. *Pensées sans ordre concernant l'amour de Dieu,* p. 149.

80. *Wating for God* (New York: Capricorn Books, 1951) p. 75.

81. J. Cabaud, op. cit., p. 71, French edition.

82. *Les Nouveaux Cahiers,* no. 26 (Autumn 1971), pp. 51–62.

83. These details are distinctly different on some points from those presented, in Rabi's article, by the witness whom Rabi calls Z. and who tells from memory what he in turn was told. According to my notes, when she realized that she was being baptized, Simone appears to have said, "Go ahead, it can't do any harm." These words would seem to express a certain indifference.

84. *Ecrits de Londres,* pp. 239–40, and *Seventy Letters,* p. 188.

85. Ibid., p. 243, and *Seventy Letters,* p. 191.

86. Ibid., p. 225, and *Seventy Letters,* p. 185.

87. Ibid., p. 236, and *Seventy Letters,* p. 186.

88. Ibid., pp. 245–46, and *Seventy Letters,* p. 192.

89. Ibid., p. 162.

90. According to a report published in the English press. See J. Cabaud, op. cit., p. 91.

91. *Cahiers,* I, p. 171: "Suicide is not permitted, except when it is only apparent."

92. *The Need for Roots,* p. 266.

93. *Ecrits de Londres,* p. 251, and *Seventy Letters,* p. 197.

94. *L'Enracinement* (Paris: Gallimard, 1949), p. 255. [French edition of *The Need for Roots.*]

95. *Seventy Letters,* p. 186.

96. Ibid., p. 192.
97. Ibid., p. 192.
98. Ibid., p. 192.
99. Ibid.
100. *Ecrits de Londres,* p. 253, and *Seventy Letters,* p. 199.
101. Ibid., p. 195.
102. Ibid., pp. 199–200.
103. Ibid., p. 194.
104. Ibid., p. 195.
105. Ibid., p. 196.
106. Ibid., pp. 196–97.
107. Ibid., pp. 200–201
108. Ibid., p. 197.
109. Ibid., p. 201.
110. The *Tuesday Express,* published in Ashford on August 31, 1943. The English text of this article is quoted by J. Cabaud in his book, *Simone Weil: A Fellowship in Love* (New York: Channel Press, 1964), p. 349.
111. See J. Cabaud, *Simone Weil à New York et à Londres,* p. 91, note 1.
112. Information gathered by May Mesnet in 1954.
113. Mme. Closon's letter to Mme. Eveline Weil, dated August 27, 1943.
114. Same letter.
115. Information collected by May Mesnet in 1954.
116. Ibid.
117. J. Cabaud, *Simone Weil: A Fellowship in Love,* p. 350.
118. J. Cabaud, ibid., pp. 348–50.

Index

Litvinov, M., 123, 165
Locke, John, 69
Lorenzo the Magnificent, 308
Louzon, R., 129, 142, 242, 247
"Love" (Herbert), 330, 340, 371, 465
"Love of God and Affliction, The," 460, 466
Lucretius, 35
Lussiaa-Berdou, P., 154
Luther, Martin, 373
Lutte de classe, La, 162
Luxembourg, Rosa, 132, 153, 176, 183, 184
Lycée Fénelon, 17, 21–2
Lycée Montaigne, 9, 15

Machiavelli, Niccolò, 69, 198, 308, 312
Magdélénat, M., 253, 256
Maine de Biran, 69, 473
Malaubre, J., 166
Malebranche, Nicolas de, 69, 341
Malraux, André, 209, 343
Manicheans, 346–7, 395, 488
Mantegna, Andrea, 301
Marcoux, Camille, 50, 57–8, 394
Maritain, Jacques, 474–5, 476, 481
Martinet, Marcel, 153, 176, 197, 247
Marx, Karl, 69, 76, 88, 120, 122, 126, 128, 146, 156, 159, 168, 176, 184, 189, 198, 205, 312, 320–3, 361, 502
Marxism, 61, 156, 158, 168, 176, 187, 195, 313, 319–22, 447, 492, 502
Masses, 183
Mathiot, Geneviève, 18
Maurin, Joaquín, 174, 270–1
Maurois, André, 34
"Meditations on a Corpse," 311
"Meditations on Obedience and Liberty," 313
Melchisedech, 457
Memorial, Le, 94, 98, 99, 100, 102, 103, 111, 113
"Memories of Belgium," 135–6
"Mer, La," 450
Mérat, 104, 108, 112
Mercier, L., 273
Mesnet, May, 490, 536, 537
Metchnikov, Elie, 11, 19, 69
Michaelangelo, 304, 306, 308, 309
Ministry of Education, 218, 249, 267, 282, 382, 390
Miravitlès, 174, 276
Moline, Suzette, 54
Molinier, Raymond, 130
Monatte, P., 47, 76, 90, 91, 129, 138, 151, 176, 177, 244
Montaigne, Michel de, 69, 359
Monteverdi, Claudio, 309, 329
"Morality and Literature," 449
Moré, Marcel, 315, 323

"Morocco, or Prescription in the Matter of Theft," 287
Mounier, Emmanuel, 290
Mouquet, 225–6, 250
Mozart, Wolfgang Amadeus, 308–9
Munich treaty, 337–8, 347, 349
Mussigmann, F., 145, 163

National Conference of the Alliance against War, 243, 247
National Confederation of Workers (C.N.T.—Spain), 271–2, 277, 280
National Council of the Resistance, 504, 505
"National Prestige and Working-class Honor," 299
National Teacher's Union, 79, 83, 84, 93, 97, 103, 113, 117, 119, 129, 316–17
Naville, Pierre, 155
"Nécessité," 450
Need for Roots, The (Weil), 492, 499, 501, 502, 503, 527
Neumand, Henri, 4
Neumand, Julie Reinherz, 4
"New Aspects of the Colonial Problem in the French Empire," 338
New Testament, 108, 498
Nietzsche, Friedrich, 69, 369, 427
Noah, 489
"Nonintervention Generalized," 281
Notebooks (Weil), 22, 39, 222, 223, 224, 373, 394, 395, 437, 445, 447, 449–50, 454, 460, 462, 464, 484, 486, 494
"Note on the General Suppression of Political Parties," 492, 504
"Note on the Penal Colony Punishment Inflicted on Foreigners," 402
"Note on the Primitive Relations of Christianity and non-Hebraic Religions," 471
Nouveaux Cahiers, 297, 315, 317, 318, 321–2, 328, 331, 337, 342, 344, 350, 356, 358, 361
Novis, Emile (pseud. of Simone Weil), 393

"Observations Concerning the Essay on Hitler," 510
"Observations on the Lessons to be Drawn from Conflicts in the North," 286
October Revolution (U.S.S.R.), 147, 172, 189
Oesterreicher, Fr., 479
Oeuvre, L', 106
Old Testament, 345–6, 395, 412, 456–7, 479, 489
Olsen, Ebba, 19–20

Index

About the Author

Simone Pétrement was one of Simone Weil's closest friends. She is a graduate of the *école normale,* a doctor of philosophy and a doctor of letters, and she participated in the preparation for publication of the majority of Simone Weil's writings. Drawing on their close relationship and with access to Weil's papers and the full cooperation of her family, Simone Pétrement has written a beautiful work that captures as no one else could the life and thought of one of this century's most extraordinary people.